Ex Libris

Miss J Shults

CITY OF CITIES

Also by Stephen Inwood

A HISTORY OF LONDON

THE MAN WHO KNEW TOO MUCH

STEPHEN INWOOD

*

CITY OF CITIES

The Birth of Modern London

MACMILLAN

First published 2005 by Macmillan
an imprint of Pan Macmillan Ltd
Pan Macmillan, 20 New Wharf Road, London N1 9RR
Basingstoke and Oxford
Associated companies throughout the world
www.panmacmillan.com

ISBN 0 333 78287 9

1 3 5 7 9 8 6 4 2

A CIP catalogue record for this book is available from
the British Library.

Typeset by Intype Libra Ltd
Printed and bound in Great Britain by
Mackays of Chatham plc, Chatham, Kent

FOR BENJI, JOE AND TOM

Contents

PART THREE: LIVING LONDON

CONCLUSION

List of Illustrations

24. An early motor show, 1900.
25. The Deptford power station, 1889.
26. The Electrophone Saloon, around 1900.
27. Repairing telephone cables, around 1900.
28. The Hôtel de l'Europe, 1900.
29. The first post-Impressionist Exhibition, December 1910.
30. Oxford Street in the 1890s.
31. Mappin and Webb in 1908.
32. Shoppers in Hammersmith, 1900.
33. New Year's Eve outside St Paul's Cathedral at the end of the century.
34. The siege of Sidney Street, 1911.
35. The Great Wheel at Earl's Court, 1894.
36. A scene from a musical comedy, 1913.
37. Filming at Hepworth studios, 1912.
38. London's first film show, 1896.
39. A horse-brake excursion, 1900.
40. Patriotic crowds in August 1914.
41. Waving goodbye, 1914.

ACKNOWLEDGEMENTS

Pictures 1, 8, 11, 14, 18, 24, 26, 28, 32 and 33 are from *Living London* (London, 1901–3).
Pictures 2, 4, 19, 30 and 35 are from *Round London* (London, 1896).
Picture 3 is from *The New Survey of London Life and Labour*, vol. 1, *Forty Years of Change* (London, 1930).
Pictures 9 and 10 are from *Britain at Work* (London, 1902).
Pictures 13 and 22 are from *Pictorial London* (London, 1906).
Pictures 15–17 are from Sir G. G. Gibbon, R. W. Bell, *History of the London County Council, 1889–1939* (London, 1939).
Picture 21 is from *London, a Souvenir* (London, 1911).
Pictures 23 and 36–9 are from *The Pageant of the Century* (London, 1933).
Pictures 12, 34, 40, and 41 are from *The Story of Twenty-five Years* (London, 1935).
Pictures 5,6 and 25 are from the author's own collection.
Pictures 7, 20, 27 and 31 are from a private collection.

Acknowledgements

Since I work alone, most of my academic debts are to people that I have never met. Historians of late Victorian and Edwardian London have at their disposal the rich materials provided by the writing and research of many modern historians, and by the labours of contemporary novelists, statisticians, investigators, commentators, autobiographers and photographers. Readers will notice the extent to which I have drawn upon the work of such people as the pioneering social investigator Charles Booth, the popular writers George Sims and Walter Besant, the statistician and historian Sir Laurence Gomme (who was responsible, as the LCC's clerk for the whole prewar period, for the excellent *London Statistics*), and the writings of the hundreds of historians so conveniently listed in the Centre for Metropolitan History's online bibliography, *London's Past Online*. The librarians at the Senate House, Guildhall Library, Kingston University and Richmond libraries, who supplied me with the books and articles I needed, also deserve my thanks.

On a more personal level, I would like to thank Heather Creaton, Professor John Armstrong and Professor Michael Ball for help and advice, my students at New York University in London for keeping me in touch with the reading public, George Morley of Pan Macmillan for giving me extra time, my editor Jason Cooper for helping me to restructure a cumbersome first draft, and my agent David Godwin for making sure that I did not write (according to Samuel Johnson's dictum) as a blockhead.

The solitary and uneventful life of a writer would not be supportable to me without the warmth and friendship of my family, and I hope that my wife, Anne-Marie, knows how much I appreciate her encouragement and support. My sons are more important to me than any number of books, and I dedicate this one to them, with love and pride.

*

Thirty Years of Change

To a man who has been long absent from the Mother of Cities the first walk must be exceedingly interesting. Change has been in every direction. During his absence narrow streets have yielded to broad, handsome thoroughfares; whole acres that were once little better than slums have been cleared, and vast hotels and splendid shops stand where, only a few years back, the thieves and ruffians of London herded, and the barrow of the costermonger supplied the 'nobility and gentry' of the neighbourhood.

From being one of the ugliest cities in Europe, London has, during the last twenty years, been transformed into one of the most beautiful, so far as shops, hotels, and street architecture generally are concerned.

George R. Sims, *In London's Heart*, 1900

This book is not a nostalgic visit to a land of muffin men and lavender girls, or to an old-fashioned Victorian city awaiting the changes that the Great War of 1914–18 would bring. This is a study of London, the world's richest and most populous city, as it experienced and pioneered a process of rapid and dramatic change involving new technology, new social and political ideas, and new ways of organizing civic and domestic life. The impression, often reinforced in films, novels, and history books, that 'Victorian' London was more or less the same in the 1880s as it had been in the 1840s or would be in the 1900s, is an illusion. London in the 1880s, it is true, still exhibited many traditional features. Horse-drawn omnibuses (introduced in 1829) were still its main form of road transport, tuberculosis and dysentery still filled its graveyards, theatre and music hall still entertained its citizens, and William Gladstone, a Cabinet minister since 1843, was still Prime Minister in 1883 and 1893.

But despite these continuities London was changing rapidly in these last Victorian decades, driven along by strong intellectual, demographic, social, and technological forces.

In the years 1882 to 1884, the time at which this study begins, the seeds of great changes were being sown. Those three years saw the publication of two sensational exposures of slum conditions which led to the establishment of a Royal Commission on working-class housing and eventually to the building of the first council flats; the foundation of London's first socialist organizations, the Social Democratic Federation and the Fabian Society, which helped to transform politics, government, and trades unionism in London and eventually contributed to the creation of the Labour Party; the establishment in Whitechapel of the Toynbee Hall Settlement, one of the seedbeds of the modern welfare state; the passing of the Cheap Trains Act, which stimulated mass commuting and the growth of working-class suburbs; the introduction of London's (and Europe's) first cable-driven tram service; the International Electric Exhibition at Crystal Palace, where Edison first displayed his world-changing inventions to the British public; the opening of Edison's Holborn electricity generating station, the first steam-powered public electric power station in the world; London's first electric-lit street, hotel, and church; the construction of a network of high-pressure water-mains pipes to power hydraulic lifts all over central London; the introduction of almost universal male franchise; the loss of the 'Ashes' to the Australian cricket team; the invention of the Welsbach gas mantle, producing the first really bright street lamps; the appointment of W. T. Stead, the creator of the popular campaigning style known as the New Journalism, as editor of the *Pall Mall Gazette*; the discovery (in Germany) of the cholera, tuberculosis, and diphtheria bacilli and London's last significant outbreak of typhus, signalling the fading power of the great killer diseases; and the start of mass immigration of Jews from Russia and Poland which transformed the East End and led, in 1905, to modern England's first immigration laws.

Sometimes single events so dominate a year that the deeper changes taking place at the same time are obscured. In 1888, the year of the sensational Whitechapel murders, male and female Londoners elected their first democratic city-wide government, the London County Council, and London got the world's first two-tier urban administration. J. B. Dunlop patented the pneumatic tyre, helping to transform cycling from an uncomfortable hobby for daredevils into a powerful force in popular leisure and transport, and preparing the way for efficient motoring. London's first

halfpenny evening newspaper, the *Star*, was started, heralding the beginning of the age of mass circulation journalism. The first Sherlock Holmes
novel, *A Study in Scarlet*, was published, and the Football League and the
Lawn Tennis Association were founded. Charles Booth completed work
on the first volume of his massive *Life and Labour of the People in London*,
the first modern study of London's economic and social life. Annie
Besant helped to organize the matchgirls' strike, a seminal event in the
rise of modern unskilled trades unionism and the women's movement.
A fourteen-storey apartment block, Queen Anne's Mansions, was built
in Victoria, giving London (briefly) the tallest residential building in the
world. Translations of three plays by Henrik Ibsen were published in
London, introducing Londoners to social and sexual ideas which challenged the most cherished Victorian values.

Other years could be chosen to represent London's interconnected
social, technological and cultural revolutions. In 1896, the speed limit
for motorized vehicles was raised from 2 to 12 mph, and London saw
the first Motor Show and the London to Brighton run. In that same year
cycling became a popular and fashionable pastime, and work on the electric Central Line, the first multi-station deep level Tube train, was started.
Lumière's first cinematograph film was shown at the Empire Theatre,
Leicester Square, and some of the earliest films of London scenes and
news events were shot. Marconi arrived in London with two bags of radio
equipment and transmitted the first public wireless signals from the General Post Office, Alfred Harmsworth published the first mass-circulation
daily paper, the *Daily Mail*, starting a revolution in London journalism,
and the new London School of Economics (founded by the Fabians in
1895 with a bequest from a rich admirer) opened the British Library of
Political and Economic Science.

London in these thirty years experienced a transition that was
technological, political, demographic, sexual, social, racial, cultural,
architectural, and spatial: it is hard to think of an aspect of urban life that
was not fundamentally transformed between 1883 and 1914. Electrification, motorization, socialism, secularism, feminism, cosmopolitanism,
family planning, suburbanization, mass entertainment, modern retailing,
democracy, state intervention were all at work in the London of the 1890s
and 1900s, as they have been ever since. This sense of rapid and momen-
tous change is not detectable only in retrospect: people living in the
period, before the horrors of the Great War created the illusion that there
had been a prewar 'Golden Age', believed that they were living in a time

of unprecedented change and modernity. In the 1880s and 1890s people spoke of the New Journalism, the New Unionism, the New Realism, the New Woman, the New Aristocracy, the New Liberalism, and they had good reason to do so. Many contemporary writers sensed that a new world was in the making in the years around 1900, though they disagreed about whether the future would be socialist (Bernard Shaw, William Morris and the Webbs), scientific (H. G. Wells), sexual (Havelock Ellis and Edward Carpenter), psychic (Conan Doyle and Annie Besant), or suburban (Ebenezer Howard and Sidney Low).

That is not to say that new ideas and new technology marched on without resistance in these thirty years. Anyone looking at London in the early twentieth century, or even today, can see that it did not go the way of Chicago or New York, embracing modern high-rise architecture without reservation. The spread of electricity, the telephone, tall buildings, the tram, the motor car, birth control, women's emancipation, democracy, and efficient government were all impeded and weakened by timidity, conservatism, or misunderstanding, with the result that London was not transformed by them as rapidly as it might have been. The modernity of the age was denounced as often as it was welcomed: the persecution and ruin of Oscar Wilde, the outrage provoked by London productions of the plays of Ibsen in the 1890s and by Roger Fry's first post-Impressionist exhibition in 1910, the powerful opposition to women's suffrage and Jewish immigration, the 2 mph speed limit on early motor vehicles, the height restriction on new office and apartment blocks, and the Churches' struggle to hold back the tide of heathenism, all indicate that two ages were in conflict, and knew that they were.

Author's notes

There are several different Londons, and I have referred to four of them:

The City, the inner business district, stretching roughly from the Tower of London to Chancery Lane, and from the Thames to Smithfield and Liverpool Street Station. 677 acres, or just over a square mile.

Inner London, or the County of London, the area under the authority of the Metropolitan Board of Works (MBW) until 1888 and the London County Council (LCC) thereafter, and stretching from Roehampton and Hammersmith in the west to Eltham, Woolwich, Bow and Hackney (the River Lea) in the east, and from Tooting and Sydenham in the south to Hampstead and Stoke Newington in the north. Nearly 75,000 acres, or 117 square miles.

Outer London, the built-up area beyond the county boundary, but within the Metropolitan Police District. Growing in area, but with an upper limit of 605 square miles.

Greater London, which is the sum of all the other three.

Londoners in these years divided their pounds into twenty shillings (s), each of which was in turn divided into twelve pence (d). Following pre-decimal practice, I have expressed smaller sums of money like this: 2s (two shillings), 10s 6d (ten shillings and sixpence, or 'ten and six'), and so on.

The 1900s, in my usage, refer to the first decade of the twentieth century, not the whole hundred years.

I move from eastern wretchedness
    Through Fleet Street and the Strand;
And as the pleasant people press
    I touch them softly with my hand,
Perhaps I know that still I go
    Alive about a living land.

John Davidson, 'A Loafer', 1894

✳

London in the 1880s

The Great Unknown

London, said the novelist Henry James in 1882, was 'the most complete compendium of the world. The human race is better represented there than anywhere else, and if you learn to know your London you learn a great many things.' Knowing this vast city well, of course, was a rare and difficult accomplishment, and one which very few Londoners achieved. Nobody could know it in the 1880s as it had been known by the historian John Stow in the 1590s, or the scientist and surveyor Robert Hooke in the 1670s, or Samuel Johnson in the 1770s. The London of Shaw, Wilde, and Wells was a city of cities, whose biggest component parts – Westminster, Islington, Stepney, Lambeth, St Pancras, West Ham – were the size of Edinburgh, Bristol, or Sheffield. Those who set about getting to know London as a whole were people with a mission, writers, reporters, social reformers, evangelists, and cab drivers, and they had to devote a lifetime to the subject. One who tried harder than most was the Liverpool shipowner Charles Booth, who began a study of the social, industrial, and cultural life of the city in 1886, and spent seventeen years and seventeen volumes on his task. But by the time he had completed his work London was no longer the city it had been when his researches began. It was, among many other things, much bigger in both area and population. Greater London's population grew more quickly (in absolute terms) in these years than at any other time in its history – at a rate of almost a million a decade between 1881 and 1901, and another nine hundred thousand by 1914. The great city had always been a moving target, but in the thirty years before the Great War, a time we often think of as a period of calm and continuity before the cataclysm that was to come, London was moving faster than ever before.

To the vast majority of Londoners, most of their own city was untrodden territory. They knew the neighbourhood in which they lived, shopped and went to church and school, and perhaps that in which they worked. But under two million Londoners were in paid occupations (in 1891), and many of these, including about three hundred thousand domestic servants, slept where they worked. Trips to London's great shopping streets in the West End, Regent Street, Oxford Street, Piccadilly, or the Strand, or to a central London theatre or music hall, or perhaps to the Regent's Park Zoo or the Crystal Palace at Sydenham, might take Londoners away from their familiar territory from time to time, but in general life in London was local and small-scale. Henry James again: 'Practically, of course, one lives in a quarter, in a plot; but in imagination and by a constant mental act of reference the accommodated haunter enjoys the whole . . . He fancies himself, as they say, for being a particle in so unequalled an aggregation; and its immeasurable circumference, even though unvisited and lost in smoke, gives him the sense of a social, an intellectual margin.'[1]

The average Londoner, according to the (incomplete) statistics gathered by the train, tram, and omnibus companies, only made about sixty-five journeys a year by public transport in the early 1880s. They did far more journeys on foot, but Augustus Hare, whose *Walks in London* went through seven editions between 1878 and 1901, was convinced that most Londoners, at least until they had read and followed his book, were ignorant of their own great city. 'Few indeed are the Londoners who see more than a small circuit around their homes, the main arteries of mercantile life, and some of the principal sights . . . Scarcely any man in what is usually called "society" has the slightest idea of what there is to be seen in his own great metropolis . . . and the architectural treasures of the City are almost as unknown to the West End as the buried cities of Bashan or the lost tombs of Etruria'. Even using Hare's thousand-page guide, the dedicated explorer would not be taken north of King's Cross into Camden and Kentish Town, or south beyond the old riverside districts of Southwark and Lambeth into the well-populated suburbs of Walworth, Newington, and Peckham. In the west, Hare accompanied his readers as far as Chelsea and the museums of South Kensington, and even to distant Fulham, but in the east he took them only to Wapping, Spitalfields, Stepney, and Shoreditch, and left them to find their own way, if they dared, through 'the populous district of Hackney', 'the black poverty-stricken district of Bethnal Green', and the 'miserable thickly inhabited districts of Shadwell and Limehouse'.[2]

There were plenty of Londoners for whom a walk with Hare's guidebook in their hand would have been an unimaginable adventure. Arnold

Bennett, watching crowds gather for a royal wedding in July 1896, was struck by the fact that there was a hidden army of Londoners, especially young women, who were rarely seen on its streets and in its omnibuses. Piccadilly that day was 'thronged with women in light summer attire – cool, energetic, merry, inquisitive, and having the air of being out for the day'.

> Judging from the ordinary occupants of the streets, one is apt to think of London as a city solely made up of the acute, the knowing, the worldly, the blasé. But, hidden away behind sunblinds in quiet squares and crescents, there dwells another vast population, seen in large numbers only at such times as this, an army of the Ignorantly Innocent, in whose sheltered seclusion a bus-ride is an event, and a day spent amongst the traffic of the West End is an occasion long to be remembered.[3]

As population growth, along with improvements in public transport and changes in patterns of work and family life, enabled and encouraged middle-class Londoners to settle in residential neighbourhoods away from the commercial and manufacturing centres of the city, their knowledge of what life was like in other parts of London, and especially in poorer districts, became thinner and more second-hand. In 1880 what most well-off Londoners knew about the lives of the London poor, apart from those of their own servants, probably came from articles in the *Illustrated London News* or *The Times*, newspaper reports from the police courts, cartoons in *Punch*, or working-class scenes from stage melodramas and romantic novels. There had been serious accounts of the London poor, from Henry Mayhew in the 1850s to James Greenwood and Thomas Wright in the 1860s and 1870s, but their influence and readership were not great. In the 1880s and 1890s a new generation of writers, including Charles Booth, George Sims, Walter Besant, W. T. Stead, Israel Zangwill, and George Gissing, told comfortable Londoners some uncomfortable truths about the city in which they lived.

One of the most active and influential of these writers was Walter Besant, the author of dozens of novels and travel pieces, the founder (in 1884) of the Society of Authors and later a prolific historian of London. One of Besant's earlier novels, *All Sorts and Conditions of Men*, published in 1882, set out to reveal the economic and cultural poverty of the East End to London's large reading public, and to propose some practical remedies.

Two millions of people, or thereabouts, live in the East End of London. That seems a good-sized population for an utterly unknown town. They have no institutions of their own to speak of, no public buildings of any importance, no municipality, no gentry, no carriages, no soldiers, no picture-galleries, no theatres, no opera – they have nothing . . . Probably there is no such spectacle in the whole world as that of this immense, neglected, forgotten great city of East London.

. . . Nobody goes east, no one wants to see the place; no one is curious about the way of life in the east. Books on London pass it over; it has little or no history . . . [4]

✳

CHAPTER ONE

CITY OF SMOKE

'Let me see,' said Holmes, standing at the corner, and glancing
along the line, 'I should like just to remember the order of the
houses here. It is a hobby of mine to have an exact knowledge
of London.'

Arthur Conan Doyle,
'The Adventure of the Red-Headed League',
in *The Adventures of Sherlock Holmes*, 1892

The common feeling that London was vast, mysterious, and unknowable
was intensified by the murkiness of its atmosphere, which was especially
dense in the 1880s. Smoke-laden fog had been a familiar and unpleasant
feature of London's environment for centuries, but the problem seemed to
get much worse in the nineteenth century, when the number of fireplaces
burning coal, and chimneys emitting smoke, increased about sixfold.
Smoke-abatement legislation introduced since the 1840s had driven some
dirty industries into the eastern suburbs, but did not control domestic coal
burning. The amount of coal used in homes and industry in London each
year increased from about 10 million tons in 1879 to over 16 million tons
in 1910. Londoners spoke of their dense fogs with a sort of affection
– to Dickens in the 1850s and 1860s a thick fog was 'London's ivy' or
a 'London particular', and to the Londoner of the 1890s it was a 'pea-
souper', and London itself was the 'big smoke'. Thick fogs could make
walking familiar London streets into an adventure. In 1900 H. G. Wells'
romantic schoolteacher, Mr Lewisham, enjoyed 'the dangers of the street
corners, the horses looming up suddenly out of the dark, the carters with
lanterns on their horses' heads, the street lamps, blurred smoky orange at
one's nearest, and vanishing at twenty yards into dim haze'. The poet and
critic Arthur Symons, in an essay on London published in 1909, took a
gloomier view of fog:

It stifles the mind as well as choking the body. It comes on slowly
and stealthily, picking its way, choosing its direction, leaving con-
temptuous gaps in its course; then it settles down like a blanket of
solid smoke, which you can feel but not put from you. The streets
turn putrescent, the gas lamps hang like rotting fruit, you are in a dark
tunnel, in which the lights are going out, and beside you, unseen,
there is a roar and rumble, interrupted with sharp cries, a stopping of
wheels and a beginning of the roar and rumble over again.[1]

Marion Sambourne, the wife of the successful *Punch* political cartoonist
Linley Sambourne, whose house in Stafford Terrace, Kensington, is preserved as a museum of late Victorian domestic and artistic life, shared
Symons' distaste for fog. Her diary in the very foggy winter of 1886–87
repeatedly refers to the unpleasantness and inconvenience of the weather.
On 23 November 1886, for instance: 'Fearful fog!!! Third day. Lin started
for *Punch* dinner but had to return'.[2]

A thick fog hid London altogether, but a moderate one made it beautiful. It lent an impressionistic charm to the city painted by James Whistler
in the 1870s and 1880s, especially his *Nocturnes* depicting the Thames at
Chelsea and Battersea, and his lovely view of Piccadilly on a foggy evening
in 1883, *Nocturne in Grey and Gold*. To Whistler, London was at its most
beautiful 'when the evening mist clothes the riverside with poetry, as with
a veil, and the poor buildings lose themselves in the dim sky, and the tall
chimneys become campanili, and the warehouses are palaces in the night,
and the whole city hangs in the heavens, and fairyland is before us'.[3]
Claude Monet painted at least a hundred pictures of London between
1899 and 1901, mostly in the fog and nearly all of the Thames, Waterloo and Charing Cross bridges and the Houses of Parliament seen from
the Savoy Hotel and St Thomas's Hospital. What interested him particularly was the way the view was altered by the autumn and winter fogs:
'My practised eye has found that objects change in appearance in a London
fog more and quicker than in any other atmosphere.' To Monet, London's
fogs and mists were a powerful justification for the impressionist approach
to the urban landscape: 'How could English painters of the nineteenth century have painted its houses brick by brick? Those fellows painted bricks
which they didn't see, which they couldn't see . . . London would not be
beautiful without the fog, which gives it its marvellous breadth. Its regular, massive blocks become grandiose in that mysterious cloak.'[4] In a
dialogue called 'The Decay of Lying', written in 1889, when London was

at its foggiest, Oscar Wilde (represented by Vivian in the dialogue) suggested that London's fogs, or at least Londoners' consciousness of them, were the creation of painters and poets:

> Where, if not from the Impressionists, do we get those wonderful brown fogs that come creeping down our streets, blurring the gas-lamps and changing the houses into monstrous shadows? To whom, if not to them and their master, do we owe the lovely silver mists that brood over our river, and turn to faint forms of fading grace curved bridge and swaying barge? The extraordinary change that has taken place in the climate of London during the last ten years is entirely due to a particular school of Art . . . At present, people see fogs, not because there are fogs, but because poets and painters have taught them the mysterious loveliness of such effects. There may have been fogs for centuries in London. I dare say there were. But no one saw them, and so we do not know anything about them. They did not exist till Art had invented them. Now, it must be admitted, fogs are carried to excess. They have become the mere mannerism of a clique, and the exaggerated realism of their method gives dull people bronchitis. Where the cultured catch an effect, the uncultured catch cold.[5]

So powerful were the suggestive effects of the Impressionists' work that a week's thick fog, like the one that descended just before Christmas 1891, could kill about 700 people. In the relatively clear Edwardian decade about 6,500 bronchitic Londoners died each year, but in 1886, probably the foggiest year of all, over 11,000 imagined themselves to death.

Useful as it was to artists, *Punch* cartoonists, and the writers of detective stories and Gothic novels, the thick yellowish fog produced by the suspension of soot and coal smoke, and especially by sulphur (oxidized into sulphuric acid), in naturally occurring fogs on still autumn and winter days corroded buildings, damaged fabrics (especially curtains and hanging washing), attacked lungs, and increased mortality in London by 5 per cent or more. The number of days on which London was foggy increased from around twenty or thirty at the start of the century to about forty-five in the early 1870s and between sixty and eighty-five in the 1880s. A run of foggy years between 1878 and 1880 (averaging sixty-nine foggy days a year) stimulated interest in the problem. Several books on air and smoke pollution in London were published in the early 1880s, and in 1882 the National Health Society put on a smoke-abatement exhibition in South Kensington. This in turn led to the formation of the London-based

National Smoke Abatement Institute, which campaigned through exhibitions and conferences for action to cleanse the London air. The frequency of thick fogs reached its peak in 1886 (eighty-six days) and 1887 (eighty-three days), and then, for no obvious reason, tailed off to about forty-five foggy days a year between 1893 and 1904, and under twenty in 1905, 1906, and 1908. Some experts believed the decline in fogs was the result of changes in London's temperature and prevailing wind, but more efficient grates and the spreading use of gas, especially for cooking, probably played a more important part in the change. In 1910, according to Laurence Chubb, secretary of the Coal Smoke Abatement Society, 'over 750,000 gas-cookers are in use in the metropolis alone, and their aggregate effect in preventing the emission of smoke from kitchen chimneys must be very great'.[6]

Before this improvement, and especially between 1878 and 1892, London was much foggier than it had been in the days of Dickens, or those of the artist Gustave Doré, whose figures seemed to live in the 1870s in a continuously foggy atmosphere. In addition to foggy days there were 'dark' days, in which 'high fog', or thick smoke-polluted cloud, completely obscured the daylight, leaving London in a state of 'day darkness'. Even London's clearer days would have seemed murky to rural visitors, or to us. 'Judged by the autographic records', the head of the Meteorological Office wrote in 1911, the London air was 'still almost opaque to sunshine strong enough to burn the card of the recorder during the winter months'.[7] In the winter of 1901–2 there was a scientific study of the frequency, intensity, and causes of London fogs by the Meteorological Office and the London County Council. On ten occasions in December and January, on days that were not classified as foggy, the director of the survey climbed to the top of London's second highest building, the Victoria Tower of the Houses of Parliament, and found that visibility was always between half a mile and one and a quarter miles. He never managed to catch sight of London's highest building, the dome of St Paul's Cathedral, a mile and a half away.[8]

Five Million Londoners

Late Victorian London was so vast, so diverse in its economic, social, and cultural organization, so complex in its government, so fragmented into socially and politically distinct neighbourhoods, that it defies brief or simple description. But some basic demographic and administrative facts will help to set the scene. At some time in 1883 or 1884 London's population passed the five million mark. In the modern world, where there are overgrown super-cities of ten million or more in Asia, Africa, and the Americas, five million does not seem an extraordinary figure, but such a vast concentration of people, living together in one continuous urban area, had never been seen before. No city in the history of the world had approached London's size, and none of London's nineteenth-century rivals could match it. There were about 2.3 million Parisians in 1883, about 1.2 million Berliners, and the same number of Viennese. The largest non-European city, New York, had just over 2 million citizens in the early 1880s, and would not overtake London in size until the 1930s. Over the next thirty years London's population carried on growing as fast as it had ever done, and faster than all its great European contemporaries. It reached 6 million in 1895, 7 million in 1907, and about 7.5 million by August 1914. There were more Londoners in 1914 than there were in 2000, living in an area about half the size of modern London, but roughly double the size of London in 1883.

Vast numbers of late Victorian Londoners were citizens by settlement, rather than birth. Of the 3.8 million people living in the London registration district (the area designated as the County of London in 1888) in the census year of 1881, over 34 per cent, 1.3 million, were born elsewhere in the United Kingdom (including over 80,000 from Ireland), and almost 107,000 (2.7 per cent) were foreign-born. The percentage of UK migrants in the County of London's population fell steadily to about 26 per cent by 1911, but the foreign-born share rose to 4.7 per cent (210,000 people) over the same period. This rise was mainly the result of the settlement of Russian and Polish Jews in the East London borough of Stepney, whose population was almost 21 per cent foreign-born in 1911. In 1898 Baedeker's guide tried to impress its readers with the immensity of London's immigrant populations: 'There are in London more Scotsmen than in Aberdeen, more Irish than in Dublin, more Jews than in Palestine, and more Roman Catholics than in Rome. The number of Americans resident in London has been estimated by a competent authority at 15,000, while perhaps 100,000 pass through it annually.'[9] In 1881, before the great influx from East Europe, the biggest foreign populations in London were German (22,000), French (8,250), Polish (6,930), American (4,300), Dutch (4,200), Italian (3,500), and Swiss (2,300). There were several distinctive areas of foreign settlement in London in the 1880s: a small Chinese quarter in Limehouse, a famous Italian community in Saffron Hill

(Clerkenwell), a cosmopolitan mixture of French, Swiss, and Italians in Soho, and a rapidly growing population of Polish and Russian Jews in Whitechapel, a district whose cheap rooms and sweated industries accomodated the very poorest settlers. In general migrants from the UK were more likely to settle in well-off West End and suburban boroughs where healthy country girls could find jobs as domestic servants – Chelsea, Hampstead, Paddington, Kensington, and Westminster.

The city's population was spreading, as well as growing. By the early 1880s, London had already spread far out into its surrounding farmland and market gardens, turning villages like West Ham, Hackney, Stoke Newington, Peckham, and Earls Court into heavily populated suburbs. London's apparently unstoppable sprawl, especially since the building of railways after the 1830s, was a constant topic of amazement or complaint. But up to 1880 the growth of London's continuous built-up area was nearly all within four miles of Charing Cross, and cab drivers charged extra to go further afield than this. Only Hammersmith in the west, Greenwich, Poplar, and Stratford in the east, and the ribbon development along the northbound Great Cambridge Road, through Tottenham and Edmonton, strayed far outside this four-mile circle. This was the metropolitan limit used by James Thorne, whose *Handbook to the Environs of London* was published in 1876, though many of the places he described were rapidly being absorbed by the spreading city. Railways had encouraged the growth of some well-populated commuter or market towns a few miles from London, places like Ealing, Enfield, Willesden, Barking, Woolwich, Penge, Norwood, Lewisham, Croydon, Surbiton, and Wandsworth, but most of these were still separated from London by open agricultural or heath land in 1880. This pattern of development reflected the nature of the transport available in the 1870s to suburban breadwinners who had to make a daily journey to work in the City, Westminster, or the East End. The poor or energetic could walk, but would only cover two or three miles in an hour. Horse-drawn omnibuses went at four or five miles an hour (and faster on a clear road) but high fares meant that only the middle class and better-paid working men could afford to use them every day. Surface trains and the steam-driven shallow underground lines (the District and Metropolitan Lines, and most of the Circle) were also too expensive for working-class commuters, except on a few lines which had been forced to run cheap workmen's trains by Parliament. But trains were fast, making it possible for well-off commuters to live in country towns like Wimbledon, Kingston,

Richmond, Sydenham, and Bromley in the south, or Harrow, Barnet, Enfield, and Walthamstow in the north.

In London's population, women outnumbered men, as they did in the country generally, and as they do today. In 1891 there were 111 females for every hundred males in Greater London, compared with 106 to 100 in England and Wales as a whole. The difference was greater in London because of the large number of female servants employed there, and was greater still in richer districts, where servants were more plentiful. Thus Hampstead and Kensington, with over 150 women to 100 men, topped the list in 1891, followed by Paddington, Penge, Hornsey, Lewisham, St Marylebone, Acton, and Wandsworth. The most 'masculine' boroughs, with few households rich enough to employ servants and many workers in male-dominated industries, were in the centre, the east (both inner and outer), and just south of the river. In Woolwich, East Ham, and Barking males easily outnumbered females, and in West Ham, Bermondsey, South-wark, Stepney, Poplar, Finsbury, and the City there was a rough parity between the sexes. This imbalance became more pronounced, as it does today, in old age, but it was significant among people in their twenties and thirties, too, and must have affected patterns of courtship, marriage, and childbirth. In Kensington and Hampstead women of twenty to twenty-four outnumbered men of the same age by two or three to one, and in the County of London as a whole there were 119 women of twenty to thirty-nine for every hundred men of that age in 1911. For various reasons, including this imbalance, 19 per cent of women in the County had not married by their mid-forties.[10]

There were striking differences between the age structure of late Victorian London's population and that of modern London. To our eyes the London of the 1880s and 1890s would have seemed very full of chil-dren, but very short of old people. The proportion of the population between fifteen and sixty-four, what we might call 'working age' today, was about 62 per cent in 1891, compared with the 2001 figure of 68.5 per cent. The great difference was that in the London (and England) of 1891 under-fifteens outnumbered over-sixty-fives by almost nine to one, while in 2001 the ratio was three to two. In modern London there are as many pensioners as there are under-tens (about 900,000 of each), but in Greater London in 1891 there were under 300,000 over-sixty-fives and nearly 1,300,000 under-tens.[11] The reasons for this difference in age struc-ture were fairly simple. In modern London, the birth rate (the number of babies born each year per thousand people) is about 12, the death rate is about 10 and life expectancy at birth is seventy-eight. In the mid-1880s, birth and death rates had already started their long decline from the peaks of the 1860s, but the birth rate was over 32 per 1,000, the death rate was about 22 per 1,000, and life expectancy at birth was about forty-two.[12] A woman who married in the 1880s and remained married for twenty-five years would, on average, produce just over five live babies, compared with a woman marrying in 1910, who would produce just over three, and a woman in the 1920s or 1930s, who would produce just over two. The demographic transition, the shift from the high birth and death rates of traditional societies to the low rates of the modern world, had begun in England in the 1870s, and by 1914 its effects on London's population structure were very great, but in the 1880s London's pattern of births and deaths was still predominantly traditional. About 180,000 babies were born in London in 1891 (to a population of 5.6 million), and probably around 150,000 of these survived to their first birthday. In the London of 2001, with a population of 7 million, 104,000 babies were born, though few of these died in their first year.[13]

Forty Governments

To some newcomers this immense city seemed to be nothing but an over-grown monster without structure or organization, or an immeasurable and uncontrollable mass of streets and houses spreading like a huge stain across the surrounding countryside. This impression was mistaken. In many respects London was, and had to be, a highly organized city. Its rapid growth since the start of the nineteenth century, and the many problems this growth created, had forced generally unwilling politicians and admin-istrators to devise new ways of making life safe and tolerable in a vast metropolis. By the mid-1880s Londoners were policed by a Metropolitan Police force of about 14,500 men (42 per cent of the policemen in England and Wales), and protected from fires by a professional and well-equipped Fire Brigade with stations all over the city. In 1883, 90 per cent of the 540,000 children of the age (five to thirteen) and class expected to go to state or Church elementary schools actually did so, though perhaps not every day. The worst problems of the 1830s and 1840s, inadequate drainage and a polluted water supply, had been alleviated by the con-struction of a modern sewer network and new controls on private water companies, and by the imposition of a range of sanitary and environmental duties on London's thirty-nine administrative units (the City, twenty-three large parishes, and fifteen district boards). Although constant supplies of clean water were not yet available to many poorer houses, the epidemic diseases caused by foul water earlier in the century, cholera and typhoid, had been driven out. Thanks to universal smallpox vaccination, growing habits of domestic cleanliness, cheaper food, rising living standards, and perhaps compulsory education, mortality from the other great infectious diseases, typhus, tuberculosis, scarlet fever, and whooping cough, was also in decline, and Londoners were starting to live healthier and longer lives.

London's magnificent main drainage system was the proudest achievement of the Metropolitan Board of Works (MBW), the nearest thing London had to a city-wide administrative authority in the early 1880s. The Board, which was created in 1855, had responsibility for main drainage, fire-fighting, building main roads and bridges, and managing some of London's larger parks and commons, and it was charged with implementing much of the public health and safety legislation passed in the 1860s and 1870s. The Board was not a directly elected body, but was composed of delegates chosen by London's elected local government bodies, the parish vestries, the district boards, and the City.

London did not exist as a county until 1888, when the London County Council (LCC) replaced the Metropolitan Board of Works. Until then, the whole of London north of the Thames and west of the River Lea was in the County of Middlesex, and London south of the Thames was either in Surrey (from Camberwell westwards) or Kent. Kentish London consisted mainly of the three south-eastern towns of Deptford, Greenwich, and Woolwich, and the growing borough of Lewisham. The newer working-class districts east of the Lea and north of the Thames, West and East Ham, Leyton, Walthamstow, Romford, Ilford, Epping, Barking, and Silvertown, were in Essex, beyond the authority of the MBW before 1888 and of the LCC afterwards. The Metropolitan Board of Works gave a sort of unity to the 117 square miles it covered, and London was already unified for policing purposes by the Metropolitan Police District, created in 1839, a rough circle about 30 miles in diameter, covering 693 square miles, including much undeveloped agricultural land. Only the City of London, which had retained its own police force in 1829, was outside the Metropolitan Police District. There was also one London-wide elected body covering the MBW area, the London School Board, which had been created in 1870 to provide elementary education for any children whose parents wanted it, and could pay the small weekly fee. To some observers working-class London in the 1880s and 1890s might have seemed to be a city of savages, but in reality nearly all of its children went to school, and so, in most cases, had their parents.[14]

London's local administration was in the hands of its long-established parishes, which had responsibility for important sanitary and environmental matters, including street lighting and cleaning, public health inspection and enforcement, and the provision of local libraries and baths. The 1855 Act that created the Metropolitan Board of Works recognized twenty-three parishes as large and efficient enough to administer these matters independently, and grouped the fifty-five smaller parishes into fifteen district boards. These amalgamations did not produce administrative units of roughly equal size or population: the St Pancras, Lambeth, and Islington vestries had populations of 240,000, 280,000, and 320,000 respectively in 1891, while the vestry of St Martin-in-the-Fields and the tiny Strand District Board had only 40,000 people between them.

By the early 1880s few people had anything good to say about the two-tier system of government that had managed London since 1855. Such was the lack of public and political interest in the vestries that many (often most) vestrymen were elected unopposed, and when elections were held a combination of a restrictive ratepayer franchise and public apathy led to very low turnouts. In the 1885 vestry elections only ninety of London's two hundred wards were contested, and in the forty wards where a full poll (rather than a show of hands) was held, thirty-two candidates topped their list with under fifty votes.[15] Probably only one in thirty of those entitled to vote in vestry elections did so in that year, and those who had to pay for public services were much more likely to vote than those who stood to benefit from them the most. The vestries and district boards represented neither the skills and power of the London elite (whose members had more important or interesting things on their minds than petty parochial duties), nor the democratic weight of the mass of citizens, who either could not or would not vote in vestry elections. Most parish vestrymen were shopkeepers, publicans, tradesmen, and members of the professions, generally members of local ratepayers' associations, who were more interested in keeping local taxes low than in extending public services. For example, parishes and district boards had been given the authority in the 1850s to open free public libraries if most ratepayers agreed to it, but by 1886 only two had done so.

The problem was exacerbated by the social and economic distinction between rich and poor vestries and boards. The West End vestries, which had the least pressing need for the social and environmental services a parish might offer, found it much easier to raise revenue through their local property tax, or rate, than poorer vestries in East and south London, which had greater need of social services but less ability to pay for them. So the rateable value (per head) of property in the richest vestries, St Martin-in-the-Fields and St James's Piccadilly, was about ten times as high in 1896 as that of the poorest vestries, Bethnal Green, Mile End Old Town, Newington, and St George-in-the-East. The City, with its vast wealth and shrinking population, was in a class of its own, over three times richer, per head, than the richest vestry. This problem was partly alleviated by the existence of London-wide ('First Tier') bodies, like the Metropolitan Police, the Metropolitan Board of Works, and the London School Board, whose services were paid for from London-wide rates, and by the Metropolitan Common Poor Fund (1867), which covered nearly half of the cost of poor relief, and into which parishes paid according to their wealth. But the disparity between vestries as far as social and sanitary spending was concerned was not alleviated at all until 1894, when the London Equalisation of Rates Act compelled vestries and district boards to subscribe to a common fund according to their rateable value. By the late 1890s this fund was worth about £900,000 a year, compared with the £1,600,000 raised directly from parish rates.[16]

The effects of these disparities were most serious in the field of sanitation, where vestries had their most important responsibilities. Poorer vestries employed fewer sanitary inspectors, used part-time Medical Officers of Health, and had hardly any headquarters staff. Their dimly lit streets were cleaned less well and less often, and sanitary nuisances were left to pollute and infect poorer neighbourhoods. In 1885 the relatively well-off districts of St Giles and St Olave's (Southwark) employed about eight times as many sanitary inspectors (in relation to their population) as Bermondsey and Mile End, two of the poorest vestries. Rateable income was not the only factor, though, because St George-in-the-East, poorer than Bermondsey, employed six times as many inspectors.[17] And sometimes the vestries ran their parishes with more vigour and commitment than their many critics, their heads filled with Dickensian stereotypes, expected them to. In October 1883, in the aftermath of the shocking revelation of *The Bitter Cry of Outcast London*, Sir Charles Dilke, one of the strongest critics of the London government system, made a brief study of sanitary and housing conditions in some of the worst slum districts, hoping to gather ammunition against the vestries. Disappointingly, he found Shoreditch much improved, Limehouse neglected, but not to a culpable degree, Bermondsey managing to reduce its death rate, and Lambeth and St George-the-Martyr better than he expected. Only conditions in parts of Clerkenwell, revealed to him in an anonymous letter, gave Dilke the sort of damaging material he had been searching for, and he and his allies used it to damn the whole system.[18]

The truth was that vestry performance was patchy and variable, and that the vestries' failures, as one might expect, have made a deeper impression on the historical record than their successes. The readers of the *Lancet* were scandalized in January 1883 to hear that in nearly 200 of 525 houses that had been inspected in Whitechapel drinking water was polluted by contact with the drainage system, and many examples of vestry inaction and penny-pinching were exposed by the Royal Commission on the Housing of the Working Classes in 1884–5.[19] In the huge parish of St Pancras, for instance, an excellent record in building public baths and converting old graveyards into public gardens could hardly compensate for the persistent failure of its vestry (a mixture of publicans, bakers, builders, and miscellaneous tradesmen) to supply its Medical Officer with an adequate staff of sanitary inspectors or to implement the 1866 Sanitary Act rules on overcrowded lodging houses and multi-occupied houses. The smaller and poorer parish of St George-the-Martyr, Southwark, had made creditable efforts to improve sanitation after a scandalous typhus epidemic in 1864, but its failure to prevent gross overcrowding in the slums of Collier's Rents was sensationally exposed by Andrew Mearns in 1883. Since the powers available to the vestry only allowed it to demolish slums and sell the cleared land to housing charities whose new dwellings were too expensive for the evicted families to rent, the vestry could rightly claim that doing nothing was better than driving the slum population from one parish to another. The active and intelligent Shoreditch vestry encountered exactly the same problem when it tried to tackle overcrowded and insanitary slums using the housing legislation of the 1860s and 1870s (the Torrens and Cross Acts), and the medical officer of another well-run parish, St Marylebone, concluded in 1884 that the laws available to vestries could only make things worse for slum-dwellers. 'Not a house is rebuilt, not an area cleared, but their possibilities of existence are diminished, their livings made dearer and harder . . . until tenements are built in proportion to those demolished at low rents, it is not humane to press on large schemes.'[20]

The Board of Works

Many of the weaknesses of the vestries were repeated and intensified in the Metropolitan Board of Works, whose forty-six members generally included the longest-serving, oldest, and most conservative vestrymen. This small and close-knit body, not answerable to an electorate or to the political parties, attracted many accusations of jobbery and corruption, which, whether they were true or not, had a damaging and cumulative effect on its reputation. Yet the MBW had been given several important new powers and responsibilities since its creation in 1855, reflecting the growth in the scope of local government in the 1870s and 1880s. As well as its original responsibilities for building sewers and major roads, it had responsibility for putting out fires, clearing slums, and selling or renting the land to the builders of working-class dwellings, building Thames bridges and tunnels, inspecting theatres, music halls, and petrol and explosives stores, supervising child minders (or 'baby farmers') and animal keepers, sanctioning tramways, controlling dangerous structures, slaughterhouses, and dairies, supervising the width of new streets and the foundations of new buildings, and naming streets and numbering houses. Its rate income, which rose from about £300,000 in the 1860s to over £1 million in 1888, was collected by the vestries and district boards, with the City and the rich West End parishes paying the largest share. To neutralize the political hostility this might cause, the MBW spent most of its income on City and West End projects, leading the outer parishes like Woolwich and Hackney to question whether they were getting value for their money. Because the MBW was not directly elected, Parliament and the Treasury exercised a tight control over its borrowing and spending. This contributed to the Board's failure to win control of London's gas supply in 1875, and prevented it from buying London's water supply from the local private water companies, as 400 smaller local authorities had done, in 1878.[21] Neither of these vital services ever came under the direct control of London's local authority, though most of the members of the Metropolitan Water Board, which took over the assets of the private water companies in 1904, were London borough and County councillors.

One of the Metropolitan Board of Works' most important and costly duties was to construct new roads to ease the flow of goods and people through London's congested streets. One of its final achievements was to

build Charing Cross Road and Shaftesbury Avenue, linking Trafalgar
Square with Tottenham Court Road, and Piccadilly with New Oxford
Street and Bloomsbury. Like so many of the Board's enterprises, these were
impeded by its lack of power, money, and democratic authority. The two
roads, which were planned by Sir Joseph Bazalgette, the Board's famous
chief engineer, and sanctioned by Parliament in 1877, generally involved
following and widening existing roads. Charing Cross Road took Castle
Street as far north as Newport Street, cut across a squalid slum district
around Newport Market (an area of butcher's shops and slaughterhouses),
and joined Crown Street at a new junction, Cambridge Circus. There was
no question that these slums, which were described in a police report as 'a
reeking home of filthy vice', and the 'veritable focus of every danger which
can menace the health and social order of a city', deserved demolition, but
the Board was obliged by the 1877 Street Improvements Act to provide
land for rehousing over 10,000 displaced tenants. The Board was not
allowed to build the new housing itself, but had the very difficult task of
finding commercial or philanthropic builders who were prepared to buy
or rent the land, and build low-cost housing on it.[22] Shaftesbury Avenue
followed and widened existing streets, mainly King Street and Dudley
Street, to reach St Giles High Street, but then cut through what was
left of the St Giles slums – the Rookery – to reach New Oxford Street,
displacing many tenants. Where it met Piccadilly and Regent Street
Shaftesbury Avenue turned a rather shapely junction that deserved to be
called a Circus into an awkward one that did not. A few years later, in
1893, the junction was chosen as a site for Alfred Gilbert's lively memorial (now called 'Eros') to the great philanthropist Lord Shaftesbury, with
a fountain that soaked anyone who stood too near it. It took the MBW
and the government about eight years to agree on the Board's responsibility for the displaced tenants, and the two new roads were not opened
until 1886 and 1887, completing the street pattern of the modern West
End, just before the abolition of the Board.

Part One

WORKING LONDON

CHAPTER TWO

*

MAKING MONEY

Londoners in the 1880s might be forgiven for believing that their city was the centre of the world. London was the place from which the world's richest and most powerful country was governed, and from which its greatest empire was administered. This empire, as any reader of the *Illustrated London News* or the *Boy's Own Paper* knew, was growing in area and population by the year, especially in Africa. By 1911 it covered about 12 million square miles, over a fifth of the land earth's surface, and held about 400 million people, a quarter of the human race. London was a great imperial capital, and had begun to acquire since the 1860s a set of impressive public buildings and thoroughfares whose size and appearance matched its status. The Home and Colonial Offices, the India Office, the Foreign Office, the Albert Hall, the Royal Courts of Justice, the Natural History Museum, the Thames Embankment, and Hyde Park Corner were built or laid out between the 1860s and early 1880s, giving London – in places, at least – the appearance of an imperial capital. A few more streets and buildings with an imperial stamp, including Kingsway, Admiralty Arch, the Imperial Institute, Tower Bridge, the Admiralty extension, the Port of London Authority building, the re-fronted Buckingham Palace, and some magnificent hotels and department stores were built over the next thirty years, but elsewhere London retained much of its unplanned and accidental quality.

The Port of London

Those who wanted to feel a sense of London's world power might stroll along Whitehall or the Mall, but to truly understand it they had to take a cab or horse bus along the Strand and Fleet Street into the City, or take a steamer, as Henry James did in the 1880s, from Westminster Bridge to Greenwich. This was a journey, he said, 'that initiates you into

the duskiness, the blackness, the crowdedness, the intensely commercial
character of London'.

> Few European cities have a finer river than the Thames, but none
> certainly has expended more ingenuity in producing a sordid river
> front. For miles and miles you see nothing but the sooty backs of
> warehouses . . . Like so many aspects of English civilization that are
> untouched by elegance or grace, it has the merit of expressing some-
> thing very serious. Viewed in this intellectual light, the polluted river,
> the sprawling barges, the dead-faced warehouses, the frowsy people,
> the atmospheric impurities, become richly suggestive. It sounds rather
> absurd, but all this smudgy detail may remind you of nothing less
> than the wealth and power of the British Empire at large.[1]

London was the world's busiest port, and its wharves and warehouses were
piled high with commodities from every part of the world: tea, coffee,
sugar, spices, rubber, wool, silk, fur, ivory, feathers, chinaware, grain,
timber, meat, fruit, and so on. Tilbury, the last and easternmost of the
wet docks that handled about a half the shipping tonnage in the Thames
(the rest went to over 300 riverside wharves), was opened in 1886.
Since the docks were surrounded with warehouses and high-security walls,
much of this trade was not visible to ordinary Londoners, except for the
20,000 who worked (when they could) as dockers. Arthur Beavan, who
wrote *Imperial London* in 1901, described the vast array of goods stored
in its docks and warehouses.

> To stroll through miles of narrow alleys in these vast storerooms,
> between chests and half-chests, and boxes of tea from India, China
> and Ceylon, arranged as closely together as they can be, the atmos-
> phere heavy with the peculiar odour from their wrappers; to be
> shown floor after floor, covered with upright bags of fragrant cinna-
> mon and packages of nutmegs, mace, and cloves, is pleasant; and with
> a 'tasting order' to explore the labyrinths of the great wine-vaults,
> may produce an exhilarating effect; but by far the most interesting
> sight in these regions is the ivory warehouse at the London Docks.
>   Just prior to one of the four annual sales, is arranged in orderly
> lots on the floor of a great room, with alley-ways between them,
> rough ivory of every shape and size – whole elephant tusks, ponder-
> ous but symmetrical; others sawn in two pieces, the larger halves
> stacked like drain-pipes one upon the other; and Siberian ivory from
> extinct hairy mammoths . . . Here the solid teeth of numerous hip-

popotami, and in special lots are many gracefully curved tusks of the walrus . . . [2]

Statistics confirmed the evidence of the eyes and nose. Of the goods imported into England and Wales in 1891, 30 per cent (by weight) and 38 per cent (by value) came into London's docks and wharves, and the capital handled nearly 23 per cent (by value) of England's exports, even though it was not itself a great producer of goods for export. Nearly twenty years later, in 1910, the Port of London still handled a third (by value) of UK imports and 18.6 per cent of its home-produced exports. It could be said without exaggeration that almost every product or commodity that was traded in the early twentieth-century world, from motorcycles to ostrich feathers, came through London's docks or wharves. Its biggest imports were the things needed to feed its five, six, or seven million mouths: tea, sugar, wheat, butter, mutton, beef, fruit, cheese, and eggs. Next, there were the materials needed to keep Londoners dressed, and to supply London's (and England's) great clothing industries: leather, furs, skins and hides, cotton cloth, silks, jute, hemp, and wool. Wool, about 40 per cent of which was re-exported, was London's most valuable import by far, representing (in 1910) over 10 per cent of its foreign imports. Then there were the raw materials London needed for its multitude of manufacturing industries: caoutchouc (unvulcanized rubber), metals (lead, copper, iron, and above all tin for London's box makers), paper, straw, wood, oil, tallow, dyestuffs, and chemicals. And London was still a great imperial entrepôt, as it had been since the late seventeenth century, handling over half of the foreign and colonial goods brought into the UK for transhipment to overseas destinations. In 1910 these re-exported foreign goods, especially cocoa, coffee, drugs, gum, hemp, jute, leather, copper, tin, nuts, rum, silk goods, spices, tallow, tea, tobacco, and wool, represented about 40 per cent of the value of London's export trade.[3]

London's position as an international port declined a little in the 1880s and 1890s, in the face of competition from Hamburg, Antwerp, Amsterdam, Rotterdam, Liverpool, New York, and other growing ports, but steadied after 1900. London merchants had an impressive ability to find new commodities and markets to replace those they were losing, and to establish London as the dominant port for goods of which it was not the major producer or consumer. London merchants were experienced, skilful, and adaptable, moving from one commodity or trading partner to another as the pattern of trade changed. There was a general movement out of trade with Europe and the West Indies towards trade with Australasia and Africa, and away from wines and spirits, grains, and textile fibres and into furs, timber, rubber, tropical produce, and miscellaneous manufactures. The movement of the Samuel brothers from shells to petroleum (without changing their company's name from Shell Transport and Trading to something more appropriate) is a famous example of this creative flexibility, and the decision in 1888 of Edward Fyffe, a Fenchurch Street tea merchant, to start importing a few bananas, is another.[4]

Several factors explain London's continuing success as a centre of world trade, despite growing competition from Germany and the USA. The presence of large numbers of settlers of British origin in some of the world's most important trading countries, including those, like Argentina, that were not part of Britain's 'formal' empire, was an important advantage, and Britain's willingness to import, free of protective duties, vast amounts of goods from all over the world was another. There were practical advantages for countries like Canada, India, Australia, Argentina, and New Zealand in buying their manufactured imports from the biggest buyer of their raw material exports, and trade and common culture built a bond of trust and understanding. Britain had a further advantage in its dominance of international shipping. The mid-nineteenth-century American challenge had been seen off, and by 1907 the British merchant fleet, at 10.7 million tons, was more than twice the combined tonnage of its three nearest competitors, Germany (2.5 million tons), France (1.4 million tons), and the USA (1 million tons). Sixty per cent of Argentina's maritime trade was carried in British ships on the eve of the Great War. Not only did this predominance give Britain and its leading port a great advantage in winning the lion's share of world trade, but it also underpinned London's control of world shipping. In marine insurance the power of the Lloyd's insurance market was unchallenged, and the sale and chartering of ships to carry cargoes throughout the world was dominated by the members of the Baltic Exchange, who moved into their grand new building on St Mary Axe in 1903. Recognizing London's primacy, shipping brokers and owners in other British and European centres set up offices, or appointed agents, in London. These shipping and insurance services, which were based on two centuries of experience and an incomparable worldwide network of agents and informants (communicating with London by electric telegraph), were an important contributor to the invisible earnings that turned Britain's large trading deficit in merchandise (usually between £90 and £170 million a year) into a healthy balance of payments surplus that rose from about £50 million in 1883 to over £200 million in 1913. Thanks to these 'invisible earnings', of which a large proportion were generated by the City of London, Britain's trading position in 1913, the end of a period usually described as one of relative economic decline, was much stronger than it had ever been before.[5]

London's unequalled network of international connections, along with its shipping and financial services and the skills of its merchants, encouraged exporters to send their goods to London for sale and transhipment to other destinations in Europe or elsewhere, sustaining its role as an entrepôt. City trading houses had the skills and capital to take the risk that the price of a commodity might fall or that customers might not be found quickly. Producers who were not sure where their goods might eventually be sold were most likely to send them to London, where transhipment was easy, information was excellent, and credit could be found more easily and cheaply than anywhere else. Australian wool came into London when the producers were ready to sell it, and was sold on when the manufacturers in Bradford and Huddersfield needed it. Sometimes ownership of the stored goods, whether they were wool, tea, coffee, carpets, copra, or copper, changed hands between several City dealers without leaving the warehouse. These transactions often took place in the many commodity exchanges that were scattered around and near the City: the Baltic Exchange for grain, timber, and Russian goods, the Coal Exchange in Lower Thames Street, the Wool Exchange in Coleman Street, the Hop Exchange in Southwark, the Metal Exchange (which moved from rooms over a hat shop in Lombard Court to a new building in Whittington Avenue in 1882), the two Corn Exchanges in Mark Lane, the Hudson's Bay Company in Lime Street for fur, and the Commercial Sale Rooms in Mincing Lane for a range of foreign and colonial produce, including sugar, tea, coffee, rice, jute, oils, spices, wine, spirits, drugs, feathers, sarsaparilla, 'rhubarb in tin-lined cases; horns containing the excretion of the civet-cat; camphor, honey, chincona, shellac, peppermint, the deadly strophanthus from Zambesi and . . . other strange and unfamiliar products of distant lands'.[6] The unfortunate Paul Bultitude, who suffered the humiliation of being turned into a schoolboy in F. Anstey's comic novel of 1882, *Vice-Versa*, made his living on the Mincing Lane Commercial Exchange.

Smaller producers relied on the skills, information and connections of City dealers to find the best markets for their goods. This is why the City, especially two streets north of Cheapside, Wood Street and Lawrence Lane, was one of the centres of the British textile trade. The biggest City firm,

Cooke's of St Paul's, handled far more business than the top Manchester company, John Rylands, and London's second biggest textile merchant, Morley's of Wood Street, sold a tenth of Britain's hosiery and knitted goods. The dominance of the Wood Street wholesalers was only threatened after about 1900, when large textile manufacturers started selling branded goods directly to retailers, especially the big London department stores.[7]

The World's Banker

London's control of international trade did not depend only on ships and cargoes entering its port. Just as important as its physical trade was the 'office trade', in which the worldwide movement of goods was controlled by City dealers and brokers receiving information and sending instructions by electric telegraph. The telegraph made it easier for cargoes to be directed to the best markets without passing through London or any other intermediary, but it also created a vital strategic role for dealers at the centre of a worldwide web of commercial information. A London coffee broker explained the value of his services to a São Paulo producer in 1903: 'We can pretty well tell you with one minute's reference anybody's price in any market in any day in any year.'[8] Britain was not a great consumer of coffee, but the City managed about 30 per cent of the world's coffee trade in 1909. The City controlled the world's rubber trade, although the USA was the dominant importer, and even the trade in manila between the Philippines and the USA was run from London. Naturally, other cities dominated particular trades (Liverpool for cotton, Newcastle for coal), but London controlled far more commodities than any of its rivals, and had a hand in almost every trade. The concentration of information, money, and expertise in London gave it unrivalled economies of scale, and attracted merchants, brokers, bankers, and agents from all over the world, redoubling its influence and power.

The City's dominant position in British banking, which had been weakened in the industrial revolution by the rise of local country banks, was restored in the nineteenth century by the local banks' need for a convenient intermediary between one region and another, a place in which funds and information could be exchanged. The introduction of the telegraph strengthened London's central role, as did the growing importance of London bills of exchange as a form of currency. When local banks merged into stronger regional combines after the Companies Act of 1862, they often moved their headquarters to London, as did the National Provincial in 1868 and the Midland in 1891. Lloyds, a major Birmingham bank with long-standing London connections, joined the London Clearing House in 1884, but only moved its headquarters to London in 1910. From the 1880s London-based banking grew rapidly, partly at the expense of local banking. By 1895 the clearings of London-based banks were nearly twenty times as great as those of provincial banks, and by 1911 London-based banks owned over half the bank branches in Britain, holding two-thirds of the nation's deposits.[9]

By the 1880s the City of London was, more than ever before, the undisputed centre of international credit and investment, Britain's and the world's indispensable banker and investor. The severe and prolonged damage done to the Bank of France and the Paris Bourse by the Franco-Prussian War of 1870 and the Commune of 1871 had removed London's only serious rival as an international financial centre. Recognizing this, European and American finance houses opened branches in the City. Although the 'City' is often taken as the ultimate symbol of top-hatted Englishness, its leading families – Rothschild, Ralli, Hambro, Cassel, Kleinwort, Morgan, Schroder, and the rest – could hardly have been drawn from a more international background. The spread of the telegraph, which placed London at the centre of a cable network that stretched, by 1872, as far as Japan and Australia, provided the flow of information through which London-based financiers could exercise their worldwide control, and the London bill of exchange was trusted across the globe.

The bill of exchange, a promise from a specific bank to pay the holder a particular sum on a certain date, was the currency through which the City financed and controlled world trade. Bills of exchange issued by London banks, a safe and easily negotiable alternative to cash, had been the most common form of currency for business and industrial use in Britain throughout the nineteenth century, and towards the end of the century, when the growing use of cheques reduced their domestic usefulness, their importance in international trade between new industrial nations and primary producers grew. Because of the universal use of the London bill, a large proportion of worldwide trading debts were settled in the City. As Sir Felix Schuster, the Frankfurt-trained Governor of the Union Bank of London, put it in 1903, 'the coffee that is shipped from Brazil into France or Italy, the cotton from New Orleans to Poland, sulphur from Sicily to

the United States, and agricultural machinery from the United States to the
River Plate, all these trades find their Clearing House in Lombard Street'.[10]

One of the institutions essential to London's national and international
dominance was the Stock Exchange, a large but outwardly unimpressive
building between Throgmorton Street and Old Broad Street, just to the
east of the Bank of England. The Stock Exchange had prospered by funding central government debt, and meeting the need for capital of a few
large-scale enterprises, including canal, railway, water, and gas companies.
Manufacturing enterprises and smaller companies did not generally seek
or need loans raised in the City, but local authorities, including the
Metropolitan Board of Works and the London County Council, did. In
addition, the overseas demand for loans raised in the City was great and
growing. On average, over 4 per cent of national income was invested overseas between 1880 and 1913, and by 1913 a third of Britain's wealth was
invested abroad. Britain's earnings from interest on these overseas investments tripled from under £70 million to £200 million a year between
1884 and 1913, helping (along with other invisibles) to convert a deficit
on visible trade into a large balance of payments surplus. About two-thirds
of this overseas investment went to Australasia and North and South
America, mostly to fund public or private infrastructure projects such as
railways, roads, tramways, water, sewerage, and power systems, or large
mining or industrial enterprises. The City's biggest merchant banks,
Rothschild, Barings, Kleinworts, and J. P. Morgan, along with the Bank of
England, the London and Westminster Bank, and the Crown Agents handled the most important loan issues.[11]

London's role as a port and information centre, in physical and office
trade, overseas investment, insurance, banking, shipping, broking, and
arbitrage (exploiting the price differences between the London and foreign
stock exchanges) gave it a unique position at the centre of international
trade and finance. An exchange between the 1886–7 Royal Commission
on Precious Metals and Bertram Currie, one of the City's most powerful
and intelligent bankers, captures the general view of London's role in the
world economy. Sir Thomas Farrer, later a London County Councillor, was
asking the questions:

> I want to understand distinctly what is the position of London as
> regards the financial centre of the world. Is it that is it a sort of clear-
> ing house to which all debts are referred and through which they are
> paid? – Yes; I think its peculiar position is, that it is the only centre

upon which bills [of exchange] from all parts of the world can be drawn. Wherever there is an exchange of any sort there is an exchange upon London. Bills upon London are always in the market; everybody has debts to pay in London, therefore everybody wants bills on London.

Just as it is the centre of the business of England it is the centre of the business of the world? – It is.

Bills from all parts can be sent to London and exchanged there? – Yes. A New York merchant wishing to buy goods in the East is obliged to supply himself with a credit upon England. This is distinctly to the benefit of London.

London becomes a sort of bank for the whole world? – Yes.

London is a sort of centre of banking which never existed before? – Yes.[12]

At night the City of London was almost deserted, except for street cleaners and carts and wagons on their way to the docks and wholesale markets. Its resident night-time population, which had been over 120,000 earlier in the century, fell from 50,000 to under 20,000 between 1881 and 1911. But every weekday morning the Square Mile was occupied by a great army of commuters – its daytime working population was 260,000 in 1881, and 364,000 (more than the population of Bristol) in 1911. These workers were employed (in 1909) in almost 40,000 manufacturing, commercial, financial, legal, retailing, and other firms. Many of them were manual workers, builders, printers, messengers, clerks, typists, and retail and catering workers, but a great and growing number were making substantial incomes from the commercial and financial work of the City, as lawyers, bankers, accountants, brokers, underwriters, merchants, agents, wholesalers, warehousemen, shippers, and so on. In 1905, 5,567 of them were members of the Stock Exchange, and over 2,000 belonged to the Baltic Exchange.

Old and New Wealth

Despite the declining prosperity of agriculture, the richest individuals in England in the 1880s were still the great landowners. Some of the very richest of these, including the Dukes of Westminster and Bedford and Viscount Portman, were the owners of large estates in London, which continued to yield high rents when farmland did not. The richest non-landowners in England, those who died with estates worth over £500,000, had more often made their fortunes in finance and commerce (the sectors dominated by London) than in manufacturing or mining. Of the 101 non-landed millionaires who died between 1900 and 1919, 54 were in commerce and finance, in London or elsewhere, and among the 260 half-millionaires, nearly half were in these sectors. Some of the rest made their money in industries and trades that were well represented in London, such as brewing, publishing, and food. London brewing millionaires and half-millionaires living (or dying) in London in the 1880s and 1890s include James Watney, Sir Henry Meux, and Robert Hanbury (all of whom died in 1883–4), Spencer Charrington, Robert Courage, Charles Combe, John Henry Buxton, and Samuel Whitbread. From publishing, there were Edward Lloyd, of the *Illustrated London News* and *Lloyd's Weekly News*, Sir George Newnes, Alfred and Harold Harmsworth (creators of the *Daily Mail* and *Daily Mirror*), George Smith (publisher of the *Dictionary of National Biography*), and Sir Cyril Arthur Pearson (who gave us the *Daily Express*).[13]

London's greatest strengths were in finance, merchant banking, insurance, trade, and retailing, and these sectors account for the City of London's impressive concentration of the rich and the very rich in the late nineteenth century. Of the 124 urban millionaires dying in Britain between 1880 and 1914, 35 worked in the City and 26 in the rest of London, and of the 311 half-millionaires, 127 lived in London.[14] Many of London's wealthiest merchant bankers were Jews: the Rothschilds, headed between 1879 and 1915 by Sir Nathan Meyer Rothschild; the Stern brothers, Herman and James, and their sons Herbert and Sydney, Baron Wandsworth; the Raphaels, the Montagues, the Samuels, the Sassoons, the Bisshoffschiems, and the Hambros. Other London millionaires, including the Schroeders and Kleinworts, were of German origin, and some, like Walter Hayes Burns of J. S. Morgan and Co., were American. One of the richest London merchant-banking families, the Barings, took a tumble in 1890, when their firm had to be rescued from bankruptcy by the Bank of England and a City consortium, but there were still plenty of wealthy and titled Barings in the City at the end of the century. The richest Londoner of all was the untitled and hardly remembered merchant banker and warehouseman Charles Morrison, who left over £11 million (five times as much as Sir Nathan Meyer Rothschild) on his death in 1909.[15]

Most of those who had not earned their money in London (or not earned it at all) came there to spend it or flaunt it. Great landowners and their families spent the spring and early summer Season (March or April to late July) in London's West End, and spent money there on entertainment, luxury goods, transport, accommodation, and professional services. The radical politician and social critic Charles Masterman included an interesting chapter on the wealthy, 'the Conquerors', in his 1909 book *The Condition of England*. To him, the London Season was

> an aggregation of clever, agreeable, often lovable people, whose material wants were satisfied by the labour of unknown workers in all the world, trying with a desperate seriousness to make something of a life spared the effort of wage-earning. It is built up and maintained in an artificial, and probably a transitory, security – security which has never been extended in the world's history to more than a few generations.

London's aristocratic elite, Masterman conceded, devoted some time and much money to philanthropic enterprises, 'shepherding its friends into drawing-room meetings to listen to some attractive speaker – an actor, a Labour Member, a professional humorist – pleading for pity to the poor. It discusses the possibility of social upheavals in that dim, silent, encompassing life in which all its activities are embedded – the incalculable populations, which set the society that matters in the midst of a rude and multitudinous society that does not count'. But the overriding aim of those who came to London for that 'orgy of human intercourse' known as the Season was to fill every moment with social activity involving others of the same class.

> For these months nobody is ever alone; nobody ever pauses to think; no one ever attempts to understand. All quick and novel sensations are pressed into the service of an ever more insistent demand for new things . . . What passes for British Art in a Royal Academy and other exhibitions; the Opera, dragging European singers to stimulate an audience numbed by the whirl of circumstance . . . But for the most part, it is talk – talk – talk; talk at luncheon and tea and dinner; talk at huge, undignified crowded receptions, where each talker is disturbed by the consciousness that his neighbour is derirous of talking to others; talk at dances and at gatherings, far into the night; with the mornings devoted to preparation for further talking in the day to come.[16]

Membership of London 'Society' was not confined to the landed classes, and new members had long been recruited from the wealthiest

London families. By the 1880s and 1890s the entry of City and urban wealth into London Society was no longer a reinforcement, but a conquest. Thanks to the decline in agricultural prices and rents since the 1870s, landed estates were no longer the great source of income and financial security they had once been, and the balance of power and numbers was swinging away from the old wealth and towards the new. London Society, measured by the number of wives and debutantes invited to Queen Victoria's formal gatherings, known as Drawing Rooms, was about three times as big in the 1890s as it had been in the 1840s, and its member-ship, overwhelmingly aristocratic at the start of her reign, was almost equally split between landed and urban wealth by the 1890s. Of the roughly 900 debutantes and wives invited to Drawing Rooms in the early 1890s, less than a half were from titled or landed families, compared with three-quarters in the 1850s. Even a title no longer implied a landed back-ground, since about a third of new peers created between 1885 and 1914 were businessmen. By the 1890s London Society was, in Beatrice Potter's words, the 'most gigantic of all social clubs', the main qualification for membership of which was 'the possession of some form of power over other people'. Landlords still set the social standard, but they had to share their social and cultural events with a crowd of lawyers, publishers, civil servants, merchants, bankers, retailers, and brewers, people for whom London was not a seasonal resort but a permanent home.[17]

Looking back in 1910 on her long career as a society hostess, Lady Dorothy Nevill concluded that 'Society, in the old sense of the term, may be said, I think, to have come to an end in the "eighties" of the last century.' 'Birth today is of small account, whilst wealth wields an unquestioned sway . . . The conquest of the West End by the City has brought a complete change of tone.' Hostesses like Lady Dorothy could of course make sure that their own lunch and dinner tables were not invaded by self-made men who talked about share prices. Her fellow host-ess Lady St Helier recalled that her Sunday luncheons in her house in Charles Street in the 1880s were 'small, but her guests were well-chosen, and no one was invited without having some claim to distinction . . . as she received all the best representatives of every kind of society, her house was one of the most agreeable in London'. Virginia Woolf, reviewing Lady Dorothy's own memoirs, took a less charitable view of a woman who 'lived for eighty-seven years and did nothing but put food in her mouth and slip gold through her fingers'.[18]

A degree of charm, tact, and 'good breeding' was generally expected in this world, but it was not essential. Unless your conduct had been particularly disgraceful, money would get you almost anywhere. In the 1890s the readiness of London Society to absorb the newly wealthy, regardless of their style or breeding, was tested by the arrival of the 'Randlords', a group of millionaires who had made their fortunes in South African gold and diamond mining, and especially in the boom of 1894–5. The most unappealing of these men was probably Joseph Robinson, who bought a lease on the Earl of Derby's Park Lane mansion, Dudley House, in 1895, and decorated it with Rembrandts and Constables. His neighbours in Park Lane included Alfred Beit, Cecil Rhodes' partner in de Beers, the diamond company, who built Aldford House, and the famous Barney Barnato, who built (but never occupied) a palace on the corner of Stanhope Gate. Barney Barnato was an East End Jew who had been a prizefighter and music-hall turn before making a vast fortune in the Kimberley diamond mines, redoubling it in the 1894–5 stock market boom in South African gold mines, and losing much of it when the shares collapsed in 1896. After Barnato had drowned himself – mad, drunk, or both – in 1897 the house was bought by the banker Sir Edward Sassoon. A few streets away, in Bath House, on the corner of Piccadilly and Bolton Street, lived Julius Wernher, a German who had made his fortune in South African mines in partnership with Rhodes and Beit.

Unlike Barnato, who was as rough as one of his newly mined diamonds, Beit and Wernher were sophisticated recruits to the London social scene, patrons of the arts and philanthropists on a heroic scale. Wernher gave £500,000 towards the establishment of Imperial College in 1907 and thereby earned the friendship of Sidney and Beatrice Webb (previously Beatrice Potter), who were involved in creating the new institution. The Webbs invited Wernher, 'a heavy, good-natured, public-spirited and scientific-minded millionaire', to meet their intellectual friends, Bernard Shaw, Harley Granville-Barker, Lord Lytton, Arthur Balfour, and Bertrand Russell, and in return Wernher invited them to meet his rich ones, at Bath House. 'Though our host was superior to his wealth', Beatrice Webb recorded, 'our hostess and her guests were dominated by it . . . The company was composed, either of financial magnates, or of able hangers-on of magnates. The setting in the way of rooms and flowers and fruit and food and wine and music, and pictures and works of art, was hugely overdone – wealth – wealth – wealth – was screamed aloud wherever one turned. And all the company were living up to it, or bowing down before it.'[19]

Men who had risen to the top of London society through business

acumen rather than accident of birth were especially welcome at
Marlborough House, the London home of Edward, Prince of Wales.
Edward did not share high society's distaste for German Jewish millionaires, and made a great friend of Baron Maurice de Hirsch, an immensely
wealthy Bavarian banker and philanthropist, whom he first met in 1886.
When Hirsch died in 1896 the Prince began an even closer friendship
with Hirsch's executor, Ernest Cassel, who became his financial adviser and
intimate confidant. Cassel, a German Jew who took British citizenship
in 1880, made a vast fortune in his twenties and thirties through his
brilliance as a banker and overseas investor, an example of City of London
finance at its best. No other man rivalled Cassel in his closeness to Edward
as Prince or King, but several other businessmen and financiers were
members of his inner circle: the Rothschilds, the bankers Albert, Arthur,
and Reuben Sassoon, Louis Bisshoffschiem and Horace Farquhar, the
philanthropic grocer Sir Thomas Lipton, and the furniture manufacturer
and retailer Sir Blundell Maple.[20]

A great deal was written in the 1880s and 1890s (and ever since) about
the poverty of London's lower classes, but we should not forget that this
was a city which generated, accumulated, attracted, and consumed wealth
on an unprecedented scale. In *Culture and Anarchy* Matthew Arnold had
denounced London, in the words Cato is said to have used of Rome, as a
place of *'publice egestas, privatim opulentia'* (public penury, private luxury), but
in Mayfair, St James's, Knightsbridge, Belgravia, and Hampstead the opu-
lence was public as well as private, and in Bermondsey and Bethnal Green
the poverty did not stop at the street door. London's vast wealth came from
its trading and financial activities, but also from its huge number of manufacturing, catering, and retailing businesses, its unparalleled concentration
of well-paid professionals, entertainers, investors, and public servants. In
1891 nearly 44 per cent of England's 2,450 joint-stock companies had
their offices in London. London's schedule D tax assessment (covering
trades and professions, public companies and foreign dividends, but not
the salaries of government employees) in 1879–80 was 10 per cent greater
than that of Britain's twenty-eight major provincial towns, though their
combined population was 5.6 million, compared to London's 3.3 million.
The City of London, the powerhouse of London's prosperity, paid more
tax that year than Manchester, Birmingham, Liverpool, Glasgow, Sheffield,
Leeds, Newcastle, and Hull combined. Ten years later the middle-class
citizens of the County of London (those earning over the £150 a year
income-tax threshold) paid 42 per cent of the income tax levied in England

and Wales, though London had only 15 per cent of the country's population.[21] Charles Booth calculated the wealth of the rich by the number of servants they employed, and using this standard we find in London a vast and prosperous propertied class, rich enough to employ as many domestic servants as there were people in Edinburgh, Leeds, or Sheffield. Measured by this or any other reasonable yardstick, the City and County of London contained a concentration of wealth and income unequalled anywhere else in the late Victorian world.

*

CHAPTER THREE

LANDLORD AND TENANT

How the Poor Lived

On 2 June 1883 readers of an illustrated London weekly paper, the *Pictorial World*, 'a class not generally given to the study of low life', were presented with the first of a series of articles called 'How the Poor Live'. The writer was George R. Sims, who was better known as 'Dagonet', the author of a light weekly column in the *Sunday Referee*, 'Mustard and Cress', and for his popular melodramas for the London stage. Sims had already tackled the subject of London poverty in his very successful play, *The Lights o' London*, which ran for almost a year in the Princess's Theatre in 1881, and in his sentimental dramatic ballads, which had sold 100,000 copies by 1879. Sims had dealt with questions of hunger and bad housing in verse in 'Billy's Rose' and 'In the Workhouse: Christmas Day', but in 'How the Poor Live' he gave a more serious account of these problems, and drew political lessons from what he had seen. Sims had been on 'a journey with pen and pencil', he said, 'into a dark continent that is within easy walking distance of the General Post Office', crossing London Bridge into darkest Southwark. His companion in this dangerous mission was the artist Frederick Barnard, who contributed gloomy and powerful drawings to illustrate the occasional liveliness and the overwhelming misery of slum life. Sims tried to enliven his weekly denunciation of the conditions of London poverty with passages of cockney dialogue and touching personal histories, but he had to admit that the story he had to tell was a repulsive and monotonous one.

> The Mint and the Borough present scenes awful enough in all conscience to be worthy of earnest study; but scene after scene is the same. Rags, dirt, filth, wretchedness, the same figures, the same faces, the same old story of one room unfit for habitation yet inhabited by eight or nine people, the same complaint of ruinous rent absorbing

three-fourths of the toiler's weekly wage, the same shameful neglect by the owner of the property of all sanitary precautions, rotten floors, oozing walls, broken windows, crazy staircases, tileless roofs, and in and around the dwelling-place of hundreds of honest citizens the nameless abominations which could only be set forth were we contributing to the *Lancet* instead of the PICTORIAL WORLD; – these are the things which confront us, whether we linger in the Mint or seek fresh fields in the slums that lie around Holborn, or wind our adventurous footsteps towards the network of dens that lie within a stone's-throw of our great National Theatre, Drury Lane.[1]

Sims provided his readers with graphic descriptions of revolting rooms, broken and dangerous stairways, filthy water butts, hideous lodging houses, babies left in the care of four-year-olds, diseased and starving families barely clinging to life, and corpses lying in crowded rooms until money could be raised to bury them.

One of the worst features of slum life, in Sims' view, was that it forced the honest poor into association with criminals, and made it almost impossible to raise decent children. Ill-judged laws allowing the Metropolitan Board of Works to demolish unfit housing without replacing it had only made things worse:

The poor – the honest poor – have been driven by the working of the Artizans' Dwellings Acts, and the clearance of rookery after rookery, to come and herd with thieves and wantons, to bring up their children in the last Alsatias, where lawlessness and violence still reign supreme . . . The worst effect of this system of Packing the Poor is the moral destruction of the next generation. Whatever it costs us to remedy the disease we shall gain in decreased crime and wickedness.

Furthermore, the poor could not travel to the suburbs in search of cheaper homes, even if the nature of their work allowed it, because of the high cost of transport. 'They herd together all in closely packed quarters because they must be where they can get to the dock, the yard, the wharf, and the warehouses without expense. The highest earnings of this class is rarely above sixteen shillings a week, and that, with four or five shillings for rent, leaves very little margin where the family is large. The omnibus and the train are the magicians which will eventually bid the rookeries disappear, but the services of these magicians cost money, and there is none to spare in the pockets of the poor.'[2]

The most hopeful sign that Sims could see, apart from the essential kindness that many people in the lowest depths of degradation showed to each other, was the impact of compulsory universal elementary education. Education could counteract the vicious influence of slum society on its children, and give members of the next generation a chance to develop into good citizens. The problem here was that acute poverty made it difficult for the very needy to take advantage of elementary schools. Many parents could not afford the fees (a few pence a week until 1891), and they often relied upon their children as breadwinners or babysitters. Since hungry or starving children were unlikely to pass the tests (fifth standard) that would allow them to leave school before they were thirteen, the most their parents could hope for was that the School Board panel would recognize their hardship and allow their children to spend their last school years as half-time scholars. Sims was full of praise for those few schools that provided crèches for toddlers, and for the charity that supplied school dinners for poor pupils.

Pictorial World readers donated about £40 to solve these problems, but Sims dismissed the value of the charitable solution, and called instead for a legislative attack on slum landlords and unfit property, the construction at public expense of cheap but decent tenement blocks with some sheds for barrows and costermongers' stock, and a system of subsidized trains and trams to encourage the poor to break free from the stranglehold of inner-city landlords by moving to the suburbs. In fact a law passed in 1883 increased the availability of cheap early morning trains for poorer commuters. Sims criticized previous legislation, especially the 1875 Artisans' and Labourers' Dwellings Act, for allowing the Metropolitan Board of Works to demolish slums without ensuring that the new homes built on the cleared sites (often by housing charities) were cheap enough for the class that had been evicted. The prosperity of Victorian London, far from benefiting the lowest classes, had evicted, isolated, and defeated them. 'It is the increased wealth of this mighty city which has driven the poor back inch by inch, until we find them to-day herding together, packed like herrings in a barrel, neglected and despised . . . It is the increased civilisation of this marvellous age which has made life a victory only for the strong . . . and left the weak, the poor, and the ignorant to work out in their proper persons the theory of the survival of the fittest to its bitter end.'

From timely reform, Sims argued, the well off would gain much more than moral satisfaction. The rookeries supplied their servants, who might bring disease and immorality into respectable households, and the next generation of working men and women. Most important, the poor, who had borne their sufferings till now with docility, might soon rise up and seize what had not been given to them. 'This mighty mob of famished, diseased, and filthy helots is getting dangerous, physically, morally, politically dangerous. The barriers that have kept it back are rotten and giving way . . . and its lawless armies may sally forth and give us a taste of the lesson the mob has tried to teach now and again in Paris.' We should not wait for a hungry dog to growl before giving it a bone, nor for the poor 'to start a crusade of their own, to demonstrate in Trafalgar Square, and to hold meetings in Hyde Park'. Three years later, as we shall see, Sims' prognostications were almost borne out by events in Trafalgar Square.

Sims pursued his crusade with another set of articles, which he called 'Horrible London', in the important and quite widely read Liberal newspaper the *Daily News*, and called upon others to take up the campaign. The most effective answer to his call came from the London Congregational Union. Its secretary, the Rev. Andrew Mearns, helped by James Munro and W. C. Preston, produced a sensational penny pamphlet, *The Bitter Cry of Outcast London*. The pamphlet borrowed material from Sims, repeated all his arguments and remedies, and drew its detailed accounts of slum life from Colliers Rents, off the Borough High Street, a part of Southwark which Sims had also investigated. But it contributed the weight of a reputable religious organization, and added shocking detail to Sims' hints of sexual malpractice in single-room dwellings: 'Incest is common; and no form of vice and sensuality causes surprise or attracts attention.'

Most important of all, *The Bitter Cry* was reprinted in one of London's most influential newspapers, the *Pall Mall Gazette*. London had six significant evening papers in 1883, most of which sought their readers among the well-off members of the West End clubs, London's traditional political class. In August 1883 John (later Viscount) Morley, having won a seat in Parliament, handed over the editorship of the *Pall Mall Gazette* to his deputy, W. T. Stead, an energetic radical who had learned his trade on the *Darlington Northern Echo*. Under Stead's editorship, which lasted until 1890, the *Pall Mall Gazette* broke away from the stuffy 'Clubland' approach of existing newspapers, and pioneered a more sensational, readable, and campaigning style that was generally called the New Journalism. Stead adapted the traditional political emphasis of the press to meet the tastes of a larger public, people who could read, think, and vote, but who were interested in sport, gossip, interviews (an American idea), scandal, and sexual misdemeanours (condemning them, not committing them), as well as parliamentary debates. Even Stead's death, on the *Titanic* in 1912, was perfectly suited to the *Pall Mall Gazette* treatment.

Like Sims, Stead was not a laissez-faire Gladstonian Liberal, but a radical advocate of state intervention in defence of the poor, and he decided to rescue *The Bitter Cry* from obscurity by printing and publicizing it in his paper. By doing this Stead started a debate in newspapers, periodicals, and the two Houses of Parliament. Edward, Prince of Wales, Queen Victoria's hedonistic and over-fed eldest son, was so moved by what he had read that on 18 February 1884 he joined Lord Carrington and the government's Chief Medical Officer, Dr Buchanan, on a tour of the slums of St Pancras and Holborn. Dressed as working men, the three explorers dismissed their police escort and went down some of the worst slum alleys in the district. In one of these they found a squalid room in which a starving woman and her three shivering and malnourished children were cowering on a pile of rags. Edward was on the point of tossing a handful of gold sovereigns to the woman, but his companions warned him that if he did so the frenzied slum-dwellers might tear him limb from limb. A few days later, in the only significant speech he ever made in the House of Lords, the Prince spoke of what he had seen, and of the urgent need for reform.[3] All this helped to create the public and political pressure that led Gladstone to set up a Royal Commission on the Housing of the Working Classes in 1884, with the Prince, Lord Carrington, Cardinal Manning, and Lord Salisbury (the Conservative Party leader and next Prime Minister) among its members. This in turn produced a report in 1885 which confirmed many of Sims' and Mearns' conclusions, and led to the passing of the Housing of the Working Classes Act, which allowed (but did not compel) local authorities, including the Metropolitan Board of Works, to raise loans to build working-class homes on cleared land, and rent them at fair but unsubsidized rents. This Act, with another in 1890, created a legal framework in which the London County Council (LCC) could start building blocks of decent council flats in the 1890s.

Slum Landlords

After the First World War municipal housing replaced privately rented accommodation as the most important type of working-class housing in London. But before 1914, in spite of the much-praised and much-studied work of municipal and philanthropic house-builders, the very great majority of Londoners still rented their homes from private landlords. In Sims' account, the slum landlords were like villains in a melodrama, neglecting repairs, seizing the furniture of rent defaulters, wringing the last penny out of defenceless tenants. Sims' artist pictured a landlord in a glossy top hat, with a gold watch-chain across his fat chest, a haughty expression on his face, and 'an air of wealth and good living all over him'. We should not accept this pantomime character as an accurate depiction of the owners of cheap housing. George Bernard Shaw, a struggling novelist who made a living by writing anonymous literary reviews for the *Pall Mall Gazette* between 1885 and 1888, was moved by *The Bitter Cry*, and inspired by it (among other influences) to begin his first play in 1884. The play, *Widowers' Houses*, which was not completed or performed until 1892, was a lesson in Fabian socialism, which suggested that slum landlords were not full-time villains but ordinary middle-class investors, drawing an income from property or mortgages instead of railway stock or the government's Consolidated Fund (Consols). The play showed (as Shaw put it) 'middle-class respectability and younger son gentility fattening on the poverty of the slum as flies fatten on filth', and ran for two nights.[4]

Much of the land of late Victorian London was owned by very substantial landlords, either aristocratic or farming families whose landed estates had been built over as London spread, or institutions such as the Church, the City Corporation, or various well-endowed schools and colleges (Eton, Westminster, and Dulwich Colleges, for instance). The Prince of Wales, as he confessed in a speech to working men when he was opening an early LCC housing estate in Bethnal Green in 1900, was a major slum landlord in Lambeth. In general these big landowners did not build and manage their own houses, but leased plots of land to speculative builders ('speculative' because they built without a specific client in mind), who built houses (often with capital from a building society mortgage) and rented them out. The rents collected by the owner had to pay interest on the mortgage, ground rent to the freeholder, rates to the local authority, and perhaps the fees of an agent or rent-collector, as well as a return on the owner's investment. If the owner wanted good tenants who would pay on time and not damage the property, he had to keep the house in good condition and set money aside for repairs and redecoration. According to one observer, the landlord does 'not make a definite attempt to exterminate vermin unless he expects a tenant of a distinctly superior class'. The owners of bad houses in undesirable streets, which could only attract the poorest tenants, were unlikely to spend money on improvements which

would increase their rents to a level their tenants could not afford, and
expected to suffer losses when their tenants defaulted on their rents and
(in the language of the day) 'did a moonlight flit'. The rents a landlord
could charge depended on the quality and location of his property, the
state of the housing market, and the degree of prosperity of the economic
group from which his tenants were drawn. When a building boom had
created a glut of empty houses rents fell, but when population growth
caught up with housing supply rents rose again. Stage landlords ignored
the hardship of their tenants, and evicted them or seized their goods when
illness or unemployment forced them into arrears, but real landlords had
to lower their rents in times of economic depression, and give their tenants time to catch up with missing payments, if they wanted to keep them.
Eviction took time and money, and an empty house yielded no income at
all. In a market economy, rents rose and fell with supply and demand, and
slum landlords, whatever their personal morality, had to recognize the
poverty of the class that supplied their customers.

The fundamental problem for slum tenants was not the quality of their
homes or their landlords, but the inadequacy of their incomes. No landlord, however benign, could provide decent accommodation for a family
earning an irregular income of ten or fifteen shillings a week. We know
this from the experience of philanthropic housing societies and the LCC
when they tried to build decent tenements in the poorest parts of London.
Housing charities like the Improved Industrial Dwellings Company and
the Peabody Trust often bought land at well under the market price (especially following slum clearance), but if they built in the poorest parts of
East and South London they had great difficulty in finding families who
could afford the unsubsidized rent on a three-roomed apartment with
decent sanitary provision. As a result of this, according to a study published in 1891, richer areas like Westminster and the City were much better
provided with philanthropic dwellings than the poorer areas that really
needed them: Southwark, Hackney, and Tower Hamlets. The East End
Dwellings Company, which was set up in the 1880s to build in these
poorer communities, soon found that it had to choose the best East End
neighbourhoods, which could supply the well-paid artisans and public servants (postmen, policemen, and so on) who could afford their rents and
keep to their rules. At the end of the nineteenth century a slum called
Falcon Court, just off the part of the Borough High Street described in
How the Poor Live and *The Bitter Cry*, was demolished, and twenty-four of
its families moved into two new LCC tenements, Borough Road Dwellings

and Cobham Buildings. They proved to be 'anything but satisfactory tenants', and 'owing to their behaviour, it was found impossible to allow them to remain as tenants for any lengthy period'.[5] So we must be sceptical about George Sims' moral certainties. It was the much-abused slum landlord, not the housing charities or the LCC, who provided cheap rooms for the residuum, London's lowest classes, and put up with their unsanitary habits, their irregular payments, their subletting, and their donkeys.

Not all landlords were rich. In 1894 Arthur Morrison, a writer who spent his childhood in Poplar and his early twenties working for the People's Palace in the Mile End Road, published a collection of stories about East London, *Tales of Mean Streets*, in which he tried to bring the realism and objectivity of the latest social research (especially Charles Booth's) to working-class fiction. One of his stories, 'All that Messuage', was an account of a frugal engine-turner who bought a house in Old Ford with £30 of his own savings and a £200 building society mortgage, repayable over twelve years, intending to rent the house out to cover his costs. The new landlord had done some simple calculations, but he had forgotten the cost of rates, taxes, repairs, and weeks without tenants, and he was soon ruined by a tenant who refused to pay his rent. The house was repossessed, and the ex-landlord ended up in the workhouse, gloomily contemplating the prospect of a pauper's burial in a cheap deal coffin.

We can understand rather more about the relations between landlords and tenants by looking at West Ham, the densely populated industrial suburb on the eastern side of Lea valley. In 1905 a group called the Outer London Inquiry Committee decided to extend Charles Booth's study of the London poor beyond the County boundary. Their report on West Ham, which by that time had a population of about 280,000, was published in 1907. The report explained how large landed estates had been sold in smaller blocks to investors or speculative builders, some of whom sold leases on to smaller jobbing builders, often lending them the capital to begin building. Skating on the edge of bankruptcy and foreclosure, the builder constructed a house as cheaply and quickly as possible, in order to rent it out or sell it and repay his debt and take his profit. Those who built better houses often found their value dragged down to those that prevailed in the district. 'It was not important to them to put up a well-built house, because tenants could readily be found, and ready money was the builder's object as well as the freeholder's. The cheapness of such building suits the demand, for in the districts where this practice prevails houses of a better class are beyond the means of the inhabitants.' Big six-roomed houses in

West Ham were soon divided into two or three smaller dwellings, usually by a process of subletting, in which a trusted tenant found sub-tenants and collected their rents in return for a small reduction in their own payments.

West Ham landlords had to let their rents fall during the housing glut of 1892–7, and again between 1902 and 1905. General rent levels in West Ham were the same in 1905 as they had been in 1888, though local rates (which were paid out of the rent) had almost doubled. Some West Ham landlords avoided the expense of repairs and redecoration and accepted poor and unreliable tenants at a low rent of about four or five shillings a week. In streets in which several houses were derelict or boarded up, this might be the sensible policy to pursue, since good tenants could never be attracted to live there. Others might choose to put their houses into good repair, re-paper the walls, deal with infestations of vermin, eject irregular or poorly behaved tenants, and carefully choose reliable new tenants by checking references and rent books and visiting them at home. By this means the landlord could increase his rent by a few shillings, and reduce his losses from arrears and 'empties'. If others in the same street did the same, they could raise the tone, and enable workers on regular earnings to live apart from those on casual or intermittent earnings. The most powerful force at work here, whether one takes the landlords' point of view or the tenants', was not villainy but economics.[6]

CHAPTER FOUR

*

THE DISCOVERY OF POVERTY

Until the 1880s knowledge of London's poorest classes had been impressionistic and anecdotal, and provided by journalists, campaigners, and sensationalists, generally people with a brief and superficial knowledge of the problems they claimed to be describing. This approach to social investigation was still alive, in the work of Sims, Mearns, and Stead, in the 1880s, and even in 1903, when Jack London's *The People of the Abyss*, the product of eight weeks spent in the East End, was published. The breakthrough to a more systematic, evidence-based, and objective understanding of the dimensions, causes, and conditions of poverty in London came in the 1880s and 1890s, with the work of Charles Booth and his team of researchers.

Toynbee Hall

Thanks in part to Sims, Mearns, and Stead, the feeling among well-off Londoners that they needed to know more – and do more – about the poorest quarters of their city was particularly strong in 1883. One of those who took advantage of this mood was Samuel Barnett, who had been rector of St Jude's in Whitechapel, one of London's poorest parishes, since 1873. Barnett warned that the growing poverty of the East End, which was rooted in physical degeneration and the rejection of thrift, could never be alleviated by money 'thrown not brought, from the West to the East'. Nothing would be achieved until the rich, who had abandoned the East End as a place to live, returned to it, bringing the leadership, knowledge, and moral example that would raise the district out of its spiritual and economic hopelessness.[1] Perhaps this was never going to happen, but there was no good reason why the well off, wherever they lived, should only know the London poor through lurid newspaper reports and music-hall songs. In November 1883 Barnett addressed a small meeting of Oxford students and scholars, urging his listeners to learn about the East End not through sensational pamphlets or brief 'slumming' trips but by coming to live, work, and teach in a 'settlement of university men' in his parish. Barnett wanted his settlers to be motivated by a new creed of active citizenship, a commitment to service, education, and understanding, not by curiosity or missionary zeal. Barnett was an experienced and well-connected advocate, and within a few months a committee had been formed, money raised, and a site on Commercial Street, about a hundred yards from Aldgate East Underground station, had been found, bought, and cleared. Toynbee Hall, which opened on Christmas Eve 1884, was named in memory of Arnold Toynbee, a young Oxford historian and advocate of middle-class service to the poor, who died in 1883. Barnett was its warden and guiding spirit for the next twenty-two years.

The purpose of Toynbee Hall was to offer education and recreation to the people of East London, to encourage enquiry into the conditions of the poor and ways of promoting their welfare, and to accommodate those wishing to help in its work. Toynbee Hall never became an East London university, as Barnett hoped, but in its college hundreds of students were taught dozens of subjects by first-class lecturers, often drawn from Balliol and other Oxford colleges. Most of its students were teachers and clerks, but a growing number of artisans took its science courses. The effects of attending these classes could be life-changing. Joseph Dent, a struggling bookbinder with a workshop in Great Eastern Street, Shoreditch, went to his first Toynbee Hall classes in 1886, when he was thirty-seven, and was (as his memoirs put it) 'literally lifted into a heaven beyond my dreams . . . My whole being was transformed.' As a result Dent progressed from book-binding to publishing, and started producing cheap editions of Lamb, Shakespeare, and Balzac in the Temple Library series. A trip to Italy with the Toynbee Travellers' Club in 1890 led to a series of books on medieval towns. In 1906, in collaboration with a London poet and essayist, Ernest Rhys, Dent started the Everyman's Library, which made good editions of some of the world's greatest writing available to poorer readers at a shilling a volume. In the first year 153 volumes were published, and the medieval verse on every title page became familiar to London readers: 'Everyman, I will go with thee, and be thy guide, In thy most need to go by thy side.' So seeds planted in Toynbee Hall spread and propagated in the wider world, just as Barnett hoped they would.

Samuel Barnett and the Toynbee Hall settlers were motivated by the belief that education, mutual understanding, and the individual influence of active and well-intentioned university men could elevate and transform even

the most degraded working-class neighbourhood. Their guiding and uni-
fying philosophy was not Christianity, socialism, or liberalism but public
service and good citizenship. They threw themselves into local community
work, taking positions on school management boards, sanitary committees,
charities, friendly societies, and boards of Poor Law Guardians that middle-
class residents would have filled in more socially mixed areas. The effects
of these experiences on the young university men who lived and worked in
Toynbee Hall could be profound. They all believed in the value of personal
contact between rich and poor, but many of them moved increasingly
towards the belief that state policy, involving limited redistribution of
wealth or compulsory insurance, was needed to alleviate the worst ills of
the East End, especially the poverty of children and the old, and the hardships brought about by unemployment, illness and bad housing. Some were
drawn into trade unionism, and helped organize the match girls' and dockers' strikes of the late 1880s; some saw socialism as the only way forward,
while others argued that a more efficient and humane form of capitalism
could rid the East End of its worst problems. Several saw greater value in
the 'scientific' investigation of the conditions and causes of poverty pioneered by Charles Booth. Following these different paths, men who had
learned their first lessons about poverty with Barnett at Toynbee Hall went
on to help reshape twentieth-century Britain. Toynbee Hall residents and
administrators between 1884 and 1914 included the great imperialist
Alfred Milner, the socialist and historian R. H. Tawney (one of the creators
of the Workers' Educational Association), the very influential editor of the
liberal *Westminster Gazette* from 1896 to 1922, J. A. Spender, the economist
and civil servant William Beveridge (whose contribution to the development of social insurance and the modern welfare state is unequalled), the
brilliant civil servant and educational reformer Robert Morant (the key
figure in the development of state education between 1895 and 1911), the
future Labour Prime Minister Clement Attlee, the social investigator and
great civil servant Hubert Llewellyn Smith (the creator of the 1911 Unemployment Insurance Act and, with Beveridge, of Labour Exchanges), and
Charles Booth's assistant Ernest Aves.

Charles Booth Lifts the Curtain

Barnett and Toynbee Hall played a vital part in making possible Charles
Booth's pioneering study of working-class London, *Life and Labour of the*

People in London. The Hall provided Booth with an East End base, Barnett gave him local advice and letters of introduction, and many of Booth's thirty-four researchers and secretaries (including Llewellyn Smith, Aves, Henry Nevinson, and Clem Edwards) were Toynbee Hall residents or associates. Booth was a Liverpool shipowner whose interest in urban poverty dated back to the 1860s, when he had investigated the streets of Toxteth. In the late 1870s he had been introduced to the pleasures and hardships of the East End by Barnett, and in the early 1880s he became convinced that the true nature of London's social and economic problems could not be revealed by the shallow sensationalism of Mearns or Stead or the abstractions of social and economic theorists. As a member of the Royal Statistical Society he was involved in the Lord Mayor's Mansion House enquiry into London unemployment in 1884–5, and this gave him experience in using data from the 1881 census and questionnaires to City institutions, both of which he later used in his own work. The leader of the Social Democratic Federation (SDF), H. M. Hyndman, who always liked to place himself at the centre of any stage, claimed that Booth's great investigation was begun as a way of proving that an SDF survey, which showed a quarter of Londoners living in extreme poverty, was an exaggeration, but Booth was already well on his way by the time he met Hyndman in February 1886, and his sources of inspiration and motivation were far more complex than Hyndman knew.[2]

Nevertheless, Hyndman's story captures an important element in Booth's motivation. Booth was influenced by a desire to clear the fog of fear, sensationalism, and guesswork that obscured the truth about East London poverty, especially after the 'unemployed' riot of 8 February 1886. Booth, unlike the Charity Organisation Society (COS) or the SDF, made no assumptions about the extent or causes of poverty, but believed that no explanations should be advanced or remedies proposed until the facts of the matter had been established. He liked nothing more than to overturn, by objective research, the assumptions of ideologues, whether they were socialists or capitalist free-traders. Booth was influenced by the Positivists Frederic Harrison and E. S. Beesly, who followed Auguste Comte in believing that society should be studied and administered by scientific methods. How could the problem of poverty be addressed or cured if its true nature and dimensions were not known? As he wrote in his study of the extent of poverty in East London in 1889:

East London lay hidden from view behind a curtain on which were painted terrible pictures:– Starving children, suffering women, over-worked men; horrors of drunkenness and vice; monsters and demons of inhumanity; giants of disease and despair. Did these pictures truly represent what lay behind, or did they bear to the facts a relation sim-ilar to that which the pictures outside a booth at some country fair bear to the performance or show within? This curtain we have tried to lift.[3]

Booth was not as free of prejudices and theories as he liked to think. In October 1886 he began a correspondence with the influential econo-mist Alfred Marshall, who shared his association with the Royal Statistical Society and Toynbee Hall. Marshall was an advocate of the view that London had created and attracted a vast population of sickly and feeble-minded degenerates, whose demand for jobs and housing drove down wages and pushed up rents, to the great disadvantage of the skilled work-ers that the city really needed. In an article in the *Contemporary Review* in February 1884, just after the publication of *The Bitter Cry of Outcast London*, Marshall argued that there were in London 'large numbers of people with poor physique and a feeble will, with no enterprise, no courage, no hope, and scarcely any self-respect', who took jobs, especially in the clothing trade, which were 'shunned by the hearty and strong', and were 'the refuge of the weak and broken-spirited'. Marshall believed that the enforcement of stricter laws on sanitation and overcrowding would force this surplus population and its employers to find new homes in the countryside, and might even induce poor Londoners to move to America, 'where the shift-less become shiftful'. Perhaps because of Marshall's influence, Booth also believed that London had a useless underclass, which damaged the eco-nomic position of the useful working class. Booth's social classification (famously illustrated in his poverty maps of London) was designed to identify this group, which he called group B, the 'very poor, on casual earnings'.[4]

Beatrice Potter

Booth's 'Board of Statistical Enquiry' first met in early March 1886, and by April a working group consisting of Booth, Jesse Argyle (one of Booth's clerks), and Maurice Eden Paul, a medical student, had been formed. One of the three others in attendance on 17 April, when Booth's 'elaborated and detailed plan' was discussed and approved, was Beatrice Potter, Booth's wife's cousin. This intelligent and wealthy woman, then in her late twenties, was suffering a period of depression associated with her father's recent stroke and an unhappy courtship. The prospect of taking part in Booth's 'gigantic undertaking' excited her: 'just the sort of work I should like to undertake – and if I were free!'[5]

Beatrice Potter is hardly a typical late-Victorian woman, but she is an interesting and important one, and in some ways her situation was not unusual. She was the eighth of the nine daughters of a wealthy business-man who had several country houses and a house in Kensington for the London Season. Like many women of her class she had little formal edu-cation, but unlike them she was encouraged to think and study for herself by a regular visitor to the house, the philosopher Herbert Spencer. Spencer was the leading exponent of a 'Darwinian' form of society, in which indi-viduals would struggle for success with the bare minimum of state intervention. In 1882, when she was twenty-four, her life was transformed by the death of her mother. 'From being a subordinate, carrying out direc-tions, and having to fit into the framework of family circumstance, studies and travels, friendship and flirtation, I became a principal, a person in authority, determining not only my own but other people's conduct; the head of a large household perpetually on the move . . . From being an anaemic girl, always paying for spells of dissipation or study by periods of nervous exhaustion, often of positive illness, I became an exceptionally energetic woman, carrying on, persistently and methodically, several sep-arate, and, in some ways, conflicting, phases of life – undergoing, in fact, much of the strain and stress of a multiple personality.'[6]

Beatrice Potter faced the choice many other well-off young women faced, between personal development and family duties. She became a society hostess, fulfilling the domestic and social duties of a wealthy late Victorian woman, giving and going to parties, entertaining friends and rel-atives, supervising servants, looking after the household finances, advising and supporting her father, making calls, and generally subordinating her own interests and inclinations to the demands of her social position. At least the Potter household was an interesting one. As well as Herbert Spencer, callers included T. H. Huxley (President of the Royal Society, 1883–5) and Francis Galton, the founder of the science of eugenics. From 1884 to 1887 Beatrice Potter was in love with the charismatic radical (and later imperialist) politician Joseph Chamberlain, but in the end the prospect

of intellectual and social subordination to his despotic personality led her
to abandon the relationship.

The women – and many of the men – involved in London Society had
no paid work to do, but, as Beatrice Potter discovered, the pursuit of pleasure could be a tiring and tiresome occupation, 'entailing extensive plant,
a large number of employees and innumerable decisions on insignificant
matters. There was the London house to be selected and occupied; there
was the stable of horses and carriages to be transported; there was the elaborate stock of prescribed garments to be bought; there was all the
commisariat and paraphernalia for dinners, dances, picnics and week-end
parties to be provided.'

> How well I recollect those first days of my early London seasons: the
> pleasurable but somewhat feverish anticipation of endless distraction,
> a dissipation of mental and physical energy which filled up all the
> hours of the day and lasted far into the night; the ritual to be
> observed; the presentation at Court, the riding in the Row, the calls,
> the lunches and dinners, the dances and crushes, Hurlingham and
> Ascot, not to mention amateur theatricals and other sham philan-
> thropic excrescences. There was of course a purpose in all this
> apparently futile activity, the business of getting married.[7]

This was not the life for Beatrice Potter. Encouraged by Herbert
Spencer, and hoping that hard work would relieve her depression, she
decided to exchange the ballroom and the dinner table for a life of mental
discipline and social study, and to find out about the world of labour
and poverty which her upbringing had hidden from her. She took her
first steps in the spring of 1883, when she visited Soho slums on behalf
of COS, the great opponent of indiscriminate alms-giving, and the advocate of personal investigation of the individuals who asked for help. She
followed this with a short period living and working incognito with
Lancashire cotton mill-hands, and then, towards the end of 1884, she
started working as a rent collector for an East End philanthropic housing association based on the ideas of Octavia Hill, one of the founders
of the COS. More than a year working in Katharine Buildings, a new
five-storey tenement with about 600 occupants near St Katharine's
Dock, taught her that the cause of London poverty was not, as the COS
argued, indiscriminate alms-giving, and that COS 'detective work' was
futile and offensive to the poor. The reaction of this wealthy but unhappy
woman to the lives of her impoverished tenants was complex. 'A drift

population, the East Enders, of all classes and races – a constantly decomposing mass of human beings, few rising out of it but many dropping down dead, pressed out of existence in the struggle. A certain weird romance, with neither beginning nor end, visiting among these people in their dingy homes: some light-hearted enough, in spite of misery and disease. More often feel envy than pity . . . Among the East Enders, in spite of their misery, misery which makes me sick to see, there seems little desire to leave life, on the whole a value in it. Perhaps they expect less than we do.'[8]

Beatrice Potter's experience in Katharine Buildings, and an article she had written for the *Pall Mall Gazette* on the question of relief work for the unemployed after the Pall Mall riots of February 1886, made her a useful assistant for Booth in his great enterprise. In the spring and early summer of 1886, when he was preparing the ground for his enquiry, Booth wrote to Potter, explaining his intention of relating individual case histories to the broader statistical picture, making sure (as Stead and Mearns did not) that specific problems, however dramatic, were not given disproportionate significance in the general account. As Beatrice Potter recalled later: 'In the course of this inquiry I had learnt the relation between personal observation and statistics . . . however vivid the picture of what was happening at the dock gates or in the sweated workshops, I was always confronted by Charles Booth's sceptical glance and critical questions: "How many individuals are affected by the condition you describe; are they increasing or diminishing in number?"'[9]

Poverty in East London

By September 1886 Booth had established a statistical framework and a methodology for his investigation, and a pilot study of Tower Hamlets had been started. He was helped by Canon Barnett, whose initial scepticism about the survey soon turned into active support.[10] Letters of introduction from Barnett were a master key that unlocked many East End doors to Booth and his interviewers. Booth's plan was to begin with the million inhabitants of the Tower Hamlets and Hackney School Board divisions, reputedly the poorest people in England, to establish the conditions in which they lived, and to study the various trades of East London, and their contribution to poverty. The district stretched about three miles east and north-east from the City boundary, to include the old East End parishes of Whitechapel, Shoreditch, St George-in-the-East, Stepney, Mile End New Town, and Bethnal Green, and the newer outlying districts of Poplar and Hackney. In time, every district and every trade in London would be studied. Booth relied upon information from the 1881 census (to which he was given privileged access), and later used the 1891 census, which included (at his request) questions on the number of rooms occupied by each household and the number of servants employed, as indicators of poverty and affluence. To supplement this bare statistical data, Booth devised a pioneering street-by-street survey, which would enable him to gather qualitative and descriptive material on working-class life, and to test the relationship between assumptions based on census data and the observed realities of poverty. A later investigator might have used sampling techniques to reduce this survey to manageable proportions, but these were not devised until after Booth's work was finished. Instead, Booth called upon the knowledge of public officials who knew the East End well. Using an idea tried by Joseph Chamberlain in Birmingham, Booth got permission to interview all sixty-six school attendance officers (or School Board Visitors) working in the East End. In these interviews, each of which took about twenty hours, Booth and his assistants (especially Booth's secretaries Jesse Argyle and George Arkell) gathered information on every family with school-aged children (three- to thirteen-year-olds) in every street. The same information was collected for Central London and Battersea, and published in 1891. The witnesses were not asked to collect information especially for the survey, but only to tell the researchers what they had already learned in the course of their work. The information was recorded in notebooks, and supplemented with information from all the other professional or educated people who worked among the poor: teachers, rent-collectors, sanitary inspectors, charity workers, clergymen, policemen, poor-law officials, and managers of philanthropic housing blocks. At first, the researchers did not visit the streets themselves until their notebooks were completed, but later, gaining confidence in their own objectivity, they visited them at the same time as they interviewed witnesses. Finally, Booth spent three periods of several weeks as an anonymous boarder, sharing houses with families of classes C, D, and E, below and above his notional poverty line. This direct but brief experience helped to give him the humane and subtle understanding of working-class life which runs through his massive work.

On the strength of these first enquiries, which mostly took place in 1887, Booth was able to divide the population of East London into eight

classes, allocating a percentage of the population to each. Booth accepted
the common idea that at the bottom of society there was a degraded and
very poor population of 'roughs', outcasts and incorrigibles, sometimes
known as a 'residuum'. These were class A, 'the lowest class of occasional
labourers, loafers and semi-criminals' (impossible to count, but roughly
1.25 per cent of the population of East London, or about 11,000 people),
and the much larger class B, those on casual earnings, which constituted
11.22 per cent of East London's population, or just over 100,000 people.
Booth was sure that class A, which also included street children, the homeless and those in common lodging houses, was not the fearful monster of
the West End's imagination.[11] Class B was a different matter – a large
group that included many widows and deserted wives and children, casual
dockers getting one or two days' work a week, and idlers and drinkers
who did not want full-time work, a sort of impoverished 'leisure class'.
Booth did not accept the extreme eugenicist position that class B was a
hopelessly degraded sub-species, bound to pass its characteristics on to its
many children. It was 'not one in which men are born and live and die, so
much as a deposit of those who from mental, moral, and physical reasons
are incapable of better work'. Its children might fall into class A, but with
education and hard work they could rise up the social scale and become
useful members of society. This class, in Booth's words, 'was at all times
more or less "in want". They are ill-nourished and poorly clad. But of them
only a percentage – and not, I think, a very large percentage – would be
said by themselves, or anyone else, to be "in distress". From day to day and
from hand to mouth they get along; sometimes suffering, sometimes
helped, but not always unfortunate, and very ready to enjoy any good luck
that may come in their way.'

Above these two 'very poor' groups there were the 'poor', families
'living under a struggle to obtain the necessaries of life and make both
ends meet'. Class C, about 74,000 people, or 8.33 per cent of East
Londoners, earned intermittent incomes in trades affected by labour surplus or seasonal fluctuations, like building, dock and wharf work, the
sweated furniture and clothing industries, and street selling. Their wives'
small earnings as charwomen, washerwomen, and needlewomen were not
enough to lift these families out of poverty. Class D (about 129,000
people, or 14.5 per cent of East Londoners) differed from class C because
their incomes were more regular. They were low-paid labourers in steady
work, perhaps in gasworks, wharves, or warehouses, or artisans in the furniture, clothing, building, or food industries. Life for these workers was a

struggle, but they were, Booth thought, 'decent steady men, paying their way and bringing up their children respectably'. Their family economy depended on the earnings of their older children as van boys, errand boys, servants, or factory hands, and on the thrift, sobriety, and domestic skills of their wives.

By carefully studying the income and expenditure of thirty families from classes B to F (the highest-paid working class) for five weeks in February, March, and April 1887, Booth tried to arrive at a practical understanding of the various degrees of poverty experienced by working-class families, and thus to establish a 'line of poverty' which would enable him to divide the population into those who were living in poverty and those who were not. Booth did not claim to have a 'scientific' notion of how much food, fuel, or clothing a man, woman, or child needed, but he believed that his examples made it fairly clear that a weekly income of four or five shillings per man (and a little less for women and children), however well used, consigned a family to the constant struggle and hardship of class B, one of seven or eight shillings involved the precarious hand-to-mouth existence of classes C and D, that nine to eleven shillings took a family into the relative security of class E, above the poverty line, and fourteen or fifteen shillings were the 'good ordinary earnings' that gave a family the basic comfort of class F.

It was not Booth's intention to follow Sims or Mearns in creating the maximum sympathy or horror among his readers by depicting working-class lives of unremitting suffering and gloom. From his own brief experience of living in the East End, Booth found that the lives of children in class E, about 46 per cent of the working class of East London and Hackney, and even in class D, were busy and happy:

> In class E they have for playground the back yard, in class D the even greater delights of the street. With really bad parents the story would be different, but men and women may be very bad, yet love their children and make them happy. In the summer holidays, when my carman had a load to carry for some building in the country, he would take two of the children with him. Supplied with bread and butter and 2d to buy fruit, they would start off early and come home in the evening happy, tired, and dirty, to tell of the sights they had seen.[12]

The great problem of these classes was the uncertainty of their economic position. Without savings or valuable skills, they were vulnerable to many personal and economic dangers: the man might fall ill, lose his job, or take to drink, the wife might start drinking and sell the furniture. The barriers between the classes were easy to breach, especially if a family was falling through them: 'Below D we have B, and below B we have the workhouse. If hand or foot slip, down they must go. "Easy the descent, but to step back is difficult'."

Mapping Poverty

In 1887, when much of the work on poverty in East London was finished, Booth recruited new assistants to help him to extend his analysis to other parts of London, including two suburbs, Battersea to the south and Walthamstow to the east, and a large part of the old West End, roughly the area enclosed by Chancery Lane, Oxford Street, Regent Street, and the Strand, plus St James's and southern Bloomsbury. Unlike the East End, this central district was a world of enormous contrasts, from the palaces and exclusive clubs of Pall Mall and St James's to the doss houses and eel-pie shops of Seven Dials and the slums and lodging houses of the streets south of High Holborn and east of Drury Lane, the remnant of London's old plague-spot, St Giles. Three of the worst of these streets, Shelton Street, Macklin Street, and Parker Street, all running east from Drury Lane, were described in detail in Booth's second volume. Booth's informants were Protestant missionaries, and their account of the lives of the 200 mostly Irish Catholic families who lived in Shelton Street's forty tumbledown houses showed as much concern for their moral and cultural condition as for their sanitary and environmental welfare:

> Fifteen rooms out of twenty were filthy to the last degree, and the furniture in none of these would be worth 20s, in some cases not 5s. Not a room would be free from vermin, and in many life at night was unbearable. Several occupants have said that in hot weather they don't go to bed, but sit in their clothes in the least infested part of the room . . . The little yard at the back was only sufficient for dust-bin and closet and water-tap, serving for six or seven families. The water would be drawn from cisterns which were receptacles for refuse, and perhaps occasionally a dead cat. At one time the street was fever-stricken . . . Gambling was the amusement of the street. Sentries would be posted, and if the police made a rush the offenders would slip into the open houses and hide until danger was past. Sunday afternoon and evening was the hey-day time for this street. Every

doorstep would be crowded by those who sat or stood with pipe and
jug of beer, while lads lounged about, and the gutters would find
amusement for not a few children with bare feet, their faces and hands
besmeared, while the mud oozed between their toes.

Dickensian neighbourhoods such as this were disappearing from central
London in the 1880s and 1890s. When Booth's account was published in
1891 Shelton Street had already been demolished, and Parker Street and
Macklin Street were awaiting destruction. Nevertheless, as Booth was to
demonstrate, extreme poverty in London was certainly not confined to the
East End, and had not been eliminated from even the richest districts.

To cover the whole of London in a reasonable time Booth and his
researchers had to speed up their work by using a street-by-street survey,
rather than the house-by-house method they had started with. By this
means, still relying on the local knowledge of School Board Visitors, missionaries, rent collectors, and other experts, Booth was able to produce a
poverty survey of the whole County of London. By allocating different
colours to each level of poverty or wealth, Booth created a graphic poverty
map of London, in which streets mostly inhabited by families of class A
were coloured black, those of class B dark blue, those of C and D (below
the poverty line) in light blue, with purple where classes C and D lived
alongside working men in regular employment (class E), pink where class
E lived with the comfortable working class (class F), red for middle-class
families employing one or two servants (class G), and yellow for the
wealthy class H, those with three servants or more.

The map, which was published in four large sheets in April 1889, made
it possible for the first time for Londoners to survey the extent and distribution of poverty throughout their city, without reading through volumes
of statistics. The map showed that London had some districts of almost
uninterrupted wealth and comfort. The whole area west of Buckingham
Palace and south of Hyde Park and Kensington Gardens (Earls Court,
Chelsea, Brompton, South Kensington, Knightsbridge, Belgravia, and
Pimlico), was reassuringly red and gold, with a few small blue patches,
and so were Bayswater, Marylebone, Bloomsbury, and (of course) Mayfair.
Wealth and comfort had spread north and west of Regent's Park, into
the suburbs of St John's Wood, Kilburn, Belsize Park, Hampstead, and
Highgate, and the lower middle classes had colonized most of the north-
ern suburbs of Canonbury, De Beauvoir Town, and Dalston. There were
black and blue patches of poverty near the railways and canals of

Paddington and to the west of Lisson Grove, and the Notting Hill and Ladbroke Grove district, beyond the north-west corner of Kensington Gardens, was extremely poor. In Westminster there was an ancient enclave of extreme poverty between the Abbey and Victoria Station, especially between Victoria Street and Horseferry Road, and right up to the First World War Westminster was not the desirable address that it is today. The uplifting influence of the new hotels and expensive mansion flats of Victoria Street, or of the Abbey and its ancient school, had not outweighed the degrading effects of Millbank Penitentiary (soon to be demolished) and several gasworks: 'the ground is packed with houses, the spaces between the streets being filled with little courts and blind alleys', wrote Jesse Argyle.

> The people look poor and vicious . . . Details obtained for half a dozen streets disclose a deplorable lack of any employments which can be dignified by the name 'industry', except indeed charing, of which there is a great deal in connection with the public offices. We hear of a street knife-grinder whose wife sells flowers: a one-legged man with a piano organ. A drunken law-writer, whose wife, too, is a flower seller. A hawker of pocket knives about offices. A seller of oranges by the fountain near the Abbey. A blind man who makes nets and sells them by St Martin's Church. A buyer of bottles and fat down area steps.[13]

Canals, railways, and gasworks nearly always created very poor neighbourhoods, because they degraded the local environment and offered plenty of unskilled work. The five or six streets trapped between the river, a gasworks, and the railway lines running into Nine Elms Station (now the site of New Covent Garden market) were especially bad, but Latchmere Grove, caught between the Waterloo and Victoria railway lines coming out of Clapham Junction, was no better. The neighbourhoods on either side of the huge area of coal stores, goods depots, and sidings behind Euston, St Pancras, and King's Cross stations were very poor: Somers Town, between Euston and St Pancras, was a famous black spot, and Pentonville, the late eighteenth-century planned suburb between King's Cross Station and Penton Street, had degenerated into very bad slums. On the other hand the main streets, not yet ruined by heavy motor traffic, generally attracted the higher classes, even in poorer districts. Cromwell Road, Bayswater Road, Victoria Street, and Brixton Road were favoured by the rich, and many others, including Oxford Street, Edgware Road, Euston Road,

Hampstead Road, Upper Street, Wandsworth Road, Old Kent Road, and Walworth Road were occupied by people with servants. In East London the main roads to Bow and Poplar, Whitechapel Road (continuing as Mile End Road) and Commercial Road, where shopkeepers lived above or behind their shops, offered the only splashes of well-off red in a sea of black, blue, purple, and pink.

Although localized areas of poverty in otherwise prosperous districts caused interest and concern, the main impression left by Booth's 1889 Poverty map is of segregated city, in which huge parts of the west, north, and south were predominantly or overwhelmingly well-off, and smaller but more densely populated inner districts were great concentrations of hardship. North of the Thames, this impoverished region started roughly at Gray's Inn Road and the Middlesex House of Correction (soon to be replaced by the Mount Pleasant Post Office), and stretched eastwards along the northern borders of the City of London from Holborn and Clerkenwell, via Hoxton, Finsbury, and Shoreditch to Bethnal Green, Whitechapel, and the dockside districts of Wapping, Shadwell, and Poplar. The section of the Regent's Canal running from the junction of City Road and Upper Street to Victoria Park acted as the northern limit of this working-class sector. North of the canal, despite some severe poverty in Islington and Kingsland and a growing slum population in Hackney (which was on the way down), classes F and G (comfortable but not wealthy) were in the ascendant.

One of the great surprises of Booth's survey and map was the intensity and extent of poverty south of the Thames. There was a thick belt of poverty from Kennington and Lambeth eastwards through Newington and Southwark to Bermondsey and Rotherhithe, which were all within daily walking distance of London's main industrial and riverside areas. South of the New and Old Kent Roads, in Walworth and Peckham, conditions were more mixed, but there were some tough streets near the Grand Surrey Canal in Peckham, and some notorious ones, Sultan Street and Hollington Street, in modestly comfortable Camberwell. Distance from the centre tended to discourage poorer settlers, because of high transport costs and the lack of unskilled local work, but this was not the case along the eastern stretches of the Thames, and there was intense poverty around the docks, wharves, and markets of Deptford and Greenwich. In fact, according to the figures on every London district or 'block' (areas with about 30,000 people) published by Booth in 1891, Greenwich (with 65 per cent in poverty) was London's second poorest district, after Southwark, with

68 per cent. Third, at 61 per cent, was the neighbourhood north of the City, between the Charterhouse and Bunhill Fields, with the notorious Whitecross Street rookery at its centre. The poorest part of the East End, West Bethnal Green, was only fourth, at 59 per cent. Booth emphasized this surprising finding with figures for each of the four inner districts, which showed that inner South London had a greater proportion of its population in poverty (47 per cent) than inner East London (44 per cent) or inner North London (43 per cent). But some of the other stereotypes were confirmed: inner West London (the West End), despite its pockets of poverty, was London's richest area (21 per cent in poverty), and the outer suburbs to the west (25 per cent) and south-east (22 per cent) were not far behind. East London differed from the other sectors because its outer suburbs, beyond the River Lea, were poor industrial and residential areas, West Ham, Stratford, Walthamstow, and Canning Town, rather than middle-class dormitories. And it was true, as Canon Barnett had complained, that the wealthy had abandoned London's poorest districts. In Booth's two sheets covering the eastern half of London, from Highbury and Hackney to Brixton and New Cross, not one street deserved to be coloured yellow, except a single crescent off the New Kent Road (the Paragon) and a few distant suburban outposts – Denmark Hill, Brixton, Lewisham, and Highbury.

In the Workhouse

Though he returned to the subject later, in his four volumes on poverty Booth wrote surprisingly little – hardly a page – on Poor Relief, the system of support and deterrence introduced in 1832. His only observation was that the system had hardened in recent years, withdrawing outdoor relief (doles to people living in their own homes), and confining its help to those who found themselves unable to avoid the shelter, discipline, and humiliation of the parish workhouse. In spite of the surprising extent of poverty he discovered, Booth was convinced that in London outdoor poor relief could be 'safely dispensed with; the result being that other agencies step in to do the work . . . While the Guardians cease to do work which should not rightly be theirs.' These other agencies were the charities, of which there were many hundreds in London, dispensing money, food, clothing, shelter, medical care, training, advice, spiritual guidance, education, admonition, and punishment in a largely uncoordinated way. By 1910 over

1,700 charities were operating in London (not counting schools with charitable status), with a total income from donations, fees, and investments of at least £12 million a year. This was over eight times the amount spent annually by the Poor Law in London, and nearly twice the national Poor Law budget. Londoners could call upon the assistance of eighty-eight charities for the blind, twenty-three for the deaf, and thirty for epileptics and incurables. Eleven London charities assisted emigrants, twenty-five protected the helpless, fifteen aided the unemployed, seventeen helped prisoners, two hundred and sixteen offered convalescence, a hundred and sixty-two gave medical aid, fifty-four dispensed drugs, sixty-five sheltered the old, and two hundred and thirty-six housed the young. Lunatics could call upon only five charities and inebriates only seven, but 'idiots', if they could find them, had eighteen. The Charity Organisation Society, which collected these figures, did its best to coordinate and control the work of all these bodies, especially to stop the growth of a class of professional spongers, but it was an uphill and ultimately impossible task.[14]

Perhaps because of this proliferation of charities, the London Boards of Poor Law Guardians were more successful (or ruthless) in refusing outdoor relief than most other Poor Law authorities in England. Outdoor relief was cheaper than workhouse relief, but it was assumed, probably rightly, that few of those refused outdoor relief would submit to the workhouse, and that workhouses would be filled, as before, with children, single mothers, vagrants, the old, and the physically and mentally infirm. The adult able-bodied, faced with the prospect of separation from their families and loss of personal freedom and dignity in a workhouse, would choose to suffer in private, apply to a charity, or take one of those jobs available in big cities to the desperate and the destitute, scavenging, crossing-sweeping, horse-holding, street-selling, or carrying a sandwich board. There had been a very steep fall in the number of Londoners on outdoor relief in the 1870s, and by 1883 only about 10 per thousand received it, compared with 23 in 1862–6 and 34 at its peak in 1868–71, and compared with a national (England and Wales) figure in 1883 of 20 per thousand. There was no significant downward trend in London until 1910, when Old Age Pensions removed about 30 per cent of outdoor paupers, but the national figure fell between 1885 and 1910 to around 16 per thousand. London, on the other hand, had far more paupers in its workhouses than the rest of England, and the gap was growing. The national average, about 6 or 7 per thousand, was fairly steady (with annual and seasonal fluctuations) from the 1860s to 1900, rising to 8 by 1910. In 1865, 10

Londoners in every thousand were in workhouses, rising to about 14 by the early 1880s and 15 by 1890. Between 1903 and 1910 the figure rose to 17.5 per thousand (more than twice the national average), falling back a little after 1910. By this time nearly 70 per cent of London's Poor Law expenditure went on indoor (workhouse) relief, and London's bill (per head of population) was nearly twice the national average, and a quarter of the national total.

At its peak, in the winter months of 1908–10, the number of people in the County of London's workhouses and other pauper institutions was about 83,000, or nearly 2 per cent of all Londoners. Of these, over 20,000 were children, either in workhouses or in children's homes, pauper schools or 'cottage homes', smaller institutions which sounded nicer than they were. About half of these children were relieved with their parents, and the rest were orphaned or alone. Of the other 60,000, about 10,000 were able-bodied adults, 7,000 were 'insane', and 40,000 were ill, unfit or old. There were another 20,000 'pauper lunatics' (not counted in these figures) living in London's County asylums. The proportion of London's population defined and confined as lunatics had increased by nearly 48 per cent between 1892 and 1911, from 45 per 10,000 to 66.5 per 10,000 Londoners.

The workhouse casual wards or 'spikes' for vagrants, which were described by James Greenwood in the *Pall Mall Gazette* in 1866 and by Jack London in *The People of the Abyss* in 1903, were a famous but statistically not very significant part of the workhouse system. On an average winter night about 1,000 vagrants were given workhouse beds, though many others were turned away. London had a much larger population of tramps and vagrants than this, but many, by the 1900s, were finding shelter at about 6d a night in one of the six houses founded by the philanthropist Montague Lowry Corry, Lord Rowton, who had been Disraeli's private secretary. Six Rowton Houses were built in London between 1892 and 1905, providing beds, sheets, and hot water for about 4,000 people in Vauxhall, King's Cross, Newington Butts, Hammersmith, Camden Town, and Whitechapel. Jack London slept in the Whitechapel Rowton House in 1902, and judged that it gave the workman 'more for his money than he ever received before'. The same hostel had a more famous visitor in 1907, when the future Joseph Stalin slept there for two weeks while he was attending the Fifth Congress of the Russian Social Democratic Labour Party in Whitechapel.[15]

Although the principle of deterrence was still generally accepted, workhouses were not, by the standards of the day, inhumane places. The Minority Report of the Poor Law Commission of 1905–9, which was written by the severest and best-informed critic of the system, Beatrice Webb (previously Potter), conceded this point. 'These institutions are, in nearly all cases, clean and sanitary; and the food, clothing and warmth are sufficient – sometimes more than sufficient – to maintain the inmates in physiological health. In some cases, indeed, the buildings recently erected in the Metropolis and elsewhere have been not incorrectly described, alike for the elaborateness of the architecture and the sumptuousness of the internal fittings, as "palaces" for paupers.' The fundamental problem with general workhouses in London and elsewhere, Webb argued, was their promiscuity, their indiscriminate mixing of men and women, young and old, healthy and diseased, virtuous and corrupt.

> In the female dormitories . . . there are no separate bedrooms; there are not even separate cubicles. The young servant out of place, the prostitute recovering from disease, the feeble-minded woman of any age, the girl with her first baby, the unmarried mother coming in to be confined with her third or fourth bastard, the senile, the paralytic, the epileptic, the respectable deserted wife, the widow to whom out-door relief has been refused, all are herded indiscriminately together. We have found respectable old women annoyed, by day and by night, by the presence of noisy and dirty imbeciles.[16]

Others took a more benign view of the workhouse regime. T. W. Wilkinson, in *Living London* (1901), described the palatial St Marylebone Workhouse, just opposite Madame Tussaud's waxworks, as a fairly comfortable shelter, at least for those singled out for better treatment. Men were no longer lumped together indiscriminately, but divided into those of a superior and rougher class, with the former being placed in dormitories that offered a degree of privacy and comfort. Ten married couples, in a workhouse population of 2,000, had rooms of their own, but the rest led an entirely communal life, whether they liked it or not. Those able to work might be found grinding flour, sawing firewood, or pursuing a craft, and the casuals (tramps in for a two-night stay) earned their bed and gruel by cleaning and oakum-picking. French-polishing had been suspended because the paupers drank the polish. Permanent residents filled their time with reading, talking, playing dominoes, or sitting in silence. The workhouse had a ward for orphans and abandoned children, and the usual preponderance of old women. There were 200 octogenarians, 'drinking tea as of old, and perfectly contented with things as they are, judging from the nodding of caps and the smiles and the whispered confidences'. The writer Arthur H. Beavan spoke glowingly of the clean buildings, the well-ventilated rooms, the plain food, of the typical workhouse.

> Throughout the winter the inmates of workhouses are treated to entertainments, concerts, magic-lantern lectures, etc., which help to break the dull monotony of their lives; and they also have the privilege, all the year round, of an occasional Sunday out. The discipline, though marked, is lax compared with that of a gaol; . . . In some Unions, such as Westminster (Soho), a most enlightened system prevails. The degrading distinctive garb has been abolished, and extra comforts in the shape of tea, sugar, and tobacco, have been granted to the aged.[17]

From Paupers to Pensioners

Workhouses were London's old people's homes, and probably half of their occupants were over sixty-five. Charles Booth published an extensive statistical study, *The Aged Poor in England and Wales*, in 1894, as a contribution to the campaign for Old Age Pensions. He found that 4 per cent of Londoners – about 170,000 people in 1894 – were over sixty-five, and of these 38 per cent were on poor relief, and 22.5 per cent, or 38,250, were in workhouses. In 1896, in his volumes on London industry, Booth published a very detailed study of the inmates of Stepney's two workhouses and its Poor Law infirmary (but not its pauper schools) in 1889. Of the 783 people whose circumstances Booth described, 446, or 57 per cent, were over sixty.[18] Some of these old people, especially those in their seventies and eighties, no doubt entered workhouses because they could no longer live alone and had no family to care for them, but others were driven into them by the distinctive London policy of refusing outdoor relief, even to the old. This must certainly have been so in Whitechapel, St George-in-the-East, Strand, St Marylebone, Kensington, Bethnal Green, and Westminster, where less than 15 per cent of paupers were given outdoor relief, compared with over half in Lewisham, Islington, Camberwell, and Poplar, and nearly 70 per cent in West Ham. The young novelist Arnold Bennett lived in Fulham in the 1890s, and used to see the old men who lived in the local workhouse walking along the Fulham Road in their 'brown coats and corduroy trousers'. 'One sees a few of them in every public house along the street. Strange that the faces of most of them afford no indication of the manner of their downfall to pauperdom! I looked in vain for general traces either of physical excess or of moral weakness. Must their helplessness in old age, therefore, be attributed mainly to mere misfortune, adverse fate? Or does society as at present constituted force them to this ignominy?'[19]

The threat of a workhouse old age and a pauper's death began to be lifted from the ageing poor in December 1908, when the first payments were made under the Liberal government's Old Age Pensions Act. This entitled needy over-seventies to a small non-contributory pension of between one and five shillings a week, depending on the size of their existing income. Those with an annual income of £21 or less got the full five shillings, and those with over £31 10s got nothing. At first, those who had been on poor relief were excluded from the pension, but from January 1911 this prohibition was lifted, and 10,000 Londoners were transformed from paupers into pensioners. The number of people in workhouses fell by about 3,000 in 1911–12, and a little more in 1913–14, though it is not clear that this was the result of the introduction of pensions. In the County of London 60,508 old people (mostly women), nearly half of London's 125,000 over-seventies, drew a pension in March 1911. Seventy per cent of pensioners were women, and nearly all of them drew the five shillings, increasing their income by at least 62 per cent.[20] So the old, a growing proportion of London's population (3 per cent in 1891, 5 per cent in 1921), entered a new world of freedom and security just before the Great War, a world in which infirmity, senility, and lack of family support might consign them to an institution, but poverty would not.

*

THE JEWISH EAST END

Although London had been from the start a city of immigrants, there had been no mass migration to London from beyond the British Isles (though plenty from Ireland) since the Huguenot settlement of the 1690s. One of the outstanding features of modern London, its ethnic, religious, and linguistic variety, can be traced back directly to the 1880s and 1890s, when parts of the East End were transformed by the arrival and settlement of nearly 100,000 East European Jews.

Asylum Seekers

This mass migration was caused by events taking place on the other side of Europe, in the Russian Empire. After the assassination of Tsar Alexander II in March 1881 there were violent attacks on Jews and their property in several towns in Russia and Russian Poland, including Kiev, Odessa, Elizavetgrad, and (in December) Warsaw. The new Tsar, Alexander III, was anti-Semitic, and the Russian government and Church encouraged or tolerated the attacks, or pogroms, which were largely carried out by illiterate and traditionally anti-Semitic Ukrainian and Polish peasants. For the rest of the 1880s the Russian government enforced new laws which prevented Jews from moving out of larger towns and villages, banned them from owning land, restricted their rights to secondary and university education, and limited their entry into the medical and legal professions, innkeeping, and the civil service. There were large-scale expulsions of Jews from Kiev in 1886 and Moscow in 1891. This brutal persecution turned a steady flow of economic migrants from East Europe to Britain and the USA into a flood of refugees in the 1880s and 1890s. There was also Jewish emigration from Germany, Austria-Hungary, and Rumania, often prompted by particular events, including Bismarck's expulsion of alien Poles from Prussia in 1886, and a dramatic 'protest march' from Rumania to the North Sea in 1899–1900. Most of the 2 million Jews who left Russia and East Europe in these decades wanted to go to America, but many travelled to Britain, either to settle there or because it was cheaper to change ships at Tilbury, Hull, or Grimsby than to sail directly to America from Bremen or Hamburg. The saving was especially great after 1902, when the fare from England to the USA was cut from £6 10s to £2, while that from Hamburg was unchanged.

Since London offered enormous opportunities for work and accommodation, and there was no restriction on the right to enter and settle in Britain, many East European Jewish refugees decided to stay in London rather than undertake a difficult and costly journey across the Atlantic. Countless others broke their journey to America in London, and stayed there for weeks, months, or years. There was an established Jewish community in London, amounting to about 45,000 people in 1881, many of whom were of Russian or Polish origin. Over 30,000 of these lived in the district immediately to the east of the City, as far as Commercial Street and Leman Street, especially in the district known as Goodman's Fields. The two main synagogues, in Duke's Place and Bevis Marks, were nearby, on the north-eastern edge of the City. Many of these families had been very successful in business, and Jews were well represented in Lloyd's, the Stock Exchange, and City banks and finance houses, as well as in shipping, wholesale and retail trading, and in some industries, including fur, ostrich feathers, meerschaum pipes, cigars, clothing, and jewellery. A study written in the 1880s concluded that three-quarters of London Jewish families had annual incomes of over £100 (a good wage for a skilled craftsman or clerk), making them far more middle-class than London's population as a whole.[1] Whether these relatively well-off and emancipated Jewish Londoners, who had spent decades accommodating themselves to the economy and culture of a Gentile society, would have much in common with Yiddish-speaking East Europeans who came to London as paupers and refugees, determined to preserve their religious orthodoxy in an alien environment, remained to be seen.

The most powerful voices of English Jewry, the Jewish Board of Guardians, the *Jewish Chronicle*, the United Synagogue, and the richest Jewish families, the Rothschilds and Montefiores, were afraid that the arrival of many thousands of impoverished and uneducated eastern Jews would swamp Jewish charities and rekindle anti-Semitism in England. Poorer Dutch and East European Jews who were already settled in Stepney and Whitechapel feared that new immigrants, willing to work for very little, would overcrowd the East End job and housing market on which they depended. In the 1880s Jewish newspapers in Eastern Europe carried warnings from English Jews that economic and political conditions in England were not what they expected. Better to stay in Russia, a paper said in 1886, than 'perish in destitution in a strange land'.[2] Those who defied this advice were not to be given assistance or hospitality when they arrived in London, in case such generosity encouraged others to follow them.

For a few months in the refugee crisis of 1882 the Lord Mayor's Mansion House Fund gave some emergency help, but after this much of the most valuable work in London on behalf of 'greeners', as newly arrived Jews were called, was done by individual Jews who defied the official policy. The most resourceful of these was a Jewish baker, Simha Becker (or Simon Cohen), who allowed newly arrived immigrants to sleep and eat in the back room of his bakery in Church Lane (now Adler Street and Back Church Lane), off Whitechapel High Street. The Jewish Board of Guardians discovered this shelter in April 1885, and had it closed down on the grounds that it was unsanitary. Some wealthy Jews who did not agree with the policy of cold-shouldering Jewish migrants, including Sir Samuel Montagu, MP for Whitechapel, and Hermann Landau, a stockbroker, provided a better building, and opened the Poor Jews' Temporary Shelter in October 1885. The sponsors of the Shelter were keen to avoid the charge that they were encouraging Jews to come to London, and limited a migrant's stay to fourteen days, with two meals a day and no money. In this way, the Shelter was able to help between 1,000 and 4,000 immigrants every year. The Shelter performed a particularly useful service by sending agents down to the wharves where immigrants disembarked, to save them from the multitude of swindlers, including some who spoke Yiddish, who took advantage of travellers when they arrived in London. Speaking only Russian, Polish, Yiddish, or German, 'greeners' were easy prey for dockside parasites who overcharged them for carrying their luggage, took them to overpriced and dishonest lodging houses, sold them worthless travel tickets, and tricked lone girls into prostitution. By 1900, according to the Shelter, most of these shysters had been driven out of the London docks.[3]

Far more Jews passed through London in the 1880s and 1890s than would eventually settle there. Almost 400,000 alien immigrants (not all of them Jewish) landed in London between 1888 and 1905, but the great majority of these were transmigrants, on their way to South Africa, Australia, South America, and especially the USA. It is thought that 15 per cent of Jews on their way to the USA travelled through London. The Poor Jews' Temporary Shelter had an arrangement with a shipping company, Donald Currie and Co., charging a small fee to look after its passengers en route to the Cape. Other migrants found themselves on a ship returning to the place they had taken such trouble to escape. Between 1880 and 1906 over 30,000 penniless Jewish migrants were helped to return to Russia or Poland by the Jewish Board of Guardians, the Poor Jews' Temporary Shelter, and other Jewish charities, on the grounds, it was said, that they had failed to establish an independent livelihood for themselves after some months in England. If the flow of migrants had to be regulated, the Jewish Board of Guardians argued, it was better for Jews to do it than to wait for the state to step in.

The number of Jewish migrants who eventually settled in London is uncertain. The census did not collect information on race or faith, but its records of places of birth suggest the size of the main flow from Russia and Poland. The number of Russian- and Polish-born Londoners in 1881, 8,709, tripled to 26,742 by 1891, and doubled again to 53,537 by 1901. Over the next ten years, when new controls came into force, the figure rose by less than 10,000. Some of the later arrivals were women and children joining their husbands, fathers, or brothers. London's Russian- and Polish-born population was only 42 per cent female in 1881, and 48 per cent in 1911. Many of these newly arrived couples wanted children, and the birth rate in the areas they settled was about a third higher than that in other parts of working-class London in the 1890s. Because Jewish mothers looked after their children well and had very high standards of domestic cleanliness, infant mortality was relatively very low in immigrant families, so the Jewish population of East London grew quickly. In 1889 Llewellyn Smith used elementary-school attendance figures to reach an estimate of between 60,000 and 70,000 Jews in East London, about half of whom were foreign-born, but this relied upon guessing the proportion of Jews attending school. A study for the Royal Statistical Society by S. Rosenbaum, based on the 1901 census and the number of Jewish weddings in 1903, produced an estimated Jewish population of 144,000, about 120,000 of whom lived in Stepney, where they made up about 40 per cent of the population.[4] In the western world, only New York and Chicago had bigger East European Jewish populations than London.

Following a familiar migrant practice, Jewish men usually arrived first, intending to make contact with friends or relatives and with their help find work and lodgings before sending for their families. Eventually most of those who wished to stay in London made their way to the established Jewish district east of Houndsditch, and found work in the local clothing, shoemaking, furniture, or cigar trades, or perhaps as bakers or street-sellers. Often, this meant accepting a reduction in status and independence for the sake of peace and safety. According to the records of the Poor Jews' Temporary Shelter, over a third of newly arrived men they sheltered in the 1880s had been self-employed traders before their flight, but Llewellyn Smith's analysis of the 1891 census concluded that only 15 per cent of working East London Jews were in trading and commercial occupations, and 80 per cent were in manufacturing, mainly making clothes and shoes. Some of these were employers, but the great majority were wage-labourers, at the lower end of London's vast working class.[5]

Jewish Whitechapel

As the Jewish population grew in the 1880s, it spread eastwards across Commercial Street (the eastern boundary of the older Jewish East End) into the rest of Whitechapel, and then into Mile End New Town, Mile End Old Town, and the southern parts of Bethnal Green, a borough that had been almost entirely British-born in 1881. There was hardly any Jewish settlement south of Cable Street, in the riverside districts of Shadwell, Rat-cliffe, and Limehouse, and the Jewish population got much thinner east of the Metropolitan Underground line between Whitechapel and Shadwell (though there were Jews as far east as Stepney Green), and north of the railway line from Liverpool Street to Shoreditch. Jewish settlers were con-centrated in an area of about two square miles, and in some small parts of Whitechapel and St George-in-the-East they created an East European Jewish world of workshops, markets, schools, and street games. In the early 1880s conditions in these districts were poor. A report by a 'special sani-tary committee' of the Lancet in May 1884 found the streets of the triangle of land between Commercial Street, Hanbury Street, and Old Montague Street crowded with little tailoring workshops in which women worked for fifteen hours or more every day, hiding when factory inspectors made their rare visits. The rooms occupied by the new arrivals were predictably appalling: broken stairs, overflowing toilets, wet walls, no beds, stinking yards, primitive sanitary habits, and intolerable overcrowding. In one block,

Shepherd's Buildings, 150 people occupied thirty-nine tenements, and in Booth Street 230 rooms had a total of 700 inhabitants.[6]

Beatrice Potter's conclusions, when she examined the state of the East End tailoring trades and the Jewish community in 1887–8, were less gloomy than the *Lancet*'s. She was sure that the Jews' intellectual training and physical and mental endurance would see them through their difficult early years in Whitechapel. 'They are set down in an already over-stocked and demoralised labour market; they are surrounded by the drunkenness, immorality, and gambling of the East-End streets; they are, in fact, placed in the midst of the very refuse of our civilization, and yet . . . whether they become bootmakers, tailors, cabinetmakers, glaziers, or dealers, the Jewish inhabitants of East London rise in the social scale.' Some Jewish men were fond of gambling, she said, but they did not drink, and in general they were 'the most law-abiding inhabitants of East London. They keep the peace, they pay their debts, and they abide by their contracts.'[7]

There is a unique record of the Jewish quarter at the end of the century, when Booth and his researchers walked round London with Metropolitan Police officers making notes on the tone and condition of every street. In March 1898 George Duckworth went with Inspector Reid around the Whitechapel neighbourhood between Cable Street, Commercial Road, Cannon Street Road, and Backchurch Street, where most streets were almost entirely Jewish. His descriptions of Boyd Street, Everard Street (parallel to Boyd Street), and Waterloo Court (near the present Golding Street) emphasized the strength of Jewish family life, and helped explain the low rate of infant mortality:

> Boyd Street, 2 st [storey], all foreign, many cannot speak or understand English . . . Children hatless but well fed, crowding, narrow street. Everard St, still narrower, 2 st ho [houses] 15 ft frontage, lamps for street lighting on brackets against the house walls. St full of all foreign, some rags but all children (crowds of them) well fed [and] happy, skipping ropes, hoops, women at doors, rough cobble roadway, almost blocked by one costers barrow . . .
>
> Waterloo Court, not coloured on map, 20 houses, inhabited by very poor Jews, only 3½ feet between the houses, mess, fish heads at entrance, feather beds hanging out to air from some of the windows, women inside houses, rocking babies in large wooden cradles, very close quarters. Quiet.
>
> General Remarks. Great improvement in this district since the incoming of the Jews. Black spots have gone. English remain in small

colonies in courts as yet unswamped by the Jewish tides. Where the
races are mixed neither is pleased & quarrels result.

Jewish children all look particularly well-fed . . .

Everard St and Boyd St are almost entirely foreign & many can
neither speak nor understand English.[8]

The neighbourhood to the north of this, in the angle between Commercial Road and Whitechapel High Street, was another largely segregated
district, messy, foreign, and improving:

> Disappearance of black and dark blue spots; Trades of district shoes,
> slippers & boots, tailoring; absorption of district by Jews: English
> remain in streets & courts which are wholly English . . . There is a
> mixture of English & Jews in some streets but friction & quarrels the
> inevitable result. The repulsion felt of one for the other is mutual.
>
> Great mess in Jewish streets – fish heads – paper of all colours –
> bread (not a great deal of this) – orange peel in abundance.
>
> The constant whirr of sewing machines or tap of the Hammer as
> you pass through the streets; women with dark abundant hair, olive
> complexion, no hats but shawls – Children well-fed and dressed.
>
> Dark beards, fur caps & long boots of men – The feeling as of
> being in a foreign town.[9]

Jewish settlement kept the population of Stepney growing in the
1880s and 1890s when those of other inner suburban boroughs were stag-
nant or in decline. One of the results of this was that overcrowding was
more severe in Stepney than anywhere else in London, and its house rents
rose more than twice as fast as the London average. When non-Jews complained about Jewish settlement in the East End the problem of high rents
often figured alongside complaints about strange East European habits,
industrial smells, and Jewish clannishness in their list of grievances. From
time to time non-Jewish residents took direct action to stop Jews from set-
tling in their neighbourhood. A blind piano tuner from Stepney told the
Royal Commission on Alien Immigration in 1903: 'there is a place just
south of where we are sitting called Wapping . . . where they will not admit
a foreigner. In fact, I lived in Old Gravel Lane for some years myself, and
on more than one occasion when the foreigners have come there to live I
have seen [sic] the native population of that place go and smash the windows and turn the foreigners out.'[10] There were other reasons for rising
rents, especially the demolition of slum streets and the building of higher-

priced municipal or philanthropic tenement blocks, but blaming immigration was always an attractive option.

The Aliens Act

To some observers the arrival of Jewish refugees seemed to make the East End a more threatening place than ever. Although it was acknowledged that Jews were hard-working and law-abiding their presence appeared to intensify the conditions that produced crime, disorder, and immorality – overcrowding, unemployment, low wages, sweating, and pauperism. It was quite widely argued, even by Booth and Beatrice Potter, that Jews were capable of living on less food, and in poorer accommodation, than English workers, and thus dragged down wages and pushed up rents. This argument, which had been used against Irish immigrants in the eighteenth century, could be developed into an attack on Jewish sanitary habits, and the suggestion that they were almost less than human. This is George Green, Secretary of the London-based National Union of Boot Clickers (cutters), speaking to a Royal Commission in 1892:

> They can live on 2d a day, whereas an Englishman would not, or could not if he would . . . they debar themselves from the common and absolutely necessaries of life. They spend nothing in soap, for instance, or anything of that kind. As for clothing, what they wear is filthy . . . If you saw them walking about you would think they were animals rather than men. They do not even know what morality means.[11]

These crude prejudices were shaped into a fairly persuasive anti-immigrant case by men such as Arnold White, an imperialist writer and politician who addressed many anti-Jewish rallies and meetings from the mid-1880s onwards. The anti-Jewish case rested on several key arguments: that Jewish immigrants were unwilling to integrate with the local population, either through marriage or by adopting English food, education, or national loyalties; that they had come to England for economic advantage, especially charitable handouts, rather than from fear of persecution; that by crowding the housing and labour markets they pauperized native Londoners; and that their poor physical condition lowered the quality of the national stock. On these grounds, it was argued that alien immigration should be restricted or stopped.

There was a strong Liberal and libertarian case against the control of immigration, which managed to hold off the demand for legislation for twenty years. The unhindered movement of people and goods was fundamental to the system of free trade that had made Victorian Britain and the world so prosperous, and a system of regulation would increase the state's power over its citizens, reducing individual freedom in a way that was inherently undesirable, in return for no clear gain. It was plainly wrong, the free-traders argued, to assume that extra population would lead to unemployment, rather than economic growth, and it was foolish to assert that someone who arrived in London penniless would become a pauper, a burden on the rates. The assertion that Jews had made the problem of sweated industry worse was effectively repudiated by the report of a House of Lords Select Committee on Sweating in 1890. After hearing 291 witnesses the committee concluded that the evils of the sweating system existed in equal measure in trades which had been entered by Jews and those that had not. It was true that Jews lived on starvation wages and worked incredibly long hours, but they were thrifty, industrious, well behaved, and self-supporting. The chief causes of the sweating system, it decided, were 'the inefficiency of many of the lower classes of workers, early marriages, and the tendency of the residuum of the population in large towns to form a helpless community, together with a low standard of life and the excessive supply of unskilled labour'.[12]

For Conservative politicians trying to win working-class votes in solidly Liberal East End constituencies, anti-Jewish feeling offered a golden opportunity. The issue first arose in 1885, when Conservative officials tried to have 1,800 un-naturalized Jews removed from the Whitechapel electoral register. In the 1892 General Election almost all Conservative candidates in the East End, including several who were themselves Jewish, played the anti-alien card. Its impact on the election is hard to distinguish from other factors, because personal loyalties, generous expenditure, and the influence of major local employers were still very powerful in working-class constituencies, and deals between Liberal and trade union or Labour candidates could be decisive. In Whitechapel, where a quarter of the population (though not a quarter of the voters) were Russian and Polish immigrants, the Liberal MP Samuel Montagu, a leader of the Anglo-Jewish community, was almost bound to win. In St George-in-the-East, where the Jewish population was rising fast in the 1890s, the Conservative candidate in 1892 ignored the aliens issue and lost the seat, but his successor won it back in 1895 and 1902 by using a combination of bribery and anti-alien propaganda. The victorious Conservative candidates in Stepney and Limehouse in 1895 were well-off Jews who supported restrictions on the immigration of pauper aliens, and in Bethnal Green south-west, where Jewish settlement was spreading, a Conservative who campaigned against immigration snatched the seat from its Liberal incumbent in 1900. In the remaining six East London constituencies Jewish settlement was not very great, and social and industrial issues were more important than the question of alien paupers.[13]

The crude anti-Semitism of some East End workers and shopkeepers was reflected in the British Brothers League, which was founded in 1901 and held its first mass meeting in the People's Palace on the Mile End Road in January 1902, when Boer War patriotism was still at fever pitch. The mood in this and later meetings, with lusty patriotic singing and Jewish protesters roughed up and bundled out by brawny stewards recruited from the local docks and chemical works, marks the League as a forerunner of London fascism in the 1930s. The League won support from employers and property owners by blaming immigrants drawing poor relief for the fact that Stepney's local property tax (the rates) had risen by 50 per cent between 1890 and 1906. Several East London Conservative MPs supported the League, and its anti-alien petition collected 45,000 signatures. Even before the January 1902 meeting the Conservative Cabinet was considering a new enquiry into immigration, and on 23 January (a week after the meeting) a Royal Commission on Alien Immigration was appointed. Though there were opponents of state restrictions on immigration on the Commission, including Baron (Nathan Meyer) Rothschild, restrictionists were in the majority, and William Evans Gordon, the anti-alien MP for Stepney, was an influential member.

Following the recommendations of the Royal Commission, the Aliens Act of 1905 imposed legal disabilities on aliens for the first time since 1870, and ended a policy of free entry that had existed for eighty years. The Act was passed at a time when a combination of an economic crisis, the threat of conscription for the Russo-Japanese War, and a new wave of pogroms in the repressive aftermath of the failed 1905 Russian revolution pushed Jewish emigration to Britain to unprecedented levels. Steerage passengers on 'immigrant ships' (those with over twenty aliens travelling steerage) had to land at ports with immigration officers, who would exclude from Britain any aliens who were considered 'undesirable'. Undesirables included those not in a position to support themselves or their family, those whose mental or physical disabilities made them likely to become a burden on the rates, and people convicted abroad of extraditable crimes. Refugees from political or religious persecution or punishment were exempted from these restrictions. Appeal was to a three-man board, not to a court of law. Furthermore, the Act allowed the Home Secretary to expel any resident alien convicted of an offence that carried a custodial punishment, or an alien who within a year of arriving in the UK claimed poor relief, became a vagrant, or was found 'living under insanitary conditions due to overcrowding' – a description that might be applied to about a third of the population of East London. Conservative politicians who generally disliked state intervention justified the measure as a way of ensuring the nation's fitness to survive in an increasingly competitive world. To achieve this, Arthur Balfour, the Prime Minister, said, 'we have a right to keep out everybody who does not add to the strength of the community'. Sir Charles Dilke, the Liberal ex-minister who dared to suggest that an admixture of Russian Jews, however miserable their present condition seemed to be, might improve the British stock rather than degrade it, received little support.[14] At the same time it was made more difficult for an alien to gain British citizenship. As well as paying taxes and obeying the law, aliens (in the words of a Home Office circular of 1905) had to prove that they could 'speak, read or write English reasonably well', as an indication that they had identified with the culture and customs of their adopted land.[15]

The Liberal government that came to power in December 1905, and won a landslide election victory in January 1906, did not enforce the Aliens Act as vigorously as the Act's supporters would have liked, and in 1906, when there were 700 pogroms in Bessarabia and the Ukraine, those claiming refugee status were given the benefit of the doubt. This indulgence was temporary, and the number of immigrants admitted to Britain as refugees fell from 505 in 1906 to a total of under a hundred in the next four years. The number of Russians and Russian Poles entering Britain was much higher than this: 12,481 in 1906, falling to 4,223 in 1910. About 4,000 were refused entry between 1906 and 1910, and unknown numbers were discouraged by the 1905 Act from even trying to enter Britain. The outcome was a significant fall in new Jewish settlement in Britain. According to estimates published in the *Jewish Year Book* the number of Jews in the UK rose by 42 per cent between 1901 and 1905, but by only 4.6 per cent between 1906 and 1911.[16] Perhaps as a result of this fall in immigration, rents in west Stepney, where Jewish settlement was concentrated, fell by 15 per cent between 1905 and 1910.[17]

Becoming Londoners

The settlement of almost 100,000 East European and Russian Jews in East London, bringing with them the customs of a strange and distant society, and determined to preserve the beliefs and observances of orthodox Judaism, raised questions of integration, conformity, and the nature of 'Englishness'. Nobody emphasized the need for the rapid Anglicization of the newcomers more than the established Jewish community, which feared that two centuries of work to achieve acceptance as patriotic Englishmen and women might be undone by a reawakening of anti-Semitism. 'Whatever they are, we are thought to be', said the *Jewish Chronicle* in October 1881. Mutual hostility between English and immigrant Jews was stronger, it was claimed in 1900, than that between Jews and Gentiles. English Jews accused the newcomers of bringing their religion into disrepute by their low sanitary habits and their practice of using foreign rabbis to perform illegal marriage ceremonies, and the strictly orthodox immigrants were shocked to find that English Jews had abandoned so many important religious beliefs and observances.[18]

The concentration of such a large population of Russian and Polish Jews in East London made it relatively easy for the newcomers to cling on to the language and traditions they had brought with them. There were hundreds of tiny schoolrooms, or *cheder*, all over the East End in which Jewish boys learned their prayers and scriptures from Yiddish-speaking teachers before and after school, and many *steibels* (little house-based synagogues) and *chevras* (religious associations), in which immigrant Jews could meet, pray, and read the Talmud in the traditional way, perhaps with others from their own part of Russia or Poland, rather than participate in the watered-down Anglicized worship they found in the bigger London synagogues. Samuel Montagu, one of the most enlightened leaders of Anglo-Jewry, grouped some of these *chevras* (the Sons of Łódź in New Castle Street, the United Brethren of Konin in Hanbury Street, and fourteen others) into the Federation of Synagogues in 1887. The Federation was funded and led by Montagu, but the Anglo-Jewish religious authority, the United Synagogue, would not accept it, and instead pursued its own ineffective efforts to establish its control over the East End. Reacting to these efforts, highly orthodox Jews based in a *chevra* in Booth Street (now part of Princelet Street) started a new community in 1891 called Machzichei HaDath (Upholders of the Religion), recognizing the leadership of its own rabbi, Aba Werner, rather than the English Chief Rabbi, Hermann Adler. In 1898 Machzichei HaDath leased an old Methodist chapel on the corner of Fournier Street and Brick Lane (built by Huguenots in 1743), and converted it into the Spitalfields Great Synagogue, which became the most popular in the East End. The community remained independent until the need for money brought it under the Chief Rabbi's authority in 1905. Today the synagogue is an Islamic centre serving the Bengali community that replaced the Jewish population of Whitechapel in the 1960s and 1970s, and which will no doubt be replaced in its turn. As the motto over the old chapel sundial reminds us, 'Umbra Sumus' – We are Shadows.

English Jews, led by the Jewish Board of Guardians and the Jewish Board of Deputies, did their best to promote the process of cultural integration, and although some of their efforts (especially the plan to disperse Jewish immigrants into other parts of London and England) were resisted, others were accepted. The Rothschild-funded Jews' Free School between Bell Lane and Middlesex Street, which had been established in 1817, was so popular with immigrant families, despite the fact that it offered a largely secular Anglo-Jewish education, that by 1900 its roll had increased to 4,300, making it the biggest elementary school in the kingdom, and probably the world. There were also many elementary schools in East London provided by the London School Board, and sixteen of these, with over 15,000 pupils (in 1902) were almost entirely Jewish, offered short Hebrew and Jewish religious lessons, and closed early on winter Fridays. Still, thousands of Jewish immigrant children had to go to Christian elementary schools, getting their Jewish education in the evenings and at weekends. Parents who wanted their sons to become more 'English' might enrol them in the Jewish Lads' Brigade or the Brady Street Club for Working Lads, both of which were founded in the mid-1890s with the aim of promoting manliness and athleticism, and (in the words of the Brigade Commander) 'ironing out the Ghetto bend'.[19]

One of the most effective ways of Anglicizing Jewish immigrants was to rehouse them in decent conditions. In 1884 the Jewish Board of Guardians set up a Sanitary Committee, which pressed the Whitechapel Board of Works to do something about the squalid conditions in which Jewish newcomers were forced to live. The Whitechapel Board replied that it was unable to cope with the flood of migrants, and the United Synagogue set up an East End Enquiry Commission, chaired by Britain's most powerful Jew, Nathan Meyer Rothschild, to find a way forward. Its conclusion was that improvement in the physical, moral and social condition of poor East End Jews could best be achieved by giving them decent homes at affordable rents, built and funded on the principles that had guided London's charitable housing companies and trusts for the past forty years. In March 1884 Rothschild gathered nineteen of London's richest and most influential Jews, and together they formed the Four Per Cent Industrial Dwellings Company, which would raise £40,000 from share-holders, and pay them a dividend of 4 per cent. In May he spent £7,000 on a large site which the Metropolitan Board of Works had cleared of slums in 1883, but had been unable to sell. The plot, a little over an acre between Flower and Dean Street, Commercial Street, Keate Street (now Thrawl Street) and George Street (now Lolesworth Street), had once been part of the notorious Flower and Dean Street rookery. By 1887 the Company had built three simple six-storey yellow-brick blocks, Charlotte de Rothschild Buildings, containing 198 flats, mostly with two rooms, a toilet and scullery, and rented at about six shillings a week. Most of the thousand people who moved into Rothschild Buildings were East European Jews.[20] The 'semi-criminal' inhabitants of the slums demolished to make way for the Rothschild Buildings moved across Commercial Street into the alleys around Dorset Street, and the streets east of the Buildings remained among the worst in Whitechapel.[21]

Jewish life in the East End was not restricted to sweatshops, syna-gogues, schools, and soup kitchens. London's Yiddish-speaking population was large enough to sustain several short-lived Yiddish newspapers, and to encourage the beginnings of Yiddish theatre in London. There were small theatre and opera troupes, and in 1886–7 a group led by the actor Jacob Adler had a theatre in Princelet Street. In 1887 they left for New York, where Yiddish theatre was thriving. Some local music halls and theatres responded to changing local demand, and under the management of Morris Abrahams in the 1880s and 1890s the Pavilion Theatre, on the corner of Whitechapel Road and Vallance Road, was famous for its Yid-dish plays and pantomimes. Abrahams had previously managed the very rough Effingham Saloon (or East London) theatre, also on Whitechapel Road, which burned down in 1879 and was reopened as the Wonderland in 1880. This showed Yiddish plays until 1894, when it was converted into a boxing saloon. Until 1911, when it burned down again, the Wonderland was the headquarters of Jewish boxing in London. Its great star was the 'Aldgate Sphinx', Ted 'Kid' Lewis (Gershon Mendeloff), who started boxing there in 1909, and won the British and European featherweight titles in 1913–14, and the world welterweight title in 1915. Other successful Jewish boxers of the pre-war years included Cockney Cohen, Aschel 'Young' Joseph, who took the European welterweight title from 'Battling' Lacroix in Paris in 1910 and lost it to Georges Charpentier in 1911, and Matt Wells, who represented Britain in the 1908 Olympics and won the world welterweight title in 1914.

Arthur Harding, who misspent his youth as a pickpocket, thief, and protection racketeer along Brick Lane in the 1890s and 1900s, remembered Whitechapel Jews as victims, competitors, and colleagues. Alongside the reputable Jewish world of tailors and market traders, there was a disreputable world of Jewish pickpockets, receivers, and mobsters. There was Mishe the Gonnoff, working Petticoat Lane as a pickpocket from his home in Old Montague Street, and Ruby Michaels, a receiver, who operated from the Three Tuns pub in Aldgate and the Warsaw restaurant at the southern – Jewish – end of Brick Lane. In the years before the First World War the East End Jewish criminal world was dominated by Edward Emmanuel, whose gang of 'terrors' included Jackie Berman, Bobby Levy, and Bobby Nark.[22]

Over time the Jewish settlement in East London, with its intriguing mixture of East European and London customs, became an accepted and picturesque part of the metropolitan cultural mix. The exotic enclave the Jews had established in Whitechapel, with its noisy Sunday market in Petticoat Lane, its Yiddish shop signs and street cries, its bearded men and bewigged women, its kosher restaurants and butcher's shops, was part of what visitors to the East End expected to see. Among the coloured pictures of familiar 'London types' illustrating George R. Sims' multi-authored three-volume study of *Living London*, which was published at the start of the new century, there were a rabbi and an 'alien street merchant' alongside the Chelsea pensioner and the pavement artist. A chapter by S. Gelberg on Jewish London described the Whitechapel ghetto, 'a fragment of Poland torn off from Central Europe and dropped haphazard into the heart of Britain', in sympathetic and sentimental terms: 'Altogether, indeed, a unique little cosmos, this East-End Hebrew colony – a poverty-stricken, wealthy, hungry, feasting, praying, bargaining fragment of a "nation of priests".' Despite their foreignness, Gelberg claimed, the East End Jews were 'patriots to their fingertips', and Jewish religious and social festivals, celebrated with fervour and delight, brought colour into the drabness of slum life. And one of the great sights of East London, the Sunday market in Middlesex Street, or Petticoat Lane, owed much of its size and vigour to Jewish traders. It was, said Gelberg,

> a howling pandemonium of cosmopolitan costerism, a curious tangle of humanity, with the Englishman (Jew and Gentile) in possession and the alien in the background. In these congested streets you can be clothed like an aristocrat for a few shillings, fed al fresco like an epicure for sixpence, and cured of all your bodily ills for a copper coin . . . The 'Lane' on Sunday is, indeed, the last home of the higher costerism. Round its stalls the coster humour reaches its finest fancies, the coster philosophy its profoundest depths, the coster oratory its highest flights. But the most abiding impression it leaves on your mind as you struggle through its seething, shouting, gesticulating, population is of infinite picturesqueness, and the life-stream tumbling like a swirling torrent along its course.

Middlesex Street was spectacular on Sundays, but for the rest of the week it was outdone by Wentworth Street, running east from Middlesex Street to Brick Lane, which was far busier, and far more Jewish. The novelist and London 'expert' Edwin Pugh described the street just after 1900:

> Each ground floor is a shop, and the kerb on either side of the road is cumbered with stalls. As you work your way through the press of people it is easy to imagine that you are in a foreign city. On every side are un-English faces, un-English wares, un-English writings on the walls. The accents of an unknown tongue assail your ears. Your companions are mostly women, Jewesses, the majority wearing the black wigs of the matron over their scanty locks . . . Fish and poultry are the articles of commerce in which trade is most brisk. At every step you come upon a woman carrying a fluttering fowl or two, or a slab of fish in a basket with kosher herbs. There is bountiful good-humour and good-nature, too, or the beggars would not be so numerous.[23]

*

CHAPTER SIX

SOCIALISTS AND THE UNEMPLOYED

The achievement of extensive (though not yet equal) voting rights for urban working men in 1867 (and again in 1884) removed the great issue that had been the focus of radical political movements in London since the late eighteenth century. But in the 1880s socialism, the ideology that replaced manhood suffrage as the rallying point for radicals and reformists, started to take root among intellectuals and some working men in London. The practical issue that attracted poorer Londoners to socialism in the 1880s was unemployment, a problem which perhaps for this reason also began to be taken more seriously by economists and mainstream politicians in the 1890s and 1900s. These were the decades, too, in which trade unionism, previously the preserve of an exclusive elite of skilled workers, started to attract a much larger body of unskilled men and women, who were more likely to look to socialists, rather than Liberals, as their natural allies. This alliance between socialists and trade unionists, which transformed political life in the twentieth century, had its origins in London and other industrial cities in the 1880s and 1890s.

Social Democrats and Fabians

Late Victorian London, the heartland of global capitalism, also sheltered some of its most vocal opponents. Karl Marx, the greatest of anti-capitalist theorists, died in his house in Maitland Park Road, Belsize Park, in March 1883, but his friend and collaborator, Friedrich Engels, lived on in Regent's Park Road until 1895, and his daughter, Eleanor Marx, was active in socialism and trade unionism until her suicide in 1898. An equally important stimulus to the growth of socialism in London was the American political economist Henry George, who made a sensationally successful tour of England in 1882. George's analysis of the ills of the industrial world began with the proposition that the 'association of poverty with progress is the great enigma of our times. It is the central fact from which spring industrial, social, and political difficulties that perplex the world, and with which statesmanship and philanthropy and education grapple in vain.' The solution, he argued in his bestselling *Progress and Poverty* (1880), was to abolish all taxes and replace them with a single tax on ground rents, which would be enough to fund all the expenses of government. The moral basis for this tax was that the land, like the air and sea, really belonged to all, and landlords were merely custodians who should pay for the privilege of occupation. Late Victorians who explained their conversion to socialism were as likely to mention *Progress and Poverty* as the works of Tom Paine, Marx, or John Stuart Mill. Henry Snell, who progressed from public speaking for secularism and Fabian socialism in London in the 1890s to Labour leadership in the House of Lords in the 1930s, said: 'I was one of the many thousands of young men whose political and social views were greatly stimulated by Henry George's famous book *Progress and Poverty*, which, if measured by the breadth and the depth of its influence on the thoughtful workmen of the eighties, must be considered as one of the greatest political documents of that generation.' The young H. G. Wells read it before he came to London, and picked up the idea that a new socialist order could be achieved without the violent revolution predicted by Marxists.[1]

Both roads to a socialist utopia, the revolutionary and the reformist, were attracting supporters in London in the early 1880s. The key figure in promoting the Marxist vision of class struggle was a wealthy businessman and *Pall Mall Gazette* journalist, Henry M. Hyndman, who had been converted by reading the French edition of Marx's *Das Kapital* in 1880. In 1881 he formed the Democratic Federation, to pursue various radical policies, including adult manhood suffrage and Irish independence. In 1883–4, thanks in part to the atmosphere created by Henry George's visit, Hyndman's new movement won some important recruits, and turned itself into an explicitly socialist organization with ten branches, its own newspaper, and a new name, the Social Democratic Federation (SDF). Edward Pease went along to one of Hyndman's meetings in July 1883: 'the oddest little gathering . . . twenty characteristically democratic men with dirty hands and small heads, some of them obviously with very limited wits, and mostly with some form of foreign accent'.[2] Some of Hyndman's recruits were to become important figures in London socialism and working-class politics. William Morris, the wealthy and very successful designer and manufacturer of textiles, wallpaper, books and furniture, converted from Liberalism to socialism in 1882, and joined Hyndman in January 1883. For nearly two years they worked together, giving out handbills, selling cheaply printed newspapers, and speaking in parks and on street corners. The SDF's inflammatory Marxist newspaper, *Justice*, was not stocked by newsagents, but its authors sold it on the Strand. 'It was a curious scene,' Hyndman recalled. 'Morris in his soft hat and blue suit, [H. H.] Champion, [R. P. B.] Frost and [James] Joynes in the morning garments of the well-to-do, several working-class comrades, and I myself wearing the new frock-coat in which Shaw said I was born, with a tall hat and good gloves, all earnestly engaged in selling a penny Socialist paper during the busiest time of the day in London's busiest thoroughfare.' New speakers were attracted to the cause, notably John Burns, a London engineer and trade unionist with a fine street-corner technique, and Annie Besant, the finest female street orator of her day. Like many other socialists, Morris found Hyndman's autocratic temperament and pro-imperialism difficult to tolerate, and their alliance was brief. After a quarrel, Morris resigned and set up his own Socialist League in December 1884, taking Ernest Belfort Bax, Eleanor Marx, and her unfaithful lover Edward Aveling with him. The Socialist League was rather fragmentary, but it had successful branches in Hammersmith, where Morris's influence was strong, in Bloomsbury, where Marx and Aveling held sway, and in Woolwich. Its newspaper, *Commonweal*, was financed by Morris, and reflected his more thoughtful and philosophical approach to socialism. Most leading members of the SDF fell out with Hyndman sooner or later. John Burns and Tom Mann, two London engineers and trade-union organizers, left in the late 1880s, and the ex-army officer H. H. (Henry Hyde) Champion, one of Hyndman's most important lieutenants, was expelled in 1887. He formed his own party around a monthly paper, the *Labour Elector*. Of all these early socialists the one who managed to put up with Hyndman for the longest was Harry Quelch, an ex-factory worker and warehouseman who had taught himself French and German. Quelch remained in the SDF until his death in 1913, and edited *Justice* for twenty-seven years. It was Quelch's letter of recommendation that got Lenin a British Library ticket in 1908, when he was in London working on a book.

London in the early 1880s seemed to be full of idealistic young men who were dissatisfied with conventional politics and religion, and searching for new ways of understanding and changing their society. Some turned to spiritualism, perhaps joining the Society for Psychical Research, which was set up in 1882 to investigate seances, clairvoyance, ectoplasm, and other apparently supernatural phenomena. Others formed earnest discussion groups, meeting in houses or teashops to formulate their new ideas. One group, calling itself the Progressive Association, met in Islington on Sunday evenings to listen to invited speakers and to discuss the moral awakening of society. Its members, who included Havelock Ellis, Edward Pearse, Percival Chubb, and Frank Podmore, fell under the influence of a charismatic Christian scholar called Thomas Davidson, who wandered between London and Italy advocating the establishment of idealistic semi-monastic communities and the search for 'the New Life'. On 24 October 1883 they met in Pearse's lodgings, along with three members of the SDF (Champion, Joynes, and Frost), and a few young civil servants and City clerks, to discuss Davidson's visionary ideas. This uncomfortable mixture of socialists and high-minded moral reformers met again in November 1883, and decided to call themselves, for the want of any better suggestions, the Fellowship of the New Life. By January 1884 the members with socialistic inclinations – those who wanted to do something practical about economic and social injustice – had driven out the moral-reform faction, those who were more interested in achieving personal moral improvement. Various defections left Pease, Podmore, and Hubert Bland, a failed businessman who dabbled in advanced ideas, in control of the group. They decided to rename it the Fabian Society (after the cautiously successful Roman general Fabius Maximus), and to work for social improvement through persuasion rather than revolution. Their first pamphlet, published in spring 1884, was called *Why are the Many Poor?*. Edith Bland, Hubert Bland's wife, who later wrote very successful children's books under her unmarried name, E. E. Nesbit, came to meetings early in 1884, and found the first Fabians 'quite the nicest set of people I ever knew'.[3] Only one of them, a house-painter called W. L. Phillipps, could be described as a working man.

As yet, the Fabians had no clear sense of direction. They were not wholehearted followers of Henry George's land-reform programme, they did not share the hostility to Christianity of Charles Bradlaugh's National Secular Society, and they found the Marxism and the street-corner politics of the SDF uncongenial. Then, on 16 May 1884, a tall Irishman with frayed cuffs, a thick red beard, 'sarcastic nostrils', and 'the face of an outlaw' came to one of their Friday evening meetings. George Bernard Shaw had arrived in London in 1876 at the age of nineteen, determined to become 'a professional man of genius'. Since then he had been living with his mother and sister, trying to make a living as a writer and failing to find publishers for five novels. Much of his time was spent wandering around London, working in the reading room of the British Museum, and attending the meetings of some of the city's many intellectual and political groups. He had joined the Zetetical Society (for sceptics, seekers, and followers of the Greek philosopher Pyrrho) in 1880 and taken the plunge into public speaking, and another liberal-minded debating club, the London Dialectical Society, in the following year. On the committee of the Zetetical Society, Shaw met an extremely intelligent and well-informed civil service clerk and Birkbeck student, Sidney Webb, a young radical who was, like Shaw, in search of a life-guiding philosophy. A little later, Shaw tried the New Shakespere Society, the Browning Society, and the Shelley Society, and in September 1882 he went to hear Henry George speak on land reform in a hall in Farringdon Street. Hearing and reading George led Shaw towards socialism, and in autumn 1883 he spent days reading the first volume of Marx's *Capital* in French in the British Museum. Its effect on him was tremendous. This book, he wrote to a friend, 'opened my eyes to the facts of history and civilisation, gave me an entirely fresh conception of the universe, provided me with a purpose and a mission in life'.[4] Shaw was also attending and speaking at SDF meetings in 1883–4, but he found the members uneducated (even in the writings of Marx), their leader unappealing and their zealotry unpalatable. Then in May 1884 Hubert Bland met Shaw in the offices of the *Christian Socialist*, the journal of the Land Reform Union, and sent him an invitation to the next meeting of the Fabians. Shaw went, and immediately transformed the Society from a rather aimless debating society into a group with a clear sense of political purpose. He gave a talk which introduced the seventeen propositions that were published as the Fabian manifesto later that year, emphasizing the need for economic reform by persuasion, legislation, and educated leadership, rather than by the mobilization of the masses. To the minutes of that evening's meeting Shaw later added these words, in mauve ink: 'This meeting was made memorable by the first appearance of Bernard Shaw'.

Voters and Intellectuals

So by the end of 1884 there were three significant socialist organizations in London (the SDF, the Fabians, and the Socialist League), where two years earlier there had been none. This fragmentation, which reflected real differences of approach as well as Hyndman's difficult personality, weakened the socialists at what appeared to be a time of great opportunity. There were a huge electoral prize to be won in 1885 if London's voters could be won over by socialist newspapers, pamphlets, and street-corner speeches. The 1885 Redistribution of Seats Act, which created single-member constituencies of roughly equal size, at last gave London something like its fair share of Members of Parliament. The City of London, with its resident population of about 45,000, got two seats, and the rest of the County got fifty-seven, or fifty-eight if London University's MP (elected by its graduates and teaching staff) is included. Outside the County there were another fourteen suburban seats, in areas like West Ham (two seats), Wimbledon, Croydon, Romford, and Kingston, and six mainly urban constituencies in Middlesex: Brentford, Ealing, Hornsey, Tottenham, Enfield, and Harrow. The Franchise Act of 1884, which defined those who could vote for these seventy-four MPs, did not create a democratic electorate in Britain, since women and more than a third of men over twenty-one were excluded from it. But the London electorate was very large, and in almost thirty constituencies working-class voters were probably in the majority. In practice this usually resulted in Liberal victories, and only two London constituencies, West Ham and Battersea in 1892, returned Labour or socialist MPs before 1914. Perhaps results would have been different if the franchise and registration rules had not excluded so many working-class men. Since voters had to occupy a separate dwelling, or lodgings worth £10 a year unfurnished, domestic servants resident with their employers, soldiers in barracks, and sons living at home were voteless. Men living in workhouses, and indeed all those in receipt of poor relief, were disenfranchised, along with lunatics, peers, and prisoners. Those lodging in rented rooms could only vote if they established their right to do so every year, and this usually only happened in closely contested seats where agents of the two big parties made sure that likely voters were on the register. A voter needed to live in his house for a year to qualify to vote, and working-class voters were much more likely to move house than richer ones. If they moved across a constituency boundary they usually lost their right to vote for at least eighteen months – a year to qualify as a resident, and over six months for the new register to come into operation. A lodger lost his residence qualification even if he moved house within a constituency, though if he moved rooms within the same house he could remain on the register. Because London rents were high, there were proportionately more £10 lodgers than anywhere else in England,

and by 1911, after two close-run elections, the party machines had registered over 100,000 of them as voters within the County, out of a total electorate of 663,648, and a County population of over 4.5 million.[5]

The first general election on the new franchise was held in November 1885, and the SDF, which had done its best to win popular support for its policies, decided to test its strength at the ballot box. At H. H. Champion's suggestion, the Federation accepted £340 for its election expenses from the Conservative Party, which hoped to split the radical and Liberal vote. The SDF's pitiful vote, twenty-seven in Hampstead and thirty-two in Kennington, along with the inevitable scandal over their use of 'Tory Gold', demonstrated the political weakness and tactical ineptitude of the SDF, and widened the gulf between the three main socialist groups. An SDF member resigned as secretary of the Fabians, allowing Sidney Webb to take his place on the Fabian executive. While the determination of John Burns, Harry Quelch, and others in the SDF to rely on street agitation and mob action rather than elections was intensified, the Fabians were confirmed in their decision to focus their efforts on the educated and influential classes. The unemployed, Shaw wrote, were a liability, not an asset, because 'the revolt of the empty stomach ends at the baker's shop'.

The ability of the Fabians to attract intellectual heavyweights in the mid-1880s owed much to the charisma and attractiveness of Shaw. One of his most interesting converts was Annie Besant, the secularist who had been tried with her mentor and lover Charles Bradlaugh for publishing a birth-control pamphlet in 1877. Secularism was one of the more active branches of radical thought in London in the 1880s, and for those interested in it there were half a dozen journals available. Foote, the publisher of three of these, the *Secularist*, the *Freethinker*, and *Progress*, spent a year in Newgate and Holloway prisons for blasphemy in 1883–4. Annie Besant campaigned for Foote's release in Bradlaugh's journal, the *National Reformer*, and in this she was helped by Edward Aveling, who edited Foote's journals when Foote was in prison. Besant was drawn towards the sexually and financially dishonest Aveling, whose allure was apparently not diminished by the fact that he had, according to Shaw, 'the face and eyes of a lizard, and no physical charm except a voice like a euphonium'.[6] Aveling and Besant used to work in the Reading Room of the British Museum, where they often met socialists like Bernard Shaw and Eleanor Marx. Aveling was increasingly attracted towards Eleanor Marx and her ideas, and in June 1884 they set up home as Mr and Mrs Aveling in his house in Bloomsbury. It was an unofficial 'free' marriage, which Marx took much more seriously than Aveling. In the end its consequences for her were disastrous.

Charles Bradlaugh was a man of famous moral courage, 'the most muscular man in England'. His campaign to take his seat in the House of Commons without swearing an oath on the Bible was at its height in the early 1880s. He was elected and ejected every year between 1880 and 1885, and finally took his seat as MP for Northampton in 1886, thanks to the support of the new Speaker, Arthur Peel. Bradlaugh was a brilliant public speaker, and often took part in debates against leading socialists. He got the better of Hyndman in St James's Hall, Piccadilly, in April 1884, and in May he appeared with Shaw in a symposium on socialism at the South Place Institute, in Moorgate. Shaw irritated Annie Besant by describing himself as a 'loafer', but she later realized that this was typical Shavian self-mockery, and by the time they met again in January 1885 at a meeting of the Dialectical Society near Oxford Circus, she had recovered from the shock of losing Aveling and had fallen for Shaw instead. Shaw gave a lecture on socialism and expected Besant, an orator of almost mystical power, to demolish him. Instead she attacked his opponents and asked him to propose her for the Fabian Society, which he did a few months later. For Annie Besant, the political was always the personal. Her disillusion with Bradlaugh and Aveling led her to abandon secularism, and her famous conversion to socialism was paralleled by her infatuation with Shaw. He apparently found her admiration rather tiresome, and broke with her early in 1887, after she had proposed that they should live together under the terms of a written contract. In the meantime, Besant helped Shaw to establish himself as a writer by serializing his rejected early novels *The Irrational Knot* and *Love Among the Artists* in her journal, *Our Corner*, and giving him his first work as an art, music, and drama critic. Unusually, she paid him for all these contributions. Besant's work for the socialist movement continued until June 1889, when she sensationally announced that she had converted to Theosophy, a psychic and spiritualist religion which enjoyed a brief vogue among London intellectuals in the late 1880s. This remained her guiding philosophy for the rest of her life.

A much more enduring friendship developed between Shaw and Sidney Webb, the well-informed young man he had met at a meeting of the Zetetical Society in 1880. Webb and his friend Sidney Olivier, in common with many other young men who were repelled by the inefficiency and injustice of untrammelled capitalism, were drawn at first to Positivism, a non-socialist philosophy which advocated a controlled industrial economy and a middle-class ethos of dedication to public service. Their conversion to socialism took place in the winter of 1884–5, when they went to meetings of the Karl Marx Club in Charlotte Wilson's converted farmhouse just north of Hampstead Heath. In these comfortable surroundings doubters like Webb, Olivier, and Pease discussed Marxism with others who had already embraced it, including Belfort Bax, John Burns, and Bernard Shaw. Webb and Olivier joined the Fabians in May 1885, and over the next two or three years, along with Shaw, Podmore, and Wilson, they used the monthly meetings of the Karl Marx Club, which was renamed the Hampstead Historic Society, to develop a Fabian version of socialism which combined a Marxist view of history with a non-Marxist economics based on the Marginal Utility theory of W. S. Jevons.[7]

Trouble in Trafalgar Square

In the mid-1880s, economic and social circumstances seemed to favour the propagation of socialist ideas. The exposure of the London housing crisis in 1883 led even some Conservative politicians to consider state and municipal solutions to a problem which had until then been left to charity and the free market. And in 1884–7 there was an unusually deep and prolonged industrial depression which hit the London economy very hard. National unemployment rates among the best-paid and most skilled industrial workers – those in trade unions – were 8, 9, and 10 per cent in those three years, and the figures among unorganized and unskilled workers (the great majority of the London workforce) were almost certainly much higher, though they are unknown. The London Chamber of Commerce told the Royal Commission into the Depression of Trade and Industry in 1886 that the metals, shipbuilding, printing, engineering, chemicals, and building industries were severely depressed, and there were also long-term problems in tanning, dock-work, watchmaking, and the sweated clothing and furniture industries. Even the agricultural depression and cheap imported food, which meant that Londoners in the mid-1880s could buy their bread, bacon, and cheese more cheaply than ever before, had economic disadvantages. Wealthy landed families who lived for part of the year in London, but drew their incomes from farm rents on their country estates, could afford to employ fewer servants, and to buy fewer carriages, gowns, jewels, and other London-made luxury goods. Charles Booth, whose study of London poverty began at the end of the 1884–7 depression, believed that over 60 per cent of the poor in East London and Hackney – nearly 200,000 heads of households – were either unemployed or inadequately employed in casual or irregular work. Some of this unemployment resulted from cyclical fluctuations in demand for labour and goods, but much was the result of the chronic overstocking of the East London labour market, and of seasonal patterns of demand for goods and labour. Most workers, except those in the fuel industries (gas, coal, and wood) and indoor entertainment (theatres and music halls), along with sweeps, furriers, and undertakers, had a slack season after Christmas. The recent influx of Polish and Russian Jews into East London intensified competition for cheap housing and unskilled work in the sweated clothing and furniture trades. A national depression like that of 1884–7, or the smaller one of 1908–10, simply added an extra degree of uncertainty to what was at best an overcrowded and irregular labour market. The common view in the 1880s was that a trade depression did something even more dangerous, by pushing 'decent' working men into temporary alliance with the degenerates, idlers, and outcasts who made up London's very large casual workforce in good years and bad.

In the winter of 1885–6 several of these sources of uncertainty came together to create a severe crisis. February was bitterly cold, forcing the suspension of most building and dock work, making other outdoor jobs scarce, and pushing up food prices. A big London sugar refinery had closed, the Millwall shipyard was in the doldrums, and there was a movement of small hardware manufacturers from London to the Midlands.[8] Taking advantage of the mood of discontent, a Conservative movement campaigning for protectionist tariffs, the Fair Trade League, organized four marches of unemployed men from South, North-west, and East London, to converge on Trafalgar Square at 3 o'clock on 8 February 1886. The SDF leaders, spotting a plot to divert working-class discontent up a blind alley, decided to take the demonstration over when it reached the Square. Forewarned of possible trouble by the League, the Metropolitan Police had about 560 extra men on duty that afternoon. By 1.30 there were already about 15,000 unemployed men in the Square, mostly builders, dockers, and sugar-refinery workers. Defying the police, John Burns managed to make a short speech urging the crowd to abandon protectionism for socialism, and waved a red flag or handkerchief given to him by someone in the crowd. When the marchers turned up an hour later, Burns, Champion, and Hyndman made inflammatory speeches from the north side of the Square (in front of the National Gallery), and scuffles broke out between socialists and free-traders. Some unpopular speakers were dumped in the fountains. Part of the crowd – 'a wholly unorganised mob', in Hyndman's words – now set off along Pall Mall towards Hyde Park, following Hyndman and Burns, who was waving his red flag on a stick, like one of the Parisian Communards of 1871. The police remained in the Square watching the bulk of the demonstrators disperse, and when a police detachment was finally sent off to guard the West End it went by mistake along the Mall towards Buckingham Palace, and thus missed all the action. The SDF's crowd, probably two or three thousand men, moved unopposed along Pall Mall, where many of the exclusive clubs whose members Burns and Hyndman had identified as the enemies of the working class were located. On the left, just after Waterloo Place, the Reform Club and the Carlton Club, the social centres of the Liberal and Conservative parties, stood side by side. Hyndman recalled servants in the Reform Club throwing shoes and nail brushes down at the crowd, and Burns said that someone at a window of the Carlton held his nose, while servants threw crusts and matchboxes. The crowd stoned the Carlton, using material from nearby roadworks, for twenty minutes or so, and then moved on, still unchallenged by the police, to St James's Street, where Arthur's, Brooks's, the Devonshire, Boodle's, and the Thatched House Clubs were damaged, along with the New University Club, which had recently expelled Hyndman for his socialism. After its tour of clubland the crowd turned left into Piccadilly, still en route for Hyde Park. In Piccadilly shops and carriages were looted, and by the time the marchers reached Hyde Park Corner some were merrier, and others better dressed, than they had been before. In Hyde Park some of the crowd dispersed, along with the SDF leaders, but the rest, between five hundred and a thousand men, went north into Mayfair, looting and breaking windows along South and North Audley Street and moving towards the plate-glass windows of Oxford Street. For ninety minutes the leaders of the Metropolitan Police, relying on chance sightings and messages sent on foot, had been unaware of the location and seriousness of the disorder, and had defended the wrong targets. When the Mayfair looters finally met determined resistance, in the shape of a baton charge by fifteen constables, they fled and went home.[9]

The full extent of the police mismanagement of the riots of 8 February 1886 was exposed by a Parliamentary inquiry, which led to the resignation of the Metropolitan Police Commissioner, Sir Edmund Henderson. The total cost of the damage done was put at almost £50,000, and 281 shops claimed compensation for broken windows and lost goods.

The riots emphasized the difference between the 'physical force' SDF and the peaceful groups, the Fabians and the Socialist League, but William Morris came forward to stand bail for Burns, Hyndman, Champion, and Jack Williams when they were charged with sedition. After a rather half-hearted prosecution at the Old Bailey the four were acquitted, and Burns, who defended himself with socialist eloquence, emerged as a popular hero – 'the man with the red flag'.

The Pall Mall riots of Monday 8 February sent shivers down the spines of well-off Londoners. This was the ogre of poverty, ignorance, and violence whose emergence from its East End lair to terrorize the respectable and vulnerable world of the West End they had so often feared, and which Sims had predicted. A thick fog on Tuesday and Wednesday added to the sense of menace, and there were rumours, reported in *The Times*, that many thousands of 'roughs' were gathering in Deptford, Whitechapel, and Bethnal Green, ready to join those still in Trafalgar Square in a concerted attack on the City and West End. On Wednesday large crowds of working men gathered in South London, in the Elephant and Castle and in Deptford, attracted by the rumours of a general rising, but the police easily dispersed them. By the following Monday the *Illustrated London News*, which ran a special supplement on the riots, felt confident that the trouble had been caused by 'a gang of common street ruffians, taking advantage of the incendiary speeches of a few Communist declaimers', and that the conduct of the disgraceful few was 'no reason for withdrawing the sympathy and compassion of benevolent persons in the middle and upper classes from the lamentable state of large numbers of unemployed working men and their families'.[10] Driven by compassion or fear, comfortable Londoners poured money into the Lord Mayor's Mansion House appeal for the unemployed, and a fund which had gathered only £3,300 in the month before the riot collected nearly £60,000 in the fortnight after it. At a political level, the February riot helped to prompt Joseph Chamberlain, who was briefly President of the Local Government Board in Gladstone's Liberal ministry, to issue a circular encouraging local authorities to use public works to relieve exceptional levels of unemployment. An article to the *Pall Mall Gazette* on the question of relief work for the unemployed in February 1886 was the first published piece by Beatrice Potter (later Beatrice Webb).

The depression continued in 1887, and Trafalgar Square was still a gathering place for the homeless and unemployed, who made good use of the fountains, and of the benches placed there at the expense of Lord

Brabazon. This miserable assembly attracted charitable workers and clergymen, and also socialists, who organized marches and demonstrations to stir the consciences of West End churchgoers. In October 1887 the level of socialist activity intensified, and the unemployed were entertained or aroused by speeches from Burns, Shaw, Besant, Morris, Henry George, and two Russian anarchists who had recently taken refuge in London, Prince Peter Kropotkin and Sergius Stepniak. Local businesses and institutions became increasingly indignant or anxious at this constant activity, and the new Metropolitan Police Commissioner, Sir Charles Warren, was worried by the growing ability of the crowd and its leaders to circumvent police controls. 'The condition of the mob is getting very disquieting,' he reported to the Home Secretary on 31 October. 'By some private signal they appear to be able to get together now to the number of 2 or 3,000 in two or three minutes.' Trouble was expected on Lord Mayor's Day, 9 November, so on the 8th Warren and the Home Office banned all meetings in Trafalgar Square, on the grounds that it was crown property. Socialist and Irish Nationalist groups called a great demonstration for Sunday 13 November to defend free speech and the right to free assembly. Warren expected trouble, and stationed 5,000 police in the Square and the approaches to it, with 200 Life Guards and a battalion of Grenadier Guards in reserve. On the afternoon of the 13th, demonstrators marched on the Square from the north, east, and south of London. Those from the north, who had assembled under Burns, Shaw, and Besant at Clerkenwell Green, were chased off by the police at Bloomsbury Street, near the British Museum. The march from the east was broken up in the Strand, but 8,000 marchers from the southern suburbs managed to force their way across Westminster Bridge and through Parliament Square. Eventually, about 40,000 men managed to reach the Square, but their assault on it was soon ended by the arrival of mounted police and troops with fixed bayonets. The violence of the police and military action, which led to hundreds of injuries and two deaths, gave the day the popular name of 'Bloody Sunday', but what stuck in Shaw's mind was the ease with which a large untrained crowd could be scattered and terrified by a few professionals. Despite a strong defence, John Burns was given six months in prison for unlawful assembly, and the ban on public meetings in Trafalgar Square was not lifted until Asquith, Burns' defence counsel, became Home Secretary in 1892.[11]

The Problem of Unemployment

Poverty in London had many causes and took various forms, but the vital issue for socialists, economists, and social analysts in the late 1880s was unemployment. The word did not enter the language of economists until Alfred Marshall used it in an essay in 1888, but there was growing agreement that a divergence between the supply of labour and the demand for it, rather than personal idleness on a vast scale, was the major cause of poverty in London. This was one of the conclusions of a Mansion House committee set up in 1885 to investigate the causes of permanent distress in London, and a Fabian tract published in 1886, written by Sidney Webb and Frank Podmore, introduced the now familiar classification of unemployment into seasonal, cyclical, and casual. These same ideas also emerged very strongly from Charles Booth's authoritative and apparently objective study of poverty in East London, which was published in 1889. The much older idea that the unemployed were divided into the deserving and undeserving, the unlucky and the idle, was still very powerful, and runs through most speaking and writing on unemployment up to the Great War, including Booth's work, but it now seemed clear that many of those suffering cyclical or seasonal unemployment were 'deserving'.

Unemployment was a massive and sometimes dangerous problem in London, and many of the expedients that were devised and implemented in England in these years originated as responses to London's difficulties. London had a persistent problem of underemployment and casual work, especially in the docks and in declining industries, and in jobs which could be easily picked up by rural migrants. It also had a problem of seasonal unemployment in building and other outdoor trades, which caused hardship every winter and acute hardship and unrest in hard winters. Thirdly, it suffered, like the rest of the country, from occasional economic depressions, which created unemployment even in industries which were not vulnerable to seasonal fluctuations or casual work. These depression years, when skilled and 'respectable' workers were out of work, along with the usual crowds of casual workers and outdoor labourers, were the times of greatest concern, which brought new ideas and expedients into play. So the years 1884–7, 1892–5, 1903–5, and 1908–9 were the ones in which unemployment went to the top of the agenda. The great size of London's problem does not mean that London's unemployment rate was higher than that of the United Kingdom as a whole. Trade union figures for London and the UK, the best index of unemployment until the introduction of compulsory unemployment insurance in 1911, are not available until 1893. From 1893 to 1902 unemployment in the more unionized industries, building, engineering, shipbuilding, and printing, was generally lower in London than the national average, but between 1903 and 1914 (and especially 1906–7 and 1911–12) London's rate was worse than the national average, especially in construction, though it did not suffer the severe problems in engineering and shipbuilding that made 1908–9 such terrible years in other industrial districts.

Different remedies for unemployment attracted different political, intellectual, and social groups. The Charity Organisation Society (COS), which had been created in 1869 to prevent the indiscriminate or unconditional distribution of alms or poor relief, in the belief that easy money demoralized and pauperized the poor, always favoured more punitive solutions which were linked to the investigation of an applicant's personal and domestic habits, preferably carried out by the COS itself. Socialists and trade unionists favoured policies which helped the temporarily unemployed without reducing them to the level of casual workers or paupers by forcing them into workhouses or relief work schemes in stone-yards, or depriving them of their vote. Some social analysts, including Charles Booth, were drawn to policies which removed large bodies of 'surplus' workers from London altogether, either resettling them in the English countryside or sending them to the colonies, to improve the chances of those above them. This appealed to those who thought urbanization had gone too far, corrupting the working men of England. The challenge was to reduce distress and disorder, to protect decent working men and their families from the physical and moral degradation that a period of unemployment might cause, but to do so without undermining the treasured Victorian principles of individual responsibility, self-help, and the free market. A further challenge was to find a remedy for unemployment that actually worked. Socialists and trade unionists were attracted to the legal limitation of working hours as a remedy for the labour surplus. The SDF had advocated this since 1883, and in 1886 one of its Battersea members, Tom Mann, formed the Eight Hours League to campaign for national legislation. By 1890 the SDF, the Fabians, the TUC, and the London Trades Council were converted to the idea, and on 4 May 1890 the League and its supporters held a vast 'eight hours' rally in Hyde Park. But when several London employers, including the shipbuilder Thames Ironworks, the Beaufoy Vinegar factory in Vauxhall, and parts of the Woolwich Arsenal, tried the eight-hour day in the early 1890s and found that it did not reduce the workers' daily output, and therefore did not make it necessary to take on more hands. These results confirmed the desirability of the reform for sake of health and economic efficiency, but ended its short life as a cure for unemployment.[12]

There was fairly widespread support for public-works schemes as a temporary relief measure, on the lines advocated (but not funded or imposed) by Joseph Chamberlain's circular in March 1886. The policy was attractive because it was punitive, involved a test of real need (as the work-house was also said to do), kept men healthy and occupied, and achieved useful results for the community that paid for it. This circular was reissued four times over the next seven years and public-work schemes were often tried by local authorities, but they hardly ever succeeded. It was difficult to find work that free labourers would not otherwise have been employed to do, and much of the work available (clearing waste land, mending roads) was not winter work. Skilled men were unwilling to degrade themselves by breaking stones or carrying sandwich boards, and the casual workers who turned up for the work, sometimes in overwhelming numbers, did not do it well, and were not its intended beneficiaries. Public and private employers who ran public-work schemes usually found that the work was done badly, and at a high cost, which the poorest London districts could not afford. The COS, which had great influence on the committee that spent the Lord Mayor's Mansion House fund after 1885, was unenthusiastic about public works, especially when organized by local authorities. The fund supported some small schemes in 1886 and in 1892–3, when 250 unemployed riverside workers were employed to convert Abbey Mills, wasteland near the River Lea in West Ham, into allotments. The COS was so wedded to the idea of individual casework and measuring personal improvement that in 1894–5, at a time of mass unemployment, it gave work to only eighty-five men at Abbey Mills. In an average year in the 1890s the COS claimed to have helped about 700 men in London to find work, and about eighty to emigrate.[13]

Match Girls and Gas Workers

There were times, mainly in the summer months of boom years in the trade cycle, when the supply of stonebreakers and sandwich-board men almost dried up. Full (or almost full) employment gave working men and women

an unfamiliar sense of the value of their own labour, and the confidence
to challenge their employers over wages and working conditions. The
boom of 1888–90, coming after the very severe depression of 1884–7,
created an atmosphere of almost unprecedented militancy in several
London industries and drew workers into labour disputes who would never
have dared to strike in normal years. The most famous example, celebrated
in West End musicals, was the strike of the women of the Bryant and May
match factory in Bow. Making matches was hard, unhealthy, and badly
paid work, which made large profits for Bryant and May and its shareholders. For between 4s a week (for unskilled girls) and 15s a week (for
the best workers), match girls cut, dipped, and boxed matches in badly
ventilated rooms, risking an extremely unpleasant disease, necrosis of the
jaw (or phossy jaw), from exposure to the phosphorus in which the
matches were dipped. Despite their hard working lives, the match workers were well known as lively girls who made the best of their sometimes
ravaged looks by dressing in feathers and high heels when they went out
on the town together. A London magistrate, Montagu Williams, wrote of
them in the early 1890s:

> Most of them have an exuberancy of spirits truly astonishing . . .
> Match girls come out very strong on a Saturday night, when any
> number of them may be found at the Paragon Music Hall, in the Mile
> End Road; the Foresters' Music Hall, in Cambridge Road; and the
> Sebright, at Hackney; . . . They seem to know by heart the words of
> all the popular music hall songs of the day, and their homeward jour-
> ney on Bank holidays from Hampstead Heath and Chingford, though
> musical, is decidedly noisy.[14]

Charles Booth's researcher, Clara Collet, studied the match girls in 1888,
around the time of their strike, and agreed with Williams: 'The super-
abundant energy displayed by the match girls when their work is over,
although they have to stand up all day at it, is inexplicable and is in striking contrast to the tired appearance of machinists.' The girls had struck
before, in 1886, and Collet found that they were better suited to trade-
union activity than most unskilled women workers:

> The match girls have always shown a remarkable power of combina-
> tion. Those in the East End are nearly all under one management, and
> therefore live near each other in Bow, Mile End, Stepney, Limehouse,
> and Poplar. They are distinguished by a strong *esprit de corps*, one girl's
> grievance being adopted as the grievance of every girl in the same

room. They buy their clothes and feathers (especially the latter) by forming clubs; seven or eight of them will join together paying a shilling a week each, and drawing lots to decide who shall have the money each week. They are fond of each other's society, and generally withdraw themselves from that of others whom they consider too aristocratic to associate with on equal terms. The difficulties in the way of trade union which would be found in every other industry are therefore much less here.[15]

Match girls were discussed at a Fabian Society meeting in June 1888, when Clementina Black spoke of working conditions in the sweated industries. H. H. Champion encouraged Annie Besant and Herbert Burrows (Besant's new man, a flannel-suited socialist) to go down to the factory and talk to them, and when they did so they found a few of them very ready to talk about the petty fines they had to pay, and indignant at the deduction of a shilling from their wages to pay for the erection of a bronze statue of Gladstone in Bow churchyard. Besant described their work in an article, 'White Slavery in London', in her new journal, The Link, and gave the girls copies of it as they came out of work. The girls were less passive than Besant expected them to be. When the foreman sacked the supposed ringleader her friends went on strike, and soon 1,400 of them were out. A delegation of over a hundred girls marched to the Link's office in Fleet Street and asked Besant for help. She was well connected among journalists and socialists, and soon turned the strike into a great public event. The Star, Echo, Daily News, and Pall Mall Gazette supported the strike and publicized the meetings Besant organized on Mile End Waste (where Shaw, Hyndman, Burns, and Besant spoke), and a public fund was established, with Shaw, Hubert Bland, and other Fabians acting as cashiers. After three weeks, following arbitration from the London Trades Council, Bryant and May gave in, and took the girls back on better terms and in safer conditions. The Matchmakers' Union, under Besant's leadership, retained over 600 members, making it the biggest all-female union in the country.[16]

The match girls' success was a demonstration of the power of publicity (in London, at least) and organization rather than the effectiveness of strike action, but it helped create an atmosphere in which bigger battles could be fought and won. Perhaps the most important victory for labour in 1889 was gained without a strike, and therefore passed almost unnoticed at the time. London gas stokers worked in two twelve-hour shifts, rather than the three eight-hour shifts that had been introduced in some other industries. As unskilled men on low rates of pay, gas workers had not been able to form a trade union to press for a three-shift system. Until 1889 it had proved impossible for workers without scarce skills and high incomes to form permanent trade unions, and use them to protect and improve their pay and conditions. Nationally, only about 10 per cent of working men, 750,000 people, were in trade unions in 1888. Most of these were members of the industrial elite, engineers, shipbuilders, coal miners, carpenters, cotton spinners, printers, bookbinders, tailors, railway-men, and the like. Except in times of exceptional demand for labour, women, unskilled men, and general labourers could not fund or organize unions, or use the threat of strikes to get their way. The London gas work-ers started to change all that. The key figure was Will Thorne, who worked at the Gas, Light and Coke Company's Beckton gasworks and was also an associate of Hyndman's in the SDF. Thorne had tried to form a union at Beckton in 1884 and 1885, but in 1889, a much more promising year, he got help from Ben Tillett, a tea porter in the docks, and from several social-ists, including John Burns, Tom Mann, and Eleanor Marx. Together, they managed to create the Gas-workers and General Labourers' Union in May 1889, and to enrol 3,000 gas workers and other labourers in it. With the support of half the workers in the gas industry, and with Eleanor Marx to write the letters, the union wrote to the gas employers in June asking for an eight-hour shift without loss of pay. Though this was the slack summer season the companies could see that their position was weak and the work-ers' demand was not unreasonable. If the gas stokers went out on strike they might not be easy to replace with competent workers in a boom year, and interruptions in supply would be dangerous in the late 1880s, a deci-sive moment in the struggle between gas and electricity companies as providers of street and domestic lighting. After a tense delay the South Metropolitan Gas Company agreed to the eight-hour day in June, and by August the other companies had fallen into line. This was a remarkable success, the more so because it was not entirely transient, as the victories of unskilled workers usually were. The South Metropolitan went back on its deal, drove out the union, and reverted to twelve-hour shifts with the inducement of a profit-sharing arrangement, but stokers in the Gas, Light and Coke Company kept the eight-hour shift. Fifteen years later, London's 17,000 gas workers still did a forty-eight-hour week, compared to sixty-five hours in Berlin and seventy-seven in New York. The companies invested in new plant and machinery to increase output and productivity, and benefited from a more committed and efficient workforce. Will

Thorne, who had come to London as an illiterate unskilled worker on the tramp in the early 1880s, went on to become a dominant figure in the labour movement. He remained the general secretary of the Gasworkers' Union, which eventually became the massive General and Municipal Workers' Union, until 1934, and represented Keir Hardie's old seat of West Ham South (the gas workers' constituency) as a Labour MP from 1906 to 1945.

The Docker's Tanner

The London gas workers' triumph was the beginning of new unionism, which drew upon the mass of unskilled workers who had always been excluded from the unions formed by the elite of skilled workers. Its example and its leaders inspired other unskilled workers to organize and seek better pay and conditions while the economic boom lasted. In August 1889, the month of the gas workers' victory, a dispute over bonuses sparked a strike in the South-West India Dock. The local leader, the tea porter Ben Tillett, called in the support of Will Thorne, John Burns, and Tom Mann, all of the SDF. Thanks to the socialist agitation over unemployment during the previous five years, these men were now experienced and skilful in political organization and outdoor oratory, and London workmen had learned to listen to them and follow their lead. Tillett and Burns managed to spread the strike to the more distant Victoria and Albert docks and to Tilbury, and to win the support of the skilled and unionized stevedores. This was vital to the union's eventual success, as the 1890 *Annual Register* recognized: 'For almost, if not quite, the first time the representatives of the skilled workmen showed a readiness to throw in their lot with . . . unskilled labour.'[17] By 22 August the whole of the dock system had been closed down by a well-organized strike of 22,000 men. The dockers wanted their hourly pay increased to sixpence, 'the full round orb of the docker's tanner', as John Burns, an early master of the sound bite, put it. In addition, they wanted an end to the unfair bonus (or 'plus') system, the abolition of the contract system that allowed gangmasters to exploit the casual dock labourers, and employment by the half-day, not the hour.

The aim of these demands was the amelioration of the call-on system, which had masses of casual workers, all desperate for a day's work, crowding and struggling at the dock gates every morning. This system sprang from the large surplus of unskilled labour in the East End and the great fluctuations in the amount of work available each day, and it suited the dock companies well enough. But most well-informed Londoners, and even readers of the *Illustrated London News*, knew that the procedure was degrading and inhumane, and with the right publicity dockers could arouse useful public support. 'For quite the first time', said the *Annual Register*, 'the sympathies of the middle classes at home, and even in the colonies, were with the men against the masters.' This support was achieved with the help of some radical and Liberal newspapers, especially T. P. O'Connor's cheap and popular *Star*, which raised £6,000 for the strikers. The union's daily press conferences were handled with skill by H. H. Champion, whose appeal to the foreign press was particularly successful. Amazingly, £30,000 of the £48,000 contributed to the strike fund came from Australian sympathizers, who telegraphed money to London in response to the press reports (also sent by telegraph) they had read. Just as important, dockers in the other great ports agreed not to handle ships from London, and workers brought down from Liverpool by the companies decided to join the strike. The union's greatest stroke was the daily midday procession in August and September from the docks and along Commercial Road to Leadenhall Street, the employers' headquarters, and Tower Hill. As they trudged through the narrow City streets with their brass bands and carrying various emblems of their trades and symbols of their poverty (a meagre docker's dinner, an underfed docker's baby), these unknown and fearsome brutes became (in the eyes of watching City men) pathetic and dignified human beings, and John Burns, the frightening 'man with the red flag' in 1886, was now the reassuring 'man in the straw hat', discussing the day's route with Superintendent Forster of the City Police. This was an image of labour and decency to replace the image of horror and degradation presented by the coverage of the Whitechapel murders just a year earlier. The City men were also watching, if they thought about it, the men who handled the cargoes that fed, warmed, and clothed their city, and the commodities on which their banks, warehouses, exchanges, shops, insurance companies, and discount houses were built. Herbert Llewellyn Smith and Vaughan Nash published an excellent eyewitness account of the strike in 1889, and described the vast crowd that followed Burns, the police, and the stevedores' brass band:

> There were burly stevedores, lightermen, ship painters, sailors and firemen, riggers, scrapers, engineers, shipwrights, permanent men got up respectably, preferables cleaned up to look like permanents, and

unmistakable casuals with vari-coloured patches on their faded green-
ish garments; Foresters and Sons of the Phoenix in gaudy scarves;
Doggett's prize winners, a stalwart battalion of watermen marching
proudly in long scarlet coats, pink stockings, and velvet caps, with
huge pewter badges on their breasts, like decorated amphibious
huntsmen; coalies in wagons fishing aggressively for coppers with
bags tied to the ends of poles . . . Skiffs mounted on wheels manned
by stolid watermen; ballast heavers laboriously winding and tipping
an empty basket.[18]

The strikers used the funds they raised to give strike pay, to pay off
blacklegs, who were offered two shillings an hour by the employers
to break the strike, and to organize thousands of pickets to persuade
strike-breakers to go home. Violence between pickets and blacklegs was
avoided, and the organization of picketing and strike relief was done with
a skill and dignity that surprised those who were accustomed to fear or
despise the East End casual worker. Opinion in the music halls, in the press,
even in the shipping companies, was on the side of the dockers, and City
men cheered Burns and Tillett when they recognized them in the street.
In early September the two sides were eventually brought together by a
Mansion House committee assembled by the Lord Mayor, which included
Frederick Temple, the Bishop of London, and Cardinal Manning, the
Roman Catholic Archbishop of Westminster, who was the most effective
peacemaker. The dockers got their tanner, but the problems of casual
labour and the call-on were not solved, and perhaps could not have been.
Dock workers were categorized as permanent employees and three grades
of casual workers, hired by the hour, with category A men being given
preference over categories B and C, and with the unclassified remainder
waiting for the crumbs.

Unlike the gas workers, the dockers did not enjoy the gains they made
in 1889 for very long. By 1892 at least half of the union's paying members were gone, and the boom conditions which allowed the workers to
prevail had been replaced by the beginnings of a depression. The dock
companies' new organization, the Shipping Federation, fitted out three
ships as floating homes for 'free labourers', and used these men to defeat
a new dock strike towards the end of 1890. During the 1890s membership of the dockers union shrank to about a thousand, and conditions for
casual workers remained much as they had been before the strike. When
Austin Freeman described the daily scene at the dock gates for Sims' *Living*

London in 1901, he did so in terms that would have been familiar in the 1880s:

> The last of the C men are passing out through the wickets; the pen is empty and we see approaching a ganger with a large handful of white slips. He is coming to take on the casual hands for the great wool ship . . . instantly a frightful change sweeps over the crowd. All human character seems to disappear in a moment. A forest of arms with outstretched hands rises into the air; the whole crowd surges forward, a moving, struggling mass; the chain seems stretched to snapping point, the posts bent over in their sockets, and the men in the front rank, crushed against the chain, crane forward with staring wolfish faces and make desperate snatches at the ganger as he passes along the line just out of their reach.[19]

The gains in working conditions made in 1889 were not all lost, and unskilled and female workers did not forget what they had learned from the dockers, gas workers, and match girls that labourers could be organized, public support could be won, and employers could be beaten when the economic circumstances were right. Although most of the new unions were destroyed or humbled by the early 1890s, this brief flowering of unskilled unionism changed the nature of trade unionism and working-class politics in London and Britain. Nationally, trade union membership doubled (to about 1.5 million) between 1888 and 1892, and rose slowly to 2 million by 1900. This was the result of unskilled groups like postmen, building labourers, busmen, vestry employees, and coal porters forming unions, and of older unions (including tailors, shoemakers, railwaymen, and compositors) widening their membership to include less-skilled workers. Its next great increase, from 2 million to 4 million, took place between 1906 and 1913. In Greater London union membership probably doubled (to about 200,000) between the 1880s and 1895, but accurate figures are not known. Ernest Aves' useful study of trade unions in the County of London, published in Charles Booth's Industry volumes in 1897, emphasized that unionism was virtually confined to manufacturing and transport workers, and had made hardly any progress among domestic servants, shopworkers, or London's 108,000 commercial clerks. Including associations of postmen and teachers, and a new union of cab-drivers, there were about 180,000 unionists in the County of London, just over 14 per cent of the working male population. The trades with the highest percentage of union members were generally those where skills and wages were highest. Printers (67 per cent unionized) topped the list, with bookbinders, plasterers, masons, stevedores, and coopers (at about 50 per cent or more) not far behind. In the middle, on between 30 and 40 per cent, came bricklayers, engineers, metal workers, carpenters, and shoemakers, and below them, in descending order, came labourers (27 per cent), railway servants, bakers, cabinetmakers, tailors (19 per cent), carriage builders, painters, glaziers, carters, seamen, and the makers of toys, musical instruments and watches (4 per cent). Milliners, dressmakers, sewing-machinists, shirt-makers, drapers, warehousemen, messengers, milk-sellers, sugar refiners, butchers, grocers, soap and chemical workers, brewers, publicans, shop assistants, stationers, newsagents, and gardeners were all part of the great majority of working Londoners who had no unions at all. There were over 200 unions in London (Aves counted 228), including sixteen each for printers, leatherworkers, and non-ferrous metal workers, fourteen for painters and glaziers, and twenty-three for cabinet-makers. Small unions commanded loyalty and tended to survive longer than big general unions, but fragmentation made effective strike action difficult, as the various building trades found when they were in dispute in 1896. In contrast, the dockers, coal-porters, and gas workers had four large unions, which helped them to make the most of their limited bargaining powers.[20] The arrival of the new unions made the socially and politically conservative Trades Union Congress (TUC) more likely to lean towards socialist allies, an inclination which led to the formation of the Labour Representation Committee in 1900 and the Labour Party in 1903. In London it radicalized the stuffy London Trades Council, and brought to prominence a set of able and articulate socialist working men, some of whom entered local and national politics, often with dramatic effects.

Socialists in Local Government

Interest in relieving unemployment subsided in the prosperous years of 1888–91, but was awoken again in the autumn of 1892, when unemployment rose and the SDF and other socialists organized rallies on Tower Hill. A torchlit march on the West End at midnight on 1 December was broken up by the police, but the Liberal Home Secretary, Asquith, who had defended John Burns in 1888, took a more relaxed view of the danger of these protests than his predecessor. In the autumn and winter of 1893–4 there were more rallies on Tower Hill, and meetings at which the secretary of the Unemployed Organisation Committee, Jack Williams, a dock labourer and SDF activist who had been acquitted of sedition in 1886, spoke of sending parcel bombs to the police. The next winter was even worse, with the frozen Thames closing the Port of London for three months, but distress did not look like turning into revolution. 'From the police point of view the whole movement is insignificant', the Chief Commissioner of the Metropolitan Police reported. 'They talk as they have always talked any time these past twenty years, stark rebellion and riot, but they don't mean to do anything.'[21]

The extension of the franchise and the election of socialists (especially members of the SDF) and trade unionists to the LCC, vestries, and Poor Law Boards of Guardians in East and South London gave working men some new ways of influencing events in the early 1890s. In West Ham, which had to cope with serious unemployment problems without the support of the Metropolitan Common Poor Fund (because it was outside the County), four trade unionists were elected to the council in 1889. After 1892 the LCC had nine elected Labour councillors and three Labour aldermen, including Ben Tillett, the leader of the 1889 dockers' strike. Will Thorne, creator and general secretary of the Gasworkers' Union, was elected to West Ham council in 1892, and held his place for the next fifty-four years. That same year James Keir Hardie of the Independent Labour Party (ILP) was elected MP for South West Ham, a seat he held until 1895, and John Burns was elected MP for Battersea. In Mile End a campaign by Will Steadman, the leader of the Bargebuilders' Union, and Tom Mann, president of the Dockers' Union, won twelve seats for Labour on the vestry in 1891. George Lansbury, elected to the Conservative Poor Law Board in Poplar alongside Will Crooks in 1892, forced them to make Poplar workhouses into decent shelters for the old and unfit, rather than grim places of degradation. Under the influence of Lansbury and Crooks, Poplar became famous for the generosity (or notorious for the profligacy) of its Poor Law provision in the 1890s. Unlike Sidney and Beatrice Webb, William Beveridge, Charles Booth and Hubert Llewellyn Smith, whose understanding of unemployment was gained through study, interviews and working at Toynbee Hall, these Labour men knew poverty at first hand, and had lost parents and children to it. Will Thorne had worked full-time since the age of six, and had tramped to London in search of work. Ben Tillett lost his mother when he was three and left home at the age of eight to join a circus. Will Crooks had been sent away from his family in Poplar to a workhouse and poor-law school in Sutton when he was eight. Keir

Hardie had been brought up in poverty in Scotland, and had worked since he was seven. Their remedies for unemployment were not always effective, but they were generally compassionate.

In 1892 Hardie started to campaign inside and outside Parliament for local authorities to buy land for the unemployed to work on, combining the idea of public works with a hint of rural settlement. West Ham started a public works scheme early in 1894, in conjunction with Poplar. Both were partly funded by Arnold Hills, owner of Thames Ironworks, a big local employer. In all, West Ham employed over 2,000 men, paying them 6d an hour for making cricket and football pitches and a lake on Wanstead Flats. In Hills' opinion the work, which cost over £2,000, could have been done at half the price by ordinary workers. These locally funded works could help only a small proportion of the unemployed. In the bitter and depressed winter of 1894–5, socialists and trade unionists counted over 10,000 unemployed men in West Ham, mostly unskilled or casual workers living in distress. In February 1895, the worst month for pauperism in London since 1871, 8,618 of these men were working in West Ham stone yards to earn poor relief. Skilled men shunned the stone yard, just as they avoided the workhouse, so those who tried to study the unemployed in such places tended to see the more hopeless and degraded cases, men who had not had a steady job for years.[22]

There was another small but important development at this time. Some London vestries, following advice from the Local Government Board in 1892, started registers of the unemployed, either in connection with relief work or to help them find paid jobs. Three vestries, Battersea, Chelsea, and St Pancras, had registries that were effectively labour bureaux, or exchanges, in 1893. In 1899 the London vestries held a conference on labour bureaux, and asked the Board of Trade to create a central London labour exchange. Then the abolition of the vestries interrupted the initiative, and the Chelsea and St Pancras bureaux were forced to close until 1902, when the Labour Bureaux (London) Act allowed boroughs to fund these offices again. By 1904 there were eleven municipal employment bureaux in London.[23]

Answers to Unemployment

There was a more radical and permanent solution to the problem of London's surplus labourers, the creation of rural settlements or labour

colonies in England or overseas. This was proposed by economist Alfred
Marshall in the *Contemporary Review* in February 1884, and picked up by
others, including Canon Samuel Barnett and Charles Booth, over the next
few years. The most powerful advocate of labour colonies was General
William Booth, the founder and head of the Salvation Army. In the late
1880s Booth decided to revive his faltering crusade by giving it a social
as well as a spiritual dimension, and in 1890 as part of this transformation
he wrote an extraordinary book, *In Darkest England and the Way Out.* William
Booth drew upon the work of Charles Booth for his statistics of London
poverty, and on the reports of his own officers for case histories illustrating individual hardship. The sensational tone, in which Darkest England
(which generally meant Darkest London) was compared with the horrors
of Darkest Africa recently reported by Henry Morton Stanley, was added
by the popular journalist W. T. Stead, who had contributed a similar flavour
to *The Bitter Cry of Outcast London* seven years earlier. After seventy pages
in which he described London's underclass, the 'submerged tenth', and dismissed the remedies already tried, Booth spent two hundred more
explaining his great rescue plan, the 'Way Out'. This involved three stages,
which were illustrated in a dramatic map at the start of the book. First the
destitute and unemployed would be given food, shelter, work, and training in City colonies, which were run on strict Salvationist lines. Some of
those taken into these colonies would be returned to the urban labour
market, strengthened in body and spirit, and others would be moved on
to a rural labour colony, where they would earn their keep in market gardening, agriculture, or a craft. Finally, some of these colonists, now fully
reformed, would be taken to overseas settlements, mainly in the British
Empire or the USA. By this means, General Booth said, apparently incor-
rigible people, 'thieves, harlots, paupers, drunkards', could be transformed
into honest and industrious Christians, a blessing to whichever community
they finally settled in.[24]

The Salvation Army opened its first City Colonies, which it called 'elevators', in Whitechapel and Battersea in 1890, a few months before the
publication of the book, and supplemented them with ten labour bureaux,
to put its graduates in touch with employers. A year later Booth bought a
3,000-acre estate in Hadleigh, near Ipswich, as his first farm colony, and
soon afterwards the Salvation Army was running assisted-emigration
schemes, some to settlements in America, others offering help on an individual basis. There were many problems with the funding of these
settlements and with the statistics issued by the Salvation Army on the

number of people they had placed in permanent work, but in the 1890s Booth's rescue schemes were regarded by many inside and outside government as a possible way forward in the treatment of poverty and unemployment. Some Poor Law unions, especially Whitechapel, had been interested in labour colonies even before 1890, and in 1895 Poplar, under the influence of George Lansbury, applied for permission to set up its own rural settlement. There were many delays, but in 1904 Poplar leased a hundred-acre farm at Laindon, near Basildon, in Essex, from a soap manufacturer, Joseph Fels, and settled a hundred men there, mostly ex-soldiers, to dig reservoirs and build chicken coops. The London Unemployed Fund leased another farm (also from Joseph Fels) at Hollesley Bay, on the Suffolk coast near Ipswich. Some trade unionists and farmers disliked settlements because they undercut the work of paid labourers, but several socialists, including the Webbs, perhaps harking back to Robert Owen and the Chartist Land Scheme, were attracted to them.[25]

In 1895 trade recovered, a building boom began, and the crisis passed. Writing in 1901, C. F. G. Masterman could talk of the social concerns of the 1880s and the unemployment scares of the 1890s as distant memories from a vanished age. 'Here an "Independent Labour Party" of pitiful dimensions testifies to the existence of that which was once regarded as a menace to society; there a Settlement drags on a starved and stunted life, witness of an enthusiasm that has almost passed away.' With the revival of trade, 'the armies of the unemployed, whose existence seemed a standing menace to society, have become rewoven into the social fabric . . . Socialism has been largely abandoned . . . The leaders who exhibited such brilliant promise have gone under or passed into obscurity.' As far as Masterman could see, the age of socialism, slumming, Salvation Army funds, and university settlements was over, though the problem of poverty was as vast and insoluble as ever.[26]

In 1903 the boom, which had been prolonged by the Boer War, came to an end, and unemployment rose again, bringing great demonstrations of the unemployed onto the London streets and reviving interest in labour colonies and public works. In October 1904, Walter Long, President of the Local Government Board, created Joint Committees (later called Distress Committees) from boroughs and Boards of Guardians, brought them together in a Metropolitan conference, and persuaded them to adopt a London-wide policy, combining casework, classification, relief works, job finding, labour colonies, emigration, and the poor law. A fund of £70,000 was established from loans and donations to the Mansion House Fund, and a Central Committee (later the Central Unemployed Body, or CUB) was created to use this to help thousands of unemployed men and their dependants. Some were found work in Hadleigh, the Salvation Army's farm colony, in the Hollesley Bay Farm Colony, or in building the new Garden City at Letchworth. Others worked in LCC parks, street-widening, tree-planting, or levelling land for allotments or playing fields, and some were found work through labour exchanges. Walter Long was keen to build on these London-wide initiatives, and incorporated them into a bill which would make such measures compulsory in London and other big cities. The resulting Unemployed Workmen Act became law in August 1905, and that autumn a new system of unemployment relief was set up in London. The Act was designed mainly for London. Every London borough had a Distress Committee, and each committee sent representatives to the CUB, which also had delegates from the LCC and the Local Government Board. Nearly all of the active Distress Committees beyond the LCC area were in the Essex and Middlesex suburbs of Outer London. The CUB was too cumbersome and understaffed to impose a common policy on the local distress committees. Its duty under the Act was to help regular workmen in temporary distress, not loafers or casual workers,' but the casework needed to establish this distinction, taken on with relish by the COS, was too slow and costly to deal with mass unemployment, and too intrusive to please the trade unions. Most applicants for employment relief were turned down by the distress committees. In January, February, and March 1910 an average of 32,700 people asked for relief in London, but on average only 4,400 were given help. Those who were taken on were given work at sixpence an hour in Hollesley Bay Farm Colony, Wanstead Flats, West Ham Park, Letchworth Garden City, women's workshops, cemeteries and parks in various London boroughs, and in the LCC parks, cleaning lakes, smoothing bowling greens, and planting trees. Some of the work they did might otherwise have gone to regular workmen, and much of it was done poorly and at a high cost. Most of the men registered for work in 1910–11 had previously worked in building, transport, or general labour.[27]

John Burns, who became Liberal President of the Local Government Board in 1905, regarded most of these local-government work schemes with the utmost distrust, and his doubts were confirmed by the scandal that broke over the more high-spending East London Boards of Guardians in 1906–7. An investigation by the Local Government Board exposed corruption in West Ham and a policy in Poplar (where Lansbury and Will

Crooks were on the Board of Guardians) of giving discretionary grants to every able-bodied applicant, which had doubled pauperism in the borough since 1894. The Poplar colony at Laindon was found to be poorly managed, expensive, and unruly, and it was discovered that colonists had been given free railway tickets to return to London for unemployed demonstrations. John Burns' opinion that Hollesley Bay was nothing more than an expensive holiday camp for the unemployed was not shared by Beatrice Webb, who found its residents 'angry with the cold wind and unaccustomed work and longing for wife and child or the Public House of the London slums'. Labour colonies continued to open and operate until 1914, but few now believed that they were the way ahead in unemployment policy.[28]

Labour-exchange bureaux, which had existed informally in London since the 1880s and with some local-authority support since 1902, seemed to be a more promising way forward, offering the possibility of decasualizing work, making labour more mobile, and making the free market in labour operate efficiently. In March 1906 the Central Unemployed Body took over the existing London labour exchanges and opened new ones, creating a system of twenty-five exchanges, with over 10,000 registrations a month. A committee chaired by William Beveridge, the Sub-warden of Toynbee Hall, was put in charge of them. A visit to Germany, which had thousands of labour exchanges, strengthened Beveridge's commitment to a centrally controlled national system, and in 1908 Winston Churchill, the new President of the Board of Trade, employed him to frame a national policy on labour exchanges in conjunction with the Board's Permanent Secretary, Sir Hubert Llewellyn Smith. Smith, a great expert on labour, had gained his first understanding of unemployment in the East End in the 1880s, living at Toynbee Hall and working with Charles Booth. The resulting piece of legislation, the 1909 Labour Exchanges Act, allowed the Board of Trade to establish or take over labour exchanges and to collect information on vacancies and people seeking work. In London the Board of Trade took over the CUB's exchanges and set up several more in the outer suburbs, giving Greater London a network of thirty-three exchanges by 1911. The exchanges started work in February 1910, just as the severe 1908–9 depression was easing. Over the next twenty-three months they placed about 218,000 applicants in jobs. Half of these were adult men, about 50,000 were women, and the rest were boys and girls. Men were mostly found work in building, transport, machinery, and Post Office Christmas work, women and girls were placed in domestic work, dressmaking, food and drink, and commercial jobs, and boys went into conveyance (mostly errands, messages, and deliveries) and commerce.

While this policy was being implemented, Beveridge and Llewellyn Smith were working on the second part of their grand plan, a system of compulsory unemployment insurance, with contributions from workers, employers, and the state, in the industries most affected by seasonal and cyclical fluctuations, but not by casual labour, shipbuilding, engineering, and construction. This system was introduced along with health insurance for wage earners by the National Insurance Act of 1911. In time these changes, along with the introduction of Old Age Pensions, would transform the lives of the poor in London and elsewhere, and begin the creation of the modern welfare state. But in 1911 and 1912 their impact was overshadowed by a series of strikes, mainly in the docks. Nationally, the strikes of 1911–12 were encouraged, as usual, by the sharp fall in unemployment following the recovery from the severe depression of 1908–9. In London the recovery was less dramatic, but it was strong enough to enable dockers to win 6d an hour again in August 1911, and to bring out 15,000 women in the Bermondsey food-processing industries at about the same time. In 1912, nationally the worst year on record for days lost in strikes, London was quiet compared to other industrial regions, where there were major strikes in railways, textiles, and especially coal-mining. Another strike in the London docks from May to July 1912 was defeated by the use of non-union (or 'free') labour, a reminder of the difficulty of winning a dispute when there were thousands of unemployed men desperate for work and with no tradition of union loyalty. The only other major strike in London in these pre-war years was in the building trade, which lasted from January 1914 until the outbreak of war, over the issue of the employment of non-union workers.

✳

INDUSTRIAL LONDON

Late Victorian London was the world's greatest centre for the making, importing, selling, and buying of goods. Its vast consumer market was served not only by merchants who imported food, raw materials, and manufactures through its vast system of railways, docks, wharves, and warehouses, but also by the biggest centre of manufacture the world had ever seen. Everyone knew about the great industrial cities of Lancashire, Yorkshire, and the Midlands, the centres of steam-powered factory production since the industrial revolution of the late eighteenth and early nineteenth centuries, but London, which was generally regarded as a laggard in the scale and technology of its industrial production, outdid them all. London was not an unusually industrialized city, by British standards, but it was vast. Greater London had about 16 or 17 per cent of the population of Great Britain (England, Wales, and Scotland), and roughly the same percentage of its manufacturing workforce. The number of people recorded as working in its factories and workshops in 1907, the year of the first census of industrial production, was 680,000, which was almost exactly the total population of Manchester, England's foremost factory city. No other city in the world – not even New York – had as many manufacturing workers as this.[1]

London's Industries

Leaving aside about a tenth of the working population whose work was unclassified, London's workers were divided almost equally between those in the service sector (including transport) and those in production (manufacturing and building). Manufacturing rose as a proportion of the total London labour force from 35 to 38 per cent between 1881 and 1911, because although there had been a rise in transport, finance, and public administration (from 20 per cent to 23 per cent of the County's workforce) in those three decades, this had been offset by a slight decline in domestic service, from 24 per cent to 22 per cent.[2]

London did not specialize in a single industry, as the Yorkshire and Lancashire textile towns did. The advantages of a London location attracted and retained many industries, especially those producing consumer goods which would be difficult or expensive to transport from a more distant centre of production, or that were made with materials that could be conveniently acquired from London's docks and wharves. Land and labour were not cheap in London, and its congested roads, polluted air, and high rates and taxes might have combined to drive manufacturers out of the city, but for many industries the metropolitan location offered advantages to offset these costs. Closeness to London's vast body of consumers allowed fashion industries (clothing, footwear, jewellery, furniture, and household ornaments) to respond quickly to the changing demands of West End shops, and London's concentration of writers, politicians, scholars, readers, and performers made it the natural home of printing, publishing, and the manufacture of scientific and musical instruments. The suppliers of food and drink gained great advantages from being so near to five or six million mouths, and the producers of gas and electricity also had to be near their consumers.

Many London producers benefited from their closeness to other manufacturers in the same or related industries. Small businesses in local clusters, such as Clerkenwell instrument-makers, Hoxton furniture-makers, or East End tailors, could gain many of the advantages of larger businesses at little or no cost. They shared information on markets, materials, and new products or techniques, drew their workers from a common pool, dealt with the same creditors, suppliers, and wholesalers, and used the same means of transport and distribution. By drawing on one large body of workers, small industries could hire and fire as their level of business fluctuated, without having to support a larger workforce than they needed. Because the range of work opportunities in London was so large, with rising demand for labour in one industry often absorbing the workers laid off by another, costly and dangerous periods of widespread unemployment were less likely in London than in cities with a narrower industrial base. Small specialized producers could gain many of the advantages of large-scale factory production by working close to related businesses. For instance in the furniture industry, timber arriving at the London docks and sawn in riverside sawmills passed through the hands of carpenters, cabinetmakers, polishers, and upholsterers before finding its way into the West

End market. Similar economies were achieved by the clustering of the clothing, footwear, carriage, light engineering and jewellery trades in particular parts of London. Some industries depended on the by-products of others for their raw materials, turning a troublesome waste product into a valuable commodity. The leather, candle, brush, soap, margarine, and glue industries used the by-products of London's vast meat and animal trades, and coal tar, a by-product of gas production, provided raw materials for the East London and West Ham chemical industry, in the manufacture of sulphuric acid, fertilizer, lubricants, rubber, linoleum, drugs, poisons, dyes, paints, ink, varnish, solvents, and explosives.[3]

Late Victorian London did not attract many industries whose main requirements were cheap coal and steampower and large factory premises. The proportion of its workforce employed in mechanical engineering and the production of metals, building materials (bricks, glass, cement, and pottery), textiles, and ships was below the national average by 50 per cent or more. In other industries, including building, and the production of food and drink, vehicles, and chemicals, London's level of employment was around the national average, in proportion to the size of its population. The industries that really thrived in London were higher value consumer goods in which a metropolitan location, closeness to the London market and fashionable society, or to the raw materials unloaded in the Port of London, were advantageous enough to overcome the higher cost of property and labour in the capital. Therefore London specialized to an unusual degree (and in descending order) in paper, printing, and publishing; leather and hides; fine instruments (mechanical, surgical, scientific, horological, and musical); woodwork and furniture; electrical engineering; clothing and footwear; and gas and electricity. These specialisms were reflected in the goods exported through the Port of London, though the port handled vast quantities of industrial goods (especially woollen and cotton cloth, metalwares, and machinery) that were produced elsewhere in the country. In 1910 the Port of London handled over half of the UK's exports of armaments, books, candles, motor cars and car parts, electrical goods, haberdashery, medicines, pickles and sauces, scientific and musical instruments, stationery, paint, jam and sweets, toys, and furniture, and over 90 per cent of its exports of cement and telephone and telegraph apparatus. Many of these were London-made, but others were produced elsewhere, especially in Birmingham and the Black Country, which had excellent railway connections with London.[4]

Pianos

An industry which combined the skills of furniture-makers, engineers, and instrument-makers was the manufacture of pianos, a business in which London had an extraordinary national dominance. In the 1840s nearly all of England's 200 piano manufacturers were in London, and of the 136 British firms listed in Alfred Dolge's *Pianos and their Makers* in 1911 all but three were not London-based. London piano-makers had a very large local market, and railway and sea connections gave them easy access to national and international markets. Pianos were complex products, and the builders of the finished instrument relied on supplies of frets, keys, strings, felts, hammers, carved wooden panels, and cases, as well as the work of polishers and tuners. In the middle of the century this community of producers and subcontractors was centred on Soho, but rents and a shortage of space pushed most of them northwards into Kentish Town, Camden Town, Chalk Farm, and Islington, and some into Hackney and Stoke Newington. Land was cheaper there, and the district's excellent rail and waterway transport, with the Regent's Canal and railway lines coming out of three main termini, gave it a vital advantage for the makers of such a bulky product. In 1911 only nine of London's 133 piano-makers were south of the Thames, though these included Henry Hicks and Son of the Elephant and Castle, which had twenty shops in South London. Some London piano-makers were small businesses, making cheap instruments for the lower middle class, but London also had some of the world's leading companies. In 1886 British (and thus London) companies produced about 35,000 pianos, about half the output of Germany, but far more than France or America. The greatest name in London piano-making was John Broadwood and Sons, a firm which had made pianos for every English monarch since George II. Broadwood's factory on the Horseferry Road in Westminster had been one of London's biggest, with over 300 employees, but the firm had declined since a disastrous fire in 1856, and moved its factory to Old Ford, Hackney, in 1902. Several of London's leading makers, including Collard and Collard, Chappell's, John Hopkinson, George Rogers, and Monington and Weston, had factories in Primrose Hill and Camden Town, near the Regent's Canal, and Arthur Allison, Barratt and Robinson, and John Brinsmead and Sons (one of the biggest London makers) were half a mile to the north, in Kentish Town. By the early twentieth century the borough of Islington, to the east of St Pancras, had about a third of London's piano-makers, including Burling and Mansfield, Ralph Allison, and John Rintoul.[5]

From the 1880s technical improvements and more efficient production and marketing were opening up a huge middle-class and even working-class market for pianos in London and elsewhere. The piano was becoming an essential possession for a respectable household, a handsome piece of furniture, a source of entertainment, and a way of demonstrating the family's accomplishments. Piano teachers were cheap and plentiful, and after 1899 an American invention, the pianola, made it possible for the untutored to play like Grieg, Debussy, or Rachmaninov, as long as they ped-alled at the right speed. Pianolas were sold in the Regent Street showroom of the Aeolian Company, and within a year or two several London firms were making pianolas or player-pianos of their own. Piano-makers, espe-cially Chappell's, did their best to stimulate the late Victorian piano-mania, by publishing easy piano music, promoting parlour songs, and organizing popular concerts. Cheap sheet music of popular songs sold in great num-bers, and songwriters like Leslie Stuart (Thomas Barrett) became famous, but not (thanks to the sale of pirated copies) wealthy. Thomas Chappell made an important contribution to London's musical life by organizing the construction of St James's Hall, Regent Street, London's main concert hall until the opening of the Queen's Hall in Langham Place in 1893. The Chappell family sponsored and organized popular Ballad Concerts ('Pops') in St James's Hall on Mondays and Saturdays, at which Londoners could hear leading performers, including Grieg, Liszt, Tchaikovsky, and Paderewski, for a shilling. These were the forerunners of the Promenade Concerts, which started at the Queen's Hall in 1895, and which were them-selves rescued from collapse by the Chappell family in 1915.

London companies tried to stimulate demand for pianos by employ-ing leading designers and architects, including Edward Burne-Jones, C. R. Ashbee, Edwin Lutyens, and Baillie Scott, to design instruments for inter-national exhibitions or aristocratic customers, and by producing cheap 'cottage pianos' which would fit into the small front rooms of clerks and skilled workers. The development of a system of hire purchase, in which the customer could rent a piano on a quarterly or monthly basis, gaining ownership after three years, made it easier for poor but aspirational fami-lies to clutter their parlours with the latest status symbol. Some of these pianos were so poorly made that they were worthless before the three years were up, but a decent piano could be bought for twenty or thirty pounds from Gamage's, Whiteley's, or the Army and Navy Stores just before the

First World War. The hire-purchase system, which is usually associated with the 1920s and 1930s, was quite widely used in the nineteenth century, especially in the sale of such costly consumer goods as sewing machines, bicycles, furniture, and pianos. When the clerk Charles Pooter, the fictional hero of the Grossmith brothers' *Diary of a Nobody*, said that his wife was playing the 'Sylvia Gavotte' on their new Collard and Collard cottage piano, bought 'on the three years system', everyone knew what he was talking about. Hire purchase was criticized by some moralists who thought that it lured the poor into spending money they could not afford on instruments they could not play, and which were in many cases not worth playing. There were also legal problems over the seller's right to force entry into a defaulter's home, and the ownership of goods sold to third parties before they had been paid for, but the latter was clarified by the *Helby* v. *Matthews* case of 1895. In 1892, when piano dealers claimed that 70 per cent of their sales were made on hire purchase, London piano-makers joined with the makers of bicycles and billiard tables to persuade the government not to limit or prohibit the system.[6]

The rise of piano ownership was encouraged by the import of cheap and well-made German pianos, produced by Bechstein, Bluthner, and more than a hundred lesser companies. More efficient and inventive German makers defeated the British in the world market, and by 1912 over £500,000 worth of German pianos were sold in England each year. The 1907 catalogue of the Army and Navy Stores listed seventy-three pianos, of which fifty-five were German-made. A good German upright piano could be had for £30, about twice the price of an English 'cottage' piano, but a buyer with £50, or about 30s a month, could have a Bechstein model 9, which was one of the best small pianos of all. Its manufacturer, Carl Bechstein, outdid Thomas Chappell in 1901 by opening a 540-seat concert hall, the Bechstein Hall, next to his showroom in Wigmore Street. During the First World War, when people ceased to believe that anything good could come out of Germany, Bechstein's London business was seized and his hall was renamed after the street in which it stood. It remains the best chamber-music hall in London, and one of the best in Europe.

Printing

The industries identified and studied by Charles Booth and his assistants as 'connected with poverty' in the East End – dock work, clothing, footwear, furniture, and the smaller sweated trades – have often been given the centre stage in histories of the London economy around 1900. But other London industries, not sources of poverty and not concentrated in the much-studied East End, should not be ignored. The paper and printing industry, London's third biggest manufacturing employer (after clothing and metals), and the second biggest manufacturing employer of women, is a good example of a thriving London industry, a source of steady work and solid sufficiency rather than short-time and starvation wages.

The market for printed matter was ever-growing. Late Victorian London had a huge reading public, the biggest concentrated market for books, periodicals, and newspapers in the world. Thanks to the work of day and Sunday schools since the beginning of the century, and state board schools since 1870, illiteracy was uncommon even in the poorer classes. The London rich and middle classes had been buying and reading newspapers and periodicals for nearly two hundred years, and the spread of newspaper reading among the Victorian poor had been hindered as much by the high price of newspapers (a result of taxation and high production costs) as by illiteracy or lack of interest. The abolition of the duties on advertisements, newspapers, and paper between 1853 and 1861, the rise of mass literacy, and a succession of improvements in the printing process opened the way for the development of the cheap popular press in the later nineteenth century, and a booming London printing and publishing industry.

To produce cheap newspapers quickly and in the large quantities demanded by this growing market, newspaper companies had to speed up the processes of typesetting, printing, and paper production, in the face of opposition from London's most well-established and politically astute unions. Composing machines in which keyboards released letters from a rack when a key was struck were available in the 1860s, but the powerful London Society of Compositors insisted that only skilled craftsmen could redistribute the type to its racks after printing. So in London only the non-union *Times*, which was usually in the vanguard of technological change, introduced keyboard-operated composing machines. When the *Sportsman* followed suit in 1891, it did so by replacing its union staff with non-union men. The most important advance in rapid printing in the later nineteenth century was the invention of the Linotype machine in the USA in the 1880s. This brilliant device, which transformed the London printing industry in the 1890s, enabled a keyboard operator to release appropriate letters from a series of magazines, the letters being forced into place by a mechanical blower or a pusher wheel, so that a slug or line of type (the line o' type) could be cast from them. When the line had been cast the individual letters, or matrices, which were all notched or nicked differently, were returned to their correct magazines by a distributor bar, each one falling into the magazine it was designed to fit without the assistance of a well-paid compositor. The metal slug was returned to the melting pot once it had been used. The lines of type were fixed into a frame from which the mould was made which would in turn produce the curved plate for the rotary press, the stereotype, which represented the layout of the finished page. The *New York Tribune* was printed using an early version of this machine in 1886, and a perfect Linotype composing machine was ready for general use by 1890. In London, the *Globe* (London's oldest evening paper) installed Linotype machines in 1892, and by 1895 they had replaced hand composition and less efficient keyboard machines in nearly all London newspaper offices. A Linotype operator could set 8,000 ens in an hour (and without the need to redistribute the type afterwards), four times as much as a skilled compositor working in the traditional way. By this time London had two training schools for Linotype operators, and a repair shop with a hundred mechanics. A later invention, the Monotype machine, in which a keyboard produced a punched paper strip, through which compressed air blew letters into place for casting, was more widely used in the book trade, which valued the paper ribbon for reprinting.[7]

The acceleration of typesetting was matched by innovations in the printing press. *The Times* introduced a flat steam press in 1814, and Edward Lloyd, founder and owner of the popular Saturday *Lloyd's Weekly Newspaper*, bought a steam-driven rotary press in 1856. By 1870 *The Times* had a steam-powered rotary press which was able to print newspapers on a continuous roll of paper and cut and fold the pages. In 1887 eight much faster American Hoe steam presses, which could print 24,000 papers of between four and eight pages in an hour, were introduced by the *Lloyd's Weekly Newspaper*. The national circulation of this paper reached a million in the 1890s, and in 1902 its owner bought even faster presses, which could each print 55,000 copies of a thirty-two-page paper in an hour. These advances, which were copied by the other London papers, led to a huge increase in paper consumption. This prompted a search for raw materials other than rags and esparto grass, and led to the development of chemical processes in the 1870s and 1880s which would produce satisfactory paper from cheap Scandinavian and Canadian wood pulp.[8] Edward

Lloyd, the pioneer of popular and local newspapers in London, led the way in the 1870s in taking control of his own paper supply, manufactured in Kent from 100,000 acres of Algerian esparto grass.

The introduction of American technology transformed the printing industry between 1890 and 1914, enabling it to produce a wider range of books, magazines, and newspapers in much greater numbers than before, and reaching a vast new market of working-class and lower-middle-class readers. This was achieved with a modest increase in the London printing workforce, from 40,000 in 1891 to 47,000 in 1911. Most of this increase was in semi-skilled women printers, whose numbers increased from about 2,000 to nearly 7,000 in twenty years. By 1900 there were about 500 newspapers and periodicals published in London, catering for almost every interest and taste, every political or religious standpoint and every degree of literacy or intellect, from the weighty and expensive *Times* (3d until Northcliffe cut its price to a penny), through the serious penny dailies (the *Standard*, the *Daily News*, the *Daily Telegraph*, the *Morning Post*, the *Daily Chronicle*, the *Financial Times*) to the newer and more popular halfpenny ones, the *Morning Leader*, the *Daily Mail*, and the *Daily Express* (1900), with the *Daily Mirror* and *Daily Sketch* following soon after.

The Census of 1907

In 1907 there was a census of factory and workshop employees in London, which, although it gives an incomplete account of London's industrial workers, provides useful information on the location of different industries. The largest industrial employer in every manufacturing borough was either clothing, metalwares (including plumbing, locomotives, mechanical and electrical engineering, and armaments), printing and bookbinding, food, drink and tobacco, or wood (including furniture, carriages, barrels, and carpentry). These five industrial groups, in that order, were the County of London's biggest industrial employers, providing about 75 per cent of its manufacturing jobs. The most central boroughs were the most heavily committed to manufacturing. Despite its white-collar image, the district with the most manufacturing workers in 1907 was the City of London, which contained 11.3 per cent of the County of London's workshop and factory jobs, including a third of those in printing and publishing, and about 14 per cent of those in clothing, textiles, and furs and leather. Next (on 8.5 per cent each) came the little borough of Finsbury (just north of the City) and Westminster, which covered the West End south of Oxford Street. Finsbury was a borough with a host of miscellaneous industries, and with about 10 per cent of the County's workers in printing, food and drink, fine instruments, and furs and leather. Together, these two boroughs had nearly 70 per cent of London's jewellery and plate industry, and Westminster also specialized in clothing, gas and electricity, fine instruments, and printing. Stepney, the biggest East End borough, had 7.2 per cent of London's manufacturing workers, including about 10 per cent of its workforce in clothing, food and drink, leather, hair and bristles (brushes), textiles, and chemicals (mainly paint, oil, soap, matches, candles, dyes, and drugs). Other inner boroughs had particular specialities: Shoreditch, the small borough north-east of the City, had over 12 per cent of London's furniture- and wood-workers, and nearly 5 per cent of all its manufacturing workforce; the tiny borough of Holborn, which included Hatton Garden, had over 12 per cent of London's jewellery workers and many printing businesses; Bermondsey, across the river from Stepney, had a third of London's leather and fur workers, and 13 per cent of its food and drink jobs; Southwark, the other inner South London borough, had a share in every important London industry, especially those using metals or paper; the East End borough of Bethnal Green was the leading district for brushmaking, but two-thirds of its manufacturing workers made clothes or furniture, in the latter of which it held second place to Shoreditch. Boroughs a little more distant from the centre were less industrial, but some had important manufacturing activities: Woolwich, with its great government arms factories, was London's biggest employer in metals and machinery; St Pancras, the centre of piano production, had 23 per cent of London's fine instrument workers; Hackney had significant employment in clothing, machinery, and fine instruments; Lambeth had a fifth of London's workers in stone, brick, pottery, and glass; and Camberwell over 22 per cent of the County's gas and electricity jobs. Some suburban and residential boroughs, including Chelsea, Deptford, Fulham, Greenwich, Hammersmith, Hampstead, Kensington, Lewisham, Paddington, Stoke Newington, and Wandsworth, had little manufacturing employment in proportion to the size of their populations, though several had small pockets of industry, especially where they bordered the Thames or the inner boroughs.[9]

In 1907 nearly a fifth of Greater London's factory and workshop workers (roughly 130,000 out of 680,000) worked outside the County boundary, mainly in Middlesex and urban Essex, but also in urban Kent and Surrey. In all these districts, though, only the County Borough of West Ham had a manufacturing workforce to compare with those in the more industrialized Inner London boroughs – 28,000 compared to Finsbury's or Westminster's 46,000, and the City's 62,000. Industrial Outer London tended to specialize in heavier and dirtier industries which were not appropriate to the inner city, because of either the pollution they caused or the large areas of land they occupied, and where closeness to the eastern docks and the River Lea was more useful than proximity to the West End stores. A quarter of London's metal and machinery workforce was outside the County (mainly in West Ham, Erith, and Enfield), along with a fifth of its furniture workers (in West Ham and Tottenham), and 38 per cent of its gas, electricity, and chemical workers (in East and West Ham).

The concentration of certain industries in particular districts of London sometimes reflected specific local advantages, such as closeness to the river, the docks, a canal or railway terminus, the availability of cheap land or labour, the importance of a local market, or the need to escape Inner London's environmental restrictions. The famous Bermondsey leather industry, the riverside sugar refineries, the glue, soap, and chemicals of West Ham, the West End carriage-builders and East End van-builders, the sweated and unskilled industries of East and South London, chose their locations in response to such practical considerations. Others, like Clerkenwell watchmaking and the remnant of Spitalfields silk-weaving, reflected the settlement patterns of immigrant craftsmen nearly two centuries earlier. Industries often gathered near the source of their raw materials, but sometimes their location was apparently a matter of chance, with manufacturers herding together in a convenient district, perhaps following tradition, or one of the leaders of their trade. Thus silk-hatters were concentrated around the Blackfriars Road, which had seventeen silk-hat factories in the 1890s, while the trimming and finishing of ladies' felt hats was mostly done in Cripplegate, in Barbican Street and Jewin Street, and cloth caps were made in Whitechapel, mostly by Jews. Zinc-workers regarded the Euston Road as their headquarters, while bicycle-makers preferred the Holborn Viaduct.

A much larger industry, the manufacture of cheap furniture, was centred on the main market and wholesaling street of the trade, Curtain Road (parallel to Shoreditch High Street). When Charles Booth's assistant Ernest Aves described the neighbourhood in 1889, Curtain Road and Great Eastern Street were full of warehouses and showrooms, and the workshops spread out into Finsbury, Shoreditch, Hoxton, Bethnal Green, as far north and east as the Regent's Canal. Gossett Street, with its sawmills and timber yards, was the centre of the Bethnal Green furniture trade, and in nearly every workshop, and in many private houses, chair-makers, cabinetmakers, turners, and carvers were at work, earning, if they were lucky, 6d an hour.[10] Charles Booth took a walk in this area, between Hackney Road and Bethnal Green Road, in March 1898, accompanied by Sergeant French of the Metropolitan Police. He found that the demolition of the notorious Old Nichol Street rookery to make way for the LCC's Boundary Street Estate had driven its worst inhabitants east across Brick Lane and into Bethnal Green, turning streets that had been coloured purple (mixed) or light blue (poor) in his 1889 poverty map into neighbourhoods that were dark blue or black, very poor or semi-criminal. Still, among the thieves, prostitutes, and gangs of young loafers there was work going on: 'the scream of the circular saw takes the place of the whirr of the Jewish sewing machine. Legs of tables, unfinished chairbacks etc. in evidence.'[11] Better-class furniture was made in workshops on and around Tottenham Court Road, for sale in big furniture stores like Maple's and Shoolbred's, and the best furniture of all was made by skilled craftsmen in the West End.

London had a reputation as a city of sweated workers, small work-shops, and traditional labour-intensive methods, rather than factories with steam-powered machinery. There was much truth in this, partly because clustering made it possible for small industries to operate efficiently. But evidence available for the decades around 1900 shows that London was also a city of factories and large industrial premises. Experts working for the 1905 Royal Commission on London Traffic compiled maps (using Home Office returns and the sixty-inch to the mile Ordnance Survey map of 1893–4) showing all London's factories and works, and indicating those with over one hundred, two hundred, or five hundred workers. These show that in the City and the Inner London boroughs (Southwark, Bermondsey, Deptford, north Lambeth, Holborn, Shoreditch, Finsbury, Stepney, Bethnal Green) there were hundreds of warehouses, wharves, engineering works, gasworks, tanneries, and factories, many of them with over two hundred workers. The factories show the enormous range of industrial activities in central London. In a small section of Whitechapel, around Commercial Street and Brick Lane, for instance, there were facto-ries making or processing spices, mustard, biscuits, chocolate, cocoa, tea, oil, feathers, fur, carts, chenille, and telephones, and in the riverside neigh-bourhood of Southwark (the streets north of Union Street, dominated now by Tate Modern) there were about fifty factories (fifteen with over a hundred workers, five with over two hundred) producing or processing wheels, engines, oil, boxes, confectionery, carts, plate glass, hats, asbestos, cocoa fibre, envelopes, lead, flour, vinegar, boilers, cement, hops, and jam. Directly across the river, on the western edge of the City, there was an extraordinary concentration of printing works and bookbinders, mostly employing over two hundred people, and in western Bermondsey, around Bermondsey Street and Tower Bridge Road (just south-east of London Bridge Station), crowded between the many leather-works and tanneries, there was an intense concentration of works making rope, cocoa, bottles, dog biscuits, meat extract, vinegar, bedsteads, felt hats, boilers, carriages, sweets, tinplate, brass, sacks, mineral water, beer, pins, dye, barrels, and electricity.[12]

Large collections of workers are not always synonymous with modern mechanized production methods, but in many London trades they were. The 1907 census of production divided London workplaces into workshops and factories, defining the latter as places in which mechanical power (steam, gas, or electricity) was used in the manufacturing process. By this definition, the County of London had 10,490 factories, with an average of thirty-seven employees, and 16,351 workshops, with an average of about ten. In the County of London 70 per cent of manufacturing workers worked in factories, and in Outer London, where there was more heavy industry, the figure was over 82 per cent. Factory inspection statistics for Greater London and its surrounding counties (including Sussex, Essex, and Oxfordshire) recorded 17,818 factories and nearly 35,000 workshops in 1910. Factory production was universal in the power-supply industries, and general in paper, printing, metals, machinery, food, drink, stone, glass, textiles, and chemicals. Only in London's biggest industry, the clothing trade, did small workshops and outworking still predominate, with just under 28 per cent of clothing workers employed in factories. Even in the City and the crowded inner-city boroughs in which clothing and furniture trades were big employers, Shoreditch, Stepney, and Bethnal Green, between 50 and 70 per cent of manufacturing workers worked in factories, or places with powered machinery. So, whatever London had been like in the 1850s, the decade of Henry Mayhew, by the beginning of the twentieth century it was, to quite a large extent, a city of factories and powered machines, with only one great industry still producing most of its goods by hand in rooms and workshops.[13]

The Sweating Scandal

The 1907 census, for all its value, missed out many thousands of manufacturing workers who worked in their own (or other people's) homes or in unregistered and uninspected workshops, or sweatshops. These outworkers and homeworkers were an important part of the workforce in the clothing trades, and were also involved in much smaller numbers in the manufacture of artificial flowers, paper bags and boxes, furniture, and brushes. The fact that the 1911 population census recorded 70,200 men and 153,600 women in the clothing and shoe industries in the County of London, while the 1907 census of factory and workshop production listed only 26,000 men and 89,000 women indicates the vast size of this uncounted workforce. Sweated labour was a phenomenon in London dating back to the early nineteenth century, when a growth in the mass market for ready-made clothes combined with the availability of a large supply of cheap (especially female) labour to break the power of the tailors' and shoemakers' craft unions and opened up the clothing trades to all comers. From the 1850s to the 1870s the introduction of new technology, especially the powered bandsaw for cutting out clothes in bulk, and the sewing machine (patented in the USA by Elias Howe in 1846), which could turn every home into a workshop, lowered the price of ready-made garments and spread the habit of buying new clothes to those who had once worn cast-offs. Rising real incomes, falling textile and raw material prices, free trade, cheaper transport, and the development of more efficient and attractive retailing all helped to create a growing mass market for clothes, shoes, furniture, and other consumer goods, inducing London producers to devise ways of responding to it. The system they developed was a form of subcontracting and division of labour, in which a few skilled or bulky tasks were carried out in a central workshop, and simpler processes were handed over to individual outworkers, or to small subcontractors who in turn employed workers as they needed them, usually in small unregulated workshops. This system was responsive to changes in fashions and levels of demand, used new technology without the expense of factory premises, and exploited the existence in London of a huge population without skills or bargaining power, who were forced either to accept low wages and long hours in unsavoury premises or to do no work at all. The master manufacturer was able to pass the costs of premises, machinery, and management on to subcontractors, avoid factory regulations, and under-mine the bargaining power of craftsmen by breaking their complex skills into small and easily learned tasks. Anyone with a room to work in and a few basic skills could enter the trade, paying for a treadle sewing machine, which was indispensable by the 1880s, on the instalment system at 2s 6d a week. For most uneducated London women who needed to work, the clothing trades were the only large-scale alternative to domestic service or laundry work, and though there were jobs for women in the shoe, food, paper, and furniture industries many of these were also in sweated condi-tions. In every census from 1881 to 1911 two-thirds of London clothing workers were women, and the true percentage, because women were always under-recorded, was higher. Nearly all the workers in dressmaking, the biggest of the clothing trades, were women, and so were about 85 per cent of seamstresses and shirtmakers, and nearly half the tailors. From the 1880s, male Jewish immigrants from East Europe poured into the sweated clothing trades, especially tailoring, both as workers and contractors, using the one marketable skill they had, and benefiting from the fact that many of the local employers shared their language and religion.[14]

London captured about 19 per cent of the British clothing industry (measured in the number of workers), using its closeness to the metropol-itan market and the flexibility and economy of the subcontracting system to equal and outdo the factories of Leeds. So the clothing trades, which supported a modest number of skilled craftsmen in reasonable comfort in the 1820s, sustained a huge number of men and women, probably a tenth of London's workers, in varying degrees of misery in the 1880s and 1890s. Some of these unlucky men and women, working all hours in horrible con-ditions for a barely living wage, might have looked back (if they had time to think) to a golden age of tailoring, but in that golden age only 20,000 of them would have been tailors. It was not working in the clothing indus-try that made them poor, but their poverty that made them work in the clothing industry.

Sweating was an old worry, but interest in it was reawakened in the 1880s. Except for brief references to children making matchboxes, *The Bitter Cry of Outcast London* hardly mentioned sweating, but the wave of concern for the lives of the London poor that followed its publication in 1883 extended to the sweated system, as well as housing, prostitution, and poverty. Concern over the entry of Jewish migrants into sweated work in the later 1880s intensified interest in the problem. A group of women trade unionists published a paper on East End sweated trades in the *Lancet* in

March 1884, John Burnett, the Labour Correspondent of the Board of Trade, carried out a careful study of the same subject in 1887, and Beatrice Potter undertook a study of the sweated clothing industry in Stepney for Charles Booth in October 1887. Potter's account was based on interviews with workers, employers, and factory and sanitary inspectors, and two days working 'under cover' as a trouser finisher in a Jewish sweatshop on the Mile End Road. The room was hot, the work exhausting and very poorly paid, and the hours long (8.30 a.m. to 8 p.m., with an hour for lunch and breaks for tea), but the atmosphere was cheerful and the 'missus' and the other girls were warm, intelligent, and friendly, sensing perhaps that Miss Potter was not what she claimed to be. The investigator did not have to live on the wages, and her main concern was that she was too slow and clumsy to do the work: 'I feel hopelessly tired, my fingers clammy and a general shakiness all over. The needle will not pierce the hard shoddy stuff; my stitches will go all awry and the dampness of my fingers stretches the linings out of place. Altogether I feel on the brink of deep disgrace.'[15] Beatrice Potter's account of her work was published as 'The Pages of a Workgirl's Diary' in the *Nineteenth Century* in October 1888, and in the first volumes of Booth's *Life and Labour* a year later.

John Burnett and Beatrice Potter were both called as witnesses before a House of Lords Select Committee on the Sweating System in 1888. The committee, which included the Archbishop of Canterbury and Lords Derby and Rothschild, was (Potter wrote) 'a set of well-meaning men, but not made of stuff fit for investigation'. Their five reports, published between 1888 and 1890, told a story of deplorable working and living conditions, starvation wages, and the easy evasion of existing factory legislation. Their half-hearted remedy, the 1891 Factory and Workshop Act, reinforced by further acts in 1895 and 1901, gave local authorities greater powers to inspect workshops and to force employers to register their outworkers. Some London authorities, notably Islington, Poplar, and Kensington, began effective inspection in the 1890s, Bethnal Green and Hackney followed suit after 1900, and a few, including Stepney, St Pancras, and St Marylebone (the centre of West End dressmaking) did little. The predictable effect of this uneven enforcement, as the 1907–8 Select Committee on Home Work was repeatedly told, was that workshops moved out of well-inspected boroughs into badly inspected ones, and the share of work done by individual outworkers in uninspected private homes increased, making conditions worse. Since many subcontractors failed to submit accurate registers of their outworkers, and female outworkers did not always record their employment on the census forms, the true extent of outworking in London is unknown. The LCC's figure of 32,236 registered outworkers (27,000 in clothing, the rest mostly in boxes, brushes, and artificial flowers) in 1910 probably misses the true figure by 60,000 or more. The figures, for what they are worth, show that three-quarters of these registered outworkers worked for employers in the City, Bethnal Green, Finsbury, Hackney, Islington, Stepney, and Westminster.[16]

The failure of the 1890s legislation to eradicate the scandal of sweated labour prompted its opponents to adopt a characteristically Edwardian way of publicizing its evils. In June 1906 the radical liberal newspaper the *Daily News* sponsored a Sweated Industries Exhibition in Queen's Hall, Langham Place. The exhibition was inspired and organized by the leaders of the Women's Trade Union League, Mary Macarthur and Gertrude Tuckwell, and administered by Richard Mudie-Smith, who had compiled the report on the *Daily News*' census of London worship in 1904. It is easy to smile at the thought of society ladies, the wives of Cabinet ministers, and members of the royal family, filling the tedious hours between shopping and the theatre by strolling along lines of sanitized mock-sweatshops, watching genuine seamstresses, box-makers, fur-pullers, cigarette-makers, tennis-ball makers, pressers, buttonholers, and machinists working at their trades. But these were powerful women, with connections in the Liberal government that had recently won the 1906 General Election by a landslide. Some of those whose consciences had been pricked joined the new Anti-Sweating League, which was led by A. G. Gardiner and George Cadbury, respectively the editor and owner of the *Daily News*, and organized by Gertrude Tuckwell, a well-connected socialist and tireless campaigner for better wages and working conditions. The issue was taken up by Sir Charles Dilke (Tuckwell's uncle) and Arthur Henderson, one of the leaders of the new Labour Party, and in 1909 a sympathetic Liberal government was persuaded to introduce the Trade Boards Bill. The 1909 Trade Boards Act established boards to set minimum wages for men and women in sweated trades, initially in tailoring, box-making, lace-making, and chain-making. In tailoring, where the new rates were imposed in 1913, the effect was to bring the wages of most male workers in these industries up to 25s for a fifty-hour week, and most women up to 13s 6½d, an average increase of over 40 per cent. A fifth of women workers were excluded from the new rates, to encourage employers to retain old and inefficient workers, and the rates did not apply directly to homeworkers. It was hoped that their rates would be dragged up too, and a quarter of

East End homeworkers questioned by the socialist academic and Toynbee
Hall resident R. H. Tawney in 1914 said that their wages had risen thanks
to the new minimum wage for workshop workers.[17]

The Electric Future

Commentators in the 1890s and 1900s, following Booth's lead, tended to
focus on London's industrial problems, its declining industries, its sweated
system and casual labour, and to miss the green shoots of industrial
renewal. Charles Booth's assistant Ernest Aves, writing at the end of the
1890s, presented a balance sheet of London's advantages and disadvantages as an industrial centre. London's main advantages included its vast
population of producers and consumers, its unrivalled place at the centre
of a national and worldwide market and distribution network, and its
unique attractiveness as a city: 'its leadership in amusement and fashion;
its historical associations; the fascination and glitter, even the gloom, of its
hurrying life – all go to swell its attractive force, and to strengthen its position as a centre of trade and manufacture'. Its dominance was moderated,
though, by some grave weaknesses, which would have crippled its industrial growth if it had been starting from scratch. Its working people, he
said, were unhealthy, its wage levels were too high, and its natural resources
were inadequate: 'Modern industry is largely dependent for economy on
cheap coal and cheap iron, and London has neither; or it may demand
ample supplies of running water and fresh air, and again London has neither; or light and space, and these are either not available or can be
obtained only at a prohibitive cost in rent.' Therefore, Aves argued, London
was doomed to lose its position in industries where fuel, iron, and steel
were important in the cost of production, and where large premises were
required, though it would hold its own in some highly skilled trades (the
finest jewellery, carriages, and surgical instruments), some finishing trades
and assembly work, industries meeting a local need (baking, brewing,
newspapers), and repair work in machinery and shipbuilding.[18]
    Less than forty years after Aves' rather gloomy analysis, London had
achieved a position of such dominance in British industrial life that a Royal
Commission (the Barlow Commission on the Distribution of the Industrial Population) was set up to work out what could be done to reduce its
industrial prosperity and influence. We can find the origins of this surprising reversal in London's industrial fortunes, its transition from sick man

to superman, in the pre-war years. Factory inspectors' reports in the early twentieth century often mentioned the appearance of new industries, especially those related to motoring. Reporting on East London in 1906, Inspector Boggis noted that 'the reclamation of rubber, chiefly from old motor tyres, is a growing industry . . . Several large engineering works are adding a motor car department, and the big clothiers have turned their attention to the making of motor clothing.' In West London there was a big new factory making composite boarding (strips of wood glued together and covered in layers of brown paper) for house partitions. In 1910 the inspectors for South-east England (including London) reported that the main growth industries were motor cars and cabs, aeroplanes, cinematograph films, filament lamps, boots, and clothing. London industry's transition from hand, steam, or gas to electric power, which would in the 1920s and 1930s allow it to compete on equal terms with the coalfield towns, was often mentioned in Edwardian inspectors' reports, especially in smaller plants and industries that needed intermittent power. 'The use of small electric motors is still increasing', and 'electric motors continue to replace gas engines, especially for smaller powers in more crowded neighbourhoods', inspectors reported in 1904 and 1905. By 1912, according to one of the inspectors for North London, 48 per cent of factories in Islington, 63 per cent in St Pancras, and 69 per cent in Holborn were electric-powered. No doubt some of these were small enterprises, defined as factories because they used electric power, but the trend is clear.[19]

London's second disadvantage, its lack of cheap space for industrial growth, was being removed, especially after 1900, when workmen's trains and cheap and fast motorized transport (electric trams, trains, the Underground, and then motor buses) pushed London's suburbs out into Essex, Middlesex, Surrey, and Kent, where rents and rates were lower and labour and factory space was readily available. With an office in central London and a factory on the industrializing outskirts of the city, a manufacturer could have the best of both worlds. The East London inspectors commented on the decentralization of London industry in 1906: 'The chief development to be noted is the continued increase in factories in what has been aptly described as "Outer London". In Walthamstow, particularly, new works of considerable size have been erected, and others are already in course of construction.' London's striking progress in the engineering and metal industries, from little more than 'a repairing shop' (Aves' words) in the 1890s to a national leader between the wars, owed a great deal to growth in the outer industrial districts, especially Woolwich, West Ham,

East Ham, Erith, and Enfield. In 1907, even before the growth of the Walthamstow motor-bus industry, Woolwich and the Outer London districts had 38 per cent of Greater London's 114,000 metal and engineering workforce, and the same share of its 49,000 workers in gas, electricity, and chemicals.[20]

In the early decades of the twentieth century the engineering and metal industries went through a process of mechanization and semi-automation which would, in the world described by Booth and Aves in the 1890s, have driven them out of the city. As Booth put it, 'in the provinces factories can be managed more successfully than in London, and work suitable for them is apt to leave the Metropolis'. But, as Hubert Llewellyn Smith explained in 1931, the rise of industrial Outer London had confounded Booth's predictions: 'the migration of work to provincial factories has now been to a considerable extent superseded by a centrifugal movement from the centre to the circumference of Greater London, the outer ring of which is becoming more and more the seat of thriving and successful factory production'. Heavy industry and shipbuilding had continued in their northward flight, but 'the new southward trend of industry has brought to the outskirts of London much fresh employment both for men and women in the newer and lighter branches of the metal trades'. The Great War temporarily diverted the engineering trades into armaments production, but the pre-war trends were resumed in the 1920s, when 'the full extent of the technical and economic revolution' that had taken place before and during the war was revealed.[21] The 1921 census shows which branches of the engineering trades London had captured or retained. Over 18 per cent of the motor vehicle and cycle-manufacturing workers of England and Wales were in Greater London, a quarter of the makers of electrical apparatus, 40 per cent of tin-box makers (mostly women), 56 per cent of the makers of electrical cables, wire, and flex, and 80 per cent of the makers of electric lamps. London's dominance of the UK export trade in telegraph and telephone apparatus and other electrical goods in 1910 shows that the state of affairs revealed by the 1921 census already existed, to a significant degree, before the Great War. Mechanized production had increased the demand for semi-skilled engineering workers (neither craftsmen nor labourers) and this, rather than the Great War, opened the industries up to women workers, who made up one third of Greater London's electrical engineering workforce in 1921.[22]

So it was in the working-class suburbs of Outer London, such places as West Ham, Woolwich, Willesden, and Walthamstow, unlovely, unvisited, ignored by guidebooks and mostly outside the County boundary, that the foundations of London's electrified industrial future were being established in the pre-war decade. Theirs were the industries that would boom in the 1920s and keep going in the Depression of the 1930s, making London the powerhouse of the interwar manufacturing economy and the envy of the industrial North.

*

New Women

The majority of women in late Victorian London did not work for money, or did not regard the casual work they did (perhaps taking in washing or mangling, or looking after other people's children) as worth putting on a census form. According to the census returns, only 40 per cent of London women over the age of ten had paid jobs, compared with 84 per cent of men. Some of these non-employed women were schoolgirls, others were too ill or old to work, and some were members of the wealthy leisured class, in which neither sex was employed. But the great majority of London's non-working women had no jobs because they were wives and mothers, and because married women did not often take jobs unless hardship forced them to do so.

Jobs for Women

In general, the work available to less educated women did not offer much personal satisfaction, and, as far as we can tell, most working women took jobs from economic necessity, not for pleasure. The great majority of working women gave up their full-time jobs when they married, even if they did not have children, either because they wanted to, or because their husbands, their employers, or society at large expected them to. According to an authoritative study of married women's work carried out in 1909–10 (but published in 1915), it was 'a general opinion and especially, perhaps, among persons of the middle class, that the working for money of married women is to be deplored'. A campaigning group called the Women's Industrial Council, which carried out this research under the direction of its president, Clementina Black, intended to find out whether the work of mothers had the harmful effects on family life and children's health that were usually attributed to it, and to examine the nature of the work these mothers did. Clementina Black's main contribution to the book was a long chapter on London, based upon a study of about 300 women working as laundresses, glovers, artificial-flower makers, jam-makers, street sellers, box-makers, boot-makers, tennis-ball sewers, wood-bundlers, book-folders, umbrella-makers and clothing workers. She found that the great majority of these women worked from necessity, because their husbands were unemployed, incapable of work, absent or dead, or did not earn enough to cover their family's food and rent. This was her conclusion:

> Women working at the sweated industries, such as brush-drawing, box-making, blouse-making, etc., or laundry work also, perhaps – take little interest or pride in their work, find it exceedingly irksome and arduous, and thankfully relinquish it on marriage if possible. When asked why they are working, the answer is almost invariably that, for one reason or another, the family cannot get on without it. The few who can command a high wage at skilled work – such as fur-stitchers, gold embroiderers, and the more expert mantle-makers – seem to view the matter from an entirely different point of view. Their work is only thoroughly mastered after years of apprenticeship and experience. They perhaps are only just entering into their full wage-earning capacity when they marry. They are proud of their ability and specialised skill, find pleasure in their work, and would regard it as the height of folly to throw aside all they have gained . . . Many of them employ servants or charwomen to do their house work, and enjoy their position of freedom and independence.[1]

A survey of fifteen married women working as milliners, feather-curlers, and fur-sewers confirmed this summary. Ten said they worked to supplement the earnings of a sick, lazy, or poorly paid husband, but four said that they worked because they wanted to: 'likes doing a little', 'no real need to work now', and 'Never gave up her work; liked to have her own money'.[2]

The range of jobs open to late-Victorian women was not very wide, and most of the better-paid and skilled jobs in transport, building, and engineering were closed to them. In 1898 Nora Philipps, the wife of a Liberal MP and the founder of the Grosvenor Crescent Club for women, published a *Dictionary of Employments Open to Women*, to inform women of the range of jobs available, the qualifications they would need, and the wages and hours they could expect. The book described more than a hundred jobs, from accountant and ballet dancer to charwoman and barmaid, in the hope that women would be directed away from the limited number of over-crowded employments that they were usually drawn into. Lack of choice was a serious problem for working women in London. According to the census of 1891, 707,000 women in the County of London and four external boroughs (West Ham, Willesden, Leyton, and Tottenham) were in paid work, and 70 per cent of these (nearly 500,000) were in domestic service or the clothing industry. The 630 women recorded as building workers in the 1891 census, and the 50 female dockers and shipwrights, were not typical of their sex, and were probably not doing the work of men. Although the census lists a total of about 11,000 women employed in such male preserves as building, transport, metals, engineering, watchmaking, and general labour, the great majority of working women found jobs in a few manufacturing industries which had traditionally employed them, or in commercial and professional work and domestic service. The textile industries (cotton, wool, linen, and silk), which employed so many women in other industrial areas, were not very large employers in London, but about 58,000 women worked in the production of furniture, chemicals, paper, books, textiles, furs, and leather, and another 42,000 made their living from the production or sale of food, drink, and tobacco, especially as confectioners and lodging- and coffee-house keepers. In only one manufacturing industry, the making of clothes, were men outnumbered by women. In 1891 London had 148,500 women working as tailors, dressmakers, seamstresses, machinists, hatters, and drapers, and 141,400 men. Most of these industrial jobs were poorly paid, and many were 'sweated' industries. The alternative, especially for young unmarried working-class women, was domestic service. In 1891 very nearly a half of all working women in London and the four nearby boroughs, 344,400 people, were employed in domestic or personal service, about 80,000 of these as waitresses, hairdressers, or laundresses, and the rest as domestic servants in middle- or upper-class households.[3] By 1911 the proportion of working women in domestic service and clothing had been reduced from 70 per cent to 59 per cent, because women's work in other industries (chemicals, paper, food, and engineering) had grown, and because so many more women had taken up professional and office work. The 'white-collar' woman was 9 per cent of the London female workforce in 1891 and 14 per cent in 1911.

Women in the Office

In mid-Victorian London it had been difficult for educated middle-class women or aspiring working-class women to find office work. In 1861, before the white-collar or 'white-blouse' revolution, there were only 2,400 women in commercial, financial, civil service, or clerical jobs in London, and almost all the higher-status jobs for women (about 50,000 in all) were in teaching, nursing, entertainment, and retailing. When the civil servant Arthur Munby met a female merchant's clerk at a dance in Soho in 1864 he considered the event a rarity worthy of an exclamation mark in his diary. But between 1861 and 1891 the number of male and female commercial clerks in London tripled from 36,000 to 108,000, and in the 1880s workers in civil service and local government offices rose from 20,000 to 27,000. Some employers tried to satisfy this enormous demand for educated clerical workers by importing German clerks, but educated young women offered a cheaper and more convenient alternative, and were drawn into clerical work in very large numbers. In the 1880s and 1890s offices which had rarely seen women without a mop and bucket now welcomed them as clerks, typists, and telegraphists. By 1891 women occupied about 12,000 civil service, clerical, and commercial jobs in the County of London, about 8 per cent of office-based work. In addition, there were 40,000 women in the professions, 7,500 in entertainment, and over 35,000 in retailing, making a sort of female lower middle class of 100,000. By 1911, the office sector (jobs in administration, commerce, and finance) had grown to 240,000, but the number of women in it had quadrupled in twenty years to 49,000, over a fifth of London's office workers.[4] So in the late Victorian and Edwardian years, women broke into the previously masculine world of the London office and counting house, preparing the way for their dominance of office work later in the twentieth century. Along with this change in practice, there was something of a change in attitudes, too. In 1898 the Daily Telegraph, which had a very wide circulation among the London middle classes, carried out a survey on its readers' attitudes towards wives who went to work. The paper received about 2,000 letters and published 206 of them (mostly from Londoners), and found, it said, 'a silent but complete revolution' in attitudes (especially among middle-class women) towards working after marriage.[5]

Although it promoted the growth of feminism, women's entry into the white-collar world was not itself the product of feminist agitation. It arose from the growing need of business and the civil service for cheap and efficient labour, willing to carry out tedious office tasks without the prospect of promotion to more interesting and well-paid work. Some of this demand reflected the growing size and complexity of commercial, financial, and governmental organizations, and the increasing need, as business became less personal, for correspondence and record-keeping. To serve this need, wooden filing cabinets began replacing shelves and pigeonholes in the 1870s and 1880s. The well-equipped Edwardian office might have metal cabinets with vertical files, which were developed in the USA in the 1890s. In addition, new office technology started to replace some traditionally 'male' clerical skills with new ones which were open to either sex. The electric telegraph, the typewriter, the telephone, and (later) the calculating machine were all seen as devices which made office work easier and more 'feminine' than it had been before. Just as this demand arose, middle-class women found themselves equipped to satisfy it. The private schools for middle-class girls that had been founded since 1848 (Queen's College, North London Collegiate School, the Girls' Public Day School Trust schools) were supplemented in the 1870s by state elementary schools, in the 1890s by municipal evening classes in commercial subjects, and after 1902 by state secondary schools. Women could get university degrees from London University from 1880, and get a university education, without graduating, in women's colleges at Oxford and Cambridge. The demand for young men and women with commercial skills, including shorthand and typing, was also met by private commercial colleges and correspondence courses. Pitmans, the leading shorthand organization, listed twelve London schools teaching its method in 1892, and thirty-nine in 1899, and the number of men and women taking the (Royal) Society of Arts examinations in commercial subjects like shorthand, typing, and book-keeping rose from about 9,000 in 1900 to over 35,000 in 1914.[6]

The mechanization of office work in the later nineteenth century created thousands of simple and repetitive tasks which Victorian employers regarded as being appropriate work for smart and quite well-educated young women. The first modern office machine, the electric telegraph, was already well established in London by 1880. The first public telegraph line in Britain, from Paddington to Slough, was laid in 1843, and the Paris and London stock exchanges were connected by land and sea cable in 1851. The first lines under the London streets – copper wires coated in Malayan gutta-percha – were laid in the 1850s, and a transatlantic line linking London and New York was completed, after much difficulty, in 1865. By the mid-1850s the Electric Telegraph Company was recruiting women clerks to operate its machines, and *Punch* was making predictable jokes about it. Male and female telegraphists were kept completely separate from each other, with their own staircases, street entrances, and dining rooms.

In 1870 London was linked by overland cable with Calcutta, and by the
1890s it was joined to the main European capitals and with the chief cities
in the African and Far Eastern empire. Under the control of the Post Office
(from 1870) the telegraph network was expanded and the cost of sending
messages was sharply reduced. As a result the number of messages sent in
the UK tripled between 1870 and 1883, and almost tripled again by 1900.
About a third of these (about 25 million a year in 1900) were sent from
London. By 1900 the main London telegraph office in St Martin-le-Grand,
easily the largest in the world, employed about two thousand men and
women in a series of 'halls', three dealing with local, national, and international telegrams, another for sending out press bulletins to other cities
using a telegraphic printing system called the Hughes Perforator, and a
fifth for sending messages across London through a network of underground pneumatic tubes. The Pneumatic Despatch system was first used in
1853 to connect the London Stock Exchange with the Telegraph Company, and by 1909 there were forty miles of 2¼in or 3in tubes in London
(running under fifty streets), operated by vacuum and compressed air provided by four steam engines. A single 3in carrier could handle up to
seventy-five messages at a time, and since unskilled tube attendants were
cheaper than skilled telegraphists the system could transmit local messages
more quickly and cheaply than the electric telegraph. Working with the
pneumatic tube was considered simple, and the room was staffed entirely
by women, while the more demanding and prestigious work of the sub-
marine cable room was carried out by men.[7]

The Telephone

The telephone arrived about a generation later than the electric telegraph.
Working from the researches of German and Italian physicists, Alexander
Graham Bell developed a practical telephone, demonstrated it at the
Philadelphia World Fair in 1876, and patented it in America and the UK
that same year. Several rivals, including the mighty Edison, challenged his
priority to the invention, and Edison's telephone was granted a UK patent
in 1877. Bell came to England with his telephone in that year, and it was
demonstrated to a meeting of the British Association by Sir William
Thomson (the future Lord Kelvin), who had brought two telephones back
with him from Philadelphia. The words used to test the telephone, 'Hey
diddle diddle, the cat and the fiddle' anticipated those used by Edison to

demonstrate his phonograph in December 1877, 'Mary had a little lamb', rather than recalling the more grandiose 'What hath God wrought?', Samuel Morse's first telegraphic message in 1844, or the strictly functional, 'Come here, Watson, I need you,' with which Bell christened the telephone in America. Perhaps Edison's greatest contribution to the development of the telephone was his suggestion that the word 'hello' should be used as a greeting when answering, instead of Bell's nautical 'ahoy ahoy'. Until 1877 halloo, hallo, and hello were only used (often shouted) to attract someone's attention, or as an expression of surprise. But the telephone established the word hello as the everyday greeting it is today, especially through its use by telephonists, or, as they were called in the 1890s, 'hello-girls'.

There was initial scepticism about the practical benefits of the telephone in the London press. The *Saturday Review* thought it 'was little better than a toy. It amazes ignorant people for a moment, but it is inferior to the well-established system of air-tubes.' With rather greater foresight, another London journalist asked 'What will become of the privacy of life? What will become of the sanctity of the domestic hearth?'[8] But the support of the British Association, *The Times*, and the *Tatler* helped the telephone get established, and so did the news early in 1878 that the Queen had ordered two telephones for Windsor Castle from Bell, after he had demonstrated long-distance calls from Osborne House, on the Isle of Wight, to London and Southampton. When the *Daily News* and the banking house of J. S. Morgan ordered telephones it became plain that the instrument had a promising commercial future in London. In 1879 Bell's Telephone Company opened its first tiny telephone exchange in Coleman Street, near the Bank of England, serving just eight subscribers from two switchboards. This was followed by exchanges in Leadenhall Street and Westminster, and by 15 January 1880, when the first London telephone directory was published, Bell had over 250 London subscribers, each paying about £20 a year. That year Bell's rival, Thomas Edison, formed his own Edison Telephone Company of London, with the intention of competing with Bell for the world's biggest potential market.

After this rapid start, only a year behind the USA, the progress of the telephone in London was delayed by the reluctance of the government and its agency, the Post Office, to allow the development of a private rival to the state-owned electric telegraph. A crucial difficulty for Bell and Edison was that they had to negotiate with property owners for permission to run wires from their buildings. In November 1879 George Bernard Shaw, struggling to make a living after the rejection of his novel *Immaturity*, took a job with the Way-Leave department of the Edison Company. Shaw had to travel the streets of the East End trying to persuade householders to allow the company to erect poles, wires, and insulators on their houses or in their gardens. Surprisingly, he found the work very difficult. 'I liked the exploration involved, but my shyness made the business of calling on strangers frightfully uncongenial; and my sensitiveness, which was extreme, in spite of the brazen fortitude which I simulated, made the impatient rebuffs I had to endure . . . ridiculously painful to me.' After six weeks of effort and embarrassment Shaw had managed to persuade just one householder and earned 2s 6d commission, but had spent over £2 in expenses. He resigned, but was instead given an £80-a-year office job supervising other door-to-door agents, 'liars, braggarts and hustlers', who were more dedicated than he was to the task of 'making slow old England hum'.[9] In June 1880 the Edison company amalgamated with Bell to form the United Telephone Company, and Shaw and his staff were sacked. The companies united to meet the threat posed by the Postmaster General, who claimed in 1880 that a telephone message was a form of telegram, and was thus covered by the Post Office's monopoly. Since most early telephone communications were not directly person to person, but involved taking written messages to or from telephone offices, there was some justice in the government's argument.

The government vacillated between the idea of making the telephone system a state monopoly and allowing competition between private companies, and chose instead to regulate, tax, and impede a private monopoly. Having won his legal case against the United Company, the Postmaster General sold it a thirty-one-year operating licence for London, but without the power to erect poles, run wires through the air or underground, lay trunk lines between London and other cities, or open public call offices. At least 10 per cent of the company's gross income had to be paid to the government as royalties. With a private and not very efficient monopoly company working under these restrictions England fell further behind America in the development of telephone services and usage, and even lost its early European lead to Germany. London had no trunk-line connections with other cities until December 1884, when the line to Brighton was opened, though there was a line between Halifax and Bradford in 1880. London was not linked to Birmingham and the Midlands by a trunk line until 1890, or to Paris until 1891. In 1885 there were only 3,800 telephone subscribers in London, and few of these were private users.

Doctors and businesses found the telephone particularly useful, but it was far from being an essential of office life. Even department stores were slow to subscribe to telephone services. Two of the first to have telephones, Peter Robinson and Swan and Edgar, only got them in the early 1890s. This was fast compared to the Bank of England, which did not subscribe until after 1900.

In 1884 the United Telephone Company was finally allowed to open call offices and erect trunk lines, and its local licence was replaced with a national one, but the company was repeatedly refused permission to lay underground wires in London, and was not given the power to run wires along streets unless it could negotiate way rights with private property owners. For the rest of the century Parliament and (from 1889) the London County Council rejected the company's requests for underground lines, impeding the development of an efficient telephone system in London. Looking back on these restrictions, Bernard Shaw saw them as representative of an English reluctance to deal realistically with technical innovations:

> electric telegraphy, telephony, and traction are invented, and establish themselves as necessities of civilised life. The unpractical foreigner recognises the fact, and takes the obvious step of putting up poles in the street to carry wires. This expedient never occurs to the Briton. He wastes leagues of wire and does unheard-of damage to property by tying his wires and posts to such chimney stacks as he can beguile householders into letting him have access to.[10]

In 1889 the London company amalgamated with other local and regional companies as the National Telephone Company, and for the next ten years the government toyed with the idea that the Post Office should buy out this private monopoly. Eventually, following a Parliamentary Select Committee report in 1898, the Post Office started its own telephone-exchange business, and municipal authorities were authorized to start their own telephone companies in competition with the National Telephone Company. Only six local authorities did so, and only two of these (Hull and Portsmouth) remained independent for more than two or three years. In London the Post Office developed a telephone system in competition with the National Telephone Company, and in 1900 obtained an injunction to stop the private company digging up roads to lay underground lines without permission from the LCC and the Postmaster General. The company then agreed to allow intercommunication between its customers and the Post Office's, and to charge the same lower rates as the GPO, in return for the Post Office providing underground lines on a rental basis. It was agreed that the government would buy out the company in 1911 at a reasonable cost.

The introduction of competition and lower charges after 1900 at last enabled the telephone to reach a huge market among London's businesses and middle-class households. In 1903 there were about 65,000 subscribers in Greater London, of whom 56,000 were with the private company. By 1911 there were 208,000 subscribers, 74,000 of whom were with the state system. This represented nearly 7 per cent of all the telephones in Europe, and almost as many as there were in the whole of France. Subscribers could pay either £17 for a line with free unlimited use, or £5 a year with calls charged at 1d or 2d each. Many of the 246 million calls made in Greater London in 1910–11 were made by people without telephones, from the 3,800 call offices (in shops, post offices, and stations), for 2d a call. To get their message to its final destination callers could use a messenger boy supplied by the District Messengers Company.[11]

When the telephone was first introduced, its value in linking one private subscriber directly with another was not generally recognized. Instead, it was regarded as a sort of broadcasting device, which could transmit songs or plays into a subscriber's drawing room. Many of the early advocates of the telephone, including Bell and Edison, emphasized this use of the instrument when they demonstrated it to prestigious customers like Gladstone and Queen Victoria. In most countries with telephone systems there were entrepreneurs using telephones as broadcasting devices in the 1890s. In Budapest in 1893 Tivadar Puskas set up a telephonic broadcasting service, Telefon Hirmondó, including a broadcast newspaper, which lasted many years and was widely admired. A London system run by the Electrophone Company was established in 1894, allowing subscribers to 'sit comfortably at home in all weathers and listen to the latest comedy, opera, or tragedy, as the case may be, by the payment of a purely nominal rental'. There were usually four sets of headphones for each subscriber, allowing a family to listen together, as they would listen to the wireless twenty-five years later. But the sound quality was poor, and by 1906 the company had only 600 paying subscribers. To serve this small group, banks of electrophone transmitters were installed behind the footlights of most London theatres and concert halls, as well as on the pulpits of many London churches (often disguised as Bibles or hassocks), including St Martin-in-the-Fields, St Margaret Westminster, and St Anne Soho.

Victoria and Edward VII were subscribers, and Queen Alexandra enjoyed electrophone relays from Covent Garden during the opera season. In 1898 the system was extended, rent-free, to the main London hospitals, where it was still in use during the Great War. At Earls Court and at the Electrophone Company's headquarters in Pelican House, Gerrard Street, Soho, there was an Electrophone Salon, where fashionable Londoners sat in full evening dress listening to a selection of West End performances on headphones, and in many London restaurants, including the Café Royal, electrophones enabled diners to listen to the latest popular music by putting 6d in a slot and winding the clockwork of the receivers. An indicator on the machine told them which theatre or music hall was connected at any particular time.[12]

Clerks and Typewriters

Like the telegraph and the typewriter, the telephone switchboard was accepted from the start as a machine that suited the special skills of women. 'The National Company', we are told in 1901, 'recruit their operators from the ranks of bright, well-educated, intelligent girls, who are, in many cases, the daughters of professional men, doctors, barristers, clergymen, and others.' The Company's 'hello-girls' (probably about 3,000 of them) worked a nine-hour day, including lunch and tea breaks, and generally gave way to the male night shift at 8 p.m. Staff had the use of dining rooms, sports and social clubs, and a company pension scheme. In the Post Office, where conditions were similar, female operators started on 11s, rising after nine years to £1 a week, and to a rarely reached upper limit of £200 a year. Only single women could enjoy a long career in telephony. At the National Company, 'Marriage terminates an operator's connection with the company, but, if specially experienced, she is registered on the reserve as a stand-by when epidemics come along.'[13] The employment of women as telegraphists and telephonists made the Post Office London's biggest employer of white-collar women in 1911, when there were 9,512 women working for the Post Office in London, representing the great majority of female civil service employees in the capital.[14]

The first modern typewriter, with individual letters pressed against an inked ribbon by keystrokes, was invented by a Milwaukee printer, Christopher Scholes, in the 1860s. Scholes also devised the Universal (or qwerty) keyboard, in order to reduce key jams by slowing down the typist.

By the time the slower 'hunt and peck' typing system had been replaced by touch typing (first demonstrated in the USA in 1888) better technology had eliminated the jamming problem. Scholes' typewriter was produced and sold commercially by a New York gun and sewing-machine company, Remington, in 1873, and in that very year one was spotted in an unusually adventurous City of London firm. Other practical machines soon followed: the very popular Remington no. 2, with a shift key, in 1878; the cheaper Yost 'Caligraph', with separate upper and lower case keys for every letter, in 1881; the heavy Underwood, an upstrike typewriter which allowed the operator to see what was being written, in 1895; and the Standard and Corona portables in 1908 and 1912. The typewriter was advertised almost from the start as a machine that was especially suitable for women to use, as important a contribution to the employment of women as the spinning wheel and the sewing machine. The early Scholes models were mounted on sewing-machine stands and had a treadle to operate the carriage return. An early typewriting manual picked up the idea: 'The type-writer is especially adapted to feminine fingers. They seem to be made for type-writing. The type-writing involves no hard labor, and no more skill than playing the piano.' For no particularly good reason, typing was soon established as women's work, and as its use in offices grew, so did the employment of female typists. Nearly all the women listed as 'clerks' in England, according to a survey in 1905–6, were in fact shorthand typists. And as shorthand typing became identified as a woman's job, men who were trained in it escaped into alternative clerical jobs, fearing the low wages, limited promotion prospects, and loss of status that always went with women's work.

Office work was not well paid or interesting, but at least it was respectable and ladylike, and could be taken without a descent into the working class. It made some use of the extended education many middle-class girls had received, and it was not seen as manual labour, although it was as physical as sewing. In many offices, women were segregated from male clerks so that no impropriety could take place, and perhaps to stop the women seeing how much more interesting the men's work had become now that cheap female labour had freed them from the dullest routine tasks. Women were confined to telegraphing, typing, taking shorthand, filing, copying, form-filling, and other simple clerical jobs, and hardly ever progressed to more demanding and better paid work, as men would have done, as they gained in age and experience. To an employer, a woman's ability to perform repetitive tasks with speed and accuracy, her tolerance of tedium and confinement, and her readiness to work without the prospect of promotion and for half the salary of a man were her chief virtues. The widely asserted weaknesses of women, their shortage of physical stamina, their inability to take complex or independent decisions, their lack of ambition, and their tendency to suffer from nervous disorders (no doubt related to the tedium of their work), were held to justify their permanent exclusion from the higher ranks of their profession. As the McDonnell Commission on the Civil Service put it in 1912, in 'powers of sustained work, in continuity of service, in adaptability to varying service conditions, the advantage lay with men'.

For ambitious and intelligent women, this confinement to the simplest office tasks was frustrating. One of the women who joined the Bank of England in 1893 was Janet Hogarth, who had studied philosophy at Oxford and passed her final exams with first-class honours. As the supervisor of the female clerks she earned the unusually high salary of £3 a week (rising to £4), but as a woman she could never reach the heights scaled by the writer Kenneth Grahame, who rose from clerk to Secretary of the Bank between 1879 and 1898. So she left in 1906, and twenty years later, in her autobiography, recalled the predicament of 'the bright intelligent girl brought in to do permanently the routine work formerly left to boys just leaving school'. 'For a time it works well. The girls show a zeal and zest which no boy thinks of emulating. But the trouble comes when they grow to be middle-aged women and are still kept at work only fit for beginners. They have become mere machines. Their task does not occupy their minds even while they are at it.'[15]

The lady clerk's hours of work were not very long, compared to those usual in manufacturing industry, and she was treated in a paternalistic way. The Prudential Insurance Company, which employed fifty women in 1874 and nearly three hundred by 1894, worked them from nine to five, with an hour for lunch in their own luncheon room, and at Baring's merchant bank, which took its first women clerks in 1873, the hours were ten to five with an hour for lunch and (after 1901) twenty-four days' annual leave. The Post Office gave its clerks of both sexes tea and bread and butter at their desks at 4.30, saving the loss of time a real tea break would have involved, and (until 1911) did not allow its female clerks to leave the building for lunch. The Bank of England, which took its first forty women in 1893–4 as part of an economy drive, gave them a free meal, twenty-seven days' leave, a modest pension at fifty, and £1 a week salary, rising to about £1 12s after ten years' service. At the Prudential, young women started on

£32 a year and might rise to £52 after several years' service. A male insurance clerk at the Prudential got £50 at eighteen and £150 at twenty-one.[16]

Clara Collet, who had worked with Charles Booth, published a study of educated working women in 1902, which found that most female City typists, on an average wage of about 25s a week, lived with their parents and travelled to work early on cheap workmen's trains. Once they had bought the smart clothes demanded by their work and contributed to the family expenses their remaining salary was hardly more than pocket money. This was satisfactory for women who regarded work as filling the gap between childhood and marriage (as most of them did), but less so for those who wanted a lifelong career. The truly independent middle-class working woman living alone needed to find at least £1 a week for board and lodging in a hostel or boarding house, and had little prospect of improvement as the years passed. In 1900 a survey by the Women's Industrial Council of five hundred salaried women in London found that their average salary was nearly £129 a year, of which over £28 went on rent. This compared very favourably with the £18 or £20 a year paid to the average domestic servant, the £24 to £40 a year earned for much longer hours by well-trained nurses, and the £20 or so earned by women in the sweated manufacturing trades, but not with men's wages in similar jobs. Among white-collar women, only school teachers earned more than clerks and typists.[17]

Women in the Saddle

Perhaps working in a typing pool or at a switchboard did not feel much like freedom, but the lives of educated middle-class London women were becoming more varied, richer in opportunities, and less dependent on the choices and wealth of men. This growing freedom took many forms. The young woman in late Victorian London who wanted to increase her opportunities to work and live more independently could learn to type and take shorthand, go to evening classes, join a club or political party, vote in local elections, use contraception, or learn to ride a bike. Women in skirts or dresses could not ride the 'ordinary' (or 'penny-farthing') of the 1870s and 1880s, but they could easily manage the safety bicycle that was introduced in the late 1880s. About a third of bicycles bought in 1896 were women's models, and women were enthusiastic participants in the cycling craze of that year. The 'Old Oriental' who returned to London in 1904 after thirty years in the East thought that this was one of the most striking social changes to have taken place in his absence: 'Girls of every rank think no more of riding a bicycle through the busy thoroughfares of London than they do of going into an A.B.C. shop for a cup of tea. Go back to 1875, and try to think, if you can, what would have been said of a woman riding a bicycle down Piccadilly on a June afternoon.'[18] The writer Eliza Lynn Linton, a diehard anti-feminist, deplored the 'unfettered freedom' cycling would bring, and the 'sturdy tramps' that young lady cyclists might meet (and then what?) on their unsupervised excursions, but H. G. Wells, in *The Wheels of Chance* (1896), celebrated the romantic opportunities that cycling would create, and Clementina Black, the suffragist and radical campaigner for women's rights, thought that the bicycle was 'doing more for the independence of women than anything expressly designed for that end. It is perhaps a mark of the change of view which has come over us, that nobody expects a woman to go cycling escorted by a chaperon, a maid or a footman.' Black was not entirely correct, because in 1896, a year after she wrote those words, the Chaperon Cyclists' Association was formed. Apparently there was not a great demand for its services. Cycling allowed women to display strength and daring without taking up tennis or hockey, and thus to challenge the predominant male perception of women as weak and unadventurous. The sight of a 'young Amazon with the auburn hair and nicely-fitting costume' cycling down Holborn on the wrong side of the road, as recklessly and fearlessly as a newspaper boy, 'dodging in and out of the mass of cabs and carts' and ignoring the policeman's signal, thrilled Duncan Lucas in 1901. 'Just when we think there will be a frightful accident she calmly crosses to the left, shaving the horses' heads. Her sangfroid is astounding.'[19]

The popularity of cycling among women gave new life to a campaign that had flourished briefly in the 1880s, for the wearing of divided skirts, 'bloomers' or knickerbockers. Some successful female cyclists, like sixteen-year-old Tissie Reynolds, who raced from Brighton to London and back in 1893, wore knickerbockers, and the Rational Dress League, founded in 1898, published its own *Rational Dress Gazette* for nearly two years. But it was immensely difficult to shift the ingrained prejudices of the majority of Victorian men, women, and children, and wearing divided skirts, however modestly cut, took courage in London in the 1890s. Cycling in knickerbockers in the London suburbs, Kitty Buckman wrote in 1897, was an awful experience: 'One wants nerves of iron . . . The shouts and yells of the children deafen one, the women shriek with laughter or groan & hiss

& all sorts of remarks are shouted at one, occasionally some not fit for publication. One needs to be very brave to stand all that.'[20] *Punch* had fun with the subject, too. A young woman cycling in bloomers in a cartoon in 1899 asked a bystander, 'Is this the way to Wareham?', and got a predictable reply. In such a climate, the arguments of cyclists and those few women who played sports were not strong enough to bring about a fundamental change in fashion, and the League gave up the struggle in 1900. Even in cycle races, Edwardian women wore straw hats and ankle-length skirts, with cages round the gears and rear wheel to stop the skirt getting caught in them. Still, the well-off lady cyclist could buy black serge cycling knickers with a chamois seat from Harrods, and a 'Rideasy Skirt' discreetly pleated and divided at the rear to make it easier to mount the saddle. And lady cyclists might benefit from Victorian attitudes, too. Thomas Hardy asked a London omnibus conductor 'if the young women (who ride recklessly in the midst of the traffic) did not meet with accidents. He said "Oh nao; their sex pertects them. We dares not drive over them, wotever they do; and they do jist wot they likes." '[21]

The New Woman

Greater freedom involved dangers and difficulties. Many working women living alone reported that they were often bothered by men who interpreted their solitude or independence as sexual availability. Sometimes, of course, the men got what they (and no doubt many of the women) wanted. Evelyn March-Phillips, writing in the *Fortnightly Review* in 1892, told her readers: 'I knew a handsome, high-spirited girl, who was receiving visits in her bed-sitting room from a man whose acquaintance she had made on the underground railways.'[22] Men's assumptions about the sexual consequences of women's economic independence were encouraged by some novels published in the 1890s, which glamorized the drab lives of salaried women in London. In George Gissing's *The Odd Women* (1893), which was set in a type-writing school, and Grant Allen's *The Type-Writer Girl* (1897), written under the pseudonym of Olive Rayner, the independence of the middle-class heroine, and the masculinity of her position, add a thrill to her eventual submission to a lover. In 1895 Grant Allen, a London-based (but Canadian-born) academic and writer, produced a novel which epitomized this rather lascivious interest in the sex lives of independent-minded 'new' women. The heroine of *The Woman Who Did*, the beautiful, dimpled

Girton-educated Herminia Barton, shocks her hostess (and Grant's readers) by telling her: 'I don't mean to say I will never fall in love. I expect to do that. I look forward to it frankly, – it is a woman's place in life. I only mean to say, I don't think anything will ever induce me to marry, – that is to say, legally.' By chapter three she had told her suitor, Alan Merrick, about her plan: 'Why, simply that we should be friends, like any others, very dear, dear friends, with the only kind of friendship that nature makes possible between men and women.' 'But do you mean to say, Herminia,' Merrick replied, 'you've made up your mind never to marry any one? Made up your mind to brave the whole mad world, that can't possibly understand the motives of your conduct, and live with some friend, as you put it, unmarried?' In the end, of course, Allen makes sure that the world has its revenge on Herminia, and her story ends in tragedy and self-administered prussic acid.

Much of the discussion of the so-called 'New Woman question' in the London press in the mid-1890s was stimulated by an article by Blanche Crackanthorpe (mother of the writer Hubert) in the *Nineteenth Century* in January 1894. The article, which was called 'The Revolt of the Daughters', spoke for young women who wanted a good education and perhaps a career, the freedom to travel and visit friends on their own, and the right to remain unmarried if they wished to. In March two rich young women wrote in the same periodical in her support. Lady Kathleen Cuffe said that young women wanted something more than the right to possess a latchkey, go to music halls, and smoke in public, the 'frivolous and evanescent pleasures of the average hobbledehoy'. She wanted the opportunity to get to know a man's ideas and character before getting engaged to him, and the right to walk the street or park and ride in a hansom unchaperoned, and go out for afternoon tea 'without the same faithful domestic walking gloomily by her side, or waiting drearily for her in alien front halls'. More fundamentally, Alys Pearsall-Smith added, daughters wanted to stop wasting their time as the appendages and servants of others, and to be allowed to choose their own lives and develop their own talents. 'How wanton is the waste continually going on in the lives of thousands of women, whose powers, by a long course of trivialities and mental starvation, deteriorate year after year, until they themselves and all their friends suffer incalculable loss.'[23]

The phrase 'New Woman', referring to the intellectually, financially, and perhaps sexually independent women of the 1890s, was first used, it is said, by Sarah Grand, a novelist and essayist whose life and interests perfectly represent the type of woman she was describing. Sarah Grand was married to a man of thirty-nine when she was sixteen, and left him when she was thirty-six (in 1890) to make her living as a novelist in London. She lectured on women's suffrage, rode a bike, wore 'rational dress', and wrote a sensational and very successful novel, *The Heavenly Twins* (1893), which denounced the sexual abuse of women within marriage by bestial, dominating, and syphilitic men. Her phrase 'the new woman' appeared in an article in the *North American Review* in March 1894, 'The New Aspect of the Woman Question', in which she contrasted the two kinds of women men readily accepted, the domesticated 'cow-woman' and the prostituted 'scum-woman', with the new woman, who had 'been sitting apart in silent contemplation all these years' and had at last found the answer to the 'woman question'. The answer, she concluded, was an equal and freely chosen marriage, for which young women should be prepared by higher education and better parenting. At present, Grand added in a later article, women were kept in utter ignorance of sex and motherhood to make them easier to dispose of in the marriage market, as she had been. 'The less girls know the more easily they are influenced in their choice of husbands.' Her article was attacked by the romantic novelist Ouida, in an article in the May edition of the *North American Review* called 'The New Woman', and it was here, used as a term of criticism, that the phrase entered the language.

For a few years in the mid-1890s the New Woman was the subject of dozens of novels, stories, and periodical pieces, and although most of the books and their authors are now forgotten, their works stimulated an unprecedented public discussion of the plight of young women, the choices they had to make between work and motherhood, sexual freedom and marital conformity, independence and security. Mona Caird, George Egerton (Mary Dunne), Sarah Grand, Netta Syrett, and Isabella Ford were the leading feminist writers, but the book that stirred up the most furious debate was Thomas Hardy's last novel, *Jude the Obscure* (1896), which challenged the value of marriage from a slightly different perspective. And all of them must yield primacy in chronology and influence to the Norwegian dramatist Henrik Ibsen, whose plays were translated and championed by the London theatre critic William Archer in the 1880s and 1890s. *A Doll's House*, dealing with a woman who abandons a suffocating marriage, was produced at the Novelty Theatre (later the Kingsway Theatre, Great Queen Street) in June 1889, and *Ghosts*, which depicted a middle-class family infected with syphilis, had a controversial success at the Royalty Theatre in March 1891. The reaction to these plays in some

London newspapers exemplifies the enormous gulf between those men and women who wanted to expose and rectify the inequalities and deceits of Victorian middle-class marriage, and those who could see nothing wrong with it. To the *Daily Telegraph*'s leader-writer, *Ghosts* was 'a dirty act done publicly', 'a loathsome sore unbandaged', a play of 'gross and almost putrid indecorum'. But Ibsen's plays excited and inspired those who wanted to challenge the sexual double standard and the male tyranny of marriage, and the new generation of English and Irish playwrights who were about to overturn the stuffy conformity and brainless farcicality of the West End stage. Shaw went to see *A Doll's House* five times (mainly because he had fallen in love with its leading lady, Janet Achurch), and gave a lecture on 'The Essence of Ibsenism' at the St James's Restaurant in 1890. The feminist socialist Edith Lees, one of the leading organizers of the socialist Fellowship of the New Life, remembered the impact of the play on a group of advanced men and women (mainly members and associates of Karl Pearson's Men and Women's Club) on its first night: 'a few of us collected outside the theatre breathless with excitement. Olive Schreiner was there and Dolly Radford the poetess . . . Emma Brooke . . . and Eleanor Marx. We were restive and almost savage in our arguments. What did it mean? . . . Was it life or death for women?' And for some of these women these ideas were for living, as well as discussing. Eleanor Marx was already involved in a disastrous open relationship with Edward Aveling, and the Fabian feminist Emma Brooke remained unmarried, making her living in London by writing novels and articles on sex and marriage. Her most important books, *A Superfluous Woman*, *In Transition*, and *Life the Accuser*, were published by Heinemann in the mid-1890s.[24] Edith Lees was soon to marry the pioneering psychologist and sexologist Henry Havelock Ellis, who managed at the same time to continue a long-running relationship with Olive Schreiner. Since Edith Lees was an enthusiastic lesbian who enjoyed sexual relationships with several women, she found Ellis's approach to marriage quite acceptable, and provided him, in herself and her friends, with the examples of female 'inverts' that he discussed in his pioneering multivolume *Studies in the Psychology of Sex* from 1897 onwards.[25]

Women in Politics

Women who wanted to enter a more public and political world could do so in several different ways. For over a century, well-off London men had been able to meet, form social and political bonds, and develop common ideas in exclusive members' clubs, from which women (and the less well-off) were excluded. In the 1880s and 1890s well-off women started to form clubs of their own, to serve their social and cultural needs. By 1900 there were about twenty women's clubs in London, mostly for upper-class women who needed places in town where they could eat, sleep, play cards or billiards, and entertain in comfort, mixing with other women of their own type. The most exclusive of these clubs, the Alexandra, the Green Park, and the Empress in Mayfair, and the Victoria near Cavendish Square, were social clubs for women of fortune, 'that class of Society which is always going on somewhere else', imitating the men's clubs of Pall Mall and St James's Street. The very large membership of these expensive clubs (the Empress had more than 2,000 members in 1898) reflected the growth of a class of wealthy women who had their own money and lived relatively independent lives in London. But others reflected changes in the ambitions and social attitudes of London women of less elevated classes. The University Club for Ladies drew its 300 members from a growing body of women graduates and students, and the Writers' Club and the Women Journalists' Club, both just off the Strand, catered for women who made a living as writers in the early 1890s, including Frances Hodgson Burnett, Mrs Humphrey Ward, and Pearl Craigie ('John Oliver Hobbes'), a successful but now forgotten novelist, critic, and playwright, and others drawn from the 400 women who listed their profession as writer or journalist in the census of 1891. The Enterprise Club served the needs of women clerks in the City, the Victoria Commemoration Club was for nurses and health workers, and the Honor Club of Fitzroy Square provided a library, a gym, a doctor, and women-only dances for respectable West End working girls. Those who wanted to share a club with men might join the Sesame Club or the Denison Club, where social issues were discussed. Probably the most important club in the development of women's political ideas and ambitions was the Pioneer Club, which was founded in 1892 by Emily Massingberd, the heir to a large landed estate, for the promotion of advanced ideas among women, and to enable poorly paid professional women like stenographers and telephonists to join in conversation and debate with women of wealth and position. The Pioneer Club, which had over 500 members in 1894, was one of the centres of the London feminist movement of the 1890s, the school in which the novelists and feminists Mona Caird and Sarah Grand practised the art of public speaking.[26] When Emily Massingberd died in 1896 the Pioneer Club split into two, and a new club of equal seriousness, the Grosvenor Crescent Club, was formed.

Some 'New Women' wanted to do far more than work a switchboard, join a club, or ride a bike in 'rational' dress. They wanted to enter public and political life, not just as hostesses and fund-raisers, but as voters, councillors, and Members of Parliament. The right to vote in parliamentary elections, which had been conceded to most men in 1884, was still denied to women, and remained so, despite the vigorous efforts of the 'moral force' suffragists and the 'physical force' suffragettes, until March 1918. But some women had the right to vote and serve in local government, and their influence on the running of London was considerable, though these rights were sometimes confused and contradictory. Women who paid property rates could vote in local vestry elections until 1872, when a court case restricted this right to single women ratepayers. This same group was able to vote in London School Board elections after 1870, but women were allowed to stand for election to the School Board whether they were qualified to vote or not, and several women of great distinction, including Elizabeth Garrett and Annie Besant, did so. Women were entitled to sit as members of London's parish vestries from 1894 (and about fifteen did so), but when the vestries were reorganized and amalgamated as boroughs in 1899 they were deprived of this right, and did not regain it until 1907. Single women ratepayers could vote in elections for Poor Law Guardians, and from 1875 a few women guardians (single or married ratepayers) sat on Poor Law Boards themselves, though the law on this had not been changed since 1834. The abolition of the property qualification for guardians in 1894, which had profound effects on the social composition of Poor Law Boards, also increased the number of women on the Boards, from forty in London in 1893 to eighty-six in 1895.[27]

The effectiveness of women on elected public bodies had already been demonstrated by the work of Elizabeth Garrett, the pioneering doctor, and Emily Davies, the future head of Girton College, Cambridge, on the London School Board between 1870 and 1873. Women won nine seats in the School Board elections of 1879, but for most of the 1880s and 1890s they only held three or four. Still, this small group, nearly all on the Liberal side, provided some of the Board's strongest and most useful members: Rosamund Davenport Hill, an expert on industrial schools and reformatories, Alice Westlake, who led the Liberal opposition to the cost-cutting Tory majority between 1885 and 1888, and Annie Besant, who represented Tower Hamlets as a socialist between 1888 and 1891. Using a mixture of eloquence, charm, and deal-making, Besant managed to persuade the Tory-dominated Board to support the imposition of fair wages clauses on its contractors, to press for the abolition of school fees in Board schools (a policy adopted by the government in 1891), and to investigate malnutrition among London schoolchildren.[28]

Although the women on London's elected bodies were well off, those who elected them were not. A survey by the *Nation* in July 1910 identified the occupations of 71,600 of the 95,000 women with votes in London's municipal elections. It found that over 36,000 of them were charwomen, office helpers, laundresses, or waitresses, over 25,000 were clothing workers, about 4,000 were lodging-house or coffee-house keepers, nearly 4,000 were nurses and midwives, and only 2,200 were teachers.[29]

In 1888 the London County Council supplanted the London School Board as the capital's largest and most powerful elected body. Assuming that those single women ratepayers entitled to vote for the LCC were also qualified to become councillors, two women stood as Liberals in the January 1889 LCC elections, with the support of a group of well-off London Liberal ladies which called itself (from 1893) the Women's Local Government Society (WLGS). Both women won, but one was unseated by an electoral petition from her defeated opponent, and the other, along with an unelected female alderman, continued attending Council meetings without voting rights. The WLGS was an effective but now generally forgotten campaigner for women's electoral rights from the 1890s onwards. Its members had extensive experience in local government as poor-law guardians and members of School Boards, and their connections by family and friendship with MPs, government ministers, journalists, and lawyers gave them influence out of proportion to their numbers. Despite its powerful friends, the WLGS was unable to prevent the opponents of women's representation in London politics from winning some important victories. Women were excluded from the LCC between 1892 and 1907 and from the vestries between 1899 and 1907. In 1904 the London School Board was abolished, and its duties were taken over by the LCC, from which women were excluded. Only the Poor Law Boards retained their women members.

The Liberal landslide in the 1906 General Election, along with a strong Labour Party presence in the House of Commons, saved the situation for the WLGS. In 1907 a government bill, promoted by the WLGS and introduced by John Burns of the Local Government Board, was passed, establishing the right of women to sit on town councils, London borough councils, and county councils, including the LCC.[30] The success of women candidates, who were mostly Progressive (Liberal) or Labour, in taking advantage of these changes was limited by the strength of the Conservatives in the LCC and the London boroughs between 1908 and 1914. Only seven women out of sixty-four candidates won seats in the borough elections of 1909, and twenty-two out of fifty-four in 1912. In the LCC elections of 1910 women candidates probably lost support because of the outburst of suffragette violence that year, and won only two seats. Some of the women involved in these campaigns, especially on the Labour side, went on to become important political figures in the 1920s. Marion Phillips and Ethel Bentham were Kensington councillors from 1912 and Labour MPs in 1929, Susan Lawrence was an LCC councillor, first Conservative, then Labour, and a Labour MP for East Ham from 1923 to 1931, and Margaret Bondfield, who failed to get into the LCC in 1910, became the first woman Cabinet minister, in the Labour government of 1929–31.[31]

The Suffragettes

The slow and unsteady progress towards full political rights being made in London and elsewhere through local government was not enough to satisfy all those who were campaigning for women's suffrage. One section of the campaign, centred on the Pankhurst family in Manchester, decided that with the argument for women's votes won the only way of pushing the Liberal government into actually extending the franchise to women was to adopt the violent methods that had (they said) won men the vote in 1832 and 1867, and enabled Garibaldi (a popular hero in Britain) to achieve Italian unification. Emmeline and Christabel Pankhurst formed the Women's Social and Political Union (WSPU) in 1903, with help and advice from Keir Hardie, but did not turn from peaceful campaigning through the Labour movement to 'propaganda by deed' until October 1905, when Christabel Pankhurst and Annie Kenney were imprisoned for refusing to pay a fine after disrupting a Liberal political meeting. The WSPU moved its headquarters to London in 1906, to increase pressure on the new Liberal government at its most sensitive point, but much of its activity took place outside London, and only about a third of its branches were in the capital. In moving to London the WSPU weakened its ties with working-class supporters and the Independent Labour Party (ILP), and became a much more middle-class movement.[32]

The WSPU's main form of direct action in 1906–8 was to heckle ministers' speeches, a device that created some lively public meetings, but alienated some politicians, including Winston Churchill, who might have supported reform. The climax came in December 1908, when Lloyd George, a supporter of women's suffrage, was heckled for two hours at the Albert Hall. After this the growing use of all-ticket meetings and the Public Meetings Act, which increased the powers of stewards to eject hecklers, reduced the value of heckling as a tactic. Frustration at the failure of constitutional forms of protest gradually drove the suffragettes (the name that distinguished the WSPU from the non-violent suffragists of the National Union of Women's Suffrage Societies, or NUWSS) towards more violent and illegal actions, often on the initiative of individual members. Window-smashing, which became a popular suffragette tactic, began in June 1908 when Mary Leigh broke windows in Downing Street because Asquith would not agree to meet a suffragette deputation. The need to keep the interest of the press also pushed the WSPU into new and more dangerous forms of direct action. The first prison hunger strike, another individual initiative, took place in July 1909, forcing the authorities to release the striker, Marion Wallace Dunlop, after ninety-one hours. Another thirty-one suffragette prisoners got themselves released by the same method, but then the government authorized forced feeding, giving the WSPU a valuable propaganda weapon. In February 1910 the Pankhursts agreed to a truce while a Conciliation Bill was considered, but when the militant campaign was resumed in November 1911, it used arson attacks on pillar boxes, a tactic first pioneered by Emily Davison. This had the advantage of avoiding confrontation with the police, who had become much rougher with suffragette protesters in 1910 and 1911. As each new form of action failed to change the government's mind, and failed even to get press coverage, more violent methods were considered. The government and the police feared assassination attempts on Asquith or another minister, and one or two suffragette speeches (especially at a meeting in Wimbledon in December 1912) flirted with this idea. Generally suffragette attacks were more upsetting than dangerous. Augustine Birrell, the scholarly Secretary of State for Ireland, had the experience of being savaged by twenty suffragettes as he was walking along the Mall to his club, the Athenaeum, in January 1911, and told C. P. Scott, the suffragist editor of the *Manchester Guardian*, about it:

Some one cried 'Here's Mr Birrell' . . . and the whole body immediately swarmed round me. I was not kicked, but they pulled me about and hustled me, 'stroked' my face, knocked off my hat and kicked it about and one whose unpleasant features yet dwell in my memory harangued me with 'Oh! you wicked man; you must be a wicked man not to help us' and so forth. I didn't like to use my fists and I couldn't swing my umbrella ... I struggled to get free and in so doing I twisted my knee (pointing to his left knee) and slipped my knee-cap ... It was excessively painful and I was in terror that they would knock off my spectacles in which case I should have been absolutely blind. I don't know what I should have done when happily at that moment Lionel ... drove up in a motor, saw [what] was taking place and jumping out scattered the women right and left and rescued me. I felt like a man attacked by pygmies who overcome him by their numbers. They then left me.

There was no attempt to do me any serious physical injury and if I had lain down on the ground I don't suppose they would have jumped upon me but it was a brutal, outrageous and unprovoked assault and it may lame me for life.[33]

What the suffragettes needed, and the government was determined not to give them, was a martyr. The notorious but effective 'Cat and Mouse Act' (or the Prisoners' Temporary Discharge for Ill-Health Act) of April 1913 enabled the government to release and rearrest hunger-striking prisoners instead of force-feeding them, and also allowed dozens of prisoners to gain their freedom by renouncing direct action or going overseas. In the end the WSPU got its martyr through the individual initiative of its most daring and persistent militant, Emily Davison, who ran in front of the King's horse during the Epsom Derby in June 1913. She was killed almost at once, and the injured horse, Anmer, was shot later. Davison's funeral was a great propaganda coup for the WSPU, though not as great as it would have been if she had been killed by the government rather than a horse.[34]

After this the WSPU used a variety of tactics, including attacking government ministers, setting fire to pillar boxes and empty houses, sending threatening or exploding letters, and vandalizing works of art. Suffragettes slashed Velázquez's *Rokeby Venus* in the National Gallery and Sargent's portrait of Henry James in the Royal Academy, and smashed porcelain in the British Museum. A bomb exploded in St John's Westminster and another was found under the coronation chair in Westminster Abbey. In the East End, Sylvia Pankhurst, who had left the WSPU and formed the more working-class East London Federation, was training an army of about a hundred women at Bow baths, mainly to protect suffragette leaders from being rearrested. Increasing violence and more effective police responses led a growing number of women away from the WSPU and into the much larger non-violent NUWSS, leaving the WSPU with a small core of perhaps a thousand committed and courageous militants, mostly young unmarried women, who were prepared to commit themselves to a dangerous and unpopular campaign of window-smashing and arson. Every escalation of WSPU violence was matched by a tightening of police controls. WSPU leaders were watched by Special Branch, their headquarters were seized, their letters intercepted and their telephones cut off. Emmeline Pankhurst was repeatedly rearrested and her daughter Christabel fled to Paris to avoid imprisonment in 1912. It was plain to most observers that the suffragette campaign was counter-productive, driving sympathetic MPs into opposition and creating public hostility towards even the NUWSS, without generating the sort of disorder that might have forced the government into making concessions. The WSPU was no Ulster Volunteer Force, and Mrs Pankhurst, despite her courage and conviction, could not match the menace of the Irish Unionist leader Sir Edward Carson. Suffragette 'outrages' were really nothing more than publicity stunts, and the power of the hunger strike had been neutralized by the Cat and Mouse Act. There was no obvious way out of this impasse until the outbreak of war in August 1914 allowed the WSPU to offer a patriotic truce, and bring a brave but ill-judged campaign to a close.

Part Two

GROWING LONDON

CHAPTER NINE

*

GOVERNING LONDON

For most of the twentieth century (until 1986) London was governed by a fairly efficient and democratic two-tier administration, in which some city-wide matters were run by a central body, the London County Council or (from 1965) the Greater London Council, and more local services were provided by borough councils. This system had its origins in the division of powers between the parishes and the Metropolitan Board of Works after 1855, but it was established in its modern form in the 1880s and 1890s, the decades in which London became a well-governed and democratic city. These were the years in which elections for London's local government became a matter of interest for the national political parties and for ordinary voters, and in which men (and sometimes women) of ability and importance sat on London's borough and County councils, with the intention of governing, not (as people said of their vestry predecessors) guzzling.

The End of the Board of Works

By the mid-1880s it seemed that the upper tier of London's two-tier system of government, the Metropolitan Board of Works, had outlasted its usefulness. The democratic reforms of 1883–5, which introduced something close to manhood suffrage and equal constituencies in national elections, made an unelected body of parish delegates look more anachronistic than ever. Furthermore, the Board appeared to be corrupt, as well as undemocratic and inefficient. In October 1886 the *Financial News* broke the sensational story that two officials of the Metropolitan Board of Works, its Assistant Surveyor (Thomas Robertson), and its Chief Valuer (F. W. Goddard), had taken very large bribes from a music-hall owner, R. E. Villiers, in return for helping him get a building lease on the Old Pavilion site on Piccadilly Circus, on the corner between Coventry Street and Shaftesbury

Avenue. The Board of Works (or the Board of Perks, as *Punch* now called it) investigated the case itself, but did so with such complacency and ineptitude that its reputation was further damaged. In February 1888 Lord Randolph Churchill secured the appointment of a Royal Commission to investigate the affair. This quickly established that Goddard and Robertson had been dealing corruptly in building sites, especially for public houses, for years, and that an important MBW architect, James Saunders, and Francis Fowler, who had represented Lambeth on the Board since 1868, had habitually taken bribes from developers who wanted to buy or lease land from the Board. It was discovered that the Criterion, the underground theatre on Piccadilly Circus, had been declared unsafe until a hundred guineas each for Fowler and Saunders reversed the decision, and that Saunders had been paid £3,500 by the hotelier Frederick Gordon for unspecified services in connection with the building of the Grand and Metropole Hotels on Northumberland Avenue in the 1870s and 1880s. The Board itself, the Commission concluded, was not corrupt, but its procedures had been lax and its distinguished chief architect, George Vulliamy, was too old to exert control over his dishonest subordinates.[1]

There was no shortage of politicians and journalists who were keen to use the corruption scandal to destroy the MBW and reform the whole system of London government. The London Municipal Reform League had over a thousand members by 1884, and its leader, Joseph Firth, had won the support of leading ministers in Gladstone's Liberal government, including the Home Secretary, Lewis Harcourt, and the President of the Local Government Board, Charles Dilke, for an elected unitary authority for London. In 1884 Harcourt introduced a government bill vesting the powers of the MBW, the City Corporation, and the vestries (but not the London School Board, the Metropolitan Police, or the Poor Law Guardians) in a new Common Council. The bill, which sought to appease the powerful City by giving it the right to choose an eighth of the new Council's members, succeeded in offending almost everyone. The vestries and district boards, which lost all their powers, were almost unanimous in opposing the bill, and though their motives were self-interested they had strong arguments on their side. Any measure which concentrated all power in a central body abolished the system of local self-government and accountability which the vestries, with all their faults, had provided, and meant that ratepayers in, say, Lewisham or Wandsworth would have hardly any control over how their money was spent or their local services provided. Centralization was not popular in London, but it was shortage of parliamentary time, not the combined opposition of the vestries, the MBW, London MPs, and the City, that stopped the 1884 London bill becoming law.[2]

When the argument was resumed under Lord Salisbury's Conservative government in 1886, London's parliamentary representation (within the Metropolitan Board of Works area) had increased from eighteen to fifty-seven, and the vestries' hostility to a single powerful London government could not be so easily ignored. C. T. Ritchie, the President of the Local Government Board and architect of the new bill, was MP for St George-in-the-East, Stepney. The unpopular idea of concentrating first- and second-tier powers in a single unitary authority was abandoned, and instead the question of London government was absorbed into the administration's plans for a reform of the whole local government system, in the Local Government Act of 1888. By this measure the 117 square miles of Middlesex, Surrey, and Kent presently administered by the MBW were designated a county, and a new directly elected London County Council, similar in its responsibilities to the other county councils created by the same act, came into being, with a Lord Lieutenant, a sheriff, and justices of the peace. The new County Council had more powers than the MBW, but it did not gain them at the expense of the parishes, which retained all their second-tier responsibilities. An almost universal dislike of the MBW brought together disparate political forces in support of a new directly elected council, briefly uniting poorer suburban Londoners who wanted a more active government and West End ratepayers who wanted a more economical one. It was generally believed that a directly elected body was less likely to become corrupt than the indirectly elected MBW, and Conservative doubts about increased democracy were stilled by their belief that they would sweep the board in the first LCC elections, just as they had won London's parliamentary seats (by forty-five to fourteen) in 1886. The idea of replacing vestries with more modern district councils was dropped, and the vestries and district boards survived with their powers intact until 1899. The City was refused the administrative independence of a county borough, but was appeased with the judicial autonomy of a quarter sessions borough, retaining its own Lord Lieutenant, sheriffs, and JPs.

The London County Council

The London County Council was not really a unified government for London. The area it covered was not the whole of London as it stood in

1888, but the much smaller area chosen by the Registrar-General for census purposes in 1851, and allocated to the MBW in 1855. Large populations of Londoners were left in the counties of Essex (East and West Ham, Walthamstow, Ilford, and Leyton), Middlesex (Tottenham, Hornsey, Edmonton, Enfield, and Willesden), Kent (Bromley) and Surrey (Croydon), and the number of Londoners living outside the County of London doubled between 1891 and 1914, from 1.4 million to nearly 3 million, as the suburbs grew. Apart from the judicial responsibilities it acquired as a County (including the duty to inspect and license most theatres, and all music halls, dance halls, and similar places of entertainment), the LCC simply inherited the powers of the MBW, along with the Board's offices in Spring Gardens. It could plan and build new roads, tunnels, and bridges, name streets and number houses, build and manage the sewers, manage many London parks and open spaces (2,800 acres in 1889), run the Metropolitan Fire Brigade, demolish insanitary slums, and provide common lodging houses. But it did not take over the powers already exercised by the London School Board, the Poor Law Guardians, the Asylums Board, and the Metropolitan Police Commissioners, and therefore had no power over London's education, poor relief, hospitals, asylums, ambulances, or policing. London's gas, water, electricity, and transport services were all privately run, but the LCC had the right to buy the private tram services, and did so in the 1890s. The LCC appointed its own Medical Officer of Health, but the vestries and district boards were London's local sanitary authorities, and lost none of the other local powers they had exercised before 1888. On the other hand, the Council acquired important additional powers after its creation, especially in public health, slum clearance and house-building, technical education, and, with the abolition of the London School Board in 1904, elementary education. These powers were great enough for the LCC to make a substantial difference to the development of London, especially its public transport, working-class housing, education, parks, and, to a limited extent, public health. But the Council and its eighteen standing committees did not have the powers or the money (even if they had had the vision) to build a New Jerusalem in London, or to overcome its great problems of poverty, ill-health, and overcrowding. The high hopes of those who welcomed its creation in 1888 were disappointed, as high hopes usually are, but more realistic expectations were not.

Despite its weaknesses, Londoners regarded the LCC as an authority worth voting for, and the national political parties saw it as a prize worth fighting for. After the shocks of the general elections of 1885 and 1886, when it won only twenty-three and fourteen out of fifty-nine London seats, the Liberal Party reorganized itself in the capital, uniting grass-roots constituency activists, leading Liberal politicians, radicals, progressive intellectuals, and prominent trade-union leaders in a campaigning organization known as the Progressives. The Conservatives formed a slightly looser and less effective organization, the Moderate Party. The Liberal cause was helped by the launching in January 1888 of a new radical half-penny evening paper, the *Star*, edited by T. P. O'Connor, and financed by a set of radical industrialists (including John T. Brunner, of Brunner Mond Chemicals). O'Connor, the Irish Nationalist MP for the Scotland division of Liverpool, set out to create a popular paper with a bold radical programme, and succeeded in doing so. It was a good year to launch a popular radical paper in London, with John Burns' imprisonment after 'Bloody Sunday' in Trafalgar Square, the Board of Trade report on sweating in January, the match girls' strike in July, the creation of the LCC, and (an editor's dream) the gruesome Whitechapel murders to keep readers happy right through the autumn. The *Star*'s circulation was 142,000 on its first day, and probably around a quarter of a million by January 1889. O'Connor hired some of the brightest radical journalists in London, including H. W. Massingham and Ernest Parke (the *Star*'s next two editors), and George Bernard Shaw as assistant leader writer. The *Star*'s causes were those of radical Liberals, with a hint of socialism: housing and land reform, free education, fair employment, and an end to vestry corruption, sweated labour, and damaging divisions between progressive liberals and respectable socialists. It demonstrated its campaigning strength in the School Board elections of November 1888, when it helped the Liberal Fabians Annie Besant and Stewart Headlam win their seats in Tower Hamlets and Hackney. In the LCC election campaign O'Connor presented a radical agenda for social reform and municipal ownership, and helped the socialist John Burns (now out of prison) to win a seat in Battersea.[3]

The LCC electorate of about half a million was based on existing parliamentary constituencies, and included householders and £10 occupiers (but not lodgers), of whom around 80,000 were women. About half these voters turned out in January 1889, exercising a right which the citizens of Manchester and Birmingham had enjoyed for decades, and gave the Progressives a decisive victory, with 73 of the 118 seats. Once elected, the councillors chose nineteen aldermen, and the fact that eighteen of these were Progressives signalled the party-political nature of the new assembly.

Of the 137 councillors and aldermen in 1889, 117 were employers, professionals, managers, or administrators (either active or retired), three were peers or their sons, and nine were men of independent means.[4] One alderman and two councillors were women – the only women elected in the English County elections that year – but one of the councillors, Lady Sandhurst, lost her seat when her election was declared invalid by the courts. Many of the new councillors and aldermen were men of national distinction, including Quintin Hogg, the sugar merchant and philanthropist, founder (in 1882) and benefactor of the Regent Street Polytechnic; Frederic Harrison, the positivist philosopher; Sir Thomas Farrer, the economist, free-trader, and leader of the Progressives; Sir John Lubbock MP, the banker, scientist, and Principal of the Working Men's College; and Lord Rosebery, the former Foreign Secretary and future Liberal Prime Minister. On the Progressive benches members of two great London landowning families, the Russells and Grosvenors, sat alongside the engineer and socialist John Burns, the LCC's only working-class councillor until others were elected in 1892.

The Vestries Reinvigorated

The creation of the London County Council did not mean the end of the vestries and district boards, or the end of the argument over how London should be governed. In the later 1880s, as public interest in the government of London grew, participation in vestry elections rose and the calibre of candidates improved. The old 'non-political' ratepayer associations were pushed aside by political groups, especially Liberal and Radical ones, who were interested in using the power and income of the vestries to pursue social policies, and keen to redeem the reputation of vestrydom. Vestries and district boards were much more likely to employ sanitary inspectors, open public libraries and wash-houses, establish recreation grounds, and build town halls in 1895 than they had been in 1885. There were only two local public libraries in 1886, but thirty-one in 1897, and most of London's roughly 200 small but important local parks, playgrounds, and public gardens were opened in the 1880s and 1890s. In Hackney the district board opened twenty-three public open spaces, a total of twelve acres, between 1883 and 1899, and crowded little Finsbury opened seven, or four acres. Some vestries in the 1890s ran technical schools, and six local authorities started their own electricity-supply enterprises between 1891 and 1899. Shoreditch, more active than most, opened technical schools, cleared and rebuilt 1.6 acres of working-class housing at Moira Place, opened eight parks or playgrounds (about six acres), gave street-cleaning work to the unemployed, and led the way in generating electricity by incinerating municipal rubbish. Charles Booth and his team, interviewing vestrymen and officials and clergy in the 1890s, were told that the corrupt and inactive old guard were gone, and that a new generation of active and efficient clerks, medical officers, surveyors, and vestrymen had taken over. Clerkenwell, they were told, 'used to be a guzzling body, but [has] now gone to the other extreme'.[5] Booth's seven volumes on London's religious life, which were published in 1902 but based on material collected before 1899, when vestries were amalgamated into boroughs, contain many comments, mostly from clergymen, on the quality of vestry administration. Not all of these were complimentary, but there was a general sense of improvement. St George's Southwark, for instance, was judged 'efficient; very quick to reply to any complaints', 'Progressive; very much better than in the past'. Booth's judgement on the vestry was generally favourable:

> They issued instructions to householders as to the treatment of phthisis and made representations to Government on the subject of tuberculosis . . . Under their regime, improvements were instituted in the system of scavenging and dust collecting; the policy of laying asphalt in side streets was adopted; wood pavement has been employed to a considerable extent in many thoroughfares; underground conveniences have been constructed; and open spaces have been secured and laid out. Altogether it seems a very fair record, and public opinion generally recognised this.[6]

In Bermondsey and Rotherhithe the vestries were much more active than before, especially in street cleaning and sanitary inspection, and in building libraries and wash-houses. In Hackney there had been useful work in slum clearance and street maintenance, but the River Lea, where Hackney boys swam, was dangerously polluted, 'refuse is still dumped on the marshes, and the children who poke about among its dirty treasures contract diseases of the skin'. In the vestries of Bow, Bromley, Poplar, and Mile End Old Town, in the outer East End, Booth noticed a significant change since 1894, when the Local Government Act's abolition of property qualifications for vestrymen and extension of the vestry franchise to lodgers broke the hold of tradesmen and ratepayers on local government, and opened it up to working men with a thirst for reform. Meetings were rather disorderly, but there was an enthusiastic approach to sanitary inspection, street cleaning, housing reform, library building, and poor relief that was in great contrast to the lethargy of the old ratepayer vestries. In the large Islington vestry 'the management of municipal affairs seems to be both honest and energetic, and shows a good deal of vigorous enterprise'. Public health was good, street cleaning, at least in the better streets, was prompt, and small parks had been opened. 'There are excellent public baths and wash-houses (three sets), and municipal electric lighting has been successfully undertaken on an extensive scale.'[7]

This improvement could not have been sustained without the Liberal government's Rate Equalisation Act of 1894, which established a common fund for London local government by collecting an annual sixpence in the pound property levy on the whole County, including the City, and distributed it according to the population of each vestry. To ensure fairness London was given a new population census in 1896, and the Registrar-General was to make annual population estimates after that. The effect of this simple Act was to take money from the City and the rich vestries and district boards around the Strand, in Holborn and the West End, and give it to the poor and heavily populated vestries in the East End, inner South London, and many of the less well-off suburbs. In fact the biggest winners, ahead of Bethnal Green, Mile End, and Poplar, were the residents of suburban Plumstead, while other cheaper suburbs, including Camberwell, Hackney, Fulham, Greenwich, Islington, Hammersmith, Lambeth, and Wandsworth, made significant gains from the new system. Four suburban vestries – Hampstead, Kensington, Paddington, and St Marylebone – made minor losses from equalization, and Chelsea broke even. The City and the West End and central London vestries felt that they were subsidizing the rest of London three times over, once by paying for the extravagance of the LCC, which spent more in poor districts than rich ones, again through the Metropolitan Common Poor Fund (over £1 million a year in the early 1890s), and now through rate equalization, which meant that East End and suburban vestries could build ostentatious libraries and town halls at central London's expense.[8]

The Metropolitan Boroughs

This state of affairs, in which nearly 70 per cent of London's local taxation went into a common fund, made the City and some rich vestries keen to sever their links with the rest of the County, and the rest of London just as keen to stop them doing so. The best way for the City to legitimize its own autonomy and reduce its isolation was to press for the division of London into a set of virtually self-governing municipalities, of which the City would be one. Because most vestries benefited from the common fund and the services of the LCC it was very difficult for the City to win support for this policy, even among the more Conservative suburban vestries. Furthermore, the break-up of London's administration would only make sense if the vestries and district boards were prepared to agree to amalgamation into reasonably sized units like Lambeth or Islington. Nobody would countenance a metropolis broken into about forty independent units which were, in six cases, under ten acres in size. To achieve the plausible division of London into large units, perhaps the ten pre-1885 parliamentary boroughs (or 'tenification', as it was called), the City and its supporters had to persuade the parishes to forget their local rivalries and to form uneasy partnerships with their neighbours: Chelsea with Kensington, Battersea with Wandsworth, the Strand parishes with Westminster, and so on. This was an uphill task, but the City gained a powerful ally in January 1894, when the Kensington vestry voted in favour of the creation of a number of independent municipalities 'with full municipal life and privileges', and sent a delegation to discuss it with the City.[9]

The Conservative Party (or the Moderates, in London local government) was also attracted to the City's plan, because the LCC seemed to be stuck in Liberal (or Progressive) control. Although the Conservatives generally won most London seats in parliamentary elections, their attack on the Progressives' expensive municipal enterprises led them to a heavy defeat in the LCC election of 1892. Middle-class suburbs like Brixton, Lewisham, and Clapham, which were Conservative in parliamentary elections, benefited from LCC spending and rate equalization and returned Progressive councillors. It was all very well for Kensington, whose total rateable value was higher than that of all English provincial cities except Manchester and Liverpool, to campaign for municipal self-government, but poorer vestries had only to look at the position of the independent county borough of West Ham, which had rates of over seven shillings in the pound, to remind themselves of the advantages of LCC services and the equalization grant. In 1894 the Conservative leadership (Salisbury and Balfour) called for the division of London into separate municipalities, and even the more advanced Conservatives of the new London Municipal Society, which favoured slum clearance and similar social programmes, fell in with this policy of decentralization. A Royal Commission on the Amalgamation of the City and County, which reported in favour of amalgamation in September 1894, preferred larger and stronger second-tier authorities with greater, but unspecified, powers. In the LCC election of March 1895 the Moderates won as many seats as the Progressives, mainly on the strength of suburban votes. This was probably not because of support for their policy of decentralization, but because the cost of LCC social programmes was being felt in the ratepayers' pockets, in the shape of a 28 per cent rise in the County rate between 1892 and 1895.[10]

The Conservative victory in the July 1895 General Election saved the City from absorption into the County, and encouraged several vestries, including some less wealthy ones, to ask the government to pass legislation that would allow them to become incorporated municipal boroughs. The new leader of the Moderates on the LCC, Lord Onslow, favoured the devolution of nearly all the Council's powers to a set of large municipal authorities, and called for a conference of the LCC, the vestries and the district boards to discuss the matter. This conference, which began in January 1896, made it clear that although many vestries resented the intrusions of the LCC, only a handful (especially Kensington and Westminster) had a real taste for independence. For the rest, the powers they wished to reclaim from the LCC did not amount to a significant shift of responsibility or expenditure, and mostly involved enforcing the building acts (on dangerous structures, sky signs, building plans, and so on), road maintenance, and control over offensive businesses and lodging houses. Lewisham, a Moderate suburban vestry, spoke for many in saying that 'for the mere honour of having these things under our own control we should not be willing to undertake extra expense'. Nor did the vestries want to be merged with their neighbours into larger units, as Onslow and the City envisaged.[11]

Following the conference, Onslow and the Moderates changed their tactics, campaigning now for the creation of second-tier bodies with a grander name and more civic dignity than the vestries, but without a great devolution of powers from the LCC. By doing this they were able to win the support of about a dozen vestries, including large ones like Islington and Lambeth and poor ones like Bermondsey, and prepare the way for true devolution when the Moderates won control of the LCC. The Moderates had high hopes of winning the March 1898 LCC election until the Conservative Prime Minister, Lord Salisbury, made a disastrous intervention. In his Albert Hall speech of November 1897, Salisbury, who knew little of

1. The City at work: top hats and bowlers in the London Coal Exchange, Lower Thames Street, around 1900.

2. The famous ivory warehouse at the London Docks, around 1895 (see page 22).

3. Shining a light on darkest London.
Homeless 'dossers' in a South London alleyway,
pictured by Frederick Barnard for George Sims'
'How the Poor Live' in 1883 (see page 36).

4. Charles Booth, London's greatest
social investigator.

5. Traders of another class. Cloth caps and
bowlers in Petticoat Lane market in the 1890s.

6. The Trafalgar Square riots of February 1886, pictured in the *Illustrated London News*.

7. Pioneers of women's trade unionism. The striking Bryant and May match girls in 1888, the year of their famous victory.

8. Dinnertime in a London workhouse, around 1900. After 1911 many of these men would become pensioners, rather than paupers (see pages 64–5).

9. Upholsterers at work in C. V. Smith's workshop in Osnaburgh Street, near Euston Road, around 1900.

10. The liquorice room in Clarke, Nickolls and Coombs' sweet factory, near Hackney Wick, around 1900.

11. Working at home. Artificial-flower makers in 1900.

12. 'Hello-girls'. Edwardian telephonists in the Central London Post Office Exchange in Carter Lane, around 1904.

13. Votes without violence. Three suffragists on the march, around 1910.

14. Well-dressed feminists listening to a debate at the Pioneer Club in the late 1890s (see page 153).

Three faces of London County Council housing

15. A slum courtyard in the Nichol area, demolished in 1890 to make way for the LCC's Boundary Street estate.

16. Arnold Circus, the centrepiece of the Boundary Street estate, with a raised garden and bandstand built on the rubble of the demolished slums. Completed in 1898.

17. A street in the LCC's new cottage estate, Totterdown Fields, Tooting. The tenants do not look like ex-slum dwellers, and probably were not.

18. A new suburban street under construction in 1900. According to the developers, most of the houses were let as soon as they were finished.

19. Walsingham House, a huge mansion block in Piccadilly, built in the Flemish Renaissance style in 1888. The block became a hotel, and was demolished to make way for the Ritz Hotel in 1904.

Old and new London

20. Wych Street and Holywell Street (Booksellers' Row) in 1900, shortly before their demolition to make way for the Aldwych.

21. The western end of the new Aldwych seen from the Strand in 1908. The *Morning Post* building is opposite Shaw's Gaiety Theatre (showing Leslie Stuart's musical *Havana*), and the Waldorf Hotel is in the centre of the picture.

London affairs, attacked the LCC, declared that London should be seen 'not as one great municipality, but as an aggregate of municipalities', and suggested that a Conservative government, in conjunction with a Moderate LCC, would abolish the LCC in favour of a set of about ten self-governing districts. However fast the Moderates retreated from this unpopular and unplanned position, it allowed the Progressives to rally support among all those who benefited from LCC policies and rate equalization, and those who wanted to retain their smaller local units, and to win a large majority on the LCC, which they retained until 1907.[12]

With the Progressives restored to power in Spring Gardens the Salisbury government set up a Cabinet committee to prepare a bill that would settle the question of London government for good. This committee agreed that there should be a general devolution of powers, but only those approved by the conference of 1896, most of which the LCC was happy to concede. In its committee stage the bill was amended by friends of the LCC, limiting the powers transferred to the second tier to road maintenance, slaughterhouse and dairy inspection, and the right to promote parliamentary bills. This made the future devolution of greater powers very difficult. Except in the case of Westminster, where the little Strand vestries were to be merged with Westminster and St George Hanover Square, the sensitive matter of amalgamating old vestries into new boroughs was left to a group of boundary commissioners led by Salisbury's nephew, A. J. Balfour. Four vestries and boards were amalgamated into the borough of Southwark, and another four (Whitechapel, Limehouse, Mile End, and St George's-in-the-East) became the borough of Stepney. Generally boroughs of the same social and economic type were joined together – Holborn and St Giles, Rotherhithe and Bermondsey, Plumstead and Woolwich – making it unlikely that the new metropolitan boroughs could ever be independent or self-financing. Several of the biggest vestries and boards (Lambeth, Camberwell, Islington, Wandsworth, Kensington, St Pancras, Hackney, Poplar) remained largely unchanged, and the local pride of some middle-sized vestries was endorsed, giving London the boroughs of Chelsea, Fulham, Hammersmith, Battersea, Stoke Newington, Hampstead, Bethnal Green, and Shoreditch. The twenty-eight new metropolitan boroughs ranged in size from Islington, Lambeth, Wandsworth, and Stepney, each of which had a population of about 300,000 or more in the censuses of 1901 or 1911, to Holborn and Stoke Newington, which had about 50,000 residents each. Smaller still was the largely self-governing City of

London, which had a resident population of 27,000 in 1901, and under 20,000 in 1911.[13]

So, after this long and complicated battle, the administrative shape of London was established for the next sixty-six years. The new boroughs were mostly bigger and all grander than the forty-one vestries and district boards they replaced, but their powers, despite all the efforts of Lord Onslow, Lord Salisbury, and the Moderates, were little changed. They cleaned, lit, and maintained the streets, removed domestic refuse, provided public baths, libraries, cemeteries, mortuaries, and small parks, appointed medical officers and sanitary inspectors, enforced some trading and nuisance regulations, and (in some cases) generated electricity. Between them the twenty-eight boroughs spent £3.6 million on local services in 1901–2, about £400,000 more than the LCC. But the boroughs did not act as a magnet for future powers as local authority duties grew after 1899. When the London School Board was abolished in 1904 the responsibility for its 521 schools, 12,000 teachers, and 550,000 children did not go to the boroughs, as it might have done, but to the LCC, doubling its annual budget. The LCC also had general responsibility for 438 voluntary (Church) schools, and ran nearly a thousand evening schools, training centres, and industrial schools. As secondary and technical education grew, the LCC's spending rose, and even before the Liberal government introduced school medical inspections and free school meals in 1906 and 1907 the LCC had taken on this work, too. The running of the new electric tram services was the LCC's responsibility, though the boroughs could veto the laying of new lines, and the growing task of registering and regulating motor vehicles also fell to the LCC. The LCC's activity in slum clearance and building working-class housing was three or four times as great as that of the boroughs. As a result of all this, and especially because of the high cost of elementary education, the LCC's expenditure in 1910–11 was over £12 million, while that of the twenty-eight boroughs was under £5 million.[14]

The Moderates in Office

London's long period of Progressive government came to an end in the election of February 1907, when the Moderates won 79 of its 118 elected seats. The Moderates' campaign, as usual, emphasized the high cost of the Progressive council, and this time managed to win over middle-class ratepayers in suburban seats which had often returned Progressives in earlier elections. In prosperous times, it seemed, ratepayers were prepared to pay for Council projects and services which, to some extent, were of value to them, but in 1907, when inflation was undermining the real value of middle-class incomes, they took a different view. An accumulation of useful but expensive projects, including the tramway system, council housing estates, the Aldwych and Kingsway development, and the establishment of technical colleges, increased the burden on ratepayers, and the abolition of the London School Board meant that the Council collected and spent the money for London's schools. A comparison of the Council's expenditure per head of population shows that spending rose fourfold, from 9s 10d in 1890–1 to 40s 6d in 1905–6, but only doubled (to just over £1) when the 20s 5d spent on education was discounted. Of this pound, 7s 10d was spent on roads, bridges, and trams, 2s 4d on drainage, 3s 6d on mental services, and the other 6s 4d on such things as parks, housing, and the fire brigade. The Moderate campaign against the Progressives rested heavily on one notorious example of Council extravagance, the short-lived steamboat service from Westminster to Greenwich. A private company had made a profit on a similar service until 1902, but the Council's enterprise was an embarrassing failure. The Council's thirty paddle-boats, bought from local shipbuilders at a cost of £195,000, were not well designed for conditions on the river, and had many collisions and accidents, including a fatal one in June 1905, on the second day of the service. The weather in 1905–6 was poor, the boats were not filled, and from October 1906 services were suspended. The enterprise cost the ratepayers nearly £400,000, and provided the Moderates with an excellent if not really representative symbol of Progressive extravagance and incompetence.[15]

Although the new Moderate council made much of its commitment to economy and retrenchment, there was not much that it could do about its large and growing budget. The rising cost of education and tramways meant that Council spending per head grew almost as fast under the miserly Moderates between 1906 and 1913–14 as it had under the profligate Progressives. In 1913–14 Council spending per head was 56s 5d, an increase of 40 per cent, or 5 per cent a year, since 1906. One of the costly projects the new Council took over from the old was the building of a new County Hall to replace the inadequate building in Spring Garden that the LCC had inherited from the MBW in 1889. After much searching, the Council chose an area of wharves and warehouses called Pedlar's Acre, on the south bank just east of Westminster Bridge. The

LCC's competition for a new County Hall was won by an unknown architect, Ralph Knott. He revised his design with advice from Norman Shaw, and building began with the construction of a huge concrete raft in 1911. County Hall was an imposing building in the 'Edwardian Imperial' style that was also used between 1905 and 1914 for Buckingham Palace, Admiralty Arch, Shaw's Piccadilly Hotel, Selfridge's, Kingsway, and Sir Edwin Cooper's Port of London Authority building on Trinity Square.[16] Most of the building, except its north wing, was completed by 1914, but before the Council could move into its grand new Hall it was requisitioned by the government for the duration of the Great War.

*

COUNCIL ESTATES

Until the 1880s the provision of housing was entirely a matter for commercial builders and privately funded housing charities. The only role for local government in this field (apart from housing paupers, criminals, orphans, and the insane in workhouses, prisons, and asylums) was the demolition of slums and the provision of building plots for the charitable housing companies. The creation of council estates, which transformed working-class housing in the twentieth century, began in the twenty-five years before the First World War, when the London County Council became London's most powerful and active landlord.

From the Nichol to Boundary Street

The 1890 Housing of the Working-Classes Act, which a London County Council deputation had requested, consolidated and clarified the housing legislation of the previous twenty years, and gave the Council responsibility for the clearance and improvement of insanitary areas, when their size or character made them of County, rather than parochial, importance. Under this and earlier acts, local authority slum clearance also carried an obligation to arrange for the building of nearby housing for those evicted from the demolished houses. The Metropolitan Board of Works (MBW) had satisfied this requirement (under the 1875 Artizans' and Labourers' Dwellings Act) by selling the cleared land to one of the many private companies or trusts that built good-quality tenement blocks for working-class families in London. In all, including the schemes completed by the LCC, the MBW had cleared over fifty-seven acres of slum land in central London between 1876 and 1887, and arranged for the construction of twenty-two estates, replacing about 13,000 rooms in slums (plus several lodging houses) with about 15,000 rooms in well-built, but higher-rented, tenement blocks.[1]

The LCC, prompted by its inability to find suitable buyers for two plots in Limehouse cleared by the MBW, decided to use its powers under the 1890 Housing Act to build council estates of its own. In March 1893, with the work increasing, the LCC recruited a permanent staff of about eight architects to its new Housing of the Working Classes Branch. This was an interesting group of young architects, most of whom had drawn their skills and ideas from design classes at the Architectural Association, where they had been influenced by a group of pioneering and socially aware architects, including William Morris, Philip Webb, Norman Shaw, and W. R. Lethaby. The careers of these architects touched and influenced each other at many points. Philip Webb's ideas had been shaped by his work for William Morris's firm, Morris, Marshall, Faulkner and Co., in the 1860s and 1870s, and Webb and Morris together founded the Society for the Protection of Ancient Buildings in 1877. This society brought together most of the important Arts and Crafts architects and designers of late Victorian London, including the architects W. R. Lethaby, Thackeray Turner, George Jack, Ernest Newton, and John J. Stevenson, the engraver and printer Emery Walker, the designer Walter Crane, the fabric manufacturer Arthur Liberty, and the sculptor George Frampton (who created *Peter Pan* in Kensington Gardens). In the 1870s and 1880s Lethaby and Newton had worked for Norman Shaw, the pioneer and popularizer of the redbrick Queen Anne style which had such an influence on the appearance of central and suburban London. Lethaby, who played an important part in transmitting Arts and Crafts ideas to the LCC in the 1890s, was himself strongly influenced by Philip Webb, from whom he learned (he wrote in 1922) that 'architecture was not mere designs, forms and grandeurs, but buildings, honest and human, with hearts in them'. Lethaby became Art Inspector in the LCC's Technical Education Board in 1894, and two years later, with George Frampton, founded the LCC's Central School of Arts and Crafts, to teach young craftsmen their skills in the spirit of William Morris and the Arts and Crafts movement. In 1913, Lethaby summarized his philosophy of art:

> A work of art is a well-made thing, that is all. It may be a well-made statue or a well-made chair, or a well-made book. Art is not a special sauce applied to ordinary cooking; it is the cooking itself if it is good. Most simply and generally art may be thought of as THE WELL-DOING OF WHAT NEEDS DOING . . . If I were asked for some simple test by which we might hope to know a work of art when we

saw one I should suggest something like this: EVERY WORK OF ART SHOWS THAT IT WAS MADE BY A HUMAN BEING FOR A HUMAN BEING. Art is the humanity put into workmanship, the rest is slavery.[2]

The London School Board, whose tall red-brick elementary schools in the Queen Anne style already dominated the skyline of working-class London by the 1880s, had shown that beauty and craftsmanship could be married to utility and economy. Their chief architect, E. R. Robson, who built or supervised 289 new board schools in London between 1871 and 1884, anticipated Lethaby's ideas in an essay, 'Art as Applied to Town Schools', in 1881: 'To do ordinary building well, using every material rightly and truthfully, is the first mark of that interdependence between building and architecture which renders the higher and more intellectual efforts of the latter at all possible . . . Architecture is not mere display, it is not fashion, it is not for the rich alone.'[3]

The architects who built the first LCC estates in the 1890s tried to follow this philosophy, as far as the tight budgets imposed by their political masters allowed them to. They got their first chance to turn their ideals into bricks and mortar in 1893, when they took charge of rebuilding a 14.85-acre site of cleared land in the western end of Bethnal Green, in the north-eastern corner of the junction between Shoreditch High Street and Bethnal Green Road. Until 1891 this had been a notorious rookery known as the Nichol, one of the blackest spots on the 1889 edition of Charles Booth's poverty map. This squalid neighbourhood was given a posthumous notoriety by the East End writer Arthur Morrison, in his successful slum novel *A Child of the Jago*, published in 1896. But although Morrison had personal knowledge of other parts of Bethnal Green, his description of the Nichol ('for one hundred years the blackest pit in London') was based upon visits he made to the area at the invitation of the local vicar, Arthur Osborne Jay, in 1894, after the LCC had demolished it. Charles Booth's brief description, written in 1889, is more reliable: 'Many cabinet makers, French polishers, carvers and chair makers, also hawkers and labourers. Several bad characters. Much poverty and dirt, many families occupying one room. Houses often very old and dilapidated.'[4]

The LCC's decision to demolish this remnant of old London in November 1890 was greeted with general approval, though probably not from the 5,719 people who lived in the 2,654 rooms earmarked for destruction. One of the leading architects in the LCC's Housing of the

Working Classes Branch, Owen Fleming, had lived for several years in a flat in a model dwelling block in Stepney, and he was determined that the Nichol would be replaced with something more imaginative and beautiful than the usual grid of barrack blocks. Instead, he designed a set of seven streets radiating from a central circular road (Arnold Circus), which enclosed a raised garden (built on the rubble of the Nichol slums) with a bandstand. By 1898 these streets, and the roads that surrounded the whole estate, were lined with nineteen five-storey blocks containing 1,044 two- and three-roomed flats, giving accommodation to 4,600 people. The designers of the Boundary Street blocks, notably Reginald Minton Taylor, Charles Winmill, and Arthur Philips, tried, with the money at their disposal, to build housing that had more in common with the Queen Anne style mansion blocks (Albert Hall Mansions and Albert Court) built in Kensington by Norman Shaw in the 1880s than with the grim tenements built by Peabody, Guinness, and other housing trusts on the land cleared by the MBW. The blocks were handsome and well designed, the flats were airy and well lit, and had their own sculleries, toilets, and gas meters, and the estate had schools, shops, gardens, a laundry, sheds, and workshops for costermongers and craftsmen. But by building to this standard, with few one-roomed flats and no subletting, the LCC and its architects took the flats out of the reach of the poor – especially the casual poor – who were evicted when the Nichol was demolished. As Charles Booth wrote a year or two after the Boundary Street estate was officially opened:

> it may be that too much was yielded to the desire to build dwellings that should at once be a credit to the London County Council and an example to others. At any rate, the cost was too great, the rents too high and, in addition, the regulations to be observed under the new conditions, demanded more orderliness of behaviour than suited the old residents. The result is that the new buildings are occupied by a different class, largely Jews, and that the inhabitants of the demolished dwellings have overrun the neighbouring poor streets, or have sought new homes further and further afield, as section after section was turned adrift.[5]

A similar story could be told of the LCC's second large development, the Millbank Estate, which was built near the Thames in Westminster between 1899 and 1902. The closure and demolition of the vast Millbank Penitentiary created space for a new National Gallery of British Art, paid for by the sugar refiner Sir Henry Tate, and an eleven-acre estate to rehouse about 3,000 people evicted by slum clearance and road improvement. The leading architect at Millbank was Reginald Taylor, and the dominant influences were W. R. Lethaby, the Arts and Crafts movement, and the experience of the Boundary Street estate. The Millbank estate used a more symmetrical layout and more uniform architecture than Boundary Street, but its emphasis on spacious gardens, decent accommodation, skilled craftsmanship, and beautiful design was undiminished. As a result, the two- and three-roomed flats cost between 7s and 13s a week to rent, putting them well beyond the reach of the unskilled or casually employed who had been evicted when the slums of Clare Market came down. As long as decent housing was unsubsidized, and especially when it was in the centre of town, the poorest Londoners, those on irregular earnings or under £1 a week, would not be able to afford it. Poverty, not bad landlordism, was their problem, and slum clearance often made their position worse.

Cottage Estates

The LCC built several small tenement estates in central London before 1914, and one larger one, the Bourne estate between Clerkenwell Road, Gray's Inn Road, and Leather Lane, for about 2,000 people. But the high cost of buying and building on sites in central London, which had already discouraged some philanthropic housing companies from building in the centre, made it very difficult to set rents that ordinary working-class families could afford, and the Council moved on to another policy. Part III of the 1890 Act gave the LCC power to purchase compulsorily land in the County for the construction of 'working-class lodging houses', which were defined as 'separate houses or cottages for the working classes, whether containing one or several tenements'. This provision, which involved building new housing, rather than rehousing those evicted by demolition, was not used at first, but in 1898 the LCC's Housing of the Working Classes Committee urged the Council to use it to tackle central London's intractable housing problem, which piecemeal slum clearance had not alleviated. An amendment to the 1890 Act in 1900 allowed the Council to buy land outside the County for new estates, and this formed the basis of the LCC's drive to move working-class families from central London slums to new housing estates on cheaper and healthier suburban land, a policy of population dispersal which the LCC pursued, with more or less enthusiasm, for the remaining sixty-five years of its existence.[6]

The idea that improved and subsidized transport might enable the working classes to benefit from the economic and environmental advantages of suburban housing was a familiar one, which had motivated the Cheap Trains Act of 1883 and been raised again by the Royal Commission on the Housing of the Working Classes in 1885. The arrival of horse-drawn trams in the 1870s and 1880s, and of electric trams, under the LCC's direct control, after 1900, gave this policy of dispersing the working classes to the suburbs a new impetus. LCC architects and planners considering this possibility could also draw upon the garden suburb ideas pioneered by Norman Shaw in Bedford Park, Acton, in the 1870s, and even (with some modification) the Garden City vision promoted by Ebenezer Howard in his seminal work *Tomorrow: A Peaceful Path to Real Reform*, which was first published in 1898. Howard's book, which was republished in 1902 as *Garden Cities of Tomorrow*, did not advocate garden suburbs, and deplored suburban sprawl, but some of his ideas, taken out of context, were useful to the suburban planner. There were practical examples of planned cottage suburbs for the working classes in George Cadbury's Bournville estate, near Birmingham, and W. H. Lever's Port Sunlight, on the Wirral. These two planned villages, which were both well advanced by 1900, were promoted in London by two influential young architect-planners, Barry Parker and Raymond Unwin, as the way forward in housing the poor. The LCC had no power to move industrial employment to new towns, but it could use its control of electric tramways to encourage working men to commute from cheap and decent suburban housing to jobs in the centre of London. With this in mind the Council bought thirty-nine acres of open land in Tooting (inside the County boundary), close to Tooting Broadway Station and the trams and buses of Tooting High Street, as the site for its first cottage estate, Totterdown Fields. The estate, which consisted of 1,229 small two-storey terraced houses with tiny front and rear gardens on a grid of eight streets, was built between 1903 and 1911. Each house had two or three bedrooms, most (unlike the Boundary Street and Millbank flats) had a bathroom, and though the houses were crowded in at over thirty to the acre the architects used individual porches, gables, and bay windows to create a sense of rustic variety. This was the only large LCC cottage estate finished before the Great War, but three others, White Hart Lane in Tottenham, the Norbury estate in Croydon, and the Old Oak estate in Hammersmith, a total of over 250 acres, were begun in 1904–6 and completed after 1918.[7]

In 1907 the Progressives lost control of the Council to the Conserv-

COUNCIL ESTATES · *183*

ative Moderates, who continued building the estates already begun but did not initiate any new ones. Nevertheless, through the schemes started between 1890 and 1907 the LCC built 26,000 rooms (excluding kitchen-sculleries), housing over 30,000 people. About 10,000 of these rooms were a net addition to the London housing stock, rather than replacements for demolished houses. This was not much in a city of 7 million, but it equalled the housing built by the four biggest housing trusts, Peabody, Guinness, Sutton, and Lewis, over a much longer period. The City Corporation, the London boroughs, and several local authorities in Outer London were also quite active house- and tenement-builders, with a total of 14,500 rooms under their control by the end of 1911. The most active local authorities were the City, St Pancras, Battersea, Camberwell, Chelsea, and Westminster within the County and Barking, East Ham, West Ham, and Hornsey outside it. The biggest of these local-authority estates, Latchmere Road, Battersea (between Battersea Park Road and the railway line from Waterloo to Clapham Junction), was built thanks to the efforts of John Burns, Battersea's County Councillor and (from 1892 to 1918) its MP. The estate, built by local-authority workmen and opened by Burns in 1903, had 315 well-built two-storey houses and maisonettes with 1,148 rooms, gathered around a recreation ground which is all that remains of Latchmere Common. Another early twentieth-century cottage estate was Grove Vale, in Camberwell, between Goose Green and East Dulwich station, which had (and still has) 649 rooms in flats or maisonettes in two-storey houses.

Those who gained least from slum clearance and rebuilding programmes were the almost 40,000 slum tenants evicted by the MBW, LCC, or borough councils between 1883 and 1914. Hardly any of them were rehoused in council flats or cottages, whose 6s or 8s rents were well beyond them, and most were left to find rooms in slums that had not yet been demolished. The people who could afford council flats or houses were of a different class, in need of good housing, but not desperate for help. When the tenants of the LCC's 10,000 dwellings were analysed by occupation in 1919 it was found that 720 were clerks, 1,390 were labourers, charwomen, or porters, and over a thousand were policemen, drivers, tailors, fitters, plumbers, or carpenters.[8] George Sims wrote an interesting chapter on 'Evicted London' for his multi-volume *Living London* of 1901. Many of those given notice to quit in preparation for an improvement scheme, he said, hung on till the last minute, and were then turned out just before their house was knocked down. The wife or one of the children guarded their piled-up possessions in the street, while the husband went off to find a room or two that he could afford. Sometimes the next shelter for an evicted family was a workhouse or a common lodging house, their children perhaps farmed out to friends or relatives. Even those who found rooms in model dwellings might not stay there for long. 'As the block becomes filled they are weeded out on some excuse or other. Slum dwellers are not wanted in nice clean buildings.'[9]

The Building Cycle

Interesting and important as these enterprises were, we should remember that they represented a small contribution to London's housing stock. Between 1901 and 1911 Greater London's population grew by 670,000 (enough to occupy 580,000 LCC rooms), and its stock of working-class accommodation, allowing for losses to demolition, rose by about 400,000 rooms. By far the biggest contribution to this increase came from private builders, not councils or philanthropic housing trusts.[10] What mattered most to working-class tenants was not the pace of local authority or charity building, but the apparently erratic behaviour of the commercial building industry. Although population growth was fairly steady, the growth of housing in London proceeded in a series of waves, with peak years producing two or three times as many rooms as trough ones. One of the driving forces behind these fluctuations was the availability of cheap capital. When capital was scarce, as it was in the 1880s, building slowed down, and when it was readily available, as in the late 1890s, the industry revived. A second factor was demand. While the building industry was depressed in the 1880s population kept rising, diminishing the stock of empty rooms created in the preceding boom. In time the shortage of housing stimulated a recovery in the building industry, as it did in the mid-1890s, when the number of empty rooms in London was unusually low. In turn, this boom created a glut of empty properties which were hard to sell or rent, and the boom therefore petered out, turning into another depression. To put some figures on these fluctuations, the average number of houses built each year in London between 1897 and 1906 was twice as high as the average number built in the building depressions of 1890–5 and 1908–13. In 1899, at the height of the boom, over 27,000 houses were built in Greater London, but this number had halved by 1909, and fallen to 8,579 by 1913. So the London housing stock, especially in the suburbs, grew through a series of imbalances, with property sometimes running ahead of population growth and sometimes falling behind it. In Wandsworth, for instance, the population grew by 75,000, or 34 per cent, between 1901 and 1911, well ahead of house-building, reducing a surplus of nearly 9,000 rooms in 1903 into a surplus of only 709 by 1912. The same thing happened in Tottenham, where building slumped after 1908, reducing its stock of empty rooms to 800. The *Building Societies Gazette* in January 1909 was critical of builders' 'feverish haste to turn orchards and market gardens on the outskirts into building land, and to run up fancy looking and often fragile houses thereon . . . The fact is that houses are not, at least in the Metropolis, built in accordance with the laws of supply and demand, but to develop, as it is called, estates, and to create ground rents.'[11]

Fluctuations in house-building, and its failure to keep pace with local population increases, produced variations in rents which had direct consequences for living standards. Rents of working-class houses (including rates), which were almost static in the 1880s, rose by about 17 per cent between 1890 and 1905. Rents in Stepney, where established residents were in competition with Jewish settlers and perhaps people displaced by slum clearances, rose by 28 per cent between 1885 and 1900. Poorer tenants responded to these increases in the usual way, by subletting and crowding into fewer rooms. Measured by Charles Booth's standard of two or more people to a room, overcrowding in the County of London had fallen in the 1890s, from 1.33 million (33 per cent) in 1891 to 1.22 million (28.6 per cent) in 1901, but improved no further by 1911. In Outer London overcrowding was less severe, but rose significantly between 1901 and 1911 (from 13.6 per cent to 17.5 per cent) as the problems of the centre spread into the poorer suburbs. In the centre, slum clearance reduced overcrowding in Holborn from 65.5 per cent of the population in 1891 to 40 per cent in 1911, but the other black spots were almost as bad as ever. About half the populations of Bethnal Green, Finsbury, Shoreditch, and Stepney lived at two or more to a room in 1911, just as they had in 1891. Finsbury, at 56.6 per cent, replaced Holborn as London's most overcrowded borough by 1891, but in absolute numbers Stepney, with 142,000 in overcrowded rooms to Finsbury's 54,000, was at the top (or bottom) of the heap.[12]

*

CHAPTER ELEVEN

A CITY OF SUBURBS

One of the outstanding characteristics of twentieth-century London was its tendency to spread far into the surrounding countryside, encouraged by improvements in motorized transport and unimpeded, until the 1940s, by any effective planning controls. Rapid suburban growth in the inter-war period attracted the greatest attention from politicians, planners, and historians, but the process became well established in the 1880s and 1890s, and accelerated in the 1900s, when modern forms of transport, the electric Tube, train, and tram, and the motor bus, made it easy for London commuters to live far beyond the County boundary.

London Spreading

The population of late Victorian London seemed to ripple outwards, impelled by a centrifugal force, leaving the older inner districts depopulated, and filling the surrounding suburban areas until they in turn overflowed and decanted their population into an outer suburban ring. So the City, Finsbury, Holborn, St Marylebone, and Westminster, and to a lesser degree Shoreditch, lost population steadily from the 1860s, and boroughs outside the old centre but within the County – Battersea, Bethnal Green, Camberwell, Fulham, Hackney, Hammersmith, Hampstead, Islington, Kensington, Lambeth, Lewisham, St Pancras, Southwark, Stepney, Wandsworth, and Woolwich – grew fast until 1895 or 1901. After the 1890s population in these crowded suburban boroughs levelled off or fell, and within the County only Fulham, Hammersmith, Hampstead, Lewisham, Wandsworth, and Woolwich experienced significant growth after 1901. The outcome of this was that the population of the County rose from 3.88 million to 4.56 million between 1881 and 1901, but then levelled off and fell. Beyond the County boundary, though, growth continued as fast as ever. The population of London's outer ring grew from under a million in 1881 to 2.7 million (equivalent to the total population of Paris) in 1911, turning parts of the counties of Kent, Middlesex, Essex, Surrey, and Hertfordshire into a metropolitan hinterland. By 1911, with 37 per cent of its population living outside the County boundary, London was truly a city of suburbs.[1]

The spread of London beyond a four-mile radius in the 1870s and 1880s was driven by population growth, and the ability of a rising percentage of this population to satisfy their desire for more space, lower rents, and all the comforts of suburban living. Middle-class Londoners, who had a well-established ambition to escape the unpleasant and overpriced centre by moving to cheaper and better houses in suburbs with good transport connections with their City offices and the West End theatres and shops, were growing in numbers and wealth. At the same time falling prices, lower fares, and better education were increasing the number of clerks and skilled workers who could realistically aspire to a terraced house in Camberwell, Hackney, or one of the other inner suburbs previously settled by the better off. Serving this demand, better train, bus, and tram services were beginning to turn areas of farmland or large 1840s villas into well-populated suburbs like Finchley, Tulse Hill, and Ealing.

New arrivals in the inner suburbs were not colonizing virgin territory, but occupying land or houses abandoned by richer suburbanites, who were moving further out to healthier, greener, and more remote suburbs, where working-class settlers could not follow them. Camberwell, an elongated South London suburban parish (or, from 1899, borough) which stretched from Peckham and the fringes of Walworth in the north to Dulwich and Sydenham in the south, more than doubled its population between 1871 and 1891, through a combination of migration and natural growth. By the late 1880s population density in the north of the parish was almost as high as that in the worst inner-city districts, and Charles Booth's 1889 poverty map of the area between Albany Road and Peckham High Street made liberal use of the light and dark blue of the 'poor' and 'very poor', very little of the red of 'middle-class', and none of the yellow of the 'wealthy'. As the poor moved in the well off moved out, perhaps taking their families to Herne Hill, where they might rub shoulders with the critic John Ruskin and the inventor Sir Henry Bessemer, or Brixton, where they might have the music-hall stars Dan Leno and Fred Karno as neighbours. Thanks to the new services stopping at Loughborough Junction the country lanes between Brixton and Dulwich were being transformed into suburban streets, and the district north of Brixton was being developed as Angell Town and Stockwell. By 1889 the fields and market gardens of North Brixton had been reduced to a fourteen-acre fragment, which the LCC bought and preserved as Myatt's Fields. Many of these suburban settlers, of course, were not refugees from the centre, but new arrivals from other parts of England, making their first London home in one of the less crowded parts of the town, where there were green spaces and fresh air to remind them of the world they had left.

Those with suburban aspirations were served by a growing number of guidebooks to the fringes of London, of which William Clarke's *The Suburban Homes of London*, published in 1881, was one of the first. Clarke was enthusiastic about almost every new district: Balham Hill was 'as pleasant a place for a promenade as we know', the new Bedford Park development in Chiswick was so well drained that it offered 'a perfect freedom from sewer gas', and Brixton, 'a creation of the last twenty-five or thirty years', was filling with fine shops, and offered excellent opportunities for new businesses. By the early twentieth century suburban guidebooks, listing average rents, death rates, and journey times to the City and West End, appeared almost annually. The Homeland Association's *Where to Live Round London*, with separate volumes on North and South London, went through five editions between 1905 and 1914.

Would-be suburbanites were unlikely to be discouraged by a sour and silly attack on the suburban ideal published in 1905 by the poet T. W. H. Crosland, Lord Alfred Douglas's friend and ghostwriter. According to Crosland, the suburban ring was populated by milkmen, postmen, drapers' assistants, Methodist ministers, and 'sluttish little girls with clean doorsteps', people who dressed like Bernard Shaw and delighted in cut-price ostentation, the plays of Jerome K. Jerome and James Barrie, the suburban science of H. G. Wells, gramophone music, tinted photographs, Harmsworth newspapers, and cheap editions of the classics. Crosland was furious that new technology and more efficient production was making available to the millions a literary culture which had once been the preserve of a privileged elite: 'Show me a house with its rows of skimpily-bound, undersized shilling or eighteenpenny volumes, and I will show you a house in which the spirit of Dalston and Clapham and Surbiton and Crouch End rules supreme.' Crosland reserved particular venom for Tooting, 'a whirling wilderness of villadom, a riot of inexpensive red brick . . . The man or woman who could be happy in Tooting could be happy anywhere, like a common goat.' And Henrietta Barnett's recent announcement of a new development, Hampstead Garden Suburb, with fine houses for the professional classes and separate quarters for the industrial classes and single women, filled him with gloom.[2]

It was all a question of attitude and perception. Arnold Bennett, writing in 1897, found a picturesque charm in the modest but fast-growing suburb of Fulham: 'Walking down Edith Grove this afternoon, I observed the vague, mysterious beauty of the vista of houses and bare trees melting imperceptibly into a distance of grey fog. And then, in the King's Road, the figures of tradesmen at shopdoors, of children romping or stealing along mournfully, of men and women each totally different from each other, wrapt up in their own thoughts and ends – these seem curiously strange and novel and wonderful.'[3] And Sidney Low, the brilliant editor of the *St James' Gazette*, shared Bennett's optimism. In an article in the influential *Contemporary Review* after the 1891 census, he argued that the fear of Darkest London, the City of Dreadful Night, that prevailed in the years after the Whitechapel murders and the Trafalgar Square riots would soon evaporate, because the London of the future would not be a city of inner-city slums, but of healthy suburbs, 'straggling far down into the depths of the home counties': 'a dozen Croydons will form a circle of detached forts round the central stronghold . . . cheap trains will whirl the artisan daily from Rickmansworth or Romford as they now bring him from Stratford or Canning Town'. The physical and mental degeneration that others had seen in the urban race would not be a problem in this new suburban London, where daily commuting sharpened the wits, and cricket, football, and cycling replaced the music hall and the pub as the leisure activities of choice. Thus, suburban life 'may do for the town artisan in future what it has already done for the clerk', making him 'more alert, more active, and more elastic than the rustic, and, as a rule, quite as tough and enduring'. Writers used the word suburban as a sneer, and housing charities and local authorities were foolishly trying to impede London's expansion by building tenements where the old inner-city slums had been, but they would do better, Sidney Low concluded, to work with the natural tendency of the age and 'to help on, by improved means of locomotion, the inevitable tendency which is leaving the costly sites in the inner circles of the towns to business and public resort' and turning us into a nation of healthy suburbanites.[4]

Shifting Centres of Growth

Low's greatest allies in this enterprise were the transport innovators and entrepreneurs (including the LCC) who staked their money on horse-drawn and electric trams, underground railways, and motor buses in the 1890s and 1900s, and the legislators who compelled train and tram operators to offer cheap workmen's fares. The transport revolution that took place in London, especially in the first twelve years of the twentieth century, beginning with the opening of the Central London Railway and the introduction of the first electric tram, enabled a greater proportion of Londoners to travel further, faster, and more cheaply and comfortably within and beyond their city than ever before. The total number of journeys in Greater London by tram, bus, and local train increased from about 850 million in 1901 to 2,255 million in 1913, or from about 130 journeys per head each year to about 300. Because the transport system had grown more extensive, the average journey was much longer in 1913 than in 1901. The increase since 1881, when the average Londoner took about sixty trips on public transport each year, is even more striking. These increases were achieved partly by changes in fares and running times which allowed working men and women to travel to work by train, tram, or bus at times that suited them. Trams offered workmen's fares, motor buses were far more useful to working men than horse buses had been, and the number of workmen's trains running each day tripled between 1899 and 1913, from 605 to 1,806.[5]

The most important consequence of the transport revolution, but also one of its causes, was the growth of London's outer suburban population in the early twentieth century. The growth of settlements on London's rural fringes enticed railway and tramway companies to invest in new tracks, but they hoped to make extra profits by enticing settlers into districts that were well served by new transport links. The existing tendency of middle-class and better-off working-class Londoners to desert central London for the suburbs, a consequence of prosperity, social aspirations, population growth, high Inner London rents, and the loss of central land to commercial and administrative buildings, was intensified and given freer rein by the development of faster and cheaper transport facilities. The population within the County boundaries had grown by 300,000 in the 1890s, but in the next decade its long twentieth-century decline began. The population of the inner nineteen square miles of the County (the City and about ten inner boroughs) fell by 136,000 between 1901 and 1911, mostly because of the loss of population from Finsbury, Shoreditch, Islington, St Marylebone, St Pancras, Southwark, Stepney, and Westminster. Only ten of the County of London's twenty-eight boroughs experienced population growth in that decade, and only Fulham, Hampstead, Wandsworth, and Lewisham, with an extra 131,000 residents, grew significantly. Further from the centre, there was vigorous growth. There were already 1,374,000 people living beyond the London County boundary and within fifteen miles of Charing Cross in 1891, without the benefit of tubes, motor buses, or electric trams. But thanks, in part, to the transport revolution this population had doubled (to 2,718,000) by 1911. The population of the three counties most affected by London's suburban growth, Essex, Middlesex, and Surrey, grew by 80 per cent (from 1,848,000 to 3,323,000), more than three times the national growth rate, between 1891 and 1911. No other county in the United Kingdom grew at anything like the speed of these three.[6]

The focus of suburban growth changed from one decade to the next, as available development land filled up and faster transport made new land accessible. In the 1880s Westminster, the City, and other very central districts lost population, but Inner London (the MBW or LCC area) gained population because of the growth of outer districts like Fulham, Camberwell, Woolwich, Wandsworth, and Hampstead. The fastest growth between 1881 and 1891 was just outside the MBW–LCC boundary, in West Ham (82 per cent) and the cheap railway suburbs of Tottenham (95 per cent), Leyton (133 per cent), and Willesden (122 per cent). In the 1890s the most rapid population growth was mostly in suburbs about five or six miles from the City, accessible by horse-drawn tram or mainline railway. Within the County boundary, the populations of the boroughs of Fulham and Wandsworth (including Balham, Clapham, Putney, Streatham, and Tooting) grew by nearly 50 per cent, and Lewisham (including Blackheath, Catford, and Sydenham) by 43 per cent in the 1890s. Beyond the County boundary to the west and north, there was rapid population growth in urban Middlesex, especially in tram or railway suburbs, such as Acton (56 per cent), Hornsey (62 per cent), Hendon (42 per cent), Willesden (87 per cent), Hanwell (70 per cent), Southall (67 per cent), Edmonton (85 per cent), and Tottenham (43 per cent). The most spectacular increases outside the County were in the urban districts of Essex, which were as close to the centre of London as Lewisham and Wandsworth were, and also had the advantage of being near the docks and the Lea Valley industrial zone. The population of Walthamstow doubled in the 1890s, while that of East Ham tripled (both reaching 95,000 by 1901), and that of Ilford, a convenient and cheap working-class and white-collar commuter suburb with good railway services to Liverpool Street, grew almost four-fold to 41,000.

Essex and Middlesex

The growing suburbs of East London housed many thousands of commuters, but they also developed significant industrial employment of their own. Walthamstow, the district to the north of Hackney Marshes which had the distinction of being described at length by Jesse Argyle in the first volume of Charles Booth's *Life and Labour of the People in London* in 1890, grew from a large village into a working-class suburb of nearly 50,000 people in the 1880s. It was breezier and healthier than the East End, but in many respects, Argyll said, the settlers who were attracted to Walthamstow by low rents and easy access to industrial London had brought the characteristics of Bethnal Green with them: 'poorly-clad, but sharp-looking children, thriving public houses, a busy Saturday night market, when the principal streets are full of stalls and redolent of naphtha lights, fried fish and vegetable refuse, . . . the same constant shifting, and not infrequently "moonlight flitting"'.[7] In the 1890s much of the parish was developed by T. C. T. Warner, one of the biggest local landowners. The Warner Estate Company built row after row of two-storeyed yellow-brick terraced houses near the railway, and some well-designed six-bedroomed 'lodges' in the more desirable northern part of the parish, near Epping Forest and Highams Park.

At the time of Argyle's account Walthamstow had very little industry, but within a few years, especially after the opening of the Blackhorse Road railway station in 1894, the position was quite different. After 1900 Black-horse Lane, running north from the station and parallel to the River Lea navigation, became a favourite location for modern industries that needed more space than central London could offer. Peter Hooker, printers' engineers, came to Blackhorse Lane in 1901, and Baird and Tatlock, makers of scientific instruments, moved there from Hatton Garden a year later. Micanite and Insulators Company, makers of insulating materials, arrived in 1902, and Fuller Electrical and Manufacturing Company, makers of electric motors and transformers, moved from West London in 1905. The Relyante

Motor Works set up its Central Cycle and Motor Works in the Lane in 1905, and the Vanguard Motor Omnibus Company and the Motor Omnibus Company came in 1906 and 1907. The Vanguard Works were taken over in 1908 by the London General Omnibus Company LGOC, which made its groundbreaking X-type and B-type buses there, near the Royal Standard public house. Under the nearby railway arches the pioneering aviator and aircraft manufacturer Alliot Verdon-Roe built his Triplane, and flew it on Walthamstow marshes, the first powered flight by a British aircraft, in 1909. To complete this picture of Walthamstow as an unlikely cradle of the modern motorized, airborne, and electrified world, the suburb was also a centre for early film production. With its open spaces, relatively clean air, and easy access to London's pool of actors and extras, Walthamstow had at least four film companies by 1914, including the important British and Colonial Kinematograph company, which occupied (as one passing craze replaced another) an abandoned roller-skating rink. Traditional industries were attracted to Walthamstow, too. Hookway, Sons and Cook, makers of collars, umbrellas, and braces, moved there from Aldersgate in 1899, and there were factories and workshops making blouses, furniture, pattern cards, mineral water, pickles, and self-adhesive sticking plasters.[8]

There was some industrial growth in Ilford, too. In 1882 a Peckham photographer, Alfred H. Harman, built the Britannia factory to make photographic dry plates in the pure air of Ilford, and by 1903, after several enlargements, his Ilford photographic-paper factory claimed to be the biggest in the world. Ilford also had a paper mill, brickworks, and the Euplyton Works, manufacturer of celluloid collars and cuffs for Ilford's white-collared workers. West Ham, though its growth was slower in the 1890s than in the previous decade, achieved the enormous population of 267,000 in 1901 (more than double its 1881 population), making it the fourth biggest port town in England, after London, Liverpool, and Bristol. Unlike most London suburbs, West Ham was not a dormitory town but a major industrial employer in its own right, a production centre for sulphuric acid, tar, naphtha, creosote, pitch, soda, synthetic dyes, gas, disinfectant, fertilizer, and insecticide.[9]

Between 1901 and 1911 the areas of greatest growth moved further out, with the help of electric trains, trams, and underground lines. Inside the County, there was still 34 per cent growth in Wandsworth (especially in Streatham and Tooting) and 25 per cent growth in Lewisham (mostly in Catford). Urban Essex was getting crowded, and grew much more slowly (at 26 per cent) than it had in the 1890s, with growth concentrated in Ilford (90 per cent), Leyton, East Ham, and Walthamstow. Middlesex, which was more affected by train, Tube, and tram extensions, experienced 42 per cent growth in the Edwardian decade, almost as fast as its 46 per cent in the 1890s. Four of its urban districts, Southall, Southgate, Wealdstone, and Wembley, doubled in population; six, Ealing, Finchley, Hanwell, Harrow, Ruislip, and Hendon, grew by more than 60 per cent; and several others, including Acton, Edmonton, Enfield, Heston, Tottenham, Twickenham, Willesden, and Wood Green, grew by over 30 per cent. The disappearance of much of rural Middlesex, so lamented in the 1920s and 1930s, was already well advanced by 1914, and Middlesex's population growth between 1891 and 1911 (by 583,000, or 107 per cent) was faster in relative terms than its growth between 1921 and 1931, when it grew by 386,000, or 31 per cent. Many of the suburban towns that replaced the Middlesex hayfields, such places as Acton, Ealing, Edmonton, Enfield, Hornsey, Southall, Tottenham, Twickenham, Willesden, and Wood Green, were almost fully grown by 1914. Hendon, Harrow, and Finchley, whose growth is usually associated with the twenties and thirties, each had a population of about 40,000 by 1911. Harrow relied on the Metropolitan Railway for its connection to central London, but Hendon, which was on the main line to St Pancras, also had three electric tram and three motor-bus services, and Finchley, which was on the main line to King's Cross, was on several electric tram routes from 1905. Even Wembley, which seemed to grow like a mushroom between the wars, had developed from a village in the 1880s to a town in 1911, with its 11,000 residents already enjoying their Metropolitan Railway station (1894), Metropolitan electric trains (1906), and an electric tram service to Paddington (1908), but still waiting for their first motor buses.[10]

Faster and more convenient routes into central London turned small Middlesex settlements into thriving suburban towns. Golders Green, north-west of Hampstead Heath, was a rural community of 8,262 people in 1901, with spacious lodges and farmhouses clustered around North End Road, which was on an hourly omnibus route from Hendon to Oxford Circus. The construction of the Yerkes' Charing Cross, Euston and Hampstead Railway began in 1902, sparking off a rush of road and sewer building, property development, and profit-taking. Agricultural land that had been worth about £200 an acre was soon being parcelled into small building plots at up to £5,000 or even £10,000 an acre, depending on their proximity to the new station. Property developers like Edward Streather built solid middle-class houses that sold for about £500 each,

setting a style in half-timbered gabled villas and semis that was repeated
in most London suburbs between the wars. One country estate after
another was bought and built over, usually at a fairly high density, quickly
obliterating the rusticity that had attracted well-off settlers to Golders
Green in the first place. By 1907, when the railway opened, Golders
Green's population was probably around 10,000, and this had risen to
16,616 in 1911, and 28,633 by 1921. By 1915 Golders Green Station
was one of the busiest in London, handling over 30,000 passengers a day.
The growing population attracted more transport routes, which in turn
made the station accessible to a bigger district and encouraged yet more
settlement. Reliable motor bus and electric tram services to Finchley began
in 1909, and by the end of 1912 Golders Green Station was in the middle
of a network of bus and tram services linking Finchley, Hendon, Childs
Hill, and West Hampstead with central London. Golders Green bus garage,
right outside the station, could hold a hundred buses. By 1914 Golders
Green was a fully-grown suburb, with two blocks of shops, including a
bank, a post office and a branch of Sainsbury's. With an interesting sense
of priorities, a luxurious 700-seat cinema, the Ionic, and a huge 3,500-
seat Hippodrome variety theatre, with a 90-foot stage and a 20,000-gallon
water tank for aquatic shows, were built in 1913, a year before Golders
Green's first primary and secondary schools were opened. Golders Green
really was, as the familiar Underground posters assured potential settlers
as early as 1908, 'A Place of Delightful Prospects'.[11]

Building the Suburbs

The builders and property developers who made these new suburbs are
only remembered in a few street names, but their contribution to the
growth of London was important, and millions of Londoners still live in
the terraces and semi-detached houses that they built. Some of them were
men with an eye for the main chance. The rascal Jabez Balfour, the founder
of the Liberator Building Society and Liberal MP for Burnley, used suburban property development as a vehicle for relieving incautious investors
of their savings in the 1880s. Balfour coaxed money out of mainly Nonconformist investors by lying about the value of the properties in Croydon
and Ilford that his many companies were developing, and got away with
it until the depression of the early 1890s exposed a £7 million deficit in
his company accounts. Thousands of small investors were ruined, James

Hobbs, Balfour's builder in Ilford and Croydon, was imprisoned, and Balfour, who fled to Argentina, was eventually extradited and sentenced to fourteen years in prison. Balfour Road, near Ilford Station, is a reminder of this piece of suburban skulduggery. In contrast, the biggest property developer in Ilford in the 1890s and 1900s, Archibald Cameron Corbett, also a Liberal MP, was an honest and efficient businessman. Corbett inherited his father's property business in 1880, and spent the next thirty years building thousands of decent houses, mainly for middle-class or skilled working-class tenants, in Lewisham, East Ham, and Ilford. Corbett completed his father's development of part of the Woodgrange estate in Forest Gate, East and West Ham, in the 1880s, giving his new roads names that might add a little distinction to a nondescript development – Windsor, Hampton, Balmoral, and Claremont. Another important developer in East Ham was the Burges family, who owned 400 acres of land in the parish and built long terraces of decent cheap housing on it between 1890 and 1914.

In 1893 Corbett moved a little north-east to a ninety-three-acre estate just south of Ilford High Road and the Great Eastern Railway's main line to Liverpool Street, and built over a thousand houses. A year later he started building 450 substantial villa houses north of the railway, on the Grange House estate. Corbett expected many of the men who bought or rented these houses to be City commuters, and persuaded the Great Eastern Railway to rebuild Ilford station to make it more accessible to the new estate. When Corbett developed the Mayfield and Downshall estates in the later 1890s, the Great Eastern, keen to pick up as much suburban traffic as it could, agreed to build two new stations, at Seven Kings and Goodmayes. By the time his work in Ilford was completed, in 1903, Corbett had developed over 500 acres of estate and market-garden land, and sold over 3,000 houses. Corbett's houses were built to typical cottage or villa designs, had between three and six bedrooms, and sold for between £217 and £520, leasehold. These prices barely covered the cost of land and building, but Corbett's profit came from ground rents. After this the demand for houses in Ilford tailed off, but by 1911 its population was 78,000, a sevenfold increase in twenty years. As Ilford's population grew, the range of transport options increased. Municipal electric trams connected Ilford High Road with Barking gas works, the Royal Albert Dock, and Poplar by 1904, and by 1911 there was an LGOC motor bus route (number 8) between Ilford and the City. The Great Eastern's new railway linking its main line at Seven Kings with its Ongar line at Woodford (now the Central Line's

Hainault loop), built in 1903, did not lead to much new housing development until the 1930s, showing that transport alone could not create a new suburb.[12]

Corbett's other main areas of operation were Catford and Hither Green in the borough of Lewisham, and Eltham in Woolwich. As in Ilford, Corbett worked closely with the local railway company to ensure that his middle-class settlers would have an easy run into central London. His 334-acre estate in Eltham was near the new railway line from Blackheath to Bexley Heath (built in 1895), and Corbett helped to pay for the new stations at Shooters Hill and Eltham Park to be built in a style that would suit commuters whose new semi-detached houses had servants' quarters. When he built the St German's estate in Catford and Hither Green between 1896 and 1914 he persuaded the South-Eastern Railway to open a new booking office in Hither Green station with an entrance from the estate, and to offer estate residents cheap season tickets. Corbett's 3,000 houses in Catford and Hither Green were intended for respectable clerks, and he made sure that they were provided with churches, schools, and libraries, but no public houses.[13] Dull neighbourhoods do not always have dull residents. The occupants of number 44 Craigton Road, on the Corbett estate in Eltham, were William and Avis Hope, a stone mason and a concert singer. They were the parents of Leslie – or Bob – Hope, who was born in Eltham in 1903.

The new houses built in the booming suburbs of the 1890s and 1900s were subject to local by-laws controlling drainage, sanitation, foundations, building density, and fire safety, but the degree to which these were enforced depended on the efficiency of the borough or urban district council. When growth was very fast in a new district where the local authority was staffed with part-timers and had developers and builders sitting on the council, slums could be the result. East Ham grew at a tremendous pace in the 1890s, faster than any other English town of a similar size. A small town of under 10,000 people in 1881, it was a dormitory suburb of 70,000, as big as Coventry or Ipswich, by 1901. In the late 1890s the East Ham council surveyor had to inspect and approve almost 2,000 new houses every year, sometimes 300 in a month, often dealing with developers who were also his political masters. One of the worst problems in East Ham, along with other parts of East London, was that the land available for working-class housing was low-lying and liable to flooding. Little Ilford Level, on the west bank of the River Roding (the border between Barking and East Ham), was developed in 1897–1900 despite

the surveyor's misgivings, and flooded in 1903. Nevertheless, there were
plenty of people in East Ham whose poverty compelled them to take rooms
or houses in the soggy slum terraces of Little Ilford Level.[14]

London's new houses were designed and built (to take the 1891
County census figures) by about 2,000 architects and about 8,000 employing builders, who could call upon a vast army of craftsmen and labourers.
There were around 140,000 masons, bricklayers, carpenters, plasterers,
painters, paperhangers, glaziers, plumbers, and locksmiths in Greater
London in 1891, and 165,000 in 1911.[15] Some builders were selected by
an architect and worked to his plans, but many speculative builders built
to standard plans, without an architect's guidance. Ernest Aves, Booth's
assistant, defended this often abused class from some of its critics:

> The speculative builder is associated in the public mind with the 'jerry
> builder', but the association is often misleading ... Many of the best
> and most fashionable parts of London have been opened up by him,
> and he is not infrequently a man who has the boldness to carry out
> great schemes and the integrity to do good work. Uniformity of style
> and a resulting architectural dullness is the charge to be laid at his
> door, rather than inferior workmanship or the use of bad materials ...
> Speculative building in the outer circle of London, especially in most
> of the poorest districts, has become a byword and a reproach to
> the whole building fraternity, [but] ... responsibility must be put
> on the right shoulders; many speculative builders who do the worst
> work are simply men of straw, the puppets of the real capitalist; who
> may be the ground landlord, the building company, or ... the
> 'money-lending solicitor'.[16]

In any case, Aves concluded, 'better Walthamstow than Whitechapel, and
better Willesden Green than Holborn'.

Suburban houses were built by the thousand in the 1890s and 1900s,
and it is not surprising that most of them were constructed without great
individuality. Only the luckiest or richest suburbanite would have a house
designed by Norman Shaw, Charles Voysey, Ernest Newton, or Ernest
George, stained-glass windows by the perfectly named Selwyn Image, or
interior design by Frank Brangwyn or (like the Wildes) Edward Godwin.
But the influence of these and dozens of other fine architects and designers were spread across the suburbs by example and imitation, through such
journals as *The Studio* (1893 onwards) and *The Burlington Magazine* (1881
onwards), books like *The Modern Home* and *The British Home of Today* (both

edited by W. Shaw Sparrow in 1904), and associations like the Art Workers' Guild (founded in 1884), which propagated progressive Arts and Crafts ideas. At a more popular level, illustrated magazines, furniture-shop displays, and exhibitions at Olympia and Earls Court (especially the Ideal Home Exhibition of 1910) alerted the public to modern styles and new domestic comforts. Machine-made building components led to a certain standardization, but they were available in such variety that the builder could create an interesting diversity of appearance in what might otherwise have been a uniform street. The features that spread most effectively were the use of red bricks and tiled roofs in the Queen Anne style of Norman Shaw and Bedford Park, red-tiled or half-timbered gables, ornamental features in terracotta or moulded brick, and bay windows on one or two floors. Stucco, a cheap painted cement coating for poor brickwork, regained popularity in the 1890s, and was transformed after about 1910 into that all-purpose metaphor for suburban London, pebbledash.[17]

Inside the houses there were factory-made fireplaces available in marble, wood, and cast iron that looked like the work of craftsmen, machine-made dados, skirting, and picture rails, mass-produced metalwork, patterned glass, and ceramic wall and floor tiles that added 'class' to a house without unduly increasing its cost. Fibrous plaster (moulded plaster on a canvas backing) was used to provide cheap and light ceiling roses and cornices, and for those who wanted to follow the fashion for whole ceilings decorated in Adam, Louis XVI, or Chippendale style, firms such as Lincrusta-Walton and Anaglypta made moulded and embossed papers that could achieve the desired effect at a fraction of the cost of real plasterwork. Frederick Walton, who invented Lincrusta relief wallpaper in 1877, had already made an important contribution to cheap interior design by his invention of linoleum (linseed oil, pine rosin, and pine flour on a flax base) in 1860. Anaglypta, Lincrusta's lighter and cheaper rival, was patented in 1887.[18]

The most important contributions of new technology to the late Victorian and Edwardian home were in the field of lighting and sanitation. Gas lighting was quite often installed in good new houses in the late 1880s, and became common in the 1890s. By 1911 there were 1,376,000 private gas consumers in Greater London, though these were not all domestic users. Gas stoves could be rented from all the London gas companies, and gas cooking was quite common in working-class Edwardian households. The Kennington labourers' wives living on weekly wages of 18s to 30s a week – poor, but not the poorest – that were studied by Maud

Pember Reeves and the Fabian Women's Group between 1908 and 1912 often spent 6d or 1s a week on gas, especially for cooking, as well as a shilling or more on coal.[19] Those who did not have a prepayment gas meter spent 6d or 8d a week on oil and candles instead, enduring a dimmer light and a much greater risk of fire, especially from cheap paraffin oil. C. H. Rolph, a policeman's son who lived in a modest terraced house in Finsbury Park from 1906 to 1910, did his homework by the light of an upright gas mantle. For richer families, inverted incandescent mantles (replacing gas jets or upright mantles) made gas lighting brighter in the 1890s, and wall switches by the door made it easier to light a room when you entered it. These improvements helped to slow the spread of domestic electricity, and by 1911 there were only 122,000 electricity customers in London. Most of these were well-off families, especially those living in recently built houses and flats in the West End and the wealthier suburbs.[20] There were gas fires on the market, but even for these richer families, heating was nearly always by coal fires, perhaps with the more efficient modern narrow grate with a firebrick back. Bathrooms were generally confined to richer households in the 1880s, but were commonplace in smaller houses by 1900. The Grossmiths did not hesitate to give their fictional bank clerk, Charles Pooter, a cast-iron bath in the early 1890s, or to have him stain himself red by painting it with enamel paint that was not heat-resistant.

Suburban Types

London suburbs varied immensely in their economic and social character, but this variety rarely discouraged writers from generalizing about the typical suburban 'type'. One quality suburbanites had in common, most of them agreed, was a snobbish sensitivity to the social superiority of one suburb to another. C. F. G. Masterman, who wrote thoughtfully about London in *The Condition of England* in 1909, regarded the 'suburbans' as a new people, 'practically the product of the last half century', whose economic and political power was growing very rapidly. It was a power that was not feared, and rarely noticed, but which could be wielded decisively when it was roused. Suburban voters threw out the Progressives in the LCC elections of 1907, in a revolt against high property taxes, or rates, and gave the Conservatives a majority in London (once a Liberal stronghold) in every parliamentary election between 1885 and 1910, except in the Liberal landslide of 1906. Masterman, a Liberal, did not find these suburban instincts very appealing: 'Listen to the conversation in the second-class carriages of a suburban railway train, or examine the literature and journalism specially constructed for the suburban mind; you will often find endless chatter about the King, the Court, the doings of a designated "Society" . . . Liberated from the devils of poverty, the soul is still empty, swept and garnished, waiting for other occupants. This is the explanation of the so-called "snobbery" of the suburbs . . . Suburban life has often little conception of social services, no tradition of disinterested public duty, but a limited outlook beyond a personal ambition.' Suburban man, 'a unit in a crowd which has drifted away from the realities of life in a complex, artificial city civilization . . . comes to see no other universe than this – the rejoicing over hired sportsmen who play before him, the ingenuities of sedentary guessing competitions, the huge frivolity and ignorance of the world of the music hall and the Yellow newspaper.' The Yellow Press, an American phrase first used in England in the late 1890s, referred to popular sensationalist newspapers, such as the *Daily Mail* and *Daily Express*.

Masterman thought that this intellectual shallowness, which was so easily exploited by the imperialistic press, stemmed from the failure of commercial work and suburban life to bring the London middle classes into contact with the problems and experiences of other social groups:

> They are the creations not of the industrial, but of the commercial and business activities of London. They form a homogenous civilization – detached, self-centred, unostentatious – covering the hills along the northern and southern boundaries of the city, and spreading their conquests over the quiet fields beyond . . . It is a life of Security; a life of Sedentary occupation; a life of Respectability; and these three qualities give the key to its special characteristics. Its male population is engaged in all its working hours in small, crowded offices, under artificial light, doing immense sums, adding up other men's accounts, writing other men's letters. It is sucked into the City at daybreak, and scattered again as darkness falls. It finds itself towards evening in its own territory in the miles and miles of little red houses in little silent streets, in number defying imagination. Each boasts its pleasant drawing-room, its bow-window, its little front garden, its high-sounding title – 'Acacia Villa' or 'Camperdown Lodge' – attesting unconquered human aspiration. There are many interests beyond the working hours: here a greenhouse filled with chrysanthemums, there a tiny grass patch with bordering flowers; a chicken-house, a bicycle shed, a tennis-lawn. The women, with their

single domestic servants, now so difficult to get, and so exacting when found, find time hang rather heavy on their hands. But there are excursions to shopping centres in the West End, and pious sociabilities, and occasional theatre visits, and the interests of home . . . You may see the whole suburbs in August transported to the more genteel of the southern watering-places.[21]

Yet Masterman did not despair of suburban Londoners. The social service ideal was making headway amongst them, and their children were well educated and well fed, 'the healthiest and most hopeful promise for the future of modern England'. In time, it was possible that a suburban culture would develop that did not consist of apeing those above them in the social hierarchy and fearing those below them, and that shilling editions of the World's Classics (first published in 1901) would replace halfpenny newspapers as the reading matter that shaped their minds.

Garden Suburbs

Ever since the Middle Ages there had been voices arguing that London was growing too large for its own and the country's good. In 1598 John Stow, London's first great historian, had lamented the loss of the fields of his childhood to the growth of Hog Lane (Petticoat Lane) and Houndsditch, just beyond the City wall. Four hundred years later Walter Besant, a great lover of late Victorian London, regretted the disappearance of the beautiful hills, heaths, orchards, and pastures to the south of London under the streets of Wandsworth, Streatham, Tooting, and Norwood. Most Londoners could no longer walk out into unspoilt countryside, as they could when Besant was a boy in the 1840s. Journals like the *Builder* and *Building News* often criticized suburban developers for building on ill-drained or marshy land, and for building so poorly and in such density that the rustic delights that initially attracted settlers to suburban neighbourhoods were destroyed. In many places all that remained of their rustic charm was their name – Shepherd's Bush, Camberwell Green, Maida Vale, Kensal Rise – and others that retained real connections with the countryside would soon lose them if the suburban tide continued to flow. But what could be done? As the *Building News* put it in 1900: 'Go where we will – north, south, east or west of this huge overgrown Metropolis – the fungus-like growth of houses manifests itself, stretching from town to suburb and village – as from the southern suburbs to Herne Hill and Dulwich, and from Streatham to Croydon . . . This is one of the social revolutions of the age.'²² More hot-headed commentators expressed their concerns in stronger terms. William Morris, in a lecture on Art and Socialism in 1884, denounced London as a 'spreading sore . . . swallowing up with its loathsomeness field and wood and heath without mercy and without hope', and even Lord Rosebery, the Chairman of the LCC, spoke of London, in 1891, as 'a tumour, an elephantiasis sucking into its gorged system half the life and blood and bone of the rural districts'. Morris's answer to the urban problem, that towns should contain more green space and at the same time use up less of the countryside, seemed to depend on a catastrophic fall in population.

Critics of the spread of ugly and uniform suburbs into London's rural hinterland could advocate one or other of two opposing policies. In the first they could call for limits to be set on London's growth, perhaps by the creation of a 'green belt' of open land protected from development by law. This was the policy advocated in the 1930s by Raymond Unwin, Patrick Abercrombie, and the Council for the Preservation of Rural England, which was founded in 1926. Very little was heard of this idea before 1914, although there were hints of it in a resolution passed by the LCC in July 1891. The LCC asked its Parks and Open Spaces Committee to consider alerting Parliament 'to the need of statutory control and direction as to the extension of building in the suburbs of the County of London and in the adjacent parts of neighbouring counties, as affecting the health and sanitary condition generally of the metropolis'. Nothing came of this, although the Chairman of the Parks Committee, Lord Meath, had written a report in 1890 suggesting that London might copy the parkways of Boston and Chicago, giving itself a narrow belt of recreational land on the edge of the presently built-up area, with further development beyond it. Meath's suggestion was intended to make London's suburbs more healthy and well supplied with parkland, not to stop them growing.²³ Ebenezer Howard, the founding father of the Garden City movement, took the argument further in his book, *Tomorrow: a Peaceful Path to Real Reform*, in 1898. Howard proposed that the remedy for the excessive growth in London's economy and population was the creation of planned garden cities, which were separate from the larger city but linked to it by rail. Howard's proposal, that cities should grow by establishing new garden cities, was an alternative to suburban sprawl, but not an explicit call for a physical limit to be placed on London's growth, and certainly not a plan for reducing the loss of countryside to urbanization. Howard's ideal was turned into reality in 1903 when a group of businessmen and others inspired by him bought a 3,800-acre estate in Hertfordshire, twenty-five miles from the outskirts of London, and built Letchworth Garden City.

The other favoured idea among those who believed that the free-market process of suburban expansion should be modified in some way was to force or encourage developers to build at lower densities, thus using more land, not less. This was the message in 1904 of the influential Inter-Departmental Committee on Physical Deterioration, which was set up after the Boer War to consider the reasons for the poor physical quality of wartime recruits to the British army. Picking up the familiar idea that urban conditions undermined individual and national health, the Committee advocated local authority planning controls to stop the reproduction of inner-city slum conditions in the suburbs. Its aim was to prevent racial degeneration through overcrowding, not to preserve the countryside. The Garden Suburb movement, pioneered by Jonathan Carr and his architect Norman Shaw in Bedford Park in the 1870s and by Henrietta Barnett and Raymond Unwin in Hampstead Garden Suburb in the 1900s, followed the same thinking. Its intention was to create suburbs which did not reproduce inner city congestion and uniformity by swamping and destroying the natural landscape, but rather used it to create suburban communities that were healthy, invigorating, and beautiful, combining the best qualities of town and country for the sake of their lucky inhabitants. There was no thought here of preserving rural England from suburban sprawl, since garden suburbs were built at low densities, using up far more of the countryside than the terraces of Tooting or Willesden.

A practical example of what could be done was set by Henrietta Barnett, the wife of Samuel Barnett, who had been rector of St Jude's, Whitechapel and Warden of Toynbee Hall in the 1880s and 1890s. Henrietta Barnett had drawn the lesson from her work in Whitechapel that well-built suburbs and cheap transport offered the poor the best way out of the slums. Her friend Octavia Hill, who had devoted her life to improving working-class housing, arrived at the same conclusion. As a campaigner for the preservation of commons (including Hampstead Heath) and one of the founders, in 1895, of the National Trust, Hill combined a commitment to eradicating slums with an equally strong desire not to do so by obliterating the countryside. Their answer was the garden suburb. In 1905–6 Henrietta Barnett and the other founders of the Hampstead Garden Suburb Trust, including Earl Grey and the Bishop of London, raised over £200,000 to buy from the Eton College Trustees a 256-acre estate in Hendon and Finchley just north of the Hampstead Heath extension. Their intention was to build a well-planned suburb which would enable working people from central London to rent cottages with gardens within a twopenny journey of their London jobs, to promote social harmony and integration by building some bigger houses for the well-off, and to preserve the natural beauty of the area by saving trees, hedgerows, and open spaces, maintaining an average density of eight houses an acre.

The suburb was begun by the Garden Suburb Development Company in 1907, and continued by Hampstead Tenants Ltd and other co-partnership societies. A special Hampstead Garden Suburb Act in 1906, and the more general 1909 Town Planning Act, gave the Trust control over the way the suburb was built. The design and building were carried out by Letchworth's architects, Raymond Unwin and Barry Parker, who showed the influence of the Arts and Crafts movement in their choice of traditional materials and Tudor, seventeenth-century, and Georgian building styles. The streets of the suburb followed the contours of the land, and used curves, cul-de-sacs, squares, and pedestrian alleys to avoid the drab uniformity of other suburbs. The central square, with two churches, two parsonages, and an Institute, all well designed by Edwin Lutyens, was intended to provide a geographical and cultural focus to the community, though the absence of pubs, shops, cafes, and entertainment (except for those who enjoyed church services) suggested that the trustees were not really in tune with those they intended to rescue from the slums. The suburb was an immediate success, and a powerful influence on the emerging town-planning movement. Even forty years later the work of Unwin, Parker, and Lutyens was impressive. Nikolaus Pevsner, not easily pleased, regarded it as 'the aesthetically most satisfactory and socially most successful of all twentieth-century garden suburbs', and Michael Robbins wrote: 'It is a pleasure to walk through with the eyes open (which distinguishes it from most suburbs); there is nothing to shock, either with ugliness or audacity. It pleases, and it does not astonish.' Henrietta Barnett's hopes for a mixed community were much less successful. The social tone of Hampstead Garden Suburb and its lack of good transport links with central London prevented it from attracting people from the London slums, and rising rents and house prices soon excluded them, whether they were attracted or not.[24]

The two parliamentary debates on the Town Planning Bill in 1908 and 1909 provide a fair reflection of prevailing views on suburban growth.

Although John Burns, the President of the Local Government Board, opened with an attack on 'the damage being inflicted upon rural England by the indiscriminate unorganised spreading, without control, of straggling suburbs', the debate itself, and the Town Planning Act that it produced, was dominated by support for low-density, land-hungry 'rustic' development exemplified by Hampstead Garden Suburb and spacious 'model' towns like Bournville and Port Sunlight. The 1909 Town Planning Act was entirely concerned with new suburban development, and promoting the growth of spacious suburbs that were well supplied with parks and gardens, and not at all with preserving the countryside. Low density was the guiding principle of the early town-planning movement, promoted in the writings of such town-planning pioneers as Raymond Unwin, and enshrined in the influential Tudor Walters standards of 1917–18, which recommended that public housing should not exceed twelve houses to the acre. The architect Trystan Edwards, who in 1913 attacked Garden Cities and Garden Suburbs as examples of fake rusticity, combining the worst of town and country and ignoring the advantages of compact and well-planned towns surrounded by undefiled countryside, was 'a lone voice, preaching what seemed barbarous heresy'. A generation later, this heresy would become the new orthodoxy.[25]

The 1909 Act, which gave important but ill-defined planning powers to the Local Government Board if suburban development proposals were presented to it, was largely ineffective, as the uncontrolled sprawl of the 1920s demonstrates. One of the few London suburbs to be developed before 1914 under the system it introduced was Ruislip–Northwood, in north-west Middlesex. Ruislip was an isolated agricultural community until the arrival of the Metropolitan Railway's Uxbridge branch in 1904. After that the largest landowner, King's College Cambridge, planned to build a 1,300-acre garden suburb, and the new Ruislip–Northwood urban district council, using its powers under the 1909 Act, increased this to a 6,000-acre development designed on the best modern town-planning principles. The outcome was judged by the historian of Middlesex to be one of 'the best examples in Middlesex of suburban development decently carried out, with reasonable conformity of new building with old and a sensible conservation of natural and historical features'.[26]

The London Society, which was formed in 1912 with the aim (among others) of persuading governments to take a comprehensive and planned view of London's future development, published a volume of essays in 1921 called *The Future of London*. By this time attitudes towards suburban expansion and its consumption of the countryside had become rather more critical. Raymond Unwin, the architect of Letchworth and Hampstead Garden Suburb, argued now that London was far too large, and in need of restriction or reduction. 'It is high time that a green belt were preserved around London to protect its inhabitants from disease, by providing fresh air, fresh fruit and vegetables, space for recreation and contact with and knowledge of nature.' Unwin recommended the decentralization of industry and population, and the creation of satellite towns and detached dormitory suburbs. His argument for a green belt to encircle and restrict London was echoed by W. R. Davidge, the Society's expert on London housing, and by David Niven, its authority on parks and open spaces. All three, in contrast to the defenders of London's vast Green Belt today, emphasized the recreational value of the protected land, and had in mind a green space that was only a mile wide, or even less, interrupting London's development, rather than stopping it altogether.[27]

*

CHAPTER TWELVE

GROWING UP

The long-standing English distaste for flats and apartments was breaking down in the later nineteenth century, especially among well-off bachelors who preferred central to suburban living but could not afford a house in the West End. Victoria Street, which was built up in the 1850s and 1860s, was the pioneer of middle-class apartment blocks (or 'mansion flats'), with flats of three or four bedrooms and servants' quarters. Almost the whole street was lined with six-storey blocks, reaching from one side street to the next, dull from the outside but comfortable within. Nearly all of these, including Westminster Chambers, Grosvenor Mansions, Windsor House ('a nightmare of megalomaniac decoration' built in 1881–3),[1] Albert Mansions (1870), and 137–67 Victoria Street, London's first mansion block, have now been demolished, but Artillery Mansions (designed by John Calder in 1895) survive to remind us of London's flirtation with apartments in the Parisian style. These blocks were high, but not dramatically different in size from others in London. But about a hundred yards north of Victoria Street, at the corner of Petty France and Broadway (opposite St James's Park station), where the house in which Milton had begun *Paradise Lost* still stood, the banker Henry Hankey commissioned an apartment block on a much larger scale. The first block of this exceptionally plain building, which was called Queen Anne's Mansions, was built nine storeys high in the mid-1870s, but in 1888 the owners added a fourteen-storey extension, which made it London's (and Europe's) tallest apartment block by far. Generally, masonry buildings of this height would need walls so thick at the base that the space gained in the upper floors would be lost in the lower ones, but Hankey's architect used brick internal and external walls that were less than three feet thick at the base, to produce a structure strong enough to survive a direct hit from a German bomb in 1940. This 180-foot monster, its plain yellow brick soon blackened by the city's smoky air, was London's highest residential building until after the Second

World War, and one of its most disliked. It was finally demolished in the 1970s to make way for the Home Office.

Going Up

The technology that made Queen Anne's Mansions and other apartment blocks possible was the hydraulic lift. Cranes and goods lifts powered by water pressure had been in general use in docks, warehouses, and factories in London and elsewhere since the 1850s, and the Colosseum in Regent's Park had a steam-powered passenger lift, or 'ascending room', in the 1830s. The first hydraulic safety lifts (made by Elisha Otis) were introduced in some New York stores and hotels in the 1850s, and similar lifts were installed in two hotels in Victoria Street in 1859 and 1862. In the simplest hydraulic lifts the passenger cage was attached to the top of a very long ram or plunger which rose and fell inside a pipe set deeply into the ground, propelled by the water pressure inside the pipe, but in most lifts the cage was connected to the plunger by a series of tackles and pulleys. Usually a steam engine forced water into the pipe to raise the lift, and a stopcock drew the water off to lower it. A counterweight moved within an iron guide to make it easier to lift the cage. There were hydraulic lifts in several big London hotels in the 1860s, and by the 1880s customers of smart hotels like the First Avenue Hotel in High Holborn and the Métropole in Northumberland Avenue expected to reach their rooms by lift. The high apartment blocks built in Victoria Street, Duke Street, Edgware Road, and Kensington in the 1870s and 1880s nearly all had lifts, and would not have attracted tenants for the upper floors without them.

These early lifts were generally operated with water tanks on the top floors of the building, with gas or steam pumps in the basement to keep them filled. But in 1882 a company was formed with the intention of laying high-pressure (700lb per square inch) water mains to supply hydraulic power (initially) to the City of London, parts of Southwark, and Victoria Street in Westminster from a steam-powered pumping station on Bankside, just to the east of Blackfriars Bridge. The advantage of this was that the power could be more efficiently generated from a cheaper site, and that the generating capacity of the company would be far less than the total needed by many localized enterprises, because the company's customers would never all want power at the same time. The company charged less than the London water companies, and their supply, unlike that of the water companies, was uninterrupted, and of a consistently high pressure. As demand for hydraulic power grew, the London Hydraulic Power Company (as it was called from 1884) gradually extended its mains network, especially into the West End, from about 20 miles in 1888 to about 100 miles in 1900 and 150 miles in 1910. The company's pipes (up to 10 inches in diameter) crossed the Thames by three bridges, the Rotherhithe Tunnel, and the Tower Subway, which the company bought. The number of machines connected to the system rose from about 4,000 in 1895 to about 8,000 in 1912, and of these over half were passenger or goods lifts in hotels, offices, apartment buildings, railway stations, and warehouses. Other users of hydraulic power included cranes and hoists, capstans, dock gates, a vacuum- and water-powered street-cleaning system known as the Silent Dustman (invented in 1910), and high-pressure fire hydrants, invented by the great tunneller James Greathead. These hydrants were installed in many buildings with a high fire risk, including New Scotland Yard, the National Gallery, and Queen Anne's Mansions.

In 1890 Waygood and Company, the biggest lift-maker in Britain, exhibited the country's first electric lift at the Crystal Palace exhibition, and in America Otis had installed electric lifts that ran as well and as economically as hydraulic ones. Electric power's higher transmission losses and the higher installation costs of electric lifts enabled hydraulic power to hold its own against the new competitor in the 1890s, but by 1900 some hydraulic lifts were being converted to electricity, and by about 1908 the number of passenger lifts served by the London Hydraulic Power Company had started to fall. The company still supplied power to nearly 4,500 goods and passenger lifts in London in 1915, and carried on pumping until 1977. In 1985 its 150-mile pipe network was sold to Mercury, the telecommunications company, as duct for its cables, and Peter Barlow's Tower Subway, which has carried cable cars, pedestrians, hydraulic pipes, and fibre-optic cables, remains as a reminder of the hundred-year journey from steam power to the Internet.[2]

The London Building Acts

Queen Anne's Mansions, and a few other tall blocks built in the 1880s, provoked a reaction in the Metropolitan Board of Works and (after 1888) the LCC against the construction of disproportionately high buildings in London. The MBW had not been inactive against over-ambitious developers, but its powers had been patchy and imprecise. The Board had managed to force Jabez Balfour and his associate, the builder James Hobbs, to reduce the height of their apartment block on Knightsbridge, Hyde Park Court, by two storeys in 1888. Others, including some MPs, were outraged that Hyde Park Court might cast a shadow over Hyde Park and the Serpentine, and campaigned for a limit of sixty feet or (on wider streets) the width of the street. The outcome of the dispute over this and Queen Anne's Mansions was the London Council (General Powers) Act of 1890, which set a limit of ninety feet plus two storeys in the roof, and the stronger and more comprehensive London Building Act of 1894, which reduced this limit by ten feet.[3] According to the 1894 Act, in streets formed after 1862 new buildings could not be higher than the width of the street, and in wider streets the maximum height of the main frontage of a building was set at eighty feet. With two extra floors set into the roof above the cornice, a builder could reach a height of about a hundred feet, or perhaps a little more with a steeply pitched roof. These regulations were amended in 1909 to take account of the introduction of steel-framed and reinforced-concrete building techniques, but the statutory height restriction remained in force until the 1950s, postponing for over half a century the arrival of commercial or residential 'skyscrapers' in London.[4]

As a result, Queen Anne's Mansions, generally considered one of the ugliest buildings in London, was unchallenged as London's tallest residential building until the 1950s, and interwar London had a skyline dominated by church spires, cathedral domes, monumental columns, and the Houses of Parliament. So the quality which Henry James, writing in 1888, had called 'the great misfortune of London', 'its want of elevation', and therefore its failure to make a striking architectural impression, was still evident over twenty years later, when another American writer, Theodore Dreiser, made his first visit. After living in Chicago and New York, he found the West End 'beautiful, spacious, cleanly, dignified and well ordered, but not astonishingly imposing', and the city as a whole surprisingly low. 'The thing that interested me about London was that it was endless and that there were no high buildings – nothing over four or five stories as a rule – though now and then you actually find eight- and nine-story buildings – and that it was homey and simple and sad in some respects.'[5] Dreiser would have found the same state of affairs all over Europe. Until the building of the Gran Via in Madrid, which was not started until 1910, none of the main European cities had anything to compare with the high-rise avenues of Chicago and New York.

The 1894 height restrictions were motivated by Parliament's and the LCC's dislike of huge buildings that cut out light, blocked views, invaded privacy, and destroyed urban proportion, and by the belief that skyscrapers could never be made safe from fires. The Metropolitan Fire Brigade's old-fashioned extending ladders could not rescue people from very high buildings, and even the motorized telescopic turntable ladders introduced in 1905 were only eighty-two feet long. There was a fire in the top floors of Hyde Park Court in 1899, without loss of life, after which an external fire escape was installed. In other countries hook ladders were used to scale very tall buildings, but the London brigade did not get these until after June 1902, when ten working women burned to death on the fourth and fifth floors of a commercial building in Queen Victoria Street, watched by a large crowd, because the stairs were on fire and the rescue ladders were too short.

Since the limits set by the 1894 London Building Act were not far short of those that could be reached by conventional masonry construction, they did not cause much controversy among engineers, builders, and architects. But in Chicago new methods were being pioneered in the 1880s and 1890s which would abolish the practical twelve-storey limit on flats and office blocks. Chicago's solution to the problem of load-bearing walls was to use an iron or steel framework, just as the builders of modern bridges did, and as Joseph Paxton had done in his Crystal Palace in 1851, and to clothe it in brick, stone, and glass. In Chicago, whose central district had been destroyed by the disastrous fire of 1871, there was a strong demand for new commercial property, and building controls and traditions were weak. In 1883 William Le Baron Jenney's ten-storey Home Insurance Building, the world's tallest office building, was constructed with cast-iron columns, and with beams of wrought iron up to the sixth floor and Bessemer steel for the rest. Brick and glass cladding protected the building, but did not support it. 'Skyscraper', a word previously used for a tall sail, man, or story, was commandeered to describe buildings over about twelve storeys in 1883, when the sky was much lower than it is today. During the 1880s Chicago architects moved from iron to steel, and made less use of brick supporting walls. Following Chicago's lead, New York got its first iron-framed building, the Tower Building at 50 Broadway, in 1888. At ten storeys and 158 feet, it was smaller than Queen Anne's Mansions, but the sixteen-storey 309-foot steel-framed *New York World* (or Pulitzer) Building, completed in 1890, was in a different class, a true skyscraper.[6] For four years, until the Manhattan Life Insurance Building beat it by forty feet, it was the tallest office building in the world.

Although London was keen to learn from Chicago's transport and retailing systems, British engineers and architects seem to have taken little interest in what was happening in the Chicago and New York construction industry in the 1880s and 1890s. When the 1894 London Building Act was passed the *Builder* did not comment on the disparity between the legal limit it set and the height to which steel-framed buildings could now safely be built, and the two or three articles on steel-framed construction in building and engineering journals in the 1890s did not suggest that it might be adopted in England.[7] London (and England) had to wait until 1906 to see its first steel-framed building, the Ritz Hotel, which was designed by the French-based firm of Mewès and Davis. Even in this revolutionary building, and the others that soon followed it, the steel structure was well hidden behind very traditional stone walls. Inveresk House (the *Morning Post* offices on the Aldwych, 1906–7), Marshall Mackenzie's Waldorf Hotel (Aldwych, 1907) and the Savoy extension on the Strand (1907–9), all pretended to be traditional buildings. The same was true of London's reinforced-concrete buildings, which used techniques developed in France in the 1880s. The first of these, all built between 1907 and 1911, were Sir Arthur Blomfield's Friars' House in New Broad Street, Norman Shaw's Portland House in Lloyd's Avenue, the King Edward Building of the General Post Office, built on King Edward Street by Sir Henry Tanner and L. G. Mouchel, and Mewès and Davis' Royal Automobile Club on Pall Mall. Only three pre-war office buildings, Sir John Burnet's Kodak House (now the Gallaher Building, Kingsway, 1911), F. W. Troup's Blackfriars House (New Bridge Street, 1913) and H. P. Berlage's Holland House (Bury Street, 1914), dared to declare the modernity of their steel framework in the rational and unadorned style of their outer stonework, though the steel-framed Selfridge's building, with nothing between its traditional Ionic columns but metal and glass, told half the truth.[8]

London's local and central politicians were conservative in matters of urban aesthetics, and so, in general, were its developers, architects, builders, and engineers. After the introduction of steel-and-concrete-framed buildings the LCC and the Local Government Board might have raised the height limit on London buildings to the twenty storeys (with a two-storey basement) that London's blue-clay subsoil could comfortably support. They consulted engineering and architectural bodies in the preparation of a revised Building Act in 1909, but the advice they got was hesitant and unclear, and although rules on wall thickness were relaxed, those on height were not.[9] The enforcement of these rules meant that while builders in Chicago and Manhattan, using steel frames, light brick and glass cladding, and fast safety lifts, reached 390 feet in the 1890s (Park Row Building, Manhattan), and almost 800 feet before the First World War (the Woolworth Building, 1913), London developers made do with buildings no higher than those they could have built in the 1880s. Even without the 1894 Act it is likely that there would have been few really tall office or residential buildings in London before 1914. Most Edwardian hotels and offices, even those with steel or ferro-concrete skeletons, stopped well short of the legal limit, and only rose towards 100 feet in the last years before the Great War. Although London's office and housing rents were high, and steel was cheap and plentiful, London was not a blank sheet, as central Chicago was after 1871, and it did not suffer the land shortage of Manhattan. For house builders, suburban development served by improving public transport offered a convenient and popular alternative to high apartment blocks, and for City businesses it was cheaper and easier to replace older three- or four-storey commercial or non-commercial buildings with six- or seven-storey offices, or to spread out from the City into Holborn, Westminster, and Finsbury.[10]

The Spreading Office World

Finsbury, the busy industrial district to the north of London Wall, began to be drawn into the City's office world in 1899–1901, when the old buildings between the southern half of Finsbury Circus and London Wall were demolished and replaced with modern six- and seven-storey offices, including Electra House, John Belcher's baroque headquarters for the Eastern Telegraph Company. Over the next few years nearly all the streets round Finsbury Circus, from Moorgate and Finsbury Pavement to Eldon Street and Blomfield Street, lost some of their old houses and gained large stone office blocks with such names as Finsbury Court and Moorgate Hall. On New Broad Street, running off Blomfield Street, all the Georgian brick houses were replaced by impressive seven-storey stone offices, designed by F. W. Marks, A. C. Blomfield, C. A. Voysey and others, after 1900. Further north, the western half of Finsbury Square was rebuilt before 1914 with offices for the London Friendly Society and the London and Manchester Assurance Company. The eastern end of the City, beyond Bishopsgate and

Gracechurch Street, had fewer large offices than the western City, but this started to change when shipping offices were built along the new Lloyd's Avenue after 1899, the new Baltic Exchange was built on St Mary Axe in 1903, and Bishopsgate's fifteenth-century Crosby Hall was dismantled (and stored for later re-erection) in 1908 to make room for the Chartered Bank of India. Before 1914 new offices began to replace old shops, houses, and offices along Bishopsgate, King William Street, and Cornhill, and on the City's north-eastern border, Houndsditch began to lose its East End flavour. Sir Paul Pindar's beautiful Jacobean house on Bishopsgate was demolished for the expansion of Liverpool Street Station in 1890, and is now partly preserved in the Victoria and Albert Museum. Further south, all the old houses between Trinity Square and Seething Lane were removed to clear a space for the vast Port of London Building, which was built between 1912 and 1922.[11]

In the western half of the City there was extensive demolition and rebuilding in Newgate Street, where the Old Bailey replaced Newgate Prison in 1907, and in the area between Giltspur Street and King Edward Street, where the seventeenth-century Christ's Hospital school was demolished in 1902 to make way for new buildings for St Bartholomew's Hospital and a concrete-framed extension to the General Post Office, King Edward Building. St Martin le Grand had already lost its old houses and the Bull and Mouth coaching inn when the main General Post Office was built in the early 1890s. This was the building from which Marconi transmitted the first public wireless signals in July 1896. Next to it, in Postman's Park, there is a reminder that not all Londoners devoted themselves to pleasure or profit. In 1887 the painter and sculptor G. F. Watts proposed a memorial to Londoners who had died in saving the lives of others as a way of celebrating Victoria's golden jubilee. Nothing came of the idea, so in 1900 Watts erected a covered gallery in St Botolph's churchyard, with the heroic deeds recorded on Doulton tiles. Watts installed the first thirteen tablets before his death in 1904, and his wife added another thirty-four. The achievements of the powerful and talented are commemorated all over London, but only in Postman's Park are we reminded of the courage of Thomas Griffin, who died trying to rescue his mate in a boiler explosion in Battersea sugar refinery in 1890; Thomas Simpson, who died after rescuing many others when the ice broke on Highgate Ponds in 1885; Elizabeth Boxall, who was killed by a runaway horse as she rescued a child in Bethnal Green in 1888; Joseph Onslow, a lighterman who drowned in the Thames at Wapping trying to save a boy in 1885; eight-year-old

Henry Bristow, who died in saving his little sister by tearing off her
burning clothes in Walthamstow in 1890; young Alice Ayres, who died
saving three children from a burning house in Union Street, Borough, in
1885; or Frederick Mills, A. Rutter, Robert Durrant, and F. D. Jones, who
died trying to save a comrade in the East Ham sewage pumping works in
1895.

On Fleet Street, which was widened to sixty feet to cope with growing traffic in the years before the Great War, late Victorian and Edwardian
offices and banks were built alongside Georgian and half-timbered seventeenth-century houses. Number 194, Sir Arthur Blomfield's Law Courts
branch of the Bank of England (1886–8), now a public house, is a fine
example of a High Victorian financial building, and other interesting
Edwardian offices, including number 6, St Bartholomew House (1900),
and number 132, Mersey House (1907), also survive. Holborn, the other
main westward route out of the City, was transformed by Alfred Waterhouse's vast red-brick and terracotta Gothic Prudential Assurance building,
which was started in 1879 and mostly built between 1899 and 1906, and
by Gamage's three buildings, which replaced a set of old houses and inns
between 1895 and 1905. High Holborn, to the west, had nothing as grand
as the Prudential, but the Pearl Insurance building (1913) and Holborn
Town Hall (1908) gave parts of the street an Edwardian appearance. In
Bloomsbury, the Georgian development north of High Holborn and New
Oxford Street, the late Victorian and Edwardian incursion came in the form
of grand hotels. On Russell Square the palatial Russell Hotel, eight exu-
berant storeys of red brick and terracotta, was built in 1898, and the
Imperial Hotel, by the same architect (Charles Fitzroy Doll) and in similar materials, followed about ten years later. The other Bloomsbury squares
kept their Georgian harmony for a few more years, but in 1911 a vast
headquarters building for the YMCA brought Edwardian baroque with a
reinforced concrete frame to Great Russell Street.

Mansion Flats

The size and style of the middle-class apartments that were built in London
owed more to Paris than to New York and Chicago. The leading creative
force in the development of the London apartment block, as he was in the
London garden suburb, was Norman Shaw. Shaw used a style that was
called 'Queen Anne', Renaissance red brick with seventeenth-century

English and Dutch features, in his seven-storeyed Albert Hall Mansions, which were built between 1879 and 1886, and this style dominated the design of middle-class flats for the next twenty years, especially those planted in the previously small-scale and leafy court suburb of Kensington. Many blocks of a similar size and design followed in the 1880s and 1890s, including the electric-lit Kensington Court (1882–1902), Albert Court (1890), a huge block near the Albert Hall, and Hyde Park Mansions and Oxford and Cambridge Mansions, which were built on Marylebone Road in the 1890s. Kensington Court, occupying a site which once contained the notorious slums known as Jennings Buildings, was begun in 1882 by Jonathan Carr, probably with money raised from the sale of the Bedford Park Estate. Carr hoped to attract tenants by providing the very latest services, including gas, hydraulic lifts powered by a London Hydraulic Power Company pumping station at the southern tip of the Court (now 35 Kensington Court Place), and electricity supplied by Crompton's generating station, which was built at the Kensington High Street end of the development (now 46 Kensington Court) in 1886. Even with all these unprecedented inducements tenants were not very easy to find, and the fine mansion blocks on the western side of the development were not built until the end of the century.[12]

Architects and developers did not always follow Shaw's stylistic lead. Frank Verity, the architect of Hyde Park Place (12 Bayswater Road) and flats in Cleveland Row (St James's) and Portland Place, preferred a Parisian style, and Alfred Waterhouse used a French Renaissance style for Whitehall Court, which was built between 1885 and 1892, at the expense first of Jonathan Carr (the developer of Bedford Park and Kensington Court), and then of the swindler Jabez Balfour, who absconded from his flat in the development in 1892. Whitehall Court survived these rather shady beginnings to become a familiar and quite distinguished feature of the riverside skyline.[13] The demand for high-quality apartments was greatest in the West End, and blocks were built in Cavendish, Hanover, Berkeley, and Kensington Squares, and in St James's and Piccadilly in the 1890s. After 1890 mansion blocks spread to the richer suburbs, especially Maida Vale, St John's Wood, Regent's Park, Earl's Court, Fulham, Paddington, and Battersea, meeting and sometimes exceeding the demand of well-off tenants for apartments near the West End. Maida Vale began to acquire a 'Parisian' appearance in the 1890s, when Maida Vale Mansions (later Cunningham Court) went up, followed between 1900 and 1908 by Aberdeen, Blomfield, Alexandra, and Sandringham Courts, and (off the main road)

Carlton, Elgin, Ashworth, Biddulph, and Delaware Mansions. The dignified atmosphere created by the aristocratic or royal names of the red-brick blocks was rather spoiled by the general gossip that rich men with mistresses used their Maida Vale flats as love-nests.[14]

Mansion flats were considered especially suited to the needs of well-off bachelors, who wanted the services available in a good hotel, often including cooked meals served in their own flats, and did not want the trouble or expense of maintaining a house and garden. The architect Edwin Hall, writing on 'Flats – British and Foreign' in 1906, thought that flats would be a permanent and growing feature of the London scene, both in the centre and the suburbs, as long as developers paid attention to the nature of their market:

> Flats have passed through the crisis of fashion and become necessary under the economic conditions of today. There has been much wild speculation, it is true. Many of the flats so hastily built in London seem to be fitted for no particular class of the community. They appeal at random to some quite indefinite public, being neither luxurious enough for the rich nor cheap enough for the immense class engaged in precarious trades and professions ... Some years ago a 'fancy' rental could be obtained for any suite of rooms if it could be advertised as a flat. But competition has grown since then, and in future a very discreet consideration will have to be given to the requirements of different sections of the public.[15]

London Vanishing

In much of central London, developers replaced unprofitable Georgian and early Victorian buildings with modern six- or seven-storey shops, hotels, tenements, apartments, or offices as the opportunity arose, contributing to the mixture of heights and styles that still prevails in the City, Holborn, Finsbury, and Westminster today. The nearest that Edwardian architects and planners came to creating an uninterrupted twentieth-century cityscape was in the LCC's Aldwych and Kingsway development, perhaps the greatest road-building project in London since the construction of Regent Street. There had been talk of making a new route from the Strand to Holborn between Covent Garden and Lincoln's Inn Fields ever since the 1830s, but the MBW had more pressing tasks, and left it to the LCC.

The LCC deferred the plan until they could find a way sharing its cost between London ratepayers and the landlords whose property values would be enhanced by the development. The Council's intentions, as they were expressed in 1892, were to make a 100-foot wide thoroughfare from Holborn to the Strand and a new crescent-shaped road of the same width from Wellington Street to St Clement Danes, relieving congestion in the Strand, one of London's busiest roads. This would also improve commu-nications between Covent Garden and Lincoln's Inn, and 'open and improve one of the most insanitary and decaying quarters of London', the streets and alleys just north of the Strand. Oddly, the chairman of the LCC Improvements Committee that presented this proposal was the positivist philosopher Frederic Harrison, who had written a powerful essay in 1884 lamenting the disappearance of old London under new streets and build-ings. After many delays, Parliament sanctioned the whole scheme in 1899, and the Council started negotiations with the owners of property along the proposed route, including the *Morning Post* and *Echo* newspapers, the Gaiety and Globe theatres, the Strand Hotel, the Freemasons, and the London School Board. The whole site was surrounded with gigantic hoardings, which were soon covered in posters advertising Bovril, Capstan cigarettes, Allsopps Pale Ale, Bird's Custard, Sandow's Embrocation, Idris lemonade, *Reynolds' Newspaper*, Nestlé's Milk, and other popular consumer products.[16]

The neighbourhood that was demolished for the Strand and Aldwych development was usually described as decaying or disreputable, but it was also one of the most interesting survivals of old London. It was a poor area, mostly dark blue, light blue, and purple (very poor, poor, and mixed comfort and poverty) on Charles Booth's 1889 poverty map, but there were much worse streets between the Strand and Holborn, especially Parker Street, King Street, and Macklin Street (all off the northern end of Drury Lane), that were not on the chosen route. Wych Street, which ran from Clement Danes to the end of Drury Lane, and Holywell Street, which ran alongside the Strand between St Mary le Strand and Clement Danes churches, were lively streets full of early seventeenth-century gabled wooden and plastered houses, which had disappeared from the City in the Great Fire of 1666 and were increasingly rare in other parts of London. Contemporaries were divided in their attitudes to these old streets. Some saw them, as we might do, as precious fragments of a vanishing pre-Fire city, which should have been patched up and preserved. Since saving them seemed almost impossible, recording them was the next best thing. The

Society for Photographing Relics of Old London had been founded in 1875 to make a record of the streets, houses, and inns that were disappearing as the modern city overwhelmed what was left of the old one. Its three photographers, Alfred and John Bool and Henry Dixon, took pictures of Wych Street and Holywell Street in the 1870s, and did not view its dilapidated Jacobean houses and shops with the distaste that London's modernizers felt for them. Philip Norman's beautifully illustrated book *London Vanished and Vanishing*, published in 1905, was an extended lament for London's old inns, shops, and houses, which were demolished with very little restraint in the later nineteenth century. Norman's painting of Holywell Street in 1900, just before its destruction, was printed as the book's frontispiece.

Holywell Street, which was condemned by two mid-Victorian antiquarians as a 'narrow, inconvenient avenue of old, ill-formed houses', and 'a narrow, dirty lane, chiefly occupied by old clothesmen and the vendors of low publications', was one of London's main centres of second-hand bookselling, inferior only to Farringdon Road in importance. The fact that some of the books and prints sold there did not meet rigorous Victorian moral standards was often mentioned, but the enforcement of the 1857 Obscene Publications Act had tamed this trade. Holywell Street had even been renamed Booksellers' Row, in the hope that this would help it shed its shameful reputation. Still, in the 1890s, was known for its 'book shops of a low class', and the future novelist and critic Frank Swinnerton, then a newspaper office boy, used to loiter in the shops, unaware (so he said) of their reputation for selling paperbound copies of the *Decameron* and *The Awful Disclosures of Maria Monk*. When demolition drove the booksellers out of Holywell Street many of them moved to Charing Cross Road and its side-alleys, where they remain (but no longer cheap!) to this day. The flagship of their trade, selling books new and second-hand, was opened by the brothers William and Gilbert Foyle in Charing Cross Road in 1904.[17]

On 26 July 1898 Charles Booth took a walk with Police Constable Tait around the doomed streets north of the Strand, making notes for the revision of his poverty map. Wych Street had moved down from the pink of working-class comfort to the purple of 'comfort mixed with poverty', and Holywell Street, narrow and crowded with pedestrians, was lined with 'second class bookshops' and 'chemists of doubtful reputation', with 'waiters and shop assistants living overhead'. These were his notes on the neighbourhood in general:

Good temper and curiosity of the inhabitants of the courts. 'Government inspector, I suppose, anyone can see what the other is.' 'Don't
pull down our houses, Guvnor, before building us up others to go
into.' 'See he's taking our pictures, look yer best, Loiza.'

A hot, thundery day. Sleepy weedy men in the courts and streets,
& stout burly Irish women – a few drawn-faced children. Many small
public houses, full today of women and children. Messy streets. No
opium dens.[18]

The Aldwych and Kingsway

In all the Aldwych and Kingsway scheme involved the displacement and
rehousing of 6,872 people, about half to make way for the two roads, the
rest for the clearance of the Clare Market rookery, between the Aldwych
and Lincoln's Inn Fields. If the demolished district represented the old
world of London, with its dark courtyards, congested alleys, overcrowded
rooms, gin palaces, cheap scruffy shops, and rickety theatres, the new
streets stood for the spacious, well-organized, well-constructed, sober, free-
flowing imperial city that London was intended to become. Fifty-one
public houses, including several ancient ones, were demolished, but no new
licences were issued. Ramshackle, rat-infested, draughty, and dangerous
theatres were replaced with grand baroque buildings designed by one of
the greatest theatre architects of the day, W. G. R. Sprague. The Olympic
Theatre, on Maypole Alley and Wych Street, was demolished and not
replaced, and the Globe and the Opéra Comique, between Holywell and
Wych Streets, were closed for good. The much more successful Gaiety Theatre, which stood on the Strand and Catherine Street, closed in 1902 with
a final speech from Sir Henry Irving, and reopened on the Aldwych in
October 1903. Its demolition caused a great swarm of rats, which poured
into the Gaiety Restaurant before finding their way into the London sewer
system. Two new Sprague theatres were built on the crescent, the Aldwych
and the Strand Theatre, which both opened in 1905, and still stand today.
Narrow streets, often impenetrable to traffic, were replaced with two great
avenues 100 feet wide and a total of 3,300 feet long, with a shallow under-
pass in Kingsway (extended to the Embankment in 1907) for the LCC's
new single-decker electric trams.

Work on the great buildings that were meant to line the two new roads
progressed slowly. It took about fifteen years to fill all the sites along

Kingsway, and the Aldwych was incomplete until its centrepiece, Bush House, was finished in the 1930s. The LCC had organized a competition in 1900 to find the best architect for the Aldwych, judged by Norman Shaw, but it proved impossible to impose a uniform design on the individual property owners on the crescent, and the buildings, although most were in what Pevsner calls an 'Imperial Palladian style', were the work of several different architects. Inveresk House, the new offices of the *Morning Post*, was built in the Parisian classical style in 1907 by Mewès and Davis, the architects who did most to promote the French style in Edwardian London. As in the Ritz, their new hotel on Piccadilly, the fancy stonework of Inveresk House disguised a modern steel-framed building. Near the western end of the Aldwych curve, the twin Strand and Aldwych Theatres, both designed by C. J. Phipps, stood on either side of Marshall Mackenzie's French-style Waldorf Hotel (1907), also steel-framed, with a Palm Court within. Mackenzie also designed the steel-framed Australia House, built between 1911 and 1918 at the eastern end of the island block, which started to give the Aldwych the imperial flavour that some of its advocates had wanted. On the southern side of this island block, the rebuilt and widened Strand, Norman Shaw designed the Gaiety Theatre and Restaurant in 1903. The restaurant failed, and the building became the headquarters of the Marconi wireless company. The large sites later occupied by Bush House and India House were still empty in 1914.

Parts of Kingsway achieved a greater uniformity, because so many of the buildings lining the road were designed by one architectural practice, Trehearne and Norman. Central, Imperial, Regent, Windsor, and York Houses were built just before the Great War, and Alexandra, Victory, Ingersoll, Princes, Crown, Africa, and Connaught Houses between 1916 and 1922. Their imposing stone fronts and giant columns gave Kingsway the desired combination of commercial efficiency and imperial dignity, but could not inspire affection or interest. On the eastern side of Kingsway there was the London Opera House, designed by Frank Matcham and built by Oscar Hammerstein of New York at vast expense in 1910. It failed, and later became a cinema, the Stoll Picture Theatre. Many of these buildings were superficially Victorian but essentially modern, with electric lighting, lifts, steel frames, and so on, but only one building on Kingsway declared its modernity in its exterior design. This was Kodak House (now the Gallaher Building), built by Sir John Burnet and Thomas Tait in 1911 for the American photographic company, without baroque stonework or classical columns, and looking like the modern steel-framed building that it was.[19]

Burnet's other work in London at this time included designing the Edward VII galleries at the back of the British Museum and supervising the building of Selfridge's department store in Oxford Street. To alleviate Kingsway's overwhelming commercialism, the Belcher and Joass partnership was commissioned to build one church in the new street. Joass produced the rather beautiful Holy Trinity, with a concave front and a domed portico, built in the Edwardian baroque style that was often used for offices, but rarely for churches. Money ran out before the church was finished, so it has no spire and most of its interior brick walls are pleasantly unplastered. The same partnership designed Whiteley's store in Queensway (1908–12) and the artificial mountains of the Mappin Terraces for the bears in London Zoo in 1914.

The Kingsway and Aldwych development seems a modest enough concession to modern architecture and town planning, compared with the skyscrapers of Chicago and Manhattan, but to some Londoners it represented the wanton destruction of old London for the sake of offices and traffic flow. Wilfred Whitten (John O'London), writing in 1913, regarded the scheme as 'the greatest evisceration of the town that has been known since the Fire of 1666', in which 'all the traditions of piecemeal change, casualness, and compromise which have made London picturesque were flouted'.[20] And one of the wittiest men of the age, Max Beerbohm, regarded the Americanization of old London, and the quality of the architects involved in it, with a gloomy contempt:

'The Rebuilding of London' proceeds ruthlessly apace. The humble old houses that dare not scrape the sky are being duly punished for their timidity. Down they come; and in their place are shot up new tenements, quick and high as rockets. And the little old streets, so narrow and exclusive, so shy and crooked – we are making an example of them, too. We lose our way in them, do we? – we whose time is money. Our omnibuses can't trundle through them, can't they? Very well, then. Down with them! We have no use for them. This is the age of 'noble arteries'.

'The Rebuilding of London' is a source of much pride and pleasure to most of London's citizens, especially to them who are county councillors, builders, contractors, navvies, glaziers, decorators, and so forth. There is but a tiny residue of persons who do not swell and sparkle. And of these glum bystanders at the carnival I am one . . .

. . . Long before the close of the Victorian Era our architects had ceased to be creative. They could not express in their work the spirit

of their time. They could but evolve a medley of old styles, some foreign, some native, all inappropriate. Take the case of Mayfair. Mayfair
has for some years been in a state of transition . . . Let me show you
Mount Street. Let me show you that airy stretch of sham antiquity,
and defy you to say that it symbolises, how remotely soever, the spirit
of its time. Mount Street is typical of the new Mayfair. And the new
Mayfair is typical of the new London. In the height of these new
houses, in the width of these new roads, future students will find,
doubtless, something characteristic of this pressing and bustling age.
But from the style of the houses he will learn nothing at all. The style
might mean anything; and means, therefore, nothing. . . . Every street
in London is being converted into a battlefield of styles, all shrieking
at one another, all murdering one another. The tumult may be exciting, especially to the architects, but it is not beautiful. It is not good
to live in.[21]

*

CHAPTER THIRTEEN

A Revolution in Transport

A city of London's vast size and population was dependent for its survival and growth on its system of transport. London's growth earlier in the century had been promoted by the introduction of omnibus services and steam-powered underground and surface railways, and between the 1880s and 1914 London was transformed by five new forms of transport, all of them based on the new technology of the late nineteenth century – the electric tram, the electric deep-level Tube, the safety bicycle, the motor car, and the motor bus.

Hansoms and Four-Wheelers

London in the 1880s and 1890s was a city full of horses. Horse-drawn omnibuses and trams had to compete for space on London's streets with a vast number of horse-drawn carts, cabs, coaches, and carriages. There were about 40,000 horses involved in the West End carriage trade in the 1890s, though the difficulty of driving private carriages on London's increasingly congested streets discouraged many well-off Londoners from keeping their own vehicles. There were at least 1,500 trams in London in the 1890s, needing about 15,000 horses, and another 40,000 were used for pulling omnibuses (about eleven per bus) in 1902. The number of trade vehicles is harder to establish, but informed observers thought that London had between 60,000 and 80,000 carts and vans, with roughly one horse each, in the early 1890s. Finally, there were about 11,000 horse-drawn carriages for private hire (or Hackney carriages), employing about 22,000 horses. This gives us a grand total of about 180,000 horses on London's streets and in its stables, allowing for a little guesswork.[1]

There were two types of horse cab for hire. In the late 1890s there were 7,000 two-wheeled 'hansoms', carrying two or three passengers, and 4,000 'four-wheelers', which could take four, with a fifth next to the driver.

Each type of cab was pulled by a single horse, but hansoms, unlike four-wheelers, usually had a change of horses during the day. Four-wheelers, also known as 'growlers', were useful for larger parties with luggage, but they were usually badly sprung, poorly maintained, and slow. Those who preferred speed, comfort, and style to safety and luggage space took a hansom, 'the gondola of London', the city's most glamorous and enjoyable form of transport. The inventor of this much-loved vehicle, Joseph Hansom, the architect of Birmingham Town Hall and the founder of the *Builder* newspaper, died in London in 1882. The special feature of the late nineteenth-century hansom was that its driver sat or stood behind the passenger compartment, taking instructions through a trap-door in its roof. The general opinion was that hansom drivers were smart and skilful, and that their horses were young and sprightly, while 'growler' drivers and their horses were usually nearing the end of their working lives. This is W. D. Howells' view of the hansom in 1905, only a few years before its extinction: 'anything more like a song does not move on wheels, and its rapid rhythm suggests the quick play of fancy in that impetuous form . . . A hansom is always cheerfully intelligent. It will set you down at the very place you seek; you need walk neither to it nor from it; a nod, a glance, summons it or dismisses . . . It takes all the responsibility for your prompt and unerring arrival; and you may trust it almost implicitly.'[2]

There were about 15,000 licensed cab drivers in London in 1902, but only two or three thousand of these drove their own cabs. All of these men were licensed by the police under the Metropolitan Public Carriages Act of 1869, and were bound to keep their vehicles in good condition and to prove to an examiner that they had a good working knowledge of London's 30,000 streets. Most drivers worked for one of London's many cab firms, which generally operated between five and ten cabs, and seven to fifteen horses. There were some bigger companies, and one, the London Improved Cab Company, had 800 employees and over a thousand horses at its stables and coachworks in Pakenham Street, near the Mount Pleasant Postal Sorting Office. A hansom and two horses was worth about £140, and most drivers paid about 12s a day to rent their vehicle, keeping the rest of their takings (perhaps 6s a day) for themselves. Out of this they had to pay £3 a year in licence fees, another 2s 6d a week if they wanted to wait for fares in the main railway termini, and small tips for the men who waited in their hundreds at hotels, department stores, churches, cab ranks, and cabmen's shelters to hold the horses' heads and perform other trivial services.[3]

Cabs were charged for by the mile (6d a mile within four miles of Charing Cross, 1s beyond this radius) or by the hour (2s for a four-wheeler, 2s 6d for a hansom), and the calculation of fares, if they were not agreed at the outset, gave ample room for trickery and dispute. Carl Baedeker's 1896 guide to London warned its readers that London cabbies were 'among the most insolent and extortionate of their fraternity. The traveller, therefore, in his own and the general interest, should resist all attempts at overcharging, and should, in case of persistency, demand the cabman's number, or order him to drive to the nearest police court or station.' The cabbies' position in this ongoing battle was strengthened when the 1896 London Cab Act (the first legal document to use the word 'cab') made 'bilking', or dishonestly avoiding paying a fare, an imprisonable offence. Uncertainties were reduced in the early twentieth century when taximeters, mechanical distance-recorders driven by a flexible shaft connected to the wheel and started by turning down a metal 'For Hire' flag, were introduced on the early motor cabs, and then quickly spread to horse-drawn ones.

Horse Trams and Omnibuses

The new force in London road transport in the 1870s and 1880s was the horse-drawn tram. The American George F. Train laid tramlines along Bayswater Road, Victoria Street, and Kennington Road in 1861, but the raised L-shaped step rails without grooves, on the Philadelphia model, were considered to be slippery for pedestrians and an obstacle to other traffic, and they were removed after a few months, before Londoners had got used to them. Train's misjudged enterprise probably helped create opposition to trams in the West End which lasted into the next century. Other private tramway bills failed in the Commons in the 1860s, but the success of trams in America, Europe, and other parts of Britain led Parliament to pass the Tramways Act in 1870, making it easier and cheaper for promoters to gain official permission to lay new lines, on condition that the relevant local authorities and over 70 per cent of affected property owners ('frontagers') gave their approval. This local authority veto allowed two parishes, St George Hanover Square and St Marylebone, to block the entry of trams into the West End. Local authorities were also given the right under the Act to buy the lines in their district at the end of twenty-one years, for the price of the tracks and tramcars. The tram companies also had to bear the cost (up to £500 a mile each year) of maintaining the roadway between their tracks and eighteen inches to either side of them, a total width of about eight feet.

Despite these restrictions three companies, with the backing of American investors, built tram lines just outside central London, stopping at the southern end of the Thames bridges or at the northern boundaries of the City and West End. South of the Thames the London Tramways Company ran trams to Clapham, Brixton, Camberwell Green, and Greenwich, and in North London the North Metropolitan and the much smaller London Street Tramways companies had lines out to Archway, Finsbury Park, Stamford Hill, and Stratford. On smooth tracks two horses could pull fifty passengers – twice as many as an omnibus could take – and fares could therefore be lower. Most tram fares were only twopence, and by the terms of the Cheap Trains Act tramway companies (because they were 'railways') had to sell cheap halfpence-a-mile tickets to working men and women at convenient commuting times (between 5 and 7 a.m. and after 6 p.m.). Omnibuses, which relied on middle-class travellers, only started running at about 8 o'clock. By attracting working people who had never commuted by public transport before, the tram companies were able to equal the passenger load (about a million passenger journeys a week) of the dominant omnibus company, the LGOC by 1875, while omnibus traffic also continued to grow.[4]

In the 1880s the three main companies and seven new competitors extended the tram network northwards into the working-class districts of Tottenham, Edmonton, and Leytonstone, east to Deptford, Woolwich, and Plumstead and south-east to Battersea, Wandsworth, and Tulse Hill. At the same time two separate suburban networks were built, one serving Norwood and Croydon, the other Shepherd's Bush, Hammersmith, Kew, and Richmond. Horse trams were cheap and frequent (every two or three minutes), and those prepared to travel two hours a day could now live up to six miles from their place of work. Working men and women with jobs in the City or West End could find cheaper houses or rooms in Peckham, Camberwell, Stockwell, Holloway, Hackney, or Stratford, pushing middle-class residents further out. But no trams ran right into the City, and the whole of West London, from Shepherd's Bush to Holborn, including Westminster, Marylebone, Bloomsbury, Paddington, Bayswater, Notting Hill, Kensington, Chelsea, and Fulham, except for a line from Vauxhall Bridge to Victoria Station, was barred to trams by local vestries and freeholders, who feared the social effects of cheap transport on their exclusive neighbourhoods. The only concession made to the tram companies before

1914 was the building of a line over Westminster Bridge, along Victoria Embankment to Blackfriars, and up the new Kingsway to Holborn, linking the North and South London systems, in 1906–8.

On some suburban lines trams drove omnibus services from the streets, but in general horse omnibuses continued to prosper, especially in the large central area forbidden to trams. Unlike the tram companies, buses could use all the central London bridges (toll-free since 1880), including two new ones built in the early 1890s, Battersea Bridge (1890) and Tower Bridge (1894). Omnibuses ran with hardly any tolls or restrictions, stopping to drop and pick up passengers wherever they liked, often in the middle of a busy road. Travellers leaving City offices or West End theatres and shops were more likely to take an omnibus, even if it cost an extra penny, than walk for ten minutes to the nearest tram route. And the cost of omnibus rides was falling, mainly because of a 15 or 20 per cent fall in the price of horse fodder (American maize) in the 1880s. Competition from trams, and from a new bus company, the London Road Car Company (founded in 1881), also helped to push down bus fares, putting them within the reach of a working man. An average bus fare in 1881 was twopence farthing, but by 1889 it had fallen by a third, to three halfpence. In the late 1890s most of London's 150 omnibus routes charged a penny for short journeys, rising to sixpence for a trip from Liverpool Street to Shepherd's Bush or Putney, and a shilling for the long haul to Richmond or Crystal Palace. Convenience, adaptability, and low costs enabled omnibuses to remain profitable in the face of almost all competition. The LGOC paid its shareholders healthy dividends, and steadily expanded the number of buses it had on the road and the number of passengers they carried.

By the early twentieth century, with the arrival of the first electric trams and the building of deep-level electric underground railways, most observers thought the days of the omnibus were almost over. The members of the 1903–5 Royal Commission on London Traffic regarded the horse omnibus as a slow and inconvenient form of transport, whose almost unrestricted right to use any street they wished, and to stop or overtake wherever they chose, was the main cause of traffic congestion in central London. Buses used unsuitably narrow streets like Bond Street, and on the major roads like the Strand and Cheapside their selfish conduct held everyone else up. In February 1903 there was a lively dispute between the Committee's chairman, the economist Sir David Barbour, and the head of the LGOC, Sir John Pound. Barbour was sure that trams acted as a regulator, causing all traffic to move more quickly and methodically, and offered the best and cheapest service to ordinary travellers. Against the evidence, Pound insisted that omnibuses could carry more people (per hour, not per vehicle) than horse or electric trams past any chosen spot, and that horse buses were as fast and cheap as their tracked rivals. Trams, ploughing dangerously along their slippery tracks, only relieved congestion by forcing other vehicles (especially cars and cycles) off the roads, and within a few years motor buses, not electric trams, would solve London's transport and congestion problems. 'I believe the ultimate solution of the difficulties of London traffic will be found in motors, and not by rails.'[5] Pound's evidence was received with scepticism or hostility, but it was his prediction, not the Royal Commission's, that turned out to be true.

London General omnibuses were run on a strange system of private enterprise, which bus companies had inherited or copied from the way stagecoach owners had traditionally rewarded their drivers. Conductors were paid an inadequate wage of 4s a day, on the understanding that they could keep some of the money they took in fares. As long as the conductor handed over a reasonable sum for his route each day, no questions were asked, but if he gave the company too little, for whatever reason, he was likely to lose his job. Conductors probably earned about £2 in an average week, and perhaps double that (Charles Booth thought) in a good one, for a fifteen-hour day, seven days a week. From their takings, conductors had to tip the driver and horsekeeper (who were also deliberately underpaid), contribute to an omnibus repair fund, and buy the black suit and bowler hat that they were expected to wear.

The tram companies used a ticket system from the start, as did the second bus company, the Road Car Company, and in March 1891 the LGOC decided to follow suit. On 31 May the LGOC introduced a punched ticket system, supplied by the Bell Punch Company, and offered conductors with a year's service an extra 6d a day, with a further 6d after three years. Bus workers had unionized in 1889 – a year in which many new unions were formed – and on 6 June 1891 they went on strike. After a week new conductors were offered an extra 6d for a twelve-hour day, with a further 6d after a year's service, and omnibuses reappeared on London's streets. Some crews later accepted longer hours in return for an extra shilling, and in the mid-1890s Charles Booth found many drivers and conductors working fifteen hours a day again, or alternating nine- and fifteen-hour days.[6]

Cheap Trains for Working Men

London had an extensive suburban railway network in the early 1880s, though almost all the lines stopped at termini outside the City and West End, as they do today. Two shallow steam-driven underground lines, the District and the Metropolitan, connected the western and north-western suburbs (Richmond, Ealing, Putney, Willesden, and Harrow) with central London, and the Inner Circle, which was finally completed in 1884, made it easier to get from one main line terminus to another. During the 1880s the Metropolitan extended its lines through open countryside to Pinner, Rickmansworth, and Chesham, but it was another twenty years or more before this ambitious north-western extension stimulated the growth of a new suburban quarter, 'Metroland'. In general, trains were too expensive for working men and shop assistants, but the Metropolitan carried most of its passengers in third class, and only charged a penny for short journeys.

The most important developments in railway commuting in the 1880s were taking place in North London, in the districts served by the Great Northern and Great Eastern railway companies. Most railway extensions approved by Parliament after 1864 had a legal obligation to run cheap workmen's trains at convenient times, to compensate the poor for the destruction of inner-city housing and to spread the working-class population. This policy had dramatic effects on the sort of passengers carried by the Great Eastern Railway, because it had to get permission to build its Liverpool Street terminus in Bishopsgate in the 1860s, but not on the Great Northern, whose trains ran into an older station, King's Cross. So the Great Northern carried thousands of clerks and similar passengers to the suburbs it served, Hornsey, Wood Green, Southgate, and Finchley, at third-class return fares in 1884 of between 8d (for Hornsey) and 1s 2d (for Finchley). The fares on the early trains on these lines – 4d return from Hornsey and 7d from Finchley – were too high for working-class commuters, and as a result the outer suburbs of Wood Green, Hornsey, Southgate, and Finchley grew in the 1880s and 1890s as middle-class and clerical neighbourhoods. Hornsey's population doubled between 1881 and 1891 (to over 44,000), and Wood Green's rose from 10,000 to 26,000. Transport arrangements thus helped to stamp a long-term social character on London's suburbs: even in 1931, clerks made up a quarter of Hornsey's working population. The suburbs just to the east of Hornsey

and Southgate – Tottenham and Edmonton – developed an entirely different character, because the early morning trains that served them were
cheaper. The Great Eastern Railway had been obliged to run early workmen's trains at 2d return in 1864, and by 1884 it carried more than a
quarter of the Londoners who travelled on workmen's tickets. The districts
it served on its main and branch lines, including Stamford Hill, Tottenham,
Edmonton, Walthamstow, Ilford, and Forest Gate, were distinctly working-class in tone, despite the fact that they were as far from central London
as such middle-class enclaves as Dulwich or Wimbledon. By 1884, the
impact of cheap fares on the suburban villages of Tottenham and Edmonton was dramatic. The General Manager of the Great Eastern Company,
William Birt, had to move out of the district, along with most of its middle-
class residents, when they were 'thrown open to the working classes' by
his own workmen's trains. As soon as the cheap trains started, he told the
Royal Commission on the Housing of the Working Classes in 1884, 'speculative builders went down into the neighbourhood and, as a consequence,
each good house was one after another pulled down, and the district is
given up entirely, I may say, now to the working man'.[7]

By 1900 the social effects of working-class settlement in Tottenham,
Edmonton and Leyton were evident. Tottenham, according to a local politician, had 'practically become another Bethnal Green . . . The place fell a
prey to the jerry-builder when cheap railway fares were introduced, and the
evils then committed have never been remedied.' In 1903 Tottenham had
by far the lowest level of church attendance in Outer London, with less than
one in six of its 102,000 residents going to church. Its nearest rival in Outer
London, Willesden (1 in 5.8), was another fast-growing working-class
suburb, and following them were the other cheap-fare settlements, West
Ham, Edmonton, East Ham, Leyton, Acton, and Walthamstow. In the clerical suburbs, Hornsey, Southgate, Finchley, and Wood Green, attendance was
almost twice as high. Tottenham's low churchgoing placed it roughly on a
par with the very poor Inner London boroughs of Stepney, Poplar,
Bermondsey, Southwark, and Battersea, and only a little higher than Bethnal
Green and Shoreditch.[8] Perhaps the working-class settlers in these cheap
railway suburbs had brought their culture with them, but other evidence
shows that they had left some of the unhealthy squalor and overcrowding
behind. Between 1907 and 1910 infant death rates, one of the most sensitive indicators of bad living conditions, were much lower in Tottenham (92
per thousand) than in Bethnal Green (130 per thousand) or Bermondsey

(135 per thousand), and Leyton's infant mortality (78 per thousand) was among London's lowest, on a par with Ealing and Lewisham.[9]

Although the 1883 Cheap Trains Act empowered the Board of Trade to compel any railway company to run cheap workmen's trains, in the early 1890s the Great Eastern was still regarded by the London County Council as the workman's railway, 'the one, above all others, which appears to welcome him as a desirable customer'. An LCC inquiry in 1892 found that the workmen's services on the London and North-Western Railway and on the Great Western were poor, despite the 1883 Act. Both ran services through Willesden Junction, but the LCC found that 'probably no part of the area of suburban London is so poorly provided with workmen's trains as the district around this junction'. Workmen living in Ealing and Hanwell had to walk four or six miles to Shepherd's Bush to pick up a cheap train to London.[10] By 1911, though, most London railway companies, including the underground lines, were running dozens of workmen's trains every day, at fares of four or five miles for a penny, about a third of the third-class fare. The Great Eastern was still a leading provider among the surface lines, with 124 workmen's trains and 130 slightly more expensive 'cheap' trains, but London and South-Western (101 workmen's trains a day), London, Brighton, and South Coast (98), and South-Eastern and Chatham (177) did their share, and the underground lines, both shallow and deep, ran more workmen's trains than all the surface lines combined. London Electric, which included the railways we know as the Bakerloo and Piccadilly lines and much of the Northern Line, ran nearly 400 workmen's trains, the Metropolitan and Metropolitan District lines (including the present Circle line) ran 427, and the City and South London (the present Northern Line from Bank to Stockwell) ran 96. The two companies criticized in 1892, the Great Western and London and North-Western, still only ran 54 workmen's trains between them.[11]

On Two Wheels

Londoners who wanted to avoid the expense of a train or hansom but to travel faster than a trotting horse had a practical alternative in the 1880s. The design of bicycles had made very slow progress in the forty years after the invention of the hobby horse in 1818, and the few people who cycled in the 1850s had to make do with iron tyres and propulsion by swinging their legs. Rubber tyres and pedals attached directly to the front wheel were introduced in the 1860s, and in the 1870s bicycles with a very large front wheel, to increase the distance travelled with each push on the pedals, were developed. The centre of innovation and production in England was Coventry, where manufacturers drew upon the skills and techniques developed in the watch and sewing-machine industries. These high or 'ordinary' bicycles (which were not called 'penny-farthings' until later), with their riders perched precariously over a four- or five-foot front wheel, were the dominant type of bicycle in the 1880s, but their instability and discomfort restricted their use to athletes, enthusiasts, and reckless delivery boys. In 1870, some of these London pioneers founded the Pickwick Bicycle Club, the world's first cycling club, and in 1884 Michael Mulhall's *Dictionary of Statistics* claimed, without giving any sources, that there were 9,800 cycles in London.[12] There were enough cyclists in England in the 1870s and 1880s to sustain several cycling magazines, including three produced by William Illiffe, a Coventry printer whose son became a leading twentieth-century press magnate. In 1886 one of Illiffe's magazines, *Bicycling News*, gave his first professional editorship to Alfred Harmsworth, one of the founders of popular journalism in England. Harmsworth had been a keen cyclist since about 1880 when, as a pupil at Henley House School, he had ridden a four-foot 'ordinary' around St John's Wood and taken trips to the country and the South Coast with members of his local cycling club. One of Harmsworth's writers for *Bicycling News* was Arthur Morrison, who later wrote two East End classics, *Tales of Mean Streets* and *A Child of the Jago*. Perhaps cycling journalism attracted writers of promise. The *Pall Mall Gazette*'s cycling correspondent in the late 1880s was the young Hilaire Belloc.

James Starley of Coventry developed chain drives and differential gears for bicycles and tricycles in the 1870s, and in 1885 his nephew, J. K. Starley, used these devices to produce the Rover 'safety bicycle', which had a chain-driven rear wheel, roughly equal-sized wheels, a frame of modern size and shape, and a saddle set well back, so that the rider would not be thrown over the top of the machine when he hit a bump on Britain's very uneven roads. The Rover was still heavy (about 50lb), its solid rubber tyres gave a bumpy ride, and since it had no free-wheel (which was not introduced until 1899) its cranks and pedals spun round quickly when the bike was going downhill. In 1888 J. B. Dunlop, a Belfast vet, invented the pneumatic tyre, and this, fitted to the safety bicycle, transformed cycling into a practical and pleasant means of transport for those without unusual courage or athleticism. Frames were designed with a low cross-bar, so that women could cycle without abandoning skirts and dresses in favour of more 'rational' outfits. In 1894 a new safety bicycle cost £4 or £5, which represented a month's wages for a working man, but was a reasonable outlay for a well-off man or woman wanting to possess one of the most useful and enjoyable of modern inventions. Working men and women could buy cheaper second-hand machines, and by the mid-1890s the cycling craze had spread to every social class, from the Prince of Wales downwards. For a while, the rich and fashionable paraded on their new bicycles in the London parks as though they were on horseback. Until 1896 Hyde Park was closed to cycles, so Battersea Park, the newer and less prestigious gardens across the river, established itself as the fashionable cyclists' favourite Sunday morning rendezvous. The rich, perhaps wearing knickerbockers and woollen socks or (for women) cycling skirts and Norfolk jackets, were helped onto their gleaming machines by their servants. By 1901, when Duncan Lucas wrote his piece on 'Cycling London' for George Sims' *Living London*, cyclists had deserted Battersea for Birdcage Walk in St James's Park and the Inner Circle of Regent's Park.

Cycling swept away the ancient distinction between the walker and the horseman, and gave working men and women the chance, for the first time, to go faster than their social superiors. Its democratic, levelling, and modern spirit appealed to London socialists. Bernard Shaw tried out a tandem tricycle with his fellow-socialist Belfort Bax, and then took some lessons at Goya's cycling school in Paddington before buying a safety bicycle in 1895. That spring and summer Shaw went cycling in the country with Sidney and Beatrice Webb, and all three of them discovered the mixture of pleasure and pain that comes from unskilled riding on rough roads. 'My God,' Shaw wrote, 'the stiffness, the blisters, the bruises, the pains in every twisted muscle, the crashes against the chalk road that I have endured – and at my age, too. But I shall come like gold from the furnace. I will not be beaten by that hellish machine . . . Yes, bicycling's a capital thing for a literary man.'[13] Literary men were falling off bicycles all over London and the Home Counties in the 1890s. On that same holiday, Shaw crashed into the philosopher Bertrand Russell, who had stopped his bike in the middle of the road to read a street sign. 'Russell, fortunately, was not even scratched; but his knickerbockers were demolished', Shaw reported to a friend.[14] Those who objected to the speed and carelessness of cyclists were sometimes irritated, also, by the fact that the dust in their eyes was thrown up by working men, 'cads on casters'. In 1896 the Duke of Teck complained about cyclists in Richmond Park, in a letter that found its way to the Home Secretary. There were more than 2,000 cycles in the park, he said, ridden by 'Maniacs, Persons in a state of madness. They went about in a pace like Lightening, looking neither right nor left . . . Many Groups, actually abreast, of from 10 to 20 or more, formed of Roughs and others apparently of members of Bicycle Clubs.'[15]

For a few years in the mid-nineties public figures who wanted to look fashionable and sporty had themselves photographed with bikes, theatre managers organized cycle parades to publicize their shows, and cycling was a popular theme for early film-makers. The most famous of many cycling songs, 'Daisy Bell' (' . . . You'll look sweet upon the seat of a bicycle built for two'), was written in 1892 by Harry Dacre, a London songwriter working in America, and turned into a London music hall hit by Katie Lawrence. Cycling also gave H. G. Wells the subject of his first comic novel, *The Wheels of Chance*, which was published in 1896, at the peak of the bicycle craze. Wells learned to cycle, and rode the route between London and the South Coast that was to be followed by his hero, the Putney drapery assistant Hoopdriver. On his ride, Wells also noted down locations for the Martian invasion he described in *The War of the Worlds*. 'The bicycle in those days was still very primitive,' he recalled later. 'The diamond frame had appeared but there was no freewheel. You could only stop and jump off when the treadle was at its lowest point, and the brake was an uncertain plunger upon the front wheel . . . Nevertheless the bicycle was the swiftest thing upon the roads in those days . . . and the cyclist had a lordliness, a sense of masterful adventure, that has gone from him altogether now.'[16]

For others, cycling was a more serious business. Cycle race tracks were built in Paddington (1888), Herne Hill (1891), and Catford, Putney, and Crystal Palace, and races between top cyclists attracted large crowds. It was said that between 1892 and 1894 the twenty-four-hour races at Herne Hill, the only nineteenth-century London track that still survives, drew 20,000 spectators. In the early 1890s popular demand for bikes created a boom in the cycle industry, which attracted many speculators and company promoters into the business, and drove up the price of shares in the bigger manufacturers, including Humber and Raleigh. Ernest Terah Hooley, a Nottingham stockbroker, bought the Dunlop tyre company, which had been started with £25,000 in 1889, for £3 million, then floated it on the London Stock Exchange in May 1896. By paying various aristocrats thousands of pounds to accept Dunlop directorships, and bribing financial journalists with cash and cheap shares, Hooley managed to whip up public demand for Dunlop shares and to sell the company for

£5 million. Hooley went on to float the Singer Cycle Company in June and the Swift Cycle Company in October, still using aristocratic stooges and corrupt journalists to excite the public into paying more than the shares were worth. Hooley went bankrupt in 1898, after promoting and floating twenty-six companies (including Bovril and Schweppes), and in his evidence to the London Bankruptcy Court revealed the tricks he and other promoters used to puff their companies and gull the public. Swindlers like Hooley – and he was not the only dishonest promoter in late nineteenth-century London – damaged investor confidence in booming new industries, including electricity and the motor car, and made it difficult for real entrepreneurs to raise capital when they needed it.[17]

By 1910 the motor car had replaced the bicycle as a status symbol and a means of transport for the smart and the rich, but cycling still played a significant part in the daily life of ordinary Londoners, who used their bikes to get to work, and for pleasure in the weekends and evenings. The pre-war streets, still relatively free of private cars, were crowded with clerks, teachers, shop assistants, and working men and women cycling to work, to the shops, to the park, or out into the countryside. Some, including policemen, postmen, delivery boys, and telegraph messengers, used their bikes in their jobs. Fleet Street newspaper boys, delivering heavy bundles of afternoon papers to London news-stands, were notorious 'scorchers', pedalling at breakneck speed through the dense central London traffic. Others used bikes to escape from London at the weekend, or packed them into padded cycle vans at Paddington or Waterloo for a day out in the country. A traffic census between May and July 1911 shows that bicycles were the most common non-commercial vehicles on most major London roads. Nearly a quarter of the vehicles crossing the twelve Thames bridges from Putney to the Tower between 8 a.m. and 8 p.m., and over a third of the traffic using the main suburban roads (Old Kent Road, Fulham Road, Uxbridge Road, Brixton Road, and so on), was pedal-powered. Cycle traffic was heaviest before 9 a.m. and between 6 and 8 p.m., when people were going to and from work. On a fine July day in 1911, just over 10,000 vehicles passed a census point on the Whitechapel Road, one of London's busiest streets. Ten per cent of these were barrows, 11.5 per cent electric trams, 5 per cent omnibuses (only one of which was horse-drawn), 46 per cent trade vehicles (all but a few of which *were* horse-drawn), 1.6 per cent cabs (mostly motorized), 1.7 per cent horse carriages, 1.6 per cent motor cars, and 22.5 per cent pedal cycles.[18] To serve this army of cyclists, there were 370 cycle factories and workshops in Greater London, employing an average of three or four men and boys. Many of these were local repair shops, but London exported nearly a million pounds' worth of cycles and cycle parts (perhaps not all London-made), 45 per cent of the UK total, in that year. Add to that the many cyclists' outfitters, cycling schools, and cycling newspapers, and it is plain that cycling gave employment to thousands of Londoners, and enabled thousands more to live in cheaper suburbs and get to jobs in central London that they could not otherwise have reached.[19]

Paving and Sweeping

In a city that was so dependent on road transport, the state of its road surfaces was of the utmost importance. Eighteenth-century London had been notorious for the appalling condition of its streets, with their thick mud, choking dust, and ankle-twisting cobbles. Although drivers and pedestrians still complained about the roads in the late nineteenth century, there had been great improvements in the 170 years since the publication of John Gay's *Trivia, or the Art of Walking the Streets of London*. Macadamization, which involved laying a surface of small granite cubes and leaving the traffic to pack them down, was introduced in London in the 1820s, and widely used thereafter, especially in Westminster and the suburbs. More important London streets, and nearly all those in the City, were paved with Aberdeen granite setts, in three- to six-inch cubes. Each surface had its disadvantages. Macadamized roads wore out and broke up quickly, and needed (but did not always get) regular repair to keep them in good condition. Granite setts were noisy, for both travellers and local residents, and unsafe for horses and pedestrians, especially in the wet. Noise and safety were important issues, but for commercial road users the efficiency of their vehicles on different surfaces was the main consideration. In the early 1880s the chief engineer to the Metropolitan Board of Works, Sir Joseph Bazalgette, supervised a test of road surfaces using a dynamometer. This showed that granite setts were the most efficient surface for hauliers, followed, some way behind, by wood blocks and asphalt, with macadam the least efficient, requiring about 50 per cent more effort than granite.[20]

The newer surfaces tested by Bazalgette, asphalt and wood, had grown in popularity in London since about 1870. Asphalt consisted of hard limestone impregnated with about 8 per cent bitumen, either occurring naturally, as it did in the Val de Travers, or created by mixing crushed stone with bitumen. A three- or four-inch coating of asphalt, rammed down onto a strong concrete base, provided a resilient, smooth, efficient, and fairly quiet surface that was quick to lay and easy to repair and clean. The first London road paved with asphalt was Threadneedle Street in 1869, but by 1871 the Val de Travers Asphalt Company had paved about twenty miles of London streets. By 1884, 28 per cent of streets in the City, and a few in Westminster, especially the narrower streets, were asphalt. Wood paving had been tried in the West End in the early 1840s, but the early wood blocks soon sank and became uneven. In 1871 a new method, using tar-impregnated blocks laid onto deal planks, was introduced, and this was improved in the late 1870s by replacing the planks with a concrete foundation. After various experiments with soft woods (which wore out quickly) and very hard woods (which were slippery) it was found that Australian hardwoods of the eucalyptus type had the best all-round qualities, though American red-gum was also widely used in London. At first wide joints filled with cement or asphalt were left to improve foothold, but this method caused deterioration, and was gradually abandoned. Some wooden roads were covered with hot pitch and sharp gravel. Wood paving was not cheap, but its quietness made it popular with West End and City residents, and cab drivers and omnibus companies liked the fact that it did not need frequent repair. By 1884 about 17 per cent of streets in the City and Westminster were wooden, though in the rest of London the vestries preferred gravel, followed by macadam and granite. Over the next twenty years granite and macadam gave way to asphalt and wood in Westminster and the City, so that by 1908 about a half of the City streets were asphalt, a fifth wood, and the rest granite. In Westminster a quarter of streets were asphalt, over a third wood, and the rest granite, macadam, or flint. Westminster's asphalt streets included the Victoria Embankment, which was resurfaced by the Trinidad Lake Asphalt Paving company in 1906–8.[21]

Once a new street had been laid, it would not be long before it was dug up again, by a gas, water, telephone, tram, or electricity company, or to put down new wood blocks or replace old macadam with new asphalt. Groups of workmen in caps or bowlers, digging a trench, banging wood-blocks into place, boiling up pitch, or eating their dinners around a little temporary hut were one of London's most familiar sights. George R. Sims, in his chapter in *Living London* called 'London "Up"', claimed that the Strand was 'a favourite field of operations for the private companies. If one part of it is down the other is up. When the up part is finished the down part is taken up again . . . The men usually work through the hours of sleep. Then great yellow flames flare up against the blackness of the night, flinging a strange and ghastly hue upon the faces of the toilers and of the wayfarers who stand at the pavement's edge and look on in silent rapture.' Children, or men with handcarts, would hang around to pick up discarded wood blocks to sell as firewood, shopkeepers would fret and complain while the works deprived them of customers, and on dark nights or foggy days warning fires or naphtha jets stopped Londoners from falling into open trenches.[22]

The maintenance, watering, and sweeping of London streets were the responsibility of the parish vestries or district boards, and of the boroughs after 1899. In dry weather streets were watered by carts or hoses to lay the dust and make sweeping easier, though it made them more slippery and prone to wear. The great problem for London authorities was the huge amount of horse dung deposited on the streets, which would turn into an offensive and slippery mess if it were not quickly removed. Most parishes used uniformed youngsters known as orderly boys to scoop up horse dung as soon as it was deposited in main roads, and adult sweepers to sweep and scour the streets after they had been watered. The 'squeegee-men' (as they were called) in their waterproofs and sou'westers swept the water-loosened mud into piles, ready to be shovelled into dustcarts. Some vestries or boroughs invested in horse-drawn sweeping and scouring machines, but the work remained labour-intensive. The City and Westminster together employed 488 sweepers and 233 orderly boys in 1905, and William Ryan, *Living London*'s expert on 'London's toilet', thought that about 8,000 people were employed in cleaning London's streets in 1901. In the central districts these men worked at night, but in the suburbs the work could be done by day, and orderly boys were also at work all day in the City, dodging among the moving traffic with a brush and scoop, wearing bright jackets to catch the drivers' eyes. The efforts of official sweepers and scavengers were supplemented by those of freelance crossing sweepers, whose worn-out brooms usually matched their worn-out bodies. Whether these men performed a useful function or were just beggars in disguise was a matter of dispute.[23]

Electric Trams

A well-ridden cycle was the fastest thing on the London roads in the 1890s, but its supremacy was brief. Two new sources of power, both capable of propelling street vehicles at dangerous speeds, were being developed in the last years of the century – electricity and exploding petrol. The idea of the electric motor goes back, like so many things, to the work of Faraday, but an efficient and practical direct current (DC) electric motor, essentially one Gramme dynamo driven by another, was not demonstrated until 1873, and motors driven by alternating current (AC) were not invented until 1888 in the USA, and 1891 in Germany. Gramme's electric motor opened the possibility of electric-powered trams and trains, for which the electricity supply could be carried along the track, or in an overhead wire. Electric cars, taxis, and buses were also possible, but they would have to be powered by batteries, which were heavy and weak, and needed frequent recharging.

Tram companies had already shown an interest in replacing horses with steam engines on their London tracks. London Tramways experimented with a steam tram, made by Merryweather and Sons, on their Vauxhall Bridge Road line in 1873, and others were tried between Stratford and Leytonstone in 1877 and in Croydon in 1884. North London Tramways used twenty-five steam trams on routes between Stamford Hill, Ponders End, Finsbury Park, and Wood Green after 1885, but the experiment was abandoned when the company collapsed in 1890. Using heavy steam engines meant laying new tracks, so London tram companies experimented with steam-wound clockwork and steam-generated compressed air as propellants in the 1880s, and lighter gas and oil engines in the 1890s. Steam-powered cable traction, which had been tried successfully in San Francisco and Chicago, was another possibility on hilly routes, but it was too expensive for general use. The Steep Grade Tramways and Works Company built a demonstration cable car up the Archway Road to Highgate in 1883–4, and this ran, without great success, until an accident forced its closure in 1892. Five years later it reopened under new management, and with automatic brakes.[24] There were other cable tramways in Brixton, Birmingham, and Edinburgh. Meanwhile, the development of Gramme's dynamo and motor, and progress in the generation of electricity for lighting, suggested another way forward. An experimental miniature electric train was demonstrated at the 1879 Berlin Trade Fair, and electric railways were installed on Brighton Beach and the Giant's Causeway in Ireland in 1883, but practical problems made these prototypes unsuitable for London streets. In the 1880s engineers in the USA, especially Frank Sprague, found effective ways of delivering current to a tramcar, introduced carbon brushes to reduce the wear caused by constant stopping and starting, and worked out how to mount the motor so that it was not damaged by the jolting of the tram. The solution of these problems led US tramcar companies to convert rapidly from horses to electric motors in the late 1880s and early 1890s. By 1892 nearly a third of US tramways were electric, and by 1897 only 12 per cent of the American system was horse-drawn. German tramways went electric in the 1890s, and American and German companies solved most of the technical problems of running an economical, safe, and reliable system. In England the shift from horses to electricity was much more hesitant, because electrification meant converting existing (and profitable) lines rather than building new ones (as in America) and because private tramway companies did not think they would be able to recoup their investment in costly electric conduits before local authorities exercised their option to buy their systems after twenty-one years, under the 1870 Tramways Act. There were experiments on the Barking Road between 1889 and 1893, and an unsuccessful line inside Alexandra Park in 1898–9, but in 1900 there were no electric trams running in London.

Their early experience in building electric tramways (over 12,000 miles by 1895) gave American companies enormous advantages over British ones in the application of the new technology to London's transport network. They had developed the most efficient, lightest, quietest, and cheapest traction motors and the best tramway generators, and had the most experience in dealing with such problems as waterproofing, insulation, dirt, and maintenance. Furthermore, the two giants, Westinghouse and General Electric (a union of Edison General Electric and Thompson-Houston) urgently needed new markets for their motors. Their keenest competitors in penetrating the English market were two German companies, Siemens and A.E.G.

Trains in Tunnels

The first steps in electric transport in London were taken underground, where the problem of electrocuting pedestrians on exposed live rails did not arise, and where the disadvantages of steam power were most intensely experienced. The Metropolitan and District companies, which ran one shallow underground line each, and shared the Inner Circle in a hostile partnership, claimed that the coal fumes and sulphuric acid gas in their tunnels helped to clear the lungs and disinfect the air, but their passengers, wheezing and gasping, knew better. A journalist riding the footplate on the Circle line in 1893 found himself 'coughing and spluttering like a boy with his first cigar' on the badly ventilated stretch from King's Cross to Edgware Road, though he breathed more easily on the rest of his journey. But the enormous cost of completing the eastern end of the Inner Circle between 1879 and 1884 (because of the need to take account of roads, houses, sewers, and gas pipes) showed that London's underground railways could not be further extended by the 'cut and cover' method. A short shallow electric line from Waterloo to Trafalgar Square was approved, but abandoned, in 1882, and a two-mile shallow line from Cheapside to Charing Cross, to be operated by the British Siemens Company, was rejected because of opposition from the Metropolitan Board of Works in 1884.

The obvious solution was to dig deep tunnels without disturbing the surface, and to use clean electric power. In 1884 the Patent Cable Tramways Corporation proposed to build a deep-level cable-driven railway running in two 10-foot tubes for almost 1.5 miles from the Monument to the Elephant and Castle. The backers of this revolutionary scheme included several railway engineers and the usual sprinkling of professional company promoters, but also the great civil engineer James Henry Greathead. Greathead had learned his craft as the assistant to Peter Barlow, the tunnelling pioneer, in the construction of a cylindrical iron tunnel under the Thames from Tower Hill to Pickle Herring Street, 7 feet wide and 1,430 feet long, in 1869. The cable railway laid in this tunnel in 1870 was a failure, but the tunnelling process itself was a great success, covering the distance in six months at a very modest cost. To achieve this Barlow borrowed and improved on a device used by Marc Isambard Brunel in building the Rotherhithe–Wapping Tunnel in the 1830s. Barlow used a tunnelling shield, a two-ton cast-iron cutting disc with a watertight door in its centre, enabling excavators to dig away the clay before the shield was forced forwards by screw-jacks. As the tunnel was cleared, its sides were lined with overlapping cast iron rings, which were bolted and cemented together to form a strong watertight tube. The space between the tube and the tunnel walls was pumped full of blue lime, which set quickly and preserved the iron. For the Monument to Southwark tunnel, Greathead used an improved version of the Brunel–Barlow shield, and adopted a compressed-air tunnelling method first used on the Hudson River Tunnel in New York in 1879–80. Work on two 10 foot 6 inch tunnels began in October 1886, and was completed in 1890. Its final destination, Stockwell, in the Lambeth suburbs, was three miles from the Monument.

Ventilation problems meant that a railway of this length and depth could not be pulled by steam locomotives. The original intention had been to draw the trains through the tunnel with a long cable, but this idea was abandoned in favour of electric motors in 1888. The contract was given to a Manchester firm, Mather and Platt, which employed Dr John Hopkinson FRS, the inventor of the Edison–Hopkinson dynamo and a man well qualified to take on this adventurous project. The whole line was built for £775,000, and public services on the City and South London Railway, the world's first electric underground railway, began on 18 December 1890. The trains, which weighed forty tons with a full load of ninety-six passengers, covered the three miles from King William Street to Stockwell (via Borough, the Elephant, Kennington, and the Oval) in about fifteen minutes. The carriages had well-padded seats and electric light, and after their journey passengers reached the surface in hydraulic lifts and left the stations through turnstiles. At the start, and for the first time in a London railway, all passengers travelled in the same class for 2d, but from 1891 fare differentials helped separate the rich from the poor and the leisured from the busy. Before 8 a.m. and between 10 and 11 p.m. the fare was a penny, but in the rush hour the full journey cost 3d.

The City and South London Railway had technical problems from the start. The voltage produced in its Stockwell generating station could not run as many rush-hour trains as the company planned, and trains struggled to climb the steep gradient from the river to King William Street. By 1900 the line was attracting just under 8 million passengers a year, far fewer than tramline it was competing against. The tunnel was too narrow and the route was too short to be profitable and efficient, but poor share performance and very low dividends made it difficult for the company to raise capital to widen and extend the line. There was plenty of cheap capital available in the 1890s, but wise investors knew that there was no profit to be expected from investing in expensive and underpowered urban railways which had to charge low fares to compete with horse buses and trams. The company had parliamentary permission to extend north to the Angel Islington and south to Clapham Common, calling at London Bridge Station instead of King William Street, but shortage of capital delayed the completion of these extensions until 1900 and 1901. At its new station at the Bank of England, where the line met the Central London Railway, the City and South London had to pay £170,000 to build its ticket office in the crypt of Hawksmoor's St Mary Woolnoth. The line was extended to Euston and King's Cross in 1907, and faster trains, more powerful generators, and better electrical equipment gave the company's passengers – now up to 22 million a year – more for their money. Nevertheless, the line remained unprofitable, and a warning to investors looking for a good place to put their money.[25]

Other projectors in the early 1890s were hoping to learn from the City's and South London's mistakes. Between 1891 and 1893 groups of investors proposed five new deep-level underground electric train routes, and won parliamentary approval for them. These were the Central London Railway from Liverpool Street to Shepherd's Bush, the Great Northern and City railway from Moorgate to Finsbury Park, the Charing Cross, Euston, and Hampstead railway (the West End branch of the future Northern line), the Waterloo and City line, and the Baker Street and Waterloo railway (the 'Bakerloo'). Only two of these lines, the Central London and the Waterloo and City, were built in the 1890s, though all five were completed, in a wonderful conjunction of engineering brilliance and financial folly, by 1907.[26]

The first of these to take the plunge was the Waterloo and City Railway, a simple 1.5-mile line for South London commuters, with no intermediate stations, from Waterloo to the Bank of England. The 'Drain' improved on the City and South London by using motorized cars instead of separate locomotives and cast-iron segments instead of bricks in its stations, but economized by using long sloping walkways rather than lifts. It opened in 1898, paid a 3 per cent dividend, and was taken over by its main sponsor, the London and South-Western Railway, in 1907. By 1910 about 8,000 commuters were using the Drain every working day, and paying about 2d or 3d a day to do so.[27]

The best of these early Tube railways, and the inspiration to those that followed it, was the Central London Railway. Following a straight east–west route from the Bank to Shepherd's Bush, it was designed to capture a share of the thousands of shoppers, theatregoers, and commuters carried by the 240 omnibuses that ran every day along Bayswater Road and Oxford Street to High Holborn and Cheapside. This excellent plan had the support of James Greathead and the other engineers working on the City and South London Railway, and financial backing some of the mighty Rothschilds, Darius Ogden Mills, founder of the Bank of California and director of Edison General Electric Company, and two important German-born City bankers, Ernest Cassel and Henry Oppenheim. A majority shareholding in this very well-connected syndicate was held by Rothschild's Exploration Company, but the all-important political and social influence was provided by Cassel, who was a member of the Prince of Wales' intimate circle of aristocratic and banking friends. With the help of a board of directors drawn from the highest social and political circles the syndicate attracted additional capital from British and European share-holders. Work on the 5.8 miles of tunnel and thirteen stations began in April 1896. Difficulties with the subways and booking hall at Bank, the eastern terminus, delayed the railway, but it was open for business between Bank and Shepherd's Bush on 30 July 1900. It was equipped with 43-ton, 568-horsepower American General Electric locomotives, comfortable and well-lit forty-eight-seat carriages from the Brush Company, and forty-nine electric lifts supplied by Frank Sprague, one of the American pioneers of fast and safe elevators. The only serious problem for the new line came from the vibrations of its powerful locomotives, which drew many com-plaints from influential West Enders. The problem was solved in 1901 by replacing the single engines with two lighter motors for each train, and introducing a geared and sprung system instead of a direct axle drive. Almost at once the Central London Railway became a familiar part of the London scene. The *Daily Mail*, which was also born in 1896, christened it the Twopenny Tube, and in the 1900 production of Gilbert and Sullivan's *Patience* the 'threepenny bus young man' of 1881 was reborn as 'the very delectable, highly respectable, Twopenny Tube young man'.[28]

The LCC's Electric Trams

At ground level the biggest, if not the fastest, investor in electric transport was London's new unitary government, the LCC, which was motivated not so much by the search for profit as by the hope of social benefits. It was a commonplace that the best way to improve the housing of the poor was to make the journey to work faster, cheaper, and more convenient. Work-men's trains offered one likely solution, but most railway companies cooperated half-heartedly with the 1883 Cheap Trains Act, and by 1890 there were only 257 workmen's trains running in London. The tram offered an equally promising possibility, especially as the LCC had inher-ited the Metropolitan Board of Works' right under the 1870 Tramways Act to buy out (though not to operate directly) any tramway company after it had been running for twenty-one years. Overcoming the opposition of the (Conservative) Moderates, who disliked costly municipal projects, the Progressive Council bought its first company, the London Street Tramways

Company, in 1895, after winning a long court battle over the price to be paid for the 4.5 miles of track. Between 1895 and 1898 Moderates and Progressives had equal representation on the LCC, and the drive to take the tramway system into municipal ownership was less intense. The Council bought the North Metropolitan Tramways Company's thirty-six-mile network within the County, but leased it back to them until 1910 in return for a share of their profits. There were even negotiations in 1895 with a group called the County of London Tramways Syndicate, which offered to form a company, with American capital and technology, to take over the whole of Central London's horse-tram network, convert it to electricity, and pay the LCC a substantial share of its profits. The proposal, which might have given London an electric system six or seven years before it actually happened, was narrowly rejected by the Highways Committee. The Progressives regained their majority in the 1898 election, and bought the London Tramways Company's twenty-six-mile network in South London, which employed 2,000 staff and carried 100 million passengers a year between Tooting, Streatham, Peckham, Greenwich, and the Thames bridges, for £850,000. This time the Council (using powers granted to it in 1896) decided to run the system itself, and set about appointing staff who knew something about the business and technology of tramways.[29]

One of the LCC's problems was that its clear understanding of the social benefits of efficient public utilities was not matched by practical experience in running electrical or transport enterprises. From 1898 until the election of 1907, when the Moderates came into power, the driving force behind the LCC's tramway policy was the Highways Committee, whose chairman and deputy were two councillors from Finsbury, John Benn and Joseph Allen Baker, men with experience of industry, but not transport. Baker was a flour miller and baker, and Benn, who chaired the Council in 1904–5, had run a furniture business on the City Road, and started a publishing company (later known as Ernest Benn Ltd) with a journal on cabinet-making. He made a small fortune in the early 1880s by giving popular illustrated lectures, and in the 1890s took charge of his brother William (the father of the future theatre and film star Margaret Rutherford), who had in a fit of madness killed their father with a chamber pot. John Benn sat as a London County Councillor from 1899 to 1922, and as a Liberal MP for St George-in-the-East from 1892 to 1895, establishing an important radical dynasty. Like Baker, he took a keen but amateur interest in transport and especially electric tramways, and visited America in 1894 to see an efficient electric system in action.

While the LCC was held back by the legal, political, and technical problems of electrifying its seventy-five miles of tramway, private and municipal enterprises beyond its boundaries showed them that it could be done. There were electric trams in Bristol, Dublin, and Middlesbrough in 1895, 1896, and 1898, using American equipment and overhead cables, and there might have been an electric route from Hammersmith to Shepherd's Bush if the LCC had not refused London United Tramways permission for an overhead cable in 1895. East Ham started its own municipal electric tram service in June 1901, and London United Tramways painstakingly gained local-authority permission to run a network of electric-tram services in the western suburbs, between Hammersmith, Acton, Kew, Southall, Ealing, Hounslow, Hampton Court, Kingston, Wimbledon, and Tooting. Making the road and bridge improvements the local authorities demanded cost the LUT around £750,000, and some, like the widening of Kew Bridge, were too expensive to undertake. Opposition to electrification came from a variety of sources. Some rich residents and estate agents in Ealing feared that faster electric trams would attract a lower class of commuter into their high-class suburb, and the scientists at the Kew Observatory complained that stray electrical currents might disturb their instruments. Only when these had been moved to an observatory in Dumfriesshire could London's first successful electric tramway be inaugurated, with journeys from Shepherd's Bush to Acton and Kew Bridge, on 4 April 1901. The LUT network, which had its tram sheds and generators in a four-acre site off Chiswick High Road, carried its passengers in 300 smart and well-upholstered double-deckers, running at three-minute intervals and at a maximum legal speed of 10 mph, more than twice as fast as a horse tram. The fare, a penny for two miles, ensured that the system was popular, and led to the subdivision of large suburban gardens into little building plots, just as the rich men of Ealing had predicted. The refusal of the West End vestries to allow horse trams into central London had greatly reduced their value to West London commuters, but the LUT electric trams ran to Shepherd's Bush, the western terminus of the Central line, which had opened in July 1900. So commuters from the expanding western suburbs could travel into the West End or the City, electric-powered all the way.

In London's north-western suburbs another firm, Metropolitan Electric Tramways, was building an electric network that would eventually stretch from Wembley to Waltham Cross. The company behind this ambitious project was British Electric Traction (BET), which had been founded in 1896 by Emile Garcke to buy and electrify horse tramways and build electric-tram networks. Garcke had been involved in the electrical industry since the early 1880s, when he had helped to save the Brush Company after the boom and bust of 1882 (see page 284). In 1893 he was called in as Managing Director to rebuild the Electric Construction Company (ECC), which had suffered a period of poor management under a Board of Directors that included Jabez Balfour, the notorious swindler. Under Garcke the ECC produced electric and petrol-driven cars, and made electrical generators and equipment for lighting and transport enterprises all over Britain. In London, the ECC provided generating equipment for electric-supply companies in Chelsea, Westminster, St Pancras, and Sydenham, and for the re-electrification of the City and South London Railway in 1900. In 1900 BET, acting through its subsidiary, Metropolitan Electric Tramways (MET), formed a partnership with Middlesex and Hertfordshire councils to construct, equip, and operate a large electric-tram network, the councils laying the track and taking about 40 per cent of the profit. The first MET trams (powered from overhead cables) ran from Finsbury Park to Tottenham and Wood Green in July 1904, and by 1909 MET electric trams covered the whole north-western quarter of Outer London, from Paddington and Wembley round to Willesden, Hampstead, Highgate, Finchley, Wood Green, Tottenham, and Edmonton, and as far north as Edgware, Barnet, Enfield, and Waltham Cross. From 1902 British Electric Traction also operated a tram system in and around Croydon, which was isolated from other South London tram routes until they spread southwards in 1906 and 1909.[30]

While its territory was surrounded by these municipal and commercial electric tramways, the LCC had particular difficulties in developing a coherent system of its own. Its tramway plans were subject to veto by the local highway authorities, the City and the new London boroughs (created in 1899), which were as insistent that LCC electric trams should not clutter the streets of central London as they had been in their opposition to private horse trams. In addition Parliament refused to sanction tramways on the Thames bridges, mainly because of the efforts of the aged Conservative Lord Chancellor, Lord Halsbury. This meant that the Council's South London tram routes, acquired in 1899, could not reach convenient central London destinations or join up with the North London routes of the commercial tram companies. When the Council tried to run its own horse buses in 1899 to link the tram routes north and south of the forbidden zone it was taken to court by the commercial bus companies, and forced to sell

off its 77 buses and 500 horses in 1902. The LCC decided that the best
way out of its predicament was to follow Boston, New York, and Paris in
building shallow tramway tunnels, as a cheaper and more accessible alternative to deep-level tubes for railways. But the Council's ambitious
proposal for a four-mile tunnel from Knightsbridge to the City was dismissed by the Royal Commission on London Traffic in 1905, and the LCC
was left with one modest tram tunnel, from the Aldwych to its new road,
Kingsway. The Royal Commission's preferred solution to the central-
London problem was a raised viaduct from Blackfriars Bridge to join
existing tram routes north of Smithfield, and two 140-foot wide roads
(enough for four tramway lines), one east–west from Whitechapel to Bayswater, the other north–south from Holloway to the Elephant and Castle.
These grandiose and unfulfilled plans sprang from a confidence in the
future of electric trams as the best and cheapest form of surface transport,
despite advances in the efficiency of motor buses. As the Commission's
1905 report said, 'we cannot recommend the postponement of tramway
extension in London on the ground of any visible prospect of the super-
session of tramways by motor omnibuses'.[31]

In spite of its failure to win 'the Battle of the Bridges' the LCC pressed
ahead with the electrification of its South London trams, starting with the
line from Totterdown Street, Tooting (where work on the LCC's new cottage estate had just begun), to the southern ends of Blackfriars and
Westminster Bridges. The opening of this route in May 1903 was attended
by three future kings (George V, Edward VIII, and George VI), who bought
their halfpenny tickets from a top-hatted John Benn. Over the next fifteen
months the routes to Camberwell Green, Brixton, Peckham, and Greenwich were electrified, and in August 1906 the LCC won an important
victory, and ran electric trams over Vauxhall Bridge to Victoria Station. In
1906 the Council paid £436,000 for the remaining four years of the
North Metropolitan Tramways Company's lease on its forty-eight-mile
horse-tram network, and in 1907 and 1908 much of this network was
electrified out to its meeting points with the outer suburban electric trams
of Metropolitan Electric Tramways, at Archway, Finsbury Park, Stamford
Hill, Lea Bridge, Bow Bridge, and Poplar. None of these routes could pen-
etrate the City beyond Holborn, Smithfield, Liverpool Street Station, or
Aldgate, none was allowed to enter the West End by going further west
than Tottenham Court Road or Kingsway, and trams on the Kingsway
tunnel route had to stop and turn at the Aldwych. The LCC had only one
further success over this policy of exclusion in December 1906, when it

started running electric trams over Westminster Bridge and along the Embankment to Blackfriars. When this route was joined to the Kingsway tunnel in April 1908, and to a new track over a widened Blackfriars Bridge in September 1909, Londoners got their first and only central-London connection between the electric tram networks of North and South London.[32]

By 1911 the LCC had bought about 108 miles of tramway from commercial companies, and had an electric-tram network, including newly constructed lines, of 123 miles. The money the LCC spent on buying and converting this system, £11.6 million, was about the same as its total annual gross expenditure on all Council services (including education) in 1910. LCC tram workers were well paid, and their sixty-hour working week (six ten-hour days) was much shorter than that of private tramway staff. LCC tram fares were kept low, at about a halfpenny a mile, for social reasons, but the system still produced a profit, after debt charges, of £100,000 in 1910–11. In 1910, 500 million passengers travelled on the LCC's 1,552 electric and 107 horse trams, nearly 700,000 return journeys every day. If we add the 260 million journeys on the private and municipal suburban trams, the number of tram journeys taken on Greater London's 344 miles of tramway in 1910–11 was greater than the total of those taken on omnibuses and local railways, for which rather inaccurate figures were kept. For those living in the suburbs, especially in South-east London, electric trams were a godsend. The Liberal politician Charles Masterman, who lived in Camberwell, believed that electric trams, along with gas stoves, were one of 'the two greatest boons which have come to our working people'. Instead of squeezing onto slow horse trams, and enduring a long and crowded journey in the dim light of a stinking oil lamp, working men and women could travel at twice the speed in well-lit electric trams, 'in which reading is a pleasure', saving an hour a day in travelling times. This, he said, was a powerful inducement for them to move out to the suburbs: 'Family after family are evacuating the blocks and crowded tenements for little four-roomed cottages, with little gardens, at Hither Green or Tooting.'[33] This seemed to many observers and experts to be the beginning of a long period of ascendancy for the electric tram, but in reality it was almost the end of a very short one, in which 1911 was the high point.

London's First Cars and Motor Buses

The motorized vehicles that brought the brief ascendancy of the bicycle
and the electric tram to an end had been developing in London and elsewhere for more than twenty years, and might have developed faster had it
not been for mid-Victorian legislation. There had been steam traction
engines on English roads since the late 1850s, and it was to control these
heavyweight vehicles that legislation was introduced in 1865, imposing,
among many other restrictions, a 2 mph urban speed limit and a rule that
every engine should be preceded by a man carrying a red flag, walking at
least sixty yards ahead, to warn and assist horse traffic. There were important advances in the design of efficient and lightweight steam carriages
with solid rubber tyres in the 1860s and 1870s, but public and political
attitudes remained hostile, and the 1878 Highways and Locomotives
(Amendment) Act retained the 2 mph urban speed limit and the insistence
on a man walking ahead to help horses, though he could now be twenty
yards ahead, and did not need a red flag. These highly restrictive rules,
which were not repealed until 1896, and which applied to all vehicles
propelled by non-animal power, naturally had a stifling effect on the development of motorized transport in England.[34]

To overcome the resistance of landlords and local authorities, designers had to produce a much lighter vehicle, which would not destroy roads
or terrify horses. To achieve this, they turned from the technology of the
steam locomotive to that of the bicycle, whose tangentially spoked wheels
and tubular steel frames gave strength without great weight. The first
British motor-powered vehicle based on cycle design was demonstrated
at a cycle-club show in New Holborn Town Hall in February 1881,
and at Westminster Aquarium a few weeks later. This 'motor tricycle' was
designed and built by two keen cyclists, Sir Thomas Parkyns of Beckenham and Arthur H. Bateman of East Greenwich. The Bateman tricycle
weighed about 220lb, and its small steam engine, heated by methylated
spirit or petrol rather than coal, could propel it at up to 12 mph, without
emitting steam or smoke. But for riding this machine through Greenwich
in April 1881 at 5 mph Parkyns was fined, and his failure to get the law
changed in favour of lighter motor vehicles discouraged their further
development in England for a decade. In France and Germany there were
no such laws, and thus many of the most important advances in motorized
transport took place there.

The two main ingredients of the petrol-driven internal-combustion engine were already available. Internal-combustion engines powered by coal gas were developed by the 1870s, but they were difficult to use on moving vehicles. There were large oil wells in the USA, Russia, and Rumania, but the early refineries produced heavy lubricating oil and kerosene for oil lamps. Petrol (or gasoline), the fuel that would eventually revolutionize the modern world, was a waste product, apparently too volatile and dangerous to have much practical value. The first man to exploit the qualities of petrol in an internal-combustion engine was Gottlieb Daimler, whose 4-stroke engine was made in 1883. Three years later, Karl Benz was road-testing the first petrol-driven car, driving at up to 15 mph on runs of fifty miles. Although the groundwork was done in Germany, the best market for motor cars proved to be France, where the roads were good and the laws favoured drivers. By the mid-1890s France had a real motor industry, with about twenty motor manufacturers and a thousand cars on its roads.[35] Road races, especially the Paris–Bordeaux race of 1895, created public interest in England, and demonstrated the superiority of internal combustion to steam. The shift from southern Germany to France meant that fashionable English tourists were more likely to experience the pleasures of motoring in Paris or on the Riviera, and to use their influence for legal reform in England. Alfred Harmsworth, who was on the verge of becoming one of England's most influential newspaper owners, rode in a petrol car in Paris in 1893, and in the same year the leader of English high society, the Prince of Wales, took his first car ride in Bad Homburg, in a French-built coke-fuelled steam car.

From 1894 to 1896 a handful of motoring enthusiasts focused their efforts on persuading the government to remove the crippling restrictions unintentionally imposed on petrol vehicles by the 1878 Locomotives Act. There was some hope that the new breed of vehicles, which were quieter, cleaner, and easier to control, would not be prosecuted for breaking the 2 mph limit. An electric parcel van, cab, and bus, all designed by Walter Bersey, had been allowed to operate without impediment in London from March 1894. To test the law on petrol engines Henry Hewetson, a Catford tea broker and probably the first man to import a European car into England, drove his Benz around the London suburbs after November 1894 preceded by a boy carrying a red ribbon on a pencil (though a red flag was in fact not required by the 1878 Act). More importantly, the Liberal President of the Local Government Board, George Shaw-Lefevre, was converted to the motor car by a visit to Paris in 1895, and had almost succeeded in getting a bill lifting the 1878 restrictions through the Commons when the Liberal government fell in June.

In 1895 several pioneering car-owners tried to provoke a confrontation with the law by driving their imported vehicles on public roads, and in October the leading campaigner, Sir David Salomons, organized a very successful and widely reported motor show in Tunbridge Wells. At this point the prospect of imminent legal reform, and the profits that might be made in the new industry, attracted the attention of a City speculator and company promoter named Harry Lawson. Between 1888 and 1896 Lawson had launched more than twenty companies, generally insurance or banking enterprises, often using the name of a titled shareholder to attract snobbish investors. Lawson was also a former racing cyclist with a long-standing involvement in the cycle industry, and in the cycling boom of the early 1890s he had joined Ernest Hooley in trying to raise nearly £1 million by selling shares in the Humber cycle company and its associates. Developments on the Continent and favourable trends in public opinion suggested that motoring offered even greater rewards. In November 1895 Lawson formed a company called the British Motor Syndicate, with the aim of buying up as many motoring patents as he could, in the hope of selling manufacturing licences at a great profit when the law was changed. His intention was not to manufacture cars, but to persuade gullible investors that he was doing so. Within a few months Lawson had bought almost every important patent except those owned by Benz, and most of the key figures in the British motor business were in his pay.

To make his killing, Lawson had to generate public and political enthusiasm for motoring, and push the government into removing the virtual ban on driving in England. To achieve this, in January 1896 Lawson and his managing director and chief engineer, Frederick Simms, formed the Motor Car Club, a campaigning alliance of motoring interests. Over the next few months, while a new and more permissive Locomotives on Highways Bill was making its way through Parliament, the Motor Car Club staged two motor exhibitions in the Imperial Institute, which had been built in South Kensington after the 1886 Imperial Exhibition. At both of these the performance of the cars was disappointing, but the guest list, which included Sir Hiram Maxim, the machine-gun and aeroplane inventor, the popular journalists George Newnes and T. P. O'Connor, and the Prince of Wales, who was given his first drive in a petrol car, was not. Taking advantage of the publicity generated by the show and the progress of the new law, Lawson tried to sell shares in a Great Horseless Carriage

Company for £750,000. The company's assets and activities were unclear, but several newspapers (including O'Connor's popular *Star*) 'puffed' its prospects and the merits of its founder. The Locomotives on Highways Bill, which exempted vehicles weighing under three tons (unladen) from the old laws and set a speed limit of 12 mph, was passed on 15 August 1896, but its implementation was delayed for three months. In these months Lawson carried on organizing parades and motor shows, and the police continued to bring prosecutions under the 1878 law. Walter Bersey, the pioneer of electric cabs and buses, was fined three times, and James Roots of Westminster Bridge Road, the manufacturer of the Roots Petro-car, was fined 10s for breaking the 2 mph limit.

On 14 November, to celebrate the end of the old law, Lawson organized a great motorized procession along Britain's busiest road, from London to Brighton and back. As the drive began, Lawson's tame aristocrat, the Earl of Winchilsea, tried to rip in half a symbolic red flag, which in fact only a few local authorities still required. An estimated 500,000 people lined the route from Whitehall to Croydon, cheering thirty-two motors, the largest collection of such vehicles ever seen in England, on their way. Lawson led the procession in the Panhard that had won the Paris–Bordeaux race, dressed in a heavily braided yachting outfit that (according to the *Engineer*) made him look like a cross between a German bandmaster and an excursion-steamer steward. Following him in another Panhard came the Earl of Winchilsea, with the humorist Jerome K. Jerome (editor of the weekly *Today*), and reporters from the *Pall Mall Gazette* and the *Daily Telegraph*. Other pressmen travelled in a Daimler charabanc, and Gottlieb Daimler himself rode in a Daimler barouche driven by Frederick Simms. There were two Duryea petrol cars from Peoria, Illinois, some commercial delivery vans (representing Sunlight Soap and Peter Robinson's department store), two French tricars driven by the Bollée brothers (the eventual winners), an electric landau full of ladies (driven by Walter Bersey), an electric cab, a Harrods' bus, and a lady in a Britannia electric bath chair. Bearing in mind the unreliability of motor cars in the 1890s, the survival rate on the first London to Brighton run was surprisingly good. Ten cars failed to get past Brixton, but twenty of the remaining twenty-two reached the finish, at least seven of these before the official 5 p.m. finishing time.[36]

Lawson regarded the London to Brighton run as a triumph, but it was soon obvious that the stunt, like one of its noisy participants, had backfired. Far from inaugurating a new automobile age, the run showed that cars were too expensive, dirty, uncomfortable, and unreliable to interest non-enthusiasts. As the *Standard* remarked, they were 'the vehicles of the future, but not of the immediate present'. Lawson tried to raise another £1 million through a new share issue in November, but the expected boom in public demand for cars did not happen, and if it had done so Lawson's companies, which did not make cars, would not have been able to satisfy it. In the last months of 1896, specialist and popular newspapers turned on Lawson, and exposed the worthlessness of the outdated patents on which his pretensions were based. The value of shares in his companies started to slide, and by Christmas the Lawson companies were in ruins, along with the fortunes of those who had invested heavily in them. In future, persuading City investors to risk their money in the car industry would not be so easy. Lawson himself escaped prosecution, but in 1904, when he and Hooley tried the same trick with an electric tramways company, they were prosecuted for conspiracy to defraud, and Lawson got a year's hard labour.[37]

There was no great motoring boom after the 1896 Act, but the gradual growth in the number of motorists – richer and more influential than the cycling lobby – created a pressure group for further liberalization of the driving laws, including a removal of the speed limit. The Automobile Club (later the RAC), founded in 1897 by Lawson's honest associate Frederick Simms, led this campaign, with useful assistance from Alfred Harmsworth, proprietor of the mass-circulation *Daily Mail* and the enthusiastic owner (from 1899) of an £800 Panhard-Levassor. The Automobile Club could count on the support of a growing number of motorists in the two Houses of Parliament, and could argue convincingly that the motor industry would soon become an important part of the British economy, but politicians also had to take account of a growing public hostility to dangerous drivers. The outcome of this conflict of interests was the 1903 Motor Car Act, which introduced car registration and number plates and raised the speed limit to 20 mph (disappointing the many motorists who wanted the limit abolished altogether), but did not impose a driving test.

The repeal of the so-called 'Red Flag' law in 1896 made it possible to introduce alternatives to the horse-drawn cab and omnibus onto the London streets, but for the first few years nearly all of them were failures. There had been a few battery-powered buses in London in the early 1890s, including a service between Charing Cross and Victoria Station in 1891, but it soon became clear that electric vehicles that had to carry their own batteries would not be a reliable form of public transport. The London

Electric Cab Company, which started with a fleet of twelve cabs in August 1897 and had over sixty by 1899, failed shortly afterwards, and London Electric Omnibus Company, which bought fourteen-seater electric omnibuses from the Electric Construction Company, never managed to run one of them for more than four hours at a time. In 1898 Harry Lawson managed to raise £420,000 for a company he called the Motor Traction Company, and began a petrol-driven bus service from Kennington to Victoria Station (over Westminster Bridge) on 9 October 1899. The service was abandoned after about a year, and a suburban service between Lewisham and Eltham, in South-east London, only ran from 1902 to 1904. The various motor buses that operated in London in 1901 and 1902, including one between Streatham and Clapham Junction, another from Piccadilly Circus to Putney, and a third from Marble Arch to Cricklewood, were all small twelve-seater wagonettes, too small to run at a profit. The biggest bus operator, the London General Omnibus Company (LGOC), whose horse-bus business had been hit by competition from the new Central line and by the loss of horses to military service in South Africa, started experimenting with horseless buses on a very small scale in 1902. The LGOC's first commercial service, an oil-fired steam bus between Piccadilly Circus and Hammersmith, started in October 1904, two days after the Road Car Company's similar service from Oxford Circus to Hammersmith. Both of them lost money, and closed down within nine months. So in 1904 the horse bus was still as familiar a sight on the streets of central London as it had ever been, and motor buses were a noisy and unreliable oddity, as likely to be steaming by the side of the road as moving with the traffic. Four or five motor buses were licensed in London in 1899 and 1900, twenty-nine in 1902, only thirteen in 1903 and thirty-one in 1904. The number increased to 241 in 1905 and 783 in 1906, but many experts and observers in 1903 and 1904 had not expected this to happen.[38]

Yerkes and Speyer

The failure of old and new bus companies to establish successful motor bus routes before 1905 had very important long-term consequences for the development of London and its public-transport system. If the full potential of motor buses had been demonstrated in 1901 or 1902, rather than 1904 and 1905, investors would have been far more cautious about putting their money into the development of deep-level electric tubes, and much of the London Underground network might not have been built. As things stood in 1900, with trams excluded from central London and bus companies dithering between horse, steam, electric and petrol power, the outlook for electric underground railways seemed very bright. The success of the Central London Railway, which carried 41 million passengers in its first full year, taking almost twice its operating costs in fares and paying a 4 per cent dividend to its shareholders, only confirmed what smart City financiers already knew. Several deep underground lines had been given Parliamentary approval in 1893, and work on some of these was already in progress in the late 1890s. The City and South London Railway was extended north to the Angel Islington (via Bank, Moorgate and Old Street) and south to Clapham, by 1901, and tunnelling work on the Great Northern and City line from Drayton Park (Highbury) to Moorgate, was completed by 1902.

The introduction of the Central Railway's faster, cleaner and more frequent service on its West End and City routes forced the Metropolitan and District Railway companies to face up to the costly and complicated task of electrifying their lines, especially the Inner Circle. To electrify the Circle, the two companies had to raise £666,000 from share issues, but there was little prospect of their getting this sum from their shareholders, who had suffered years of poor dividends and falling share prices. In February 1901 the position was transformed by the intervention of a syndicate led by Robert Perks, a solicitor, company promoter and Member of Parliament who had been associated with the Metropolitan Railway since the 1870s. Perks' main interest was in promoting the unity and financial strength of the Methodist Church, but his knowledge of London railways, finance, Parliament and the Liberal Party made him a powerful force in the reshaping of the Underground in these few years. Business creates unlikely partnerships, and Perks' main associate in 1901 was a man of an altogether different type, the American financial fixer and transport entrepreneur Charles Tyson Yerkes. Yerkes had made, lost and remade a fortune in stockbroking and financial speculation in Philadelphia in the 1860s and 1870s, and spent seven months in prison there for embezzlement in 1872. In 1881 he moved to Chicago, and quickly spotted the possibility of making a fortune from promoting the development of urban electric transport networks, usually with other people's money. By 1886 he had gained control of the North Chicago Street Railroad Company, and in the 1890s he took over two of the city's three elevated railroad companies. Yerkes was very effective in raising money and obtaining franchises to extend his networks and exclude competitors, but his notorious use of bribery, sexual entrapment and blackmail made him too many enemies, and in 1899 he sold his shares for $20 million and abandoned Chicago for his palatial mansion on Fifth Avenue, New York. Within a year he was in London, determined to apply his business philosophy ('buy up old junk, fix it up a little and unload it upon other fellows') to the biggest transport system in the world. Yerkes had been to London in 1898, when he discussed the future of the District Railway with Perks, and it might have been Yerkes that Dame Henrietta Barnett spoke to in 1896, when she met an American with 'a proposal . . . to convey all London about in tunnels' and to build a station next to Hampstead Heath. Yerkes was certainly interested in the proposed Charing Cross to Hampstead line in September 1900, when, using Perks as his intermediary, he paid £100,000 for control of the Charing Cross, Euston and Hampstead Railway, which had parliamentary approval for its underground line but, until Yerkes' arrival, no capital to start construction.

Unlike the men he had taken over from, Yerkes did not believe in wasting time. By December engineers and a construction company had been appointed, and bills were before Parliament to extend the line south to Victoria and north to Highgate and Golders Green, in defiance of those who thought a railway more than 100 feet beneath the ground would damage the trees on Hampstead Heath. In May and June 1901 a parliamentary Select Committee considered these bills, along with proposals for extensions to three existing schemes and plans for six completely new lines, and suggested (in vain) that London's emerging Underground system should be designed with a view to the best interests of Londoners, and with closer supervision by Parliament, the City, the LCC and the Board of Trade, rather than in response to uncoordinated commercial proposals. Meanwhile Yerkes had collected American backers for his new line, and for the electrification of the District Railway, and in July 1901 the formation of the Metropolitan District Electric Traction Company, with £1 million capital subscribed by Boston and New York businessmen, was announced. This company also held the rights to the approved but unbuilt Brompton and Piccadilly Circus Railway, paid £131,000 to the Great Northern for the right to build the Great Northern and Strand Railway (from the Strand to Finsbury Park), and took over Yerkes' rights to the Charing Cross, Euston and Hampstead Railway. By March 1902 Yerkes' Traction Company had bought the Baker Street and Waterloo Railway, which the near-bankrupt London and Globe Finance Corporation had begun but could not complete, for under £200,000. In doing this, the Traction Company was taking over the line from Warwick Wright, a financier and company promoter whose dealings were even shadier than Yerkes'. Wright had raised his capital largely on the strength of his mining interests in Western Australia, whose likely yields were overstated by a bribed financial press. While the City had confidence in him he lived the life of a lord of the manor in Surrey, but his fortunes crashed in December 1900, perhaps because of the actions of a hostile City syndicate, but also because he seemed to have over-reached himself in undertaking to build the Baker Street and Waterloo Railway. Wright fled to Paris and New York, but was brought back to face trial for fraud at the Old Bailey in January 1904. He was convicted and sentenced to seven years' penal servitude and then, like the heroine of a 'new woman' novel, finished himself off with potassium cyanide.[39]

Wright's downfall might have acted as a warning to those thinking of investing in railways, but the continuing success of the Central Railway ensured that Yerkes would not be the only American financier hoping to profit from London's underground boom. In December 1900 the powerful American banking house of J. S. Morgan and Company, which had interests in the American firm General Electric and the British branch of the Siemens Brothers electrical company, took a leading part in two underground proposals, the Piccadilly and City Railway and a line from the City to Tottenham. In 1901 Morgan entered negotiations with London United Tramways, which had plans for two underground railways to join up with its new electric tram routes in West and North London, which were excluded from the City and the West End. This gave Morgan an interest in a proposed thirty-eight-mile network of underground lines, including a line running north to the working-class suburbs of Southgate and Tottenham, which did not in fact appear on the Tube map until the 1930s and was not completed until the 1960s.

To meet this powerful challenge, Yerkes enlisted an international banker of his own, Edgar Speyer, the senior partner in Speyer Brothers. Edgar Speyer was born in New York of German Jewish parents, and educated in Frankfurt, the German headquarters of the family banking firm. He came to London in 1887, took British citizenship in 1892, married a professional violinist, and became a generous patron of the arts in London. The Whitechapel Art Gallery, which opened in 1901 to bring good paintings to the East End, relied heavily on his patronage, and without Speyer's financial support the popular but unprofitable Promenade concerts at the

Queen's Hall might not have survived, and Captain Scott's 1910–12 expedition to the Antarctic might not have taken place. Most of the deep-level railways that sheltered Londoners from German bombs in both world wars were built with money invested or raised by Speyer. Yet in 1915 public hostility to Germans forced him to move to New York, and after the war he was stripped of his British citizenship and his membership of the Privy Council for trading (indirectly) with the enemy, as many businessmen did in the early years of the Great War.

Yerkes met Speyer in March 1902, and by April they had agreed that Speyer Brothers of London, Speyer and Company of New York, and the Old Colony Trust of Boston would together give financial backing to a new company, the Underground Electric Railways Company of London (UERL), replacing the underfunded Traction Company with a £5 million company capable of building three underground railways and electrifying the District Railway. Yerkes remained the chairman of the company and its largest individual shareholder, but Speyer and the bankers were in control. Among the shareholders, East Coast Americans outnumbered British investors by almost two to one. The Speyer and Morgan syndicates presented their rival proposals to a House of Lords Committee in the spring of 1902, each trying to outdo the other in the frequency, speed, and cheapness of the services they would offer. Things seemed to be going Morgan's way in July 1902, but during the summer parliamentary recess Yerkes and Speyer took advantage of divisions between Morgans and London United Tramways, and pulled a trick that threw the Morgan proposals into disarray. On 21 October it was announced that Speyer Brothers had bought a controlling interest in London United Tramways, Morgan's partner in their underground bid. By this brilliant masterstroke (or piece of skulduggery, depending on your point of view) Speyer and Yerkes destroyed the Morgan plan, took control of a large part of the Outer London tram network, and deprived Parliament of the opportunity to shape London's underground railway system by choosing between rival proposals.[40]

Building the Electric Tube

The LCC had been pressing the government for some months to establish a public authority which could exert a degree of control over the development of London's underground railways, which seemed otherwise to have fallen under the control of business interests which were not concerned with the public good. Lord Ribblesdale, who had chaired one of the House of Lords committees on the new underground proposals, thought that the LCC itself should be the regulatory authority: 'Unlike the American financier or City of London financier, the London County Council is always here. It is in the constitutional sense of the word responsible.' The Conservative government instead decided to appoint a Royal Commission on London Traffic to examine the question in its widest context. The Royal Commission did so, sitting from February 1903 to July 1905 and producing eight large and highly informative volumes of evidence. Among other things, it dismissed the LCC's claim to supervise London's public-transport system. How could a body which ran its own large tram network exercise impartial authority over competing transport companies, and how could the LCC, whose powers did not extend beyond the County boundary, oversee the transport facilities of the much larger Greater London area? Instead, the Royal Commission agreed with Yerkes that a small body of experts, the London Traffic Board, should examine all London transport bills, prepare local schemes, and promote joint operation between private concerns. Like most of the Commission's proposals, this was never implemented, and by the time the Liberal government turned its mind to the matter in 1907, the LCC, now under Moderate (Conservative) control, no longer wished to become London's transport authority. So the government created an almost powerless body, the London Traffic Branch of the Board of Trade, and the development of London's transport system in these vital years was left mainly in the hands of private enterprise.

While the Royal Commission left most new underground proposals in abeyance between 1902 and 1905, the Speyer–Yerkes syndicate had a free hand to press on with its already approved lines. Thanks to the skills of Yerkes and Speyer, the company had the capital it needed for this stupendous enterprise. Since investors proved unwilling at first to risk their money on shares in the new underground lines, the Underground Group had to raise most of the capital it needed in early 1903 by selling Profit Sharing Notes (as Yerkes enticingly called them) worth £7 million, half in the UK, half in America, with a guaranteed tax-free interest rate of 5 per cent, and redeemable in 1908. Another £3,350,000 was raised by the sale of debentures in 1904 and 1905, bringing the total amount raised by the UERL to about £15 million. Some of this vast sum was secured against the company's assets, especially the huge power station it was building in Lots Road, on Chelsea Reach, but most of it was dependent on the UERL's ability to sell its shares, which would depend in turn on whether the new railways made the healthy profits their promoters were predicting. Costs were increased, meanwhile, by new regulations requiring fireproof trains and platforms and escape routes from tunnels and stations, after a fire killed eighty-four passengers in the Paris Métro in August 1903.[41]

The Yerkes railways were finished with astonishing speed. The tunnels, which were generally 11 feet 8¼ inches in diameter, over a foot wider than the inadequate City and South London tunnels, were dug with Greathead shields, driven through the soil with hydraulic rams. Their cost, according to Yerkes, was £35 a yard, which was well under a tenth of the cost of the cut-and-cover tunnelling used on the Whitechapel to Bow extension of the Metropolitan Railway in 1899–1902.[42] Compressed air was used to stop water rushing into the tunnel under the Thames, where it had to go through water-bearing gravel. On the Piccadilly line the shield was fitted with an electric-powered rotary excavator, with six revolving arms carrying blades to cut the clay and buckets to empty it into a chute. This doubled the tunnelling speed from about 73 feet a week on the Baker Street line to 160 feet on the Hampstead line, and a maximum of 180 feet on the Strand line. Tunnelling was no faster than this in the 1930s, though by 1965 tunnels could be cut at over 450 feet a week. The Baker Street to Waterloo tunnels were finished by November 1903, and by the end of 1905 the stations, tracks, lifts, and power supply were ready, and the rolling stock was ordered. The first passengers went from Lambeth North to Baker Street in March 1906, and on to Edgware Road a year later. Nearly all the tunnelling for the Great Northern, Piccadilly, and Brompton railway (which went as far west as Hammersmith) was also done by October 1905, though the tunnel down to the Strand was delayed for a year because the new road, Kingsway, was being built above it. The line between Hammersmith and Finsbury Park was opened by David Lloyd George in December 1906, and extended to the Strand (later Aldwych) a year later. The Charing Cross, Euston, and Hampstead line was finished by April 1906, and public trains ran from Charing Cross to Hampstead and Archway in June 1907. As Yerkes had emphasized before the Royal Commission on London Traffic, all three UERL tubes were designed to operate as one system, with convenient underground passageways enabling travellers to change from one line to another at Piccadilly Circus, Leicester Square, Tottenham Court Road, Euston, and other shared stations.[43]

At the same time the older shallow underground companies, the Metropolitan and the Metropolitan District (which was controlled by Yerkes), were converting from steam to electric traction. The Metropolitan's power plant at Neasden was operating by the end of 1904, its first public electric trains ran in January 1905, and a full service to Harrow, with British Westinghouse locomotives, was running a year later. On the District Railway, an electric train ran from Mill Hill Park and Bow Road in March 1905, and public services from Ealing to Whitechapel started that July. By the end of that summer, the District Railway to Richmond, Putney, Wimbledon, and East Ham, and most services on the Circle, which were shared between the two companies, had converted to electricity.[44]

Those who had invested so heavily to make the creation of this new electric Underground possible had been led to expect a revolution in the travelling habits of Londoners. Electric trains were faster, quieter, cleaner, and more frequent than steam trains, and on their routes through central London their only competitors were horse-drawn buses and cabs, which were often caught up in heavy traffic. But on longer commuter routes the new lines were in competition with the Twopenny Tube and cheap electric trams, and the Metropolitan and the District railways had already been forced to cut their fares to hold onto their suburban passengers, who could go from Richmond or Ealing to the Bank by tram and Central Railway for 4d. To make a profit on fares of 3d and 4d, the new electric lines had to carry a vast number of passengers. But electrification hardly increased the number of people using the Metropolitan Railway in 1905 and 1906, and only increased those using the District by 10 per cent, instead of the 100 per cent predicted in 1903. Yerkes had found an expert who anticipated that 145 million passengers would use the three UERL tubes, but in their first full year only 71 million people used the Piccadilly, Hampstead, and Bakerloo railways, despite the fact that they were fast, frequent, and cheap. The highest fare, from Hammersmith to Finsbury Park, was only 4d, the fare from Charing Cross to Archway or Hampstead or Elephant and Castle to Baker Street was 3d, and many central London fares were only a penny. These low fares reflected Yerkes' hope that a 2d flat fare on all his railways would enable working men to move out to healthy suburban homes built on green-field sites (as they had in Chicago), but they did not generate the traffic or the profits that his highly capitalized companies needed. He died in New York at the end of 1905, leaving his own fortune, and those of the investors who had believed in the profitability of his underground railways, almost in ruins. Whatever his shortcomings as a husband and a financier, Yerkes left London the legacy of an efficient deep-level underground railway network which would probably never have happened without the help of his unscrupulous business methods, and for which private investors, not London ratepayers, had paid the bill.

Sir Edgar Speyer, who was left with the responsibility of rescuing the UERL and the District Railway from collapse, hired George Gibb, the only experienced railwayman who had sat on the Royal Commission on London Traffic, as managing director of the UERL and the District Railway. In an effort to reduce the company's £100,000 annual loss and stave off bankruptcy Gibb introduced through tickets between the three tubes, the District, and LUT trams, increased some fares, and started a drive to publicize the new services with posters, maps, and timetables. He was assisted from February 1907 by a young general manager, Albert Henry Stanley, an English-born American whose work in running trams in New Jersey had impressed the UERL's anxious American shareholders. Stanley replaced Gibb as managing director in 1910, and (as Lord Ashfield) ran the UERL, and then the London Passenger Transport Board, until 1947, except for a period in Lloyd George's Cabinet from 1916 to 1919.[45]

All the underground railway companies were suffering the effects of too much competition and the burden of debt. The UERL considered selling out to the LCC, and Speyer discussed the idea with the Progressive Party leader, Thomas McKinnon Wood, at Sidney and Beatrice Webb's house in April 1906. Perhaps it would have happened if the Progressives had not lost power in 1907. Instead, Speyer Brothers had to pay out £475,000 in December 1907 to save UERL from bankruptcy. The Metropolitan, which carried more passengers than the three UERL tubes combined, cut its dividend from 3 per cent in 1905 to 0.5 per cent in 1907, and the Central London, which carried fewer passengers in 1910 than in 1901, was forced to increase its famous 2d flat fare to 3d for longer journeys in July 1907. This eased the pressure on the District, which already charged 3d from the suburbs, and allowed the Metropolitan to do the same. The Central London's change of policy helped to draw the underground railways together to fight the challenge of the bus companies, which were threatening to introduce halfpenny fares for short journeys in 1907. All the underground companies except the Waterloo and City agreed in February 1908 to market their railways as one system, with standardized signs, and wall and pocket maps showing all the London lines. At the same time the railway companies demonstrated the benefits of electricity by running their trains faster and more often. The journey time from Ealing or Wimbledon to the City, which had been over forty-five minutes by steam train, was cut to under thirty-five minutes, and at

peak times some lines ran thirty-five or even forty trains an hour. To reduce
waiting times, the UERL introduced cut-price strips of tickets in 1908, and
installed escalators at Earls Court in 1911. The Metropolitan, whose passenger numbers had only risen by 3 per cent between 1906 and 1910,
tried to increase its business by encouraging suburban development in the
Middlesex countryside, which would be served by fast trains from its stations at Wembley, Pinner, Ruislip, Harrow, and Northwood. Some of the
suburban surface railways, whose business had been severely damaged by
the arrival of electric trams, motor buses, and the electric underground,
tried to regain their lost passengers by electrifying their lines. The Brighton
company, which had lost millions of passengers to trams, buses, and tubes
on its suburban services between Victoria or London Bridge and Peckham,
Brixton, Balham, Streatham, Crystal Palace, Battersea, and Clapham Junction, won them back by introducing electric trains and cutting journey
times by half in 1910–12. To hold or regain their suburban traffic, which
was at least as great as that of the underground railways, several main-line
railway companies rebuilt or extended their London termini: Waterloo and
Victoria were almost doubled in size in 1908–9, and extra tracks were laid
at London Bridge, Euston, and Paddington.[46]

3,000 Buses Come at Once

At the very moment when the new electric railways were trying to establish themselves a powerful new rival appeared on the streets of London. A
thirty-four-seater double-decker petrol bus, a British chassis on a Berlin-
built Daimler engine, which Tillings ran from Peckham to Oxford Circus
on 30 September 1904, was a success, and the company ordered another
twenty-four. The Atlas and Waterloo Association ran a similar bus between
Waterloo and Baker Street in October 1904. In December 1904 a group
of businessmen and provincial bus owners raised about £500,000 by
floating two companies, the London Motor Omnibus Company (LMOC)
and the London and District Motor Bus Company, on the Stock Exchange
early in 1905. Investors were excited by new government regulations in
March 1905 which increased the maximum unladen weight of motor buses
with rubber tyres from 3 to 5 tons, making bigger and more economical
buses possible. Early in 1905 two major horse-omnibus companies, Tillings and the Road Car Company, decided to start replacing horses with
motor buses, and by September 1905 these two, along with LMOC, had

78 motor buses in operation, out of London's total of 132. These early motor buses were unreliable and expensive to run and repair, especially with London's rough roads and untrained drivers (usually from horse buses) who liked to tinker with their engines. Constant stopping and starting, and getting stuck in heavy traffic, tested their primitive clutches and cooling systems to destruction. So in the middle of this scramble the LGOC's wily chairman, Sir John Pound, with twenty-five years' experience of running the company, held back until motor technology had improved. In mid-1905, judging that he could delay no longer, Pound ordered about a hundred motor buses, and by March 1907 the LGOC had 171 in service, almost as many as the LMOC. The dramatic rise in the number of motor buses in these two or three years is confirmed by the number of licences issued by the Metropolitan Police. Four or five motor buses were licensed in London in 1899 and 1900, twenty-nine in 1902, only thirteen in 1903, and thirty-one in 1904. Then the boom began, with 241 in 1905, 783 in 1906, and about 1,200 for each of the next four years. Horse buses held their own until 1905, when the number of annual licences issued started to fall. There were over 3,600 licences issued annually from 1899 to 1903, and still about 3,500 in 1905, but only 2,964 in 1906, 2,155 in 1908, and 1,103 in 1910, when they were outnumbered for the first time by motor buses.

The population of London was rising, and the number of journeys taken by each Londoner was increasing too, but not fast enough to fill the large number of extra seats available for them in 1906 and 1907. The position of the London bus companies, competing against each other as well as trams and the new tubes and electric underground lines, was very difficult. The LGOC, which made a gross profit of £65,000 in 1905, sustained a £147,000 loss in 1907–8, and the other motor bus companies, which had smaller reserves, did just as badly. The companies' main competitive devices, fare cuts and more frequent services, made their position even worse, and several smaller companies were forced into liquidation in 1907–8. Four larger companies joined forces as the Vanguard Motorbus Company in April 1907, and in 1908 they began negotiations with the Road Car Company and the LGOC to form a single company to compete against tubes and trams. Predictably, the much richer LGOC absorbed the other two, forming a company with about a thousand motor buses. Another firm, the Great Eastern, joined in 1911, leaving Tillings as the main independent company.

The amalgamation made the LGOC's position much stronger, but their real breakthrough was their decision in 1909 to develop their own motor bus, which would withstand the challenges of the London roads and traffic without the frequent breakdowns that bedevilled earlier services. At the Vanguard's Walthamstow works in the Lea Valley, the LGOC's chief motor engineer, Frank Searle, designed a new lightweight bus, the X-type, followed by another, the famous B-type, the world's first mass-produced bus, which was first made in October 1910, and was light enough to meet a new 3.5-ton limit introduced in March 1910. Almost every component of the B-type was made at Walthamstow, and the utmost care was taken to make sure its parts were interchangeable. By 1911 the factory was producing twenty B-types a week, at a cost of £300 a vehicle, less than the cost of a horse bus and its horses. The B-type, which gave a bumpy, solid-tyred ride to thirty-four passengers (eighteen of whom sat on the open upper deck), was not the last word in comfort, but it was a reliable and economical bus, well suited in its speed, size, and handling to the nature of the London roads. From this moment, the horse omnibus, which had held its own against trains and trams for eighty years, was obsolete. The LGOC ran its last one in October 1911, from Moorgate Street and London Bridge, and the number operating in London fell from 1,103 in 1910 to 376 in 1912. The number of motor buses, which had stagnated at about 1,200 from 1907 to 1910, reached almost 2,000 in 1911 and 2,900 by 1912. The great majority of these were B-types, bearing the LGOC's identifying name, 'General', on their side, and crewed by men wearing the LGOC's cap and jacket. Tillings ran the last London horse bus from Peckham Rye to Honor Oak on 4 August 1914, after which its horses were conscripted for military service in France.

The new buses could reach over 16 mph (though the limit was 14 mph), enabling them to run services deep into the outer suburbs, and beyond them to such places as Chessington, St Albans, Hounslow, and Reigate. On Sundays they carried Londoners even further, to Leatherhead, Dorking, and Maidenhead. By 1914 London had 112 motor-bus routes, covering a total of 1,106 miles, nearly four times the distance covered in 1911. The long-standing law limiting omnibuses to an area within fifteen miles of the centre of London was repealed in 1912. Most of the routes began in central London, or passed through the centre between one suburban extremity and another, but there were also many completely suburban routes (like the 105 between Ealing and Surbiton, or the number 37, for people from Peckham Rye who fancied a day out in Richmond or Isleworth), and routes that connected suburban railway or Underground stations with London's rural outskirts. It was cheaper and easier for motor buses to try out new suburban routes, and thus open up fresh areas to settlement, than it was for trains and trams, which had to carry a much heavier traffic to justify the outlay on new tracks, and could not change their minds so easily. In the centre of London, motor buses achieved a saturation which was apparently as great as that achieved by horse buses around 1900. In summer 1913 motor buses passed Selfridge's, the vast new department store in Oxford Street, about every thirteen seconds in each direction between 7 a.m. and 8 p.m., and the Ritz, the new hotel in Piccadilly, every eighteen seconds.[47]

The development of an efficient motor bus by the LGOC brought to an end that brief period in which the electric tram seemed to be the answer to London's transport problems. The number of tram journeys in Greater London reached its pre-war peak of 820 million in 1911–12, and had declined a little by 1913–14, while the omnibus nearly doubled its passenger journeys (from 400 million to 756 million) between 1911 and 1914. The previously profitable London United Tramways was in serious trouble, paying no dividends, in 1910, and the LCC's electric-tram network, which made a good profit in 1911–12, only managed to break even in 1912–13, and lost nearly £90,000 in 1913–14. The LGOC, on the other hand, almost doubled its profits between 1910 and 1911. After the Great War, tram and bus journeys each stood at about 1,000 million a year, but while tram journeys remained at roughly that figure, the number of journeys by motor buses surged ahead, reaching 2,000 million by 1930. The foundations of this ascendancy were laid before 1914.[48]

By 1911 the LGOC had almost complete control of London motor bus services. They had bought the Great Eastern Company in March 1911, and had a working agreement with the last significant independent operator, Tillings, limiting it to 150 motor buses. At this point the leaders of the UERL, Edgar Speyer and A. H. Stanley, entered negotiations to unite the two companies, to end or at least control the competition that had so undermined the profits of trams and trains. The UERL's generous offer for LGOC shares was accepted in February 1912, and a single company, soon to be called the London Traffic Combine, was created, with Stanley as its managing director. Over the next year the new company swallowed up most of London's smaller transport operators, including Emile Garcke's Metropolitan Electric Tramways, which had extensive tram routes in North and North-west London and was on the point of starting its own bus services. Of London's four remaining independent bus companies, all except

Tillings had yielded control of their services to the Traffic Combine by the end of 1913. The only independent electric-tram operator left was the LCC, but LCC trams carried over 500 million of the 800 million tram passengers in Greater London in 1913–14. The Traffic Combine's control of trams, buses, and tubes gave it an armlock on the remaining underground railways, which were struggling for profits and customers. The Central London Railway, which had extended to Liverpool Street in 1912 to gain new traffic, and the City and South London, the oldest electric underground railway, were taken over by the Traffic Combine on 1 January 1913. Now only the Metropolitan Railway, which had more passengers and more miles of track than any other underground line, and the small Waterloo and City Railway remained outside the Traffic Combine's control of the underground network. The Metropolitan retained its independence until 1933, when the whole system was taken over by the London Passenger Transport Board, under the chairmanship of Lord Ashfield, who had once been the Traffic Combine's A. H. Stanley.[49]

The Impact of Motor Transport

The breakthrough years for motor cabs in London were 1906 and 1907, about twelve months behind the start of the motor-bus boom. There were still 11,000 licensed horse cabs in London in 1905 (with hansoms outnumbering four-wheelers by seven to four), and only 19 motor cabs. But 96 motor cabs were licensed in 1906, 723 in 1907, and 6,397 in 1910. Hansoms declined fastest, down to 2,000 by 1910 and 386 by 1913, when there were 8,387 motor cabs and 1,547 four-wheelers. By 1911 twelve companies ran three-quarters of the London motor cabs, and one, based in Brixton, had 1,400 cabs, nearly a fifth of the total. In the longer run, though, the larger companies failed, and individual operators and small firms predominated.

Probably half of London's 180,000 horses had vanished by 1914. Nearly all the 75,000 horses involved in public transport were gone, except for 4,000 cab horses, and by 1911 (according to the LCC's traffic survey) most people who ran private carriages had bought horseless ones. This still left a large number of commercial horse carts and vans, which outnumbered motorized vans and lorries by about seventeen to one in 1911 and by seven to one in 1913, according to London traffic surveys. At three or four tons each, 180,000 horses deposited about 650,000 tons of droppings on London's street in the 1890s, giving London's twenty-eight Metropolitan boroughs a costly and messy job. Street cleaning cost the twenty-eight boroughs (not including the City) £712,000 in 1908–9, nearly 15 per cent of their total annual spending. Between them, the boroughs collected about a million tons of street refuse and 'gully slops' that year, from 2,191 miles of roads, but the task was getting smaller. The Westminster authorities collected 60,000 tons of street refuse in 1905–6, but only 29,000 tons in 1911–12. The cost of cleaning London's streets fell by very nearly a third between 1905–6 and 1909–10, and about 13 per cent in 1908–9 to 1909–10 alone.[50] The decline in horse traffic also reduced the need for street orderlies, with their dustpans and brushes, and undermined the prosperity of shoeblacks. The reduction in the amount of horse dung on the streets and piled up awaiting collection also had an impact on the health of London's population, especially because of the decline in flies and fly-borne diseases. Annual deaths from diarrhoea and dysentery, important killers of young children, fell more sharply than those from any other major cause between 1900–4 and 1910, from 3,567 (the 1900–4 average) to 1,368, a fall of over 60 per cent, when London death rates in general fell by only 22 per cent over the same period. The other disease for which mortality declined by over 60 per cent, typhoid, could also be spread by flies, though its more common cause was polluted water.[51]

The coming of electric and motorized transport made London healthier and sweeter-smelling, but also made it a far more dangerous place for the cyclist and pedestrian than it had been before. By 1910 there were 1,200 motor buses, 2,411 electric trams, 6,400 motor cabs, 1,900 motorcycles, and just over 7,000 motor cars licensed or registered in the LCC area. In the same year, but in the much larger Metropolitan Police District (excluding the City of London, which had nineteen deaths), road accidents killed 367 people, about a third of the national total. Of these deaths, only 49 were caused by horse vehicles or cyclists, and 318 were caused by cars, vans, and motorized cabs, buses, and trams. To put this into perspective, the annual number of deaths on London's far busier roads in the years around 2000 was under 300. Motor buses, which killed 61 people, were considered particularly dangerous, compared to electric trams, which were twice as numerous but caused only 26 deaths. Motor cabs, which killed 32 people, were much safer than private cars and vans, which killed 197. The only advice that Muirhead's *Blue Guide* could offer to visitors to London was to take 'considerable care' in crossing streets and getting off trams or omnibuses: 'a busy street should be crossed only at a point where an "island refuge" is provided in the middle'. At a few busy junctions there were subways provided by the underground railway companies, but elsewhere London's inexperienced pedestrians had to take their chance against London's untrained and often deadly drivers. There had been an experimental gas traffic light outside the Houses of Parliament in 1868, but it had exploded, injuring a policeman. The first electric traffic lights were not installed in London until 1926, Belisha beacons appeared in 1934, and zebra crossings were not introduced until 1951.

Motorists and their organizations usually blamed pedestrians for their carelessness in crossing roads, and it is true that films of London streets at the start of the twentieth century show people wandering casually between moving vehicles in a way that made sense when carts and buses went at walking pace, but which was courting disaster in a motorized world. Others blamed a new class of drivers, those who drove cheap Ford and Morris cars without the 'gentlemanly' good manners that had restrained the well-bred motorists of the first generation. Like cycling, *The Times* said in 1901, driving had attracted low-bred 'cads' who had to be taught to behave properly behind the wheel. 'There is no turning a cad into a gentleman, but there is such a thing as making even cads fear the law.'[52] The new American name for these selfish drivers, 'road-hogs', first used to describe cyclists in the early 1890s, gained currency in England after 1900.

London had long suffered from congested streets and 'traffic blocks', and various street-widening and traffic-control measures had been taken to improve the flow of vehicles. In 1899 the police used new powers to ban cabs from 'crawling' along Piccadilly, the Strand, and Bond Street looking for passengers, though it was generally thought that trade vehicles loading and unloading, and omnibuses picking up customers in the middle of the road, were the worst causes of congestion. Several witnesses to the Royal Commission on London Traffic had predicted that the transition to motor transport would reduce traffic congestion, because horse vehicles were bigger, slower, and less manoeuvrable than motorized ones. A table of road-obstruction factors produced by the Board of Trade in 1919 maintained that horse-drawn vehicles were generally twice as obstructive as their motorized equivalents. A motor car or cab had a factor of one, horse cabs and carriages were rated at two, slow heavy lorries were given a five, but slow two-horse carts were the most obstructive vehicles on the road, with a ten. Electric trams (nine) ran them close, but these were huge vehicles, and there were no longer any horse trams to compare them with.[53] The Metropolitan Board of Works had built and widened many roads to improve the flow of traffic in London, but the LCC after 1888 was much less active, mainly because they had failed to win renewal of the coal and wine duties that had contributed about £325,000 a year to the MBW's public-works fund. Only one of the LCC's road projects, the construction of Kingsway and the Aldwych, matched the work of the MBW. Of the major intersections that caused the greatest delays – Piccadilly Circus, Ludgate Circus, Trafalgar Square, Mansion House, Elephant and Castle, and Hyde Park Corner – only the last (and busiest) was redesigned, when Piccadilly was widened opposite Park Lane in 1902. The need to undertake consultation and win the approval of affected property-owners meant that some street-widening schemes progressed at a snail's pace. Improvements in the Strand and Piccadilly, begun in 1897 and 1903, were still unfinished in 1938, and the construction of flyovers at busy junctions, which was first suggested by Sir John Wolfe Barry (the engineer of Tower Bridge) in 1898, had still not taken place forty years later. The abolition of the ancient hay market that cluttered the whole length of Whitechapel High Street, one of the City's main eastern exits, was recommended in 1905, but did not happen until 1929.[54] The Royal Commission on London Traffic's recommendation in 1905 that two great avenues, each 140 feet wide (as wide as Whitehall, London's widest street), should be built to carry trams, trains, and vehicles across London from east to west (from Bayswater Road to Whitechapel) and north to south (from Holloway to the Elephant and Castle) was not acted upon. But recognition that the growth of motor traffic would put intolerable pressure on some of the narrow main roads out of London (Brentford High Street, Uxbridge Road, Shooter's Hill, and so on) led the Board of Trade to organize a series of Arterial Roads Conferences between 1913 and 1916, which began to plan the construction of wider roads and bypasses after the Great War. Western Avenue, from White City into North-west London, and Eastern Avenue, from Leytonstone into Essex, were conceived before 1914, and born in the 1920s.

Building Bridges

There was a spate of bridge rebuilding and repair in the 1880s, when the MBW's chief engineer, Sir Joseph Bazalgette, rebuilt the Hammersmith suspension bridge, replaced the wooden bridges at Putney and Battersea with less romantic but sturdier structures of granite and cast iron, and overhauled the Albert Bridge. James McNeil Whistler's series of paintings and etchings of the old wooden bridges at Putney and Battersea in the 1860s and 1870s remind us of their rickety charm, but they were too weak for the burden of heavy traffic (including electric trams) they would have to carry as London expanded westwards. It was Whistler's study of Battersea Bridge by night, *The Falling Rocket, a nocturne in black and gold*, which was described by the critic John Ruskin as 'flinging a pot of paint in the public's face'. Foolishly, Whistler sued Ruskin for libel in 1878, won a farthing damages without costs, and was reduced to bankruptcy. As a result he had to sell the White House in Tite Street, Chelsea, which had been built for him by Edward Godwin. The LCC replaced the cast-iron bridge at Vauxhall with a steel and granite bridge between 1895 and 1906, but delayed work on its other old bridges (Chelsea, Lambeth, and Waterloo) until the 1920s and 1930s.

The most spectacular addition to London's collection of bridges was the work of the City Corporation. There had been talk of a bridge at the eastern end of the City for years, and Bazalgette had drawn up a plan for the MBW in 1878. Thames shipping interests and ferry owners opposed the bridge, and the government's refusal to extend the Board's income from coal duties forced it to drop the idea. A Select Committee examined the Board's alternative plans for a road tunnel (to replace Barlow and Greathead's 1869 pedestrian tunnel) in 1884, and discovered that the City Corporation's Bridge House Estate, the ancient fund from which it covered the costs of maintaining the three City bridges, had a healthy surplus. So the Corporation took over the task of building a new bridge, and employed the civil engineer John Wolfe Barry, the son of the architect of the Houses of Parliament, and the City Architect, Horace Jones, to design it. They came up with a 940-foot suspension bridge with a bascule bridge (with two opening leaves, or bascules) in its central span. When these bascules were raised there would be an opening 200 feet wide and about 140 feet above high water (up to the high-level footbridge) for ships to enter or leave the Pool of London. Tower Bridge was built between 1886 and 1894, and like much London building in these decades it was an odd combination of the ancient and modern. The two massive steel towers that held the steam engines, water tanks, and hydraulic machinery that could raise the two massive bascules in 90 seconds were cased in Gothic stonework that protected the steel from corrosion and disguised the modernity of the mechanism within. Purists objected to the deception involved in clothing late-nineteenth-century machinery in medieval masonry, but the great

Gothic gateway to London, which reflected the combined efforts of Jones (who died in 1887) and the Scottish architect George D. Stephenson, satisfied the tastes of most Londoners, and has done ever since. The bridge and its approaches, about half a mile in length, cost around £1.5 million, but provided a very useful river crossing, mainly for trade vehicles and omnibuses. According to the 1911 traffic census, Tower Bridge carried more commercial carts, wagons, and vans than any other Thames bridge, though Battersea and London Bridge ran it close.[55] But unhappy Londoners lost a convenient and popular means of killing themselves when the upper walkway was closed to the public in 1909.

The growth of population and industry beyond Tower Bridge made river crossings further downstream essential, and it was clear that tunnelling, rather than bridging, was the practical way to link the Essex and Kentish halves of East London. The experience of building the City and South London railway tunnel near London Bridge between 1886 and 1890 encouraged tunnellers to undertake more ambitious underwater projects. The Blackwall road tunnel, linking the Lea Valley with Greenwich and South-east London, was dug through over 3,000 feet of clay and water-bearing gravel, using a very large shield with movable shutters, between 1892 and 1897. Though the tunnel was built for horse traffic, it has given pleasure to generations of motorists. It also began to stimulate a little development in Bugsby's Marsh (or Greenwich Marsh), the desolate piece of land in the bend of the river opposite the Lea which is now the home of the Millennium Dome. The Rotherhithe road tunnel, built between 1904 and 1908, was 4,863 feet long and 27 feet across, with 1,400 feet directly under the river, making it the biggest underwater tunnel in the world. Since they joined London's poorer industrial districts, it is not surprising that over 90 per cent of the vehicles using the two tunnels in 1911 (apart from cycles and a few handbarrows) were carts, wagons, and other trade vehicles. On a typical day, only fourteen cabs passed under the river in East London, along with fewer than a hundred private cars and carriages. Foot passengers preferred to use the Greenwich pedestrian tunnel, which opened in 1902, and the LCC's free Woolwich ferry (1889), which carried about 24,000 passengers and 2,400 vehicles a day (in 1911) between Woolwich, Plumstead, and Royal Arsenal in the south and North Woolwich, Silvertown, and the Royal Docks in the north.[56]

Looking back on the social and cultural impact of the transport revolution twelve years after the Great War, the *New Survey of London Life and Labour* argued that cheap travel for women and the working class had broken down the isolationism and local loyalties prevalent at the time of Charles Booth's researches in the early 1890s. 'Once acquired for the purpose of getting to and from work, [the habit of travelling] has been extended both by men and women to their leisure hours, whether for purposes of education, amusement, or for visiting friends, and by women especially for their shopping expeditions.' Working-class consumers were less dependent on local pubs, music halls, shops, and markets, but used cheap fares to visit West End theatres and music halls, better street markets in Bermondsey and Fulham, and bigger department stores and multiple shops, either in the West End or in local centres like Brixton and Peckham. This led to the growth of specialized shopping centres, the decline of local shops, and a standardization of prices and quality across London. Furthermore, the *New Survey* argued, there had been a decline in class and local distinctions in dress, accent, and habits: 'Chokers, Derby coats and ostrich feathers are rarely to be seen. The dress of the younger generation of working men and women, so far from having any distinctive note of its own, tends merely to copy, sometimes to exaggerate, any particular fashion current in the West End . . . The Cockney dialect and rhyming slang are slowly disappearing while the Cockney twang is spreading to other classes. In fact the whole demeanour of the different social classes has tended towards a close approximation in the past generation.' Of course, many other influences, including the Great War, the BBC, the Hollywood film, and the shorter working day, must have contributed towards these trends, but it is important to remember that the transport revolution of 1890 to 1914, which helped to make London physically so much bigger, made it, in the cost and duration of journeys, smaller too.[57]

*

THE END OF DARKEST LONDON

Gaslight

In the early 1880s London was still a gaslit city, as it had been since the 1830s and 1840s. London's supplies were dominated by two big companies. The Gas Light and Coke Company, the oldest gas company in the world, supplied gas to most of London north of the Thames, and the smaller South Metropolitan Company had most of the South London market. There were several smaller companies, reduced to five by amalgamations by 1911, the biggest of which was the Commercial Company, serving part of East London. The two major companies produced and distributed about 80 per cent of London's gas supply, and their huge gasholders, rising and falling in their cast-iron framework as supply and demand waxed or waned, had been a familiar feature of the London skyline since the 1840s. The greatest gasholder of all, with six moving sections (or lifts), a diameter of 293 feet and a full height of 180 feet, was built by the South Metropolitan Company in Greenwich in 1892. The Gas Light and Coke Company's Beckton works – the biggest gasworks in Europe – had created a riverside industrial zone producing gas, tar, creosote, ammonia, and other gas by-products between the Royal Docks and Barking Creek, where the northern outfall of the London sewage system reached the Thames. The company had other riverside works in East London at Silvertown and Bow, on the Regent's and Grand Union Canal at Haggerston, St Pancras, and Kensal Green, and further west on the Thames at Fulham, Nine Elms, Pimlico, and Westminster. The South Metropolitan's six works in South London were on the Thames at Greenwich, Rotherhithe, and Bankside, on Greenwich Creek, on the Surrey Canal by Old Kent Road, and at Vauxhall, near the Oval sports ground.

Gas lighting was common in public buildings and better private houses, and thousands of London theatres, hotels, stations, workhouses, shops, offices, and churches were lit with gas jets in the 1880s. The gas lamps that lit the London streets in the 1880s and 1890s were essentially naked coal-gas flames shaped by the cut of the burner into a flat fishtail or cockscomb, in which the light was produced by the incandescence of the particles of carbon in the gas. The best and brightest gas burners in the 1880s were regenerative burners, which used an arrangement of concentric chimneys to heat the air before it came into direct contact with the flame. The most efficient regenerative gas burner available in the 1880s could give about eight or nine candle units of light per cubic foot of gas, four times as much as a simple fishtail gas burner, and nearly three times as much as the London Argand, the best burner in the 1870s. The gas companies enriched their coal gas with various types of oil gas (benzol and naphtha) to increase its illuminating power, but gas street lamps in the 1880s were still dimmer than a modern 25 watt electric bulb. In the West End and favoured main streets, where lamps were not placed too far apart, gas street lamps and shop lights could light a street adequately, and visitors from darker cities often marvelled at the brilliancy of London's lights. But these early gas lamps created patches of brightness in the surrounding darkness, rather than turning night into day.[1]

The contrast between the well-lit streets of the West End and the murky darkness of East End backstreets, where gas lamps were poorly maintained and too far apart, became a lively issue in the autumn of 1888, after the horrific Whitechapel murders of that year. In late October a *Daily News* correspondent took a walk around the neighbourhood in which the killings had taken place, and noted the contrast between Whitechapel High Street and Mile End Road, the main street, with its gas lamps and gaslit shops and pubs, and the dark backstreets where the women had died. The main streets were almost as bright as the West End, but when he turned down a side street the correspondent entered another world.

> The street is oppressively dark, though at present the gloom is relieved somewhat by feebly lighted shopfronts . . . Now round the corner into another still gloomier passage. This is the notorious Wentworth Street . . . How black and unutterably gloomy all the houses look! How infinitely all the moral and physical wretchedness of such localities as these is intensified by the darkness of the streets and the houses. It is wise and astute of Mr. Barnett to give emphatic expression to the cry that has so often been raised for 'more light' for lower London. If in this one matter of light alone, the streets and houses of the West End were reduced to the condition of the East, what would

life become there? Oh, for a great installation of the electric light, with which, as the sun goes down, to deluge the streets and lanes, the dark alleys and passages, the staircases and rooms of this nether world. Homes would become cleaner, and more cheerful and attractive; life would become healthier, whole masses of crime would die out like toadstools under sunlight, and what remained would be more easily dealt with. The Cimmerian darkness of lower London indoors and out constitutes no small part of its wretchedness, and the brilliant lighting of the public-house gives it much of its attraction. Even the repute of many of these shady localities is due in great measure to their impenetrable gloom after nightfall.[2]

The most promising technological solution to the problem of darkness in the late 1880s was not electricity, but an improved form of gas lighting, in which the heating action of gas, rather than the light from a simple flame, was exploited. It had been known for decades that some substances would glow brightly when heated by a gas flame, but their value in gas lamps was limited by their tendency to be eroded by the heat. Lime, or calcium oxide, shone brilliantly in a hot gas flame without decomposing, and was used to light theatrical stages in the 1860s and 1870s, until electric arc lights replaced it in the 1880s. But lime was too bulky for other forms of lighting, and a practical and efficient incandescent gas lamp was not available until the Clamond mantle, an inverted cone of threads of calcined magnesia in a platinum cage, was demonstrated at the Crystal Palace exhibition of 1882–3. In 1885 an Austrian, Carl Auer (later Baron von Welsbach), patented the first commercial gas mantle, made of cotton soaked in various metallic salts, which had been burned so that the cotton was replaced with metallic oxide. He experimented with many different substances until he discovered that thorium oxide (thoria) mixed with just under 1 per cent of ceria (cerium oxide) produced the brightest light with the least deterioration, and patented this perfect mixture in 1886. The Welsbach incandescent mantle, which was first advertised in England in 1890, saved gas lighting from the oblivion that had threatened it when Edison and Swan invented the electric filament lamp in 1879 and 1880, and prolonged the power struggle between gas and electricity into the 1920s and 1930s. Once the cotton had been burnt off, the Welsbach mantle was too delicate to handle. Welsbach solved this problem by dipping the thoria net into collodion (guncotton dissolved in ether, alcohol, and castor oil). This coating protected the mantle in transit, and was burned off when it was first used. Welsbach mantles were an instant success, and most people with simple gas lighting converted to the incandescent alternative in the 1890s. Further improvements followed, as the gas companies struggled to keep up with electricity, including wall switches (introduced into England in 1903), street lamps with pilot lights and time switches (making the famous lamplighter redundant), and inverted mantles (1905) which prevented the fitting from being discoloured by combustion, and provided a more attractive light. New mantles, using different mixtures of metallic oxides and high-pressure gas, provided brighter and cheaper light, maintaining gas's competitiveness with electricity right up to the First World War. While old-fashioned burners had yielded between one and three candlepower per cubic foot of gas in the 1870s, the Welsbach mantle and inverted burners gave between fifteen and twenty, and high-pressure burners gave twenty-two to thirty-six.[3] The first gas mantles were used in London street lights in Kensington in January 1895, and they spread quickly through London over the next ten years. If the streets of London were brighter and safer in 1914 than they had been in 1888, this owed more to the Welsbach mantle than to the Swan or Edison lamp. Even in the early 1930s, about half of London's streets were lit by gas.

The continuing prosperity of the gas industry owed a great deal to the development of the incandescent mantle as a real rival to the electric lamp, but a second device, the prepayment slot meter (invented by T. S. Lacey in 1870) played almost as great a part, by opening up a vast market for gas lighting, cooking, and heating among working-class families who could not be trusted to pay their bills. Prepayment meters were installed in vast numbers in the 1890s, and the gas collector became a regular monthly visitor to poorer homes. By 1911 nearly two-thirds of London's 1.4 million gas customers were on prepayment meters.

The First Generation

There were few gas-company shareholders who would have predicted, in the early 1880s, that their industry had so many years of prosperity, even in the field of lighting, ahead of it. Progress in the production and use of electricity was so sudden and rapid between about 1877 and 1882 that a complete revolution in lighting and power seemed imminent. This was the culmination of a century of scientific advance. A practical electric battery, based on the work of Alessandro Volta, was demonstrated in London in 1800, and a giant battery was used to power the arc light demonstrated to the Royal Institution by Sir Humphrey Davy in 1808. But the electric generator that transformed the streets of Edwardian London was not the battery, but the dynamo. The dynamo, or self-excited electromagnetic generator, which converted mechanical activity into electricity by rotating a coil of wire around a magnet, was based on the principle of electromagnetism discovered in the 1820s by Michael Faraday. In the late 1860s several scientists, including Henry Wilde, S. A. Varley, E. W. von Siemens, and Charles Wheatstone, contributed to the development of a working dynamo, but it was a Belgian working in Paris, Z. T. Gramme, who in 1870 produced the first really practical commercial dynamo. In 1873 a Gramme dynamo was used, as a public demonstration of its effectiveness, to light the Westminster clock tower, and it was widely used in lighthouses. Gramme and Siemens dynamos produced a direct current, but more efficient generators, producing an alternating current (and thus called alternators) were demonstrated at the very influential Paris Exhibition of 1881. The development of electricity generation opened the way for practical applications that began the transformation of the modern world in the second half of the nineteenth century. First there was the electric telegraph, which developed in the 1830s and 1840s, then the telephone and electric lighting in the 1870s, and electric motors for industry and transport in the 1880s. The impact of these innovations on the economic, social, and cultural life of London was, as we shall see, dramatic and extensive, but not immediate.

Arc lights, in which an electrical arc jumped from one carbon electrode to another when they touched and were then pulled apart, had been known since 1808, and were used in lighthouses in the 1860s. But it was Gramme's dynamo that made smaller-scale arc lights, suitable for use in stations and theatres, a practical proposition. The Paris Gare du Nord was lit with arc lights in 1875, and in London John Hollingshead used six arc lights to illuminate the facade of the Gaiety Theatre on the Strand. Although arc lights sparked off a frenzy of interest in electric lighting in England around 1880, they had many disadvantages. They were very bright, they flashed and flickered, they were very expensive to run, they needed careful attention to make sure that the gap between the two carbon electrodes remained constant as they wore down, and at first they needed a separate dynamo to run each light. A modified arc light, or 'electric candle', invented and demonstrated in Paris in 1876 by Paul Jablochkoff, a Russian army engineer, had more practical uses. One Gramme dynamo could operate several circuits, with six lamps on each circuit, and each lamp, instead of giving the dazzling light of a lighthouse beam, produced a more manageable 150 to 200 candlepower. Jablochkoff 'candles' were used to light the Avenue de l'Opéra in Paris in July 1878, and the French Société Générale de l'Electricité did its best to promote their use in London. They had already been tried in the West India Docks and a Shoreditch ironworks, and the company installed them in Billingsgate fish market in November 1878, and shared the cost of installing sixty lamps on the Victoria Embankment (about a mile either side of the northern end of Waterloo Bridge) with the Metropolitan Board of Works that December. Jablochkoff's inefficient and unreliable candle lamps were expensive to run and they could not be relit if they went out, without wasting half-used carbons. In 1884 the Embankment reverted to old-fashioned and cheap gaslight, but the initial display was impressive, so the City of London decided to light Holborn Viaduct and the outside of the Mansion House with arc lights for a few months, and in 1881 the Commissioners for Sewers, who were responsible for lighting the City of London, launched a one-year trial of different electric lighting systems in the City.

Just as the London public was enjoying its first sight of arc lighting, a second type of electric light, the incandescent bulb, in which light was emitted from a substance heated by electricity, made its public appearance. As far back as the 1850s the English scientist Joseph Swan had realized that running an electric current through a carbon filament in a good vacuum would produce a long-lasting incandescent light, but his work was delayed by the inability of existing vacuum pumps to completely evacuate a glass bulb. The demonstration of an effective mercury vacuum pump in 1865, followed by the invention of Gramme's dynamo, led Swan to resume his work. He produced a carbon-filament incandescent lamp in December 1877, and was ready for commercial production at his factory in Newcastle by the beginning of 1881. Swan joined forces with Rookes E. B. Crompton, the English pioneer of arc lighting, and before the year was out there were Swan incandescent lamps lighting the House of Commons and in the newly built Savoy Theatre, the first public building in London, and the first theatre in the world, to be lit entirely by electricity. The Savoy, which staged the very popular Gilbert and Sullivan comic operas, provided Swan with excellent publicity. It used about 1,200 lights, for the auditorium as well as the stage, powered by a Siemens generator and several steam engines. When the lights were first lit on 11 October 1881 (for a performance of *Patience*) they were (said *The Times*) 'cheered to the very echo', though the seating was better lit than the stage, a problem that was corrected on 28 December, when the whole stage was lit with Swan lamps. The lamps needed no attention, and unlike gas lamps they did not make the theatre unpleasantly hot. In the few years after the success of this experiment nearly all major theatres in London (and elsewhere) converted from gas to electricity, and those that had not changed did so after the disastrous fire in the Theatre Royal, Exeter, which killed 150 people in 1887. Success in the Savoy helped Swan to win some important new contracts in 1882, including the new Royal Courts of Justice in the Strand, the Mansion House, the British Museum, and the Royal Academy.

Swan faced powerful American competition from Thomas Edison, whose company patented his own version of the incandescent filament lamp in November 1879. The lamp, with a filament of carbonized Japanese bamboo, was in commercial production by 1880. Moving quickly to win a share of the huge London market, Edison made a deal with the City of London to light Holborn Viaduct and its nearby streets using electricity produced in a steam-powered generating station on the Viaduct, at number 57. By 12 January 1882 the world's first public steam-powered electricity-generating station was in operation on Holborn Viaduct, using two Jumbo generators sent by Edison from New York. (The power station opened in Godalming at the end of 1881 was water-powered.) Because the viaduct was an open iron structure it was possible to run supplies to street lamps and private customers without digging up roads, and by April the station was powering 164 street lamps of sixteen candlepower (much brighter than the best available gas burner) from Holborn Circus to Newgate Street, and nearly 1,000 lamps in shops, hotels and restaurants along the route. The incandescent lighting of the General Post Office on Newgate Street and the huge new Nonconformist chapel, the City Temple, attracted particular attention.[4] Though it was successful as a showpiece, the Holborn station never made a profit. Edison and his London representative, Edward H. Johnson, decided to hide the fact that the cost of an hour's electric light was three or four times that of a gas burner by setting his prices at the same level as gas. Within two or three years the cost of running Holborn station at a loss had become too great for the company, and it was closed down and abandoned in 1886.[5]

These problems were not widely foreseen in early 1882, when the excitement caused by the electrification of the Savoy, the arc lights on the Embankment, and the opening of the Holborn Viaduct electricity station was reinforced by the International Electric Exhibition at Crystal Palace. Here, in vast electric-lit halls, the wonderful range of Edison's inventions, including a complete and practical electrical system, was on display. Alongside twelve steam dynamos, there were service boxes, circuit breakers, meters, rheostats, current regulators, filament lamps, telephones, and everything else needed to create the electric house or street. Aristocrats with London properties, including the Duke of Sutherland and the Duke of Westminster (the biggest landlord in the West End), were particularly impressed by the Edison system. There were also important improvements in arc lighting in the early 1880s, mainly thanks to the work of an American, Charles Brush, whose arc lights were manufactured and marketed in England by the Anglo-American Brush Electric Lighting Company. The advantage of the Brush lamp was that it came with its own high-voltage dynamo that could run sixteen arc lamps in series, providing lighting for streets, shops, or factories that was cheaper and more robust than Jablochkoff's.

In May 1882, these advances, exaggerated or 'puffed' by journalists, self-interested company promoters, and Edison's London agents, created a brief stock-market boom in electricity shares. In a few frantic weeks several million pounds were invested in a large number of electricity companies, some of which had no useful patents and no hope of success, by investors who had no idea of the technical and commercial problems facing the industry. Over a hundred new companies were formed in 1882, more than twice the number created in the previous two years.[6] At the centre of the boom was the Brush company, which floated several sub-licensed companies on the Stock Exchange, including the Metropolitan Brush Company, which was promoted by the ubiquitous company promoter H. Osborne O'Hagan. *The Economist* warned its readers that electricity would not turn investors into millionaires, and the *Electrician* was appalled at the sight of people throwing their money into good and bad companies indiscriminately, excited by exaggerated promises of an imminent electrical revolution: 'This speculative gambling is a curse to true enterprise. Rotten companies, not worth the paper their prospectuses are printed on, are always started when the public lose their heads, as they seem to have done now, to the loss of the ultimate holders of shares.' The pilot schemes begun by the Brush sub-concessions quickly turned out to be unprofitable, because electricity costs were well above those for comparable gas lights, and hardly any customers were interested. O'Hagan, one of the more principled promoters, blamed a group of Stock Exchange 'bears', men who had gambled on share prices falling, for spreading rumours about the faults in the Brush system, and panicking speculators into selling electricity shares as fast as they had previously bought them, but there were real difficulties with marketing electric lighting in the early 1880s, which investors had been encouraged to ignore. Not for the first time or the last, City professionals, company promoters, and stockbrokers chose to exploit investors rather than guide them, and in so doing inflicted serious and long-term damage on an important new industry by destroying the public's confidence in electrical enterprises. Later in the 1880s, when promising electrical entrepreneurs like R. E. B. Crompton and Sebastian de Ferranti investigated the possibility of raising capital through a Stock Exchange flotation, they found the City as cold as it had once been hot.[7]

Power Struggle

The stagnation of the electricity industry between 1883 and 1887 was exacerbated by the general economic downturn of the mid-1880s, and by the government's attempt to legislate for the future of the industry. Shortly after the collapse of the so-called 'Brush boom', Parliament passed the 1882 Electric Lighting Act, which had been promoted by Joseph Chamberlain of the Board of Trade, with the aim of strengthening local authorities against the growth of private monopolies. The Act allowed electricity companies with a Board of Trade licence or a provisional order to dig up the streets to lay cables, but in return the companies had to accept price controls and were made subject to compulsory purchase by local authorities after twenty-one years. Electricity companies later claimed that this buyout clause was suppressing investment in the industry, and as a result the twenty-one-year period was doubled in 1888. The industry's real problem, though, was the cost of the supply, and the fact that advances in gas lighting in the later 1880s and especially in the 1890s (when incandescent gas lamps were first available) had greatly reduced the advantages of the costly electric lamp over the cheap gas one. The strength and inventiveness of the well-entrenched gas industry in Britain, rather than the 1882 Act, was the main reason for the slow advance of electricity in Britain compared to the USA, where the gas industry was weaker. Electricity suppliers cut the cost of an hour's lighting from about 0.65d in 1882 to about 0.42d in the early 1890s and 0.24d in 1900, but at the same time incandescent gas lighting was getting cheaper, brighter, and more reliable.

So in the 1880s demand for electricity was generally limited to the richer parts of London, and to fashionable London clubs, shops, and theatres, for whom cost was not the main consideration. In Grosvenor Square, one of London's richest addresses, wealthy families shared the cost of a private generator, and Whitehall Court, an eight-storey apartment block built on the Victoria Embankment in 1884, was lit by a private supplier that grew in the 1890s into one of London's bigger companies, the Metropolitan Electric Supply Company, supplying Covent Garden, Lincoln's Inn, Bloomsbury, and St Marylebone. Several major London companies developed in this way, from small localized concerns. Kensington Court, a private estate completed in 1883, was lucky enough to have the electrical pioneer Rookes Crompton as one of its residents. In 1886 Crompton erected a generator behind his own house, Thriplands (number 40), and made Kensington Court the first private estate in Britain to have its own electricity supply. Crompton's Kensington Court Company expanded to become the Kensington and Knightsbridge Electric Lighting Company, supplying customers in Kensington and Westminster. By running cables through subways Crompton avoided breaking up the roadway, and thus escaped the controls imposed by the 1882 Act. Crompton's original generator house is still there, behind the house he lived in for forty years.[8]

These local stations produced a direct or continuous current (DC), which it was expensive and inefficient to distribute over a wide area. Direct current produced by high-speed engines at between 100 and 200 volts could not be transmitted more than a mile, because of losses caused by resistance (and thus heating) in the cables. When plenty of customers could be found within that radius DC was practical, but the way ahead for cheaper supplies covering a wider area was in the development of alternating current (AC), which could be transmitted further than DC at much higher tension (or voltage) and lower current (amperage) with much less loss of power, because power loss is proportional to the square of amperage. The problem of converting very high voltages into the lower ones needed by domestic or street lamps could be overcome by the use of local transformers, which could be set to meet the requirements of particular groups of consumers. Faraday had established the principles of transformers earlier in the century, and efficient and practical machines had been developed in England and Hungary in the early 1880s. The unlikely pioneer in this was the Grosvenor Gallery, in Bond Street, which had been lit with arc lamps powered by its own backyard generator since 1883. The art gallery and the generator were owned by Sir Coutts Lindsay, whose brother, Lord Wantage, was married to the heiress to Lord Overstone's vast banking fortune. Gradually the gallery extended the supply to its neighbours through overhead lines, and in 1885 the Grosvenor station was built, with more than 300 customers throughout the West End, from Regent's Park to the Thames.

The growth of the company was due largely to the inventiveness of Lindsay's brilliant young engineer, Sebastian de Ferranti, who was employed in 1885 to redesign the Grosvenor station. Ferranti installed powerful alternators and a Hungarian Ganz transformer in the station, but he was convinced that the way forward was to follow the gas companies in moving their plant to cheaper sites on the edge of London, where access to coal and cooling water was easier, and where there were no objections to the noise and smell of powerful generators. In 1887, following Ferranti's advice, the Lindsays raised over £500,000 to start the London Electricity Supply Corporation (LESCo) and build a revolutionary electricity-generating station at Deptford, on the Thames next to Deptford Creek. The Lindsays invested in Ferranti because they saw him as England's Edison, but Ferranti's engineering brilliance was not married, as Edison's was, to a sound sense of the practical and the profitable. Hardly any of the equipment needed for this unprecedented enterprise had been developed, so Ferranti had to design machine tools, lathes, alternators, transformers, and cables to generate and transmit power at 10,000 volts, at least forty times the usual DC voltage. Many of these were made in Ferranti's new factory in Charterhouse Square. After initial difficulties Ferranti arrived at some solutions which set the standard for the development of high-voltage power stations in the future. His improvised device of insulating his cable with spirally-wound waxed brown paper became the industry standard, and his double copper tubing mains (running alongside railway lines) were still in use in London in the 1920s. Ferranti convinced the Board of Trade that the mains were safe by having an assistant hold a chisel while another hammered it into the live cable, causing a fuse to cut the supply. The steel ingots for the crankshafts of the Deptford steam engines were the biggest ever made in Britain. Ferranti's gigantic alternators, his 10,000-horsepower steam engines, and his 10,000-volt transformer were engineering miracles, but commercial failures. The Deptford station could deliver 10,000 volts, but not with the reliability its customers demanded. A fire destroyed the Grosvenor Gallery in November 1890 when an attendant pulled out a high-voltage plug switch and caused an arc, and the next month all the Grosvenor station transformers burned out, cutting the supply for three months and forcing three-quarters of the company's customers to switch to the smaller suppliers operating in the company's territory. Even when it was working smoothly, the whole enterprise was on too large a scale for the electricity market as it existed in the early 1890s. If the Deptford station had been completed as Ferranti planned, with the five huge 7,500 kW alternators all working at full power, it could have lit a million electric lamps, probably twice as many as there were in the whole of London. The other electricity companies had no intention of yielding their shares of the London market to LESCo, and they got support in 1889 from the Board of Trade inspector, Major Marindin, who rejected the idea of entrusting a large area of London to one electricity company or to alternating current (which he feared would interfere with telegraph and telephone services), and decided that even in its own district LESCo should compete with smaller DC suppliers. In May 1891 work on Ferranti's planned 7,500 kW alternators was halted, and a few months later he was dismissed. The company struggled on, but it was forced into receivership in 1894, and did not pay a dividend to its shareholders until 1905. This commercial failure obscured the fact that Ferranti had solved many of the difficulties in the way of the suburban generation of high-voltage electricity on a large scale, and allowed a dispute between proponents of DC (including Lord Kelvin, Crompton, and Edison) and AC (Ferranti and the American George Westinghouse), the so-called 'battle of the systems', to continue into the 1890s. Even in 1911, forty-eight of the sixty-nine municipal and private companies generating electricity for London were supplying direct or continuous current.[9]

Circumstances favoured electrical enterprises in the late 1880s. The Welsbach gas mantle was not yet available in England, and the 1888 Electric Lighting Act increased the period a company could operate before becoming subject to a local authority buyout. At last, the *Illustrated London News* declared in October 1889, London might start to catch up with lesser cities in Europe and America, which had been enjoying electric lighting for several years. Four new electricity supply companies were established in 1889, all serving the richer parts of town: the Brompton and Kensington, the Metropolitan, the St James and Pall Mall, and the Chelsea. Another four, the Westminster, the City of London, the Charing Cross, West End, and City, and the Notting Hill, followed in 1890–1. These were significant companies, but their power stations were local and small-scale, using batteries to store electricity for peak times. The Westminster Electric Supply Corporation, which became one of London's biggest companies, began

supplying Belgravia and Mayfair from small generating stations in Eccleston Place, Davies Street, and Millbank in 1890, collecting rainwater from the roof of Victoria Station to cool its steam condensers. The biggest of the new companies, the Metropolitan, had six generating stations in the West End, enough to supply 300,000 lights in the Strand, Holborn, and Westminster. At the other extreme, the Gatti brothers, owners of a famous restaurant on the Strand, and of the Adelphi Theatre nearby, built a small generating station in a little alley between Maiden Lane and the Strand in 1889 to serve their own enterprises.

London's new lights, either electric or the latest gas mantles, gave its streets a brilliance which some observers found particularly thrilling. Alice Meynell, whose essays, London Impressions, were published in 1898, loved to see the new electric lights against the evening or night sky: 'Light grey sky and thrilling lamp together make – or so it seems to me – one of the most beautiful sights that eyes can see – the most refined, most severe, and most exquisite. This carbon electric light was so much disliked because, no doubt, it was first seen under the glass and iron of a railway station. Seen with the sky it cannot but be seen to be most beautiful. The golden lights – electric or gas lamps – have the beauty of fire, but the white lamp has the beauty of light.'[10] And the poet Richard Le Gallienne, whose Ballad of London appeared in 1895, seems to have been particularly moved by the newly installed electric lights on the Strand:

Ah, London! London! our delight,
Great flower that opens but at night,
Great City of the midnight sun,
Whose day begins when day is done.

Lamp after lamp against the sky
Opens a sudden beaming eye,
Leaping alight on either hand,
The iron lilies of the Strand.

Like dragonflies, the hansoms hover,
With jeweled eyes, to catch the lover;
The streets are full of lights and loves,
Soft gowns, and flutter of soiled doves.

The human moths about the light
Dash and cling close in dazed delight,
And burn and laugh, the world and wife,
For this is London, this is life!

For electricity to beat gas in the power struggle of the 1890s it had to be produced more cheaply. An important advance towards this goal was the invention of the steam turbine by Charles Parsons in the late 1880s. Parsons' turbines, which were first installed in power stations in Newcastle in 1888 and Cambridge in 1892, used no more coal than steam engines, and also took up less space and caused less vibration, important advantages for power stations in residential parts of London. The Metropolitan Company's Manchester Square power station in Marylebone, which installed 350 kW Parsons turbines (the biggest yet built) in 1894, had been taken to court by its neighbours because its conventional steam engines vibrated too much. When steam turbines were installed in Deptford in 1912, they were nearly one twentieth the size of the steam-engine-driven alternators Ferranti had originally planned. By this time, nearly all the new generating capacity installed was powered by turbines, rather than steam engines.

The development of big and economical suburban power stations serving a large number of customers over a wide area was inhibited by the Electric Lighting Acts of 1882 and 1888, which tried to prevent the development of electricity monopolies by insisting on local generating stations and banning amalgamations between companies. The development of local-authority power companies, encouraged by the Lighting Acts, also pushed the electricity industry towards fragmentation, rather than efficiency. A further problem for electricity companies was that electricity, unlike gas, could not easily be stored, and therefore generators had to be large enough to meet the peak evening demand, though this meant remaining idle for much of the day. It was difficult to increase the daytime market for electricity for industrial production and transport, because steam power was cheaper. When transport enterprises started using electricity after 1900 they generally preferred to build their own generating stations. The massive generating station built by the Underground Electric Railways Company between 1902 and 1905 at Lots Road, by Chelsea Creek, to serve the new electric underground railway, was second in size only to the Deptford station.[11]

During the 1890s nine of these local electricity companies grew into substantial public suppliers, and at the end of the decade three more were founded to supply Lambeth, Camberwell, Southwark, Bermondsey, and Greenwich. In 1897 one of the biggest, the Metropolitan, began building a big new suburban power station in Willesden, on the Grand Junction Canal and several railway lines, to deliver AC electricity to its central

London customers at 10,000 volts. At about the same time local parish
vestries started their own municipal enterprises, to supply street lighting
and private customers. St Pancras led the way in 1892, but Islington,
Hampstead, and Hammersmith soon followed in 1894–7. Shoreditch,
which started in 1897, was the first to generate some of its electricity from
incinerating municipal waste, demonstrating that municipal parsimony
could have beneficial results. By 1911 seven boroughs, including Hackney,
Stepney, Poplar, and Fulham, had followed Shoreditch's lead in this. In
Greater London, Kingston (1893), Ealing (1894), Leyton (1896), and
West Ham (1898) were the first municipal electricity producers. By 1903
fifteen of Inner London's twenty-eight boroughs, eight of its suburban
municipal corporations, and sixteen of its urban district councils generated
their own electricity, alongside thirteen private companies in Inner London
and ten in the outer suburbs (mostly founded after 1900), each of which
had its own designated area of operation.

Lightest London

After almost twenty years of disappointment, progress was at last being
made. Arthur Beavan's *Imperial London*, published in 1901, claimed that
electricity was 'bidding fair to oust its rival from the field of illumination',
and Desmond Young, writing at the same time, agreed that the balance
was at last swinging in electricity's favour. Streets were 'up' all over London
for the laying of electric cables, and the lamplighter, with his familiar stick
and ladder, was giving way to the less romantic figure who replaced the
worn-out carbon rods in arc lamps. Electric lights had at last returned to
the Victoria Embankment, where they 'formed a beautiful curving chain
of illumination from Westminster to Blackfriars'. The statistics issued by
the LCC confirm these impressions. The annual cost of electricity used in
public lighting rose from £35,504 in 1898 to £61,386 in 1900, and over
£220,000 in 1911, at a time when unit costs were falling. By 1911 there
were 32,000 public electric lamps in Greater London, over 70 per cent of
which were incandescent, and there were 184,650 public and private electricity customers. Total electricity-company revenues in Greater London
rose from about £1 million in 1899 to over £3 million by 1911. London's
slow start meant that it was still far behind New York, where electricity
consumption per head was nearly seven times as high as London's in
1911.[12]

Yet gas was still dominant in the home and on the street, if not in the workplace. There were still about 90,000 gas lamps in London in 1911, as many as there had been in 1900, and lamps were now much brighter and more economical than before. The number of gas customers had risen from 640,000 (out of about 1.5 million families) in 1900 to 1.4 million in 1911, thanks to the installation of 892,000 prepayment meters. These private consumers bought nearly all the fifty billion cubic feet of gas the companies made each year, since gas consumed by works and offices accounted for a little over 1 per cent of output, and that required to supply London's gas street lamps was only 3 per cent of gas sales.

By the standards of the day, and especially by the standards of the past, London in 1911 was well lit, with 121,000 public gas and electric lamps that gave a much brighter light than the old gas burners could ever manage. But the adequacy of local lighting depended on the willingness or ability of individual local authorities to pay for it, and as a result some parts of London were much gloomier than others. As one might expect, the City of London and Westminster were the brightest, spending £478 and £405 a mile respectively (more than twice the metropolitan average) on lighting their streets. Shoreditch, Holborn, St Marylebone, St Pancras, and Islington were some way behind, but all spent well over the London average of £173 a mile. Stepney, whose dark and dangerous alleys still haunted the public mind, now spent £187 a mile, much the same as Chelsea, Hampstead, and Kensington. The gloomiest boroughs in 1911, measured in money spent per street mile, were Stoke Newington, Bethnal Green, Deptford, and Lambeth, which (at £90 a mile) was the worst of all.[13] This, as sensationalists and social explorers liked to say, was Darkest London.

The piecemeal growth of electricity supply since the 1880s left London with an unusually fragmented and illogical system, in which most consumers had to buy their supply from an inefficient local generator. Legislation forbade amalgamations, preventing the growth of the large and efficient companies like those that served Chicago or Berlin. Those two cities were each served by six power stations with an average capacity of 30,000 kW, but London in 1911 had seventy-two electricity authorities, sixty-six generating stations with an average capacity of 4,670 kW, and dozens of different frequencies and voltages. Most of these stations were situated in expensive and inconvenient central sites, without room for expansion and without convenient access to coal or water. The application of electric power to industrial production had been slow, and without cheaper electricity, the government feared, industry would continue to desert London, exacerbating its poverty and unemployment. In the early twentieth century several leading experts urged the government and the LCC to bring London's electricity supply and usage to the level of that of the most advanced Western cities. One of the leading British electrical engineers and consultants, Charles Merz, who had experience of large-scale electricity generation in Newcastle, turned his mind to the London situation around 1900. In 1905 he presented a bill to Parliament for the establishment of a new company, the Administrative County of London and District Electric Power Company, to provide East London industries and lighting and transport throughout London with bulk electricity supplies from a 20,000 kW power station. Merz had the support of 250 London manufacturers but he was opposed by the London local authorities, the private electricity companies, and the LCC, which wanted to establish its own company. Merz's bill passed its committee stages, but was lost when the Conservative government fell in December 1905. When it was introduced again in 1906 it was in competition with an LCC bill for a municipal power company. Lloyd George, President of the Board of Trade, negotiated a compromise in which the proposed private company would be supervised and eventually bought by the LCC, giving London ratepayers the benefits of an efficient system without the initial risk of setting it up. This public–private partnership was favoured by the LCC, which had a Conservative majority from 1907 onwards, but was disliked by Liberal MPs (the great parliamentary majority from 1906 to 1910), who thought that it would deliver London's electricity supply into the hands of a private monopoly, and opposed by the London boroughs, whose own electricity enterprises were expanding rapidly. So the technological and commercial case for efficient power generation in the world's largest city was overwhelmed by the political issues of local-authority independence and the conflict between municipal and private enterprise. Bills intended to put the Lloyd George scheme into effect were defeated, and instead two ineffective bills encouraging cooperation between borough and private companies were passed in 1907 and 1908, leaving London with an inefficient system based on small local generators. Merz continued to campaign for a unified system, and eventually played a central part in establishing the national grid in 1925. But for the moment he could only warn the LCC, as he did in 1913, that London was in danger of falling further behind its international rivals, especially in the industrial use of electricity: 'We use . . . an absurdly small amount of electricity . . . We ought to be first, not second, or third, or last: and I am afraid that at the present rate of progress there is a very great danger of our not only being last, but of our remaining last.'[14] Perhaps Merz was too pessimistic. Factory inspectors' reports, as we saw in an earlier chapter, showed that many London manufacturers, undeterred by high costs and inefficient supplies, installed small floor-mounted electric motors in the ten years before the Great War, preparing the way for London's surprising industrial regeneration in the 1920s and 1930s.

Part Three

LIVING LONDON

CHAPTER FIFTEEN

*

DYING LONDON

Diseases in Retreat

Of all the changes that took place in the lives of Londoners in the thirty years before the Great War, none was of greater significance than the shift from the high birth and death rates and low life expectancy of the 1870s and 1880s towards the much lower birth and death rates and longer lives of the twentieth century. Such fundamental changes are rarely rapid, but compared to the snail's pace of earlier years the changes that took place in these decades were dramatic. London's death rate averaged a little over 20 per thousand in the 1880s, and only fell to 19 per thousand in the 1890s, according to the calculations of the LCC's Medical Officer of Health (MOH), Sir Shirley Murphy. But between 1899 and 1910 the death rate fell by nearly 30 per cent, from about 19 to about 13.7 per thousand. Comparing the 1890s average with 1910, every age group up to forty-five enjoyed a fall in its mortality rate of 30 per cent or more, and for babies and children up to ten the fall was over 40 per cent.

These improvements reflected national trends, especially in the decline of mortality from infectious diseases, but in several respects they were more striking in London than in other parts of the country. Whooping cough, for instance, killed 6 out of every thousand under-fives in London in the 1870s, but only 3.65 in England and Wales as a whole. By the 1890s London's under-fives death rate had fallen to 4.2 per thousand, while the national rate was still 3.1. Smallpox, a disease which seemed to be in rapid retreat in the face of vaccination in the 1850s and 1860s, recovered in the 1870s to kill an annual average of 457 per million Londoners, about double the national rate. But in the 1880s and 1890s it was driven back, so that by 1900 London's mortality rate, 10 per million, was as low as the national figure, and in 1910 there were no smallpox deaths in London at all. Typhoid death rates were halved in London and nationally between the 1870s and 1890s, and fell by another two-thirds (to 43 per million in

London) by 1910. Typhus, a great killer of slum-dwellers in the 1840s and 1850s, had a final flourish in 1881 and 1882, before being driven into insignificance in the late 1880s and virtual extinction in the 1890s. Scarlet fever, which killed nearly 6 in every thousand under-fives in London in the 1860s, was already almost halved by the 1870s, and killed about 1 under-five in a thousand by the 1890s. Tuberculosis, a much greater killer than any of the other infectious diseases, began its steady decline in the 1880s, when it killed more than 2 Londoners out of every thousand each year. By 1900–4 the death rate had fallen to 1.7 per thousand, and by 1910, it was down to 1.2 per thousand, half the rate of the 1870s. Unlike smallpox, typhus, cholera, and typhoid, tuberculosis was far from being a conquered disease, seen more often in the textbook than in the flesh. In 1900–4, nearly a tenth of Londoners who died were killed by tuberculosis, which remained the second biggest killer in London, after 'diseases of the brain, nervous and circulatory system', but ahead (just) of bronchitis and pneumonia, and well ahead of the other major killers, cancer, diarrhoea and dysentery, digestive diseases, prematurity birth, old age, and measles.[1]

Two diseases, both of which specialized in killing young children, resisted the social, medical, and sanitary advances of the later nineteenth century, and did not decline before 1900. One of these was measles, an endemic and epidemic disease that prospered in crowded cities like London. It declined in the 1870s, but grew again in the 1880s and 1890s, killing nearly 5 out of every thousand under-fives every year. Its long twentieth-century decline did not start until 1917, and it can therefore be counted as the one major disease whose defeat was initiated by the political or social circumstances created by the Great War. The other resistant disease was diphtheria, which killed about 120 per million Londoners in the 1870s, but double that number in the 1880s, and over 600 per million at its peak in 1893–6. Deaths fell in the later 1890s, so that only 250 per million died in 1900–4, and only 100 per million (back to the 1870s level) in 1910. The persistence of these two diseases, along with whooping cough (declining but still powerful), tuberculosis, bronchitis, pneumonia, diarrhoea, and dysentery, helps to explain the refusal of the mortality rate of infants (under one year old) to fall in the 1880s and 1890s, when the health of every other age group improved.

In the last twenty years of the nineteenth century enormous advances were made in Europe in understanding the causes, prevention, and cure of infectious diseases. Robert Koch discovered the bacilli that caused tuberculosis in 1882 and cholera 1884, and Theodor Klebs identified the diph-theria bacillus in 1883. A diphtheria antitoxin was developed in 1890, and was widely used in London hospitals (their first foray into bacteriology) by 1895.[2] Important as these achievements were in the long term, the early decline in the main infectious diseases was not much affected by them. The effects of Klebs' antitoxin were disappointing, and the decline of diph-theria mortality after 1896 seems to be the result of the appearance (or reappearance) of a less virulent strain of the disease. This is also the most likely explanation of the pattern of deaths from scarlet fever, a disease for which no effective treatment was introduced but which declined precipi-tately nonetheless.

Where human actions reduced the incidence of disease, plumbers and engineers should share the credit with doctors and politicians. Water-borne typhoid was uncommon in London in the 1880s and 1890s because of the improvement in the quality of piped water in the 1870s, and of the growing availability of continuous supplies, which made it unnecessary to rely upon unsafe cistern-stored water. The East London Water Company pioneered continuous supplies in the 1870s, and had extended them to all its customers by 1883. Unfortunately, and probably for other reasons (including Jewish settlement), the 750,000 East Enders served by the com-pany had the highest typhoid death rate in London in 1894.[3] Better water closets with stronger flushes, installed by trained plumbers, played their unsung part in making typhoid a rarity by 1900. The outbreaks that still occurred were mostly the result of poor personal hygiene, fly-infected food, bad shellfish, infected milk (which killed thirty in St Pancras in 1883 and twenty-three in Plumstead in 1895), and transmission by carriers, London's anonymous equivalents of New York's infamous 'Typhoid Mary' Mallon.

Active and well-informed local authorities could make a real differ-ence, too. Vestries that followed the example set by Eugene Poubelle in Paris in 1884, and replaced traditional open dust-holes, breeding grounds for germ-carrying flies, with modern covered dustbins in the 1890s, and emptied them frequently, and the LCC, with its tougher by-laws on the storage and removal of horse dung, played an important a part in reduc-ing deaths from typhoid, as did the bus, tram, and cab companies that switched from horsepower to petrol or electricity. The London death rate from diarrhoea and dysentery, one of the main killers of infants, fell by 60 per cent between 1900–4 and 1910, though it rose sharply and briefly in the hot summer of 1911. This decline saved over 2,000 lives a year, mostly the lives of infants (under ones), in the County of London.[4] Local-authority sanitary policies were important, also, in clearing out the last of the squalid districts that harboured the remnants of typhus in London in the 1870s and 1880s, so that when fever reappeared in isolated pockets – Camberwell in 1885, Southwark in 1890, Kensington in 1898 – it could not re-establish itself, as it would once have done, in its natural slum habitat.[5]

Much of the best work of vestries, borough councils, and the LCC was done by their Medical Officers of Health (MOHs) and sanitary inspectors, the most active of whom continued the war against filth and disease that had been launched by Edwin Chadwick in the 1840s. Medical officers acted efficiently in 1890 to stamp out localized outbreaks of smallpox by removing sufferers to isolation hospitals. An outbreak among Swiss waiters in 1892 was not allowed to turn into an epidemic, and an epidemic that started in Salvation Army shelters in October 1892, which spread to Spitalfields, Stepney, Bloomsbury, Edgware Road, Peckham, Bermondsey, Woolwich, Stockwell, and Vauxhall, was brought under control by the end of 1893. Vagrants, who slept in cramped conditions in shelters and common lodging houses and wandered all over London, were recognized as the main carriers of smallpox in the epidemics of 1893, 1895, and 1901–2, and it was the work of MOHs to identify and isolate the victims and disinfect the reservoirs of infection. MOHs, and especially Shirley Murphy, the LCC's first MOH, were also active in the campaign against tuberculosis. Murphy campaigned in the 1890s to establish the connection between tuberculosis and overcrowding, and to force doctors and medical officers to accept the implications of the unsettling discovery (in 1882) that tuberculosis was an infectious disease, transmitted by (among other things) the dust of dried sputum. Local MOHs became more active in disinfecting and demolishing infected houses in 1898 and 1899, at the time when the Prince of Wales gave his patronage to the new National Association for the Prevention of Tuberculosis. It is not possible to attribute the fall in London's tuberculosis death rate between the 1890s and 1910 (from 1.8 per thousand to 1.23 per thousand) to these efforts alone, but it is the view of one of the leading historians of the subject that 'the efforts of London's MOHs, in terms of demolishing old housing stock, cleaning houses, improving domestic ventilation, and educating the public, seem to have played a critical role in reducing the impact of the disease'.[6]

One of the MOH's main weapons in the late nineteenth-century battle against infectious disease was the isolation of sufferers in hospitals. London had about ninety privately run general and specialist hospitals, mostly supported by endowments and donations, especially from King Edward's Hospital Fund for London (established in 1897), and the Metropolitan Hospital Sunday Fund. About twenty-five of these were little cottage hospitals in the suburbs, dealing with a dozen patients a day, and others were large and well-funded hospitals with prestigious medical schools, including Guy's, St Bartholomew's, St Thomas's, the Middlesex, and St George's. London's biggest hospital, the London, had 800 in-patients on an average night (in 1910), and dealt with half a million out-patients every year. London's publicly managed and funded hospitals were run by the Metropolitan Asylums Board (MAB). Although the MAB was an offshoot of the poor law boards, which chose most of its members, treatment in a MAB hospital did not (after 1883) stigmatize the patient as a pauper, and from 1887 entry was not restricted to the poorer classes. The Board ran several smallpox hospitals, and eleven fever hospitals, for the treatment and isolation of those suffering from the notifiable infectious diseases, scarlet fever, diphtheria, typhus, and typhoid. The great majority of admissions to these MAB hospitals, and to the London Fever Hospital in Islington, were scarlet-fever patients, who had usually had plenty of time to propagate their disease before its symptoms landed them in hospital. Isolation was probably as ineffective with the other important notifiable disease, diphtheria, but at least the hospitals' surgeons were able to save some of their patients from suffocation by giving them tracheotomies. In the 1870s MAB's smallpox hospitals had been regarded by local residents as dangerous centres of infection, and research by some MOHs showed that the areas in which they were located suffered high rates of smallpox. Following the report of a Commission on Smallpox in 1882, the MAB moved its smallpox hospitals from heavily populated parts of London to Dartford in Kent. This led to a sharp fall in smallpox cases in London, and proved that the 'nimby' ('not in my back yard') spirit is not always wrong.[7]

A Dangerous Age

The general decline in mortality in the 1880s and 1890s therefore reflects a variety of environmental and medical factors, as well as changes in the virulence of some infectious diseases. Broader social and economic changes, including reductions in the price of basic foods, slight improvements in housing, great advances in education and literacy, and falling family size, all contributed to the falling death rate, affecting different diseases in different ways. Better nutrition increased resistance to infection, and reduced the incidence of rickets (caused by a shortage of sunlight and vitamin D), a condition which made people more vulnerable to whooping cough and tuberculosis. The modest reduction in overcrowding achieved by council, philanthropic, and private housebuilding in the 1890s and 1900s probably helped reduce mortality from tuberculosis, whooping cough, and scarlet fever, and a decline in the number of foggy days contributed to a fall in deaths from bronchitis to about 5,000 (still over 8 per cent of all deaths in the County) by 1910. But one group, the very young, was strangely resistant to the benefits these changes brought to other age groups, both in London and the rest of England and Wales. In London the mortality of infants in their first year was as high between 1894 and 1899 as it had been in the 1860s, and actually higher than it had been between 1875 and 1893. Statistically speaking, it was more dangerous to be under one than over seventy-five in the 1890s, and about a quarter of all funerals in London were those of babies. Infant mortality was so high, nearly always over 150 per thousand in the 1880s and over 160 per thousand in the later 1890s, that it prevented the overall death rate from falling below about 18 per thousand in the 1890s.

The refusal of infant mortality to fall in the 1890s, when the life expectancy of every other age group improved, and its sudden decline after 1899, from about 160 per thousand in 1899 to 90 per thousand in 1912, has always been something of a puzzle. The long-term factors generally and rightly credited with causing the improvement, including better-nourished and better-educated mothers, falling family size, improved urban and domestic hygiene, better housing, and rising real incomes, cannot account for the lateness and suddenness of the change, since they were all present in the 1880s and 1890s, too. One important factor in the 1880s and 1890s, rising real incomes, did not apply after 1900, when prices rose and real incomes fell. Improvements in midwifery, health visiting, and milk depots to provide uninfected cow's milk to mothers who could not breastfeed were too local and too late to account for the beginning of the change in 1899–1900, though they were probably important in the longer term, and the same can be said about the fall in the number of horses and therefore flies in London. Overlaying, or being suffocated in bed by one's parents, was a significant and declining cause of infant deaths in Edwardian London. The number of infants recorded as dying from this cause fell from about 570 a year (about 4 per cent of infant deaths) between 1900 and 1904 to 310 (2.6 per cent of infant deaths) in 1910. But probably the most convincing explanation for the fall in infant mortality is climatic. Leaving aside prematurity and congenital defects, which did not change much from one decade to another, the most important and some of the most volatile causes of death among infants were diarrhoea, dysentery, and gastro-enteritis. In the hottest years, nearly a third of infant deaths might be caused by these infections, and in cooler ones, less than a sixth. After the very cold 1880s, the 1890s were generally much warmer, especially after 1895, and these hot dry summers meant high levels of diarrhoea and enteritis, and therefore high infant mortality, despite a modest underlying decline in infant deaths from other causes. Temperatures fell after 1898, the hottest year of the late nineteenth century, and the Edwardian decade was the coldest of the twentieth century. As a result, deaths from diarrhoea and dysentery fell by 60 per cent between 1900–4 and 1910, allowing the underlying improvements in infant health to produce a dramatic 35 per cent fall in infant mortality. The year 1911 was hot, with average temperatures in July and August about 4 degrees Celsius higher than those in 1909 and 1910. That same year, infant deaths from diarrhoea, dysentery, and gastro-enteritis rose almost fourfold, pushing the whole infant death rate up by about 30 per cent. The following year was colder and healthier, with infant mortality falling to 90 per thousand for the first and only time before the Great War, then two warm years, 1913 and 1914 (the golden pre-war summers that romantic historians like to talk about), repeated the effects of 1911, but on a less dramatic scale.[8]

These London averages conceal some striking local variations, generally reflecting the levels of crowding and deprivation in different London boroughs and districts. In 1910, infant mortality in Hampstead and Stoke Newington was about 40 per cent below the London average, and that in Shoreditch (the only London borough whose figures put it among the fifty worst towns in the country) was more than 40 per cent above. The rate of infant deaths in Bermondsey, Deptford, Finsbury, and Poplar was about 50 per cent higher than that in Lewisham, Wandsworth, and Westminster in 1910. Variations in overall death rates were less spectacular, but in 1910 the poor and crowded boroughs of Finsbury, Bermondsey, Shoreditch, and Southwark suffered late Victorian death rates of about 18 per thousand, while the spacious suburban boroughs of Hampstead, Lewisham, and Wandsworth enjoyed late twentieth-century rates of under 11 per thousand. Even in the poorest boroughs, Londoners were beginning to abandon traditional ways of dying – in infancy or childhood, and of bronchitis or an infectious disease – and to discover the modern way of death, in middle or old age, of cancer, heart disease, pneumonia, or 'old age'. Those who really wanted to embrace the modern age could be run down and killed by a motor vehicle or electric tram, as over 300 Londoners were in 1910.[9]

*

CHAPTER SIXTEEN

SEX AND SCANDAL

Vice and Vigilantes

London had always been regarded as a place of vice and sexual danger, and its gigantic size and fearsome reputation made it easy for commentators to believe and repeat the most ludicrous estimates of the number of prostitutes walking its streets. The many London societies for the suppression, rescue, shelter, or reform of prostitutes tended to publicize inflated estimates of 100,000 or more, while the Metropolitan Police, who liked to claim that London's problems were firmly under their control, asserted that the true figure was less than a tenth of this number. Prostitution in itself was not illegal, but about 5,000 prostitutes were arrested each year (about fourteen a night) for soliciting, indecency, loitering, or riotous behaviour.

The notorious nightly parade of prostitutes on Piccadilly, the Haymarket, and other fashionable West End streets was past its mid-century peak, but open soliciting on pavements and in music halls still provided compelling evidence that behaviour of the capital's men and women fell far short of the Victorian ideals of unmarried chastity and marital fidelity. Rudyard Kipling, who arrived in London from India in 1889, was disgusted to find that street prostitution in the area round Charing Cross was worse than anything he had seen in the East, with families having to walk 'through four packed miles of seething vice thrust out upon the street'. This was only the most visible part of the trade. London also had unnumbered brothels, some of them masquerading as massage parlours and nursing homes, where 'nursing nymphs, . . . clad in the flimsiest of costumes, minister to the desire of elderly gentlemen'. In 1913 the police raided a school for elocution and deportment and seized nineteen canes, three sets of handcuffs, a mask, and a number of obscene books.[1]

Accounts of prostitution in London, whether statistical or literary, were always highly subjective, depending on the assumptions of the observer and the point that he or she was trying to make. The editor of the *Pall Mall Gazette*, W. T. Stead, was a great campaigner against child prostitution, but he did not agree with Kipling on the state of the West End. Although the condition of Regent Street at midnight was shocking, he wrote in 1885, many of the stories about the extent of prostitution on London's streets and about the bad behaviour of professional streetwalkers were grossly exaggerated:

> I have been a night prowler for weeks. I have gone in different guises to most of the favourite rendezvous of harlots. I have strolled along Ratcliff-highway, and sauntered round and round the Quadrant at midnight. I have haunted St James's Park, and twice enjoyed the strange sweetness of summer night by the sides of the Serpentine. I have been at all hours in Leicester-square and the Strand, and have spent the midnight in Mile-end-road and the vicinity of the Tower. Sometimes I was alone; sometimes accompanied by a friend; and the deep and strong impression which I have brought back is one of respect and admiration for the extraordinarily good behaviour of the English girls who pursue this dreadful calling. In the whole of my wanderings I have not been accosted half-a-dozen times, and then I was more to blame than the woman.

As an ally of Josephine Butler, who had been working for years for the repeal of the Contagious Diseases Acts, Stead was utterly opposed to increasing the powers of the police to control adult prostitutes, and thus to extort money from them.

> The power of a policeman over a girl of the streets, although theoretically very slight, is in reality almost despotic ... A girl's livelihood is in a policeman's hand, and in too many cases he makes the most of his opportunity. To increase by one jot or one tittle the power of the man in uniform over the women who are left unfriended even by their own sex is a crime against liberty and justice ... If we say that the policeman is constantly tempted to transmute his power into cash, we only say that he is human and that he is poor. But it is too bad to convert the truncheoned custodians of public order into a set of 'ponces' in uniform, levying a disgraceful tribute on the fallen maidens of modern Babylon.

William Caine, a puritanical temperance reformer and radical MP for Barrow in Furness, took a different view. He complained to the Home

Office in 1887 that during a short walk from the Reform Club in Pall Mall to Regent Street he was 'accosted by 42 women, chiefly French or Belgians, not merely a nod, a wink or a touch, which one could pass by, but the women walked by his side and spoke in their native tongue, inviting him to go home with them, and see them dance naked on a table &c.'. The Metropolitan Police, who were accused by Caine of taking bribes from prostitutes to allow them to conduct their trade without hindrance, tended to regard such accounts as exaggerated. Caine lived alongside Clapham Common, and in 1886 had helped to form a Vigilance Association whose aim was to clear prostitutes off the Common. The Common, he told the Home Secretary in 1886, was 'literally infested by prostitutes of the lowest type. Not only is solicitation openly and offensively practised, but actual fornication is shamelessly committed on the numerous benches.' The police inspectors and superintendents who investigated the complaint told another story. Five or six solitary and sober prostitutes used the Common in that way, generally accosting men who had gone there deliberately to meet them. There was no doubt that 'when prostitutes and their admirers find a retired place where they can practise their trade without detection, they do so on Clapham Common just as in other parts of London not far removed from some of the most fashionable quarters of the Metropolis', but it would take a determined snooper to catch them at it. Caine and his vigilantes, the police said, jumped to conclusions about young women who walked on the Common with men. 'There are a great number of well-dressed "courting couples" (apparently respectable), who roam about the Common after dark, and many of them are frequently to be seen sitting on the seats caressing each other', but 'it would be unfair to assume that in all cases the women are common prostitutes'. Fifteen years later, Charles Booth agreed with the police view. 'The use of open spaces for immoral purposes is by no means limited to professional vice . . . Boys and girls wander off out of sight, and mischief ensues which might otherwise have been avoided: and young men and women who are keeping company deliberately make use of such opportunities.'[2]

While the National Vigilance Association, the London Council for the Promotion of Public Morality, and the Church of England Purity Society agitated for the strict enforcement of laws against brothels and street prostitution, the Metropolitan Police generally argued for a more modest and pragmatic policy, putting public order before moral purity. Sir Charles Warren, who was briefly Metropolitan Police Commissioner in 1887-8, believed that raids on brothels tended to drive prostitutes onto the streets,

or into other neighbourhoods: 'As long as there is a demand for prostitutes on the part of the public there is no doubt they will exist in spite of
the vestries and Vigilance Societies, and the more they are driven out of
their brothels . . . the worse it becomes for law and order and decency.'
When the police worked in willing cooperation with the purity campaigners, as they did between 1901 and 1906, they could make life very
uncomfortable for prostitutes and brothel-keepers. In those years there was
a concerted campaign, also involving Westminster Council and other local
authorities, against brothels and streetwalkers, made easier by the 1898
law against living on the earnings of a prostitute. Between 1893 and 1903,
when the rate of prosecutions for other serious offences fell by nearly 20
per cent, the number of prosecutions for brothel-keeping, living on prostitutes' earnings, and solicitation and similar offences almost quadrupled.[3]
Whether these prosecutions really reduced the number of prostitutes,
rather than forcing them to use different streets and premises, nobody
knew, but the morality campaigners were sure they had made a real difference. William Coote, Secretary of the National Vigilance Association,
claimed that London in 1907 was like 'an open-air cathedral', compared
to its vicious condition in the 1860s.[4]

The Middle Ground

The policeman's interpretation of what was happening on Clapham
Common's secluded benches is supported by recent research on the records
of the London Foundling Hospital, which took in the illegitimate infants
of otherwise respectable women who had been seduced, tricked, or
coerced into premarital intercourse. Françoise Barret-Ducrocq's work in
the 1990s on the hospital records of 1850–80 reveals a much freer and
more varied sexual world than the one we find in Victorian novels. The
girls' stories show that young men could easily befriend servants, barmaids,
and shop girls, chatting to them in the street, at their place of work, or in
a park or music hall. After a month or two friendship might lead to inti-
macy and eventually to sexual intercourse, perhaps at home or at work, or
in one of suburban London's many parks, where it might have been wit-
nessed from behind a bush by William Caine MP. The girls said they
agreed to intercourse because they 'fancied' the man, or because they were
talked into it, or because they did not know that it was wrong. Sometimes
they submitted because their lover promised to marry them, or because

they had agreed that they would marry if a baby was conceived. Very often these promises were kept, and many firstborn legitimate children had been conceived out of wedlock. But when the girl was 'let down', as nearly all the Foundling Hospital applicants were, they were generally not 'ruined' as they would have been in a Victorian melodrama. Families usually stood by their unlucky daughters, and even employers were ready to take them back into service, as long as the Hospital took care of the baby. 'The discovery of illicit sexual relations did not usually lead to exclusion from the family or social group; exclusion and blame, when they did appear, were directed against social ineptitude rather than moral failing.'[5]

Women who felt that they had been tricked into sexual intercourse by false promises of marriage could, if they chose, take their lover to court for breach of promise. A recent study of these cases, drawn from all parts of late nineteenth-century England, reached the conclusion that 'premarital intercourse was an accepted part of courtship in the lower middle and "respectable" working classes, but only in long-term relationships and infrequently even then'. Once couples had learned to trust each other they might make love on odd occasions if the opportunity presented itself, but 'intercourse was an important step and a big risk, not to be taken lightly, though not taboo'. It was hard for most courting couples to find a suitably secluded place (thus the popularity of Clapham Common), and the methods used to prevent conception were primitive and uncertain. Women 'gave in', it was assumed, to bind their chosen partner more closely to them, and to make marriage more certain. When they brought breach of promise cases against lovers who had deserted them these women were not treated with disapproval, and the strongest moral condemnation was directed at the man's betrayal, not the woman's compliance. Only those women who seemed to be sexually experienced (a widow or a woman with more than one lover), and those who had sex too soon and too willingly, were likely to be have their cases dismissed.[6]

So London's sexual world was more ambiguous and complicated than Caine and Kipling thought, and there were several gradations of sexual behaviour between innocence and utter corruption. There was not just one kind of man and two kinds of women. In the West End there was a loose world in which prostitutes, mistresses, showgirls, and 'fast' women mingled with free-spending men in casinos, dance halls, theatres, and music halls. Its heyday had been in the 1860s, before the closure of the most notorious night houses, such as the Holborn Casino and the Argyll Rooms, but there were lively nightclubs in the 1880s. Looking back on the West

End of the 1880s after the Great War, Ralph Nevill had nostalgic memories of the Bohemian clubs and music halls where 'men about town' could spend their evenings in harmless enjoyment, and 'where pleasant female acquaintances were easily to be made'. Some of the women to be met in such places as the Gardinia in Leicester Square and the Corinthian in York Street, Nevill admitted, were prostitutes, but 'their manner was always unobtrusive, while they very seldom spoke to anyone who had not addressed them first. Not a few of these ladies were fairly educated and of quite a good class, the result of which was that a good many of them ended by marrying well.' Others, he was sure, were looking for a good time rather than an income, and were just throwing off the stifling restrictions imposed on young women by the Victorian moral code.[7] The memoirs of Compton Mackenzie, a young man about town in Edwardian London, confirm Nevill's opinion that there were plenty of women in London who lived their lives in the extensive territory between prostitution and respectability. There were the girls who made love to their boyfriends on the boxed back stalls of Terry's Theatre, a cinema on the Strand, and women like Mackenzie's friend Daisy, whose rent and expenses in her flat in Great Coram Street were paid by a commercial traveller. She was a kept woman, not a prostitute, but her commitment to her keeper did not prevent her from going with Mackenzie to the Café de Provence in Leicester Square and teaching him all a young novelist needed to know about London's demi-monde.[8]

The image of Victorian London as a place of extreme sexual contrasts, a Jekyll and Hyde world of laced-up Christian respectability in the home and readily available commercial sex on the streets, with nothing between them except hypocritical gentlemen scuttling from the marriage bed to the brothel, is difficult to eradicate, but hard to believe. The Victorian convention that women were either Madonnas or Magdalenes, either fallen or bolt upright, is questioned now. It is plain that plenty of women, especially in London, broke strict taboos on premarital or extramarital sex, not to earn money, but because they wanted pleasure and excitement, or just to be with the partner of their choice. So we should be careful not to accept the image of respectable late Victorian society that was promoted in novels, plays, and contemporary moral writings. The absence of sexual adventure and pleasure-seeking from Victorian literature can hardly be taken as conclusive evidence that these things did not exist in real life. There were enormous pressures on novelists from critics, publishers, and commercial circulating libraries not to depict young women who broke the rules on premarital sex without suffering a suitable punishment – suicide, death in childbirth, or descent into prostitution. Playwrights, who were subject to rigorous and narrow-minded censorship by the Lord Chamberlain's office, were even more tightly controlled, and could hardly mention anything that would disturb a bank clerk. Shaw's play depicting an intelligent and moral prostitute, *Mrs Warren's Profession*, written in 1894, was first performed in a private club eight years later, and was not allowed on the public stage until the 1920s. Thomas Hardy, who treated 'fallen' women with sympathy in *Tess of the D'Urbervilles* and *Jude the Obscure*, was so fiercely attacked by the critics in the 1890s that he abandoned novel-writing altogether, and even in the easier atmosphere of 1909 H. G. Wells found himself condemned by critics, clergymen, and moralists after the publication of *Ann Veronica*, 'in which the youthful heroine was allowed a frankness of desire and sexual enterprise, hitherto unknown in English popular fiction'. In these circumstances, the absence from late Victorian and Edwardian literature of non-commercial premarital sex, or sexual enterprise or enjoyment by women who were not prostitutes, does not tell us much about the real world, especially about life in the world's greatest city, London, where social and sexual rules were most likely to be broken.

Birth Control

Since we do not share the much-publicized but far from universal Victorian belief that sane women did not desire or particularly enjoy sexual intercourse, we have no reason to think that women who had sex outside marriage were motivated only by money. Many of them no doubt found prevailing moral restraints intolerable, and broke them for pleasure. If the world was as respectable clergymen, doctors, journalists, and novelists liked to depict it, the ready availability of contraceptive sponges and syringes and abortion-inducing drugs by mail order or from London chemists' and barbers' shops is a little difficult to explain. Many men and women – and not only married couples – knew a good deal about contraception, thanks in part to the prosecution of Charles Bradlaugh and Annie Besant in 1877 for publishing a dated but informative pamphlet on the subject, Charles Knowlton's *The Fruits of Philosophy*. The prosecution failed on a technicality, and thanks to the publicity hundreds of thousands of copies of the pamphlet were printed over the next few years. In the twelve years after the trial about 175,000 copies of Annie Besant's book *The Law of*

Population were sold, and any reader who wanted to find out how to have sex without getting pregnant could do so. There is no reason to assume that those who bought Knowlton's pamphlet, or used the sponges and rubber syringes it recommended, were all married couples, though birth-control propagandists implied that this was the case.

The devices available to well-informed couples were more numerous and effective in the 1880s than they had ever been before. The development of the vulcanization process for rubber in the 1840s led to the availability of rubber condoms in the 1850s, but they were not especially cheap, comfortable, or respectable. Efficient, comfortable, and cheap latex condoms were not available until the 1930s. The rubber diaphragm, or 'Dutch cap', which was described in the early 1880s, was more trustworthy, especially when intercourse was followed by douching with a tube attached to a fat rubber bulb (a common practice), but it had to be fitted by a doctor. For those without access to a cooperative doctor there were various cheap spermicides (to make sponge barriers more effective) on sale in chemists' shops in the 1880s. A London chemist and freethinker, W. J. Rendell, began making and selling cheap quinine and cacao-butter pessaries in his shop in Clerkenwell in the 1880s, and well-informed women could buy their own spermicides and smear them over the traditional sponge. The many encounters described in the memoirs of Frank Harris, the boastful and sexually active editor of the *Evening News* and *Fortnightly Review* in the 1880s, usually involved some simple contraceptive precautions, especially douching. Commonest of all, there was the withdrawal method, which was denounced in an American manual published in London in 1894 as 'conjugal onanism' which 'soiled the conjugal bed' (as it no doubt did). By the 1890s the Anglican clergy had begun to attack those who used contraceptive devices. In 1905 Arthur Foley Winnington-Ingram, the popular (and unmarried) East End clergyman who became Bishop of London in 1901, wrote to the London clergy denouncing artificial contraception: 'It is all part of the miserable gospel of comfort that is the curse of the present day, and we must learn ourselves and teach others to live the simpler and harder lives our forefathers lived.'[9]

We do not know how widespread these methods were. The fact that the birth rate started to fall in the 1870s, shortly after the Bradlaugh–Besant trial, is suggestive, but far from conclusive. Although London no doubt had its share – more than its share – of sexual sophisticates, we should not lose sight of the probability that most London couples who restricted their family size did so by traditional methods which involved restraint, abstinence, and a degree of sexual frustration. Low-birth-rate groups, including lawyers, doctors, clergymen, civil servants, clerks, teachers, businessmen, and domestic servants, usually married late, and then tended to space their pregnancies out to achieve a family of three, four, or five. Couples did not talk openly about how they achieved this, but from time to time the matter was investigated through surveys, questionnaires, and censuses. In 1946–7 the Royal Commission on Population interviewed 3,281 women, 42 per cent of them being from London, about the birth-control methods they had used during their married lives. Of those married between 1900 and 1909, only 2 per cent said they had ever used 'appliances', and 13 per cent said they had used 'non-appliance' methods. For those married in the next decade the figures were 9 per cent and 31 per cent respectively. Interviewers explained that 'non-appliance' methods could mean coitus interruptus, the 'safe period', or abstinence, and E. Lewis-Faning, who conducted and analysed the research, reported that in nearly every case the 'non-appliance' method used was coitus interruptus, rather than abstinence. The women questioned were told that 'abstinence' meant going without sex for periods of six months or more, therefore much shorter periods of abstinence (a week or fortnight, say), which can have very significant effects on the spacing of pregnancies, were ignored. Since the birth-rate figures for 1900–9 show that a much higher percentage of couples limited their families than the 15 per cent who admitted to having done so, it is probable that a large number restricted their pregnancies by making love less frequently than they might have done in other circumstances. Perhaps husbands exercised restraint without telling their wives, who therefore did not report it as a form of family limitation to the Royal Commission on Population survey. Other national studies of falling fertility, especially a survey of women graduates in 1914, confirm that 'continence' or 'abstinence' was the most common method of family limitation, followed by coitus interruptus, condoms, and pessaries. Abortion, which was dangerous and illegal, would have been a useful backup when these methods failed, but very few women questioned in these surveys admitted to it.[10] Finally, twentieth-century evidence, such as the letters written to Marie Stopes between the wars, and the National Survey of Sexual Attitudes and Lifestyle published in 1994, does not suggest that there was a significant growth in sexual knowledge or sophistication before the Great War, or at any time before the 1950s or 1960s.[11]

The general effect of the efforts of many couples to limit their family

size, whether by traditional or modern methods, was a 23 per cent fall in
the birth rate in London and England between 1881–5 and 1906–10.
This decline, which we now regard as a vital advance along the path to a
healthier and more affluent society, caused great concern at the time. Politicians who were worried about a future shortage of soldiers or workers, and
thinkers who believed the 'lower' classes and races would start to outbreed
and defeat the 'higher' ones, could call upon the new 'science' of eugenics, the study of the factors responsible for the improvement of the human
breed, which was named and virtually invented by the anthropologist
Francis Galton in his book *Human Faculty and its Development* in 1883.
Galton endowed a research fellowship in eugenics at London University
in 1904, and the subject excited much interest among late Victorian and
Edwardian imperialists, social reformers, and scientists, who agreed that
there was a problem, but not what caused it or what should be done about
it. These concerns shaped many of the inquiries into poverty, health, and
fertility that took place between the 1880s and the First World War,
including Charles Booth's study of London, and the important Inter-
Departmental Committee on Physical Deterioration of 1903–4, which was
set up to investigate the poor quality of military volunteers and recruits in
the Boer War. Some of those who were interested in fertility differences
between different classes believed that the urban poor, especially in
London, were a degenerate breed, incapable of producing healthy or intelligent offspring. This theory of irreversible urban degeneration produced
some unpleasant proposals for compulsory sterilization or segregation of
the lowest urban class, the residuum, but it was overwhelmed after 1900
by a more optimistic environmentalist view, which held that improvements
in education, housing, and income, and especially the provision of social
services for children, could reverse urban degeneration, and enable the
children of the poor to grow into healthy and intelligent citizens.[12]

Stead and the Maiden Tribute

If Londoners knew too little about ordinary sex lives, they knew a great
deal – perhaps too much – about extraordinary ones. In the 1880s a succession of shocking scandals, enthusiastically reported (and to some extent
created) by the livelier newspapers, taught Londoners that their sexual
world was more complicated and much more squalid than they had previously believed. The biggest scandal came from a growing concern among

feminists and moral reformers about the problem of child prostitution. The revelation that young English girls were being supplied to licensed brothels in Belgium prompted a Quaker, Alfred Dyer, to set up the London Committee for Suppressing the Traffic in British Girls in 1880. Helped by Josephine Butler, the formidable campaigner for the repeal of the Contagious Diseases Acts, the London Committee persuaded the government to set up a House of Lords Select Committee on 'the law relating to the protection of young girls from artifices to induce them to lead a corrupt life'. The Select Committee found that the real problem was not the traffic in girls to Belgium, but child prostitution in England, and proposed a new law to raise the age of sexual consent for girls from thirteen to sixteen. This measure, the Criminal Law Amendment Bill, passed through the House of Lords but failed in the Commons in 1883. The weakness of the existing law was demonstrated in May 1885, when Dyer's committee brought a private prosecution against a high-class Chelsea brothel-keeper, Mary Jeffries, who was suspected of using thirteen-year-old girls. Mrs Jeffries was a large-scale operator, with four brothels in Chelsea, one in Kew, and houses for those with more specialized tastes in Hampstead and Euston. Jeffries pleaded guilty to keeping a disorderly house to prevent embarrassing evidence being heard, and her £200 fine was paid by her grateful clients after (or perhaps during) a whip-round. The rumour in London was that Jeffries was saved from worse punishment by her professional association with Edward, the Prince of Wales, and his loose-living Marlborough House set.[13]

After this failure Butler and her allies decided to arouse public anger against sexual corruption and parliamentary apathy by enlisting the support of the inventor and master of the campaigning 'New Journalism', W. T. Stead of the *Pall Mall Gazette*. Stead agreed, and set up what he called a 'Secret Commission of Inquiry' to 'shed light on these dark places' and shame the Commons into passing the Bill. In the belief that a dramatic 'stunt' would stir up more interest than a weighty dossier of evidence, Stead prepared a plan. After consulting two of London's leading churchmen, Bishop Temple of London and Cardinal Manning, the Roman Catholic Archbishop of Westminster, Stead asked the Salvation Army to provide him with a woman who knew the ways of London's sexual underworld. A reformed brothel-keeper, Rebecca Jarrett, helped Stead to find a mother who was prepared to sell her thirteen-year-old daughter into prostitution for £5. Stead took the girl, Eliza Armstrong, to a procuress and 'midwife', Madame Mourez, to certify her virginity, and then handed her over to a Salvation Army officer, who had her examined by a doctor, and took her into their care in Paris.

Stead ran his sensational account of this escapade, along with a more general description of the trade in young girls in London, in four very long articles in the *Pall Mall Gazette* in July 1885. His overall title, 'The Maiden Tribute to Modern Babylon', suggested a parallel with myths of human sacrifice, and allowed him to depict London as a Cretan Labyrinth, with wealthy debauchees as the Minotaur at its centre: 'I am not without hope that there may be some check placed upon this vast tribute of maidens, unwitting or unwilling, which is nightly levied in London by the vices of the rich upon the necessities of the poor. London's lust annually uses up many thousands of women, who are literally killed and made away with – living sacrifices slain in the service of vice.' Using narrative and descriptive techniques familiar to patrons of the melodrama or readers of Gothic horror stories or Victorian pornography, Stead painted a lurid and probably exaggerated picture of the trade in girls, with plentiful references to bondage, flagellation, aristocratic entrapment, and White Slave Traffic. Like Mearns' research for *The Bitter Cry*, Stead's investigations were brief and anecdotal, relying on conversations with policemen, brothel-keepers, prostitutes, 'gentlemen', and others who seemed to know London's sexual underworld well. Stead made a virtue of this superficiality: 'Awful as are the revelations which we have brought to light, they are far less awful than the actual facts. We have but skimmed the surface of the subject. All that has been done has been done in six weeks, at a total outlay of not more than £300 in expenses – less than a rich man will spend in procuring the corruption of a single shop girl of the better class.' Perhaps Stead's researches were brief, but they were also, he assured his readers, heroic:

> For four weeks, aided by two or three coadjutors of whose devotion and self-sacrifice, combined with a rare instinct of investigation and a singular personal fearlessness, I cannot speak too highly, I have been exploring the London Inferno. It has been a strange and unexampled experience. For a month I have oscillated between the noblest and the meanest of mankind, the saviours and the destroyers of their race, spending hours alternately in brothels and hospitals, in the streets and in refuges, in the company of procuresses and of bishops. London beneath the gas glare of its innumerable lamps became . . . a resurrected and magnified City of the Plain, with all the vices of Gomorrah.

Stead's audience was told how London procuresses hunted and ensnared guileless virgins, using techniques which had apparently not changed much since the days of Fielding, Defoe, and Hogarth.

> When a keeper has spotted a girl whom she fancies will be 'a good mark' she – for in most cases the creature is of the feminine gender – sets to work to secure her for her service. Decoy girls are laid on to tempt the girl with promises of dress and money. The ordinary formula is that if you come with us you will live like a lady, have plenty of fine clothes, have your own way in everything and do as you please. If the girl listens, she is lost. The toils [nets] close round. She calls upon her friends. Some night she stops out after the time her mistress locks the door. She is obliged to return to seek shelter, and before morning she is done for.

One of the procuresses explained her modus operandi:

> Young girls from the country, fresh and rosy, are soon picked up in the shops or as they run errands. But nurse-girls are the great field ... Every morning at this time of the year my friend and I are up at seven, and after breakfast we put a shawl round our shoulders and off we go to scour the park. Hyde Park and the Green Park are the best in the morning; Regent's Park in the afternoon. As we go coasting along, we keep a sharp look out for any likely girl, and having spotted one we make up to her; and week after week we see her as often as possible, until we are sufficiently in her confidence to suggest how easy it is to earn a few pounds by meeting a man. In the afternoon off goes the shawl and on goes the jacket, and we are off on the same quest.

Once the girls had been trapped, they were (in Stead's words) 'seduced' by high-paying clients, often with great brutality: 'When means of stifling a cry – a pillow, a sheet, or even a pocket handkerchief – lie all around, there is practically no danger. To some men, however, the shriek of torture is the essence of their delight, and they would not silence by a single note the cry of agony over which they gloat.' When a girl's highly marketable virginity had been lost, it could be 'restored' by the same 'midwives' who had verified it in the first place.

There were several roads to ruin in Stead's Babylonian city. Even worse than the fashionable West End brothels, he said, were 'the great drapery and millinery establishments of the metropolis', and some of its theatres.

Stead was probably referring to William Whiteley, the notorious philanderer who owned London's first and largest department store:

> Some theatrical managers are, rightly or wrongly, accused of insisting upon a claim to ruin actresses whom they allow to appear on their boards; and it is to be feared that a certain persistent report is not ill founded, and that the head of a great London emporium regards the women in his employ in much the same aspect as the Sultan of Turkey regards the inmates of his seraglio, the master of the establishment selecting for himself the prettiest girls in the shop.

Whatever Stead's shortcomings as a social observer, his skills as a publicist were beyond dispute. His articles were denounced in the House of Commons, banned from W. H. Smith's bookstalls, seized by the City Chamberlain, and attacked in the London press, but praised by feminists, radicals, and morality campaigners. Letters of support came from leading Christians and public figures, including Lord Shaftesbury, William Booth (the founder of the Salvation Army), the great popular preacher Charles Spurgeon, Cardinal Manning, and George Bernard Shaw, who offered to join the many vendors who were selling the *Pall Mall Gazette* on the streets. Demand for the 'Maiden Tribute' issues was so high that the printers ran out of white paper, and had to use pink paper intended for the *Globe*, London's oldest afternoon paper. Public pressure was so great that the Criminal Law Amendment Act, which had been delayed for years, passed through both Houses of Parliament by 10 August. By this Act the age of consent for women was raised from thirteen to sixteen, brothel-keeping and procuring women for prostitution were made illegal, and indecency between males in public or private was made punishable by up to two years in prison. This last clause, introduced at the committee stage with very little discussion by Henry Labouchère, significantly extended the law's reach into the private lives of homosexuals by criminalizing all sexual touching between men, and played its part in one of the great dramas of the 1890s.

To maintain the momentum of this morality crusade Stead and his allies organized a huge rally in support of the new Act in Hyde Park on 22 August. The crowd, estimated at 250,000, contained many working men, taking the opportunity to remind the well off that the East End did not have a monopoly on vice. There were also large numbers of women, including many who had been involved in the struggle for the repeal of the Contagious Diseases Acts. One contingent, tempting London's roués almost beyond endurance, brought along a wagonload of young virgins dressed in sacrificial robes. The impact of the morality crusade Stead had stirred up extended far beyond the matter of child prostitution. The National Vigilance Association (NVA), formed in 1885 to help enforce the new Act, campaigned against London's pornographic book trade, and also against the uninhibited depiction of sex in plays, songs, novels, and paintings. The movement also opposed the dissemination of birth-control and abortion information and devices, and encouraged the police to use the 1885 law to close brothels and other places where prostitutes met their clients in relative safety. One of the results of the police campaign against brothels, which took place in other big cities as well as in London, was to drive women like Rebecca Jarrett and Madame Mourez out of business, and to deprive prostitutes of the protection and companionship brothels had given them. Instead they found rooms in cheap lodging houses, and their customers on the streets, parks, and alleyways. Isolated and vulnerable, they were now more likely to fall under the control of pimps, and even – as several unlucky women did in 1888 – into the hands of murderers.

The dramatic outcome of the 'Maiden Tribute' scandal is well known. Stead was brought to trial at the Old Bailey for abduction and indecent assault (the virginity test on Eliza), along with Bramwell Booth (a future leader of the Salvation Army), the reformed brothel-keeper Rebecca Jarrett, the 'midwife' Madame Mourez, and two others. Eliza's mother, who had been beaten by her husband and castigated by her neighbours for what she had done, was a persuasive witness for the prosecution, and Jarrett's dishonesty and evasiveness cast doubt on Stead's story. Stead was sentenced to three months' imprisonment with hard labour, and Jarrett and Madame Mourez, the procuress and 'midwife' who had carried out the virginity test, got six months. Mourez died in jail, but Stead spent two comfortable and happy months in Holloway, with daily visitors and newspapers, and meals delivered from a local tavern. He left Holloway in January 1886 as a national figure, and commemorated his imprisonment by wearing his Holloway uniform one day a year for the rest of his life. He edited the *Pall Mall Gazette* for another four years, and spent most of the following twenty pursuing his interest in psychic research and as a campaigner for world peace. A headliner to the end, he was last seen on the deck of the *Titanic* on 15 April 1912, calmly helping women and children into the lifeboats as the great liner went down.

Cleveland Street

Three years later, in 1889, Londoners who believed that male lust, and especially upper-class lust, was running out of control in their sinful city, were provided with shocking evidence. In 1889 the Metropolitan Police were investigating a theft from the Central Telegraph Office, and questioned a telegraph boy, Thomas Swinscow, about 18s he had in his pocket. Swinscow told them he had earned it by going to bed with two men in a homosexual brothel in Cleveland Street, near Fitzroy Square, and that others had done the same. On 6 July Inspector Frederick Abberline called at 19 Cleveland Street to arrest Charles Hammond, the householder, and Anthony Newlove, the young man who had introduced Swinscow to Hammond, on the charge that they 'did unlawfully, wickedly, and corruptly conspire, combine, confederate and agree' to find young men 'to commit the abominable crime of buggery'. Warned by his lawyer, Hammond escaped to the Continent, but Newlove was arrested, and under questioning he named Lord Arthur Somerset, superintendent of the stables of Edward, Prince of Wales, and the Earl of Euston, and implicated Prince Edward's oldest son, the feeble-minded and dissolute Duke of Clarence ('Prince Eddy'). The full extent of the scandal was kept quiet, and Lord Arthur Somerset was allowed to escape to Germany. But in the autumn, after Newlove had been sentenced to four months' hard labour, Ernest Parke, editor of the radical *North London Press*, broke the story of an apparent cover-up, named Euston and Somerset as customers of the brothel, and implied that someone very 'highly placed' – Prince Eddy – was involved. Euston sued Parke for libel, and the editor, protecting his sources, went to jail for a year, three times as long as Newlove. The conspiracy (if there was one) was not exposed, but the public was left with the impression that homosexuality involved the exploitation of innocent lads by rich men with protectors in the highest places. This suspicion seemed to be confirmed in 1895 when Oscar Wilde, the most successful wit and dramatist of his day, was brought down by his love affairs with teenage boys.

*

CHAPTER SEVENTEEN

BOHEMIA AND GRUB STREET

Aesthetes and Bohemians

Late Victorian London was home to dozens of literary and artistic groups, clubs, cliques, and coteries, many of which seemed mightily important to their members at the time, and most of which are now almost completely forgotten. In the early 1890s a mainly Irish poetry group, the Rhymers Club, met nightly in an upper room of the Cheshire Cheese, an old Fleet Street eating house. This group was founded by a young Irish poet, W. B. Yeats, and a Welsh poet and editor, Ernest Rhys, who later (from 1906) edited almost a thousand volumes for Joseph Dent's Everyman's Library series. Yeats was the leading figure of the group, but the poets Ernest Dowson, Lionel Johnson, John Davidson, and Richard Le Gallienne, and Selwyn Image, the artist and designer of stained glass, were regulars, and Arthur Symons, the poet, editor, and literary go-between, came from time to time. Oscar Wilde was invited to the Cheshire Cheese, but he 'hated Bohemia' (he told Yeats), and would only join them when they met in a private house. Drinking ale and smoking clay pipes, the Rhymers read their poems to each other, taking their turn in alphabetical order, and held rather uneasy conversations which were sustained by the more voluble Irish members. Yeats recalled that the group shared 'an opposition to all ideas, all generalisations that can be explained and debated'. When Yeats raised such ideas, he said, 'a gloomy silence fell upon the room'. Most of them dressed like gentlemen rather than 'Bohemians'. Only Yeats, in 'a brown velveteen coat, a loose tie and a very old Inverness cape', Symons, whose Inverness cape was newly bought, and Le Gallienne, who wore the loose tie and knee breeches of a Gilbert and Sullivan aesthete, really looked the part. Lionel Johnson, Selwyn Image, and another Rhymer, Herbert Horne, lived together off Fitzroy Square (not yet 'Fitzrovia'), sharing a manservant and living the artistic life in what Yeats thought was a rather self-conscious way.[1]

In 1888 Yeats met Oscar Wilde at a Sunday evening gathering of writers and talkers in Chiswick, at the home of William E. Henley, the critic, writer, and editor. Kenneth Grahame, a conscientious and successful clerk at the Bank of England whose literary aspirations were being fostered by Henley, was also there. Wilde was about nine years older than the rest of Henley's guests, and Yeats found his conversational fluency astonishing. 'I never before heard a man talking with perfect sentences, as if he had written them all over night with labour and yet all spontaneous.' Wilde seemed like 'a triumphant figure, . . . an audacious Italian fifteenth-century figure', whose brilliant conversation 'could pass without incongruity from some unforeseen stroke of wit to elaborate reverie'. Like Dr Johnson, Wilde was above all a conversationalist, and (Yeats thought) 'his plays and dialogues have what merit they possess from being now an imitation, now a record, of his talk'. Wilde and Henley exchanged experiences of editing magazines, and briefly became friends, but they grew apart, and in Wilde's moment of humiliation Henley joined the onslaught upon him.[2]

Despite this visit to Chiswick, Wilde's preferred stamping grounds were the West End and Chelsea, which was becoming the aesthetes' suburb of choice. A favourite meeting-place for Wilde and his friends, and for very many of London's more 'advanced' writers and artists, was the Café Royal, at the Piccadilly Circus end of Regent Street. In the famous Domino Room, Wilde, Max Beerbohm, Richard Le Gallienne, Aubrey Beardsley, and Arthur Symons might meet the painters Walter Sickert, Will Rothenstein, and James Whistler. In October 1893, Will Rothenstein, a brilliant Oxford undergraduate, introduced a fellow student, Max Beerbohm, to the haunts of literary and artistic London. They visited Sickert in Chelsea, Beardsley in Pimlico, and the offices of the publisher Bodley Head in Vigo Street (off Regent Street), and drank vermouth in the Domino Room of the Café Royal. Twenty years later, Beerbohm recalled the impression the room made on him:

> There, on that October evening – there in that exuberant vista of gilding and crimson velvet set amidst all those opposing mirrors and upholding caryatids, with fumes of tobacco ever rising to the painted and pagan ceiling, and with the hum of presumably cynical conversation broken into so sharply now and again by the clatter of dominoes shuffled on marble tables, I drew a deep breath, and 'This indeed,' I said to myself, 'is life!'[3]

On less formal occasions London writers and artists preferred the theatres and music halls around Leicester Square or the Strand, and the lively public houses in the nearby streets. A favourite was the Crown, on Cranbourne Street, by Charing Cross Road, where Rothenstein, Beardsley, Beerbohm, Johnson, and Wilde might meet the Christian Socialist priest Stewart Headlam, or the writer George Moore, and listen to Arthur Symons extolling the beauty of the latest music-hall dancer to take his fancy or watch Ernest Dowson drinking himself to death. This is where Wilde drank hot port after performances of *Lady Windermere's Fan* in 1892, and where Arthur Symons, in company with the publisher John Lane in 1893, first met Aubrey Beardsley, 'the thinnest young man I ever saw, rather unpleasant and affected'.[4] Other favourite meeting places in this Bohemian world included the Cock in Shaftesbury Avenue, and several restaurants in Soho, especially the Poland, where Dowson wooed Adelaide, the owner's daughter.

The group of writers and artists loosely associated with Wilde, some of whom were also involved in the Rhymers' Club and (in 1895–6) the *Yellow Book*, are often called the Decadents or Aesthetes. This group is sometimes taken to represent the spirit of the last fifteen years of the century, partly because its world-weary tone and mockery of conventional moral and social values seem to exude an appropriately fin-de-siècle spirit, and perhaps because the deaths of so many of its members, notably Wilde and Beardsley, coincided so neatly with the end of the century. The 'Decadent' group of writers and artists in late 1880s and early 1890s London was really a junior branch of the French avant-garde, replenishing its spirit by frequent visits to Paris and the Normandy seaside resorts. Its ideas and inspiration came from Charles Baudelaire and the French 'Symbolist' writers, Arthur Rimbaud, Joris Karl Huysmans, Stéphane Mallarmé, and Paul Verlaine, and with additional influences from the writings of the critics John Ruskin and Walter Pater, especially Pater's *Studies in the History of the Renaissance* (1873). The group had an intriguing moral and sexual ambiguity. Its leading members, Oscar Wilde, Aubrey Beardsley, Ernest Dowson, Arthur Symons, and Max Beerbohm, subscribed to Théophile Gautier's 'art for art's sake' doctrine, that a work of art should be judged for its beauty rather than its usefulness or moral content. The Rhymers' unwillingness to discuss serious issues was symptomatic of the same outlook, though Le Gallienne, despite his 'aesthetic' appearance, joined Yeats in rejecting it. As Wilde put it in the preface to his only novel, *The Portrait of Dorian Gray*: 'There is no such thing as a moral or an immoral book. Books are well written, or badly written. That is all.' If these views were taken to apply to life as well as art, as the prosecuting counsel in Wilde's trial assumed they did, their implication was that morality did not matter, and that one mode of life was as acceptable as another, as long as it was aesthetically pleasing.

In general members of the Wilde set were beautifully dressed, languid, witty, and fastidious, with the bored air of 'people imprisoned in a waiting room during a block on the railway, or in a country house on a wet Sunday'.[5] In the case of Beardsley, this languor was symptomatic of the tuberculosis that led to his early death, but for others it seemed to be a kind of fin-de-siècle affectation, a rejection of the late Victorian ideal of sporty, imperialistic 'manliness' that was extolled by such writers as Rudyard Kipling and Rider Haggard, and exemplified by politicians like Joseph Chamberlain and Lord Salisbury. Knee breeches, silk shirts, and soft hands were not really indications of effeminacy or homosexuality, any more than the muscular virility of English public schools was a sign of robust heterosexuality, but in a society where a sexual relationship between men was an offence punishable (after 1885) by up to two years' imprisonment with hard labour, it could be dangerous to arouse suspicions, and disastrous to confirm them. As the Marquess of Queensberry said in his famous confrontation with Wilde in Tite Street in June 1894: 'I do not say you are it, but you look it, you pose as it, which is just as bad.' And after the trial, when the hunt was on for sexual deviants, Aubrey Beardsley was disturbed to discover that he too 'looked like a sodomite'.

A Double Life

Oscar Wilde settled in London in 1879 when he was twenty-four, after moving from Dublin and graduating from Oxford. He lived first in lodgings in Salisbury Street, off the Strand, and then in rooms in Tite Street, Chelsea. Soon he was friends with Mrs Lillie Langtry, who became the Prince of Wales' mistress in 1879, the actress Ellen Terry, whose great association with Henry Irving at the Lyceum had just begun, and the artist James McNeill Whistler, recently returned to England after his ruinous libel suit against John Ruskin. Wilde and Whistler, who were neighbours in Tite Street in 1880–1, were (according to Ellen Terry) 'more instantly individual and audacious than it is possible to describe'. Soon they were the talk of the town, caricatured by *Punch*'s leading cartoonist, George du Maurier, and ridiculed as lily-wielding aesthetes by Gilbert and Sullivan in their 1881 musical comedy *Patience*. Whistler's friendship soon turned into a witty but hurtful rivalry, and then into malicious hostility. In the early 1880s Wilde tried to make a living by giving public lectures in France, England, and America, and in May 1884 he married Constance and soon moved into 16 Tite Street. Over the next two years Wilde had two sons, wore his hair short, gave up velveteen and large turned-back cuffs, kept up an increasingly unfriendly exchange of cruelly witty newspaper articles with Whistler, became a favourite guest at London dinner parties, and won a reputation a London's best conversationalist. Following the example of the hero of Huysmans' *A Rebours* (*Against Nature*), a book much admired by the English Decadents, Wilde had his house in Tite Street decorated at great expense under the supervision of the 'aesthetic' architect Edward Godwin, and discovered a real world of incompetent builders and unpaid bills that he had not found in Huysmans' fiction. Yeats visited Wilde's 'House Beautiful' and it struck him that 'the perfect harmony of his life there, with his beautiful wife and his two young children, suggested some deliberate artistic composition'. Wilde liked the company of handsome young men, especially university undergraduates, but he had not yet given in to his physical desire for them. When he saw young male prostitutes in Piccadilly Circus while he was shopping with Constance in Swan and Edgar's, he recalled later, 'Something clutched at my heart like ice.' But in 1886, on a visit to Oxford, he was seduced by a seventeen-year-old, Robert Ross, and his sexual relationship with his wife came to an end.

After this Wilde led a double life, as a storyteller, essayist, and playwright of growing wealth and reputation, and as a homosexual whose criminal relationships with young men became increasingly indiscreet. Between 1887 and 1889 Wilde wrote around a hundred book reviews, mainly for the *Pall Mall Gazette*, became acquainted with Bernard Shaw (who 'has no enemies, and none of his friends like him'), and edited a women's magazine. Wilde persuaded Cassell's, the owners of the magazine, to change its name from *The Lady's World: a Magazine of Fashion and Society* to *The Woman's World*, and to replace some of its fashion coverage with articles on literature, history, feminism, and women's suffrage. But Wilde's interest in the project (though not in the £6 a week he earned from it) soon flagged, and he rarely made the underground train journey from Sloane Square to his office in Belle Sauvage Yard, off Ludgate Hill. As for dealing with the editor's correspondence, Wilde avoided it at all costs: 'I have known men come to London full of bright prospects and seen them complete wrecks in a few months through a habit of answering letters.'[6]

In the late 1880s Wilde wooed various Oxford undergraduates,

befriended Max Beerbohm (the younger brother of the theatrical producer
Herbert Beerbohm Tree), and fell in love with an aspiring young writer,
John Gray. In the autumn of 1889, not long after his affair with Gray had
started, Wilde was asked to dinner by J. M. Stoddart, the American publisher of *Lippincott's Monthly Magazine*, who hoped to persuade Wilde to
write a novel for serialization. One of Wilde's fellow guests was a Southsea general practitioner, Arthur Conan Doyle, who had recently had a great
success with a long detective story, *A Study in Scarlet*. Doyle had moved on
to more ambitious historical novels, but Stoddart wanted to talk him into
reviving his detective as a serial character for his magazine. The outcome
of this highly successful dinner was Doyle's *The Sign of Four*, which established Sherlock Holmes and Dr Watson as popular heroes, and Wilde's *The
Picture of Dorian Gray*. Dorian Gray's now familiar story revolves around a
hidden portrait that is steadily disfigured by the sins of its amoral subject,
who remains ageless and unblemished until the picture is destroyed. *Dorian
Gray* caused a tremendous sensation when it was published in June 1890,
but its sympathetic presentation of homosexual love ('such love as Michael
Angelo had known, and Montaigne, and Winckelmann, and Shakespeare
himself') was too much for many late Victorian stomachs. The Conservative MP George Curzon made a scarcely veiled attack on Wilde's
homosexuality, Macmillan refused to publish the story in book form, and
W. H. Smith, the station bookseller and self-appointed guardian of middle-
class sensibilities, would not sell it.

Wilde had set out on a journey, as one of his reviewers warned him,
that would end in Bow Street. But not yet. Towards the end of 1890 the
new manager of the St James's Theatre, George Alexander, asked him to
write him a play on a modern theme. The result was *Lady Windermere's Fan*,
which opened to mixed reviews and full houses in February 1892 and
made Wilde £7,000 in its first year. On the first night, which was attended
by Lillie Langtry, Bernard Shaw, Henry James, and Frank Harris, Wilde and
his coterie of young admirers all wore green carnations (a symbol of homosexuality in Paris), and Wilde made a curtain speech which many found
offensive. Wilde's circle (or cenacle, as he liked to call it, referring to the
gathering of Apostles at the Last Supper) now included the poet Richard
Le Gallienne ('Shelley with a chin') and the young artist Aubrey Beardsley, whose face was 'like a silver hatchet'. Beardsley was befriended by the
Wildes in 1891 at the home of the Pre-Raphaelite painter Edward Burne-
Jones, and two years later Wilde helped to advance his brief and
extraordinary career by asking him to illustrate his banned play, *Salome*. In

April 1893 Wilde had another great success with *A Woman of No Importance*, which was produced at the Haymarket Theatre by Herbert Beerbohm Tree. Joseph Chamberlain and Arthur Balfour were at the first night, and the Prince of Wales, who liked Wilde's plays as much as Henry James hated them, at the second.

Oddly, Wilde was not asked to contribute to the most important literary periodical of the Decadents and others in the 1890s, the *Yellow Book*. This quarterly in book form was conceived by a New York-born writer, Henry Harland, and the artists Charles Conder and D. S. MacColl in Dieppe (literary London's favourite French holiday resort) in the summer of 1893. They were visited there by Beardsley and John Lane of Bodley Head, a publisher on the lookout for profitable and exciting projects. It was decided later that Harland should be the magazine's editor and Beardsley its art editor, and that Oscar Wilde should be kept out of it altogether. Beardsley wanted a magazine that would showcase the most daring and avant-garde writers and artists and shock respectable middle-class readers, but Harland was more conventional in his tastes. The title suggested parallels with popular and sometimes indecent yellow-covered French novels of Zola and others, but it was the *Yellow Book* itself which made yellow the colour of fin-de-siècle Decadence. John Lane and his partner Charles Elkin Matthews used their influence and connections to enrol many of London's leading literary and artistic talents, 'Decadent' or not, and to generate enormous advance publicity for the magazine. New and disturbing talents like Beerbohm, La Gallienne, Symons, George Moore, and Beardsley appeared in the first volume alongside such respectable figures as Henry James, Edmund Gosse, Sir Frederick Leighton (President of the Royal Academy), and A. C. Benson, a son of the Archbishop of Canterbury. The next two volumes included Ernest Dowson, Kenneth Grahame, and the illustrators Walter Crane and Wilson Steer.

When we look at the *Yellow Book* today it seems to be innocuous enough, but in the 1890s critics were so sensitive to mild sexual innuendo and gentle mockery of their moral and cultural values that some of them reacted to the first edition with horror and contempt. Beerbohm's ironic defence of cosmetics, Symons' poem 'Stella Maris' about a meeting with a prostitute (based on ample personal experience), and especially Beardsley's drawings were singled out for abuse. Beardsley's pictures showed handsome and assertive women in ambiguous or puzzling situations, at a time when public anxiety over the 'New Woman's' rebellion against Victorian subjection was becoming intense. The picture of a smartly dressed woman playing a grand piano in a field on the *Yellow Book*'s title page was upsetting, and his 'Night Piece', showing a beautiful woman – was she a prostitute? – walking alone in London by night was offensive. Beardsley's cover picture, of a plump laughing woman wearing a mask and a beauty spot with a rather sinister masked man behind her, was denounced by *The Times* as insolent and repulsive. J. A. Spender, assistant editor of the intelligent Liberal evening paper the *Westminster Gazette*, proclaimed that the drawings contained 'excesses hitherto undreamed of' and suggested that such works should be outlawed, and the Academy's reviewer found them 'meaningless and unhealthy'. These reactions may seem excessive, but a glance at the reproductions of dreary and sentimental paintings of kittens, Cavaliers, and water mills that the *Illustrated London News* provided almost weekly for its many readers helps us to appreciate the extent of the gulf that separated Beardsley from conventional London art-lovers.[7]

Despite – or because of – the scandal it caused in respectable London, the *Yellow Book* was a great success, selling over 7,000 copies of its early editions at the very high price of 5s an issue. Its success was interrupted, though, by a dramatic change in the fortunes of the writer excluded from its pages, Oscar Wilde. As Wilde's literary reputation rose in the early 1890s his personal one sank. It was a divergence as dramatic and dangerous as that between Dorian Gray's face and his portrait. In the spring of 1892 Wilde began a love affair with Lord Alfred Douglas ('Bosie'), an unstable and impulsive Oxford undergraduate who was already being blackmailed by another young man over an indiscreet letter. Encouraged by Douglas, Wilde began meeting boys in their late teens, who slept with him in return for money, gifts, and dinner. These boys, who were mostly introduced to him by Alfred Taylor, were clerks, grooms, and paper-boys, not the sort of companions who would have interested him socially or intellectually. All were prostitutes, and several were blackmailers, perhaps working together. They found him an easy and generous victim. His affairs were well known at the Savoy, the Albemarle Hotel, Mayfair, and at the Café Royal. In May 1893 Wilde and Douglas shared a room at the Savoy without any attempt at concealment, and that October they narrowly avoided a scandal involving a sixteen-year-old boy. Wilde's unsuccessful efforts to rid himself of Douglas's dangerous friendship only drove the young man into wilder indiscretions. In June 1894 Douglas's father, the Marquess of Queensberry, a hot-tempered and violent man who had lately tried to attack Lord Rosebery (probably the lover of his eldest son) with a dogwhip, turned up at Wilde's house in Tite Street in the company of a prizefighter, and threatened to thrash him if he saw him with Douglas in a public restaurant. The death of Queensberry's eldest son in October (probably suicide because he feared a scandal over his affair with Rosebery) dashed Wilde's hopes of pacifying the Marquess. On 14 February 1895, at the glittering opening night of *The Importance of Being Earnest*, Queensberry planned a to make a scene in the St James's Theatre, but the police would only allow him to leave the prop he had planned to use, a 'grotesque bouquet of vegetables', at the stage door. Queensberry was determined now to ruin Wilde, and a few days later he left him this famous and often misquoted note at the Albemarle Club: 'To Oscar Wilde posing Somdomite'. For some reason Wilde, who had courted scandal and mocked Victorian moral standards so often, found this attack insupportable: 'My whole life seems ruined by this man. The tower of ivory is assailed by this foul thing.' Wise friends told him to do nothing, but Douglas goaded him to act, and Wilde went to Marlborough Street Magistrates' Court and had Queensberry arrested for criminal libel. Wilde believed his opponent would rely for his defence on literary evidence and some suggestive letters, but Queensberry's solicitor used private detectives to search in the West End for evidence – which was plentiful – of Wilde's involvement with boy prostitutes. In 13 Little College Street, Westminster, they broke into the top-floor flat of Alfred Taylor, who had a list of the names and addresses of the boys he had introduced Wilde to since 1892, and a collection of trousers with slits instead of pockets. Before he knew of this devastating evidence, Wilde lunched at the Café Royal with Frank Harris and Bernard Shaw, who had almost persuaded him to drop the case when Douglas came in and stiffened Wilde's resolve.

Queensberry's trial took place at the Old Bailey in early April 1895. His defence counsel was Edward Carson, a brilliant young barrister who was later famous for rallying Ulster Protestants against Irish Home Rule. Carson and Wilde sparred inconclusively about literature and letters, but when the defence declared that it would call as witnesses several of the boys and young men Wilde had met through Taylor and slept with at the Savoy and elsewhere, it was clear that the case was lost. The jury was instructed to conclude that Queensberry was justified in calling Wilde a sodomite in the public interest, and Queensberry's solicitor sent the witness statements and trial notes to the Director of Public Prosecutions. Wilde had several hours to pack and escape to France, as his friends urged him to do, but indecision, courage, or self-destructiveness held him back, and just after 6 p.m. on 5 April he was arrested at the Cadogan Hotel and taken to Bow Street Police Station. Wilde's trial involved three Bow Street hearings, a first Old Bailey trial (with Taylor as his co-defendant), which left the jury split, and a final trial, from 21 to 25 May, which ended in his conviction for indecency and sodomy, and a sentence of two years' imprisonment with hard labour. In the first trial Wilde spoke eloquently in defence of the love of an older for a younger man, 'the love that dare not speak its name', but the evidence of a succession of male prostitutes, blackmailers, landladies, and Savoy chambermaids, reinforced by the opinions of judges who seemed to regard homosexuality as almost worse than murder, convinced the second jury of Wilde's guilt. All the London newspapers except the radical *Reynold's News* were hostile to Wilde, and few of Wilde's friends who had not left the country dared to speak up for him. Rosebery, who was now Prime Minister, decided that helping Wilde would draw hostile attention to his own sexuality. W. B. Yeats offered him the support of many Irish writers, and Stewart Headlam, the Christian Socialist curate of St Matthew's, Bethnal Green, who hardly knew Wilde, provided half of the £2,500 bail he needed to keep out of jail between his two trials.

To late Victorian eyes Wilde's trials exposed the ugliness beneath the cult of loveliness, and showed what had really been going on in the 'house beautiful'. Wilde's exposure and conviction dealt an almost fatal blow to the Decadent movement, of which he (along with Beardsley) was the personification. In the atmosphere of triumphant puritanism and anti-aestheticism during and after the trials it took courage to speak out on Wilde's behalf. Frank Harris, Bernard Shaw, Robert Ross, Ernest Dowson, William Rothenstein, and Max Beerbohm were not afraid to do so, but others, especially those dependent on the London public for their livelihoods, hurried to distance themselves from Wilde and his work. Wilde's name was removed from the two theatres where his plays were running, and soon the plays themselves were closed down. He had already been declared bankrupt, and his furniture, books, papers, and pictures had been sold off at bargain prices in a poorly organized public auction in Tite Street.

Leonard Smithers and the 'Tragic Generation'

Wilde's arrest was especially worrying for John Lane and all those involved with the *Yellow Book*. Although Wilde had never written for it, and claimed to have thrown the first edition out of a train window, he was seen carrying a yellow-covered book when he was arrested at the Cadogan Hotel on 5 April 1895. 'A' yellow book soon became 'the' *Yellow Book*, and the publishers, who had done their best to avoid being associated with Wilde, were caught up in the scandal. The Bodley Head shop in Vigo Street, the literary headquarters of Decadence, was pelted with mud and stones by a mob, and two of Lane's bestselling authors, William Watson and Alice Meynell, urged on by the popular novelist Mrs Humphrey Ward, demanded that Beardsley's drawings should be removed from the next edition of the *Yellow Book*. After a brief hesitation Lane decided to put profit before principle, and dismissed Beardsley from the art editorship. The magazine carried on for another nine volumes without its best and most controversial contributor, and lost the power to shock.

Beardsley was rescued from unemployment and penury by Leonard Smithers, a disreputable publisher of erotic books and prints. Smithers suggested that Beardsley should work with Arthur Symons on a new quarterly, even more daring and advanced than the *Yellow Book*, and the three spent much of August 1895 planning the project in Dieppe. The magazine was to be called the *Savoy*, a name that suggested modernity, luxury, and perhaps – remembering the evidence brought against Oscar Wilde – a touch of sexual impropriety. Leonard Smithers, now unjustly forgotten, played a vital part in preserving the Decadent movement after Wilde's fall. In the later 1880s, working in Sheffield as a solicitor, he had been attracted into the world of high-quality erotic publication by contact with the great explorer Sir Richard Burton, whose translations of the *Kama Sutra* and the *Thousand and One Nights* had been published in London in expensive scholarly editions in 1883 and 1885–6. Smithers came to London in 1891 and started a business with a partner, Harry Nichols, which involved publishing translations of erotic French and classical works, under the cover of dealing in antiquarian books and prints. Their Soho premises, in Wardour Street and Dean Street, were in the district already occupied by other underground publishers, like the notorious Edward Avery, who operated from Greek Street. Smithers' publications in the early 1890s included a twelve-volume translation of Casanova's *Memoirs*, various editions of Burton's *Thousand and One Nights*, and *Teleny*, a homosexual novel said to have been written collaboratively by Wilde and his circle of young men. This was a risky business in a puritanical and repressive society, as the trial and imprisonment in 1888 of Henry Vizetelly, Emile Zola's London publisher, had shown. But it could also be profitable. Burton made £10,000 from his *Thousand and One Nights*, and Smithers had made enough money by 1896 to open a smart Mayfair bookshop in Royal Arcade, Old Bond Street, and to move his family into 6a Bedford Square, one of the best houses in Bloomsbury, and for many years the home of Lords Chancellor.

By 1895 Smithers already knew the Crown Tavern and Café Royal sets pretty well, and when the Wilde trial and John Lane's retreat left London's avant-garde without a publisher he seized the opportunity to expand his business and reputation. He published Arthur Symons' collections of poems, *London Nights* and *Silhouettes*, when nobody else would take them, and gave the ill and impoverished young poet Ernest Dowson a steady income as a writer and translator from 1895 to 1899. Those who came to rely on Smithers as a publisher and paymaster after 1895 were divided in their attitudes towards him. Symons spoke of his 'diabolical monocle', and his 'pasty white face, and blanched hands which always seemed to need washing'. The artist Will Rothenstein, who sued Smithers over a disputed payment in 1896, regarded him as 'a bizarre and improbable figure', and blamed him for encouraging Beardsley and the artist Charles Conder (Rothenstein's close friend) in their most destructive vices, in both London and Dieppe. 'I thought Smithers had an evil influence on Beardsley, taking him to various night haunts, keeping him up late into the night, which was bad, too, for Beardsley's health . . . In Smithers, Conder found a boon companion who encouraged his worst excesses, excesses which brought on an attack of delirium tremens, which thoroughly frightened Conder.' Wilde joked that Smithers' taste in women, appropriately for a book-dealer, favoured 'first editions', and he was probably right. Yeats was particularly upset by his affair with the Irish poet and artist Althea Gyles in 1899: 'Althea Gyles, after despising Symons and [George] Moore for years because of their morals, has ostentatiously taken up with Smithers, a person of so immoral a life that people like Symons and Moore despise him.' Smithers abandoned Althea Gyles in 1900, having reduced her, according to Symons, to a state of friendless desperation.[8] But others admired Smithers' courage, his contempt for the moral and sexual sensibilities of respectable Victorians and his readiness to 'publish anything that the others are afraid of'. Robert Ross, Wilde's loyal friend and first lover, described him as 'the most delightful and irresponsible publisher' he had ever met, and Ernest Dowson, who relied very heavily on Smithers' money and friendship, thought him 'all round, the best fellow I know'. Whatever the truth about his obscure private life, Smithers was the only significant London publisher willing after May

1895 to bring the work of Beardsley, Dowson, Symons, and Wilde before the public, and to keep the flag flying for Decadence and the avant-garde. If it had not been for Smithers much of Beardsley's late and best work would not have been produced or published, and Wilde's final years in France would have been even more desolate and penurious than they were. Most of the money to pay Wilde's hotel bills in the late 1890s came from Smithers, who published his *Ballad of Reading Gaol* and two hitherto unpublished plays, *The Importance of Being Earnest* and *The Ideal Husband*. The outrageously erotic pictures Beardsley drew in his last years, especially his enormously phallic illustrations for *Lysistrata*, were produced for Smithers, and daringly published by him in secret limited editions.

The *Savoy*, whose first edition appeared in January 1896, did not shock or interest London readers and reviewers as the *Yellow Book* had done. Although Beardsley's writings and illustrations were still disconcerting, the general tone of the magazine was not disreputable, and if it represented a literary movement it was not Decadence, but symbolism, with its emphasis on suggestion and impression rather than realistic description. Its very diverse contents included essays, criticism, and stories by Shaw, Yeats, Havelock Ellis, and Joseph Conrad, as well as pieces by Symons, Beerbohm, Dowson, and Hubert Crackanthorpe. Critical reaction, hostile at first, grew more friendly, but the *Savoy* was expensive to produce, and at a low cover price of 2s 6d it had to sell in large numbers to break even. Sales were not helped by the decision of the prudish but powerful manager of W. H. Smith's, who had his 'young ladies' to think about, not to stock the third (July 1896) edition of the magazine. His pretext, oddly, was a drawing by William Blake, a symbolist favourite. Damaged by this decision, by editorial conflicts, and by public indifference, the *Savoy* closed after a short but brilliant run at the end of 1896.

Smithers did not profit much from his association with Wilde and Beardsley, and very few of the works he published in the late 1890s sold enough copies to cover his expenses. After an illness he was declared bankrupt in 1900, and most of the copyrights and prints he had accumulated were snapped up by his rival, John Lane. Smithers moved his shop from Mayfair to Covent Garden and his home from Bedford Square to Maida Vale, and scraped a living by publishing erotic French translations, pirated versions of the works of Wilde and Beardsley, and fake limited editions. As illness, poverty, drink, and opiates dragged him down, he moved to cheap rooms in Holborn, Islington, and finally Fulham, where he died of cirrhosis of the liver in December 1907, at the age of forty-six. His funeral expenses were paid, it was said, by Lord Alfred Douglas.[9]

As it turned out, the air of weariness, morbidity, and decline with which London Decadents and aesthetes liked to surround themselves was more than an affectation. Yeats had once complained to his Rhymers that there were too many of them, but within a few years of Wilde's trial, alcoholism, tuberculosis, suicide, madness, and misfortune had thinned the ranks of London's avant-garde to an extraordinary degree. Hubert Crackanthorpe killed himself (aged thirty-one) in 1896, Beardsley died of tuberculosis (aged twenty-five) in 1898, Wilde died (aged forty-six) in Paris, probably from a syphilitic infection, and Dowson died (aged thirty-three) from drink and tuberculosis in 1900. The poet Lionel Johnson (aged thirty-five) fell down drunk in Fleet Street and suffered fatal head injuries in 1902, Henry Harland died (aged forty-four) in 1905, Smithers in 1907, Conder (aged forty-one) in 1909, and John Davidson drowned himself (aged fifty-two) in Penzance that same year. To complete the disappearance of the movement from the London scene, Le Gallienne went to America in 1901, Symons had a disastrous mental breakdown, from which he never fully recovered, in 1908, and Max Beerbohm moved to Italy in 1910. No wonder W. B. Yeats, one of the few London-based writers of the 1890s whose career lived up to its early promise, later spoke of them as a 'Tragic Generation'.

Writing for the Millions

One of the problems for the avant-garde writers of the 1890s, and for their publishers, was that so few readers and play-goers were interested in what they wrote. Wilde enjoyed a brief success before his disgrace, and another (with *The Ballad of Reading Gaol*) after it, but the sales of the rest of the members of the 1890s generation were small, and Leonard Smithers was nearly always left with unsold stock. The *Yellow Book* enjoyed a certain *succès de scandale*, but the *Savoy* sold in disappointingly small numbers, and so did Beardsley's works. To understand the tastes of the London reading and theatre-going public of the 1890s we have to look not at the *Savoy* or *Yellow Book* but at George Newnes' *Strand Magazine*, the novels of Marie Corelli, Hall Caine, and Mrs Humphrey Ward, George Edwardes' musical comedies, Harmsworth's *Daily Mail*, and T. P. O'Connor's London evening paper, the *Star*.

As Charles Knight and John Cassell discovered in the 1840s and 1850s, there were fortunes to be made in producing popular books and periodicals for the ordinary London reader. One of these early Victorian pioneers, Edward Lloyd, the founder and owner of *Lloyd's Weekly News* and the *Daily Chronicle*, was still active in the 1880s, and left a large fortune when he died in 1890. By this time a new generation of publishers had arrived in London, anxious to grasp the opportunities offered by the growth of a mass urban readership and improvements in printing technology. One of the first and most important of these was George Newnes. Newnes had been sent to Manchester by a London fancy goods company, and decided in 1881 to start a magazine for busy working people, which would contain nothing but useful or amusing tit-bits reprinted from other publications. The reader of his magazine, Newnes assured his first customers, would 'have at his command a stock of smart sayings and a fund of anecdote which make his society agreeable'. Nobody would back Newnes' instinct, so he used £500 of his own money (earned from running a vegetarian restaurant), and hired the Manchester Boys' Brigade to distribute his penny weekly, which he called *Tit-Bits*. Newnes moved *Tit-Bits* to London in 1884, and used a succession of competitions and special promotions, including free railway accident insurance (a winner with his commuter readership) and a prize of a house in Dulwich ('*Tit-Bits* Villa'), to push its circulation above 500,000, and even (in 1897) to 670,000. As these prizes suggest, *Tit-Bits*' core readership was drawn from the middle class and aspiring working class, not from the poorest and least educated.[10]

If *Tit-Bits* was designed for clerks and commuters who wanted something lively to read on the bus or train, Newnes' next important publication, the *Strand Magazine*, 'a monthly magazine costing sixpence but worth a shilling' (as Newnes' slogan claimed), was aimed at a more educated and leisurely middle-class readership. The first edition of the *Strand*, which was published in December 1890, sold over 300,000 copies, thanks to Newnes' reputation and his extensive advertising in *Tit-Bits* and on hoardings and billboards around the country. It was also cheaper, brighter, and less highbrow than the established shilling monthlies, the *Cornhill*, *Temple Bar*, and *Cassell's Magazine*. Early editions of the *Strand* relied on translated stories by Pushkin, Maupassant, and others, but soon Newnes was able to call upon some Britain's most popular writers, several of whom are still read today: Max Pemberton, Edith Nesbit, Walter Besant, George R. Sims, Rudyard Kipling, H. G. Wells, P. G. Wodehouse, W. W. Jacobs, E. W. Hornung, Grant Allen, Somerset Maugham, and Jerome K. Jerome.

Above all, Newnes bought the English rights to the most popular stories of the 1890s, the Sherlock Holmes tales of Arthur Conan Doyle.

Conan Doyle's first Sherlock Holmes story, a short novel called *A Study in Scarlet*, was completed in April 1886, when Doyle was a general practitioner in Southsea. He had spent a few weeks in London, but in Edinburgh he had studied medicine under the surgeon Joseph Bell, whose investigative turn of mind helped to inspire the character of Holmes. *A Study in Scarlet* was rejected by the *Cornhill Magazine*, but published in *Beeton's Christmas Annual* in November 1887, and as a book in July 1888, a few weeks before the first victim of the Whitechapel murderer was found. Its success led to a commission for another long serialized story (*The Sign of Four*) in an American magazine, *Lippincott's Monthly*, in 1890, and the contract with Newnes for a series of complete stories, each featuring the same two characters, Holmes and his plodding but reliable friend, assistant, and amanuensis, Dr Watson. By this time Conan Doyle was represented by Alexander P. Watt, the world's first literary agent, who also managed the affairs of Kipling, Henry James, Rider Haggard, Walter Besant, and (until his death in 1889) Wilkie Collins. The enormous success of the Holmes stories, which increased the *Strand*'s circulation by 100,000 in 1891, enabled Doyle to give up medicine, buy shares in *Tit-Bits*, and move from his lodgings in Montague Place (at the back of the British Museum) to a suburban villa in South Norwood, with sixteen rooms and a tennis lawn. By the end of 1891 Doyle was one of London's great literary names, sharing dinner tables with J. M. Barrie, Jerome K. Jerome, Eden Philpotts, and Anthony Hope, and Sherlock Holmes of 221B Baker Street, cocaine addict, violinist, master of disguise, and the world's first scientific detective, was London's most famous fictional inhabitant. His cloak and deerstalker hat were contributed by Sidney Paget, who illustrated the *Strand* stories. Conan Doyle's tales established the *Strand* as England's favourite monthly magazine, and created a popular image of Victorian London which has been almost as powerful and enduring as that created by Dickens earlier in the century. But unlike Dickens, Conan Doyle did not know London well, and relied on street maps and his experience of Edinburgh and Portsmouth to compensate for his lack of local knowledge. Like Arthur Sullivan, the musical partner in the famous light operatic partnership, Conan Doyle yearned for recognition through his more serious work, rather than his lighter popular successes. So, ignoring Newnes' entreaties, he threw Holmes down the Reichenbach Falls in December

1893. Sherlock Holmes did not return to the *Strand* until 1901, when a huge fee from Newnes persuaded Doyle to bring him back to life again.

The *Strand* had many imitators in the 1890s, including the *Idler* (edited and briefly owned by Jerome K. Jerome in the 1890s), the *Pall Mall Magazine* (founded by the millionaire William Waldorf Astor in 1893), and *Pearson's* (1896), all of them hungry for novels to serialize. Most London novelists, from such great figures as George Meredith, Thomas Hardy, Henry James, H. G. Wells, Robert Louis Stevenson, Marie Corelli, Rudyard Kipling, George Gissing, and Joseph Conrad to an army of forgotten journeymen, relied on monthly magazines for much of their income. Another literary form, the short story, came into fashion in the 1890s, mainly because it suited the requirements of the illustrated monthly magazines, and several London writers, including P. G. Wodehouse, G. K. Chesterton, Rudyard Kipling, and W. W. Jacobs, made their names as short-story specialists.[11]

As well as giving well-paid employment to dozens of novelists and essayists, Newnes began the Fleet Street careers of two of late Victorian London's most important popular newspapermen. Arthur Pearson got his first job on *Tit-Bits* as a competition prize, and went on to found a similar magazine called *Pearson's Weekly* (1890), whose half-million weekly sales helped to finance the launch of the mass-circulation *Daily Express* in 1900. Alfred Harmsworth, 'the Napoleon of Fleet Street', got his first taste of journalism in the early 1880s when he edited the school magazine at Henley House, a private school in Kilburn which was owned and run by A. A. Milne's father, and which employed H. G. Wells as a science teacher in 1888. After this Harmsworth earned a living by submitting freelance pieces to various London publications, including the *Hampstead and Highgate Express* and Cassell's *Saturday Journal*. In 1885 he started selling short descriptive pieces to *Tit-Bits*, and realized that Newnes had invented a new type of popular journalism, presenting easily digestible tips and stories to busy and newly educated readers. After a short spell in Coventry, editing *Bicycling News*, Harmsworth returned to London and in June 1888 launched a popular magazine, *Answers to Correspondents*, that would imitate though not outsell *Tit-Bits*. In the 1890s, when *Tit-Bits* and its many rivals and imitators competed for readers with prizes, treasure hunts, and special offers, London seemed to be full of young men who were guessing the amount of gold coin in the Bank of England (to win a pound a week for life), hunting for buried sovereigns, and filling in the 'missing words' in blank spaces in magazine articles. In the early 1890s Harmsworth pro-

duced successful publications for specific but large groups of readers –
Comic Cuts, Chips, Marvel (featuring Sexton Blake, the poor man's Sherlock
Holmes), *Union Jack*, and *Boys' Friend* for children, *Forget-Me-Not* and *Home
Chat* for women, the *Sunday Companion* for churchgoers, and so on. Finally,
in May 1896, Harmsworth launched London's first halfpenny morning
newspaper, the *Daily Mail*, and changed the face of British journalism. Perhaps it was true, as Lord Salisbury said, that the *Daily Mail* was 'written
by office boys for office boys', but Harmsworth made money, and in doing
so freed himself from party political subsidies and achieved a degree of
independence which the owners of more traditional London newspapers
could only dream of. By 1914 Harmsworth was Lord Northcliffe, the first
and greatest of the 'press barons', and owned the *Daily Mail*, the *Daily
Mirror*, which was started by Harmsworth and his brother as a paper for
women in 1903, and *The Times*, which he had bought in 1908. His political and public influence was substantial, though perhaps not as great as
he thought it was. In a world in which politicians needed to speak to a
mass audience, and (more importantly) producers and retailers needed to
find customers by the million, newspapers like Harmsworth's were the ones
they would turn to. Those London newspapers that followed Harmsworth's
lead, cutting their price to a halfpenny and trusting to a mass circulation
and advertising revenue to make them a profit, prospered and survived,
while those that relied on selling small numbers to well-off readers in West
End clubs fell into debt and died off, either before the Great War or soon
afterwards.

Academicians and Outsiders

The art establishment of London and England was represented by the
Royal Academy. Its summer exhibitions were a highlight of London's
social and artistic calendar, and its leading members commanded high
prices, and received high honours. The President of the Royal Academy
from 1878 to 1896, Frederick Leighton, was the first painter to be given
a peerage, though he only lived one day to enjoy it. His more enduring
honour was to be the inspiration for Professor Higgins in Shaw's *Pygmalion*,
with his favourite model, Dorothy Dene, as Eliza Doolittle. His
magnificent house in Holland Park Road, the fruit of his early commercial success, is now a museum and gallery. Several other artists, including
John Millais, Edward Poynter, Lawrence Alma-Tadema, Edward Burne-

Jones, and George Frederic Watts, gained (or in Watts' case refused) knighthoods or baronetcies. The most highly regarded portraitist of his day, John Singer Sargent, was only prevented from achieving the same recognition by his American citizenship. More advanced artists who had come under the influence of Whistler and the French Impressionists and dismissed the old-fashioned academic style of painting so admired by the Academy were mostly members of the New English Art Club (NEAC), which was founded in 1886 by Sargent, Philip Wilson Steer, Frederick Brown, George Clausen, and others. Fifty artists were represented in the NEAC's inaugural show in April 1886, and the club attracted some of the best and most adventurous young artists in the 1890s and 1900s, including Walter Sickert, Charles Conder, Henry Tonks, William Rothenstein, Roger Fry, Augustus John, Max Beerbohm, William Orpen, Jacob Epstein, and Spencer Gore. In the 1890s the NEAC became more conventional, and many of its members eventually joined the RA, treating the club as a halfway house on the road to social respectability and commercial success. Those most determined to remain independent of the RA joined Walter Sickert, Spencer Gore, Harold Gilman, Will Rothenstein, and Lucien Pissarro in the Allied Artists' Association, a group that met in a jointly rented studio at 19 Fitzroy Street in 1907. This developed into the Camden Town Group (including Augustus John and Wyndham Lewis) in 1911, and the bigger London Group, which included women artists, in 1913.

The artists of the New English Art Club and the Fitzroy Street Group might not command high prices or find their pictures reproduced in the *Illustrated London News*, but their work did not often shock or outrage Edwardian taste, and nor in general did their lives. As Ian Dunlop says, 'the spirit of revolt, of defiance of authority, of change for change's sake, of anarchy and restlessness that had affected every major city in Europe – Munich, Dresden, Berlin, Brussels, Paris and Moscow, in particular – is almost totally absent from the London artistic world'. The Chelsea of the 1890s, as described by William Rothenstein, was no Montmartre or Montparnasse, and the painters who lived or worked there, Walter Sickert, Philip Wilson Steer, Charles Ricketts, Charles Shannon, Charles Conder, did not live or paint like radicals.[12]

Sickert, the most gifted of all these London artists, had studied under Whistler and been greatly influenced by the French Impressionists, especially Degas, whom he met often in Paris and Dieppe in the 1880s. Sickert's belief that places of popular entertainment were a worthwhile subject for an artist was reinforced by the use of similar locations by Degas,

Manet, and Renoir. He had an unusual hankering for the dreary and the squalid, both in what he painted and where he lived and worked, and his subject matter, music halls, dingy North London interiors, and plump nudes on iron bedsteads, struck many critics and fellow painters as unsuitable. The old Royal Academician Sir William Richmond was mortified by Sickert's 1911 exhibition of drawings of drab domestic subjects: 'they are abominable. Ugly Dirt is odious. Sexualism in Art can only be redeemed by grand treatment. This is worse than Slum Art, worse than Prostitution, because it is done by a man who should know better.' The lesson for any artist seeking success in Britain, Sickert wrote, was not to 'depict a scene dealing with anyone lower in the social scale than, say, a University Extension lecturer and his fiancée, or to set it in a "Lokal" as they say in Germany, less genteel than a parlour'. His own view, expressed in his essay on an exhibition of the work of the London Impressionists in December 1889, was that 'Nature', as a subject which could be rendered beautiful in art, did not stop where London began. 'For those who live in the most wonderful and complex city in the world, the most fruitful course of study lies in a persistent effort to render the magic and the poetry which they daily see around them.'[13] It is odd, if this was his view, that Sickert rarely painted outdoor scenes in London, as he did in Dieppe and Venice. In the early 1890s he lived and worked in Chelsea, but after 1905, on his return from seven years in Europe, he moved northwards, first to Fitzroy Street, then to a long succession of studios in and around Camden Town – Mornington Crescent, Harrington Street, Harrington Square, Augustus Street, Brecknock Road, Gloucester Crescent, and three addresses in Hampstead Road. He was particularly interested in the murder of a prostitute, Emily Dimmock (the notorious 'Camden Town Murder'), in September 1907, and drew or painted the scene as he imagined it several times.

'On or about December 1910 . . . '

Until 1910, Sickert, as the main representative of Impressionism in England, was the leader of the London avant-garde. His position was usurped in that year by the artist and critic Roger Fry, who had found something far more interesting than Impressionism. Artists and critics in Edwardian London knew virtually nothing of the group of painters now called post-Impressionists (a term invented by Fry) – Cézanne, Matisse, Gauguin, and Van Gogh. Fry, never a great admirer of the Impressionists, was first awakened to the work of Cézanne when he saw two of his paintings (a still life and a winter landscape) in a London exhibition in 1906. For the next three years Fry used articles and lectures to publicize the genius of Cézanne, and in 1910 he and the critic Desmond McCarthy went to Paris, Munich, and Holland to collect paintings for an exhibition to be held in November and December 1910 at the Grafton Gallery in Mayfair.

The exhibition, which Fry decided to call 'Manet and the Post-Impressionists', had nine Manets, twenty-one Cézannes, thirty-five Gauguins, twenty-two Van Goghs (including *Dr Gachet* and *Crows over a Cornfield*), and some Matisses (including *Woman with Green Eyes*), Derains, Vlamincks, and Picassos. Fry included Manet, already an 'old master', because of his influence on Cézanne. Many of the paintings in the exhibition were about twenty years old, but to many London artists, critics, and connoisseurs, who had hardly come to terms with Impressionism, they were virtually incomprehensible. Their reactions to works that are now regarded as masterpieces reveal the vast gulf that had developed between English and French taste in painting since the 1880s. Ebenezer Cook of the *Pall Mall Gazette* thought the works on display were like 'the outpourings of a lunatic asylum', and Robert Ross of the *Morning Post* suggested that the paintings should be destroyed, like plague-carriers. The critic J. Comyns Carr, the director of the New Gallery, saw in Post-Impressionism 'a wave of disease, even of absolute madness; . . . A sort of combined endeavour to degrade and discredit all forms of feminine beauty.' The *Daily Telegraph*'s reviewer, the curator of the Wallace Collection, was more circumspect: 'Those who come to scoff will perhaps remain, not to pray, but to wonder at this new art, and at the time of which it is in a sense the reflection . . . We wait and watch; declining to howl with the crowd, or to rhapsodise with the excessive eulogists.' It was not simply a case of insularity. The poet and diplomat Wilfred Scawen Blunt, an intrepid traveller through India and the Arab world, was one of the scoffers:

> The exhibition is either an extremely bad joke or a swindle. I am inclined to think the latter, for there is no trace of humour in it. Still less is there a trace of sense of skill or taste, good or bad, or art or cleverness. Nothing but the gross puerility which scrawls indecencies on the walls of a privy.
>
> The drawing is on the level of that of an untaught child of seven or eight years old, the sense of colour that of a tea-tray painter, the

method that of a schoolboy who wipes his fingers on a slate after spitting on them. Apart from the frames, the whole collection should not be worth 5 pounds and then only for the pleasure of making a bonfire of them.

Arnold Bennett had lived in Paris, and found London's reaction to paintings whose quality was generally accepted in France an embarrassment: 'The mild tragedy is that London is infinitely too self-complacent even to suspect that it is London and not the exhibition which is making itself ridiculous . . . in twenty years London will be signing an apology for its guffaw.' The reaction of the leading Academicians, including Sargent, was predictably hostile, but artists who liked to think of themselves as advanced, the members of the NEAC and Sickert's various groups, were in two minds. Tonks and Steer disliked the elevation of a new set of heroes, but Augustus John was won over to the work of Van Gogh, though not to that of the 'charlatan' Matisse, during the course of the show. Sickert already knew and admired the work of Gauguin, Cézanne, and Van Gogh, and had been influenced by it, but he resented the sudden elevation of Cézanne's reputation over that of the great Impressionists on the strength of an exhibition thrown together by a latecomer to the appreciation of modern art, Roger Fry. He also suspected, at first, that post-Impressionism was an art dealers' plot, to enable incompetent works to be sold for high prices. If they succeeded, he wrote in 1912, 'Picassos and Matisses would be painted by all the coachmen that the rise of motor traffic has thrown out of employment'.[14]

Some of Fry's strongest support came from the group of writers, artists, critics, and intellectuals which he had joined through his friendship with a wealthy businessman, Clive Bell, in 1910. At the centre of this group, which met in a house in Gordon Square, Bloomsbury, were Thoby, Vanessa, and Virginia, the three children of the philosopher and editor of the *Dictionary of National Biography*, Sir Leslie Stephen, who had died in 1904. Vanessa was married to Clive Bell, and Virginia married Leonard Woolf in 1912. Through Thoby, the Stephens befriended a set of brilliant Cambridge scholars who had been influenced by the philosopher G. E. Moore, and called themselves 'the Apostles'. These included the economist John Maynard Keynes, the novelist E. M. Forster, the critic Lytton Strachey, and Leonard Woolf. The group was characterized by an intellectual contempt for Victorian taste and moral values, and a cool detachment from the social and political hurly-burly. Looking back on the group, Keynes described them as 'water-spiders, gracefully skimming, as light and reasonable as air, the surface of the stream without any contact at all with the eddies and currents underneath.' The Bloomsbury artists Duncan Grant and Vanessa Bell were great supporters of the exhibition, and Fry found himself in the position once occupied by Sickert, 'the central figure round whom the most advanced young painters grouped themselves'.[15]

Perhaps it is too much to say, as Virginia Woolf did in 1924, that 'on or about December 1910 human character changed', but Fry's exhibition was certainly an important moment in London's entry into the modern cultural world. The parallel with the impact of militant suffragism at the same time was too obvious to miss. A writer in the *Daily Herald* in 1913 declared that socialists and suffragettes 'were both Post-Impressionist in their desire to scrap old decaying forms and find for themselves a new working ideal'. Even in their hostility, the London public took an interest in modern art they had not displayed before. Laurence Binyon, writing in the *Saturday Review*, was impressed by the fuss: 'What scorn, what noble rages, what talk, what clouds of dust. One would think that art had really got hold of the nation at last, so bitter and so heartfelt is the language used.' Over the next two years London was introduced to cubism and Italian Futurism, so that when Fry's second post-Impressionist exhibition opened in October 1912, Cézanne seemed like a familiar friend among the more shocking new works of Picasso (mostly from his cubist period), Derain, Vlaminck, and Matisse, whose thirty-odd paintings dominated the show. The main impression left by this exhibition was that the modern English painters represented in it, including Grant, Fry, Spencer Gore, Stanley Spencer, and Eric Gill, seemed tame and derivative next to their European masters. Of the English artists in the show only Wyndham Lewis, who would shortly become a Vorticist, had the power to shock.[16]

Fry's period of unchallenged leadership was brief. In 1913 he took a lease on 33 Fitzroy Square (helped by a £250 donation from Bernard Shaw) and established Omega Workshops, in which young artists would paint and decorate (but not make) furniture, pottery, lamps, clothes, textiles, and carpets, especially (but not exclusively) in post-Impressionist and cubist styles. In 1913 the Ideal Home Exhibition provoked a dramatic split in the new group. The *Daily Mail*, hoping to excite its visitors with a glimpse into the world of modern art, commissioned a domestic interior designed by Omega Workshops for its 1914 show. Fry and his friends, including Vanessa Bell and Duncan Grant, disliked the influence of mechanization on domestic artefacts, but a faction within the group, led by

Wyndham Lewis, took the opposite view, and argued that art should recognize and celebrate the power of the modern machine. Through a
misunderstanding, both factions believed that they had been commissioned to make the Ideal Home's 'Post-Impressionist sitting room', and the
group split acrimoniously in two over the quarrel. Lewis called his new
group the Vorticists, and launched a vitriolic attack (the only sort he knew)
on Fry's 'aesthetes' and their attachment to 'prettiness' and 'Post-What-
Not fashionableness', rather than the 'rough and masculine work' that
would shape the modern world. The Omega Workshops soldiered on without Lewis and his faction, but their work was confined to expensive houses
and fashionable clubs. As Shaw warned Fry in 1914, 'It is all very well to
live in a quiet London square and look like an Orthopaedic Institute, but
the price you pay is that your business remains the secret of a clique.'[17]
Lewis found a sympathetic ally in the American poet Ezra Pound, who had
arrived in London in 1909 and established himself as a leading figure in
W. B. Yeats' literary circle. In 1914 Lewis founded the Rebel Art Centre
and joined Pound in publishing a Vorticist journal, *Blast*. Over the following four years their appetite for 'rough and masculine' action was well fed
but not sated, and in the 1930s both of them declared their support for
Adolf Hitler.

*

A City of Shops

Late Victorian London offered entrepreneurs and salesmen the largest, wealthiest, and most accessible market the world had ever known. Centuries of ostentation, imitation, and fashion-consciousness had made London, and especially West London, a city of shoppers and spenders, a society devoted to conspicuous consumption before the phrase had been coined (by the economist Thorsten Veblen in 1899). Rich tourists and wealthy families in town for the late spring season regarded spending money on fashionable clothes, household goods, and West End entertainments as one of the main purposes of their visit, and no doubt there was an element of mimicry in the spending of middle-class men and women who crowded into West End theatres and department stores. As well as the thousands of shoppers who bought things because they wanted them, there were millions of Londoners who bought things because they needed them, the buyers of bread, cheese, milk, tea, eggs, bacon, soap, and shoes.

Street Sellers

To meet the needs of all these consumers, London was a city full of shops. Every type of retailing, from the street hawkers and stalls that had been serving Londoners since the Saxons, to department stores and chain stores that are still familiar names today, was carried on in late Victorian London. Although more traditional methods of selling were probably in relative decline, street sellers, hawkers, costermongers, and market traders were still very familiar figures in 1883 or 1914. Henry Mayhew, in his great study of the London poor, thought that there were about 45,000 street traders in London in the 1850s. If we believe his figures, which were based on guesswork, then London's street-selling population had fallen sharply by 1891. But Charles Booth's analysis of the census suggests, on the contrary, that costers and street sellers were one of the fastest-growing occupational groups in London in the 1880s, having risen from 9,350 to 12,900 (38 per cent) between the censuses of 1881 and 1891. By 1911 there were 18,760 London street sellers, a further increase of 45 per cent, though they were more likely to be selling newspapers, milk, and ice-creams than the pigs' trotters and watercress they sold in Mayhew's day. The true figure was probably much higher than the census figure. As part of its enforcement of the 1903 Employment of Children Act, the LCC issued badges to 15,441 boys and over 1,000 girls under sixteen engaged in street trading in 1910–11.[1]

Booth's assistant Harold Hardy, writing in 1896, described an economy in which the costermonger and hawker were still an essential part of the distribution system, especially for the poor. Some still pushed their barrows from street to street, but most had settled on a regular time and pitch, forming unauthorized but tolerated street markets, mainly in the poorer parts of London. Hardy counted 106 street markets, with a total of over five thousand stalls. Most sold perishable goods (fruit, vegetables, fish, flowers, cakes, sweets, meat, eggs, coffee, and cats' meat), but clothes, furniture, crockery, books, toys, and second-hand goods were also traded. The biggest and most famous of these street markets was the one in Wentworth Street and Petticoat Lane (Middlesex Street), Whitechapel, but Hoxton Street in Shoreditch, Crisp Street in Poplar, White Cross Street in St Luke's, Watney Street in St George-in-the-East, Leather Lane in Holborn, Chapel Street in Clerkenwell, and Brick Lane in Bethnal Green were all big and thriving markets. In South London, Southwark Park Road in Bermondsey, Lower Marsh by Waterloo Station, and East Lane (or East Street) in Walworth, where Charlie Chaplin was born in 1889, were the biggest street markets. These markets were not threatened by a loss of public interest, but by vestries and district boards, which were tempted to close them or move them to new sites, because they impeded the flow of traffic and pedestrians, and were (in Hardy's words) 'an offence against a rather visionary idea of civic order'. In 1894 the Court of Appeal spoke up for the costers:

The unauthorized street markets of London undoubtedly fulfil a most useful purpose. They are practically confined to poor and crowded neighbourhoods, and are largely the means by which the surplus produce remaining unsold in the authorized markets is distributed amongst the poorer classes. Costermongers are keenly alive in ascertaining when produce is at exceptionally low prices, and are always ready to purchase and distribute an almost unlimited quantity when this is the case.[2]

Some costermongers owned their own barrows, and even a donkey to pull it, but many rented them by the week, or worked on commission for more successful traders. Like many other London workers, they were vulnerable to the weather and seasonal fluctuations, and had to adapt their merchandise to changing demand. The switch from summer lemonade or ice-cream to winter roast chestnuts or hot coffee was a popular one. Their average age, Booth calculated, was above that of London workers, because 'the old and broken down of other trades sometimes take to street selling as a last resource'.

Multiple Stores

The rise of chains of stores under single ownership, selling a small range of standardized products, began in the 1860s and 1870s. Two early pioneers, the W. H. Smith chain of station bookstalls and the Singer sewing machine shops, opened in the 1850s, but Walton, Hassell and Port, the first London grocer's chain, and E. H. Rabbits and Pocock Brothers, London first footwear multiples, were established by about 1870. Over the next twenty years the number of multiple stores in these two trades, grocery and shoes, grew quite quickly in London, and some familiar names appeared on London streets, including Freeman, Hardy and Willis, and Lilley and Skinner (both in shoes), and the grocers George Carter, Home and Colonial, the International Tea Company, Thomas Lipton, and the Maypole Dairy. From the 1890s multiples entered other markets, including the Aerated Bread Company and J. Lyons (in bread and cakes), Maynards (sweets), Salmon and Gluckstein (tobacco), Boots of Nottingham and Timothy White's (chemists), George Mence Smith and Davis and Evans (oil and colour merchants), John Sainsbury and David Greig (groceries), and Hope Brothers, Dunn and Company, Hepworths, and Montague Burton, in the growing field of men's clothing.[3] The greatest multiple of all, the retail wing of the Co-operative movement, was weaker in London than in its northern heartland, where the steady habits of saving through spending, and earning the loyalty dividend, had been easier to establish. But the Co-op was nevertheless an important and growing retailer of groceries, household goods, and clothes in London, having made 'astonishingly rapid progress' in

London, according to the 1898 *Baedeker's* guide, with about thirty shops
'carrying on an immense trade'. In all, London shoppers probably bought
about a fifth of their goods in Co-operative, multiple, and department
stores by 1914, and the challenge to the independent shopkeeper had
begun.[4]

Large-scale retailing grew in London (and in the rest of Britain) because
it enjoyed clear economic advantages over traditional methods. The later
nineteenth century was a good time for retail expansion, because the spending power of the London working class was growing thanks to the falling
prices of essential foodstuffs, especially bread, enabling them to buy a
greater variety of food and other goods with money that once would have
gone on bread, milk, potatoes, tea, and cheese. Working-class Londoners
began to buy things regularly which once would have been occasional luxuries: jam, fish, pickles, coffee, sugar, eggs, fruit, new shoes and clothes,
newspapers. This was a small-scale local market, but multiple stores were
able to take advantage of it because their operating costs were lower, and
because they could buy their stock more cheaply in bulk. Bulk-buying was
only possible when goods were being produced in large quantities by factories or organized systems of sweated production, or imported on a large
scale. Multiples therefore had the advantage in buying and selling factory-
made shoes, clothes, pharmaceuticals, cigarettes, chocolate, margarine
(invented in the 1860s), jam, tinned milk, canned and bottled fruit, pickles, and spreads, and also in a growing range of imported foods, including
butter, bacon, meat, and dried fruit. Sometimes, as in the case of the Co-
op, the Aerated Bread Company, Liptons, and Maypole Dairies, the retailer's
own factories or plantations produced the goods they sold. Where supplies
were small-scale and local, independent retailers were still able to buy and
sell at a reasonable price, and held their own against the multiples. That is
why independent butchers, greengrocers, and fishmongers held their dominant position far longer than independent grocers and shoe shops. They
took their carts to Smithfield, Covent Garden, or Billingsgate every morning, traded on the same terms as the employee of a multiple store would
have to do, and probably did so with more skill and commitment.

Department Stores

Another innovation in retailing, the department store, had developed in
London and other big towns and cities since the 1860s. These stores

22. Staff and passengers at Bank Station, on the Central London Railway (the Twopenny Tube), soon after its opening in 1900.

23. London's first motor taxi, a Hansom body on a four-wheeled chassis, in 1904.

24. The latest models on display. An early motor show, around 1900.

25. Powering the electric age. Sebastian de Ferranti's revolutionary electricity-generating station at Deptford in 1889 (see page 287). From the *Illustrated London News*.

26. Enjoying a West End performance by telephone, in the Electrophone Salon in Gerrard Street, around 1900 (see page 143).

27. A National Telephone Company lineman repairing London's rooftop cables, around 1900.

28. Parisian elegance in Leicester Square. A night out in the brasserie of the Hôtel de l'Europe in 1900.

29. *Gauguin and Connoisseurs*, Spencer Gore's impression of Roger Fry's first post-Impressionist exhibition, in December 1910 (see page 343).

30. Oxford Street, looking east from near Oxford Circus, in the mid-1890s. The Princess's Theatre, on the left, opened in 1840 and closed in 1902.

31. The jewellers Mappin and Webb, built in 1906, a few yards west of the Princess's Theatre, brought a new style of retailing in Oxford Street, with plate-glass window displays instead of sunshades.

32. Suburban shoppers on a Saturday night. A crowded food store in Hammersmith in 1900.

33. A vast crowd assembled outside St Paul's Cathedral towards midnight on New Year's Eve – Watch Night – at the end of the century.

34. Scots Guards, Metropolitan policemen, Winston Churchill (in a top hat) and an innocent bystander at the siege of Sidney Street in January 1911 (see page 396).

35. The first 'London Eye': the Great Wheel at Earl's Court soon after its construction in 1894. The steam-driven wheel was 300 feet high and carried 1,600 passengers (see page 412).

36. A lively scene from the musical comedy hit of 1913, *The Girl in the Taxi*, at the Lyric, Shaftesbury Avenue. Its stars were Yvonne Arnaud and Arthur Playfair.

37. The early days of the London film industry. Rehearsing a scene at the Hepworth Studio, Walton-on-Thames, in 1912. The producer is clapping a rhythm for the dancers (see page 447).

38. The programme for Félicien Trewey's film show at the Regent Street Polytechnic in February 1896, the first public cinema performance in Britain (see page 446).

PROGRAMME

Will be selected from the following subjects, and will be liable to frequent changes, as well as ADDITIONAL PORTRAYALS

Lecturer   FRANCIS POCHET.

Bathing in the Mediterranean.

Arrival of a train in a country station.

Trewey (under the hat).

Fall of a wall.

Babies playing.

A quiet game of ecarte.

Russian Views.

London Street Niggers.

Racecourse Scene.

Cavalry horses led to be watered.

PROGRAMME. Continued.

Surf boat leaving harbour.

Ludgate Circus.

Change of Guard—St. James' Palace.

Hyde Park at noon.

Spanish Life.

Blacksmith at work.

Breakfast on the lawn.

Travelling Photographer.

Charge of Cavalry.

Tit for Tat.

Champs Elysees (Paris).

Place des Cordeliers (Lyons).

Teasing the gardener.

Arrival of the Mail Boat at Folkestone.

The Tuileries, Paris.

39. London women dressed up for a grand day out. A horse-brake excursion, perhaps a works outing, in 1900.

August 1914

40. Patriotic crowds outside Buckingham Palace (around the new Victoria Memorial) celebrating the outbreak of the Great War.

41. Goodbye to all that.

catered for the growing middle-class market, especially for goods which
would not be bought on a daily basis, such as women's and children's
clothing, drapery, footwear, and furniture. Their sales of everyday goods
like food, stationery, sweets, and tobacco, where closeness to the customer
was important, were small, though one of London's biggest department
stores, Harrods, started as a grocer's in 1849, and was still famous for its
food. Many of the London department stores had started much earlier as
drapery or women's clothing retailers, including Debenhams (1778),
Dickins and Jones (1803), Swan and Edgar (1812), Shoolbred's (1814),
Peter Robinson (1833), and Marshall and Snelgrove (1837), and added
extra departments later in the century. John Maple, of Tottenham Court
Road, started in 1841 selling carpets, clothes, and drapery, but specializing in furniture. The true London department store began with William
Whiteley's of Bayswater in 1863, and with the Civil Service Supply Association in the Strand (1866) and the Army and Navy Co-operative Society
store in Victoria Street (1871). These last two were cooperative department
stores, serving only their own subscribers, who had to be civil service or
military families and their friends. The Army and Navy Stores had its own
factories and workshops, a members' restaurant, a sales and manufacturing
staff (in 1887) of 5,000, and annual sales in the 1890s of nearly £3 million. By the 1870s Harrods had also achieved junior department store
status, having expanded from groceries into crockery, medicines, and stationery. When it burnt down (as common a fate for department stores as
it was for theatres) in 1883 it had over a hundred staff.

Most London department stores grew by expanding into neighbouring properties, hoping eventually to acquire a whole block. This was not
easy. To get its full site in Oxford Street, Bourne and Hollingsworth had
to dislodge over thirty tenants, including a cigarette factory, a beauty parlour, a palmist, a backache-pill shop, a 'nest of Polish tailors', a chapel, and
a brothel, and in Kensington High Street it took John Barker from 1870
to 1902 to get control of all but one of the small shops between Young
Street and Derry Street, and Charles Derry and Charles Toms from 1869
to 1912 to take over the next block, from Derry Street to High Street Kensington Underground station.[5] Once this was achieved, it was possible to
replace their ramshackle enterprises with purpose-built stores, on the lines
of the one built for Bon Marché in well-off suburban Brixton in 1877. In
fact, all the early purpose-built department stores in central London were
Edwardian. Harrods great terracotta-fronted store was built between 1901
and 1905, Barkers between 1904 and 1914, Debenham and Freebody

between 1906 and 1907, Whiteley's between 1908 and 1912, and Self-ridge's between 1908 and 1909. John Barnes of Finchley Road (1900), Arding and Hobbs of Clapham (1910), Burberry's of the Haymarket (1911–12), and Waring and Gillow, the Oxford Street furniture store (1901–6), were all built in the decade in which the big London store was born. Other big stores, like Liberty's and Gamages, the 'People's Popular Emporium' in High Holborn, just linked smaller properties together, leaving their customers to find their way from one department to another along ramps and passages.

These big stores prospered because the market for ready-made clothes (as opposed to clothes made at home from shop-bought fabric) was growing, and because they could offer middle-class women a much wider range of styles, colours, and sizes than smaller shops. Economies of scale and sometimes production in their own clothing or furniture workshops kept their prices down, but variety and quality, not cheapness, gave them the edge over local shops. For well-off women in the 1890s and 1900s, shopping in the big department stores, drapers, and furniture stores was a pleasure, a way of passing long workless days in comfort and safety. Although *Baedeker's* still recommended Cheapside, Ludgate Hill, and Fleet Street in the late 1890s, the best streets for female shoppers were Regent Street (Swan and Edgar, Dickins and Jones, Liberty's, Mappin and Webb), Bond Street (for jewellers and other luxury shops), Tottenham Court Road (Shoolbred's, Maples), perhaps Piccadilly, for Fortnum and Mason and the little shops of the Burlington Arcade, and above all Oxford Street, which by 1914 had Waring and Gillow, Peter Robinson, D. H. Evans, Marshall and Snelgrove, Bourne and Hollingsworth, Swears and Wells, and Self-ridge's, all in a row. Whiteley's made Bayswater worth a visit, but although the success of this great store had attracted other smart shops to West-bourne Grove it was not quite the 'new Regent Street' that some said it was. Kensington High Street, with Derry and Toms, Barkers, and Pontings, and Brompton Road and Knightsbridge, with Harrods, Harvey Nichols, and the National Fur Company, had as strong a claim to this title. Marion Sambourne kept a diary that listed her shopping trips in Kensington (where she lived) and the West End. In the 1880s she favoured Whiteley's, Shoolbred's, Maples, Gamages, Marshall and Snelgrove, Barkers, Pontings, the Baker Street Bazaar, Harvey Nichols, and Harrods, a 'dirty place though cheap'.[6] The best suburban shopping centres had department stores of their own: Jones Brothers of Holloway, Peter Jones of Sloane Square, Bon Marché of Brixton, Pratt's of Streatham, John Barnes of South

Hampstead, Bentall's of Kingston. As Booth explained, there was a clear pecking order in shopping centres: 'Walworth is as much above Bermondsey New Road as Lewisham or Holloway would consider themselves above Walworth; and a widening gulf separates these from shops in Kensington, in Oxford Street and in Regent Street.'[7]

It would not be long before Regent Street would itself become the 'new Regent Street'. Plans to demolish and rebuild parts of John Nash's great curving terraces were put forward in the 1880s by individual shopkeepers, who found their existing shops too cramped and poorly built, but most had come to nothing. The continuity of Nash's terraces, which few late Victorian critics valued highly, was broken by the replacement of the Hanover Chapel with a much higher building in 1896, and two years after this Arthur Cates, chief architect to the Office of Land Revenues, prepared a plan for the rebuilding of the whole street, with blocks of shops that were sixty feet high to a parapet or balustrade, topped with dormer windows, pavilion roofs, towers, mansards, cupolas, and other fashionable features. In 1904 the greatest architect of the day, Norman Shaw, was called in to design a finer replacement for Nash's street. He produced a beautiful plan for a new Quadrant modelled on (and improving on) John Carr's Georgian Crescent in Buxton, but Regent Street's tenants, worried that the loss of shop space and the lack of plate-glass windows would lose business for the street, united to defeat the plan. The fact that the shops on the Regent Street frontage of the Piccadilly Hotel, built to Shaw's design in 1906–8, could not find tenants strengthened the shopkeepers' case, and Shaw, who was eighty, gave up the struggle. Nothing more was done until the shops' ninety-nine-year leases ran out in 1919. If this tiresome dispute achieved anything, it alerted some Edwardian critics and architects to the forgotten merits of John Nash and his stucco facades.[8]

When it could be difficult for respectable women to walk around London alone, the department store had particular attractions. Walking around Bayswater, a timid housewife might feel vulnerable, but inside Whiteley's, so long as she did not meet the proprietor (a notorious womanizer), she was safe. One of the great problems for women shoppers, the difficulty of finding a public toilet, was solved if she shopped in a department store. Seaman, Little and Company, drapers, which opened in Kensington High Street in the 1870s, seems to have led the way in providing customers' toilets, but the new Edwardian department stores all had them. Debenham's boasted of its Ladies' Club Room, in which shoppers could 'read the papers and magazines, telephone, write letters, or meet their friends', and from 1905 Harrods offered 'retiring rooms for both sexes, writing rooms with dainty stationery, club room, fitting rooms, smoking rooms, etc., free of charge or question'.[9] Many women joined West End clubs so that they could rest, have tea, and use the toilet when they were enjoying a day's shopping, but late Victorian tea rooms and big Edwardian stores offered the same facilities for nothing. From the mid-1890s, there were tea shops run by the Ladies' Tea Association, and from 1888 the 'Dorothy' ladies' restaurant identified 'weary shoppers' as its target customers. In 1909, its opening year, Selfridge's urged women to use its free ladies' club instead of the costly alternatives, and Harrods, fighting back, claimed that it was 'a recognised social rendezvous; in fact, one of the few smart rendezvous acknowledged and patronised by Society'. In the same year the *Pall Mall Gazette* claimed that by these tactics 'the whole of London's shopping centres, from Knightsbridge to Tottenham Court Road, has of late been transformed into a vast feminine club'. In time, as department stores, tea shops, and restaurants catered for the needs of their female customers, West End clubs for lady shoppers faded away.[10]

A visitor to London in 1900, the American banking millionaire Andrew Carnegie, neatly summarized the shortcomings of the big West End stores, before they had been rebuilt: 'Just look at the jumble of windows . . . so much stuff that you cannot take it all in. And when you go into a shop they treat you most indifferently. You are scowled at if you ask for goods out of the ordinary, and you are made to feel uncomfortable if you do not buy. These shop people drive away more people than they attract . . . What London wants is a good shaking up.' The man who was destined to provide this shaking up arrived in London in 1906. Like Charles Tyson Yerkes, Gordon Selfridge had made his reputation and fortune in Chicago, and came to London with the intention of conquering the world's biggest market through the introduction of new American methods. Selfridge had been retail manager of Marshall Field of Chicago, and claimed to have introduced some of its most successful marketing devices. He retired in 1904, and came to London with £350,000 and the conviction that he could teach Whiteley, Harrod, Marshall, and the other London store-owners some lessons in modern retailing techniques. Sadly William Whiteley, who was shot dead in his office in 1907 by a man claiming to be his illegitimate son, did not live long enough to learn these lessons.

The new Harrods, Barkers, and Debenhams stores had already started to make shopping in London a more welcoming and enjoyable experience, but Selfridge's outdid them all. Only the eastern section of Selfridge's vast steel-framed building was built at first, but its huge Ionic columns and three-storey windows, its gigantic clock and statue of the Queen of Time, set the store apart from the jumble of smaller shops in Oxford Street, and even from London's other new department stores. Selfridge's windows, which were lit till midnight, were dressed like stage sets by the top Chicago window-dresser, not over-stuffed with goods as his competitors' were. Unlike William Whiteley, Gordon Selfridge was a great believer in advertising, and bought ninety-seven pages of newspaper space to excite public interest in his opening week in March 1909. Though Harrods discovered that its golden jubilee, an event to be celebrated with galas and special displays, fell in the same week, and D. H. Evans and Derry and Toms announced rival events, a huge crowd filled Oxford Street on Selfridge's opening day. Selfridge was an instant household name, and the efforts of its rivals to spoil the party were compared by the *Advertising World* with 'the feeble attempts of a few small boys to arrest the legions of an invading army'.[11] The American invader had several new tactics with which to complete his conquest. Carpets, wrapping paper, and delivery vans were all in the store's colour, 'Selfridge Green'; staff were trained to assist, not to badger customers into making purchases; an ice-cream-soda fountain and a bargain basement drew in the greedy and the stingy, and cosmetics counters near the main entrance attracted women in from Oxford Street. But this was not a one-man revolution. Selfridge was refining a concept of the self-contained department store and shopping as entertainment which William Whiteley, Charles Harrod, Richard Burbidge (General Manager of Harrods from 1891), James Marshall, John Barker, and others had created, and most of the technology available to Selfridge had been pioneered in London by other retailers. Harrods was first with the moving staircase, the Junior Army and Navy Stores in Waterloo Place was probably the first London shop with passenger lifts, and John Barnes of Hampstead and Bon Marché of Brixton were among the first (in 1900) to install pneumatic-tube systems, or cash railways, for carrying money and orders from one department to another. Arding and Hobbs installed a cash railway in 1910, and still uses it.

Shopworkers

Retail and distribution work, for either big department stores or small independent or multiple shops, was a great and growing area of employment in London, especially for women and school-leavers. According to statistics given to Parliament in 1899, about 40 per cent of boys leaving school in London became errand boys or van boys, and another 14 per cent went into shopwork, though most were dismissed in their late teens, when they would have to be paid as adults.[12] Because the census did not make a clear distinction between making, handling, and selling goods it is impossible to count the number of shopworkers in London. The 1911 census listed 10,600 miscellaneous shopkeepers and 17,870 workers in general and multiple shops in the County of London, but most of the 37,400 drapers and many of the 172,650 bakers, confectioners, grocers, oilmen, butchers, and fishmongers listed were essentially shopkeepers or shop assistants. In 1891, by Booth's calculations, there were over 27,000 shopworkers in drapery and hosiery shops, but for other commodities he was unable to make the distinction between makers and sellers. So the large number of employees in London department stores (about 6,000 in Whiteley's or Harrods in 1914, for instance) included manufacturing, warehousing, office, and delivery workers as well as sales staff.

The enforcement of legislation helps clarify the picture. Until the 1912 Shops Act, which gave all shop assistants a weekly afternoon off, the only legislation on working conditions in shops applied to women and children. In its enforcement of the 1892–5 Shop Hours Acts (which limited under-eighteens to seventy-two hours a week), in 1907–11 the LCC inspected about 78,000 wholesale and retail shops (and about 6,500 pubs and beer houses) each year, and checked on the working conditions of about 30,000 boys and girls who worked for them. The Council also enforced the 1899 Seats for Shop Assistants Act, which directed that there should be one seat to every three female assistants. In 1910–11 it inspected over 14,000 shops, which employed 39,500 women. This is not inconsistent with the 35,526 women listed as working in retail and distribution in 1891. These figures suggest the extent of the employment of women and children in retailing in Edwardian London, without establishing its precise dimensions.[13]

The lives of the late Victorian shop assistant were often described in the early novels of H. G. Wells (*The Wheels of Chance, Kipps*), whose own working life began with two years in a draper's shop in Southsea. Wells knew of 'the intrigues and toadyism, the long tedious hours, the wretched dormitories, the insufficient "economised" food, the sudden dismissals, the dreadful interludes of unemployment with clothing growing shabby and money leaking away'. Charles Booth's assistant, George Arkell, gave a very full account of the work of a draper's assistant in the 1890s. They worked from about seven thirty or eight in the morning until about eight thirty or nine at night, and sometimes until ten in the suburbs, where shops were open longer. In a suburban shop that stayed open late on Fridays and Saturdays the assistants' weekly hours might be seventy-five or more, including mealtimes, though sixty-five to seventy was more usual. The work was unsettled and insecure, and many shopworkers did not stay in one job long enough to take the fortnight's paid holiday that long-serving assistants enjoyed. Moving from one job to another was often a better way to increase one's salary than staying put. Assistants' wages might be as low as £12 or £15 a year, or as high as £40 or £50 for senior staff in big stores. At the top of the profession was the shopwalker in a department store, who might earn between £150 and £200 in the West End, or £100 in the suburbs. Women, the majority of shop assistants, usually left work to marry before reaching these heights, which in any case were rarely open to them. Thirty pounds a year was considered a good wage for a female assistant. Assistants could add perhaps 30 per cent to their salary through commissions, with the senior salesman getting his choice of customers and juniors only serving when those above them were busy. In bigger shops, the unmarried assistants slept and ate on the premises or in a lodging house supplied by the employer. Food and accommodation varied, with smaller shops offering more homeliness and friendship, the larger ones better facilities. In the 1880s Charles Booth classified two-thirds of the 21,500 male shop assistants of Hackney and East London as class E (comfortable, with regular standard earnings), with the rest either classes B to D (very poor or poor) or F (higher paid labour). In general, Arkell thought, shop assistants lived about as well as domestic servants in good families, working harder, but enjoying higher social status and greater freedom in the evenings and at weekends. In both domestic and shop service, Arkell believed, 'the comforts afforded continually increase, following that general rise in the standard of life which is so marked a feature of the present time'.[14]

Most Londoners bought most of their needs in small independent shops, whose prolonged twentieth-century decline was only just beginning in the 1890s. There were about 78,000 wholesale and retail shops on the LCC inspectors' registers in 1907–11, serving a resident population of 4,500,000. Allowing for a slightly higher concentration of shops in the centre than in the suburbs, the 2,750,000 people of Outer London might have had another 42,000 shops, giving Greater London around 120,000 shops (and shopkeepers) in all.[15] All but about 5,000 of these were independent shops, run by the shopkeeper who owned or rented the premises, perhaps with the help of an errand boy, a few assistants, and family members. Even in these shops the nature of the work was changing. Some traditional retailing skills (blending tea, curing and slicing bacon, killing animals, grinding sugar and coffee, and so on) were fading, as groceries started to arrive already weighed, packaged, and priced, and the old producer-retailer, selling what he or she had made, was dying out. Instead, the modern shopkeeper had to learn how to market his goods by displaying them in his windows or on poles outside the shop, writing enticing slogans, giving out handbills, and making good use of gas or electric light.[16]

These shopkeepers were a substantial section of London's middle classes, occupying the same income levels as skilled artisans, policemen, foremen, small employers, publicans, clerks, and schoolteachers. In his poverty survey of the late 1880s, Charles Booth counted over 8,000 male shopkeepers in Hackney and East London, which had a total population of 890,000. He categorized the smaller shopkeepers, without assistants, as predominantly (83 per cent) comfortable working-class (classes E and F) with the rest either poor (class D) or lower middle-class (class G). Shopkeepers who employed assistants, Booth said, were divided between classes F, G, and H, upper working-class, lower middle-class, and upper middle-class. These were the people whose shops lined the main streets all over London, giving those streets, even in the roughest districts, the red of solid prosperity in Booth's coloured poverty maps.[17]

To add to the usual problems of running a small business, late Victorian shopkeepers had to worry about the growing competition from Co-operative shops, multiples, and department stores. Even in Bromley, beyond the suburban sprawl but with a convenient railway line to Victoria, H. G. Wells' parents' hardware shop started losing customers to well-organized London competitors in the 1870s and 1880s: 'Presently the delivery vans of the early multiple shops, the Army and Navy Co-operative Stores and the like, appeared in the neighbourhood to suck away the ebbing vitality of the local retailer. The trade in pickling jars and jam-pots died away.'[18] Inside London, where the threat to small shops was even more intense, independent retailers formed local associations in the 1880s and 1890s to defend their trades, without any clear idea of what form this defence should take. Some believed that compulsory early closing on one day each week would allow them to save money without losing business to their competitors, and others argued that fixed minimum prices, set by manufacturers, would stop cooperatives like Civil Service Stores from undercutting small shops by accepting low profit margins which independent retailers could not match. Most small businessmen did not welcome state intervention, and clung to their right to compete on price and service, even if they were doomed to be beaten in the end. In the long run the spread of fixed pricing, or resale price maintenance (RPM), was an important change, and one that probably helped independent retailers in their battle with multiple stores, but it did not make much progress before 1914, except in books, pharmaceuticals, and tobacco. Probably only 3 per cent of goods sold in 1900 were fixed price (compared to 30 per cent in 1938), leaving shopkeepers to set most prices as they chose.[19]

The Art of Advertising

One of the things that helped London's 100,000 and more small shop-keepers to survive was the late Victorian consumer boom, which was based on falling basic food prices, rising real incomes, and a growing range of cheap and desirable processed and manufactured products. The boom was stimulated, to some degree, by the growth of advertising. Thrifty Londoners who had been brought up to buy only what they needed, and to seek out the cheapest goods in street markets and second-hand stores, found their careful habits challenged and undermined in every newspaper and on almost every street corner. Commercial advertising was not new in London. In the 1840s and 1850s 'Professor' Thomas Holloway made enough money by advertising and selling Holloway's Pills to enable him to build and endow a women's college in Egham. But the mass market for publications, entertainments, cigarettes, and branded foods and medicines was bigger than ever before, and advertising campaigns in the 1880s and 1890s were therefore more aggressive, expensive, and universal. The mass-circulation newspapers and magazines of the period, selling at much less than their cost of production, relied on advertisers for their profits, and most trams and omnibuses carried advertisements on their fronts and sides, making it difficult sometimes to make out their destinations. Advertisements in newspapers and magazines, posters on trams, buses, railway platforms, walls, and hoardings, and leaflets handed out in the street alerted late Victorian Londoners to the new products and branded goods that were available to them: Bovril (Johnson's Fluid Beef), Nestlé's condensed milk, Hovis bread, Colman's mustard, Cadbury's cocoa powder, Remington typewriters, Coventry bicycles with Dunlop tyres, Kodak cameras, Pears soap, Player's cigarettes, and so on. Posters announcing the latest plays and entertainments covered every available hoarding. After a rainy day, bill posters toured the London streets, replacing wet and bedraggled posters with fresh ones. Armies of sandwich men, with their high boards strapped to their shoulders, having been banned from the pavements, marched along the gutters of busy streets, advertising a nearby shop or the latest show. Many of these men, the *Big Issue* sellers of their day, operated from a head-quarters in Ham Yard, which is still off Great Windmill Street, just north of Piccadilly Circus. H. G. Wells, with his sharp eye for contemporary issues, satirized the advertising boom in his 1909 novel *Tono-Bungay*. His narrator, newly arrived in London, was struck by the extent of street adver-tising ('the very hoardings clamoured strangely at one's senses'), and found that his uncle, who had made a fortune from making and marketing the useless 'tonic' that gave the book its title, was a great advocate of the power of advertising in the modern economy:

> Advertisement has revolutionised trade and industry; it is going to revolutionise the world. The old merchant used to tote about com-modities; the new one creates values. Doesn't need to tote. He takes something that isn't worth anything – or something that isn't partic-ularly worth anything – and he makes it worth something. He takes mustard that is just like anybody else's mustard, and he goes about saying, shouting, singing, chalking on walls, writing inside people's books, putting it everywhere, 'Smith's Mustard is the Best.' And behold it is the best!

In Paris in the 1880s and 1890s, the years of the so-called *affichomanie* (poster mania), commercial posters, 'the art of the streets', were exhibited, analysed, and republished as if they were high art, and the work of the greatest pioneers of poster art, Jules Chevet and Henri de Toulouse-Lautrec, justified this attention. London advertisers of the 1880s liked to promote their products by associating them with paintings by Royal Aca-demicians (Sir John Millais' *Bubbles*, used by Pears' soap, is the most famous example), but in the 1890s the work of such artists as Walter Crane (the William Morris socialist and book illustrator), Aubrey Beardsley, Maurice Greiffenhagen, Dudley Hardy, and the so-called 'Beggarstaff Brothers',

William Nicholson and James Pryde, began to appear on walls and hoardings. Hardy's famous posters for the Savoy Theatre, the Gaiety Girls, and
Jerome K. Jerome's weekly magazine *Today*, Greiffenhagen's posters for
the *Pall Mall Budget*, and Nicholson's woodcuts for the Lyceum Theatre,
Rowntree's Cocoa, Kassama cornflour, and *Harper's Magazine*, with their
bold and simple designs and large areas of flat colour, took English poster
art far beyond the imitation of Chevet and Lautrec, and helped give
London streets a distinctive appearance. The Beggarstaff Brothers, whose
influence on the development of poster art in England and Germany was
very great, only worked together from 1894 (for an exhibition at the
Westminster Aquarium) until 1896. After this, Nicholson went on to produce sets of woodcuts for the publisher William Heinemann, including
London Types (1898), which, with poems by William Henley, is one of the
most powerful evocations of the late Victorian city. Here, along with three
soldiers, a mounted policeman, a newsboy, a flower girl, a bus-driver, a
hawker, a dubious 'lady', a cockney Liza ('a stupid, straight, hard-working
girl'), a blue-coat (charity-school) boy, and a barmaid, there was the
sandwich-man, in his rotten boots and greasy old hat, who 'trails his
mildews towards a Kingdom-Come / Compact of sausage-and-mash and
two-o'-rum'. Nicholson went on to a long and distinguished career in
painting and the theatre, including, in 1904, designing the costumes for
the first production of James Barrie's *Peter Pan*.

Of course, not every street advertisement was a work of art, and the
almost uncontrolled proliferation of posters, illuminated signs, and gigantic wooden names and slogans projecting above the London roofline
(known as sky signs) provoked a hostile reaction in the 1890s. In 1890
public pressure forced a soap company to take down a sky sign that
obscured the view of St Paul's Cathedral from Fleet Street, and the next
year there were injuries when a great storm blew down hoardings in Hyde
Park. In 1893 a spate of letters to *The Times* led to the creation of the
Society for the Checking of Abuses in Public Advertising. The Society
shortened its name to SCAPA (a pioneering acronym fifty years before the
word for them was invented), got the future Poet Laureate, Alfred Austin,
to write them a sonnet, and campaigned for local authorities to be given
powers to prevent the desecration of town and countryside. SCAPA faced
opposition from advertisers and the United Bill Posters Association, which
argued that posters enhanced the urban landscape, turning ugly hoardings
into open-air art galleries. SCAPA's quarrel was not with work of high
quality, but with cruder excesses, like sky signs and the projection of

magic-lantern advertisements onto public buildings. On Trafalgar Day 1894, for instance, slogans for pills and blacking were projected onto Nelson's Column and the National Gallery. Alice Meynell, the poet and essayist, enjoyed the effect of electric beams on London's night-time scene: 'A search-light suddenly draws the eye up to the chimney-pots (sweetly touched, they too, on the westernmost of their squalid sides) and to the unbroken sky; and then at once the eye travels down its shaft, revealing clouded air; . . . or the search-light makes the programme of a music hall to shine black and white upon the wall; anon, an advertisement is written in light, and perpetually among the even progress of the carriage lights flit the lamps of bicycles.'[20] In 1894 the London Building Act banned all sky signs, including advertisements on 'any balloon, parachute or similar device', as well as advertising signs which were visible above buildings and against the sky. A little later, an LCC by-law banned the use of flashlights and searchlights to illuminate or project advertisements, because of the danger to traffic. These restrictions did little to slow the growth of the advertising industry, and by 1910 there were in London about 350 advertising agents, about a hundred of whom ran substantial businesses. And they did nothing to prevent the shopkeepers with facades on the Shaftesbury Avenue corner of Piccadilly Circus from renting their walls to advertising companies, who erected large electric signs on them. By 1910 there were advertisements for Van Raalte cigars, Mellins foods, Perrier water (on the famous Café Monico), Schweppes, and Bovril, and the circus had started to acquire a little of its familiar twentieth-century appearance.[21]

*

CHAPTER NINETEEN

IGNORANT ARMIES

In 1867 Matthew Arnold, the poet, critic, and school inspector, published 'Dover Beach', a poem that lamented the fact that the Sea of Faith was ebbing away, leaving bare shingle where once there had been a full, all-encompassing high tide of Christian belief. But almost twenty years later, as far as London was concerned, there was evidence that the decline in Christian worship had slowed or stopped, perhaps because of the vigorous efforts of Churches and missionaries over the previous thirty years. The enormous success of the American evangelists Moody and Sankey, whose revivalist meetings in London were attended by over 2.5 million people in 1875, might have halted the advance of Hardy's 'ignorant armies', at least for a few years. A survey of churchgoing commissioned by William Robertson Nicoll for publication in his new Nonconformist journal, the *British Weekly*, revealed that on Sunday 24 October 1886, a cold but clear day, 1,167,312 Londoners, almost 30 per cent of Inner London's population of just over 4,000,000, went to church. This was a well-organized amateur survey using several thousand volunteer observers, producing much more reliable results than the national religious census of 1851, which had relied entirely on figures supplied by the clergy. The 1886 survey's weaknesses were that it counted attendances on a single (perhaps untypical) day, did not distinguish between men, women, and children, omitted all attendances before 11 a.m., and missed out smaller missions, whose own figures were added a year later. Still, its results were widely accepted, and seemed to show that the Churches' nightmare of a huge heathen city had been averted, or at least postponed.

Building More Churches

The effort to rechristianize working-class London, and to prevent its more prosperous parishes from sinking into apathy, continued in the 1880s and

1890s. The building of churches and chapels progressed at a steady pace, especially in the growing suburbs, but it depended on each denomination's ability to raise money from its supporters. In prosperous suburbs this was not so difficult, but in poorer areas worshippers often had to make do with converted houses or plain huts. Suburban church-building almost kept pace with population growth. Camberwell, which had 26 churches and chapels in 1851, enough to seat 30 per cent of its population, had 156 in 1903, with pews for a quarter of its inhabitants. On two occasions in the year, harvest festival and watchnight, the very popular New Year's Eve service, it was possible that all these seats might be full. For London as a whole, the 1886 survey had counted about 1,500 places of worship, but by 1903 there were over 4,000 (including small missions), spread over a much larger population and area.

Some of the new churches were places of real distinction or importance. The Roman Catholic Church, whose poor Irish congregations had generally had to worship in drab huts, at last managed to build some impressive churches in the 1880s and 1890s. The first of these, the London (or Brompton) Oratory in South Kensington, was wider than St Paul's Cathedral, and designed in an appropriately Italian style by Hubert Gribble. Cardinal Manning, the Archbishop of Westminster from 1865 to 1892, a famous philanthropist and friend of the poor, resisted the devotion of money to huge churches when it might be spent on educating Catholic children. On his death in 1892 his successor, Cardinal Vaughan, authorized the construction of Westminster Cathedral on a site just off Victoria Street, and commissioned John Francis Bentley, a Catholic convert, to design it. The Gothic style was no longer obligatory, and Bentley went to Italy to study the best examples of Italian and Byzantine church architecture. The result, which was not quite finished when Bentley died in 1902, was a fantastic late Victorian interpretation of the Byzantine style, in the striped red brick that had recently been used by Norman Shaw for New Scotland Yard, the police headquarters on Victoria Embankment. This modified Byzantine style became an identifying characteristic of other early twentieth-century Catholic churches.

The Anglicans achieved nothing quite so spectacular, but some impressive parish churches were built, especially for the new congregations of subdivided suburban parishes. Many were in traditional Gothic style, but some demonstrated the influence of new aesthetic trends. Holy Trinity, Sloane Street, designed by J. D. Sedding at the end of the 1880s, showed what the Arts and Crafts movement could do to enliven Gothic church architecture. Sedding's assistant was Henry Wilson, of the Art Workers' Guild, and Holy Trinity's stained-glass windows were the work of Edward Burne-Jones and William Morris & Company. Henry Wilson also designed St Peter's in Ealing, and Norman Shaw, the architect whose work inspired the formation of the Art Workers' Guild, built Holy Trinity, Latimer Road, and St Mark's, Cobourg Road, off the Old Kent Road. One of the most prolific church-builders of the period was W. D. Caroe, architect to the ecclesiastical commissioners. In London, Caroe built churches in Edmonton and Walthamstow, working-class suburbs in which the churchgoing habit was not firmly established. Pews were likely to be fuller in Hampstead, where Edwin Lutyens, consulting architect to the new Garden Suburb, built St Jude's for Anglicans and the Free Church for Nonconformists. Nonconformists were also busy building new churches, both in the centre and in the suburbs. The Methodists' ornate Parisian-style Central Hall (1905–11), next to Westminster Abbey, was intended to enable their best preachers to address mass audiences, as Wesley had once done, and as the Congregationalists and Baptists now did in their temples and tabernacles. Its capacity, 2,700, was almost the same as that of St James's Hall, Piccadilly Circus, a concert hall which also held London's biggest Methodist services until its demolition in 1905. Other notable places of worship constructed in these years include the Congregationalists' huge Union Chapel in Islington (1876–89), and their King's Weigh House Chapel, built by Alfred Waterhouse on Grosvenor Square, the Baptist Tabernacle at Peckham, and the High Anglican church of St Cuthbert's in Kensington, whose ritualistic Anglo-Catholic services infuriated some Low Church Anglicans.

Some of the money for the Church of England's new suburban churches came from the City of London, whose shrinking population no longer needed sixty parish churches, and where development sites could be sold for a high price. Three Wren churches, St Matthew Friday Street, St Olave Jewry and St Mary Magdalene, Old Fish Street, were sold and demolished in the 1880s, three more, All-Hallows-the-Great, St Michael Bassishaw, and St Michael Wood Street, in the 1890s, and one, St George Botolph Lane, in 1904. The process was easy, because the Union of City Benefices Act allowed the amalgamation of City parishes, and Wren's churches, some of which were too simple and unadorned for Victorian taste, did not command the almost universal public admiration that protects them today. Opening them for private prayer presented some problems, too. The rector of St Mary Woolnoth complained that the privilege was abused: 'dozens and dozens of times men women have actually made a public convenience of the sacred building; others have come in and stripped themselves nearly naked in the darker corners, for what reason no one can say; others come for the sole purpose of altercation with the attendant . . . and when I first became rector of the parish the church, between one and two o'clock, was regularly used as a luncheon room'.[1]

Knees on Hassocks

In prosperous suburbs churches might almost fill themselves, but in poorer parishes, including the working-class suburbs created in the 1880s by cheap workmen's trains, clergymen often felt like missionaries, taking the gospel into territory where the natives were hostile or indifferent. The danger of relying on bricks and mortar and neglecting the quality of the clergy was illustrated by the experience of Bethnal Green, where there was a vigorous church-building programme in the middle of the century. In the 1890s Charles Booth found six of the seven parishes between Hackney Road and Bethnal Green Road, with a population of over 40,000, in a state of pitiful neglect, with demoralized, apathetic, or absentee vicars and empty churches. The vicar of St Peter's Bethnal Green, Bishop Beckles of Sierra Leone, lived in Eastbourne, and the clever and unprincipled absentee vicar of the neighbouring parish of St James's, E. F. Coke, confined his parish activities to performing cheap three-shilling weddings, at the rate of about eight a week. For almost fifty years his bishop had been unable to remove him, but death eventually did so in 1898. A measure of success was possible in the East End slums, but generally this was social, not religious. Osborne Jay, the vicar of Holy Trinity, the parish which contained the notorious slum area or rookery known as 'the Nichol' until its demolition in the 1890s, ran a very successful lodging house for his poorest parishioners, and a club below his church, where they could smoke, box, and play bagatelle or cards. But the club members 'seldom if ever tread the stairs that lead to the church above'. Jay's poorest parishioners, the 'submerged tenth', might have been surprised to hear that he favoured sending them to single-sex penal settlements, to prevent them doing further damage to the national stock.[2]

Some Anglican clergymen relied on the appeal of traditional High Church ritual and vestments, sometimes provoking Low Churchmen into unseemly protests. A few ritualistic churches built up large congregations in the most unpromising territory. St Katharine's, Rotherhithe, a ritualistic church founded in 1882, had a congregation of 800, along with a Sunday school of 600, a large temperance society, a cricket club, and an orchestra in a community of dockers, sailors, and factory workers. High Church clergymen sometimes had radical social views, and Charles Booth and Charles Masterman thought that it was their social concern, rather than their candles and fancy clothes, which won over the poor. Christian Socialism, which began with the work of Frederick Denison Maurice and Charles Kingsley in the 1840s and 1850s, was revived in London in the 1870s and 1880s, especially by Stewart Headlam, who worked in poor London parishes until 1884, after which the Bishop of London prevented him from finding a parish. Headlam studied under Maurice at Cambridge, but he was also influenced, like many other socialists, by the American land reformer Henry George when he visited London in the early 1880s. He joined the Fabians in 1886, and remained a member for the rest of his life. Headlam never had a parish position after 1884, but he was elected (along with Annie Besant) to the London School Board in 1888, and represented Bethnal Green, one of his old parishes, on the London County Council from 1907 until his death in 1924. Headlam founded a small Christian Socialist organization, the Guild of St Matthew, in 1877, but many socially concerned Anglicans found Headlam's views, especially his public support for Charles Bradlaugh and Oscar Wilde and his defence of stage dancing, too strong to swallow. They preferred to join the moderate Christian Social Union, founded in 1889 by Henry Scott Holland, a canon of St Paul's, and to draw attention to social injustices in a tone that would not antagonize the Anglican hierarchy as Headlam had done.

Another Anglican minister who combined a love of ritual with a deep commitment to the interests of his working-class parishioners was 'Father' Robert Dolling, who worked in a mission in Stepney in the early 1880s, spent twelve years in Portsmouth, and finished his career in 1898 to 1901 as vicar of St Saviour's, Poplar. In the East London 'water famine' of 1898, Dolling denounced the greed and incompetence of the East London Water Company, and became a well-liked figure in Poplar in the last years of his life. This popularity helped to fill his church, which was one of only two Anglican churches in Poplar to have a bigger congregation in 1903 (just after his early death) than in 1886. Dolling was a wonderful preacher, and when Booth's researcher heard him speaking in a City church, denouncing the apathy of the rich like a modern Savonarola, many in the congregation were moved to tears. But Dolling was despondent about the state of religion in his own large parish. 'Religion', he said, 'has, so to speak, gone to pieces. There is no opposition. We do not care enough to oppose. God is not in any of our thoughts; we do not even fear Him.'[3]

Outstanding preachers did not need to embrace socialism to attract huge crowds. Some of London's most successful and popular preachers proclaimed a traditional biblical and social message, but did so in a robust and enjoyable way, using vernacular language and theatrical oratory. The Baptist preacher Charles Spurgeon, an unyielding old-fashioned Calvinist but a great self-publicist, was able to attract 3,000 listeners to his Metropolitan Tabernacle at the Elephant and Castle every Sunday until his oratorical powers faded in the years before his death in 1892. The *British Weekly* churchgoing survey credited Spurgeon with 10,589 listeners for his Sunday services on 24 October 1886. When Charles Booth and his assistants visited the churches of Walworth and Newington in 1902 Spurgeon's influence was still very strong. His son still drew about 4,000 a week to the Tabernacle (just rebuilt after a fire), though Booth's researchers thought the worshippers were mostly middle-class or lower middle-class. The network of missions, Sunday schools, Bible classes, benefit clubs, and temperance societies established by Spurgeon was still thriving, giving the Baptists a special place in this part of South London.

Spurgeon was unmatched in his charismatic popular appeal, but there were other very successful Nonconformist preachers in the 1890s. After Spurgeon's death the greatest Baptist preacher in South London was Frederick Meyer of Christ Church, Westminster Bridge Road, who attracted Sunday audiences of 2,000. In North London, Dr John Clifford, Spurgeon's successor as President of the Baptist Union, was the minister of Praed Street Baptist Chapel, Paddington, from 1858 to 1923. His congregation, which had to be housed in a new building in Westbourne Park, was over 2,000 in 1903, as it had been in 1886. Unlike Spurgeon, Clifford embraced new scientific and political ideas, and tried to identify Baptism with advanced reformist causes. He joined the Fabians, welcomed Darwinism, supported the 1889 dock strike, opposed Anglican control of state schools, and supported the Liberal Party's programme of social and industrial reform. There were two very successful Baptist Tabernacles in East London, the East London Tabernacle in Mile End and the Shoreditch Tabernacle near the junction of Hackney Road and Shoreditch High Street. These two, Booth believed, had the largest popular congregations in London, of two or three thousand each. But even these drew their supporters from the upper working class. In Shoreditch, 'there is among them no appearance of poverty. All are well dressed, and of that their pastor is rightly proud.'[4] Another Baptist, Archibald Brown, attracted over 2,000 to the Metropolitan Tabernacle, and John Wilson had similar numbers at the Woolwich Tabernacle.

The Wesleyan circuit system prevented individual ministers from building up a large personal following, but in 1885 the Wesleyan Conference introduced a new London Wesleyan Mission, to enable outstanding ministers to stay longer in a particular district, on the Baptist model. They built six big mission churches in the eastern boroughs, north and south of the river, and filled them all with large congregations which seemed to be predominantly working class. One of their greatest stars was Henry Meakin, minister of the Locksfields Chapel in Rodney Road, Southwark, in the 1890s, and of Methodist Great Central Hall on Star Corner (the junction of Long Lane and Bermondsey Street), near Bermondsey Leather Market, from 1898. Total attendance at Meakin's Central Hall in 1903 was just over 3,000, but nearly half of these were children. Meakin's success in difficult working-class districts was based on a range of crowd-pleasing methods. He gave lantern-slide lectures on the day's events, sent a brass band round the streets, used young men to 'buttonhole the stranger and invite him in', and young women to visit homes and deliver free meals. Arthur Baxter went to one of Meakin's services on Charles Booth's behalf in 1901, and described an event that was 'half concert, half religious meeting', in which Meakin 'attacked, assaulted and battered our feelings and emotions, appealing to our hopes and fears, especially our fears'. There were a few top hats, but 'the general impression was of solid working-class comfort: obtrusive poverty was of course almost absent', though just in front of him there was a collarless man and a woman 'with the dowdiest of shawls thrown on a threadbare dress'. Booth had his doubts about the religious effectiveness of these methods. 'Attendances, always a crude test, are more than usually so when lantern slides and attractive orchestral music are freely used as auxiliaries.'[5]

The Congregationalists' greatest preacher was probably Dr Joseph Parker, whose sermons, racy in style but teetotal and traditional in content, attracted congregations of about 3,000 in the 1880s and 1890s to the City Temple on Holborn Viaduct, the first church in the world to be lit by electricity. Clergymen came from all over London, and even from America, to study Parker's techniques. He claimed that his sermons were extemporized from a few notes, but Charles Booth doubted their spontaneity: 'the whole service is an exquisite performance . . . Of course it was not what he said, but the way he said it that as remarkable – and I can only repeat that he brings to the pulpit all the arts of the stage.'[6] Parker died in 1902, but his successor at the City Temple, Reginald Campbell, seems to have inherited his congregation. When church attendance was counted in 1903 the City Temple's 7,000 (over two services) was easily the biggest in London.

The man voted the greatest Anglican preacher in England by *British Weekly* readers in 1887, H. P. Liddon, who regularly attracted congregations of over 2,000 to his services in the nave of St Paul's Cathedral, where he was canon, also did so without making concessions to doctrinal or social modernity. For twenty years Liddon's sermons were 'a central fact of London life . . . All ranks and conditions of men were there.' They did not come to learn anything radical or new, but to hear their old beliefs powerfully expounded and confirmed. Henry Scott Holland, who wrote Liddon's entry in the *Dictionary of National Biography*, said that 'he bent himself in his sermons to exclude originality of idea; he spent himself in the effort simply to prove and to persuade. And to this effort everything in him contributed – his charm of feature, his exquisite intonation, his kindling eye, his quivering pose and gestures, his fiery sarcasm, his rich humour, his delicate knowledge of the heart, and his argumentative skill.' Good music was always an attraction, and at the end of the century the music in St Paul's was probably the finest in England.

Reaching Out to the Heathen

It is not clear whether these famous preachers drew new members into the churches, or simply attracted existing worshippers from other churches, where the services were duller. Masterman was convinced that, in South London at least, they did not increase the total number of worshippers, which was a fixed or diminishing figure. 'You may, by special effort of preaching, music or excitement, draw a large and active congregation; but you have done so by emptying the churches of your neighbours. The water is not increased in quantity, but merely decanted from bottle to bottle.' Actual harm might be done, he thought, by using 'the methods of the circus and the music-hall' to whip up interest in gigantic non-denominational services, like the one held at the Peckham Theatre during the *Daily News* census, which drew a crowd of 3,764. 'People who had attended humble churches and chapels, often miles away, were drawn to this new spiritual excitement. In many cases they never returned to their old membership, finding the old methods humdrum and unstimulating.'[7]

Charles Booth and his assistants, in their comprehensive survey of the state of religion in London between 1897 and 1902, visited many successful ministers with large congregations, but their overall impression was not optimistic. Over and again they spoke to clergymen who had been defeated by the impossibility of interesting the poor in the delights of Christian worship or in the eternal punishment that awaited the unrepentant sinner. In the inner districts of South London, which were being rapidly abandoned by the well off and even the artisan class as transport improvements made the outer suburbs more accessible, the position seemed almost hopeless, especially in Anglican churches. In Southwark 'a feeling of doubt and discouragement prevails'; in Bermondsey 'we hear of ingrained apathy and contentment, such as makes the despair of the missionary and the reformer, pervading life to the very end', and 'the people are ready to do anything they can for you – short of coming to church'. Working-class churchgoers were regarded by their neighbours as 'cadgers and beggars, and, by implication, hypocrites'. A new vicar in the costermonger quarter of Walworth, near the East Lane market, was despondent: 'On Sunday morning "crowds surge past"; the "fancy" market being at his very door; the church remains empty. The people are exceedingly accessible and friendly and exceptionally easy to gather into any social function, but on the spiritual side almost hopeless. The instinct of worship seems lost.' Vicars who had not given up the fight devoted much of their time to 'running things': organizing free breakfasts, umpiring cricket matches, presenting entertainments, running clubs, and supervising crèches and Sunday schools. In Booth's view, these social activities were successful 'almost exactly in the degree that they are not religious'. Churches and missions in London's poorest quarters gave out free breakfasts, suppers and cups of cocoa by the thousand, and looked after tens of thousands of children in Sunday schools while their parents read the papers or went back to bed, but it was not clear to the clergymen Booth spoke to that any of this brought true spiritual gains. Nevertheless, children were fed and educated, men gambled and played billiards in church halls, families were taken on trips, and the harsh experience of slum life was softened. As one vicar told Booth, he hated 'the whole system of bribery by treats, but yet wishes the women to have their outing, and hear the cuckoo again'.

The belief that Christians should not wait for the poor to come to church but should reach out to them through street-corner services and brass-band music had its advocates in most denominations by 1900, but its most famous and effective exponent in these years was the Salvation Army. The movement was founded as the Christian Mission by the Methodists William and Catherine Booth in Whitechapel in the 1860s, and took on its new name, along with the hierarchy, uniforms, and terminology of a military organization, between 1878 and 1882. By the early 1880s the Army had its familiar blue uniforms and Hallelujah bonnets, its tambourines and brass bands playing hymns and music-hall tunes, its newspaper, the *War Cry*, and its militant teetotalism, but it was still an evangelizing movement, without a social programme. A Salvation Army home for prostitutes opened in London in 1884, but the Army first came to public notice as a rescue organization in 1885, when William Booth's son, Bramwell, helped W. T. Stead to buy and look after Eliza Armstrong, the prize exhibit in the *Pall Mall Gazette*'s exposure of child prostitution, and went on trial for his part in the affair. The Army had been trying to win favour within the established Churches, but now it saw a new way forward, and relaunched itself as an organization that would work with those forgotten and rejected by almost everyone else – tramps, prostitutes, ex-prisoners, and the homeless. In 1890 William Booth's book, *In Darkest England and the Way Out*, which was written in collaboration with W. T. Stead, set out the Army's new agenda. Playing on the idea that urban England, especially London, was as savage, cruel, and impenetrable as the Darkest Africa recently described by the journalist and explorer Henry Morton Stanley, Booth presented his readers with a colourful and depressing account of life in the slums. Drawing on the conversations of Salvation Army officers with prostitutes, convicts, casual dock workers, and rough sleepers, William Booth presented a picture of outcast London that was reminiscent in its language of *The Bitter Cry* (also 'ghosted' by Stead), though its focus was on the streets and alcohol, not the houses and rents. William Booth's solution to the problem, expressed in an extraordinary pictorial map, was to establish 'colonies' in which urban drunkards, prostitutes, and paupers would be sheltered and reformed. With the terrifying troubles in Trafalgar Square still fresh in the public mind, there was a generous response to Booth's appeal for money, and the Army collected £100,000 for its great social mission. William Booth established shelters, food depots, and work stations in London and other cities, and a 3,000-acre farm colony for 300 people in Essex, and when Charles Booth's assistants visited these places they reported that they were well-run and useful institutions which made a modest contribution to the care of the 'submerged tenth', and even set a few on a path towards self-reliance.[8]

Though the Salvation Army was a worldwide organization, its chief recruiting ground and the main beneficiary of its social work was London. So visible – and audible – was the Salvation Army in London in the 1890s that its apparent failure as an evangelizing organization came as something of a surprise. Writing in 1902 Charles Booth (assisted by Ernest Aves) was sure that the Army had done its best, and failed. 'Of the genuineness and honesty of the attempt there can be no question. Moreover, the mark was hit. The Army has been entirely successful in bringing the Gospel of Salvation freshly and simply to the notice of all, especially to the notice of the classes standing aloof. This being so, it becomes the more remarkable that, as regards spreading the Gospel in London, in any broad measure, the movement has altogether failed.'[9]

The *Daily News* Census

Charles Booth's impression that this and many other Christian efforts to stop the spread of irreligion and indifference in working-class London had been unsuccessful was dramatically confirmed in 1903, when a Liberal newspaper, the *Daily News*, published the results of a comprehensive census of religious worship in Greater London. This was a far more thorough survey than those of 1851 and 1886, making it very difficult to compare attendances in the three years. The *Daily News* employed 400 enumerators and superintendents, mostly from a military or naval background, and organized a careful count of Sunday worshippers in every church, chapel, and mission (and Jews attending a synagogue at the beginning of Passover week) in Greater London. Care was taken to identify 'Twicers' – those who attended two Sunday services – and men, women, and children were counted separately. The count was spread over a year, usually at the rate of one borough each week, and covered the outer suburbs as well as the Inner London area counted by the *British Weekly*. In all, 2,688 places of worship in Inner London and 1,338 in Outer London were watched and counted. The results were published first in the *Daily News*, and then in much fuller form, with graphs, statistics, and analytical essays, in a book edited by the superintendent of the census, Richard Mudie-Smith.

The bad news for Christians was that the decline in churchgoing feared but apparently averted between 1851 and 1886 had come to pass between

1886 and 1903. The population of Inner London had risen from 4 million to over 4.5 million, but the number going to a place of worship had fallen from 1,167,312 to 832,051 (omitting Twicers). Even if those too young, old, ill, or busy to attend were excluded, this meant that almost two-thirds of London's potential churchgoers had decided not to bother. In the outer suburbs, there were 420,383 worshippers in a population of 1,770,032, and for London as a whole there were about 1,252,000 worshippers (excluding Twicers) in 1903 in a population of about 6,700,000. For one reason or another – age, illness, indifference, bad weather, work, shopping, holidays – four out of five Londoners did not go to church.[10] Comparing 1886 with 1903, the Nonconformists or Free Churches had done the best, almost holding the number of attendances steady, but the Anglicans had lost over a quarter of their worshippers.

When the statistics collected in 1902–3 were analysed borough by borough, and (even more revealingly) by individual neighbourhoods, it became clear that churchgoing was commonplace, though declining, in London's well-off suburbs, but confined to a small minority in poor districts. In the East End, out of a population of over 900,000, there were only about 117,000 regular worshippers, of whom 12,627 were Jews. As in the rest of London, women attended in greater numbers than men, and middle-class neighbourhoods had far more churchgoers than poorer districts, Nonconformists easily outnumbered Anglicans, and about a third of worshippers were (or looked) under fifteen. Only 23,000 non-Jewish men (aged over fifteen) went to church in East London, and most of these, it seemed, were clerks, shopkeepers, and skilled artisans. Working-class children in vast numbers were sent to Sunday schools, but once they were in a position to make their own decisions they abandoned places of worship, except for two traditional services, harvest festival and watchnight. Conformism and the desire to share the life and values of one's friends and neighbours might draw suburbanites to church or chapel, but in the London backstreets men found fellowship and approval in pubs and music halls, and those who opted for Christianity and its usual associate, teetotalism, often had to endure mockery or isolation in their own communities.

Charles Masterman, the future Liberal MP and Cabinet minister, produced a valuable study of the figures for inner South London, whose 1,750,000 population was a reasonable cross-section of London as a whole. In South London one man in six and one woman in five went to church on the census day, but attendance was nearly five times higher in the rich suburban district of South Dulwich and Forest Hill than in the poor and densely populated neighbourhood between Walworth Road and Old Kent Road. Masterman, who knew the district well, was sure that the 6.5 per cent of adults in Newington and Walworth who worshipped on a Sunday were nearly all drawn from the lower-middle-class residents of the main streets, shopkeepers, clerks, and craftsmen, not the struggling population of its backstreets. He drew these conclusions from the South London census:

> The working man does not come to church. A few small communities of Primitive Methodists, Baptists, Salvationists, and similar bodies, as a general rule represent his contribution to the religious life of the nation. The tradesmen and middle class of the poorer boroughs exhibit an active religious life, mainly gathered in the larger Nonconformist bodies, especially the Baptists. The residents in the suburbs crowd their churches and chapels, and support with impartiality and liberality all forms of organised religion.[11]

The indifference of the London poor to religion had not been overcome by the efforts of the many Christian missions that had established themselves in the London backstreets in the last twenty or thirty years. Masterman agreed with Charles Booth (whose seven-volume study of London's religious life was published in 1902–3) that the Christian mission system, in which well-off congregations paid for the erection of mission huts in slum streets, had been a dismal and deserved failure, attracting tiny and demoralized congregations into dilapidated tin halls to listen to ignorant and inarticulate ministers and sing breezy hymns to the accompaniment of cheap harmoniums. The inability of the Salvation Army to attract the poor to its indoor services, even by bribing them with soup and cocoa, was one of the most interesting findings of the *Daily News* survey. In East London, the Salvation Army's heartland, its attendances had doubled from 3,123 in 1886 to 6,376 in 1903, but both figures were extremely disappointing. About 450 of the 1903 worshippers were living in Salvation Army shelters (and therefore bound to attend), and over 3,000 went to two Salvation Army halls in Hackney, the richest part of East London. They might 'come to scoff', as General Booth used to say, but in Poplar, Stepney, Shoreditch, and Bethnal Green only 2,350 people (including Twicers) 'stayed to pray'. In the whole of Inner London there were about 22,000 attendances at Salvation Army services, but the Army did rather well in Outer London, giving it a total London attendance of nearly 40,000. Strangely, its mission to the suburbs was more successful than its mission to the slums. Masterman was impressed by the success of the Catholic Church in maintaining its working-class congregations, the adaptability of well-established Anglican parish churches in the face of the transformation of their middle-class parishes into working-class neighbourhoods, and the ability of eloquent Baptist and Congregationalist preachers to attract vast audiences to their halls and tabernacles. In the whole of inner South London, Masterman said, he had 'only seen the poor in bulk collected at two places of religious worship – Mr Meakin's great hall in Bermondsey, and St George's Roman Catholic cathedral at Southwark'.

The results of the *Daily News* census were not as bad as some Christians, including Masterman, had expected, and modern churches would be happy to have even half as many worshippers as those counted in 1903. But after decades of vigorous evangelical effort by the Salvation Army, the Anglican Church Army, the Evangelisation Society, the Open-Air Mission, the Baptist, Congregationalist, and Wesleyan preachers, and the Pleasant Sunday Afternoons movement ('Brief, Bright, Brotherly'), the sense of disappointment and failure was intense. The London working class seemed to be too big, too impermanent, too poor, and too preoccupied with work and survival to yield to Christian appeals. Most of the 'new' methods advocated by commentators on the 1903 census had already been tried, generally to little effect. 'The Churches are practically powerless to attract the outside masses . . . The immense battalions of non-churchgoers are before the eyes of Christians, and even at their church doors, degenerating into materialism on the one hand and paganism on the other.'[12]

Six years after the *Daily News* census Charles Masterman looked again at the state of religion in London, and found nothing to change his view that urban religious beliefs (but not moral values) were in steady decline, and that there was nothing the Churches could do about it:

> I think there can be no doubt that . . . present belief in religion . . .
> is slowly but steadily fading from the modern city race. Toleration,
> kindliness, sympathy, civilization continually improve. Affirmation of
> any responsibility, beyond that to self and humanity, continually
> declines . . . The Churches . . . labour on steadily amid a huge indif-
> ference. The very material of their appeal is vanishing.[13]

Of course, giving up churchgoing did not mean that working-class Londoners had become entirely secular and rationalistic in their beliefs. The mental world of most Londoners included the songs and stories picked up in Sunday school or morning assembly, along with an inherited set of superstitious beliefs and fears that were as likely to involve a rabbit's foot, a horseshoe, or a sprig of lucky heather as a Bible or a crucifix. The popularity of some church services, especially watchnight, was connected with the belief that they were 'lucky'. Men and women left the pubs just before midnight on New Year's Eve and took their fish and chips into the local church, but this was a matter of superstition, not Christian faith. A. W. Jephson, the vicar of St John, Walworth, told Booth's survey: 'At present the people come to church to this extent; for marriage, churchings and baptism, for the last night of the old year and for Harvest thanksgiving but all this is mainly from superstition; they do it to keep or change their luck.'[14]

So in the two decades after 1886, as far as we can judge, poorer Londoners moved decisively towards that rejection of religious beliefs and observances that has characterized the modern city. Despite the best efforts of Anglican clergymen, tabernacle preachers, and Salvationists, Londoners turned away from the church and towards the godless comforts of the public house, the football match, the street market, and the Sunday paper. Puzzlingly, for those Christians who believed that the natural savagery of poor was only kept in check by their belief in the Ten Commandments and the fear of damnation, public behaviour (measured by falling crime and illegitimacy rates) seemed to improve alongside the fall in churchgoing.

*

'THE SAFEST CAPITAL'

For most of the nineteenth century London had been regarded as a dangerous and crime-infested city, in which the Metropolitan Police, for all its professionalism, was barely holding the line against the forces of savagery and immorality. Crime statistics, for what they were worth, were high, and it was generally believed that a criminal class of thieves, swindlers, muggers, beggars, and prostitutes lived and thrived in the city, especially in those sordid and almost impenetrable districts known as 'rookeries'. London guides and travel books devoted long chapters to the tricks that 'sharp' Londoners played on 'flat' visitors, and Henry Mayhew and his associates, writing of London in the 1850s, devoted 500 large pages to describing London's vast and complex community of prostitutes, thieves, robbers, burglars, coiners, cheats, receivers, and beggars. This literary tradition survived in the later nineteenth century, and reached a much wider audience through the popular press in the 1880s and 1890s, but a growing body of informed opinion believed that it no longer reflected the realities of life in London.

Counting Crime

Criminal statistics, which were more complete and accurate after 1856, seemed to show that crime of almost every kind had fallen (in proportion to London's growing population) between the 1850s and 1880s, and that the wave of crime and disorder that had apparently threatened to overwhelm London in the 1830s and 1840s had somehow been beaten back. In the late 1860s about 22,000 felonies relating to property were reported to the police, representing just over 6 offences for every thousand Londoners. In 1884, after a substantial fall in the 1870s and a short-lived rise in 1880–3, the figure was 21,311, about 4 per thoudand Londoners. For the rest of the century the total number of reported property felonies only rose above the 1884 figure once (in 1888), and by the late 1890s there were only 2.5 felonies per thousand Londoners, a fall of 40 per cent since 1884 and 60 per cent since 1867.[1] David Jones' work on the Metropolitan Police Criminal Returns shows that the London figures for offences against the person, including murder, manslaughter, and common and indecent assault, showed similar reductions between the 1850s and 1880s.[2] Arrests for drunkenness and drunken and disorderly conduct, a very subjective category, reflecting changing police policies and public standards, have a more erratic pattern, varying from about 9 per thousand Londoners in the early 1850s to under 6 per thousand in the 1860s and over 7 in the late 1870s. Between 1884 and 1889 arrests were very low, under 5 per thousand, but in the late 1890s they rose again to over 8, reflecting a police drive against the drunkard rather than a true rise in heavy drinking.[3]

As a result of these impressive statistics there was a general mood of satisfaction among politicians and senior Metropolitan Police officers in the early 1880s. The Director of the Metropolitan Police Criminal Investigation Department, Howard Vincent, reported in 1882 that 'London . . . is the safest capital for life and property in the world', and *The Times*, speaking of the national figures for 1881, announced that 'property, at the present day, is safer than it has ever been against depredations of every sort'. Five years earlier L. O. Pike, the great authority on the history of crime, declared that despite London's 'lingering and flickering tradition' of the old sanctuaries and similar resorts, 'any man of average stature and strength may wander about on foot and alone, at any hour of the day or night, through the greatest of all cities and its suburbs, . . . and never have so much as a thought of danger thrust upon him, unless he goes out of his way to court it'. England's apparent triumph over crime was held up by American and European experts as a lesson to their own governments, and Edmund du Cane, England's leading prison administrator, told the readers of *Murray's Magazine* in 1887 that while Lord Liverpool had often changed his route through London in the 1820s to avoid robbers, Gladstone, the present Prime Minister, could travel with his wife in an open carriage from Westminster to Dollis Hill House, in Willesden, in perfect safety.[4]

The Mystery of Jack the Ripper

The crimes that are assumed to typify a particular time and place are very often not typical at all. Murder was rare and getting rarer in the 1880s and

1890s, and usually took place within the family. In the five years from 1883 to 1887 there had been sixty-two known murders in Greater London, and in nearly every case, except where the murderer committed suicide, the supposed culprit was caught and convicted. But nothing represents the London of the 1880s to modern readers more powerfully than the extraordinary Whitechapel murders, generally called the Jack the Ripper killings, of 1888. The discovery of the mutilated corpses of at least six Whitechapel prostitutes between August and November 1888, each one apparently killed by a man with a savage hatred of women, naturally aroused intense public interest. The murder of a prostitute was not very unusual. On 7 August, over three weeks before the first generally agreed 'Ripper' victim was murdered, the corpse of Martha Tabram (or Turner) was found in George Yard Buildings, near the Whitechapel High Street and Aldgate East Underground station, with multiple stab wounds. The murder was reported without great excitement. Prostitution was a risky trade, and Whitechapel was a dangerous place to pursue it. The discovery of the partly disembowelled and almost decapitated body of Mary Ann Nichols in Buck's Row (now Durward Street), an alley behind Whitechapel Station, early in the morning of 31 August, was another matter. *The Times* and the *Daily Telegraph* thought the two murders might be the work of a brutal protection racket, but the *Star* and the *Globe* decided that their readers would be more entertained by the idea that a maniac, a Mr Hyde 'who goes about killing for the mere sake of slaughter', was at work. Robert Louis Stevenson's *The Strange Case of Dr Jekyll and Mr Hyde* had been published in 1886, and this speculation brought fact and fiction excitingly together. On 8 September, just as this story was fading away, the discovery of the body of Annie Chapman, mutilated even more savagely then Nichols', in Hanbury Street, less than half a mile from the other two murders, brought it back to life. Now the newspapers were sure that a monster was on the loose, and that (in the words of a *Pall Mall Gazette* headline) there would be 'More to Follow'. The less squeamish papers gave lurid accounts of the nature of Annie Chapman's horrific injuries, and suggested that the killer might be a Marquis de Sade figure with a knowledge of anatomy, rather than the usual East End ruffian.[5] Material from the two inquests, along with mockery of the incompetence of Chief Commissioner Warren and the Metropolitan Police, and discussions of the danger that Whitechapel's moral decay might pose to London as a whole, kept the story going until 30 September, when two dead prostitutes, one (Elizabeth Stride) with her throat cut, the other (Catherine Eddowes, Kelly or

Conway) revoltingly mutilated, were discovered. The first was in a yard alongside Berner Street (now Henriques Street), off Commercial Road, and the second was in Mitre Square, near Aldgate, inside the City. The sensational impact of this double killing was intensified by the publication in early October of a letter and bloodstained card from a man claiming to be the killer, and signed 'Jack the Ripper'. In view of the fact that the district in which the murders took place had been heavily settled by Jewish immigrants over the previous few years, it is not surprising that the police and public hunt for the killer, who had been described as dark or foreign, should have concentrated on the Jewish population of Whitechapel. The racial element in the Ripper panic might have been even greater if a chalked message over a doorway in Goulston Street, where a piece of Catherine Eddowes' bloody apron was found, saying 'The Jewes [or Juwes] are not the men who will be blamed for nothing', had not been sponged off on the instructions of the Metropolitan Police Commissioner, Sir Charles Warren. News of the message soon got out, but Warren's aim, he said, was to avert an anti-Semitic outburst in the panic following the discovery of the two bodies. 'I do not hesitate myself to say that if that writing had been left there would have been an onslaught upon the Jews, property would have been wrecked, and lives would probably have been lost.'[6] Despite the intense public anxiety and the anti-Semitic rumours there was no major outbreak of mob violence against Jews in 1888, something that may tell us as much about Whitechapel society as the murders themselves.[7]

Over the following month a steady flow of letters from people claiming to be the killer, including one that contained a piece of kidney cut – the writer said – from the body of Catherine Eddowes, kept the story alive. Press criticism of the efforts of the police and of its disappointingly un-Holmesian commissioner became more intense, and speculation about the killer's identity continued, with a ritualistic Jew, a mad doctor, and an unhinged aristocrat among the favoured candidates. Stead of the *Pall Mall Gazette* had been attacking the Metropolitan Police for its incompetence and corruption since its mishandling of the Trafalgar Square riots of February 1886, and now decided that Warren, the new chief commissioner, was as bad as his predecessor. On 9 November the body of Mary Jane Kelly, appallingly mutilated, was found in her room in Miller's Court, a squalid lodging house at the back of 26 Dorset Street (later Duval Street), between Spitalfields Market and Whites Row. At twenty-four or twenty-five, Kelly was about twenty years younger than the other victims, and had been a West End prostitute with well-off customers. This was the murder that led Warren to resign and prompted Queen Victoria to urge Lord Salisbury to reform the detective force and install gaslights in dark alleys. It was also the last of the Whitechapel murders, though two middle-aged prostitutes murdered in Whitechapel in June and September 1889 were represented as Ripper victims in some newspapers.

Because the murderer was never caught, speculation about his identity and motives has continued ever since, with the finger still pointing at obscure East European immigrants and deranged aristocrats, doctors and men-about-town, as it did from the start. The urge to pin the crimes on someone famous has led various writers to name Lewis Carroll, the Prince of Wales' idiotic son the Duke of Clarence ('Prince Eddy'), the homeless poet Francis Thompson, the Queen's physician Sir William Gull (in a fanciful Freemasons' plot), and the painter Walter Sickert as the Whitechapel murderer. The latest of these celebrity theories, Patricia Cornwell's *Portrait of a Killer. Jack the Ripper: Case Closed*, which revives the case against Sickert, is as unconvincing as any of its predecessors.[8]

It is very probable that this serial killer, like most of his kind, was an otherwise obscure person, with little to distinguish him from his five million fellow-Londoners except his urge to kill. In his note on the murders in February 1894, Sir Melville Mcnaghten, later the head of the CID, proposed three chief suspects: the failed barrister Montague Druitt, who drowned himself in December 1888, and two Polish Jews with 'homicidal tendencies', Dr Michael Ostrog and Aaron Kosminski (though Mcnaghten only used the latter's surname). Ostrog, an insane thief who was released from prison in March 1888 and sent back to prison on 18 November 1888 and to an asylum in 1891, is a plausible candidate. We might add to this list Severin Klosowski (George Chapman), a Polish immigrant with surgical experience who lived in Whitechapel and was hanged in 1903 for poisoning his three wives; Jacob Levy, a Whitechapel butcher who died in a lunatic asylum in 1891; Joseph Barnett, Mary Kelly's lover; and Francis Tumblety, an American quack doctor who came to Whitechapel in June or July 1888, fell under police suspicion, and fled to avoid prosecution on indecency charges in late November 1888.

The Decline of Crime

No doubt those who declared in the early 1880s that the Metropolitan Police had conquered urban crime would have chosen their words more carefully at the end of the decade, after the scares of the Trafalgar Square riots and the unsolved murders in Whitechapel, but the underlying statistical trends would have justified their optimism, nevertheless. Reported felonies involving property, by far the largest category of serious crime, rose a little in 1888, perhaps because the police were diverted from their London-wide duties by the troubles in the West End and Whitechapel, but fell by 30 per cent between 1883 and 1893. In 1893 the method of recording crime statistics was altered, making comparisons before and after that date uncertain, but statistics between 1893 and 1913 show a very clear fall in almost all categories. Among reported indictable offences (serious crimes that would be tried before a jury), burglary and housebreaking declined by 20 per cent, robberies fell by two-thirds, aggravated and minor larcenies (by far the largest category) were almost halved, and murders fell from 9 per million to 7. Edwardian Londoners who died by deliberate violence were ten times more likely to have committed suicide (as over 500 did every year) than to have been murdered. Burglary (housebreaking by night), which did not fall as fast as other crimes, and actually increased by 10 per cent between 1893 and 1903, was seen as a professional crime which benefited from some of the changes that were taking place in London society. The Metropolitan Police Commissioner's report for 1908 blamed the rising figures on burglary insurance, which made householders more careless, ornamental leaded glass, which made it easier to open doors, and 'rapid and cheap transit by Tube and motor bus, which enables a professional housebreaker to live an orderly life in one part of London, and commit his offences in another, where he is quite unknown'. The police believed that a few hundred skilled criminals, never using violence, were responsible for the great majority of the 2,000 or so burglaries and housebreakings that were reported in London each year.[9] The only indictable crimes that became more common in London between 1893 and 1913 were fraud, false pretences, receiving stolen goods, and 'unnatural offences'. There were always new victims ready to fall for old tricks, but London fraudsters also invented new swindles to meet changing business conditions. For example the 'long firm', first named in 1868, involved using credit or false references to obtain goods without payment, and then selling them quickly and disappearing with the money. Among non-indictable offences (cases heard before magistrates) the more serious crimes, including assault, malicious damage, and unlawful possession, fell by 54 per cent, suggesting the development of a society in which disputes were settled with words rather than blows. The less serious offences, including betting, drunkenness, soliciting, begging, and infringements of the Education Acts, most of which reflected the efforts of legislators and the police to enforce a broader moral code, rose by a quarter, mainly because arrests for drunkenness increased by two-thirds, and highway offences, uncommon in 1893, were on their way to becoming (by 1923) the most common offence of all.[10]

Unless Londoners had become much less willing to report crimes to the police, or the efficiency of the Metropolitan Police in law enforcement and record-keeping had seriously declined (neither of which appears to have happened), London was a much safer and more orderly city in 1913 than it had been in 1883, and a very much safer one than it been in the 1850s. The mid-century criminal class that (if Victorian novelists and social observers are to be believed) had spent its days in low pubs and flash-houses (brothels) and its nights robbing, swindling, or enticing honest citizens, was a feeble remnant by the 1880s and 1890s. Its chief recruiting agents had been ignorance, poverty, and parental neglect, not real-life Fagins, and rising living standards and compulsory education had been cutting off its sources of supply since the 1870s. Charles Booth's study of the East End, London's criminal heartland, in the 1880s concluded that about 11,000 of the 909,000 inhabitants belonged to Class A, 'the lowest class of occasional labourers, loafers and semi-criminals'. These people were economic and social failures, Booth said, but not, in general, professional or habitual criminals. 'Their life is the life of savages, with vicissitudes of extreme hardship and occasional excess. Their food is of the coarsest description, and their only luxury is drink . . . these are the worst class of corner men who hang round the doors of public-houses, the young men who spring forward on any chance to earn a copper, the ready materials for disorder when occasion serves.' The streets in which these wretched people lived were not safe places for respectable Londoners to walk in, but the inhabitants did not threaten London as a whole. 'The hordes of barbarians of whom we have heard, who, issuing from their slums, will one day overwhelm modern civilization, do not exist. They are barbarians, but they are a handful, a small and decreasing percentage: a disgrace but not a danger.'[11]

Booth's poverty maps show us the last enclaves of this vanishing species, mean and narrow streets marked in black. In East London in 1889 there were about a dozen patches of black, often grouped round a road that was notorious for squalor and vice – Old Nichol Street and Mount Street in Shoreditch, Great Pearl Street, Flower and Dean Street, Thrawl

Street and Dorset Street in Whitechapel, and London Street in Ratcliffe. South of London Bridge, there was a rookery around Marshalsea Road and Mint Street, one of the old sanctuaries, another in Tabard Street and its side alleys (now Tabard Garden Estate), and several bad streets around St George's Circus. In central London, where the most feared rookeries had been situated in the 1840s, there were still some dangerous streets and alleys in the late 1880s. Between Drury Lane and Lincoln's Inn Fields, Parker Street and Macklin Street were best avoided, and across High Holborn, Eagle Street was almost as bad. The Colonnade, a few yards from wealthy Russell Square, the alleys off Cromer Street, near King's Cross station, the streets between Barnsbury Road and Copenhagen Street (now the Barnsbury Estate), and several streets between Lisson Grove and Edgware Road, just south of St John's Wood, were isolated northern outposts of this semi-criminal world. Booth walked most of these streets again in 1897 and 1898, in the company of a local policeman. Many of them, including the Cromer Street alleys and the Colonnade, had been cleared and rebuilt since 1889, but others retained their old character. Tabard Street was still 'much used by prostitutes and shady people generally', and Macklin Street, still black, was occupied by 'market porters, shoeblacks, costers', and the like. In the Cromer Street area London School Board schools and rebuilding had brought great improvement but in a little court called Bryan Vale the old way of life was still hanging on. It was 'a great place for Sunday gambling. Very difficult of approach for the police as they always have "cocks" and "crows" posted for the alarm. Police always come in plain clothes, as working men, pretending to be drunk, etc.' Campbell Road, which later gained notoriety as North London's worst street, had already slipped into criminality by December 1897, when Booth visited it with Inspector Ogball. 'Thieves in the common lodging houses at 4d a night, and prostitutes generally two together in a single furnished room, which they rent at 4/6 and 5/-. They are the lowest class of prostitute whose business is done in the back streets.' There was a Congregational mission nearby, but, said Inspector Ogball, 'they don't touch Campbell Road at all'.[12]

Charles Booth knew better than almost anyone that each of the poorest parts of London bred its own distinctive social problems. In Bermondsey, in streets smelling of jam, glue, and leather, heavy drinking, and therefore violence, was the main concern. 'At night', he was told, 'they are hanging about the streets, or going about in hooligan gangs.' Bermondsey, Booth explained, 'has not the Whitechapel Jew, the Hoxton burglar, or the Notting Dale tramp, nor is it, like parts of Fulham, a receptacle and dumping

ground for the rejected from other quarters. It has not even the Spitalfields
dosser in full force. It is neither vicious nor criminal in any marked degree;
it is simply low; but for debased poverty aggravated by drink this portion
of Southwark and Bermondsey falls below any other part of London.' To
observe 'brutality within the circle of family life' the social explorer could
have done no better (or worse) than visit the old Nichol Street neighbourhood (Arthur Morrison's 'Jago') before its demolition for LCC flats in the
early 1890s. But for real professional crime, Booth said, the specialist
neighbourhood was Hoxton, 'the leading criminal quarter of London, and
indeed of all England'.

> Of professional thieves, there are two distinct kinds: those who live
> day to day by the more casual kind of depredations, and those who
> lie low while making elaborate plans for some great haul. The latter
> may maintain a life of apparent respectability, pursuing ostensibly
> some regular calling, and they bring to bear upon their operations
> much forethought and some skill. They perhaps have had the train-
> ing of a carpenter, a blacksmith, or a locksmith. They live the life of
> the lower middle class. The number of first-class burglars is said to
> be very small; with most, daring takes the place of skill . . . The rela-
> tions of these men with the police are curious, regulated by certain
> rules of the game . . . Violence is a breach of these rules, or perhaps
> the result of their breach by the other party, but if 'fairly' taken no
> ill-will is borne. These men are generally known to the police, and
> so are the receivers into whose hands they play. Gold or silver stolen
> anywhere in London comes, it is said, at once to this quarter, and is
> promptly consigned to the melting pot. Jewellery is broken up,
> watches are 'rechristened'. The 'fences' . . . are of all grades and serve
> every sort of thief; and in Hoxton thieves of every kind seem to be
> represented.[13]

Drunkards and Gamblers

The battle between policemen and gamblers in Bryan Vale, off Cromer
Street, was typical of the social or moral policing that Metropolitan Police
officers, sometimes against their better judgement, had to undertake in late
Victorian London. Of the almost 117,000 people (one Londoner in fifty-
five) apprehended by the Metropolitan Police in 1898, only 14,774 were
arrested for what the police returns called 'criminal offences' (mostly prop-

erty crimes), and only 3,234 were committed for a jury trial. Over 54,000 were apprehended for drunkenness and drunk and disorderly conduct, and the rest were accused of 'divers other offences', mainly disorderly prostitution, assault, not sending their children to school, betting, begging, and cruelty to animals.[14] In this great campaign to 'civilise' London, the police were the often unwilling agents of politicians who did not understand the practical difficulties of imposing middle-class values on a vast working-class population. Police action against particular offences rose and fell in response to particular pressures, incidents, and legal judgements. Pressure from purity campaigners kept the number of arrests for prostitution offences high in the 1880s, at about 6,000 a year, until the embarrassing arrest of an innocent dressmaker, Elizabeth Cass, in Regent Street in June 1887 forced the chief commissioner to issue new guidelines to his officers, which cut the number of arrests by about 40 per cent. So 1888, the year in which prostitutes were most likely to be murdered, was also the year in which they were least likely to be arrested. Arrests increased again in the late 1890s, but never reached 5,000 in any year between 1888 and 1914. Arrests for drunkenness were at a much higher level, and involved a greater police intrusion into working-class life. Under pressure from the temperance movement, and especially from its political representatives in the Liberal Party and the Progressives on the LCC, the Metropolitan Police increased its annual haul of drunkards from about 25,000 in the 1880s to 30,000 in the early 1890s, about 50,000 between 1900 and 1910 and over 70,000 in 1913 and 1914.[15]

Gambling, which some moralists identified as a vice which was as damaging to the national spirit as prostitution or drinking, was particularly difficult to police without appearing to punish in one class what was condoned in another. Almost every popular newspaper printed horse-racing news, including the odds on which illegal street bookmakers and their customers made their bets, and in 1900 London had over twenty papers devoted entirely to sport. Popular newspapers ran competitions to attract new readers, most of which were effectively lotteries. Was filling in a missing word in a *Pearson's Weekly* competition, or guessing the monthly number of births and deaths in London for the *Rocket* magazine, anything more than a game of chance? The courts decided that the first was an illegal lottery in 1893, but that the second was not in 1898. The Prince of Wales was a gambler and racehorse-owner, and those with the time and money to go to the races could place bets legally, except between 1897 and 1899, when race tracks came briefly under the terms of the 1874

Betting Houses Act. But under the terms of the Licensing Act of 1872, the Betting Houses Acts of 1853 and 1874, the Metropolitan Streets Act of 1867, and the Vagrancy Act of 1873, the police were bound to try to suppress betting in London. The police made some effort to close some fashionable West End gaming clubs, especially when the evangelical Robert Anderson was the head of the CID in the 1890s. A few were raided and prosecuted, notably the Field Club of St James's in 1889, but club owners soon amended their rules to conform to the letter of the law. The suppression of cheaper betting houses in 1872 had driven working-class gamblers onto the streets, where policemen tried to catch them at it by turning up in disguise. Bookmakers employed scouts to watch out for plainclothes policemen, and even to track them from the police station. 'We could disguise ourselves in any way we like [but] they would know us,' a constable told a Royal Commission in 1908. West Ham and the LCC passed by-laws in 1896 and 1898 to make it easier to get convictions, and the Street Betting Act of 1906 allowed the police to arrest a person loitering for the purpose of betting or paying or receiving winnings. This act increased the number of arrests in London by about a quarter, but most bookmakers found new ways of getting round the law, by using coded betting slips and well-guarded alleyways, employing shopkeepers as agents, or, probably most effective of all, bribing policemen. So the outcome of this moral crusade was a more demoralized, corrupt, and unpopular police force, a more professional body of bookmakers, and probably no great change in the amount of illegal betting going on in London's backstreets.[16]

The great majority of those convicted of minor offences were fined, but even in 1910 nearly 1,000 London drunkards, 1,700 misbehaving paupers, 630 prostitutes, and 4,000 beggars and rough sleepers were sent to jail. In general the period from the 1890s to 1914 was one in which the worst excesses of the mid-Victorian penal system, long prison sentences with solitary confinement and labour on the hand-crank and treadwheel, were replaced by a system that was more responsive to the needs of individual offenders, emphasized education and reform, and relied increasingly on non-custodial treatment, especially for children. Thanks especially to the 1907 Probation of Offenders Act and the introduction of Borstals in 1908 the number of people in England and Wales sent to prison each year fell from 200,000 in 1905 to 57,000 in 1914. Most of London's oldest and most primitive prisons had been closed and demolished in the 1870s and 1880s, especially following the abolition of imprisonment for debt (except non-payment of fines, rates, or maintenance) in 1869. Tothill Fields Bridewell was pulled down in 1885, and Coldbath Fields (or Clerkenwell) House of Detention in 1889. Millbank, the gigantic penitentiary opened in 1821, was closed in 1890 and dismantled to make room for the Tate Gallery, which occupies about a quarter of its vast site. Newgate Prison, the last survivor of London's medieval prison system (though it had been rebuilt in 1780), was demolished in 1902, making way for an enlarged Central Criminal Court, the Old Bailey. London was left with five local prisons, all built in the nineteenth century, and mostly reflecting in their designs the cellular system favoured in the 1840s and 1850s. In 1910 Brixton (1820), Pentonville (1842), Wandsworth (1851), Holloway (1852), and Wormwood Scrubs (1874–90) had a total capacity, at one prisoner per cell, of 5,600, and an annual intake, mostly of men and women on remand or serving short sentences, of about 60,000.[17]

Even in its improved condition London was, as Edward Troup of the Home Office wrote in 1888, 'the centre of crime and vice, not for its own area alone but for the whole country', and the rate of recorded indictable crime was about 25 per cent higher in the capital than in England and Wales as a whole. Comparisons are imprecise because each English police force recorded crime in its own special way. In London property reported stolen was often entered in a 'Suspected Stolen Book', rather than being recorded as a crime known to the police. When this system was abolished in 1932 recorded property crime in London almost doubled, taking it well above the national average.[18] London's higher crime rate may also reflect the fact that it was more than twice as heavily policed as the rest of England, making it more difficult for wrongdoers to escape attention or arrest. In 1886, 42 per cent of the policemen in England and Wales (14,696 of 35,015) were in the Metropolitan Police, watching over 18 per cent of the country's population.[19]

Hooligans

Although London was a far more law-abiding and controlled city in the 1890s than in the 1850s or 1860s, and the 'criminal classes' had far more to fear from the forces of law and order than 'respectable' Londoners had from crime, public interest in London's criminal underworld was as intense as ever. Several writers, in a tradition that stretched back via Dickens and Henry Fielding to Geoffrey Chaucer, took their readers into London's murky and exciting underworld of scuttlers, cracksmen, smash-and-grab raiders, impostors, and fences. Some of these writers created an entirely fictional world of cerebral detectives and criminal masterminds. Although Arthur Conan Doyle's great detective, Sherlock Holmes, was contacted at 221B Baker Street by many gullible readers, his cases bore no relation to the real world of London crime, and his great opponent, Professor Moriarty, was no more typical of the London lawbreaker than Raffles, the 'amateur cracksman' and cricket star (the creation of Doyle's brother-in-law E. W. Hornung), or Flambeau, who was hunted in one implausible story after another by G. K. Chesterton's priestly detective, Father Brown. Clarence Rook, who claimed to be an expert on London's juvenile street gangs, came closer to the real London underworld with his stories of fights and petty theft. Rook's 1899 book, *The Hooligan Nights*, popularized a word which had started appearing in police court reports in London newspapers in the summer of 1898. It is possible that the word 'hooligan' was drawn from a comic music-hall song about an Irish family, but it was applied to street ruffians, especially in gangs, regardless of their ancestry, and immediately produced a set of derivative verbs, nouns, and adjectives. The *Pall Mall Gazette* reported in January 1899 that 'the proprietor of Lord Tennyson (in wax) says that it was a certain young man, who, with others . . . when called upon to desist, Hooliganed about and threw the late Laureate's head at him'.[20] In a city of six or seven million there was no need to invent stories, only to select them. To some commentators incidents like these were examples not of the age-old roughness and rebellion of adolescent boys, but of a worrying new disorder, a symptom of urban physical and moral degeneration.

A new word did not imply a new phenomenon, and the gangs of ragged, unemployed, underfed, and undersized youths described by Rook, gambling, fighting, stealing, and larking about, might have existed at any time in the previous century. In 1901 Rook took the readers of *Living London* on a tour of 'Hooligan London', from the Elephant and Castle, through Lambeth and Chelsea to Notting Hill, along the Euston Road to Pentonville, Bethnal Green, and the Commercial Road, and south to the Old Kent Road, Walworth, and the Borough, to introduce them to the breed in its natural habitat. He described a fight between the Borough and Pentonville gangs, with belts, buckles, iron bars, knives, and even cheap pistols, and explained how youthful lawlessness could turn into real crime. 'From cracking heads for love to bashing "toffs" for gain is a short step', and the sandbag, an American import, was a cheap and effective alternative to the bludgeon or the pistol. For recreation, hooligans took their girls to cheap music halls, and watched or joined back-alley boxing contests which might, for the best of them, be a stepping stone towards a fight in the Whitechapel Road Wonderland, or even the National Sporting Club. Rook's piece was illustrated with frightening sketches of old men in evening dress being attacked by thugs, and a more reassuring photograph of four glum little urchins in oversized jackets and pudding-shaped cloth caps.[21]

Charles Booth heard many stories of these juvenile gangs from vicars and schoolteachers in his research for his series on the religious life of London, first published in 1902. Talking of Hoxton, he said that 'one of the most notorious developments of juvenile crime has been that of bands of boys, called after this or that street and making themselves the terror of the neighbourhood. It is said that the bus and tram car "cock horse" boys, and those who hang around to share their work, provide some of the worst examples. Of these gangs and their fierce quarrels among themselves, turning on the favour of the girls who consort with them, we have heard strange accounts. One of our informants, a schoolmaster, speaks of the terror exercised by the leaders of these boys over their followers. Sitting safe at home the follower hears the whistle and turns pale, but obeys the summons.' The streets were quiet when Booth visited them, but he attributed this to a recent fight in a 'belt and pistol gang' in nearby Haggerston, in which a girl was killed and heavy sentences imposed.[22]

Those who wanted to see criminal London had to walk the streets by night, as most of London's policemen did. Robert Machray, a novelist and *Daily Mail* journalist, wrote a lively and well-informed account of *The Night Side of London* in 1902, at about the time that Charles Booth's great enterprise reached its conclusion. Like Wordsworth, Machray thought that London was at its best in the dead of night, especially between two and four o'clock, when 'there is a lull, a quiet, a hush, a vast enfolding, mysterious awe-inspiring silence'. After four 'the city begins to awake, and the great silence, which has wrapped it round like a garment, is gone – swiftly swallowed up in the roar of the streets, growing and swelling even as the day and its business grows and swells'. In these dark hours the streets of central London were given over to vagrants, young and old, sleeping on benches and in doorways, prostitutes, cabbies, night workers, and policemen. Most of these people were to be found hanging around coffee stalls, of which there were many dozens on the streets of central London, competing for business with whelk counters and hot-potato carts. Watching a typical coffee stall in New Oxford Street for a few minutes, Machray saw two young prostitutes, a group of five young men, two cabbies, four workmen, two drunken couples, and two young ruffians eating cake and hard-boiled eggs. These, Machray knew, were 'Hooligans . . . a curse, and a pest, and an altogether damnable feature of London life at the present time'. A policeman was watching the group from across the road. In Euston Road, Whitechapel, and the Borough the scene was almost the same, 'the stall, its lamp shining on a group of figures standing about its counter, and, not far away, a watchful policeman'. Perhaps Machray's description was a composite based on many visits, but his account of the dangers lurking around coffee stalls was not fanciful. John Burns, MP for Battersea, drew attention to coffee-stall lawlessness in a letter to the *Daily Chronicle* in 1901. Over the previous year a young man had been stabbed at one in Waterloo Road, a policeman and an old woman killed in separate brawls, a porter's head cut open in a fight, and a labourer assaulted and slashed across the throat by two women.[23]

Anarchists

Most of the work of the Metropolitan Police was mundane stuff, controlling traditional wrongdoing by the well-established method of walking the streets in uniform, especially at night. A small detective force had been created in 1842, and disbanded in 1877 after a major corruption scandal involving collusion with horse-racing fraudsters. A reorganized and renamed detective force, the Criminal Investigation Department, was created in 1878, with 240 men. The main duty of the detective force was to gather information on London's habitual criminals, using informers, visits to prisons and criminal districts, and the study of police records. By 1886 there were 32,000 habitual criminals (not all London-based) on the Metropolitan Police registers, and under some sort of police supervision. A long-standing objection to plain-clothes detectives was the possibility that they might be used to spy on the government's political opponents and undermine individual liberty, as they were on the Continent. Ever since the collapse of Chartism in 1848 there had been general agreement that the British political system was safe from the threats from socialists, anarchists, and republicans that troubled less stable regimes in Europe, and London had become a haven for radical refugees from more repressive governments in France, Russia, Austria, Italy, Germany, and elsewhere. Despite the requests of foreign governments, these people were never extradited for trial abroad, and rarely watched or arrested. When the London police wished to know the intentions of Karl Marx, one of Europe's leading revolutionary theorists and propagandists, and a Londoner from 1849 until his death in 1883, they wrote him a letter. The closest Marx got to being arrested was when he got drunk with two fellow German exiles and started smashing street lamps in Tottenham Court Road. London welcomed the Paris Communards (including Gustave Brocher and Louise Michel, the 'Red Virgin') after 1871, German Social Democrats (including Johann Most and Sebastian Trunk) after Bismarck outlawed them in 1878, and Russian socialists and anarchists, including Aron Lieberman, Varlaam Cherkezov, and the leading philosopher of anarchism, Prince Kropotkin, who lived in London from 1876 to 1917. The expulsion and flight of Jews after the Tsar's assassination in 1881 added to the gathering of revolutionaries in London. Even when there was a spate of attempted and actual political assassinations in Europe and America in 1878–81 (in which Tsar Alexander II and President Garfield died, both in 1881), the relaxed British attitude towards radical exiles persisted, though with some reservations. The prosecution and imprisonment in 1881 of the German anarchist Johann Most, whose London newspaper, *Freiheit*, had celebrated the assassination of Tsar Alexander, was an unusual concession to foreign pressure. The thirty revolutionaries and anarchists who gathered in London (in a pub near the Euston Road) for an international congress in July 1881 could do so without fear of arrest or expulsion. Life was so quiet that some anarchists preferred to go where the authorities and the public took an interest in what they were doing. As Kropotkin put it in 1882, 'Better a French prison than this grave'.[24]

The change of mood came from a different quarter. In January 1881 American-based Irish Republicans known as Fenians exploded a bomb in Salford, killing a boy. There were minor explosions in Chester and Liverpool, and on 16 March a bomb outside the Lord Mayor of London's residence, the Mansion House, was defused by a policeman. These incidents were fairly harmless compared with the Fenian explosion at Clerkenwell jail in December 1867, which had killed twelve people. But on 15 March 1883 a more dangerous campaign began, with bombs outside the *Times*' offices and in Whitehall. At this point the Home Secretary, William Harcourt, set up a thirteen-man Irish Bureau within the Metropolitan Police, to gather intelligence on Fenian activity, and keep a watch, either openly or in disguise, on suspected terrorists. This little force, the

future Special Branch, doubled in size over the next year, and its efforts
were supported (or possibly undermined) by the work of a shadowy group
of spies or agents under the command of Edward Jenkinson, who had been
involved in anti-terrorist work in Ireland. Undeterred, the Fenians switched
to mass civilian targets, planting bombs in the underground tunnels at
Westminster Bridge Station and Praed Street on 30 October 1883, injuring seventy passengers. Between February 1884 and January 1885, Fenian
targets in London included Victoria, Charing Cross, Paddington, and
Ludgate Hill railway stations, the Junior Carlton Club, Scotland Yard,
Nelson's Column, London Bridge, and the Underground at Gower Street.
Some of these bombs were defused, some did minor damage, and the one
on London Bridge killed three bombers. On 24 January 1885 the Fenians
staged their most impressive attacks, exploding bombs in the Tower of
London, Westminster Hall, and the Chamber of the House of Commons.
These attacks introduced a more repressive tone into the press and political debate on terrorism, but hardly anyone suggested the expulsion of
European refugees who advocated violence, or the outlawing of socialist
or anarchist groups. The press took comfort from the fact that the only
terrorists active in England were Fenians, and that their efforts had produced neither panic nor significant damage. 'They have not killed a
creature, blocked a railway, destroyed a building, or in any way checked
for a moment the even flow of English life', said the *Pall Mall Gazette*,
tempting fate.[25]

It was much easier for terrorists to cause mayhem in the 1880s than
it had been twenty years earlier, thanks to the work of the Swedish indus-
trialist Alfred Nobel in the development of stable high explosives.
Nitroglycerine, a liquid explosive discovered in 1846, was much more
powerful than gunpowder, but too volatile for the average bomb-planter
to use. In the 1860s Nobel found that three parts of nitroglycerine mixed
with one part of kieselguhr, charcoal, or some other inert and absorbent
substance – a mixture he called dynamite – could be handled easily, and
was safe until detonated.

Fenianism was quiet in London for the next two years, but an apparent plot to plant bombs to disrupt Victoria's Jubilee service in June 1887,
which the Special Branch and other police secret agents foiled, seemed to
justify keeping this 'spying' network in existence, although it went against
the principles of open deterrent policing established at the time of
Sir Robert Peel. When there were no Fenians to watch, the Special
Branch kept an eye on Russian nihilists and European revolutionaries and

anarchists. It seems that these police agents were not interested in home-grown socialists, and left the policing of the unemployed riots of 1886 and 1887 to uniformed men. The London public and press seem to have had an ambivalent attitude towards undercover policing. They were desperate for the police to find Jack the Ripper, and when Sherlock Holmes put on a sailor's disguise in *The Sign of Four* (the story written by Conan Doyle after his meeting with Oscar Wilde and Joseph Stoddart) his many readers were happy enough, but policemen in false moustaches seemed underhand and un-English, except (perhaps) when they were watching foreigners.[26]

In the later 1880s and the 1890s, when anarchists who advocated 'propaganda by the deed' committed acts of violence all over Europe, London offered a refuge, and was generally not the target of terrorist activity. The frequency of terrorist outrages in France, Spain, Italy, and the USA in the 1890s generally provoked complacency, rather than anxiety, in England. Some of the foreign anarchists living in London were inoffensive – even admirable – intellectuals like Prince Kropotkin, the Italian Errico Malatesta, or the German Rudolph Rocker, who spent years doing social work in East End Jewish sweatshops. They were believers in a society without state-imposed laws, not in acts of terror directed against politicians or people sitting in cafes, theatres, and railway carriages. Others were dangerous in Paris, Madrid, or Chicago, but harmless in London. Sergei Kravchinski, the Russian revolutionary who stabbed the chief of the Tsarist secret police to death in 1878, lived and wrote peacefully in London, calling himself Stepniak, from 1885 until 1895, when he died violently, but non-politically, on a level crossing near his home in Bedford Park. Perhaps G. K. Chesterton had Stepniak in mind when he made Bedford Park ('Saffron Park') a hotbed of anarchism in his 1908 satire on plotters and policemen, *The Man Who Was Thursday*. Louise Michel, a heroine of the Paris Commune, spent some of her exile in London from 1881 to 1895 running a school for the children of political refugees, as well as speaking at anarchist meetings in Soho or Trafalgar Square. It was not a crime to be an anarchist in England, and London was home to several anarchist journals and clubs, watched but not molested by the Metropolitan Police. The Autonomie Club produced a German paper, *Die Autonomie*, and held its meetings, dances, and concerts in Charlotte Street, near Fitzroy Square. One of the members of the club in the early 1890s, Emile Henry, had left a bomb in Paris which killed five policemen and a secretary in 1892, and was arrested for throwing a bomb in a Paris cafe in 1894.

Freedom, the most important and long-lived anarchist journal published in London, was produced in the late 1880s by Kropotkin, the Italian Severio Merlino, and the wealthy Fabian anarchist (an unusual hybrid) Charlotte Wilson, whose money kept it going. Dante Gabriel Rossetti's nieces published a revolutionary journal, *The Torch*, in the early 1890s, from various addresses in North London. They had a special affinity with Italian anarchists, and gave shelter to about twenty Italian refugees in their printing works in Ossulton Street (near St Pancras Station) in 1895.[27]

Foreign anarchists and revolutionaries resident in London did not want to alienate their protectors by organizing violent incidents in England, even while they were endorsing the use of direct action in other parts of Europe, and sometimes providing the explosives. The one true anarchist bombing incident in London in the 1890s, in which a young French tailor, Martial Bourdin, blew himself up with his own device in Greenwich Park in February 1894, is well known to us from Joseph Conrad's 1907 novel, *The Secret Agent.* Conrad presented the explosion as part of the Russian Embassy's attempt to discredit revolutionaries, rather than an anarchist act, but it is unlikely that he had evidence that this was the case. Bourdin was a member of the Autonomie Club, and had a room in Fitzroy Street and a tailor's shop in Soho. He left Soho on the afternoon of 15 February with a bomb in his overcoat pocket and took a tram to Greenwich. The police knew he was up to something, but lost track of him and put a watch on likely targets, which included railway stations, but not Greenwich Observatory. Bourdin's inquest found that his bomb had exploded in his left hand about forty-five yards from the Observatory, causing such grave injuries that he was dead within thirty minutes. Why he chose this unlikely target, and under whose instructions he was acting, have never been discovered.[28] After this the authorities took a more serious view of anarchist activity. In April 1894 a French anarchist, Théodule Meunier, was arrested and extradited for throwing bombs in French cafes, and two Clerkenwell-based Italians were given very long sentences for making bombs which they intended, it was said, to throw into the Stock Exchange. At the end of June 1894, a week after the fatal stabbing of President Carnot of France, two English anarchists, including the printer of *Freedom*, were sentenced to six months with hard labour for inciting violence against the royal family at the opening of Tower Bridge.[29]

There was a further influx of anarchist refugees in the later 1890s, because of increased repression in France, Italy, and Spain, and a succession of dramatic assassinations in Europe and America between 1898 and

1901, in which the Empress of Austria, the King of Italy, and the President of the USA were killed. In London anarchists were relatively inactive, depressed perhaps by the final split between anarchism and socialism in 1896, and by a growing popular hostility to their movement. In 1904 the Metropolitan Police Commissioner reported that anarchism in London was 'practically quiescent', and anarchist journals struggled for inspiration and funds.[30] Prince Kropotkin, living in respectable Bromley, spent some of his last years in London writing articles for the 11th edition of the *Encyclopædia Britannica*, including a piece on anarchism that did not mention its use of violence. The two best-known Edwardian novels on anarchism, *The Secret Agent* and *The Man Who Was Thursday*, made light of the anarchist threat, focusing instead on the way it had been exaggerated and exploited by its opponents.

In January 1909, as if to prove them wrong, two Latvian 'anarchist' refugees, Paul Hefeld and Jacob Lepidus, staged an armed raid on a car carrying the wages for Schnurrman's rubber factory on Tottenham High Road, at the corner of Chesnut Road, near the local police station. When they were confronted by the police the robbers decided to shoot their way out, killing a boy and PC Tyler. There followed an anarchic 'Keystone Cops' chase across Tottenham marshes, in which the killers used an electric tram, a milk cart, and a grocer's horse and cart with its brake on, and the police chased them for six miles in an advertising cart (until the Latvians shot the pony dead), on bicycles, and in a second tram going in reverse. Using their pistols without restraint, the two men fired over 400 rounds, injuring twenty-seven people, including seven policemen. Finally the two were cornered, and used the last of their ammunition to shoot themselves. Lepidus was found dead and Hefeld died three weeks later, without explaining whether 'property is theft', or simply theft, was the motivation for the 'Tottenham outrages'.[31]

It is possible that the Tottenham raid was intended to raise money for a political cause, but it is just as likely that it was a robbery pure and simple. There were many refugees from the Russian Empire in London, and their numbers had increased following the failure of the revolt against Tsarist rule in 1905. East Londoners, especially Jewish tradesmen, were said to be plagued by gangs of protection-racketeers and extortionists from Bessarabia, Odessa, and elsewhere, who were often in brutal competition for the same pickings. Occasionally these gangland crimes came to court. Several Bessarabians received long sentences for killing an Odessan rival in 1902, and in March 1911 a gang fight took place outside Worship Street magistrates' court. The most dramatic incident involving East European criminals or anarchists began on 10 December 1910, when local people reported hearing hammering and drilling coming from an empty house next door to a jeweller's shop in Houndsditch (number 119). When PC Bentley went into the house he was shot dead, and in the battle that followed three more constables were killed and one of the Latvians was fatally wounded by his companions' bullets. The other three Latvians escaped, dropping off the dying man, Gardstein, in the house of Rosa, a friendly anarchist. On 2 January 1911 the police were tipped off that two of the other three men were hiding in 100 Sidney Street, between Whitechapel Road and Stepney Way. Early the next morning the police surrounded the house, and called in the Scots Guards when the trapped men started shooting. The Latvians barricaded their windows, and the young Home Secretary, Winston Churchill, who always enjoyed front-line activity, turned up to supervise the siege and satisfy his curiosity. At about 1 p.m. the house started burning, ignited by either the Latvians or their besiegers. Later, two burned bodies were found, and identified as Fritz Svaas and Joseph Marx, two of the three Houndsditch killers. The third man, and the supposed ringleader of the gang, Peter Piatkov or 'Peter the Painter', was never found, and thus joined Jack the Ripper as one of London's undiscovered killers. The other alleged members of the gang were tried, but acquitted after a botched prosecution. Another murder, perhaps unrelated to the activities of the Latvian gang, took place on 1 January 1911, when the battered body of an immigrant slum landlord, Louis Beron, was found on Clapham Common. A mark that looked something like the letter S was scratched on Beron's forehead, perhaps suggesting that he had been killed as a Russian government spy. Steinie Morrison, an ex-convict who worked in a baker's shop in Lavender Hill, was tried and convicted (rather unconvincingly) of the murder, and imprisoned for life.[32]

Chesterton might make fun of the fear of anarchist plots, but the Tottenham and Houndsditch killings, the mysterious Clapham Common murder, and the assassination of the Secretary of State for India's aide de camp by an Indian nationalist at the Imperial Institute in July 1909 all suggested that London's immunity from extreme political violence was coming to an end. In addition, there was a growing belief in police and government circles that the Germans might have agents in London, trying to stir up trouble among trades unionists and aliens. Responding to (or taking advantage of) this threat, the Liberal government created a Secret

Service Bureau (later known as MI5), set up an interdepartmental committee to plan a response to civil disorder in London in the event of war (both in 1909), and increased the level of Special Branch surveillance on aliens, strikers, and socialists.[33]

*

CHAPTER TWENTY-ONE

A City of Showmen

For most of its history, London had been a centre of leisure and consumption, a place where wealth was spent as well as created. The twelfth-century writer William Fitzstephen, in the first substantial description of social life in London, devoted nearly half of his text to the sports and pleasures of the city. The almost insatiable appetite of Londoners for books, newspapers, clothes, luxuries, exotic foods, and entertainments had played an important part in the rise of printing and publishing, the commercial theatre, the modern novel, colonial trade, industrial production, and the growth of modern retailing. In the later nineteenth century London's vast and increasingly prosperous population consumed more luxuries and diversions than ever, and the city became the centre of a mass entertainment industry on a completely new scale. Its huge and affluent middle class joined the leisured elite in theatres, opera houses, department stores, and tennis clubs, and a substantial proportion of its immense working class at last found that they had time and money to spend somewhere other than the pub and the street market. As always, there were entertainers and entrepreneurs ready and able to sell Londoners the goods and services they wanted, exploiting every available technological and commercial device to create and satisfy their demand for pleasure and instruction. William Caxton, Ben Jonson, James Burbage, Daniel Defoe, William Almack, Madame Tussaud, and Charles Knight had their late Victorian and Edwardian successors in George Newnes, Richard D'Oyly Carte, Henry Wood, Imré Kiralfy, H. G. Wells, Oswald Stoll, Gordon Selfridge, Alfred Harmsworth, George Edwardes, and Robert Paul. Thanks to the combined efforts of customers and providers, there was probably no city in the late nineteenth-century world that offered its rich, middling, and poor citizens a greater variety of ways to spend their time and money.

Entertainment for Free

Londoners' entertainment started on the streets. The concentration of population in its inner districts, the density of its traffic, the vigour of its commercial life, created the wealth of incident and activity that made a walk down one of London's busy streets an experience to savour. For Henry James, who arrived and settled in London in the 1870s, the Strand still had the bustle and variety that had excited Samuel Johnson and Charles Lamb: 'It appeared to me to present phenomena, and to contain objects of every kind, of an inexhaustible interest.' For the aimless saunterer or flâneur (a word first introduced into English in the 1870s), London presented an abundance of distractions. Horse-drawn transport offered several possibilities for amusement. Crowds gathered round fallen horses, or offered advice to carters or cab-drivers whose horse was refusing to go on. Street fights, fires, burst water mains, escaped pets, weddings, and funerals always drew a crowd, and watching a heavy safe being hoisted from a wagon to the upstairs window of a shop or office, with exciting possibilities of broken ropes and unplanned impacts, was an irresistible attraction. Alexander Paterson, an Oxford graduate who spent several years living and working in Bermondsey, teaching and running boys' clubs, described these street pleasures in *Across the Bridges*, a study of South London first published in 1911. 'There is a great genius for watching among all Londoners . . . a fire engine, an arrest in the street, an epileptic in a fit, the short quick appearance of friends at the police-court, are scenes in melodrama not a bit less moving than the sensations pumped up for sixpence at a theatre . . . A group of boys leaning against the wall, or over the counter of some ice-cream shop, will discuss league football or county cricket from nine o'clock till midnight.'[1]

After the accidental entertainers there were those whose intention was to amuse: street musicians, singers, dancers, and performers of all kinds. Londoners were diverted by street actors or Pierrots, Irish, Scottish, and one-legged dancers, men with performing monkeys, bears, birds, or rats, and people who could swallow fire, swords, pebbles, nails, broken glass, and almost anything else. These swallowers usually drew a crowd by setting their chosen diet on a table and aroused their onlookers' interest and generosity by repeating a standard piece of jocular patter before passing round a hat. Some street musicians were simply beggars in disguise, singers, tin-whistlers, and fiddlers who were paid from pity rather than admiration. But there were real professionals on the streets, too: one-man-bandsmen, cornettists, accordionists, German bands, harpists, and singers with decent voices. Several music-hall stars, including Gus Elen, Harry Champion, and Jenny Hill, claimed to have started as street singers. Then there were players of mechanical instruments, of which London had great variety. True hurdy-gurdy men were rare, because the archaic instrument, which was a sort of violin operated by turning a handle and pressing keys, had been supplanted by mechanical street pianos and organs, in which a revolving barrel with pins activated the hammers or opened the pipes. An innovation of the 1890s, the punched-paper roll or card to replace the barrel, allowed street piano and organ players to produce a greater variety of tunes, with no skill except the ability to turn a handle at a steady pace. These mechanical piano and organ grinders, many of whom were Italian, generally hired their instruments by the day from one of several companies that kept them in good repair and supplied the latest music-hall tunes. Before the spread of the phonograph, which was invented and developed by Thomas Edison in the 1870s and 1880s, these mechanical instruments were one of the main ways in which new songs were made familiar to the London public.[2]

Patriotic Diversions

Beyond these everyday diversions, there were special public events for Londoners to enjoy. The most popular officially provided spectacles, public hangings, had been abolished in 1868 (the Irish Fenian Michael Barrett was the last to die in public), but others still survived. Royal excursions, state or civic ceremonies, royal levees and receptions, visits from foreign statesmen, Old Bailey trials, military processions, and marching bands all contributed to the passing show. Londoners loved a parade, and turned out in force to watch Buffalo Bill Cody and his cowboys riding through the West End to Earls Court in 1887, or Fred Karno's comedy troupe driving through South London to Epsom on Derby Day 1895. Taking their lead from these showmen, late Victorian governments decided to move some royal ceremonies from the private to the public sphere, using the street parade to revive affection for the monarchy and to stimulate public interest in imperial adventures. The climax of Victoria's Golden Jubilee in 1887, with which Disraeli hoped to restore the reputation of a gloomy and reclu-

sive royal widow, was a spectacular street procession from Buckingham
Palace to Westminster Abbey and back again on 21 June, with three European kings, crown princes by the dozen, including the heir to the German
Empire, all the colonial prime ministers, and Victoria's children and grand-
children riding behind her open landau. Indian cavalry accompanied the
Queen Empress's carriage, and soldiers strung out behind it so that the
whole procession, according to Mark Twain, 'stretched to the limit of sight
in both directions'. 'Everything was done – even to the appropriation of a
Parisian popular tune for street and barrel-organ use – to make people
think of the Jubilee and nothing else. Shops placarded it, villages feasted
it, errand boys whistled it,' wrote the London editor of the *Manchester
Guardian*. Although many in the vast watching crowd were injured in the
crush, the event was judged a huge success, a newly discovered instrument
of imperial and royal propaganda. As a permanent memorial to the Jubilee
the government established the Imperial Institute in South Kensington,
using a subscription from all parts of the Empire and the profits from the
very successful Colonial and Indian Exhibition of 1886. The Imperial
Institute was a huge exhibition building in the Italian Renaissance style,
with galleries intended to explain and illustrate the economic benefits of
the Empire. It was opened in 1893 with another grandiose royal parade,
and demolished to make way for the expansion of Imperial College in
1963. Only its impressive 280 foot Collcutt (or Queen's) Tower remains.

The Diamond Jubilee of 1897 was even more imperial than its predecessor, with more emphasis placed on the eleven colonial prime ministers
than on European rulers, and the imperialist Joseph Chamberlain setting
the tone. It was a tourist attraction, too, with souvenir maps, programmes,
crockery, and books for sale on every street corner. 'London is simply
packed and double-packed', reported Rudyard Kipling, who was back in
town after four years in America. 'There are stands and seats everywhere;
and like the embassies the police are praying for the day to be over without accidents. Estimates say between eight and ten million people will
attend. There are an extra 80,000 Americans in town; and Cook the tourist
man has practically chartered all the suburbs of Richmond for their accommodation.'[3] Kipling escaped to Rottingdean to write his Diamond Jubilee
poem, 'Recessional', which created a sensation when *The Times* published
it in July. The destination of the procession this time was St Paul's, and the
ageing Queen stayed in her carriage during the thanksgiving service on
the west steps of the Cathedral. Great crowds had walked the Queen's decorated route through London in the days before the ceremony, though

there was not quite such a rush for early places as there had been in 1887. After the service Victoria's carriage crossed London Bridge and went through Southwark and Lambeth to Westminster Bridge, Whitehall, and the Palace. 'No one ever, I believe, has met with such an ovation as was given to me, passing through those 6 miles of streets', the Queen recorded. 'The cheering was quite deafening & every face seemed to be filled with real joy. I was much moved and gratified.' For those who saw it, the Jubilee procession was an unforgettable experience. It was one of the first events that Harold Macmillan, the future Prime Minister, remembered: 'We watched it from Mr Bain's bookshop in the Haymarket. I remember, too, being taken to see the lights in the evening. My father carried me most of the way – down Piccadilly and St James's Street – and somehow home. I was only a few months over three years old, but I recall it vividly.'[4] Those who wanted to relive the Jubilee could see it on film in their local music hall, or flick through the pages of their souvenir 'flicker book', to make a little film of their own. The permanent memorial of the Diamond Jubilee was the Prince of Wales' Hospital Fund for London (later the King's Fund), which aimed to re-endow the main London voluntary hospitals with £100,000 a year, drawn from public and City donations. Nothing stimulated generosity as much as royal patronage, and soon the Fund was the biggest contributor to London's hospitals, easily outstripping the Metropolitan Saturday and Sunday Funds and the League of Mercy.

The London crowd did not fill the streets only when the authorities called upon them to do so. There was intense public interest in London in the progress of the war against the Boer settlers in South Africa in 1899–1902, and especially in the besieged towns of Ladysmith and Mafeking, the second of which was defended for seven months by the heroic and irrepressible Colonel Robert Baden-Powell. Huge crowds gathered spontaneously when sailors who had served in Ladysmith arrived in London, and on the evening of 18 May 1900, when news came that Mafeking had been relieved, an immense crowd, out of all proportion to the military significance of the event, filled the streets of central London, from the Royal Exchange to Fleet Street, along the Strand and into Trafalgar Square, Pall Mall, Regent Street, Piccadilly, and Oxford Circus. Young Harold Macmillan's nanny, who had been with him in Hyde Park when the crowd started to gather, hurried him quickly home to Cadogan Place, and Llewellyn Woodward (the future historian), whose father kept him on the omnibus, all the way from West Hampstead to the Elephant and Castle, to avoid stepping out into the riotous crowd, was left with a permanent

distrust of mobs. 'For a long time I used to listen in my bed at night thinking that I might hear the rush and roar of a mob up the hill from Finchley
Road station.' Theatre and music-hall shows were interrupted by the happy
announcement and the National Anthem, and drunken and patriotic men
took cabs to wake up the suburbs with the news. The frenzy – known
afterwards as mafficking – lasted for several days, and then interest in the
event, and in the war itself, subsided. Thoughtful commentators were surprised and disturbed by the Mafeking demonstrations. Working men in
caps might be expected to forget themselves and to react with emotion,
even hysteria, to good or bad news, but men in bowler hats and straw
boaters (the predominant headgear in the crowd) ought to know better.[5]

For the radical Liberal Charles Masterman, who edited and introduced
a book of essays, *The Heart of Empire*, in the autumn of 1901, mafficking
was yet another sign of the mental, spiritual, and physical degeneration
brought about by the growth of great cities. Britain, he told his readers,
was 'face to face with a phenomenon unique in the world's history':

> Turbulent rioting over our military successes, Hooliganism, and a cer-
> tain temper of fickle excitability has revealed to observers during the
> past few months that a new race, hitherto unreckoned and of incal-
> culable action, is entering the sphere of practical importance – the
> 'City type' of the coming years; the 'street-bred' people of the twen-
> tieth century; the 'new generation knocking at our doors.'
>   . . . The England of the future is an England packed tightly in
> such giant aggregations of population as the world has never before
> seen. The change has been largely concealed by the perpetual swarm
> of immigrants from the surrounding districts, which has permeated
> the whole of . . . London with a healthy, energetic population reared
> amidst the fresh air and quieting influences of the life of the fields.
> But in the past twenty-five years a force has been operating in the
> raw material of which the city is composed . . . The second genera-
> tion of the immigrants has been reared in the courts and crowded
> ways of the great metropolis, with cramped physical accessories, hot,
> fretful life, and long hours of sedentary or unhealthy toil . . . The
> result is the production of a characteristic *physical* type of town-
> dweller: stunted, narrow-chested, easily wearied; yet voluble,
> excitable, with little ballast, stamina, or endurance – seeking stimulus
> in drink, in betting, in any unaccustomed conflicts at home or abroad.

The old evils of urban life – crime, ignorance, slums, and sweatshops –
were destined in time to pass away, Masterman said, but new problems had

arisen in their stead. Elementary education and urbanization had created a population hungry for sensational newspaper stories but ignorant of religion and the spiritual world.[6]

Although the Mafeking celebrations suggested that the government's efforts to arouse public interest in the Empire and the monarchy had been a little too successful, the policy was not abandoned. The Queen died in January 1901, and her funeral procession through London to Paddington Station was as grand and well attended as the two Jubilees. The German Emperor, four kings, and the heirs to six European thrones rode behind the gun carriage that carried the dead Queen and the Crown Jewels. Harold Macmillan, nearly seven now, remembered the 'vast blackness of it all – black clothes, black ties, black crepe; the slow march of the soldiers; the muffled bands; King Edward VII; the Kaiser'.

King Edward was far happier at the centre of royal ceremonial than his mother had been. He revived the state opening of Parliament, riding down Whitehall in his gilded glass coach, and made London a royal capital again. Victoria's homes had been Osborne and Balmoral, and the Jubilees had been important just because she had virtually abandoned the capital, and royal ceremonies were so rare. Edward, as Prince and King, maintained a proper distance between himself and the public, but he humanized the monarchy by openly enjoying the pursuits of a London man about town, living his life of race-going, card-playing, dining, dancing, and play-going in the public eye. By his example he helped to lift the dead weight of 'respectability' from the shoulders of those who took their moral code from the top, and in his social circle he broke down the barriers between landed and City wealth. The King lived in London from December to February, and again for the London Season in May and June, and levees, courts, Privy Council meetings, and daily changing of the guard ceremonies started to mean something again. Londoners who enjoyed a royal occasion saw far more of them under Edward than under Victoria, starting with his aborted coronation in June 1902 (abandoned because he was ill), an unparalleled gathering of crowned heads, Indian princes, and colonial troops. To wander in the London royal parks and see Malays, Hausas, Fijians, Chinese, and British regulars camped out in row after row of tents, with their guns and horses nearby, like an Earls Court show in real life, was one of the great pleasures of the year. The delayed coronation took place in August, and for the next eight years Edward continued to give Londoners good value until his final appearance, in a non-speaking role, on the traditional black-draped gun carriage on 9 May

1910. 'Everyone in London, rich and poor, felt King Edward's death as a personal loss', Compton Mackenzie remembered. 'The death of Queen Victoria had awed London, but there was no feeling of grief like that roused by the death of the son she had always resented.'[7]

London's main shortcoming as an imperial and royal capital, it was widely agreed, was its lack of a magnificent processional route like the Champs-Elysées. The Adam brothers' Portland Place and John Nash's Regent Street, which inspired Baron Haussmann in his much-admired restructuring of Paris in the 1850s and 1860s, were grand enough, but they led to Oxford Circus and London Zoo, not St Paul's or the Houses of Parliament. London, the capital city of a far greater empire than that ruled by Paris, Berlin, or St Petersburg, was too cluttered, too devoted to the everyday business of making money, to provide an appropriate stage for the theatrical displays of imperialism. In 1901 a committee was set up to plan a fitting memorial for the dead queen, and decided that what London needed was a grander, more imperial road from Buckingham Palace to Trafalgar Square and Whitehall, fit for a coronation or state opening of Parliament. Aston Webb, the architect of the Victoria and Albert Museum, was chosen to widen the Mall, to reface Buckingham Palace in a fittingly dignified style, and to build at the other end of the Mall a noble archway, Admiralty Arch, through which royal coaches could pass into Trafalgar Square and Whitehall. At the western end of the Mall, in front of the Palace, would be the Victoria Memorial, Thomas Brock's statue of the late Queen surrounded by smaller sculptures symbolizing the qualities of British colonial rule: motherhood, truth, justice, peace, progress, prosperity, courage, and so on. Most of this was achieved by 1911, in time for George V to ride in his golden state carriage along the newly widened Mall and under Admiralty Arch on his way to Westminster Abbey and his coronation.[8] Webb's refronting of the Palace was finished by 1913, and before long the Victoria Memorial had developed from an imperial showpiece into a precarious grandstand for people wanting a better view of the changing of the guard.

Fairs and Freaks

Until the early nineteenth century Londoners of all classes had found amusement at the traditional annual fairs that took place all over the city, but few of these were left by the 1880s. At least eight London fairs were suppressed in the 1820s, and others, notably the Camberwell, Greenwich, Stepney, and Bartholomew Fairs, were closed down by police and magistrates in the 1850s. Several suburban fairs, including Blackheath, Charlton, Harrow, Fairlop (Barkingside), and Harlow Bush, were closed in the 1870s, and by the 1880s there were only a few survivors on the outer fringes of London, where their agricultural connections helped to preserve them. Fortunately for fairgoers, the Liberal Home Secretary from 1880 to 1885, Sir William Harcourt, had a tolerant and aristocratic approach to popular amusements, and ruled that fairs should be protected where they relieved the tedium of working-class life without threatening public order. The Metropolitan Police, which had good relations with the commercial showmen who increasingly ran these fairs, shared the Home Office's pragmatic approach. The eight-hundred-year-old Barnet Fair, a favourite with costermongers from North and East London, came under sustained attack in 1888, but it was an important commercial event in this cattle- and horse-trading town, and the Metropolitan Police sided with the local interests that petitioned for its survival. The local police superintendent, apparently not sharing the public-order anxieties that followed the Trafalgar Square riots of 1886 and 1887, reported that the fair, which attracted about 20,000 London and country folk per day in early September, offered harmless pleasure to the poor and benefited the local economy. In 1894 the local Metropolitan Police superintendent played a similar part in saving the Pinner Fair, which was looked forward to, he said, 'by several hundred of the poorer classes living in and around Pinner, as their only holiday in the year'. Fairs at Croydon (specializing in walnuts), Chertsey (famous for black cherries, geese, and onions), and Mitcham also survived into the twentieth century, and until the present day.[9]

The surviving fairs offered an interesting combination of traditional and modern entertainments. As well as the sale of animals and farm produce, there were boxing booths, menageries, sideshows exhibiting people of unusual size or appearance, or deformed animals, living or (more often) dead. Perhaps the most famous attraction in the 1880s was Joseph Merrick, the unfortunate 'Elephant Man', whose face, deformed by monstrous growths, was his fortune. In November 1884, soon after the start of his career as a professional 'freak', Merrick was brought to London by a showman, Tom Norman, and exhibited in the Bell and Mackerel public house, and in a house in Whitechapel Road (now number 259). He was seen by two doctors who worked with Frederick Treves of the nearby London Hospital, and Treves negotiated to show him before the London Pathological Society. In 1886, after various misadventures, Merrick was given sanctuary in two rooms in the London Hospital under Treves' protection, and lived there as a minor social and medical celebrity until his death, aged twenty-eight, in 1890. Tom Norman continued his successful career as a travelling showman, managing less troublesome clients, including John Chambers the Armless Carpenter, Mary Anne Bevan the World's Ugliest Woman, and Leonine the Lion-faced Lady. The well-equipped fair might also have a waxwork show, and a collection of exotic or wild animals, perhaps Bostock and Wombwell's travelling menagerie or one of its rivals. Showmen were quick to use new technology to add to the excitement and novelty of their attractions. Steam-driven merry-go-rounds were common in late nineteenth-century fairs, and before the Great War some fairgrounds had electric scenic railways. The greatest innovation, though, was the travelling cinema or bioscope. The great showman Randall Williams incorporated a bioscope into his ghost show at the Islington World's Fair in December 1896, only a few months after the first London cinema show in the West End. Other showmen, including Alf Ball and Billy Biddall, had travelling film shows in London fairs, complete with giant cinema organs, but most of these died out in the years before the Great War, because of competition from permanent cinemas, some of which were owned by fairground showmen.[10]

An Age of Exhibitions

While seasonal outdoor fairs were in decline, permanent showgrounds and halls, presenting traditional entertainments or prestigious exhibitions, were on the increase. Joseph Paxton's Crystal Palace, which had been moved from Hyde Park to high ground in Sydenham a few years after the Great Exhibition of 1851, was probably London's most popular exhibition and concert hall. As well as a menagerie, theatre, amusement park, fountains, firework displays, and grounds in which huge prehistoric beasts (in painted stone) hid in the bushes, the Crystal Palace had a concert hall with London's only permanent orchestra. The Crystal Palace orchestra was created in the 1850s by George Grove (later the author of the famous *Dictionary of Music and Musicians*), and its Saturday afternoon winter concerts, conducted from 1855 to 1901 by the German August Manns, were a highlight of London's musical scene. On the other side of London there was Crystal Palace's less impressive commercial rival, Alexandra Palace,

which was rebuilt in 1875 after a fire. Alexandra Palace had its most successful season in 1888, when the American balloonist 'Professor' Thomas
Baldwin demonstrated parachute jumps from a tethered balloon, and hopeful crowds waited in vain for the parachute (and consequently its
passenger) to disintegrate, as Robert Cocking's had in 1837. After this the
palace became less profitable, and it was eventually converted into a public
trust, with free entry except on a few special days.

Islington's Royal Agricultural Hall, built in the 1860s, was the main
venue for horse, dog, and dairy shows, and staged the Royal Military Tournament, which began in 1880 as the Grand Military Tournament and
Assault of Arms (complete with a competition to 'cleave the Turk's head')
in 1880. 'Lord' George Sanger, Victorian Britain's most famous showman,
used the Agricultural Hall as one of the winter homes for his circus, which
spent the rest of the year travelling in Britain and Europe. Sanger's main
London performances were in Astley's Amphitheatre on the Westminster
Bridge Road (just over the bridge), the home of London circus since the
1790s. Sanger's circuses were not the animal-free shows we see today, but
full-blown spectaculars teeming with wild beasts. His pantomime in
Astley's in the winter of 1884–5, *Gulliver's Travels*, used seven hundred
men, women, and children, thirteen elephants, nine camels, fifty-two
horses, and an assortment of lions, ostriches, kangaroos, pelicans, deer, and
buffaloes, and his show depicting the death of General Gordon at Khar-
toum involved a hundred camels, two hundred Arab horses, and three
hundred Grenadier and Scots Guardsmen. The rumour that his Siberian
wolves had run wild and killed a performing mare thrilled Londoners in
February 1888. Sanger sold his amphitheatre for demolition in 1893, but
continued to tour until 1905, when his seventy-year career came to an
end.[11]

Sanger had rivals in West London. There was a large exhibition ground
in South Kensington between Exhibition Road and Queens Gate (behind
the Natural History Museum), where the Royal Horticultural Society had
its gardens until 1882. Every year from 1883 to 1886 there was an exhibition on the site, attempting to combine education, entertainment, and
profit. The International Fisheries Exhibition of 1883 was followed by
exhibitions on Health, Inventions, and India and the Colonies, the last
before the dilapidated buildings were demolished. When the South Kensington site was redeveloped in 1886, two new West London showgrounds
opened. A huge new National Agricultural Hall, known as Olympia, was
built on the site of the Vineyard Nursery on the Hammersmith Road, in

1884. The hall, 'brilliantly illuminated with Electric light', held 9,000 spectators. Its first great show, at the end of 1886, was staged by the Paris Hippodrome Circus, and involved four hundred animals, horse and chariot races, a mock stag hunt, performing elephants, Olympic races, and a pantomime. In short it was, according to its advertisements, 'devoid of one single element of vulgarity'. In 1890, catering for the latest London craze, Olympia's owners spent £6,000 on a maple-floored roller-skating rink. Olympia was outdone, though, by a new showground laid out 'with magical quickness' in 1887 on a twenty-three-acre triangle of waste railway land between three railway lines, and known as Earls Court. Unlike Olympia, which was on a branch line, Earls Court was served by three Underground lines and three stations. The site was first laid out for a great American Exhibition, which included twelve acres of ornamental pleasure gardens and music pavilions, a diorama of New York harbour, switchback and roller-toboggan rides, and an art gallery. Its centrepiece was Buffalo Bill Cody's Wild West Show, 'an exact reproduction of daily scenes of frontier life', including buffalo hunts, a rodeo, an Indian attack on the Deadwood stage and a brave rescue by Cody and his Rough Riders, an Indian war dance, the sharpshooting of Annie Oakley, and re-enactments of famous incidents in the conquest of the American West. The *Illustrated London News*, which gave this and other exhibitions continual publicity, reported that that Wild West Show had room for 40,000 spectators, and that the gardens were lit by 250 electric lights and 9 spotlights, the equivalent of half a million candles. This was one of the events of the London season, and received visits from Gladstone, the Prince of Wales, and Queen Victoria, in her Golden Jubilee year.[12]

There was an element of imperial propaganda in these late Victorian and Edwardian shows, and Londoners were no doubt fascinated to see in the flesh representatives of the peoples whose lands had been absorbed into Britain's Asian and African empires. But these spectacular shows were popular all over Europe, Australia, and the United States, from Melbourne, Chicago, and St Louis to Brussels, Berlin, and Budapest, and their themes were as often historical, commercial, technological, or national as they were imperial.[13] The dominant theme in the large national fairs and exhibitions was commerce, technology, modernization, and the propagation and popularization of new products and ideas, rather than imperial expansion. In the process of informing consumers of new inventions and persuading them to buy them, the London exhibitions played a significant part. The 1884 International Health Exhibition, for instance, set out the

ways in which old London would be transformed in the decades to come
by new technology, especially electric power. Life in an old London street
was contrasted with model shops and houses, and new products and
brands (Pears, Schweppes, and so on) were promoted. The 1885 Inventions Exhibition pursued the same theme, and so did the various national
exhibitions (representing in turn Italy, Spain, France, and Germany) held
at Earls Court between 1888 and 1891, and the Anglo-French Exhibition
of 1908. The 1887 American Exhibition, which is remembered for Buffalo Bill, was mainly a showcase for American products, including
industrial and agricultural machinery, canned food, and watches and
clocks, and its purpose was to stimulate trade and investment. Olympia ran
a string of modernizing exhibitions in the early twentieth century. There
had been poorly attended motor shows at Crystal Palace in 1903 and
1904, but the first large Motor Show, attracting hundreds of thousands of
visitors, was held at Olympia in 1905 (organized by Kiralfy and the RAC)
and annually thereafter. The 1907 Building Trades Exhibition, the first of
Olympia's many trade shows, promoted new housing styles and domestic
fittings to the building profession, and the Daily Mail Ideal Home Exhibition, beginning in 1908, taught middle-class householders what to look
for in a new house, by presenting rooms furnished by the best London
stores and decorated by its leading designers. The exhibition was not
wholeheartedly committed to modernism (its first 'ideal home' was a
thatched cottage), but its intention was to introduce consumers to the
advantages of labour-saving devices, the electric kitchen, and everything
(as the *Daily Mail* put it) that would improve 'the comfort, convenience,
entertainment, health and well being of home life'.

The main aim of West London exhibitors was to sell goods and make
money, and of the customers to enjoy themselves. For the price of a bus
or train journey to Earls Court and a shilling or two entry fee city-bound
Londoners could fancy, for an afternoon, that they were in Venice, Peking,
or the Kasbah, enjoying a combination of spectacle, shopping, and self-
improvement as tourists do today. Successful London shows ran for months
in the winter and spring, and attracted hundreds of thousands of ordinary
Londoners, as well as the fashionable set. 'Parties to Olympia are the latest
distractions in society', the *Illustrated London News* told its readers in October 1887. Roughs might be rioting in Trafalgar Square, but in Olympia,
where the electric lighting was bright and the atmosphere warm and comfortable, 'order and discipline prevail everywhere'. In the real world defeat
was a possibility (the death of General Gordon in the Sudan in January

1886 was a dramatic recent example) but in the West London arenas the cavalry always arrived on time and the French Zouaves fought off the Arab hordes every night.

Men who could produce successful and long-running shows were in demand in all the great Western cities. Hippolyte Houcke, who filled Olympia with French acrobats and wild animals in 1886 and with Moors, Zouaves, Whirling Dervishes, and dancing girls in 1887, was one such star, and John Robinson Whitley, who organized the first five seasons at Earls Court, was another. The greatest showman of them all, Phineas T. Barnum (1810–91), brought his famous Barnum and Bailey Circus to Olympia in December 1888, and again in the two following seasons, establishing a Christmas circus tradition that lasted until the 1960s. A popular feature of the Barnum show that opened in Olympia in November 1889 was *Nero, or the Fall of Rome*, a spectacular play produced by Imre Kiralfy. Imre Kiralfy and his brother Bolossy were Hungarian Jews who had learned their showmanship in Paris, Brussels, New York, and Philadelphia, and crowned their careers with two triumphant decades in London. The Kiralfys followed up their Roman success with a Venetian pageant at Olympia in 1891–2, with five acres of gardens, a hundred gondolas, and Venetian glassblowing demonstrations. The eight-year-old Compton Mackenzie was there, and remembered the thrill seventy years later: 'The whole floor of the great building was flooded and one could be given marvellous rides in gondolas down the canals . . . Finally there was a great spectacle in the main arena, where Venetians and Genoese fought a tremendous battle. Over 1000 performers were called upon and it was a pageant of moving colour that the most elaborate coloured films of sixty years later never surpassed.' The writer Arnold Bennett, who was twenty-two years older than Compton Mackenzie, enjoyed the Earls Court Exhibition of 1897 in a different way: 'All the men enjoy more or less the close presence of these thousands of girls in their summer attire and white shoes, the smiles and light laughter coming from behind veils of spotted muslin'.[14]

In 1892 the Grand Canal reappeared as the Bosphorus in a show called 'Constantinople or the Revels of the East', and the next year Kiralfy's subject was the Orient. After this Kiralfy set up his own company, London Exhibitions Limited, and moved his productions to Earls Court, which could accommodate larger shows and bigger audiences. Kiralfy staged a spectacular show at Earls Court every year from 1895 to 1903, beginning with the Empire of India exhibition and continuing with shows devoted to India and Ceylon, the Victorian era, women, the army, and Paris, and two more general 'International' or 'Universal' exhibitions. Earls Court's main new attraction was a Great Wheel, which was erected for the 1894–5 season and eventually taken down in 1907. The Wheel, an enlarged copy of the one in the Chicago Exhibition, was built (in part) by Maudslay, Son and Field of Greenwich, was powered by two 50hp electric motors, and weighed, with its eight supporting columns, over 1,000 tons. Its forty cars could carry 1,600 passengers, took twenty minutes to complete a rotation, and reached a height of 300 feet, over two-thirds as high as the London Eye, built a hundred years later. In the vast expanse of London suburbs such landmarks provided valuable reference points for travellers and novelists. Toward the end of G. K. Chesterton's comic novel *The Man Who Was Thursday* (1908), six Scotland Yard detectives chased the President of the Central Anarchist Council (who was riding on the back of a runaway elephant) from London Zoo to the Earls Court Great Wheel, where he escaped by untethering and flying off in the Kiralfys' 'captive balloon'.

Better-off visitors could enjoy the bands and fairy lights in seclusion from the holiday crowds by joining Earls Court's own club, the Welcome Club. The schoolboy Compton Mackenzie, who lived between Olympia and Earls Court and was a frequent visitor to both, remembered the excitement when the wheel got stuck one night, earning the stranded passengers generous compensation, and encouraging schoolboys to gamble their sweet and cigarette money on riding the wheel in the hope that it would get stuck again. In 1899 he bought himself a 10s 6d season ticket so that he could enjoy the pleasures of Earls Court, the 200-foot belvedere tower, the captive balloon, the bandstand, the panorama of Hungary, the Empress Theatre, and that year's show, on the theme of Greater Britain, as often as he liked. Living near the two showgrounds had other advantages. Playing billiards in the Bell and Anchor in Hammersmith in 1899, Mackenzie saw two of the 'freaks' then performing in Barnum and Bailey's show at Olympia. One of these was the Living Skeleton, and the other was a man with the body of a child growing from his middle. 'To see him walking round the billiards-table with that pendulous burden in front of him and lifting it on to the table to make certain shots' was 'as macabre a sight as ever I saw'.[15]

Inventive showmen often found ways of feeding Londoners' appetite for new thrills without going to the expense of staging elaborate and costly shows. This was the great age of the 'stunt'. The word, meaning an athletic feat or deliberately eye-catching action or event, made its way from American college slang to English newspapers during the 1890s, at the same time as the word 'rubberneckers', meaning people who drive slowly past accidents or gawp at oddities, crossed the Atlantic. The king of Edwardian 'stuntists' was Harry Houdini, the American magician and escapologist, who played his first London season in 1900. Houdini and his agents stirred up public interest in his ability to escape from almost any form of captivity by inviting and accepting challenges from popular newspapers. At the Alhambra in 1900 he was challenged by a press reporter who had lately exposed the tricks of the Georgia Magnet and the Bullet-Proof Man, and satisfied him by escaping from heavy slave-irons. Four years later, when Houdini was appearing at the Hippodrome (a combined music hall and circus with a vast water tank for aquatic shows), the *Daily Mirror* challenged him to escape from a pair of newly devised handcuffs which 'no mortal man could pick'. It took Houdini over an hour, in front of a full house, to open the lock, but by doing so he confirmed his reputation as the 'Handcuff King', and helped Alfred Harmsworth's *Daily Mirror*, whose circulation had fallen to 25,000 since its first publication in October 1903, to gain a mass readership. Houdini's most famous London performance was in 1908, when he accepted a 'challenge' from Cantonese seamen, who strapped and chained him by the neck, wrists, and ankles to a fiendish Chinese torture rack known as a sanguaw in the Oxford Music Hall (in Oxford Street). Stretched, twisted, and almost strangled by the machine, Houdini somehow managed to free himself using his teeth and by contorting himself like a circus acrobat.[16]

Stunts could be built of much flimsier materials than Houdini's skills. Charles B. Cochran, an agent and impresario who started his London career in 1899, was engaged in 1906 to create a popular event in Olympia, after the failure of indoor football and a pelota championship. He set about creating a 'Mammoth Fun City', with all the usual fairground attractions, a menagerie, a circus, a troupe of wrestlers, an old-fashioned mumming booth (supplied by Fred Karno), a record-breaking non-stop juggler, and a band of Congolese pygmies from the Ituri Forest. The great crowd-pullers, though, were the Sacred Bull of Benares (a heavily costumed hump-backed Indian bull in a mysterious Sinhalese temple), and Sacco, 'the Fasting Man', who spent fifty-two days living on water in a sealed glass house. When public interest was flagging, Cochran arranged to attempt to evict Sacco, whose lawyers, forewarned of the stunt, successfully resisted the challenge. Thanks to the publicity this staged event generated, Cochran was able to increase the fee for seeing Sacco from 6d to 2s 6d.[17]

In the early 1900s, when Imre Kiralfy's exhibitions began to outgrow Earls Court, he dreamed up and created a new exhibition centre a little further west, on 140 acres of open land alongside Wood Lane, between Shepherd's Bush and Wormwood Scrubs. This vast development, which Kiralfy called White City, was built to accommodate the great Anglo-French Exhibition of May 1908, a celebration of mutual trade and friendship to cement the Entente Cordiale of 1904. White City consisted of a huge sports stadium, an impressive Court of Honour with a lake and illuminated cascade, half a mile of waterways, ornamental gardens, a hundred and twenty exhibition halls, and twenty thematic 'palaces', all designed in an amalgam of Indian, Spanish, and baroque styles and built on iron frames in concrete covered in white stucco. The flip-flap machine (two gigantic metal arms in a V-shape, swinging backwards and forwards), and the spiral and scenic railways made it much more exciting than Earls Court. Some critics thought Kiralfy's dream city was vulgar, but the *Architectural Review*'s critic described the Court of Honour as 'a vision of dazzling whiteness, with its tiled court and plashing cool waters, its pointed arcades and lattice windows. At night it is equally effective with its thousands of lights and the rainbow colours of the cascade.' The Anglo-French Exhibition, which was opened in May by Edward VII and the French President, was a great success, attracting 8,400,000 visitors in under six months. This was more than the great exhibitions of London in 1851 and Paris in 1867, but much less than the vast exhibitions held in Paris in 1878, 1889, and 1900. The Central London Railway (the modern Central line) extended its track from Shepherd's Bush to White City especially for the Anglo-French Exhibition, and increased its fare income in 1908 by 20 per cent, despite competition from new motor-bus services.

Spectator Sports

In 1906, while the Anglo-French Exhibition was being planned, the Italian government declared that it could not afford to stage the 1908 Olympic Games (the fourth since their revival in 1896) in Rome. A group of aristocratic English sportsmen and members of the British Olympic Association, led by the heroic all-rounder Lord Desborough (William Henry Grenfell), offered to save the games by staging them in London. Desborough contacted Kiralfy and persuaded him to include in his buildings for the 1908 Exhibition a modern sports stadium with running and cycle tracks, grass pitches, a swimming pool, and changing rooms. Kiralfy agreed to spend at least £44,000 on all this, in return for 75 per cent of the Olympic ticket sales. He did even more than he had promised, and within a year provided the finest stadium the world had seen, from which 93,000 spectators could watch athletics, swimming, gymnastics, and wrestling without leaving their places. The Olympic committee's share of the costs was raised through a campaign in the *Daily Mail*, and various individual gifts, including £1,500 from the professional strongman and bodybuilder Eugen Sandow. Edward VII opened the summer games on 13 July 1908, and over 2,000 athletes, representing twenty-two countries, took part in the first Olympic opening ceremony, marching (in most cases) behind their national flags. The summer games lasted two weeks, but autumn sports, including rugby, football, and boxing, were contested in October. The games were soured by repeated disputes between American officials and British judges, especially over British footwear in the tug of war (won by the City of London Police) and the result of the 400 metres, which was won by a British athlete running alone after American withdrawals. The only really memorable and popular event of the games was the marathon, whose course from Windsor Castle to White City established the present race distance of 26 miles 385 yards. This was the race in which the Italian runner, Dorando Pietri, collapsed on his final lap and was helped over the line by track officials. Pietri was disqualified, but he became a popular hero and was given a special trophy by Queen Alexandra. Although there was some American disquiet at the fact that Great Britain (which provided all the judges) won half the gold medals, and over 40 per cent of all the medals awarded, it was generally recognized that between them Desborough and Kiralfy, given only a year to plan and build, had staged the first well-organized modern Olympiad, and saved the Olympic movement from collapse.[18] After this triumph, Kiralfy produced an International Imperial Exhibition at White City in 1909 and a Japan–British Exhibition in 1910, but the crowds did not fill his Olympic stadium again until greyhound races were held there in the late 1920s.

As an alternative to the fair, the street show, and the exhibition, late Victorian Londoners could go to professional sporting events, some of which, like boxing matches, had developed first as fairground sideshows. Professional boxing began to make its way out of the fairground booth and public house with the establishment of the National Sporting Club in Covent Garden in 1891, the Wonderland boxing saloon in Whitechapel Road in 1894, and the Ring on Blackfriars Road (near the Old Vic) in

1910. There was still a touch of the sideshow about professional boxing stars. The American champions John L. Sullivan, Gentleman Jim Corbett, Bob Fitzsimmons, and Jack Johnson all appeared on the London stage between 1888 and 1914, and so did the Stepney-born local favourite Bombardier Billy Wells and the popular French fighter Georges Carpentier. There was public anxiety over the introduction of American promotional methods into boxing, which threatened to return it, opponents said, to the days of prizefighting and brutal knock-outs. In 1911 a proposed fight between Jack Johnson, the black American, and Bombardier Billy Wells was cancelled when the LCC threatened to withdraw the licence of Earls Court, the planned venue. The fact that many women were expected to be in the crowd, smoking cigarettes and generally behaving in a manly fashion, was advanced as an argument for stopping the fight.[19]

The spectator sport that surpassed all others in popular appeal (especially among young working-class men) by the end of the century was football. Amateur football was already well established in England by 1883, the year that a working-class team, Blackburn Olympic, first beat a public-school one, the Old Etonians, in the FA Cup Final. The Football Association was founded in 1863, and had been offering its annual Cup since 1871, and several successful modern clubs (but not London ones) were established in the 1870s. Three of London's modern professional clubs, Fulham, Tottenham, and Leyton Orient, began as amateur teams in the early 1880s, and three more, Millwall, Queen's Park Rangers, and Arsenal, started in 1885–6. Three years after the FA accepted professionalism in 1885, the Football League was founded to organize games between twelve professional clubs, all of them from the Midlands or Lancashire. By 1914 the League had grown to contain forty clubs in two divisions, but no London club was included in it until Arsenal (London's first professional team) was elected in 1893, followed between 1905 and 1908 by Chelsea, Fulham, Clapton (later Leyton) Orient, and Tottenham. Arsenal (in 1904) and Chelsea (in 1907) were the only London teams to get into the First Division before the Great War. Most London teams joined the Southern League, which was founded in 1894 by (among others) Millwall, London's second professional club. Tottenham, Queen's Park Rangers, and West Ham entered the Southern League in the later 1890s, and Brentford, Fulham, and Crystal Palace joined soon after 1900. Some of these Southern League games drew crowds of 20,000, but the biggest crowds went to Football League matches at Chelsea and Tottenham Hotspur, which had average attendances of 37,000 and 28,000 in the

1913–14 season. Teams with a good winning record, a well-populated working-class home territory, and a convenient railway station tended to draw the biggest crowds. The station near Stamford Bridge helped fill Chelsea's stands, and the move from Plumstead to the more heavily populated Highbury in 1913 increased Arsenal's fan base. The greatest event in the football calendar was the FA Cup, which was usually played at the Kennington Oval until 1892 and at Crystal Palace from 1895, although it was dominated by Midlands and northern teams. Only one London club, Tottenham Hotspur, won the FA Cup before 1915, and it did so in 1901, before it had joined the Football League. The growth of the FA Cup final crowd, from 17,000 at the Oval in 1888 to 120,000 at Crystal Palace in 1913, is a measure of the growing importance of football in England's sporting life, an importance recognized by King George V, who watched Aston Villa beat Sunderland in 1913.[20]

The People's Palace

There were plenty of Londoners who were too poor to participate fully in this growing world of commercialized leisure. In 1882 Walter Besant, a professional journalist and playwright, wrote a novel of East End life, *All Sorts and Conditions of Men*, which had an unusually strong impact on the minds of the London reading public. In it he criticized the barrenness and tedium of social and cultural life in the East End, and described a fictional Palace of Delight which transformed the lives of millions of poor East Londoners. Capitalizing on the initial impact, he started a campaign to raise £70,000 by public subscription to turn this dream into a real People's Palace, in which the London poor could enjoy (as he put it in the novel) 'music, dancing, singing, acting, painting, reading, games of skill, games of chance, companionship, cheerfulness, light, warmth, comfort – everything'. In an article in the *Contemporary Review* in March 1884, Besant tried to explain the narrowness of the cultural and educational opportunities available to poor Londoners. Certainly, working-class men had the tavern or public house, the essential leisure institution of the poor: 'the circle which meets there is the society of the workman; it is his life'. They could take trips on steamboats and excursion trains, perhaps to the seaside or one of the 'holiday' suburbs, Kew, Greenwich, Richmond, or Epping. They could spend their Sundays in the local park, if they lived near one. Besant advised those who felt gloomy about the working class to 'pay a visit to

Battersea Park on any Sunday evening in the summer'. They could go to
the music hall, or visit one of the cheap popular theatres, but there were
only six of these in the poorer parts of London. Beyond that, there was
very little to do. Working men did not generally play cricket, tennis, or
football, they did not make music, paint, swim, act, or read. Working-class
women, Besant said, apparently had no leisure pursuits at all. The amusement of London factory girls seemed 'to consist of nothing but walking
about the streets, two and three abreast, and they laugh and shout as they
go so noisily that they must needs be extraordinarily happy'. The facilities
which might allow them to broaden the range of their activities simply
did not exist. In 1884 London had just six free libraries, including only
one in East London (at Bethnal Green) and another in South London. Of
institutions for teaching arts and accomplishments to the working class,
there was 'not one, anywhere in London'. Perhaps most depressing of all
was the fact that 'in the whole of this vast city there is not a single place
where a couple, so minded, can go for an evening's dancing', except for a
hall in North Woolwich. Two years later, with his campaign in full swing,
Besant painted a rather darker picture for the readers of the same periodical. The problem of children aged thirteen to eighteen (the word teenager
was not yet available) who had left school but had no social institutions
was particularly worrying. They forgot their schooling, and spent all their
spare time on the street. 'The love which these children have for the street
is wonderful; no boulevard in the world, I am sure, is as much loved by its
frequenters as the Whitechapel Road, unless it be the High Street,
Islington.' But on the street 'their favourite amusements and their pleasures, they grow yearly coarser; as for their conversation, it grows
continually viler'. Fortunately, Besant added in February 1887, the
People's Palace was now being built. 'The Palace is going to take that boy
out of the streets: it is going to remove both from boy and girl the temp-
tation – that of the idle hand to go away and get married. It will fill that
lad's mind with thoughts and make those hands deft and crafty.'[21]

The main hall of the People's Palace, the Queen's Hall, was opened by
Queen Victoria when she 'descended into purgatory' as part of her Golden
Jubilee celebrations in May 1887. After that, the completion of the project depended on funding from the Drapers' Company, which paid for a
clock tower (1893) and a classical facade that looked more institutional
than palatial. Under the Drapers' influence, and to Besant's distress, the
educational functions of the 'Palace of Delights' began to outweigh the
recreational ones, and in *Living London*, published in 1901, it was described

in the chapter on 'Institute London', along with London's other poly-
technics and technical colleges: 'after undergoing considerable vicissitudes,
the People's Palace has settled down to a strictly educational work, which
it carries on with singular success'. Besant's original intention was preserved, though, in popular concerts in the great hall, a winter garden for
promenading, a gymnasium and swimming pool, and a free library. Eventually, in 1934, the East London Technical College became Queen Mary
College, one of the colleges of London University.[22]

Besant's bleak account of working-class Londoners whose main leisure
activities, until the opening of the People's Palace, consisted of drinking,
wandering the streets, and having coarse conversations, needs to be bal-
anced against the growing popularity of football as a spectator and
participant sport, the continuing prosperity of the music halls, the popularity of cycling, and the enormous crowds using London's parks on
weekends and holidays. A survey on Whit Monday 1893 counted over
900,000 visitors to twelve LCC parks, mainly Victoria Park, Battersea
Park, Southwark Park, Brockwell Park, Clissold Park, and Finsbury Park.
These parks, which constituted a sixth of the 6,200 acres of public open
space within the County of London (excluding Richmond Park, and Hainault and Epping Forests) were probably more heavily used than most,
because they were situated in areas of high population density. Parks in or
near such overcrowded boroughs as Stepney, Shoreditch, Southwark,
Finsbury, Holborn, and Islington, whose 1,119,000 residents (in 1901)
only had 116 acres of open space (nearly 10,000 people to the acre) were
bound to be well used. Still, the fact that nearly a million Londoners went
to these twelve parks that day (and probably millions more to the others),
walking, boating, lying down, playing football or cricket, flying kites,
eating picnics, and making friends, needs to be set alongside those grim-
mer images of Londoners wheezing in thick fogs, rioting in Pall Mall,
labouring in sweatshops, and dying in workhouses that sometimes domi-
nates our picture of life in late Victorian London.[23]

The London Stage

For people with money in their pockets – a great and growing proportion of Londoners – London was a city which offered a huge variety of
pleasures and entertainments. For the serious-minded, there were the
British Museum, the National Gallery, and the three museums at South

Kensington. One of these, the Natural History Museum, had moved into its magnificent new terracotta building on the Cromwell Road, designed in the Romanesque style by Sir Alfred Waterhouse, in 1881. For serious music, Londoners could go to the Crystal Palace, the home of London's only permanent orchestra, and orchestral concerts could often be heard in St James's Hall in Piccadilly, where Tchaikovsky, Dvořák, Grieg, and Liszt performed in the 1880s. The Albert Hall, a vast echoing amphitheatre in South Kensington, also staged concerts, along with exhibitions, mock battles, and charity balls. Its organ was the largest in the world. In addition, London had the Royal Opera House, Covent Garden, which had specialized in Italian opera since the 1840s.

Above all, Londoners had the theatre and the music hall. At the end of the 1870s, according to John Hollingshead, manager of the Gaiety Theatre, there were fifty-seven theatres in London and its suburbs, with seats for about 126,000 people. These ranged from the two long-established Covent Garden 'patent theatres', the Theatre Royal Drury Lane and the Royal Opera House, and the fashionable West End theatres of Haymarket and the Strand, to the cheap working-class theatres of the poorer suburbs, like the Britannia in Hoxton, the Standard in Shoreditch, and the Pavilion in Whitechapel. Theatres were vulnerable to fires, and in the 1890s Edwin Sachs, a campaigner for safer theatres, calculated that the average life expectancy of a theatre was only twelve years, and that a London theatre burned down about every three years. These averages must have been affected by the unlucky Grand Theatre in Upper Street, Islington, which was destroyed by fire in 1882, 1887, and 1900. Nevertheless a few pre-1850 theatres, notably the great Theatre Royal, Drury Lane, the Haymarket Theatre, the Lyceum, the Olympic, Princess's (on Oxford Street), and Sadler's Wells, survived in the 1880s. There was a spate of theatre building and rebuilding in the late 1850s and 1860s, starting in 1858 with the new Adelphi in the Strand, which set new standards in size, visibility, luxury, and architectural sophistication. Other products of the 1860s boom were the Royal Pavilion, Whitechapel ('the Drury Lane of the East'), the Marylebone (or West London), the Globe and the Opéra Comique (the 'Rickety Twins') in side streets off the Strand, and the Vaudeville and the Gaiety, both on the Strand. The concentration of theatres on and near the Strand increased with the building of the Savoy Theatre in 1881 and Terry's in 1887. There was a second cluster of theatres around Leicester Square and the Haymarket, most of which were built or rebuilt in the early 1880s: the Comedy in 1881, the Empire and the Alhambra in 1883, the Prince of Wales (in Coventry Street) in 1884, the Garrick (on Charing Cross Road) in 1889, Daly's in 1891, and the Duke of York's in 1892. A third focus was Shaftesbury Avenue, a new street opened in 1886. At the Piccadilly Circus end of the road there was the new Criterion Theatre, rebuilt with electric lighting by the great actor–manager Charles Wyndham in 1884. Next there were the Lyric and the Shaftesbury, both built in 1888, and where the new road crossed Charing Cross Road at Cambridge Circus there was Richard D'Oyly Carte's Palace Theatre (1891), which failed as an opera house but succeeded under the veteran Charles Morton, 'the father of the music hall', as a Theatre of Varieties. Four new theatres, the Apollo, the Globe, the Prince's, and the Ambassador's, were built on Shaftesbury Avenue after 1900, confirming its status as one of London's two great theatrical streets. In all, according to the LCC's figures for 1911, there were fifty-four theatres in the County of London (twenty-nine in Westminster), with seats, calculated in line with the Council's stringent licensing regulations, for about 67,000 people. London's fifty music halls and variety theatres held another 74,000.

In the early 1880s the London theatre was at the end of one important change and the beginning of another. Since the 1860s the growing popularity of music halls had drawn some of the rowdier working-class elements away from West End theatres, enabling some theatre managers (especially the Bancrofts at the Prince of Wales Theatre) to increase seat prices and win back the respectable classes who had abandoned play-going over the previous fifty years. In 1877, Henry James was struck by the high price of theatre tickets and by the dull respectability of London play-goers, compared with Parisians. The London audience was

much more 'genteel'; it is less Bohemian, less blasé, more naïf, and more respectful—to say nothing of being made up of handsomer people. It is well dressed, tranquil, motionless; it suggests domestic virtue and comfortable homes; it looks as if it had come to the play in its own carriage, after a dinner of beef and pudding. The ladies are mild, fresh-coloured English mothers; they all wear caps; they are wrapped in knitted shawls. There are many rosy young girls, with dull eyes and quiet cheeks—an element wholly absent from Parisian audiences. The men are handsome and honourable looking; they are in evening dress; they come with the ladies—usually with several ladies—and remain with them; they sit still in their places, and don't go herding out between the acts with their hats askew.[24]

The Bancrofts left the Prince of Wales Theatre for the Haymarket in 1880, and provoked a riot there by abolishing the pit, where the cheapest seats had been. The drive for respectability was pursued in the 1880s by John Hare at the Royal Court (Chelsea) and the St James's, Henry Irving at the Lyceum, Richard D'Oyly Carte and William Gilbert at the Savoy, and Charles Wyndham at the Criterion.

In general, these well-dressed play-goers were presented with the plays that had dominated the London stage for most of the century – melodramas with spectacular surprises and special effects in place of credible stories or characters, burlesques that relied heavily on Londoners' enjoyment of puns, and comedies and dramas translated and adapted from French originals. Thomas Robertson, a writer whose plays (*Society, Ours, Caste, Play, and School*) brought an unusual touch of intelligence and realism to the theatre in the later 1860s, was not emulated until the 1890s. When Henry James came to London and took lodgings in Piccadilly in 1876, after a year in Paris, he was surprised and disappointed by the low quality of the theatre. The plays of Sardou and other French dramatists, translated, 'adapted', and bowdlerized for London audiences (and the Lord Chamberlain) had nothing valuable to say about English society, and transplanted from French to English soil 'they bloom hardly longer than a handful of cut flowers stuck into moist sand . . . They are neither English nor a drama; they have not that minimum of ponderable identity at which appreciation finds a starting-point.' James had seen the most admired actor in London, Henry Irving, playing Richard III and Macbeth at the Lyceum, and was deeply disappointed: 'That an actor so handicapped, as they say in London, by nature and culture should have enjoyed such prosperity, is a striking proof of the absence of a standard, of the chaotic condition of taste.' James was only slightly more impressed the much-admired leading lady of the Court Theatre, Ellen Terry, who was soon to join Irving at the Lyceum: 'She is intelligent and vivacious, and she is indeed, in a certain measure, interesting . . . Miss Terry has all the pleasing qualities I have enumerated, but she has, with them, the defect that she is simply not an actress.'[25]

No doubt Henry James misunderstood the demands of West End audience. When, in 1894, his own play, *Guy Domville*, was produced by another great actor–manager, George Alexander, at St James's Theatre, the first night of its one-month run was a disaster. James wrote to Compton Mackenzie's mother, 'I was hooted at myself by a brutal mob, fruitless of any of the consequences for which I had striven . . . simply the most horrible experience of my life'. 'The only thing they understand, or want here, is one kind of play – the play of the same kind as the unutterable kind they already know. With anything more delicate they are like a set of savages with a gold watch. Yet God knows I have tried to be simple, straightforward & British.' He continued trying – and failing – to write a successful West End play for the next ten years.[26] Alexander, who ran the St James's Theatre from 1890 until 1918, was one of the finest actor–managers of his day. He avoided the French farces that monopolized many theatres, and instead promoted English dramatists including Wilde and Pinero. His management was efficient as well as enterprising. Arnold Bennett went to St James's to see Pinero's *His House in Order* in 1906, and though he thought the play was 'thoroughly pretentious, sentimental and dull', and the acting 'mediocre and worse', he found the theatre 'organised and worked with the perfection of a battleship. An air of solidity, richness, cleanliness, decorum; punctuality, short entr'actes; general care for the public. Such a difference from Parisian theatres.'

Ellen Terry joined Henry Irving when he took over as manager of the Lyceum in 1878, and between them these two dominated the London stage until Irving's tenancy at the Lyceum expired in 1901. Terry's acting was generally thought to be much finer than Henry James believed it to be, and Irving's, although it was too exaggerated and melodramatic for some tastes, had a hypnotic intensity that fascinated his audiences. His distinctive vocal and physical mannerisms, which seemed to colour every role he played, irritated some critics, but most admired his intellect, vigour, and versatility. Shaw, who loved Ellen Terry and disliked Irving, thought that Irving had 'never in his life conceived or interpreted the characters of any author except himself'.[27] Irving's rival and successor as London's greatest actor–manager was Herbert Beerbohm Tree, who was manager of the Haymarket Theatre (which had been remodelled by the Bancrofts) from 1887 to 1896, and of his own theatre, Her (or His) Majesty's, from 1897 to 1915. Tree produced and performed in Shakespeare, Wilde, and Ibsen at the Haymarket, excelling in character and comedy roles like Falstaff and Iago, but his most famous role was Svengali in a dramatization of George du Maurier's novel *Trilby* in 1896. At Her Majesty's, Tree produced and performed in eleven Shakespeare plays, cheerfully adding his own words and characters (a dog for *Richard II*, extra Malvolios in *Twelfth Night*) to improve on the original. Tree's improvisations (especially when he forgot his lines), his comical gestures, and his lavish and realistic sets helped to make Shakespeare popular with London audiences, and enabled him to run a series of successful Shakespeare seasons from 1905 onwards. There was a comical clash of personalities between Tree and Shaw when *Pygmalion* was staged in 1914. Shaw, who directed his own plays and knew exactly what he wanted, had to battle against Tree's love of props, disguises, and pantomime 'business'. As Michael Holroyd tells us, the role of Professor Higgins, who did not have a beard or an ear trumpet, or speak with a strong regional accent, left Tree disappointed and puzzled: 'In vain did he plead with Shaw to let him take large quantities of snuff, to use a Scots accent, to vault on the piano from time to time, to indicate an addiction to port by walking with a limp and a stick.' When Shaw went to the hundredth performance of *Pygmalion* in July he was horrified to find that Tree had embellished the play with dozens of crowd-pleasing devices and gestures. 'I should have resented it more, but [Tree] was so utterly innocent of the meaning of the play, and so pleased with himself as Eliza's lover, that he had no idea of the outrage to me.'[28]

Irving used Shakespeare and high drama to fill London's biggest theatre, but Augustus Harris, 'Druriolanus', used very different methods to fill its second biggest. Harris took over the management of the Theatre Royal, Drury Lane, in the early 1880s, when it was close to bankruptcy, and restored its fortunes by putting on spectacular melodramas, grand operas, and lavish pantomimes, with the great music-hall star Dan Leno as the pantomime dame. Harris died in his forties in 1896, but his successor Arthur Collins, who ran the theatre until 1923, stuck with the same recipe, taking stage spectacle and special effects to new extremes, partly in an effort to outdo films. In his production of *Ben Hur* in 1902 there was a chariot race on stage, with real horses galloping towards the audience on treadwheels, a huge revolving cyclorama to give the impression of speed, and fans to whip up dust around the spinning chariot wheels, and in *The Whip*, in 1909, about a plot to kidnap a racehorse, there was a horse race and a thrilling train crash. Most of London's greatest theatrical events, including Henry Irving's last season in 1905, Ellen Terry's golden jubilee celebration in 1906, and Johnston Forbes-Robertson's farewell to the stage in 1913, took place at Drury Lane.

Musical Comedy

Perhaps Henry James would have written less despondently in 1877 if he had seen the first work of a partnership that brought a new originality and intelligence to the London theatrical world in the 1870s and 1880s. William Gilbert had written several successful comedies and dramas, mostly for the Royal Court Theatre, in the 1870s, and he had collaborated briefly with Arthur Sullivan, a serious composer with a taste for light comedy, in 1871. Their true partnership began four years later, when the manager of the New Royalty Theatre in Dean Street, Soho, Richard D'Oyly Carte, suggested that they work together on a short comic opera, *Trial By Jury*. The next three Gilbert and Sullivan operettas, *The Sorcerer* (1877), *H.M.S. Pinafore* (1878), and *The Pirates of Penzance* (1880), were so successful that D'Oyly Carte was able to use his one-third share of their profits to build a theatre devoted almost exclusively to Gilbert and Sullivan productions. The result, in 1881, was the Savoy Theatre, the first public building in the world to be lit entirely by electric light. Three years later, with his share of the profits from the first Savoy operas, *Patience* (1881) and *Iolanthe* (1882), D'Oyly Carte built the Savoy Hotel, and employed César Ritz and Auguste Escoffier as manager and chef, to make sure that it would be the best in London. The run of successes at the Savoy lasted for the rest of the 1880s, despite frequent disputes between the three men over money, management, and artistic ambition, and an almost terminal row over the cost of a new carpet for the Savoy in 1890. Gilbert and Sullivan operas provided middle-class audiences with a witty and conservative commentary on the main political and cultural issues of the day: mock medievalism, artistic squabbles, 'miminy-piminy, je-ne-sais-quoi young men', and the 'unmanly oddities' of Oscar Wilde in *Patience*; politics and the House of Lords in *Iolanthe* (1882); female emancipation and university women in *Princess Ida* (1884); bureaucracy, the legal system, and modern fads in *The Mikado* (1885); and melodrama in *Ruddigore* (1887). Sullivan wanted to be England's Wagner, not its Offenbach, and constantly fretted over the limitations Gilbert's words and silly stories imposed on his creative genius. He expressed his frustration in his diary: 'How am I to get through this year's work? Do they think me a barrel-organ? They turn a handle and I disgorge music of any mood to order.'[29] Still, Sullivan enjoyed the wealth and social position that commercial success brought him, and Gilbert made so much money that he was able to build his own theatre, the Garrick, in 1889. The pair produced three further hits, *The Yeomen of the Guard* (1888), *The Gondoliers* (1889), and *Utopia Limited*, and the less successful *The Grand Duke* (1896), before their creative partnership ended. Both men continued working with other collaborators until their deaths

(Sullivan's in 1900, Gilbert's in 1911), but they never achieved the success alone that they had enjoyed together.

One factor in the decline of Gilbert and Sullivan was the rise in the 1890s of a new type of theatrical show, the musical comedy, which achieved longer runs than the Savoy operas with thinner material. Its main London home was the Gaiety Theatre, on the Strand, which was taken over by George Edwardes when John Hollingshead retired in 1886. Edwardes had been business manager at the Savoy Theatre until 1885, and his early independent productions were operettas in the Gilbert and Sullivan style. His first great success was *Dorothy*, a comic opera composed by Alfred Cellier, who had been D'Oyly Carte's conductor until 1878. Dorothy ran for 931 performances (mostly at the Prince of Wales Theatre) between 1886 and 1889, 259 more than *The Mikado*, the most successful Gilbert and Sullivan opera, which was at the Savoy at the same time. Its leading actors, Marie Tempest and Hayden Coffin, remained important London stars for the next twenty years. Trying to repeat this winning formula, Cellier wrote two modest successes for the Lyric, *Doris* and *The Mountebanks* (with words by Gilbert), before his early death in 1891.

When the popularity of the Savoy operas waned after 1890, George Edwardes saw the possibility of producing a musical entertainment that would attract both music-hall and operetta audiences by inserting tuneful songs of the music-hall type into a play with a thin and cheerful plot, and decorating the whole thing with the proverbial beauty of the famous Gaiety Girls. His cast would be dressed in the most fashionable suits and dresses, not the tights and comedy clothes of music hall, and his scripts would be stripped of the tiresome puns that characterized the comical plays, or burlesques, which had been standard fare in the Gaiety. He also borrowed some ideas from New York's Broadway, where Ned Harrigan and Tony Hart had been producing light musicals since 1879. In 1892 Edwardes staged a 'musical farce', *In Town*, starring the popular music-hall comedian Arthur Roberts, at the Prince of Wales Theatre, and then at the Gaiety. In 1893 *In Town* was followed at the Prince of Wales by *A Gaiety Girl*, the first London show to be billed as a 'musical comedy'. Over the next twenty years Edwardes produced dozens of successful musical comedies, usually with 'girl' in the title, either at the Gaiety or at Daly's Theatre, Leicester Square, which he built in 1892–3. The musicals had predictable romantic plots, and settings which ranged from London department stores to the exotic east. Shows with oriental themes seemed to do particularly well. *A Chinese Honeymoon* ran for over a thousand performances at the

Royal Strand Theatre in 1901–3, and *Chu Chin Chow* broke all records during the Great War, with 2,238 performances at His Majesty's Theatre. Such London musical shows as *The Geisha*, *The Circus Girl*, *Floradora*, and *The Arcadians*, which are hardly remembered today, dominated the musical theatres of America and Europe, even after the great success of Franz Lehar's Viennese operetta *The Merry Widow* in 1906–9. *The Geisha*, with songs by Sidney Jones and Lionel Monckton, was an enormous hit in Germany, France, Austria, Italy, and even Russia, where it featured in Chekhov's 1899 story 'Lady with a Lapdog'. The leading musical-comedy performers, Marie Tempest, Letty Lind, Huntley Wright, George Grossmith (a Savoy star), Gertie Millar, Seymour Hicks, and Ellaline Terriss, were major London stars, influencing fashions in dress and speech, as well as musical tastes. In 1904, when the shapely Camille Clifford was such a success in *The Catch of the Season*, every young woman wanted to look like 'the Gibson girl', and in 1913 London's favourite catch phrase, 'If you can't be good, be careful', was taken from that year's musical comedy hit, *The Girl in the Taxi*. When soldiers marched in military processions at the end of the century, they might well do so to 'The Soldiers of the Queen', a song written by Leslie Stuart for Sidney Jones' musical comedy *The Artist's Model*, the hit show of 1895.[30]

The composers of West End musical-comedy scores, Leslie Stuart, Ivan Caryll, Sidney Jones, Paul Rubens, Howard Talbot, and Lionel Monckton, are not household names today, but they began a musical tradition that led on, in England, to the musical revues of C. B. Cochran, and the work of Noel Gay, Ivor Novello, and Noel Coward, and in America to the great musicals of Jerome Kern, Irving Berlin, Vincent Youmans, and Richard Rodgers. Every year from 1905 to 1910 the aspiring songwriter Jerome Kern came to London, where he got his musical training from George Edwardes and Seymour Hicks, and worked with the young P. G. Wodehouse, who later wrote the books and lyrics for many Broadway shows. One of their earliest joint successes was a light political song, 'Oh, Mr Chamberlain'. Kern contributed songs with an American appeal to dozens of West End musicals between 1902 and 1914, most famously adding one of the twentieth century's most popular love songs, 'They Didn't Believe Me', to Sidney Jones' *The Girl from Utah* in 1914. Kern drew early inspiration from one of the greatest British composers of music-hall and musical-comedy songs, Leslie Stuart. Stuart, to compound these transatlantic influences, drew ideas and rhythms from the US black-face minstrel shows that visited London, and especially from his work with Eugene

Stratton, a white American who built a successful career in London music halls in the 1880s and 1890s by singing 'plantation' songs with a blackened face. Many of these 'minstrel' songs, supposedly from the American South, were composed by Stuart, including 'Lily of Laguna', 'Little Dolly Daydream', and 'The Cake Walk'. Leslie Stuart's musical comedy *Floradora*, which ran at the Lyric for 455 performances in 1899–1901, was one of the first to add minstrel, cakewalk, and almost ragtime rhythms to a musical, and had a significant influence on Kern, George Gershwin, and Richard Rodgers. Its best song, 'Tell me, Pretty Maiden (are there any more at home like you?)', was a hit in the West End and on Broadway.

Ibsen and Shaw

W. S. Gilbert commented on Victorian society in his own way, but for more serious discussion of social, moral, and political issues on stage, Victorians had to wait until the 1890s, when two writers of farces and melodramas, Henry Arthur Jones and Arthur Wing Pinero, began to produce more serious society dramas. The great interest excited in 1893 by Pinero's *The Second Mrs Tanqueray*, which dealt with Aubrey Tanqueray's marriage to a woman with a sexual 'past', says a great deal about the moral emptiness of the theatre up to that point, though it also owed much to the impact made by Mrs Patrick Campbell in her first great role. Oscar Wilde's brief and brilliant theatrical career blossomed at the same time, between 1892 and 1895, though the minor scandals that formed the subject matter of his plots were soon overshadowed by the much greater scandal of his personal life.

The great force that awakened English theatre from its slumber in the 1890s was the dramas of Henrik Ibsen, which dealt skilfully and honestly with such difficult, uncomfortable, or forbidden issues as the inequalities inherent in nineteenth-century marriage, venereal disease, business ethics and corruption, and duty in public life. Ibsen was virtually unknown in England until William Archer's translations of *Pillars of Society* and *Ghosts* and Eleanor Marx's translation of *An Enemy of the People* were published in 1888. The following year two young actors, Janet Achurch and her husband Charles Charrington, managed to raise the money for a one-week production of *A Doll's House*, in Archer's translation, at the Novelty, a scruffy theatre in Great Queen Street. The play was denounced by more conservative critics, but praised by others, including George Bernard Shaw, who saw the play five times, and fell in love with the leading lady. *A Doll's House* showed Shaw that drama could be used for a serious social or moral purpose. 'I find people enjoying themselves there who have been practically driven from the other theatres by the intolerable emptiness of the ordinary performances . . . I see people silent, attentive, thoughtful, startled – struck to the heart, some of them.'[31]

Ibsen's great year was 1891, when Jacob Grein, a Dutch-born London critic, publisher, and tea merchant, founded the Independent Theatre of London, for the performance of non-commercial plays with artistic value. Supported by Thomas Hardy, George Meredith, George Moore, Henry Arthur Jones, Pinero, and others, Grein organized the first English staging of Ibsen's *Ghosts* at the Royalty Theatre, Dean Street, in March. This was the production that the *Daily Telegraph*'s critic Clement Scott, who was not used to finding syphilis, incest, and euthanasia in his cup-and-saucer comedies, described as 'a dirty act done publicly'. *Hedda Gabler*, performed at the Vaudeville in April and May 1891, aroused less hostility (Scott said it was 'like a visit to the Morgue'), and ran for more than a month. Ibsen's champion, William Archer, regarded the performance as the 'second great step towards the popularization of Ibsen in England', and Shaw, who saw Ibsen as a battering ram against Victorian hypocrisy and narrow-mindedness, published his long Fabian lecture on 'The Quintessence of Ibsenism'.

Grein, who was looking for something to follow *Ghosts*, agreed to stage Shaw's first play, *Widowers' Houses*. The play, which had two performances at the Royalty in December 1892, was a failure, more like 'a pamphlet in dialogue' or a manifesto for the Progressives in the forthcoming LCC elections than a piece of theatre, but it began Shaw's career as a professional playwright. His second effort, *The Philanderer*, was considered unstageable, and his third, *Mrs Warren's Profession*, a study of London prostitution which married the researches of W. T. Stead and Charles Booth to the dramatic techniques of Ibsen and Pinero, was so indecent (by Victorian standards) that its first public production was delayed until 1925. But his fourth, *Arms and the Man*, which saw the folly of war through a child's eyes, ran from April to early July 1894 at the Avenue Theatre, Northumberland Avenue (rebuilt in 1907 as the Playhouse Theatre), though the audiences were small and padded out with people with free tickets. The play did well in America, and Shaw's royalties were enough to persuade him to give up some of his journalism and stake his future on the theatre.[32]

Shaw's optimism was premature, since his next three plays, *Candida*, *The Man of Destiny*, and *You Never Can Tell*, were not staged in London, and he did not achieve success in the West End for another ten years. Instead, in December 1894 he accepted Frank Harris's invitation to become dramatic critic of the *Saturday Review*, which Harris had just bought for £5,600. This put Shaw in a position to mock the standard diet of farces, melodramas, and snobbish and artificial dramas that West End and suburban theatre managers were still feeding to their audiences in the later 1890s, on the assumption that it was 'impossible to underrate the taste and intelligence of the British public'. Only the plays of Henry Arthur Jones escaped Shaw's general contempt for West End drama. Shaw also took the opportunity in 1895 to greet the death of the Lord Chamberlain's Examiner of Plays, E. F. Smyth Pigott, 'a walking compendium of vulgar insular prejudice', in 'the most abusive article ever written on a recently dead man'. Unfortunately G. A. Redford, the retired bank manager who took over the post for the next sixteen years, was as determined as Pigott had been to keep any honest discussion of sexual issues off the London stage.[33]

To see plays that challenged prevailing moral or commercial judgements, serious-minded Londoners had to wait until 1899, when the Stage Society was created. Its founders, Charles Charrington and other Fabians, intended to carry on where Jacob Grein's Independent Theatre had left off seven years earlier, staging uncommercial plays for society members in West End theatres. The Society gave their first performances to several of Shaw's 1890s plays, including *You Never Can Tell* (in a performance interrupted by a police raid), *Captain Brassbound's Conversion, Man and Superman, Candida*, and *Mrs Warren's Profession*. One of the young actors in these plays, Harley Granville Barker, struck up a close friendship with Shaw. In 1904 Barker was asked to produce *Two Gentlemen of Verona* in the Royal Court Theatre in Chelsea, and he did so on condition that he could also stage matinees of Shaw's *Candida*. These were so successful (and even profitable) that Barker was able to persuade the manager of the Royal Court, J. E. Vedrenne, to run a season of matinee productions of challenging plays. The Barker–Vedrenne seasons lasted from 1904 to 1907, and helped to transform the London theatre. Barker staged thirty-two plays by seventeen authors, including Ibsen, Maeterlinck, Euripides, John Galsworthy, Granville Barker himself, and especially Shaw. Eleven of Shaw's plays were performed at the Royal Court, and 701 of the 988 performances were of Shaw plays. This was a real breakthrough for Shaw and the advocates of intelligent modern drama, because the audiences were not stuffed with Fabians, feminists, and friends of the cast. Beatrice Webb persuaded the Prime Minister, Arthur Balfour, to come to *John Bull's Other Island* (which mocked British policy in Ireland) in November 1904, and Balfour brought the Liberal leaders Campbell-Bannerman and Asquith along to it. At a command performance in March 1905 the extremely portly Edward VII broke his inadequately reinforced chair because (it was charitably explained) the play made him laugh so much. Shaw's reputation was made. *Man and Superman, Major Barbara,* and *The Doctor's Dilemma* were all staged at the Royal Court, and when the Barker–Vedrenne season ended there were successful productions of *Getting Married* at the Haymarket and *Fanny's First Play* at the Little Theatre. When Sir Herbert Beerbohm Tree, who generally preferred Shakespeare to modern works, produced and starred in *Pygmalion,* Shaw's play about class and phonetics, at His Majesty's in 1913 (with Tree as Professor Higgins and Mrs Patrick Campbell as Eliza Doolittle) it was plain that Shaw had achieved an acceptance in the West End, which disturbed him almost as much as his previous exclusion. It was true, of course, that London audiences still preferred musical comedy, light society dramas, spectaculars, melodrama, and pantomime. In 1910 the American impresario Charles Frohman, who had achieved commercial success in London with musical comedies and J. M. Barrie's *Peter Pan,* decided to run a repertory season at the Duke of York's Theatre, giving brief runs to serious modern plays such as Shaw's *Misalliance,* John Galsworthy's *Justice,* and Granville Barker's *The Madras House,* but audiences were much smaller than he expected, and Frohman was glad to be able to use the King's death to bring the season to an end after ten weeks.

In the early twentieth century melodrama no longer monopolized the London theatre, but it was certainly not dead. As far as ordinary London theatregoers were concerned, the brothers Walter and Frederick Melville, playwrights, managers, and theatre-builders, were just as important as Shaw or Irving. The Melvilles owned and managed the Standard Theatre, Shoreditch, from 1896 to 1907, and Terriss's Theatre, Rotherhithe, from 1901 to 1907, and staged a new melodrama every autumn, running it for seven or eight weeks before taking it on tour. In 1907 they sold their two East End theatres to Walter Gibbons' syndicate and moved to the West End, where they took control of the Lyceum from 1909 to 1939, built the Prince's Theatre in 1911, and leased the Aldwych Theatre from 1909 to 1911. The Melvilles also ran the Brixton Theatre from 1907. Many of the melodramas that were staged in these theatres were written by the Melvilles themselves. Between 1898 and 1914 they wrote twenty-nine so-called 'wicked woman plays', mostly for the Standard and Terriss's, with such titles as *A Disgrace to her Sex, The Sins of London, The Shop-soiled Girl, The*

Ugliest Woman on Earth, and *The Girl Who Took the Wrong Turning*. These are deservedly forgotten now, but they might tell us as much about Edwardian attitudes to women and sex as *Candida* and *The Second Mrs Tanqueray*.[34]

From time to time offstage events in London's theatrical world matched those in a Melville melodrama. Nothing in *Married to the Wrong Man* (Elephant and Castle Theatre, 1908) could have outdone the shocking descent of Oscar Wilde from West End idol to social outcast in 1895, and the plot of *A Drunkard's Story* (Terriss's Theatre, 1906) could hardly have been more dramatic than the fate of the great Adelphi star, William Terriss, whose name was commemorated in that Rotherhithe theatre. Terriss was a very popular leading man in melodramas at the Adelphi and Shakespearean roles at the Lyceum, admired for his breezy manner and vigorous performances. Shaw, who made fun of the plays he regularly appeared in, wanted him to star in *The Devil's Disciple*. On 16 December 1897 Terriss was stabbed through the heart at a back entrance of the Adelphi, in Maiden Lane, by a deranged and failed actor, Richard Prince, who had apparently got the mistaken idea that Terriss was barring his way to stardom. Terriss's murder created a sensation in London, and his funeral attracted a huge crowd.[35]

By 1914 West End audiences had come to terms with Shaw and Ibsen and were used to seeing the tiny glimpses of reality offered them by Jones and Pinero. In general, though, their diet was almost as insubstantial as it had been thirty years earlier. In the last spring before the Great War, London theatres offered several Anglicized French farces, musical comedies, burlesques, light comedies of manners (including a revival of Wilde's *An Ideal Husband*), two translated Sardou dramas from the 1860s and 1870s, and a spectacular show, *Sealed Orders*, complete with battleships and aerial scenes, at Drury Lane. The modern world was represented by occasional references to cars, telephones, and feminism, by Shaw's *Pygmalion* at His Majesty's, J. M. Synge's *Playboy of the Western World* at the Royal Court, Somerset Maugham's *Land of Promise* at the Duke of York's, and Jack Hulbert's new musical comedy, *The Cinema Star*, starring Cicely Courtneidge and Fay Compton, at the Shaftesbury.

A Variety of Music Halls

Theatre's main competitor, until the arrival of the cinema after 1900, was music hall. Since the early nineteenth century Londoners had been able to listen to professional singers while they ate or drank in pubs and 'song and supper rooms'. In the 1850s and 1860s entrepreneurs built halls with the primary purpose of selling entertainment, rather than refreshment, and called them music halls. Charles Morton, who earned the title 'father of the halls' by building a separate hall for musical performances alongside his pub on Westminster Bridge Road, the Canterbury Arms, in 1849, and who opened the first West End music hall, the Oxford, in 1861, was still active in the 1890s, when he helped to lift the London Pavilion and the new Tivoli out of the doldrums. Some of the biggest and most important halls in the 1880s and 1890s dated from the 1850s and 1860s, and were still going strong. The Canterbury, at the junction of Westminster Bridge Road and Upper Marsh (behind Waterloo Station), was rebuilt in grander scale in 1876, and staged prestigious ballets as well as hiring the greatest music-hall stars. Morton's second hall, the Oxford, at the eastern end of Oxford Street, remained a typical music hall, where men could watch the show from the bar, even after it was taken over and rebuilt in 1891–2 by a syndicate that also owned the Tivoli and the London Pavilion. The Royal Holborn, on High Holborn 150 yards east of Southampton Row, built as Weston's, one of the first West End halls, was famous for W. B. Fair's imperishable hit, 'Tommy, Make Room for your Uncle', and survived, as the Holborn Empire, until 1941. The London Pavilion, on Piccadilly Circus, where 'jingoism' was born in 1878, was rebuilt in 1885, and thrived as the main home of the great cockney comedian Dan Leno, until overwork helped to drive him to insanity and an early death in 1904. The Middlesex, at the northern end of Drury Lane, which had developed from a sing-song pub, the Great Mogul, into a large and popular music hall, was one of the last to retain its chairman, or master of ceremonies, and the South London Music Hall, in the London Road between St George's Circus and the Elephant and Castle, one of the oldest halls, was famous for ballet and spectacle.

Music halls are not easy to define. At one extreme, the great West End halls were often called variety theatres, and sometimes crossed and recrossed the line between music hall and theatre. For instance, the Alhambra, on the east side of Leicester Square, had been a theatre, a music hall, and a circus before 1883, when it was burned down and rebuilt in the Moorish style as a theatre. It soon became a music hall or theatre of varieties again, but went over to revue, with connected shows rather than individual 'turns', in 1911. Theatre managers like George Edwardes and Augustus Harris also ran music halls, and music-hall stars quite often appeared in theatres. In the early 1880s there were about 400 places in London that might be called music halls, because they were licensed to sell drink and play music, but only about forty large permanent music halls employing well-known performers. Elizabeth Pennell (wife of the artist Joseph Pennell), writing in praise of music halls in the *Contemporary Review* in 1893, claimed that there were 189 in London, and five years later *Baedeker's* guide told its readers that London had 500 music halls, entertaining about 300,000 visitors every night, but the LCC only licensed forty-two (seating 50,000) in 1891 and 1901, and fifty (seating 74,000) in 1911. Some of the *Baedeker's* halls were hardly more than public houses where drinkers could sing, not very different from the first music halls of the 1840s and 1850s, and most held fewer than 300 people.[36]

The humorist and novelist Thomas Anstey Guthrie (F. Anstey, the author of *Vice Versa*), who knew the London music hall well, wrote in 1891 that they could be divided into four types: the more aristocratic West End halls around Leicester Square, the lesser West End halls, the middle-class suburban halls, and the minor halls of working-class London. In the best halls men wore evening dress, and spent most of their time in the audience promenade or at one of the refreshment bars. Most of the women on the promenades were prostitutes, but generally behaved with decorum. The evening's entertainment, to which little attention was paid, consisted of a series of turns, and two half-hour ballet performances. The middle-class suburban halls, Anstey said, had a faded gaudiness, with entrances decorated with plaster statues and coloured lamps, and walls lined with gilded trellises or tarnished glass. Some still had a chairman with an auctioneer's hammer to announce each performer, as the old halls used to do. Most of the patrons of such places were respectable and comfortably off, including family parties and courting couples. 'Taken as a whole, the audience is not remarkable for intelligence; it is seldom demonstrative, and never in the least exacting, perfectly ready to be pleased with dull songs, hoary jokes, stale sentiment, and clap-trap patriotism.' This was just as well, because in a typical South London music hall visited by Anstey the show consisted of a woman in a glass tank who could eat and drink under water, a conjuror, a vocalist singing the virtues of 'Bovril – Hot Hot Hot', a novelty musician, and a sentimental sketch, 'The Little Stowaway'.

In Anstey's opinion, the working-class halls offered more enjoyment, though much less physical comfort, than the suburban ones. The evening's two shows might consist of a mimic impersonating bigger music-hall stars, about thirty songs, comic, romantic, patriotic, dramatic, or sentimental, and

several short plays or sketches, either melodramatic or farcical. The audience, mostly young men, greeted the comical sketches with the utmost
appreciation. 'They rock with laughter, the whole pit swaying like a field
of wheat in a breeze. Those who assert that the London poor are a joyless
class, incapable of merriment, should see this crowd when genuinely
amused, and consider whether there is not some exaggeration in descriptions of their hopeless gloom.' As for the songs, most were instantly
forgettable, and only a few – one or two a year – would ever be played or
whistled in the street. Since performers with good voices soon rose to the
better halls or the musical theatre, the singers in these cheap halls did not
sing well. The women, Anstey said, 'cannot sing in tune, their playfulness
is of a kind to cause a shiver, their voices are metallic, and even their personal appearance by no means prepossessing, as a rule; but still they are
always greeted with applause, and parted from with reluctance. It would
be infinitely more difficult to fail than succeed in satisfying a music-hall
audience'.[37]

In the West End, at least, the late Victorian music halls were not very
cheap, and had to attract middle-class customers to fill their better two-
shilling or five-shilling seats, and even their cheaper ones. By the 1890s
some of the most elaborate halls, like the London Pavilion or the Tivoli
Theatre of Varieties in the Strand, had no seats for less than a shilling, the
same price as gallery seats in most West End theatres. Working men could
pay sixpence to get into Collins' Music Hall on Islington Green or one of
the big East End and South London halls, like the Paragon Theatre of Varieties in the Mile End Road, or the vast 5,000 seat South London Palace
of Amusements near the Elephant and Castle. Men with only threepence
or fourpence to spare would have to go to one of the cheapest public-house
music halls, the non-alcoholic Royal Victoria Music Hall and Coffee
Tavern (the once and future Old Vic), or one of the cheap and popular
melodrama theatres in the poorer parts of town, such as the Standard
in Shoreditch, the Pavilion Theatre in Whitechapel (mainly for Jews), the
Britannia in Hoxton, or the Surrey in the Blackfriars Road.

Turns and Critics

The music hall was in its heyday in the 1880s, and some of the 'turns'
(a word first used in this sense around 1890) whose songs, dances,
and comedy routines topped the bills of the bigger halls were great stars,

popular heroes whose songs were known to a million Londoners. The twice-nightly system, introduced in the 1880s and widespread by 1900, and the associated practice of sending popular performers from one hall to another, made the top stars richer and more famous, but sometimes burned them out. Dashing from hall to hall, and perhaps drinking heavily, they often died young. The big names of the early 1880s were George Leybourne ('Champagne Charlie'), and his rival 'swell' or lion comique, 'The Great Vance' (Alfred Stevens), G. H. Macdermott ('We don't want to fight, but by Jingo if we do . . .'), Charles Coborn ('Two Lovely Black Eyes' and 'The Man who Broke the Bank at Monte Carlo'), G .H. Chirgwin ('The White-Eyed Kaffir'), and one of the first big female stars, Jenny Hill, 'The Vital Spark', whose spark went out in 1896, when she was forty-four. In the 1880s the great comedians Dan Leno and Harry Randall, and the male impersonator and singer Vesta Tilley ('Burlington Bertie'), were on their way to the top, and the stars of the Edwardian music hall, Albert Chevalier, Gus Elen, Harry Champion, Little Tich, George Robey, Vesta Victoria, and Marie Lloyd, were starting their stage careers. At the other extreme there were the obscure performers, enjoying a brief prosperity on a few pounds a week until loss of looks, drink, declining skills, or changing fashion caught up with them. Charlie Chaplin's mother and father, a singer with a failing voice and a baritone who drank too much, were fairly typical examples of the uncertainties of the profession.

The search for a larger and richer audience led music-hall owners to broaden the range of 'turns' they put on stage. From the 1880s the comic songs were interspersed with a greater number of novelty acts such as strongmen, clever animals, acrobats and jugglers, and short dramatic or comical scenes. 'Sketches', which the *Daily News* defined in 1892 as 'the new name for small or condensed, and in some cases mutilated, stage plays, the acting time of which shall not be more than 40 minutes', became a mainstay of music-hall shows, and helped turn music hall into 'variety', its more commercial twentieth-century successor. Sketches were not subject to the Lord Chamberlain's censorship until 1912, and thus a new form of dramatic comedy was able to develop in the 1890s and 1900s. They were not always comical. George Gray had a great success with his short anti-drink melodrama, 'The Road to Ruin', and his sketch against bullying, 'The Fighting Parson', which filled the Royal Holborn for 159 nights in 1903. The Holborn, which had been in apparently terminal decline, did so well with Gray's moral sketches that it recovered its prosperity, and survived as the last variety music hall in the West End until it was destroyed in the

Blitz. One of the early masters of this developing art form was Harry Tate (Ronald Hutchinson), who had a series of sketches about the misfortunes of a man trying his hand at golfing, fishing, gardening, motoring, and flying. By 1914 Tate's disaster sketches were so familiar that anything that was badly run in the war (the army or navy, for instance) was given 'Harry Tate's' as a prefix. Other popular sketches revolved around a single comical creation in a series of predicaments. Charles Austin's sketches about an inept policeman, Parker, PC, were among the most successful of these.

The master of the comic sketch was Fred Karno (Frederick Wescott), an illiterate circus and music-hall gymnast who turned a talent for devising silent sketches into a very lucrative career. Karno's first sketches, 'Love in a Tub' and 'Hilarity', were drawn from circus and pantomime traditions, and made him enough money to start his own business. From 1901 Fred Karno's Fun Factory, based in two houses in Vaughan Road, Camberwell, supplied stars and sketches to music halls all over London. Karno knew how to use the streets of London to generate public interest in his sketches, and had his companies (sometimes four or five of them) set off for the various music halls dressed for their parts and riding in appropriate vehicles. Karno's use of a Black Maria prison van to carry the cast of *Jail Birds* to the Paragon Theatre of Varieties in Stepney in 1901, with the costumed actors escaping and chasing each other, was a famous publicity coup. Karno's sketches started or promoted the careers of several great music-hall and comedy stars, whose later work, especially in silent films, reminds us of the sort of material he used on the London stage. Fred Kitchen, Billy Reeves, and Harry Weldon, famous stars in their day, were Karno players, and Will Hay joined him in 1914. Charlie Chaplin and Stan Laurel, names still famous today, got their early experience with Karno. A brilliant Karno sketch, 'Mumming Birds', in which drunken swells in music-hall boxes heckle and eventually fight with incompetent stage performers, went to America as 'A Night in an English Music Hall' in 1910 with Charlie Chaplin and Stan Laurel in the cast, helping both of them to start their American stage and film careers. As their stars rose, Karno's fell. In 1912 he spent most of his fortune on building a magnificent hotel, the Karsino, on Taggs Island, in the Thames near Bushey Park. Karno employed London's leading theatre architect Frank Matcham to design the hotel, which had a grand ballroom and concert pavilion, and opened it with star-studded celebrations in May 1913. By 1925 bad weather, the Great War, and mismanagement had driven Karno into bankruptcy and an obscure old age in the West Country.[38]

In the early days of the music hall it was said that its middle-class fans were the less respectable members of their class – bohemians, medical students, and young 'swells' on the look-out for women. In the 1890s, though, the big halls attracted a more mainstream middle-class clientele, including men who brought their wives. The singer Albert Chevalier had fans among London's ruling elite, including Lord Salisbury, Lord Rothschild, and the Dean of St Paul's, who liked his impersonation of the cheerful cockney costermonger, and perhaps took it for the real thing. Many other music-hall stars achieved fashionable success, performing for the Prince of Wales or appearing in West End plays. Dan Leno, 'the King's Jester', and George Robey were society favourites, and Vesta Tilley married well and grew old gracefully in Monte Carlo. Music halls were especially popular with poets and artists, who relished their faintly dissolute atmosphere, and used them as a source of ideas and images. For those who wanted to see and understand the 'real' London, the ordinary Londoner at ease, going to the Canterbury or the Middlesex was a pleasant alternative to tramping the streets with Charles Booth or taking up residence in Toynbee Hall. Arthur Symons, a particular enthusiast, filled such works as *London Nights* and *London: A Book of Aspects* with references to music halls, and fell in love with girls from the *corps de ballet*. Rudyard Kipling used to go to Gatti's in Villiers Street when he was alone in London in 1889, and his *Barrack Room Ballads*, published in 1890, were written to music-hall tunes and seem to owe their version of the cockney dialect to Albert Chevalier.[39] Walter Sickert was especially keen on the Old Bedford music hall, in Camden High Street, which he painted many times in the 1890s. According to his friend Will Rothenstein, Sickert

preferred the exhausted air of the music-hall, the sanded floor of the public house, and the ways and talk of cockney girls who sat to him, to the comfort of the clubs . . . Night after night Sickert would go to the Bedford or Sadler's Wells, to watch the light effects on stage and boxes, on pit and gallery, making tiny studies on scraps of paper with enduring patience and with such fruitful results. Incidentally he memorised the songs, storing his mind with the pregnant nonsense of music-hall doggerel and tunes . . . While for Sickert the music-hall was a workshop, for the rest of us it was a pleasant dissipation. The Empire Promenade was the orthodox place to go to. I remember meeting Le Gallienne there . . . At the Empire, or the Tivoli, other[wise] the Oxford, one would surely meet Arthur Symons, Ernest Dowson, Herbert Horne, Selwyn Image, Beardsley, or Max.[40]

Fortunately, the music hall did not become completely respectable. Marie Lloyd, the daughter of a Hoxton artificial-flower maker, was probably the most popular and successful female performer from the 1890s to the Great War, earning up to £600 a week. Her active and newsworthy love life, with three husbands and plenty of adultery, probably endeared her to the London public, and certainly gave an edge to her suggestive songs ('Oh, Mr Porter', 'She'd never had her ticket punched before', and many others), but prevented her from becoming a favourite of high society. Inevitably, she was not invited to appear alongside George Robey, Harry Tate, Little Tich, Vesta Tilley, George Chirgwin, Harry Lauder, and the great juggler Paul Cinquevalli at the first Royal Music Hall Performance at the Palace Theatre in July 1912. Even Vesta Tilley's trousers, essential for a convincing performance of 'Algy, the Piccadilly Johnnie with the little glass eye', caused Queen Mary some embarrassment. Marie Lloyd was one of the stars Arnold Bennett saw at the Tivoli on New Year's Eve, 1909: 'Little Tich was very good, and George Formby, the Lancashire comedian, was perhaps even better. Gus Elen I did not care for. And I couldn't see the legendary cleverness of the vulgarity of Marie Lloyd . . . All her songs were variations on the theme of sexual naughtiness. No censor would ever pass them, and especially he wouldn't pass her winks and her silences.'[41]

Critics were not all persuaded that the music hall had contributed a great deal to English culture. One of the most influential, William Archer, who had helped Anstey with his research in 1891, wrote a ferocious article for the *Contemporary Review* in March 1895, in which he dismissed talk of the artistic value of music halls as 'pseudo-aesthetic cant'. He accepted that London music halls had the best acrobats and jugglers in the world, because they paid the highest wages – Cinquevalli the juggler, the Schafer family of gymnasts, Morris Cronin and his Indian clubs, the Selbini cycling troupe. But in other respects the English music hall was 'the home of rampant, blatant and incredibly brainless vulgarity'. Of the thousands of songs written every year for music-hall singers, 'not one song of them all, not one verse, not one line from them, has passed into literature! They contribute a few cant phrases to the journalism of the moment, then pass away and are heard no more . . . Their philosophy is a mean and shallow knowingness, their patriotism is cheap and empty bluster.' Even in the much-praised 'cockney' songs of Albert Chevalier and Gus Elen, the 'representations of coster life are either absolutely trivial or grotesquely sentimentalised; they never get anywhere near the essence of their subject'.[42]

Archer's attack ignores the real pleasure and excitement the music hall brought to its audiences, but it is a useful corrective to those who have presented music-hall songs as a vehicle for the expression of popular discontent over high rents, the workhouse, or the class structure. Many of these songs were not written by their apparently (and sometimes truly) cockney performers, but by professional composers like George W. Hunt and Alfred Lee, the most prolific songwriters of the 1870s, and Joseph Tabrar, who wrote many thousands of songs in his office near Waterloo Station from the 1880s to the 1920s. Many very popular songs depicted a social world that was lower than that to which the majority of music-hall customers belonged, and it is possible that audiences were cheered up by being shown a life that was more deprived, though perhaps more lively, than their own. This is what Max Beerbohm, who knew music hall well, thought: 'The aim of the music hall is, in fact, to cheer up the lower classes by showing them a life uglier and more sordid than their own.'[43] The impact that music-hall songs could have did not have much to do with the truth or significance of their lyrics. It is hard to imagine a sillier song than 'Ta-ra-ra-Boom-de-ay', Lottie Collins' great hit of 1891, but its popularity in London and beyond was enormous. The *Manchester Guardian*'s London correspondent remembered its irritating ubiquity in the early 1890s:

> The tasteless and irrepressible air was at the time a universal annoyance; it appears now almost a portent . . . The very sound of the tune was jeering, as well as ludicrous . . . Its penetrating shrillness warned people that nothing was going to be taken seriously. The street-boy whistled it; the junior clerk sang it . . . even the cashier and the junior partner thought it . . . It had no individual interest whatever; it was the voice of the crowd asserting itself.[44]

Whatever the reason for their popularity, the best music-hall songs were loved and remembered for a century, transmitting to later generations a memory of late Victorian and Edwardian London as a strange world of rag-and-bone men, penniless monocled toffs, costermongers, moonlight flits, wives who bullied their husbands, couples on two-seater cycles, and working men who loved to gorge themselves on 'Boiled Beef and Carrots' or (to quote one of Harry Champion's less catchy titles) 'Hot Meat Pies, Saveloys and Trotters'.

The Battle for the Empire

The LCC, the licensing authority after 1888, was not particularly interested in the cultural value of music-hall entertainment, but it was extremely
concerned about the problems of fire, drink, and sex. The enforcement of
fire regulations was especially damaging to smaller halls in poor districts,
many of which lost their licences in the 1890s. There was a justified suspicion, voiced by the hall owners and Conservative newspapers, that
puritanical and anti-drink Progressives on the Council wanted to use their
licensing powers to suppress immoral songs and indecent behaviour in
music halls. The LCC's attack on the selling of drink in music-hall auditoria was a serious challenge, because many halls, especially those that were
little more than pubs, relied heavily on drink sales. The Council refused
several drink licences in its first few years, and by 1894 it had a general
policy of refusing new music and dancing licences to applicants who also
wished to sell drink. By 1911 only twenty-four of the fifty licensed music
halls (mostly the prestigious West End halls) had liquor licences, and drinking in the auditorium was usually forbidden. Luckily for their thirsty
customers, many music halls had a pub next door, and at least one, the
Hackney Empire, had a secret doorway connecting to it. The appointment
in 1890 of twenty-three LCC inspectors to report on music-hall performances and audiences, as well as structural matters, opened a third line of
attack on unruly halls. By 1892 the LCC Theatre and Music Halls Committee had a collection of 1,200 inspectors' reports, and used them when
licences came up for renewal. The owner of the Middlesex music hall
thought this was a 'ridiculous system of uneducated espionage', but the
inspectors' reports provide some interesting snapshots of the character of
different halls. Collins' music hall on Islington Green was 'a place of entertainment that I would not hesitate to take my wife and family to' (1890);
in the Canterbury, a year later, 'there were policemen and attendants in
every part of the house . . . the audience were principally tradespeople,
and their wives, working men, lads and girls, and considering the neighbourhood, well-behaved'; in Gatti's in Charing Cross, also in 1891, 'the
audience was respectable – there were "prostitutes" in the hall, but there
were none "soliciting"', but if there had been a fire the outcome would
have been 'something appalling'.[45]

London music-hall owners fought back, using the London Entertainments Protection Association and their sympathizers in the anti-Progressive press, but they also tried to defend themselves by imposing their own censorship on the singers, dancers, and comedians they hired. It was not always clear to the inspectors, proprietors, or the LCC committee whether particular entertainments were indecent or not. 'The borderline which divides the legitimate from the objectionable is not well-defined,' an inspector wrote in 1897. Were the 'skilful and artistic representations of well-known paintings and sculptures' by women in tights at the Palace Theatre of Varieties improper or not? Why was the refined art of ballet so extraordinarily popular? What was the significance of the words Lottie Collins ('not too bad and not too good') sang in her great hit of 1891, describing what she did with men when her father's back was turned – 'Ta-ra-ra Boom-de-ay', eight times over, with high kicks? What did Marie Lloyd, dressed as a schoolgirl, mean when she asked a schoolboy 'What's that for, eh?', at the Oxford music hall in 1896, and (to leap ahead to 1915) why was the great cockney singer Harry Champion so fond of his 'little bit of cu-cum-cu-cum-cu-cum, little bit of cu-cumber'? Richard Knowles, who came to London from America in 1891, was a great popular favourite, pacing the stage in his opera hat, black frock coat, and white trousers, but his material bothered the committee and its inspectors. He made fun of Mrs Ormiston Chant, the purity campaigner, and his patter about marital relations was 'altogether racy and insinuating – without expressing actual facts in plain words – but acting, winking, pointing to leave no doubt to what they mean'. Avoiding direct indecency, but implying the worst by gesture and innuendo, was one of the music-hall performer's most cherished skills, and getting the unspoken joke was one of the audience's greatest pleasures.[46]

In this war between 'respectable' or prudish London, represented by the Progressive/Liberal Party on the LCC, the temperance movement, and Christian morality campaigners of the National Vigilance Society, and 'racy' or realistic London, represented by music-hall owners, performers, and customers, the most famous battle was fought over the Empire, Leicester Square. The Empire was one of London's most famous music halls, and it was well known that its promenade was the resort of high-class prostitutes, never accosting but always available, and that its female ballet dancers did not wear many clothes. Mrs Laura Ormiston Chant, a leading figure in the campaigns for women's suffrage, temperance, and moral purity, had reported on London music halls for the *Vigilance Record*, the journal of the National Vigilance Association, in 1888–9. In 1894 she went to see what went on in Leicester Square for herself, and challenged the renewal of the Empire's licence in October. Several leading feminists (but not the great Josephine Butler) spoke on her behalf, and the Empire only kept its licence on condition that its manager, George Edwardes, agreed to stop selling drink in the auditorium and to erect a barrier between the music hall and the notorious promenade. The response from the Empire's friends and customers was powerful and well orchestrated. The *Daily Telegraph* printed 170 letters of protest against prudery and the 'New Woman', Arthur Symons and Bernard Shaw wrote to the anti-prudery *Pall Mall Gazette*, and young bucks, including Winston Churchill, pulled down the flimsy barrier erected by the Empire management. The Empire employed 647 people, and claimed to give work to another 3,000, and many of these people, the painters, actors, ballet dancers, scene shifters, choristers, and cab-drivers, met in protest against the decision, supported by the London Trades Council, the railway union, and Stewart Headlam's Church and Stage Guild. The women evicted from the Empire crowded the promenades of the Tivoli, the Alhambra, and the Oxford, and hardly anyone believed that a useful victory over vice had been won. The following year the Empire got its full licence back again.[47]

Frank Matcham and the Great Theatres

Strictly enforced safety regulations finished off many of the smaller music halls, but helped to create a new generation of large, luxurious, and well-built theatres and halls between 1880 and 1910. The building boom of these years was a response to the growth of the London market, but also to the Metropolitan Building Act of 1878, which imposed stringent safety regulations on London theatre and music-hall owners, preventing them from dangerously extending and adapting old buildings, as they had done before. The career of the leading specialist theatre architect of the 1870s and 1880s, Charles Phipps, who had designed about twenty London theatres and music halls, including the Savoy, the Prince of Wales, the Shaftesbury, the Tivoli music hall, and three surviving theatres, the Lyric, the Garrick, and Her Majesty's, was damaged by his admission after the Exeter Theatre fire of 1887, in which 140 people burned or suffocated to death, that his plans 'did not allow for smoke'. Frank Matcham, who had taken over his father-in-law Jethro Robinson's practice in Holborn in 1878 and had been involved with Robinson in advising the government on the new regulations, was well placed to succeed Phipps as London's leading theatre architect. Matcham's second London theatre, the Grand Theatre in Islington (1883), was praised for its good sightlines, acoustics, and ventilation, its economy of space and cost, and its ample fire-escape routes. This was just as well, since it burned down in 1888 and 1900, both times being rebuilt by Matcham. In 1885 Matcham was commissioned by the London Syndicate, which owned the Canterbury, the Tivoli, the Oxford, the London Pavilion, and suburban halls in Brixton, East Ham, Walthamstow, and Chelsea, to build the Paragon Theatre of Varieties, a very big music hall with a generous promenade and good ventilation, in Mile End Road. In 1890 Matcham rebuilt the Canterbury for the Syndicate, and later in the decade he built theatres and music halls for various clients in Shoreditch, Hammersmith (the Lyric), Brixton, Stratford, Crouch End (the Queen's Royal Opera House), Walham Green (the Granville Theatre), and Richmond. In 1899 he built the 3,000-seat New Cross Empire for Edward Moss, the owner of nationwide chains of theatres and halls. In 1900 Moss formed a partnership, Moss Empires, with another provincial owner, Oswald Stoll, and they began an assault on the London theatrical world, using Matcham as their principal architect.[48]

Matcham's first project for the Stoll–Moss Syndicate was the Hippodrome at Leicester Square, a combined water circus and music hall, complete with a 100,000-gallon tank operated by a hydraulic ramp. For nine years, until the tank was removed in 1909, an audience of 3,000 could watch elephants sliding down chutes into the water, and up to seventy polar bears swimming in it, as well as variety shows and circuses with large numbers of wild animals. Matcham's London Coliseum, built in St Martin's Lane for Stoll in 1904, had three revolving stages driven by electric motors at up to 20 mph, useful for simulated horse races and high-speed chases, and also for quick scene changes. In Drury Lane, Matcham rebuilt the Middlesex music hall (the Old Mogul) as the New Middlesex, a variety theatre which caused a scandal in 1914 by putting on a French revue featuring an apparently naked woman, 'the Girl with the Muff'. Most of the rest of Matcham's work for Stoll was in the suburbs, where he built a succession of 'Empire' variety theatres, in Hackney (1901), Shepherd's Bush (1903), Finsbury Park (1910), Chiswick (1912), and Wood Green (1912). And he still worked for the London Syndicate, which commissioned him to design the Holborn and Willesden Empires in 1906–7, the Lewisham Hippodrome in 1911, and the Palladium, a rival to the Coliseum and Hippodrome, in 1910.

In all, Matcham built or rebuilt thirty theatres and music halls in central and suburban London (and nearly a hundred elsewhere in the United Kingdom), for Stoll–Moss, Gibbons, and several independent owners. Bertie Crewe and W. G. R. Sprague, who worked for Matcham before opening practices of their own, built most of the rest. Matcham's use of steel cantilevers to support his huge sweeping galleries meant that there were no pillars to obscure the views of those in the stalls, and allowed him to construct efficient and impressive auditoria that still work well today. He built cheaply, quickly, and well, using oddly shaped city centre sites with skill, and his lavish use of fibrous plaster, along with his lack of academic training, allowed him to adorn his theatres with a fantastic variety of classical, Renaissance, baroque, rococo, Moorish, and oriental statues, balconies, and decorations. This pleased men like Stoll and Walter Gibbons of the London Syndicate, and probably delighted his equally untutored audiences, but it earned Matcham the contempt or condescension of his profession. Many of Matcham's buildings became cinemas, and those that escaped the Blitz were mostly demolished in the early 1960s, when cinema attendances collapsed. Now Matcham's reputation has revived, but few of his London theatres survive. Three of his West End theatres, the Palladium, Coliseum, and the Hippodrome (now mutilated as a night club), still exist, along with two of the Stoll Empires, at Hackney and Shepherd's Bush, the Victoria Palace and the beautiful theatre in Richmond. The Hammersmith Lyric was demolished in 1969, but its interior was reconstructed in a new building ten years later. W. G. R. Sprague, Matcham's pupil and rival, has fared better, because more of his buildings were true theatres, rather than theatrical music halls. Eight of the theatres Sprague built between 1899 and 1916, including St Martin's, Wyndham's, the Albery (once the New Theatre), the Strand, the Aldwych, the Gielgud (once the Globe), Queen's, and the New Ambassadors, are still in business.

Electric Palaces

The cinema, which helped to destroy the music hall after the Great War, began its public life in London as a variety show 'turn'. If we leave aside the Kinetoscope Parlour that opened at number 70 Oxford Street in October 1894, showing little films in a peepshow machine, the first public showing of a screened moving film in England took place on 10 January 1896, when the pioneering inventor and film-maker Birt Acres showed a film to his local Lyonsdown Photographic Society in Barnet. A few weeks later, on 20 and 21 February, a French music-hall performer, Félicien Trewey, who had the exclusive right to use the Lumiere brothers' Cinématographe (a combined movie camera and projector) in Britain, put on a movie show at the Marlborough Hall of the Regent Street Polytechnic, first for the press, then for the paying public. On 9 March Trewey moved to the Empire Theatre of Varieties, Leicester Square, where his Lumière film show became one of the evening's main attractions. We have Trewey to thank for some of the earliest films of London scenes. In spring 1896 he filmed the crowd outside the Empire, traffic at Piccadilly Circus and on Westminster and Tower Bridges, tigers at London Zoo, riders in Rotten Row, cyclists and riders arriving at a house in Hampstead, two girls dancing to a barrel organ, and one of the other acts at the Empire, a black-face minstrel troupe, dancing in the street. Though their content would seem tame to us, these little films were a great success, and were advertised prominently outside the hall. On 26 March the Empire's neighbour and rival, the Alhambra, had its own film show, this time featuring the films and equipment of London's own cinema pioneer, Robert Paul. Paul, one of the greatest and most versatile innovators in the early history of cinema, was born in Highbury, educated in the City and Guilds technical college in Finsbury, and trained in Elliott Brothers electrical shop in the Strand. In his electrical-instrument business in Hatton Garden, Paul made the movie camera which Birt Acres used between March and June 1895 to produce some of the first films ever shot in England, including the 1895 University Boat Race, a boxing match, and the arrest of a pickpocket. At first these were shown through peepshow Kinetoscopes (also made by him), but then he made his own 35mm projector, the Theatrograph, which he demonstrated in February 1896 at his Finsbury college and the Royal Institution. In March 1896, exploiting the commercial and entertainment possibilities of his wonderful and ever-improving machine, Paul gave film shows at the Egyptian Hall in Piccadilly (19 March), Olympia (21 March), and the Alhambra music hall, Leicester Square, on 25 March. While he was at the Alhambra he used its roof and one of its actors, Fred Storey, to shoot his first short fiction comedy, 'A Soldier's Courtship'. On 3 June Robert Paul shot the first true news film, a movie of the last moments of the 1896 Derby, which was won in a very close finish by the Prince of Wales' horse Persimmon. The film was shown the next day at the Alhambra and the Canterbury and was a terrific hit, demonstrating for the first time the commercial potential of the newsreel.[49] A year later, at least a dozen cinematographers filmed Queen Victoria's Diamond Jubilee procession, using equipment made by Paul, Lumière, and Gaumont, and between 1900 and 1902 audiences could watch the mighty British army making heavy weather of beating the Boers in the first filmed war. In 1901 and 1902 films of Victoria's funeral procession and her son's coronation were shown in music halls all over London.

Since it was such a vast market for films, and the home of several of the pioneers of the cinema, London quickly became a centre of film production, too. In 1898 the American Charles Urban formed a film-production company, the Warwick Trading Company, in Warwick Court (between High Holborn and Gray's Inn), which excelled in news films and documentaries. Nearby, Gray's Inn Road became an early centre of film production, with the optician Alfred Wrench's film developing and printing shop, Will Barker's Autoscope Company (1900), and the Topical Film Company (1911) all at number 50, and the Edison Phonograph Company at number 52. The outer suburban Thames Valley, so important for film production after the Great War, was already attracting film makers. Cecil Hepworth, the son of a magic-lanternist, was sacked by Charles Urban in 1899 and set up his own production company, Hepwix (later the Hepworth Manufacturing Company), in Walton-on-Thames. He concentrated on short and well-made fiction films, produced at the rate of about three a week. His early output included the famous *Rescued by Rover* (6 minutes, 1905) and its sequels, a series of slapstick comedies featuring Tilly the Tomboy, with Alma Taylor and Chrissie White, who became big stars in the 1920s, and one new technology's comment on another, *How it Feels to be Run Over* and *The Explosion of a Motor Car*, both made in 1900. By 1914, Hepworth's studio had made several hour-long feature films, including *Oliver Twist* and *Hamlet*, using stars of the West End theatre. Twickenham, Ealing, and Elstree, great names in film production between the wars, already had film studios by 1914.[50]

Film shows became a popular and familiar feature in music halls and fairgrounds, and businessmen and film-makers used a wide range of convenient buildings, including shops, schools, local halls, and skating rinks, to accommodate paying audiences in London. The LCC's records suggest that it licensed two 'Electric Theatres' for public entertainment in 1903, and eighteen in 1910. Which of these places might be called London's first true cinema is a matter of dispute and definition. The Balham Empire, a converted swimming bath, concert hall, and theatre which opened as a Pathé cinema in 1907, is a strong contender, but the Daily Bioscope, at 27–28 Bishopsgate Street, beats it. The Bioscope opened on 23 May 1906 with a bill that included film of the San Francisco earthquake and the Athens 'Interim' Olympics and two short comedies, and tickets at 2d and 4d for a twenty- or thirty-minute show. The syndicate owning the Daily Bioscope promised its customers a waiting lounge, an auditorium 'sumptuously upholstered in red and gold', quick lunch-hour shows, continuous programmes from noon till 9 p.m., and the latest Gaumont equipment, 'the Chrono, king of bioscopes', by which 'the objectionable flicker, so tiring to the eyes, has been entirely eliminated'.[51]

Projectors were hot, nitrate film was highly combustible, and crowded halls were hard to escape from. In January 1908, sixteen children were killed in a panic in Barnsley, and 160 died in an explosion and fire in Boyestown, Pennsylvania. Following these accidents the Cinematograph Act of 1909 was passed, and cinemas had to be licensed by the local authority, like theatres and music halls. From the start of 1910 all places showing films had to have a fireproof projector in a fireproof projection room. Licensing made film houses safer, and also easier for us to identify and count. Within the County, there were ninety-four licensed or provisionally licensed cinemas in November 1911, with seating for 55,000 people. A few of these were converted theatres or music halls, like Terry's in the Strand and Gatti's in Westminster Bridge Road, and others were halls with sloping floors, tip-up seats, a white-plastered screen, and an attractive front announcing that it was a 'Picture Palace', 'Electric Theatre', or cinema. There were already three cinemas with a thousand seats, the Premier Electric Theatre in Highbury, the Streatham Empire Picture Palace, and the Maida Vale Cinematograph Theatre, but most were about half that size. Unlike theatres, picture palaces were not concentrated in the centre of London. There were eight in Westminster and four in Tottenham Court Road, but twelve in the borough of Wandsworth, five in Stepney, six in Hackney, four each in Fulham and Brixton. There were probably about another sixty cinemas in the City and the outer suburbs, beyond the County boundary, and dozens more were opened by 1914.[52] For a show lasting sixty or ninety minutes, usually with a piano accompaniment, cinemas charged from 3d for benches at the front to 1s for padded seats at the back, with reductions for children. These were prices to attract poorer families and the lower middle class, who were just beginning to regard the picture palace, rather than the music hall, as their entertainment of choice. Over the next ten years, when longer feature films largely replaced 'shorts', cinema advanced from this beachhead, deep into territory till then held by music halls and theatres. By 1921 there were 266 licensed cinemas in the County, and only 94 licensed theatres and music halls.[53]

Music and Dancing

Music hall and musical comedy were the main source of the songs Londoners enjoyed hearing and singing in the 1880s and 1890s, and indeed many of them became so deeply embedded in English culture that they are still familiar today, when the halls and their stars are long gone. But there were other suppliers and purveyors of popular songs, including schools, churches, street singers, and municipal bands. The County of London, according to the census of 1891, had 10,425 professional musicians (half of them women), earning their livings in streets, concert halls, theatres, music halls, classrooms, churches, dancing academies, and bandstands.[54] The LCC gained powers to spend money on providing music in its parks in 1890, and took over the task from the National Sunday League. By 1911 there were three LCC bands (about 115 musicians in all), and sixty-four smaller bands hired for the summer season. Seventy London parks had permanent or temporary bandstands, and on a warm Bank Holiday nearly 100,000 Londoners would attend one or other of these performances. Some of London's best-known songs were popularized by sheet-music sales and parlour performances: Sir Arthur Sullivan's 'The Lost Chord', Michael Maybrick's 'The Holy City', Henry Bishop's 'Home Sweet Home'. London had nearly a hundred music shops in 1888, and it was the centre of the business of music publishing in England. In popular music, the leading London companies were Chappell, Boosey and Company, Ascherberg, and Francis, Day and Hunter, the pioneers of mass-produced sheet music with pictorial covers. Music publishers were not concentrated in a particular neighbourhood, as they were in New York's 28th Street ('Tin Pan Alley'), but when Francis, Day and Hunter moved to Charing Cross Road in 1897 and Lawrence Wright (the publisher and prolific songwriter also known as Horatio Nicholls) started his business round the corner in Denmark Street in 1911, this district began to look like the centre of the London music-publishing industry.

Music-lovers could also hear famous voices recorded on cylinders or discs. Edison's wax cylinder phonograph and Emile Berliner's gramophone, which used a flat wax disc, were good enough for commercial musical recordings by the 1890s. Progress was fastest in America, but in

London a branch of Berliner's Gramophone Company, with its famous 'His Master's Voice' trademark of a dog and a gramophone trumpet, was established in 1898, the year in which the Hotel Cecil Orchestra made its first dance record. The gramophone and phonograph popularized the operatic voices of Chaliapin, Caruso, and Nellie Melba, but the performers that dominated the London record catalogues just before the Great War were music-hall stars like George Robey, Harry Lauder, Harry Fragson ('The Caruso of the Halls'), the tenor Burt Shepard ('The Laughing Song'), Eugene Stratton, the banjo virtuoso Olly Oakley, and Dan Leno, whose famous clog dancing was captured on wax not long before his death in 1904.[55]

There were very close musical links between London and New York. All the West End musical comedies went to Broadway after their West End runs, initiating a process of cross-fertilization between London and New York that continued throughout the twentieth century. In return, American composers wrote some songs which, when sung in music halls or West End shows, seemed terribly British, including 'After the Ball', 'Down at the Old Bull and Bush', and the Boer War favourite 'Goodbye Dolly Gray'. In the 1890s the flow of influence was generally westwards, from London to New York, but the channels of communication also meant that new fashions in American music would reach London without much delay. The cakewalk, an African-American plantation dance, was popularized in London by Will Marion Cook's all-black song-and-dance show, *Clorindy, or the Origin of the Cakewalk*, which came to London from New York in 1899, and by the dancing of Bert Williams and George Walker in the first all-black musical, Cook's *In Dahomey*, which ran for 251 performances at the Shaftesbury Theatre in 1903–4. Ragtime, a syncopated musical style (with the main notes of the melody on the off-beat) based on the cakewalk, developed in America in the 1890s, and became commercially popular early in the twentieth century. Ragtime songs were sung and recorded in London before 1900, and in 1912 a great ragtime 'invasion' took place, when the American Ragtime Octette came to London, bringing with them such songs as 'Waiting for the Robert E. Lee' and 'Ragtime Cowboy Joe'. Within a year there were about 130 American ragtime bands playing British music halls, as well as ragtime banjo players and brass bands that had picked up the ragtime style, though not the true jazz musician's ability to improvise. Ragtime songs were popularized in London revues, plotless assortments of songs, dances, and sketches that were popular in some big West End theatres and music halls in the last pre-war years. In

1912 and 1913 ragtime songs and American singers featured in musical revues at the Alhambra, the Hippodrome and the Empire Leicester Square – *Everybody's Doing It, Kill That Fly!, Hello, Ragtime!, Keep Smiling,* and *Hello Tango* – and by 1914 the new American singing style was very familiar to London audiences. The songs they learned from these shows, 'Everybody's Doing it', 'Row, Row, Row', the 'Hitchy-Koo', 'That's A-Plenty', 'Get Out and Get Under' (the 'Daisy Bell' of the automobile age), and the Irving Berlin hit 'Alexander's Ragtime Band', announced the arrival of a new age of American popular music, tinged with the rhythms of ragtime and jazz. So when the Original Dixieland Jazz Band and Will Cook's Southern Syncopated Orchestra came to London in 1919, and played their jazz at the new Hammersmith Palais de Danse, they were resuming a process that had begun before – and been interrupted by – the First World War.[56]

The new music helped to revive popular interest in dancing, which had hardly moved on from waltzes, polkas, and the lancers since the middle of the nineteenth century. Masked balls, which had fallen out of favour in the mid-nineteenth century, had been revived at Covent Garden Theatre in the 1890s, and those who could afford a guinea (one pound and a shilling, a workman's weekly wage) could dance from midnight till 5 a.m. to the music of Dan Godfrey, the famous military bandmaster. The wearing of masks and fancy dress was optional, and in decline. Dancing teachers and promoters did their best to satisfy the demand for new dances, preferably ones that involved a fair amount of bodily contact, with new inventions and American imports. The schottische and the two-step were brought over from America in the 1890s, the veleta was invented in 1900 as an entry for the annual St James's Hall contest to find a new sequence dance, and the cakewalk caught on after *Clorindy* in 1899. Several easy 'one-step' walking dances based on syncopated ragtime rhythm, including the 'Bunny Hug' and the 'Grizzly Bear', arrived in London from America around 1910, and one, the 'Turkey Trot', was popularized by Irving Berlin's ragtime song, 'Everybody's Doing It' in the London show of that name in 1912. The refinement of the 'animal dances' into the graceful fox-trot and quickstep, the dances that filled the London dance halls in the 1920s, was mainly the work of the Anglo-American dancing partnership Irene and Vernon Castle, who introduced the 'Castle Walk' in New York in 1912, and the others over the next five years.[57]

In 1912, when Compton Mackenzie went to a Covent Garden ball, the change from waltz to one-step had already begun. 'Ragtime was beginning to reduce the number of waltzes. The fox trot had been invented . . .

There was also a dance called the bunny-hug.' For those who could not afford a guinea, there were local 'hops', costing from threepence to a shilling, in commercial and municipal halls all over London. The Holborn Town Hall hop, every Monday, Thursday, and Saturday in the winter months, was one of the most popular, and was described at length by Robert Machray in 1902. The master of ceremonies, a dancing teacher or 'professor of dancing', acted as chaperon and instructor, and young men and women, mostly drawn from 'the exceeding great army of shop assistants', mixed with each other freely. They danced well and seriously to the music of an eight-piece band, to the tunes that would be heard at a society ball – waltzes, lancers, barn dances, a cake walk, and more waltzes.[58] Walter Macqueen-Pope, a theatre manager who wrote several books of reminiscences about pre-war London, remembered these dances as lively but decorous occasions, in which courtship took second place to the display of dancing skills. Price and location determined the social class of the young participants – threepenny or sixpenny hops in a shed or a room above a shop for working men, clerks, and shop girls, and one- or two-shilling dances with supper and dance cards in a tennis club or local hall or 'assembly room' for the middle classes. Dress might vary from class to class, but dancing skills and styles did not. Waltzes predominated, but there were polkas, barn dances, the Paul Jones, the valeta, the lancers (the high spot of the evening) and, from about 1904, the cakewalk. The local hall played many parts in middle-class suburban life. 'It was to this hall that parents might take you to political or other meetings, to lectures to improve your mind, to wedding breakfasts, coming-of-age parties, to bazaars, for it was the hub of the social life of the suburb.'[59]

The LCC's licensing records show that there were hundreds of places where dances could be held in Edwardian London. Thirteen assembly rooms, including large ones (seating a thousand or more) in Balham, Putney, and Highbury, had music and dancing licences in 1911, and so did twenty-five church halls, eighteen municipal halls, and forty-two other public or commercial halls. Twelve skating rinks and eighteen swimming baths, mostly with seating for over a thousand, had dancing licences, enabling them to fit temporary dance floors when their sport was out of season. In 1914 the *Illustrated London News* noticed a new fashion for dancing after supper, either in cabaret clubs like the Four Hundred Club in Leicester Square, or in the Winter Garden of the Savoy, but the LCC's records show that many hotels and restaurants already had dancing licences in 1911. Seventeen hotels, including the Ritz, the Savoy, the Cecil, the Waldorf, the Piccadilly, and the Strand Palace, and eleven restaurants, including Café Monico, the Connaught Rooms, the Criterion, the Trocadero, Frascati's, and the Holborn Restaurant, were licensed for dancing. In all, the LCC issued 253 music and dancing licences in 1911, and although not all of these places were used for regular dances these figures suggest that the dance-free city described by Besant in 1884 had disappeared, and that the popular dancing culture that we associate with the 1920s and 1930s had already taken root in London, along with the cinema, the gramophone, and the musical, in the ragtime years before the Great War.

Conclusion

CHAPTER TWENTY-TWO

✳

LONDON BEFORE 1914

A New World

The First World War, which began, as far as the United Kingdom was concerned, on 4 August 1914, seemed to bring the world described in this book to an end, and for 750,000 British men, including about 124,000 Londoners, this was literally true. The idea that the War was a 'deluge', a great divide between the Victorian and Edwardian world and the modern age, is a powerful and attractive one, which gives due acknowledgement to the horror of the conflict and recognizes its terrible impact on those who took part in it. A leading exponent of the view that the Great War is the watershed between the traditional and the modern age puts it like this: 'In destroying the old, the war helped the rise of the new: out went gold sovereigns, chaperones, muffin men, and the divine right of private enterprise; in came state control, summer time, a new prosperity and a new self-confidence for families long submerged below the poverty line.'[1]

Of course, the War brought about many temporary changes, including a dislocation of international trade and finance, a much greater government control over work, food, and prices, the recruitment of women into manual and skilled jobs previously (and subsequently) barred to them, a rise in the number of married women working, a shift in industrial production towards munitions and other war industries, the end of unemployment, the suspension of sporting events and the tightening of licensing laws, dimmer street lights, fewer buses and cars, a sharp fall in the birth rate, a rise in illegitimacy and the mortality rate of one- to four-year-olds, and the government or military occupation of many hotels, parks, and clubs. Some wartime changes were permanent, or left a permanent residue: the rise in prices and wages, the increase in trade union membership, shorter working hours, higher taxation, a more active state, an acceleration in the technology of flight and wireless broadcasting.

But the Londoners who marched off to France in August 1914 were not leaving behind them a gas-lit, horse-drawn city, hardly changed from the days of Dickens and Mayhew. It is true that London was still, in its worst parts, an impoverished world of slums, workhouses, sweatshops, prostitutes, dying infants, and men and women coughing with tuberculosis or bronchitis. But the changes that had taken place since the 1880s were enormous, and had touched almost every life. Mortality, including infant mortality, had fallen by over a third, and the deadly power of infectious diseases over the population was being broken at last. Almost the whole population had been through elementary education, and many had gone further. Basic foods were much cheaper, and the level and variety of nutrition had much improved. Families were smaller, and women of all classes were starting to escape from the servitude of repeated and unlimited childbirth. The working lives of women, contrary to the common impression, changed more fundamentally and permanently in the pre-war decades than in the war and the 1920s. London's female workforce grew by 176,000 between 1891 and 1911, and only 34,000 between 1911 and 1921. The employment of married women and the entry of women into skilled engineering and munitions work was much greater in the war, but the employment trend that most affected women in the longer term, the growth of white-collar work in shops, offices, and some of the professions instead of work as servants and needlewomen, made its greatest strides in the pre-war decades. The 'New Woman', going to secondary school and perhaps university, earning her living, asserting her social and political rights, challenging Victorian sexual standards, riding a bicycle, going out unchaperoned, marrying for love, limiting her family, voting in local elections, was already a familiar figure in the 1890s and 1900s.

The twentieth-century city has been dominated by the application of new technology, especially electric power, lighting, communication, motorized transport, the cinema, and broadcasting. All these except the last were commonplace in London before the Great War. Electric- and petrol-driven transport dominated London's roads, sharing them with bicycles and horse-drawn goods vehicles. More Londoners were killed by motorized transport in the last pre-war years than in an average year in the 1990s. A few roads fit for the new transport had been built, and the inter-war network of bypasses and circular roads had already been planned. Many London streets and houses were lit by electricity, and the others had modern gas lamps which gave a similar light. Cinemas were spreading fast, starting to challenge theatres and music halls, which were themselves greatly altered in appearance and quality from those of the 1870s.

Telephones were in widespread use in offices, if not yet in homes, and mass-produced national papers were sold by the million. On a Sunday, Edwardian Londoners were far more likely to read a popular newspaper than they were to go to church. As the power of Christian teaching declined, they might be influenced now by ideologies which Londoners of the 1870s would probably not have heard of, socialism and feminism.

In the field of architecture, London had few 'skyscrapers', and continued to be a low-rise city even in the 1930s, but thousands of poorer Londoners lived in council flats, and richer ones in apartment blocks with electric lifts, and many office workers and hotel guests, although they did not know it, were working or living in steel- or concrete-framed buildings. Many of the great department stores that dominated West End retailing in the twentieth century were already built, and chain stores were already threatening the prosperity of the independent shop. London's suburban sprawl, which is usually presented as an interwar phenomenon, was very far advanced by 1914, when nearly 3,000,000 Londoners lived beyond the County boundary, and such distant places as Golders Green, Ilford, Ealing, Hendon, Finchley, Wimbledon, West Ham, and Beckenham were well established as London suburbs. In some of these places new industries, based on electricity and mechanization, were already thriving, establishing the basis for London's industrial dominance in the interwar years. The first mutterings of discontent from those who wanted to encircle London with a green girdle or green belt were beginning to be voiced, though it took another thirty years for their views to achieve their late-twentieth-century grip.

In the years between the 1908 Olympics and the outbreak of the Great War the sense of rapid change, of the hatching of a new world, was intense. This anticipation was fostered by the writings of popular prophets, especially H. G. Wells, whose Edwardian novels and stories dealt with germ warfare, air combat, mutated animals and food, moon landings, and the sexual revolution. Reality could not match this fiction, but it was not so far behind. In these few years great advances in mechanical transport transformed the experience of travelling in London. The new deep electric Tube lines, the Piccadilly, Northern, and Bakerloo, started operating in 1906 and 1907, and over the next six years motor buses and taxis drove horse-drawn omnibuses and cabs from the London streets. The White City showground, with its electric lights, scenic railway, and flip-flap ride, the arrival of ragtime music and dancing, and the building of Selfridge's, symbolized the arrival of a new popular culture with an American flavour. The outbreak of militant suffragette protests in Westminster, beginning with heckling in 1907 and reaching a climax of arson, window-smashing, and bombing in 1912–13, declared that the process ran deeper than mere technological advance, and involved a fundamental rethinking of relations between the sexes. The introduction of Old-Age Pensions in 1908, and of limited unemployment and sickness insurance in 1911, initiated a state-led social revolution, recognizing that the country might gain more from rescuing the old, sick, and unemployed from the worst consequences of their poverty than by punishing them for their improvidence.

Change in the Air

Flight and the wireless, two technologies that developed very quickly during the Great War, both made their mark on London in the last years of peace. Guglielmo Marconi had arrived in London to apply for his first wireless patent in 1896 (the year of the first London film show and the launching of the *Daily Mail*), and over the next ten years valves, tuning devices, and the other components of a practical broadcasting were developed in Europe and America. The Marconi Company prospered, and sparked a political crisis in 1913 when several Liberal ministers were accused of dishonest dealing in its shares. In that same year the company started making experimental speech and music broadcasts from Marconi House in the Strand, which could be picked up by wireless enthusiasts all over London.[2] The wider public were more aware of the use of wireless as a means of communication at sea, especially through two sensational stories, the arrest of Dr Crippen and the sinking of the *Titanic*. In July 1910 the headless and largely boneless body of Cora Crippen (a singer with the stage name Belle Elmore) was found buried in the coal cellar of 39 Hilldrop Crescent, near Holloway Prison. Peter Crippen, an American who dealt in patent medicines and called himself a doctor, went missing with his mistress, but was captured on a steamship heading for Montreal, thanks to a Marconi wireless message from its captain, which read as follows: 'Have strong suspicions that Crippen – London cellar murderer and accomplice are among Saloon passengers. Moustache taken off – growing beard. Accomplice dressed as boy. Voice manner and build undoubtedly a girl.' Crippen's flight, capture, trial, and execution were the newspaper story of 1910. In April 1912 wireless helped to save lives in the *Titanic* disaster, though many more might have been saved if its SOS signals had been picked up and answered promptly by nearby ships, as those sent by the sinking emigrant ship the *Volturno* were eighteen months later.

Advances in heavier-than-air powered flight were extremely rapid in the six years before the Great War. The French flier Henri Farman made the first one-kilometre circular flight in Europe in January 1908, and Colonel Samuel Cody, an American-born showman in a 'ten-gallon' hat, made the first flight in Britain at Salisbury that October. The early British flights were made in Salisbury, Bournemouth (where Charles Rolls was killed in 1910), and Brooklands in Surrey. But in 1910 one of the early English fliers, Claude Grahame-White, bought a 200 acre estate in Hendon, in North-west London, as a commercial aerodrome and a site for air shows that would stimulate and exploit the interest of Londoners in the new technology. Using money won in races in the USA, Grahame-White went into partnership with Louis Blériot, the first man to fly across the Channel, and Hiram Maxim, the inventor and aeronaut, to develop the site. From the spring of 1912 there were tournaments and shows every weekend at Hendon Aerodrome, and the paying public could watch skilled fliers doing the tricks and stunts that they would be using in combat within two or three years. In collaboration with Lord Northcliffe and the *Daily Mail*, Grahame-White, who was as much a showman as a businessman and flying ace, popularized flight by flying over London and dropping rose petals on the city. London's other great flying ace was Alliott Verdon-Roe, who built and flew planes on the Lea Marshes, near Walthamstow, from 1909 to 1910, when he moved to Manchester to manufacture aircraft. Flight was publicized in newspaper articles, films, music-hall songs, and sketches, and in stories and stage melodramas, some of which raised the terrifying possibility that Britain might be bombed or invaded from the air. Hendon's air shows became more dramatic and popular, with demonstrations of looping the loop and flying upside down by the first Englishman to master these tricks, B. C. Hucks. In July 1912 the artist Spencer Gore took a party of painters of the Camden Town group to Hendon, where they went up in Blériot planes. Gore's picture of this outing, *Flying at Hendon*, is one of the first paintings featuring an aeroplane. The *Daily Mail* also stimulated the development of longer distance commercial flight by offering a prize for the first flight from London to Manchester in under twenty-four hours. Grahame-White took up the challenge in April 1910, flying by night to make up for time lost with engine trouble, but he was beaten in a race by Louis Paulhan, who did the journey with only one stop, and won £10,000.[3]

Three years after the opening of the London Aerodrome at Hendon, Londoners who had been thrilled by aerobatic stunts and mock fights and bombing raids got an unpleasant taste of the real thing, when London was bombed, first, from 1915 to 1917, by airships, and then, from 1916 to 1918, by aircraft. London was not driven back into a pre-industrial age, as H. G. Wells had imagined in his 1908 novel *The War in the Air*, but 670 of its citizens died, nearly 2,000 were injured, and many more took refuge in the deep-level Tube, using one new technology to mitigate the effects of another.

The *London Symphony*

So this was London just before the outbreak of the 'war to end wars' – a city of unparalleled size and complexity, a city of cities, with 4,500,000 people in its twenty-eight metropolitan boroughs, and another 3,000,000, enough to fill any other city in Europe, spilled over into its five suburban counties. Those who want to feel the power and beauty of London in these last years of peace, its haunting combination of night-time stillness and frantic daytime activity, of miserable poverty and unimaginable riches, of ancient buildings and traditions alongside the jarring intrusions of an electrical and motorized modern world, could do worse than listen to a piece of music and read the final pages of an Edwardian novel. In 1909 Ralph Vaughan Williams spent an evening with his friend and fellow composer George Butterworth, playing music and smoking. Stimulated by Butterworth's suggestion that he should write a symphony, Vaughan Williams struck on the idea of writing a piece that reflected his feelings about London, his adopted city. The work took him several years to complete, and it was not finished until the end of 1913, or performed until March 1914, in the Queen's Hall, Langham Place. The *London Symphony* does not attempt to describe London or to mimic its sounds (except in one or two brief passages), but rather to capture its spirit, and to evoke its mood in particular places or at particular times of day. 'It is in no sense descriptive', Vaughan Williams wrote in 1925, 'and though the introduction of the "Westminster chimes" in the first movement, the slight reminiscence of the "Lavender Cry" in the slow movement, and the very faint suggestion of mouth organs and mechanical pianos in the Scherzo give it a tinge of "local colour", yet it is intended to be listened to as "absolute" music', perfectly comprehensible to those with no knowledge of London. Still, he went on to explain that the allegro section of the first movement 'may perhaps suggest the noise and hurry of London, with its always underlying calm'. The title sometimes given to the slow second movement, 'Bloomsbury Square on a November Afternoon', serves as a clue to the music, Vaughan Williams said, but not its explanation. On the third movement, a scherzo (nocturne), the composer wrote: 'If the hearer will imagine himself standing on Westminster Embankment at night, surrounded by the distant sounds of the Strand, with its great hotels on one side, and the "New Cut" on the other, with its crowded streets and flaring lights, it may serve as a mood in which to listen to this movement.' The fourth movement ends with the Westminster chimes again, and a coda which took its inspiration, Vaughan Williams said, from the final pages of H. G. Wells' 1909 novel of modern city life, *Tono Bungay*.

This last section of *Tono Bungay*, 'Night and the Open Sea', describes the narrator's voyage down the Thames to the sea, on a destroyer just completed in the last Chiswick shipyard, a voyage in which he seemed 'to be passing all England in review'. From the aristocratic, Anglican, and sporting England of Kew, Putney, and Hurlingham, the ship went 'past the long stretches of muddy meadow and muddy suburb to Battersea and Chelsea'. In Battersea Reach

> there come first squalid stretches of mean homes right and left and then the dingy industrialism of the south side, and on the north bank the polite long front of nice houses, artistic, literary, administrative people's residences, that stretches from Cheyne Walk nearly to Westminster and hides a wilderness of slums. What a long slow crescendo that is, mile after mile, with the houses crowding closelier, the multiplying succession of church towers, the architectural moments, the successive bridges, until you come out into the second movement of the piece with Lambeth's old palace under your quarter and the houses of Parliament on your bow! Westminster Bridge is ahead of you then, and through it you flash, and in a moment the round-faced clock tower cranes up to peer at you again and New Scotland Yard squares at you, a fat beef-eater of a policeman disguised miraculously as a Bastille.
>
> For a stretch you have the essential London; you have Charing Cross railway station, heart of the world, and the Embankment on the north side with its new hotels overshadowing its Georgian and Victorian architecture, and mud and great warehouses and factories, chimneys, shot towers, advertisements on the south.

The northward skyline grows more intricate and pleasing, and more and more does one thank God for Wren. Somerset House is as picturesque as the civil war, one is reminded again of the original England, one feels in the fretted sky the quality of Restoration Lace.

Then the ship passes the Inns of Court and passes under Blackfriars road and railway bridges

and just between them is the finest bridge moment in the world – and behold, soaring up, hanging in the sky over a rude tumult of warehouses, over a jostling competition of traders, irrelevantly beautiful and altogether remote, Saint Paul's! . . . Only the tall warehouses and all the roar of traffic have forgotten it, every one has forgotten it; the steamships, the barges, go heedlessly by regardless of it, intricacies of telephone wires and poles cut blackly into its thin mysteries, and presently, when in a moment the traffic permits you and you look round for it, it has dissolved like a cloud into the grey blues of the London sky.

. . . The third movement begins, the last great movement in the London symphony, in which the trim scheme of the old order is altogether dwarfed and swallowed up. Comes London Bridge, and the great warehouses tower up about you, waving stupendous cranes, the gulls circle and scream in your ears, large ships lie among their lighters, and one is in the port of the world.

Past the Tower of London and under 'the vulgarest, most typical exploit of modern England, the sham Gothic casings to the ironwork of the Tower Bridge', and on towards the port and the open sea:

One goes down the widening reaches through a monstrous variety of shipping, great steamers, great sailing-ships, trailing the flags of all the world, a monstrous confusion of lighters, witches' conferences of brown-sailed barges, wallowing tugs, a tumultuous crowding and jostling of cranes and spars, and wharves and stores, and assertive inscriptions. Huge vistas of dock open right and left of one, and here and there beyond and amidst it all are church towers, little patches of indescribably old-fashioned and worn-out houses, riverside pubs and the like, vestiges of townships that were long since torn to fragments and submerged in these new growths. And amidst it all no plan appears, no intention, no comprehensive desire. That is the very key of it all. Each day one feels that the pressure of commerce and traffic grew, grew insensibly monstrous, and first this man made a wharf and that erected a crane, and then this company set to work and then that, and so they jostled together to make this unassimilable enormity of traffic. Through it we dodged and drove eager for the high seas.

MAPS

1. The growth of London between 1850 and 1914.

Reproduced from the Royal Commission on Local Government in
Greater London, 1957–60, with the permission of the
Office of Public Sector Information.

2. A plan of Kingsway and the Aldwych.

C. Gordon, *Old-time Aldwych, Kingsway and Neighbourhood* (London, 1903).

3. London's underground railway system in 1910.

401 Views of London (London, n.d.)

4. The distribution of large factories in the County of London, 1898.

Reproduced from the Royal Commission on London Traffic, 1905–6.

5. Central London in 1899.

J. G. Bartholomew's *Royal Atlas of England and Wales* (London, 1900).
Maps 5a to 5d cover the northern half of central London from west to east,
and maps 5e to 5h cover the southern half.

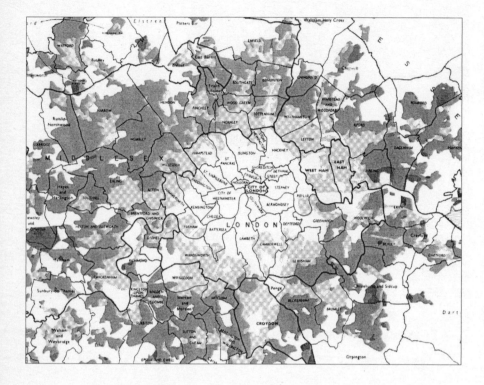

1. The growth of London. The white central area is London as it was in 1880 and the light grey represents its growth by 1914. The darker greys show suburban growth between 1914 and 1955.

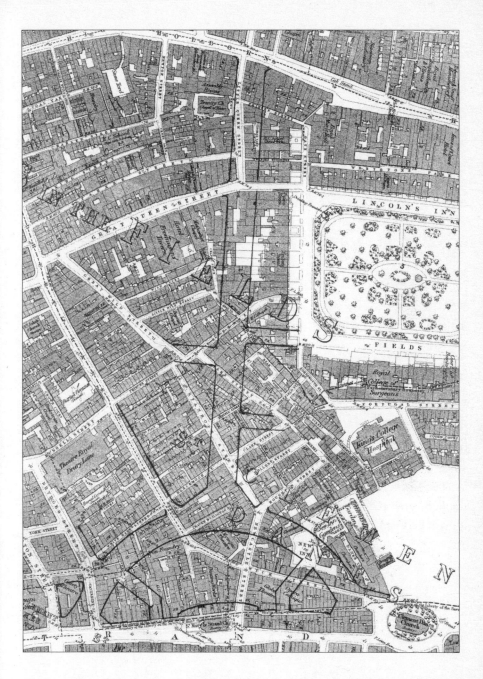

2. The route of Kingsway, the Aldwych and the widened Strand superimposed on a map of the streets to be demolished. Holywell Street (alongside the Strand), Wych Street, four theatres, a printing works and an iron foundry were cleared to make way for the Aldwych.

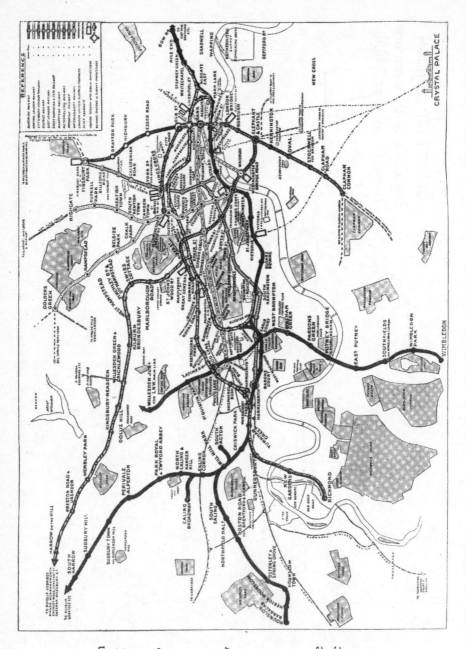

3. London's underground railway system in 1910, including the new deep level 'tube' lines, the Central, Bakerloo, Piccadilly, Hampstead, City and South London, and Waterloo and City lines. The map shows some suburban electric tram lines, and London's open spaces and football clubs.

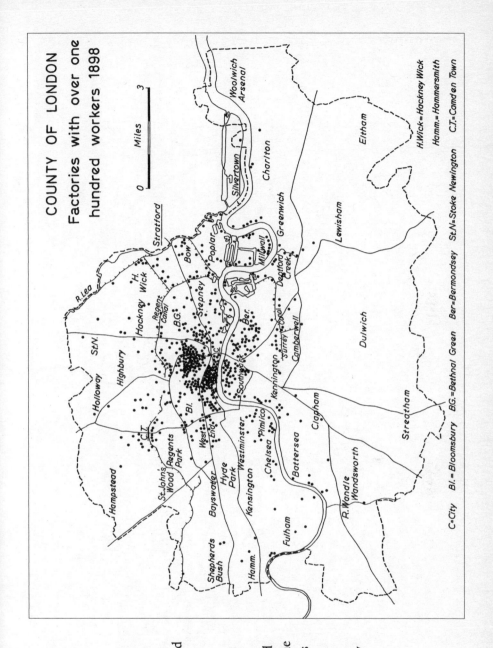

COUNTY OF LONDON
Factories with over one
hundred workers 1898

0 Miles 3

Woolwich Arsenal
Silvertown
Charlton
Greenwich
Deptford Creek
Millwall
Poplar
Bow
Stratford
R. Lea
H. Wick
Hackney Wick
Regent Canal
Stepney
B.G.
St.N.
Highbury
Holloway
Bo.
C.
Bl.
C.T.
Southwark
Surrey Canal
Camberwell
Kennington
West End
Westminster
Pimlico
Chelsea
Battersea
Clapham
Dulwich
Lewisham
Eltham
Streatham
St. John's Wood
Regents Park
Hyde Park
Bayswater
Kensington
Fulham
R. Wandle
Wandsworth
Hamm.
Shepherds Bush
Hampstead

C=City   Bl.=Bloomsbury   B.G.=Bethnal Green   Ber=Bermondsey   St.N=Stoke Newington   C.T.=Camden Town
H.Wick=Hackney Wick
Hamm.=Hammersmith

4. A map from the 1905–6 Royal Commission on London Traffic, based on Home Office returns, showing factories within the County of London with over a hundred workers in 1898. The main concentrations were in the City, Holborn, Finsbury, Shoreditch, Stepney and Southwark.

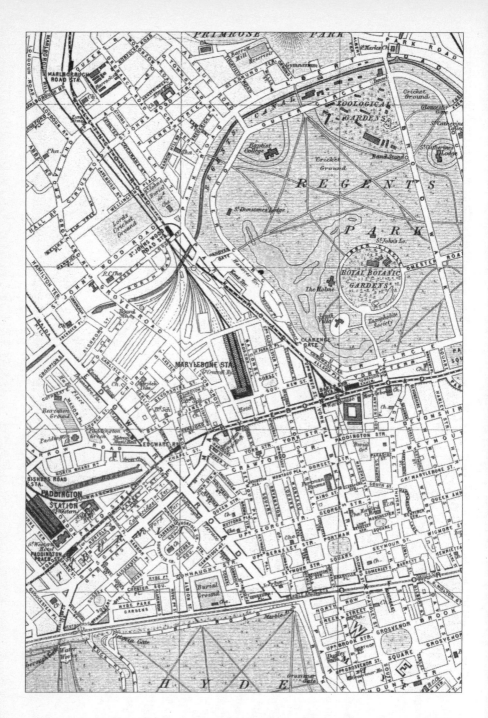

5a. Bayswater, St Marylebone and St John's Wood. The workhouse opposite Baker Street station is the one described on pages 63–4. The Royal Botanic Society's gardens in Regent's Park closed in 1932, when their lease expired. Marylebone Station opened in 1899.

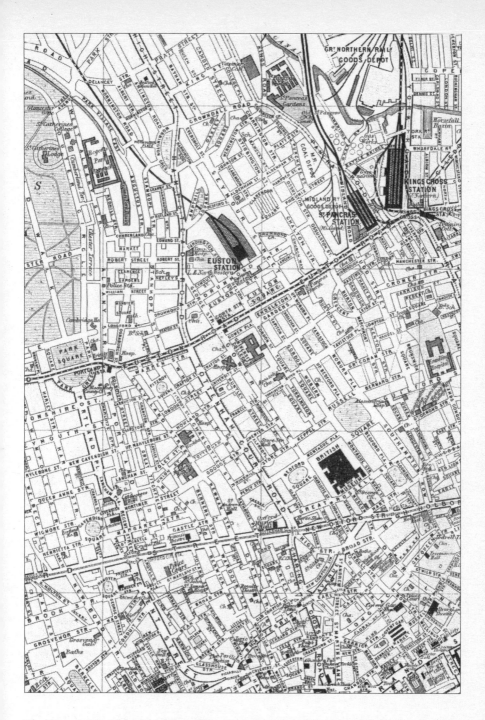

5b. Euston, St Pancras, Bloomsbury, and parts of St Marylebone, Soho and St Giles. The Central London Railway is marked along Oxford Street, and the older District and Circle lines run under Marylebone and Euston Road. Horse-trams were excluded from the West End, but are visible in this section along Hampstead, St Pancras, Caledonian and Gray's Inn Roads.

5c. Holborn, Clerkenwell, Finsbury, and parts of the City and Islington. Christ's Hospital (on Newgate Street) was demolished in 1902, and the Foundling Hospital in 1926. Kingsway and the Aldwych had not been built. There are horse-tram routes on most main streets, but only as far south as Holborn.

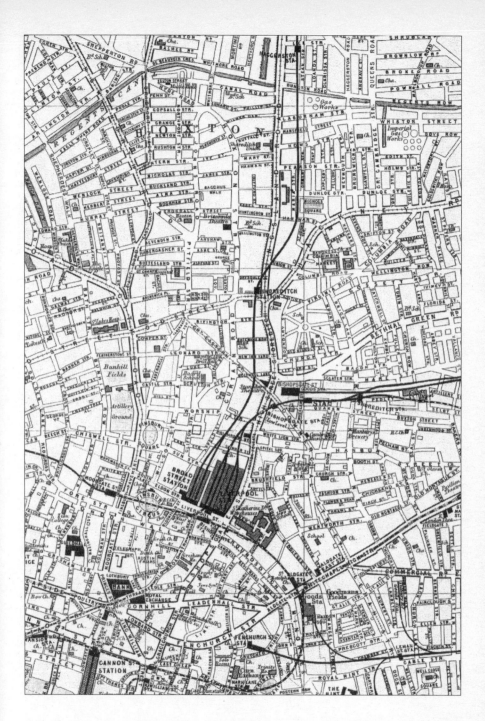

5d. Hoxton, Shoreditch, Whitechapel and parts of the City and Bethnal Green. The Jews' School on Bell Lane (east of Liverpool Street Station) was the biggest elementary school in the country, with over 4,000 pupils, and the LCC's Boundary Street estate, east of High Street Shoreditch, had just replaced the Old Nichol rookery (see pages 78 and 180).

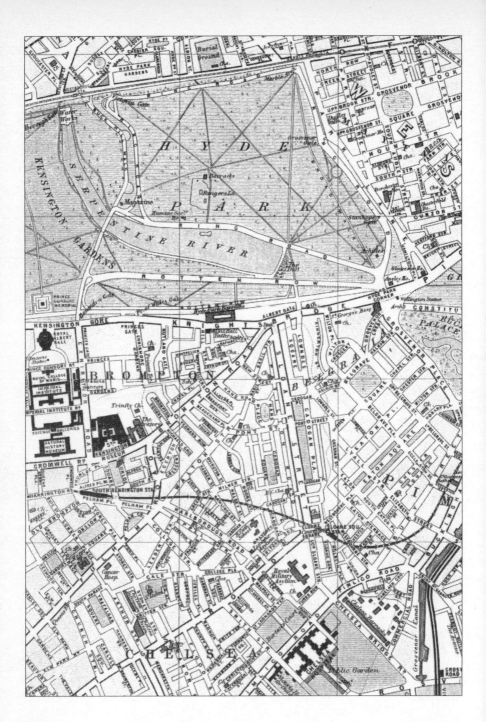

5e. Brompton, South Kensington, Belgravia, Chelsea and part of Mayfair. The Imperial Institute (demolished in 1963) had been open for six years, and the South Kensington Museum was on the point of being renamed and rebuilt. Park Lane and South Audley Street, east of Hyde Park, had several aristocratic mansions, which were demolished in the 1920s and 1930s.

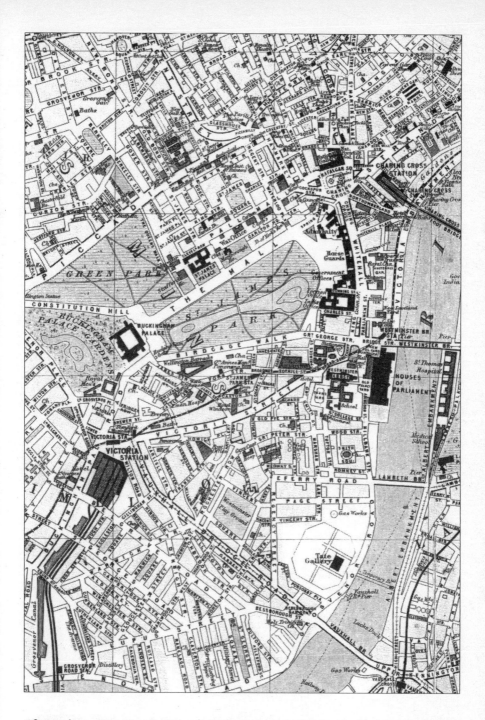

5f. Pimlico, Victoria, St James' Park, Leicester Square and part of Mayfair. The West End's only tram line ran along Vauxhall Bridge Road, just south of the Tate Gallery (1897), which stood in the space left by the recently demolished Millbank Penitentiary. West of Westminster Abbey, the huge Royal Aquarium on Tothill Street had not yet been replaced by the Methodist Central Hall (1906).

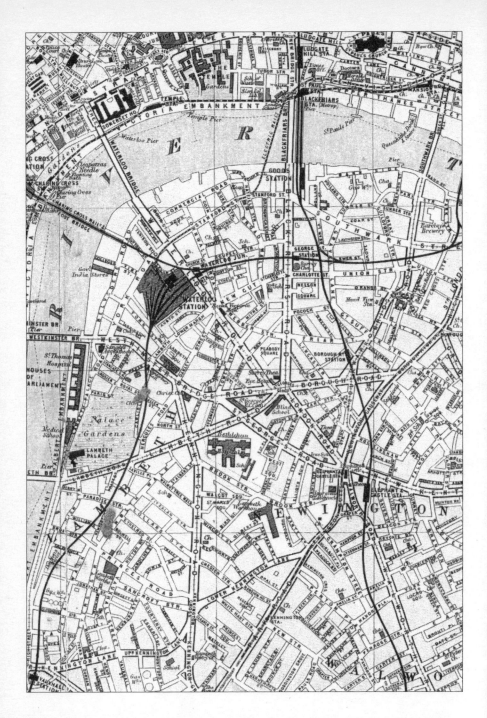

5g. Southwark, Newington, and parts of Lambeth and Kennington. The Waterloo and City railway, which opened in 1898, is marked, and so is Sanger's Amphitheatre (previously Astley's, next to St Thomas' Hospital), although it had been demolished in the mid-1890s. There are horse-tram routes along every main street, but none on the bridges.

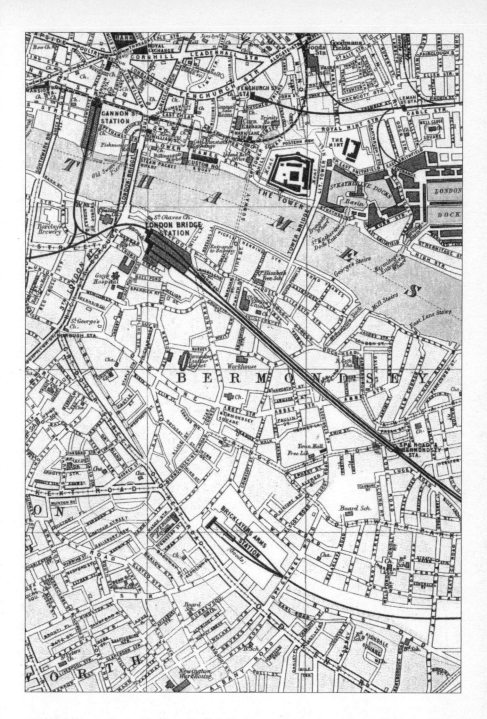

5h. Bermondsey and parts of Walworth and the City. The railway running from King William Street under Borough High Street and through the Elephant and Castle is the City and South London, the world's first electric underground railway (1890). The pedestrian subway near the Tower was built by Barlow and Greathead in 1869, and closed after the opening of Tower Bridge in 1894.

NOTES

INTRODUCTION: LONDON IN THE 1880s

1 H. James, *English Hours* (London, 1905, 1960), 6–7.
2 London County Council, *London Statistics*, vol. 22, *1911–12* (London, 1912), 432.
   A. Hare, *Walks in London* (London, 1884), vol. 1, xiv, 317, 419.
3 F. Swinnerton (ed.), *The Journals of Arnold Bennett* (London, 1954), 20–1.
4 W. Besant, *All Sorts and Conditions of Men* (London, 1882), 18.

ONE: CITY OF SMOKE

1 H. G. Wells, *Love and Mr Lewisham* (London, 1900). The foggy walk is in ch 15.
   A. Symons, *London: a Book of Aspects* (London, 1909).
2 S. Nicholson, *A Victorian Household* (Stroud, 1994), 83.
3 Whistler's Ten o'Clock lecture, 1885, quoted in J. House, 'London in the art of
   Monet and Pissarro', in *The Image of London. Views by Travellers and Emigrés,
   1550–1920* (London, 1987), 77.
4 Ibid., 184–5.
5 R. Aldington (ed.), *Oscar Wilde. Selected Works* (London, 1946), 54.
6 *Encyclopædia Britannica* (11th ed., New York, 1910), 'Smoke'.
7 Ibid., 'Smoke' and 'Fog'.
8 H. T. Bernstein, 'The mysterious disappearance of Edwardian London fog',
   189–206, in *London Journal*, vol. 1 (ii), 1975, 198–9. There are good accounts of
   London fog in P. Brimblecombe, *The Big Smoke* (London, 1987) and A. S. Wohl,
   Endangered Lives: Public Health in Victorian Britain (London, 1983).
9 *Baedeker's London and its Environs* (11th ed., Leipzig, 1898), 95.
10 B. R. Mitchell, P. Deane, *Abstract of British Historical Statistics* (Cambridge, 1962),
   12. S. Szreter, A. Hardy, 'Urban fertility and mortality patterns', 652–3, in
   M. Daunton (ed.), *The Cambridge History of Urban Britain*, vol. 3 (Cambridge,
   2000).
11 London County Council, *London Statistics*, vol. 3, *1892–3* (London, 1893), xl.
12 S. Szreter, G. Mooney, 'Urbanization, mortality, and the standard of living debate:
   new estimates of the expectation of life at birth in nineteenth-century cities', in
   Economic History Review, vol. 51 (1998), 84–112.

13 *The New Survey of London Life and Labour*, vol. 1, *Forty Years of Change* (London, 1930), ch. 2.

14 Ibid., 245–69.

15 J. Davis, *Reforming London. The London Government Problem, 1855–1900* (Oxford, 1988), 20–30.

16 Ibid., 33–40, 168–75, appendices 1, 3.

17 D. Owen, *The Government of Victorian London, 1855–1889* (London, 1982), 223.

18 J. Davis, *Reforming London*, 89–90.

19 Ibid., 37–40. W. J. Fishman, *East End 1888* (London, 1988), 40.

20 D. Owen, *The Government of Victorian London, 1855–1889*, 342. And see chapters 10–15 (written by David Owen and Frances Sheppard) for the work of individual London vestries.

21 J. Davis, *Reforming London*, 44–50.

22 B. Weinreb, C. Hibbert (eds), *The London Encyclopaedia* (London, 1983), 565.

TWO: MAKING MONEY

1 H. James, *English Hours* (ed. A. L. Lowe, 1960), 102–3.

2 A. H. Beavan, *Imperial London* (London, 1901), 236–7.

3 London County Council, *London Statistics*, vol. 3, *1892–3* (London, 1893), xlii. London County Council, *London Statistics*, vol. 22, *1911–12* (London, 1912), 438–43.

4 R. Mitchie, 'The City of London and international trade, 1850–1914', 34–40, in D. C. M. Platt (ed.), *Decline and Recovery in Britain's Overseas Trade, 1873–1914* (London, 1993), 21–64.

5 D. C. M. Platt, *Decline and Recovery in Britain's Overseas Trade, 1873–1914*, 65–76. B. R. Mitchell, P. Deane, *Abstract of British Historical Statistics* (Cambridge, 1962), 334–5.

6 A. H. Beavan, *Imperial London*, 232.

7 S. D. Chapman, *Merchant Enterprise in Britain. From the Industrial Revolution to World War I* (Cambridge, 1992), 167–90.

8 R. Mitchie, 'The City of London and international trade, 1850–1914', 34–40, in D. C. M. Platt, *Decline and Recovery in Britain's Overseas Trade, 1873–1914*, 41.

9 M. Ball, D. Sunderland, *An Economic History of London, 1800–1914* (London, 2001), 338–41, 344–6.

10 D. Kynaston, *The City of London*, vol. 2, *The Golden Years* (London, 1995), 380–1.

11 M. Ball, D. Sunderland, *An Economic History of London, 1800–1914*, 354–5. S. D. Chapman, *Merchant Enterprise in Britain. From the Industrial Revolution to World War I*, 231–61.

12 D. Kynaston, *The City of London*, vol. 1, *A World of its Own* (London, 1994), 392–3.

13 W. D. Rubinstein, *Men of Property* (London, 1981), 86–110.

14 W. D. Rubinstein, *Elites and the Wealthy in Modern British History* (Brighton, 1987), 23–6.

15 T. Nicholas, 'Businessmen and land ownership in the late nineteenth century', *Economic History Review*, vol. 52 (1999), 36.

16 C. F. G. Masterman, *The Condition of England* (London, 1909), 37–41.

17 N. W. Ellenberger, 'The transformation of London "Society" at the end of Victoria's reign: evidence from the court presentation records', in *Albion*, vol. 22 (4) (1990), 635–53.

18 Lady St Helier, *Memories of Fifty Years* (London, 1909), 210–11. V. Woolf, *The Common Reader*, First Series (London, 1975) 249.

19 B. Webb, *Our Partnership* (London, 1948), 268, 300, 311, 346–7. J. Dowsing, *Mayfair. A Guide to its History and Landmarks* (London, nd), 10–11.

20 P. Magnus, *King Edward the Seventh* (London, 1964), 247, 273–5, 320–3. J. Camplin, *The Rise of the Plutocrats. Wealth and Power in Edwardian England* (London, 1978), 41–54, 101–5.

21 London County Council, *London Statistics*, vol. 3, *1892–3* (London, 1893), xlii. W. D. Rubinstein, *Elites and the Wealthy in Modern British History*, 56–64. W. D. Rubinstein, *Men of Property*, 108–10.

THREE: LANDLORD AND TENANT

1 G. R. Sims, F. Barnard, 'How the Poor Live', ch. 6, *Pictorial World*, 7 June 1883, in 21.

2 G. R. Sims, F. Barnard, 'How the Poor Live', ch. 2, *Pictorial World*, 9 July 1883, in 637.

3 P. Magnus, *King Edward VII* (1964; Penguin, 1967), 226–8.

4 M. Daunton, *House and Home in the Victorian City. Working-class Housing 1850–1914* (1983), especially chs 4–7, is an excellent discussion of private rented housing, though its emphasis is not on London.

5 R. Dennis, '"Hard to let" in Edwardian London', *Urban Studies*, vol. 26 (1989), 77–89.

6 E. G. Howarth, M. Wilson, *West Ham. A Study in Social and Industrial Problems* (1907), 9–15, 113–18.

FOUR: THE DISCOVERY OF POVERTY

1 *The Nineteenth Century*, November 1886.

2 R. O'Day, D. Englander, *Mr Charles Booth's Enquiry Life and Labour of the People in London Reconsidered* (London, 1993), 12–32.

3 Quoted in H. Glennerster, J. Hills, D. Piachaud, Jo Webb, *One Hundred Years of Poverty and Policy* (York, 2004), 18.

4 S. Szreter, *Fertility, Class and Gender in Britain, 1860–1940* (Cambridge, 1996), 97–114.

5 N. and J. MacKenzie (eds), *The Diaries of Beatrice Webb* (London, 2000), 69–70.

6 Beatrice Potter, *My Apprenticeship* (1926; Penguin ed., 1971), 130–1.

7 Ibid., 70–1.

8 N. and J. MacKenzie, *The Diaries of Beatrice Potter*, 8 March, 12 April 1885.

9 Beatrice Potter, *My Apprenticeship*, 341. R. O'Day, D. Englander, *Mr Charles Booth's Enquiry Life and Labour of the People in London Reconsidered*, 35–7.

10 R. O'Day, D. Englander, *Mr Charles Booth's Enquiry Life and Labour of the People in London Reconsidered*, 42

11 C. Booth, *Life and Labour of the People in London* (London, 1889), Poverty series, vol. 1, 29.

12 Ibid., 160–2.

13 Ibid., 244.

14 London County Council, *London Statistics*, vol. 22, *1911–12* (London, 1912), 95–6.

15 J. London, *The People of the Abyss* (London, 1903), 110–35, 275–82.

16 *The Minority Report of the Poor Law Commission* (London, 1909), part 1, 6–7.

17 G. Sims (ed.), *Living London*, vol. 2 (London, 1901), 100–6. A. H. Beavan, *Imperial London* (London, 1901), 199–201.

18 C. Booth, *Life and Labour of the People in London* (London, 1902), Industrial series, vol. 4, 311–80, 394–473.

19 F. Swinnerton (ed.), *The Journals of Arnold Bennett* (Harmondsworth, 1954), 15 June 1896.

20 London County Council, *London Statistics*, vol. 22, *1911–12*, 97–112, 603–6. *The New Survey of London Life and Labour*, vol. 1, *Forty Years of Change* (London, 1930), 361–88. C. Booth, *The Aged Poor in England and Wales* (London, 1894), 23–5.

five: THE JEWISH EAST END

1 D. Feldman, *Englishmen and Jews. Social Relations and Political Culture, 1840–1914* (London, 1994), 21–3.

2 L. P. Gartner, *The Jewish Immigrant in England, 1870–1914* (London, 1960), 24–6, 54–5.

3 Ibid., 36–7.

4 D. Feldman, *Englishmen and Jews*, 155–8, 171–2. L. P. Gartner, *The Jewish Immigrant in England, 1870–1914*, 171–2.

5 D. Feldman, *Englishmen and Jews*, 160–5, 185–214.

6 D. Englander (ed.), *A Documentary History of Jewish Immigrants in Britain, 1840–1920* (London, 1994), 19–21, 85–90.

7 C. Booth, *Life and Labour of the People in London* (London, 1902), Poverty series, vol. 3, 186–92.

8 Booth notebooks, B351, pp. 62–81, on www.booth.lse.ac.uk.

9 Ibid., pp. 47–9.

10 D. Englander (ed.), *A Documentary History of Jewish Immigrants in Britain, 1840–1920*, 92–3.

11 Ibid., 271–2.

12 Fifth report of the House of Lords Select Committee on Sweating, paragraph 185, p. xliii. PP 1890, vol. XVII.

13 H. Pelling, *Social Geography of British Elections, 1885–1910* (London, 1967), 42–8.
14 D. Feldman, 'The importance of being English. Jewish immigration and the decay of Liberal England', 78–9, in D. Feldman and G. S. Jones (eds), *Metropolis – London. Histories and Representations since 1800* (London, 1989).
15 D. Feldman, *Englishmen and Jews*, 371–2.
16 D. Englander (ed.), *A Documentary History of Jewish Immigrants in Britain, 1840–1920*, 15.
17 D. Feldman, *Englishmen and Jews*, 179.
18 C. Russell, H. S. Lewis, *The Jew in London. A Study of Racial Character and Present-Day Conditions* (London, 1900), quoted in Englander (ed.), *A Documentary History of Jewish Immigrants in Britain, 1840–1920*, 101.
19 L. P. Gartner, *The Jewish Immigrant in England, 1870–1914*, 174–5.
20 J. White, *Rothschild Buildings. Life in an East End Tenement Block, 1887–1920* (London, 1980), 24.
21 C. Booth, *Life and Labour of the People in London*, Poverty series, vol. 3, 80 (Llewellyn Smith).
22 R. Samuel, *East End Underworld. Chapters in the Life of Arthur Harding* (London, 1981), 125–40.
23 G. Sims (ed.), *Living London*, vol. 1, 365 (E. Pugh, 'Representative London Streets').

SIX: SOCIALISTS AND THE UNEMPLOYED

1 H. Snell, *Men Movements and Myself* (London, 1936), quoted in www.Spartacus.schoolnet.co.uk. H. G. Wells, *Experiment in Autobiography*, vol. 1 (London, 1934), 179.
2 N. and J. MacKenzie, *The First Fabians* (London, 1977), 19.
3 Ibid., 24–9.
4 M. Holroyd, *Bernard Shaw, volume 1, 1856–1898, The Search for Love* (London, 1988), 126–30.
5 N. Blewett, 'The franchise in the United Kingdom, 1885–1918', 27–56 in *Past and Present* vol. 32 (December 1965), 36–43.
6 M. Holroyd, *Bernard Shaw*, vol. 1, 154.
7 N. and J. MacKenzie, *The First Fabians*, 63–4.
8 *Illustrated London News*, 13 February 1886, 186.
9 H. M. Hyndman, *The Record of an Adventurous Life* (London, 1911), 400–3. D. C. Richter, *Riotous Victorians* (Ohio, 1981), 103–20.
10 G. Stedman Jones, *Outcast London* (Oxford, 1971), 292–4. *Illustrated London News*, 13 February 1886, 186.
11 D. C. Richter, *Riotous Victorians*, 133–62.
12 J. Harris, *Unemployment and Politics. A Study in English Social Policy, 1886–1914* (Oxford, 1972), 58–73.
13 Ibid., 73–9, 106–15.
14 M. Williams, *Round London: Down East and Up West* (London, 1892), 16–17.

15 C. Booth, *Life and Labour of the People in London* (London, 1902), Poverty series, vol. 4, 285–8: Clara E. Collet, 'Women's work'.

16 A. H. Nethercot, *The First Five Lives of Annie Besant* (London, 1960), 270–4. N. and J. Mackenzie, *The First Fabians*, 91–2. J. D. Walkowitz, *City of Dreadful Delight* (London, 1992), 76–9.

17 Quoted in J. H. Clapham, *An Economic History of Modern Britain*, vol. 3 (London, 1938), 485.

18 J. Pudney, *London's Docks* (London, 1975), 121–2, quoting H. Llewellyn Smith and V. Nash, *The Story of the Dockers' Strike 1889*.

19 G. R. Sims (ed.), *Living London* (London, 1901), vol. 1, 169–73: R. A. Freeman, 'In the London docks'.

20 C. Booth, *Life and Labour of the People in London*, Industrial series, vol. 5, 136–181.

21 J. Harris, *Unemployment and Politics*, 80–3.

22 Ibid., 84–90.

23 W. Beveridge, 'Unemployment and its treatment', in *The New Survey of London Life and Labour*, vol. 1, *Forty Years of Change* (London, 1930), 341–60.

24 W. Booth, *In Darkest England and the Way Out* (London, 1890; reprinted 1970).

25 J. Harris, *Unemployment and Politics*, 126–43.

26 C. F. G. Masterman (ed.), *The Heart of Empire* (London, 1901), 3–7.

27 J. Harris, *Unemployment and Politics*, 150–84. London County Council, *London Statistics*, vol. 22, *1911–12* (London, 1912), 114–19. W. Beveridge, 'Unemployment and its treatment'.

28 J. Harris, *Unemployment and Politics*, 192–9.

SEVEN: INDUSTRIAL LONDON

1 New York's population in 1910 was 4.75 million (compared to Greater London's 7.25), and the proportion of its working population in manufacturing, 37 per cent, was roughly the same as London's.

2 M. Ball, D. Sunderland, *An Economic History of London, 1800–1914* (London, 2001), 61–4.

3 Ibid., 16–29, 74–7, 293–319.

4 London County Council, *London Statistics*, vol. 22, *1911–12* (London, 1912), 440–1. Thanks to Professor John Armstrong of Thames Valley University for discussing this point with me.

5 D. Wainwright, *The Piano Makers* (London, 1975), 133–6.

6 C. Ehrlich, *The Piano: A History* (Oxford, 1990), 98–103.

7 J. Child, *Industrial Relations in the British Printing Industry* (London, 1967), 155–83.

8 *Encyclopædia Britannica* (11th ed., New York, 1911), 'Printing' and 'Typography'. C. Singer, E. J. Holmyard, A. R. Hall, T. I. Williams, *A History of Technology*, vol. 5, *The Late Nineteenth Century, c. 1850–1900* (Oxford, 1958), 684–8, 694–701, 713.

9 London County Council, *London Statistics*, vol. 22, *1911–12*, 76–85.

10 C. Booth, *Life and Labour of the People in London* (London, 1902), Industrial series, vol. 1, 180–5.

11 LSE Charles Booth Archive, notebook B351, pp. 178–199. www.lse.ac.uk/Booth.
12 M. Ball, D. Sunderland, *An Economic History of London, 1800–1914*, 80–1. Royal Commission on London Traffic, vol. 5, plan F, PP. 1906 xxxxiii.
13 London County Council, *London Statistics*, vol. 22, 73–88, 225–8.
14 J. A. Shmiechen, *Sweated Industries and Sweated Labor. A History of The London Clothing Trades, 1860–1914* (London, 1984), 24–43. M. Ball, D. Sunderland, *An Economic History of London, 1800–1914*, 294–308. C. H. Lee, *British Regional Employment Statistics, 1841–1971* (Cambridge, 1979), tables for 1881–1911 (unpaginated).
15 N. and J. MacKenzie (eds), *The Diaries of Beatrice Webb* (London, 2000), 99–106.
16 J. A. Schmiechen, *Sweated Industries and Sweated Labor*, 140–7. London County Council, *London Statistics*, vol. 22, *1911–12*, 88.
17 J. A. Schmiechen, *Sweated Industries and Sweated Labor*, 164–77.
18 C. Booth, *Life and Labour of the People in London*, Industrial series, vol. 5, 87–94.
19 J. H. Clapham, *An Economic History of Modern Britain*, vol. 3 (London, 1938), 194. PP1907, x, Annual Report of Chief Inspector of Factories and Workshops, 1906, 6–7. PP1911, xxii, Annual Report of Chief Inspector of Factories and Workshops, 1910, 2. PP1913, xxiii, Annual Report of Chief Inspector of Factories and Workshops, 1912, 2. PP1906, xv, Annual Report of Chief Inspector of Factories and Workshops, 1905, 4–5.
20 PP1907, x, Annual Report of Chief Inspector of Factories and Workshops, 1906, 6. London County Council, *London Statistics*, vol. 22, *1911–12*, 76–9.
21 *The New Survey of London Life and Labour*, vol. 2, *London Industries 1* (London, 1931), 24, 41.
22 Ibid., 202, 204.

EIGHT: NEW WOMEN

1 C. Black (ed.), *Married Women's Work* (London, 1915), 1, 103–4.
2 Ibid., table preceding 259.
3 *The New Survey of London Life and Labour*, vol. 1, *Forty Years of Change* (London, 1930), 410–21.
4 Ibid., 414–21. C. Booth, *Life and Labour of the People in London* (London, 1902), Industrial series, vol. 5, 60.
5 D. Rubinstein, *Before the Suffragettes. Women's Emancipation in the 1890s* (Brighton, 1986), 42.
6 G. Carnaffan, 'Commercial education and the female office worker', in G. Anderson (ed.), *The White Blouse Revolution* (Manchester, 1988), 68–87.
7 *Encyclopædia Britannica* (11th ed., New York, 1910), 'Pneumatic Despatch'.
8 H. N. Casson, *The History of the Telephone* (Chicago, 1910), ch. 8.
9 M. Holroyd, *Bernard Shaw, volume 1, 1856–1898. The Search for Love* (London, 1988), 77–8.
10 Ibid.
11 London County Council, *London Statistics*, vol. 22, *1911–12* (London, 1912), 460–5. *Encyclopædia Britannica* (12th ed., New York, 1922), 'Telephone', 713.

12 J. Wright, 'The Electrophone', in *The Electrical Engineer*, vol. 10 (September 1897), 343–4. A. Briggs, *The History of Broadcasting in the United Kingdom*, vol. 1, *The Birth of Broadcasting* (London, 1961), 42–4.
13 H. Thompson, 'Telephone London', in *Living London* (ed. G. R. Sims, London, 1901–3), vol. 3, 115–19.
14 London County Council, *London Statistics*, vol. 22, *1911–12*, 460.
15 J. E. Hogarth (Courtney), *Recollected in Tranquillity* (London, 1926), quoted in S. Dohrn, 'Pioneers in a dead-end profession', in G. Anderson (ed.), *The White Blouse Revolution*, 63.
16 Ibid., 56–61.
17 G. Anderson (ed.), *The White Blouse Revolution*, 9.
18 D. Rubinstein, *Before the Suffragettes. Women's Emancipation in the 1890s* (Brighton, 1986), 73.
19 C. D. Lucas, 'Cycling London', in G. R. Sims (ed.), *Living London*, vol. 3, 250.
20 D. Rubinstein, *Before the Suffragettes*, 216–19.
21 A. Adburgham, *Shops and Shopping, 1800–1914* (London, 1964), 227–9, 264–5. J. Mackenzie (ed.), *Cycling* (Oxford, 1981), 59.
22 Quoted in D. Rubinstein, *Before the Suffragettes*, 75.
23 *Nineteenth Century*, March 1894. D. Rubinstein, *Before the Suffragettes*, 12–14.
24 K. Daniels, 'Emma Brooke, Fabian, Feminist and Writer', in *Women's History Review*, vol. 12, (2), (2003), 153–67.
25 L. Bland, *Banishing the Beast. English Feminism and Sexual Morality 1885–1914* (London, 1995), 293–5.
26 D. Rubinstein, *Before the Suffragettes*, 222–6. G. R. Sims (ed.), *Living London*, vol. 1, 114–18; Sheila Braine, 'London's Clubs for Women'. Mary H. Krout, *A Looker-on in London* (London, 1899), 79–99.
27 P. Hollis, *Ladies Elect. Women in English Local Government, 1865–1914* (Oxford, 1987), 38–47.
28 Ibid., 71–119.
29 M. Pugh, *The March of the Women* (Oxford, 2000), 200.
30 P. Hollis, *Ladies Elect. Women in English Local Government, 1865–1914*, 306–36.
31 Ibid., 411–19.
32 G. R. Searle, *A New England? Peace and War, 1886–1918* (Oxford, 2004), 457.
33 T. Wilson (ed.), *The Political Diaries of C. P. Scott, 1911–1928* (London, 1970), 36–7.
34 B. Harrison, *Peaceable Kingdom* (Oxford, 1982), 26–81: 'The act of militancy. Violence and the Suffragettes, 1904–1914'. M. Pugh, *The March of the Women*, 171–223.

NINE: GOVERNING LONDON

1 D. Owen, *The Government of Victorian London, 1855–1889* (London, 1982), 175–92.
2 J. Davis, *Reforming London. The London Government Problem, 1855–1900* (Oxford, 1988), 68–95.
3 P. Thompson, *Socialists, Liberals and Labour. The Struggle for London, 1885–1914* (London, 1967), 97–101. S. Koss, *The Rise and Fall of the Political Press in Britain* (London, 1990), 307–10.

4 G. Clifton, 'Members and Officers of the LCC, 1889–1965', in A. Saint (ed.), *Politics and the People of London. The London County Council 1889–1965* (London, 1989).

5 J. Davis, *Reforming London,* 156–66.

6 C. Booth, *Life and Labour of the People in London* (London, 1902), Religious series, vol. 4, 52–3.

7 Ibid., vol. 1, 59–68, 105–8, 156–7.

8 J. Davis, *Reforming London,* 168–75.

9 Ibid., 177–184.

10 Ibid., 187–200.

11 Ibid., 208–17.

12 Ibid., 217–33.

13 Ibid., 234–47.

14 London County Council, *London Statistics,* vol. 22, *1911–12* (London, 1912), 8–9, 158–69. Sir G. Gibbon, R. W. Bell, *History of the London County Council, 1889–1939* (London, 1939), 591–600.

15 Sir G. Gibbon, R. W. Bell, *History of the London County Council, 1889–1939,* 181–201, 612–14.

16 N. Pevsner, J. M. Richards, *The Anti-Rationalists* (London, 1973), 203.

TEN: COUNCIL ESTATES

1 London County Council, *London Statistics,* vol. 22, *1911–12* (London, 1912), 158.

2 W. R. Lethaby, 'Art and workmanship', in *The Imprint,* vol. 1, (January 1913).

3 S. Beattie, *A Revolution in London Housing. LCC Housing Architects and their Work, 1893–1914* (London, 1980), 23, 31.

4 C. Booth, *Life and Labour of the People in London* (London, 1902), Poverty series, vol. 2, appendix, p. 24 (first published 1891).

5 Ibid., Religious series, quoted in S. Beattie, *A Revolution in London Housing,* 54.

6 A. S. Wohl, *The Eternal Slum. Housing and Social Policy in Victorian London* (London, 1977), 250–5.

7 S. Beattie, *A Revolution in London Housing,* 85–119. A. Saint, '"Spread the people": the LCC's dispersal policy, 1889–1965', in A. Saint (ed.), *Politics and the People of London. The London County Council, 1889–1965* (London, 1989), 215–35.

8 Sir G. Gibbon, R. W. Bell, *History of the London County Council, 1889–1939* (London, 1939), 369–75.

9 G. Sims (ed.), *Living London* (London, 1901), vol. 1, 203–9.

10 London County Council, *London Statistics,* vol. 22, *1911–12,* 170–3.

11 S. B. Saul, 'House building in England, 1890–1914', *Economic History Review,* vol. 15 (new series) (1962), 124–36.

12 H. Llewellyn-Smith and L. C. Marsh, 'House Rents and Overcrowding', 143–70 in *The New Survey of London Life and Labour,* vol. 1, *Forty Years of Change* (London, 1930), ch. 5.

ELEVEN: A CITY OF SUBURBS

1 H. A. Shannon, 'Migration and the growth of London, 1841–91. A statistical note', in *Economic History Review*, vol. 5 (1934–5), 79–86.

2 T. W. H. Crosland, *The Suburbans* (London, 1905).

3 F. Swinnerton (ed.), *The Journals of Arnold Bennett* (London, 1954), 11 January 1897.

4 Sidney Low, 'The rise of the suburbs', in *Contemporary Review*, October 1891, 545–8.

5 T. C. Barker, M. Robbins, *A History of London Transport*, vol. 2 (London, 1974), 191.

6 *The New Survey of London Life and Labour*, vol. 1, *Forty Years of Change* (London, 1930), 71–7.

7 C. Booth, *Life and Labour of the People in London* (London, 1902), Poverty series, vol. 1, 254–71.

8 *Victoria History of the County of Essex*, vol. 6, ed. W. R. Powell, 244–5, 270–2. M. O'Brien, J. Holland, '"Picture shows". The early British film industry in Walthamstow', in *History Today*, vol. 37 (February 1987), 9–15.

9 *Victoria History of the County of Essex*, vol. 2, ed. J. H. Round, W. Page (London, 1907), 495.

10 M. Robbins, *Middlesex* (London, 1953), 188–200, and gazetteer entries on various places. I. C. R. Byatt, *The British Electrical Industry, 1875–1914* (Oxford, 1979), 41–4.

11 A. A. Jackson, *Semi-Detached London* (London, 1973), 70–89. *The New Survey of London Life and Labour*, vol. 1, *Forty Years of Change*, 189.

12 *Victoria History of the County of Essex*, vol. 5, ed. W. R. Powell (Oxford, 1966), 188–9, 251. A. A. Jackson, *Semi-Detached London*, 59–70.

13 A. A. Jackson, *Semi-Detached London*, 229. www.ideal-homes.org.uk, Suburbia in Focus.

14 *Victoria History of the County of Essex*, vol. 6, ed. W. R. Powell, 21–3.

15 C. Booth, *Life and Labour of the People in London*, Industrial series, vol. 1, 46, 49. *The New Survey of London Life and Labour*, vol. 1, *Forty Years of Change*, 329.

16 C. Booth, *Life and Labour of the People in London*, Industrial series, vol. 1, 51–2.

17 H. C. Long, *The Edwardian House* (Manchester, 1993), 78–83.

18 *Encyclopædia Britannica* (11th ed., 1910–11), vol. 10, 'Floorcloth', 567.

19 M. Pember Reeves, *Round About a Pound a Week* (London, 1913), 58–9, 77–87.

20 London County Council, *London Statistics*, vol. 22, *1911–12* (London, 1912), 471, 483. I. C. R. Byatt, *The British Electrical Industry, 1875–1914*, 24–6. H. C. Long, *The Edwardian House*, 89–95.

21 C. F. G. Masterman, *The Condition of England* (London, 1909; 1960 ed.), 57–8.

22 D. Olsen, *The Growth of Victorian London* (London, 1976), 197–207.

23 Sir G. Gibbon, R. W. Bell, *History of the London County Council, 1889–1939* (London, 1939), 503.

24 M. Robbins, *Middlesex*, 258–9. N. Pevsner, *The Buildings of England: Middlesex* (Harmondsworth, 1951), 59–64. W. Ashworth, *The Genesis of Modern British Town*

Planning (London, 1954), 160–3. H. Meller, *Towns, Plans and Society in Modern Britain* (Cambridge, 1997), 41–5.

25 W. Ashworth, *The Genesis of Modern British Town Planning*, 171–90.

26 M. Robbins, *Middlesex* (London, 1953), 322–3. W. Ashworth, *The Genesis of Modern British Town Planning*, 192.

27 Sir Aston Webb (ed.), *London of the Future* (London, 1921), 181–2, 200, 243–5.

TWELVE: GROWING UP

1 N. Pevsner, *The Buildings of England: London I, The Cities of London and Westminster* (Harmondsworth, 1957), 578.

2 The three preceding paragraphs are based on Ralph Turvey's interesting article, 'London lifts and hydraulic power', in *Transactions of the Newcomen Society*, vol. 65 (1993–4), 147–64.

3 *Survey of London*, vol. xlv, *Knightsbridge* (London, 2000), 55–7.

4 R. Turvey, 'London lifts and hydraulic power', 151. Sir G. Gibbon, R. W. Bell, *The History of the London County Council, 1889–1939* (London, 1939), 520–7.

5 H. James, *English Hours* (London, 1905, 1960), 10–1. T. Dreiser, *A Traveller at Forty* (New York, 1913), 57–8, 80.

6 P. Hall, *Cities in Civilization* (London, 1998), 770–5. E. G. Burrows, M. Wallace, *Gotham. A History of New York City to 1898* (Oxford, 1999), 1049–53.

7 M. Bowley, *The British Building Industry* (Cambridge, 1966), 11–12.

8 S. J. Murphey, *Continuity and Change. Building in the City of London, 1834–1984* (London, 1984), 42–61. N. Pevsner, J. M. Richards, *The Anti-Rationalists* (London, 1973), 203–8.

9 M. Bowley, *The British Building Industry*, 22–5.

10 *High Buildings in the United Kingdom* (London, nd [1954?]), 25.

11 H. Clunn, *London Rebuilt, 1897–1927* (London, 1927), 12–50.

12 *Survey of London*, vol. xlii, *South Kensington: Kensington Square to Earls Court* (London, 1986), 67–76.

13 E. Harwood, A. Saint, *Exploring England's Heritage: London* (London, 1991), 115.

14 Sir J. Summerson, 'London, the artefact', in H. J. Dyos, M. Wolff, *The Victorian City. Images and Realities* (London, 1973), vol. 1, 311–32. T. F. T. Baker (ed.). *A History of the County of Middlesex, vol. 9. Paddington: Maida Vale* (London, 1989). British History Online, http://www. british-history.ac.uk/report. asp?compid=22667.

15 W. S. Sparrow (ed.), *Flats, Urban Houses and Cottage Homes* (London, 1906), 82–3.

16 C. Gordon, *Old-time Aldwych, Kingsway and Neighbourhood* (London, 1903), 3–14, 23–4.

17 P. Norman, *London Vanished and Vanishing* (London, 1905), 243–5. E. Walford, *Old and New London* (London, 1883–5), vol. 3, 33–5, quoting Thomas Allen and Peter Cunningham. F. Swinnerton, *The Bookman's London* (London, 1951), 3–4, 72.

18 Charles Booth notebooks, B354, pp 128–33, seen at http:booth.lse.ac.uk.

19 N. Pevsner, *The Buildings of England: London, I. The Cities of London and Westminster*,

296–3, 311–12, 321–2. J. Schneer, *London 1900. The Imperial Metropolis* (London, 1999), 19–27. H. P. Clunn, *The Face of London* (Feltham, 1970), 109–16.

20 W. Whitten, *A Londoner's London* (London, 1913), quoted in N. G. Brett-James, *A London Anthology* (London, 1928), 251–2.

21 M. Beerbohm, 'The naming of streets', reprinted in M. Beerbohm, *Yet Again* (London, 1909).

THIRTEEN: A REVOLUTION IN TRANSPORT

1 F. M. L. Thompson, 'Nineteenth-century horse sense', in *Economic History Review*, vol. 29 (February 1976), 60–81.

2 W. D. Howells, *London Films* (London, 1905), 50–2.

3 *Britain at Work. A Pictorial Description of Our National Industries* (London, 1902), 326–331: P. F. W. Ryan, 'The cab industry'.

4 T. C. Barker, M. Robbins, *A History of London Transport*, vol. 1 (London, 1963), 178–97.

5 PP 1906 xl, Minutes of Evidence to the Royal Commission on London Traffic, vol. 2, 631.

6 T. C. Barker, M. Robbins, *A History of London Transport*, vol. 1, 277–88.

7 Ibid., 217. J. R. Kellett, *Railways and Victorian Cities* (London, 1969), 376–7, 386–7.

8 R. Mudie-Smith, *The Religious Life of London* (London, 1904), 339–42, 443. H. McLeod, *Class and Religion in the Late Victorian City* (London, 1974), 299–300.

9 Parliamentary Papers, 1913 xxxii, 42nd Annual Report of the Local Government Board. Second Report on Infant and Child Mortality, by the Medical Officer of the Board, Arthur Newsholme.

10 M. Robbins, *Middlesex* (London, 1953), 81.

11 London County Council, *London Statistics*, vol. 22, *1911–12* (London, 1912), 433.

12 A. Briggs, *Victorian Things* (London, 1988), 36.

13 M. Holroyd, *Bernard Shaw, volume I, The Search for Love, 1856–1898* (London, 1988), 267–8.

14 Quoted in J. Mackenzie (ed.), *Cycling* (Oxford, 1981), 52, 55, 59.

15 W. Plowden, *The Motor Car in Politics in Britain* (London, 1971), 7.

16 A. Horrall, *Popular Culture in London, c. 1890–1918* (Manchester, 2001), 54–64. H. G. Wells, *Experiment in Autobiography* (London, 1934), vol. 2, 543.

17 D. Kynaston, *The City of London*, vol. 2, *The Golden Years, 1890–1914* (London, 1995), 142–5, 179–82.

18 London County Council, *London Statistics*, vol. 22, *1911–12* (London, 1912), 438, 440, 406–20.

19 G. R. Sims (ed.), *Living London* (London, 1901), vol. 3, 248–53: C. D. Lucas, 'Cycling London'.

20 R. Turvey, 'Street mud, dust and noise', in *London Journal* vol. 21 (2), (1996), 131–148.

21 Ibid. *Encyclopædia Britannica* (11th ed., New York, 1910), 'Roads and Streets'.

22 G. R. Sims (ed.), *Living London*, vol. 3, 184–9: G. R. Sims, 'London "up" '.
23 G. R. Sims (ed.), *Living London*, vol. 2, 196–201: P. F. W. Ryan, 'London's toilet'. R. Turvey, 'Street mud, dust and noise'.
24 T. C. Barker, M. Robbins, *A History of London Transport*, vol. 1, 293–5.
25 Ibid., vol. 2, 53–4.
26 Ibid., 36–7.
27 D. F. Croome, A. A. Jackson, *Rails Through the Clay. A History of London's Tube Railways* (2nd ed., London, 1993), 31–4.
28 T. C. Barker, M. Robbins, *A History of London Transport*, vol. 2, 44–7. D. F. Croome, A. A. Jackson, *Rails Through the Clay*, 34–7.
29 T. C. Barker, M. Robbins, *A History of London Transport*, vol. 1, 268–70; vol. 2, 22–5.
30 T. C. Barker, M. Robbins, *A History of London Transport*, vol. 2, 30–4. I. C. R. Byatt, *The British Electrical Industry, 1875–1914* (Oxford, 1979), 29–45, 189–91.
31 Quoted in T. C. Barker, M. Robbins, *A History of London Transport*, vol. 2, 103–4.
32 Ibid., 91–5, 100–1.
33 Ibid., 99.
34 T. R. Nicholson, *The Birth of the British Motor Car, 1769–1897*, vol. 2, *Revival and Defeat, 1842–93* (London, 1982), 275–81.
35 Ibid., 312–23.
36 T. R. Nicholson, *The Birth of the British Motor Car, 1769–1897*, vol. 3, *The Last Battle, 1894–97* (London, 1982), 455–65.
37 Ibid., 465–75. D. Kynaston, *The City of London*, vol. 2, *Golden Years, 1890–1914* (London, 1995), 145–9
38 T. C. Barker, M. Robbins, *A History of London Transport*, vol. 2, 188–26.
39 Ibid., 60–70. D. Kynaston, *The City of London*, vol. 2, *Golden Years, 1890–1914*, 173–4, 216–9.
40 T. C. Barker, M. Robbins, *A History of London Transport*, vol. 2, 70–85.
41 D. F. Croome, A. A. Jackson, *Rails Through the Clay*, 64–5. T. C. Barker, M. Robbins, *A History of London Transport*, vol. 2, 113–15.
42 PP 1906, xl. Minutes of Evidence to the Royal Commission on London Traffic, vol. 2, 745, Yerkes' evidence, 24 March 1904.
43 D. F. Croome, A. A. Jackson, *Rails Through the Clay*, 65–70.
44 T. C. Barker, M. Robbins, *A History of London Transport*, vol. 2, 104–9.
45 Ibid., 113–17, 137–42.
46 Ibid., 142–63.
47 Ibid., 184–5.
48 Ibid., 190, 214.
49 Ibid., 170–87.
50 London County Council, *London Statistics*, vol. 22, *1911–12*, 153, 520–1; *London Statistics*, vol. 24, *1913–14* (London, 1915), 206.
51 London County Council, *London Statistics*, vol. 22, *1911–12*, 64–5.
52 W. Plowden, *The Motor Car and Politics in Britain* (London, 1971), 27.
53 F. M. L. Thompson, 'Nineteenth-century horse sense', 77.

54 Sir G. Gibbon, R. W. Bell, *History of the London County Council, 1889–1939* (London, 1939), 441–50.

55 London County Council, *London Statistics*, vol. 22, *1911–12*, 418–20.

56 Ibid., 420.

57 *The New Survey of London Life and Labour*, vol. 1, *Forty Years of Change* (London, 1930), 189–93. The chapter on Travel and Mobility was by G. Ponsonby and S. K. Ruck.

FOURTEEN: THE END OF DARKEST LONDON

1 L. Nead, *Victorian Babylon: People, Streets, and Images in Nineteenth-century London* (London, 2000) has a good discussion of the impact of gas lighting in London in the 1860s.

2 Quoted in *Littell's Living Age*, 3 November 1888, 313–15.

3 *Encyclopædia Britannica* (11th ed., New York, 1910), 'Gas' and 'Lighting'. B. Bowers, *Lengthening the Day. A History of Lighting Technology* (Oxford, 1998), 44–54, 127–34.

4 B. Bowers, *Lengthening the Day. A History of Lighting Technology*, 102–3.

5 I. C. R. Byatt, *The British Electrical Industry, 1875–1914* (Oxford, 1979), 22–3. T. P. Hughes, *Networks of Power: Electrification in Western Society, 1880–1930* (Baltimore, 1983), 54–7, 62.

6 H. H. Ballin, *The Organisation of Electricity Supply in Great Britain* (London, 1946), 6, says £23 million, L. Hannah, *Electricity before Nationalisation* (London, 1979) 5–6, prefers £1.5 million, and D. Kynaston (see n. 7) suggests £7 million.

7 D. Kynaston, *The City of London*, vol. 1, *A World of its Own, 1815–1890* (London, 1994), 340–3, 403–8. I. C. R. Byatt, *The British Electrical Industry, 1875–1914*, 17–21.

8 T. P. Hughes, *Networks of Power*, 234–5.

9 L. Hannah, *Electricity before Nationalisation*, 11–12. I. C. R. Byatt, *The British Electrical Industry, 1875–1914*, 100–4. C. M. Jarvis, 'The generation of electricity', in C. Singer et al. (eds), *A History of Technology*, vol. 5, *The Late Nineteenth Century. 1850–1900* (Oxford, 1958), 197–202.

10 Quoted in A. H. Hyatt (ed.), *The Charm of London* (London, 1920), 96–7.

11 I. C. R. Byatt, *The British Electrical Industry, 1875–1914*, 109–12. *Encyclopædia Britannica* (11th ed., New York, 1910), 'Electricity Supply'.

12 A. Beavan, *Imperial London* (London, 1901), 328–9. G. R. Sims, *Living London* (London, 1901), vol. 2, 274–80. London County Council, *London Statistics*, vol. 11, *1900–1* (London, 1902), lx. London County Council, *London Statistics*, vol. 22, *1911–12* (London, 1912), 478–505.

13 London County Council, *London Statistics*, vol. 22, *1911–12*, 401, 520–1.

14 T. P. Hughes, *Networks of Power*, 249–61. H. H. Ballin, *The Organisation of Electricity Supply in Great Britain*, 69–94.

FIFTEEN: DYING LONDON

1 London County Council, *London Statistics*, vol. 22, *1911–12* (London, 1912), 64.
2 A. Hardy, *The Epidemic Streets* (Oxford, 1993), 102–3.
3 Ibid., 182, 207–8.
4 Ibid., 181–90. London County Council, *London Statistics*, vol. 22, *1911–12*, 64–5.
5 A. Hardy, *The Epidemic Streets*, 205–10.
6 Ibid., 142–8, 233–66. The quote is from p. 265. London County Council, *London Statistics*, vol. 22, *1911–12*, 64.
7 London County Council, *London Statistics*, vol. 22, *1911–12*, 137–49. A. Hardy, *The Epidemic Streets*, 60–7, 94–102, 137–42.
8 R. Woods, *The Demography of Victorian England and Wales* (Cambridge, 2000), 247–309, especially graphs on p. 275. London County Council, *London Statistics*, vol. 22, *1911–12*, 59–69. www.metoffice.com/research/hadleycentre.
9 London County Council, *London Statistics*, vol. 22, *1911–12*, 60–1, 435.

SIXTEEN: SEX AND SCANDAL

1 P. Bartley, *Prostitution. Prevention and Reform in England, 1860–1914* (London, 2000), 161, 169.
2 The National Archives: PRO copy, HO45/9666/A45364, correspondence between W. S. Caine and the Metropolitan Police, 1886–7. C. Booth, *Life and Labour of the People in London* (London, 1902), final volume, 130–1.
3 *New Survey of London Life and Labour* (London, 1930), vol. 1, *Forty Years of Change*, 400–2.
4 L. Bland, *Banishing the Beast* (London, 1995), 334, note 44.
5 F. Barret-Ducrocq, *Love in the Time of Victoria* (London, 1991), 165–81.
6 G. S. Frost, *Promises Broken. Courtship, Class, and Gender in Victorian England* (1995), 98–117.
7 R. Nevill, *Night Life* (London, 1926), 46–61.
8 C. Mackenzie, *My Life and Times, Octave Three* (London, 1964), 235–6.
9 H. McLeod, *Class and Religion in the Late Victorian City* (London, 1974), 157.
10 S. Szreter, *Fertility, Class and Gender in Britain, 1860–1940* (Cambridge, 1996), 398–409.
11 S. Szreter, 'Victorian Britain, 1831–1963: towards a social history of sexuality', 142–3, in *Journal of Victorian Culture*, vol. 1 (1996), 136–49.
12 S. Szreter, *Fertility, Class and Gender in Britain, 1860–1940*, 182–237.
13 P. Bartley, *Prostitution. Prevention and Reform in England, 1860–1914*, 165.

SEVENTEEN: BOHEMIA AND GRUB STREET

1 W. B. Yeats, *Four Years* (Churchtown, Dundrum, 1921), 58–68.
2 Ibid., 12–28, 59

3 M. Beerbohm, *The Incomparable Max* (ed. S. C. Roberts, np, nd), 166. D. Cecil, *Max. A Biography of Max Beerbohm* (London, 1964), 93.

4 W. Rothenstein, *Men and Memories. Recollections of William Rothenstein, 1872–1900* (London, 1931), 238–41. S. Calloway, *Aubrey Beardsley* (London, 1998), 142.

5 E. T. Raymond, *Portraits of the Nineties* (London, 1921), 193.

6 R. Ellmann, *Oscar Wilde* (London, 1987), 276.

7 S. Calloway, *Aubrey Beardsley*, 100–18.

8 K. Beckson, *Arthur Symons. A Life* (Oxford, 1987), 210. J. G. Nelson, *Publisher to the Decadents* (Pennsylvania, 2000), 268–73.

9 J. G. Nelson, *Publisher to the Decadents*, 257–83. K. Beckson, *Arthur Symons. A Life*, 127–8.

10 K. Jackson, *George Newnes and the New Journalism in Britain, 1880–1910* (Aldershot, 2001), 56–7.

11 P. Keating, *The Haunted Study* (London, 1989), 39–43.

12 I. Dunlop, *The Shock of the New: Seven Historic Exhibitions of Modern Art* (London, 1972), 125–6.

13 R. Shone, *Walter Sickert* (Oxford, 1988), 56, 36. W. Baron, R. Shone (eds), *Sickert Paintings* (London, 1992), 59.

14 J. Rothenstein, *Modern English Painters* (London, 1962), vol. 1, 117–18, quoting Sickert's article in the *English Review*, January 1912.

15 W. Rothenstein, *Men and Memories*, quoted in I. Dunlop, *The Shock of the New*, 158.

16 F. Spalding, *Roger Fry. Art and Life* (London, 1999), 145–54.

17 Ibid., 165–82.

EIGHTEEN: A CITY OF SHOPS

1 London County Council, *London Statistics*, vol. 22, *1911–12* (London, 1912), 229. C. Booth, *Life and Labour of the People in London* (London, 1902), Industrial series, vol. 5, 60.

2 Ibid., vol. 3, 260–71. London County Council, *London Statistics*, vol. 3, *1892–3* (London, 1893), xxxviii–xxxix.

3 J. B. Jefferys, *Retail Trading in Britain, 1850–1950* (Cambridge, 1954), 21–7 and passim.

4 *Baedeker's London and its Environs* (Leipzig, 1898), 32.

5 A. Adburgham, *Shops and Shopping, 1800–1914* (London, 1964), 278. *Survey of London*, vol. xlii, *South Kensington: Kensington Square to Earls Court* (London, 1986), 87–9.

6 S. Nicholson, *A Victorian Household* (Stroud, 1994), 85.

7 C. Booth, *Life and Labour of the People in London*, Industrial series, vol. 3, 68–9.

8 A. Saint, *Richard Norman Shaw* (London, 1976), 374–91. Donald Install Associates, *Regent Street History and Conservation* (London, 2002), 17–20. www.regentstreetonline.com/crownhistory.asp.

9 A. Adburgham, *Shops and Shopping, 1800–1914*, 164, 272–3.

10 E. D. Rappaport, *Shopping For Pleasure: Women in the Making of London's West End* (Princeton, 2000), 101–2.

11 E. S. Turner, *The Shocking History of Advertising* (Harmondsworth, 1965), 144–6.

12 G. S. Jones, *Outcast London* (Oxford, 1971), 69–70.

13 London County Council, *London Statistics*, vol. 22, *1911–12*, 232–4. G. S. Jones, *Outcast London*, 359.

14 C. Booth, *Life and Labour of the People in London*, Industrial series, vol. 3, 68–80.

15 London County Council, *London Statistics*, vol. 22, *1911–12*, 232–4, 254–5. The 1892 Act defined shops to include public houses, but I have subtracted them from the number of properties registered by the LCC.

16 J. B. Jefferys, *Retail Trading in Britain, 1850–1950*, 36–8.

17 C. Booth, *Life and Labour of the People in London*, Poverty series, vol. 1, 33–5.

18 H. G. Wells, *Experiment in Autobiography* (London, 1934), 65.

19 J. B. Jefferys, *Retail Trading in Britain, 1850–1950*, 37–8, 54.
G. Crossick, 'Shopkeepers and the state in Britain, 1870–1914', in G. Crossick, H. Haupt, *Shopkeepers and Master Artisans in Nineteenth-century Europe* (London, 1984), 239–69.

20 A. Meynell, *London Impressions* (London, 1898).

21 *Encyclopædia Britannica* (11th ed., New York, 1911), 'Advertisement' (by H. R. Haxton). P. Jackson, *Walks in Old London* (London, 1993), 22–4.

NINETEEN: IGNORANT ARMIES

1 P. Fitzgerald, *Picturesque London* (London, 1890), 238.

2 C. Booth, *Life and Labour of the People in London* (London, 1902), Religious series, vol. 2, 74–80.

3 Ibid., vol. 3, 61. C. F. G. Masterman, *The Condition of England* (London, 1909; 1960 ed.), 207.

4 C. Booth, *Life and Labour of the People in London*, Religious series, vol. 2, 81; vol. 7, 123.

5 H. McLeod, *Class and Religion in the Late Victorian City* (London, 1974), 109.
C. Booth, *Life and Labour of the People in London*, Religious series, vol. 3, 82–4, 109–10.

6 C. Booth, *Life and Labour of the People in London*, Religious series, vol. 3, 63–5.
H. McLeod, *Class and Religion in the Late Victorian City*, 162.

7 R. Mudie-Smith, *The Religious Life of London* (London, 1904), 204.

8 C. Booth, *Life and Labour of the People in London*, Religious series, vol. 6, 173–85.

9 Ibid., vol. 7, 326.

10 R. Mudie-Smith, *The Religious Life of London*, 1–18.

11 Ibid., 201.

12 Ibid., 314.

13 C. F. G. Masterman, *The Condition of England*, 205–6.

14 S. C. Williams, *Religious Belief and Popular Culture in Southwark c. 1880–1939* (Oxford, 1999), 55–86, 93–4.

TWENTY: 'THE SAFEST CAPITAL'

1 Report of the Commissioner of the Metropolitan Police, 1899, table 31, p. 72. PP 1900 XL.

2 D. Jones, 'Crime in London: the evidence of the Metropolitan Police, 1831–92', in *Crime, Protest, Community and Police in Nineteenth-century Britain* (London, 1982), 117–43.

3 Report of the Commissioner of the Metropolitan Police, 1899, table 34, p. 75. PP 1900 XL.

4 L. Radzinowicz, R. Hood, *The Emergence of Penal Policy in Victorian and Edwardian England* (Oxford, 1990), 115–29.

5 L. P. Curtis, *Jack the Ripper and the London Press* (London, 2001), 109–39.

6 Warren's letter to the Home Office, 6 November 1888. The website www.casebook.org has this and much more material on the Whitechapel murders.

7 L. P. Curtis, *Jack the Ripper and the London Press*, 259–60, contradicting J. R. Walkowitz, *City of Dreadful Delight* (London, 1992), 214.

8 Sickert used to visit music halls and brothels in the East End and elsewhere, had what seems to us a rather unpleasant attitude towards women, and painted some pictures around 1905 showing the Ripper's victims as they appeared in the post-mortem photographs. Since these photographs were published in France in 1899 (a fact apparently unknown to Cornwell), Sickert's ability to reproduce them is not as incriminating as she claims. Cornwell decorates this flimsy case with some completely worthless DNA evidence, a comparison of common watermarks on paper used by Sickert and in some of the many 'Ripper' letters (which Cornwell is almost alone in regarding as genuine), and some amateur psychology. She asserts, on no good evidence, that Sickert had a painful penis defect (his real problem was probably piles) which made him impotent (thus the frequent visits to brothels) and filled him with rage against women. Sickert had three wives, many love affairs, and a reputation for sexual promiscuity, but this, Cornwell asks us to believe, was just a cover for his inadequacy. Cornwell mixes all this up with some discredited material invented in the 1970s by a man claiming to be Sickert's illegitimate son, an assertion of Sickert's love of violence based upon his youthful fondness for Punch and Judy shows, and an account of the seedy tastes and bohemian lifestyle that Sickert shared with most English and French painters of his day. The fact that Sickert was in Normandy from late August to early October, when four of the murders took place, and would have had to make secret and hasty trips back to London, was not allowed to spoil the predetermined outcome of her researches. It seems likely that this misguided exercise will leave Patricia Cornwell's reputation more damaged than Sickert's.
P. K. Crossley, 'Cornwell rips Sickert. How bad is it?', at www.tonsethhouse.net/DB/CornRip.html, answers the Cornwell case very well.

9 PP 1892 XLI, Annual Report of the Commissioner of the Metropolitan Police, 4–5. T. R. Gurr, P. N. Grabosky, R. C. Hula (eds), *The Politics of Crime and Conflict. A Comparative History of Four Cities* (London, 1977), 110–27.

10 *The New Survey of London Life and Labour*, vol. 1, *Forty Years of Change* (London, 1930), 389–408: Sir Edward Troup, 'Crime in Greater London'.

11 C. Booth, *Life and Labour of the People in London* (London, 1902), Poverty series, vol. 1, 29.

12 Charles Booth Online Archive, www.booth.lse.ac.uk. Booth's notebooks, 1897–9, B354, 47–51; B349, 21–3, 149–61; B364, 21.

13 C. Booth, *Life and Labour of the People in London*, Religious series, vol. 2, 111–12.

14 Report of the Commissioner of the Metropolitan Police, 1899, table 17. PRO 1900 XL.

15 S. Petrow, *Policing Morals. The Metropolitan Police and the Home Office, 1870–1914* (Oxford, 1994), 215.

16 Ibid., 239–93.

17 London County Council, *London Statistics*, vol. 22, *1911–12* (London, 1912), 271–96.

18 S. Petrow, *Policing Morals*, 13. T. R. Gurr, P. N. Grabosky, R. C. Hula (eds), *The Politics of Crime and Conflict. A Comparative History of Four Cities*, 111.

19 London County Council, *London Statistics*, vol. 3, *1892–3* (London, 1893), xli.

20 *Oxford English Dictionary*, supplement to the 1933 edition, 475.

21 G. Sims (ed.), *Living London* (London, 1901), vol. 2, 229–35, C. Rook, 'Hooligan London'. C. Rook, *The Hooligan Nights* (London, 1899, 1979). G. Pearson. *Hooligan. A History of Respectable Fears* (London, 1983). S. Humphries, *Hooligans or Rebels? An Oral History of Working-class Childhood and Youth, 1889–1939* (Oxford, 1981).

22 C. Booth, *Life and Labour of the People in London*, Religious series, vol. 2, 112–15.

23 R. Machray, *The Night Side of London* (London, 1902), 22–43.

24 H. Oliver, *The International Anarchist Movement in Late Victorian London*, 10–17.

25 B. Porter, *The Origins of the Vigilant State* (London, 1987), 25–34.

26 Ibid., 91–7.

27 H. Oliver, *The International Anarchist Movement in Late Victorian London* (London, 1983), 42–50.

28 Ibid., 99–108.

29 Ibid., 108–16.

30 B. Porter, *The Origins of the Vigilant State*, 154–5.

31 D. Rumbelow, *The Houndsditch Murders and the Siege of Sidney Street* (London, 1973), 17–29.

32 W. J. Fishman, *The Streets of East London* (London, 1979), 105–10.

33 B. Porter, *The Origins of the Vigilant State*, 161–74.

TWENTY-ONE: A CITY OF SHOWMEN

1 Sir Alexander Paterson, *Across the Bridges* (London, 1911; new ed., 1914), 38–9.

2 P. A. Scholes, *The Oxford Companion to Music* (London, 1938), 'Mechanical Reproduction'. A. Horrall, *Popular Culture in London, c. 1880–1918* (Manchester, 2001), 12–18.

3 C. Carrington, *Rudyard Kipling: His Life and Work* (London, 1955, 1978, 1986), 309.

4 H. Macmillan, *Winds of Change, 1914–1939* (London, 1966), 34.

5 Ibid. E. L. Woodward, *Short Journey* (London, 1942), 26. R. H. Gretton, *A Modern History of the English People, 1880–1922* (London, 1930), 527–31.

6 C. F. G. Masterman (ed.), *The Heart of Empire* (London, 1901; reprinted 1973), 7–9.

7 C. Mackenzie, *My Life and Times*, Octave 3 (London, 1964), 92.

8 T. Smith, '"A grand work of noble conception": the Victoria Memorial and imperial London', in F. Driver, D. Gilbert (eds), *Imperial Cities. Landscape, Display and Identity* (Manchester, 1999), 21–39.

9 H. Cunningham, 'The Metropolitan fairs: a case study in the social control of leisure', in A. P. Donajgrodski, *Social Control in Nineteenth-century Britain* (London, 1977).

10 Articles by Vanessa Toulmin on the website of the National Fairground Archive, Sheffield University, www.shef.ac.uk/nfa/index.php.

11 G. Sanger, *Seventy Years a Showman* (London, 1910), 234–42.

12 *Illustrated London News*, 1 January 1887, 16 April 1887.

13 For a full list of national and international exhibitions from 1851 to 1911, see the article on 'Exhibition' in *Encyclopædia Britannica* (11th ed., New York, 1911).

14 C. Mackenzie, *My Life and Times*, Octave 2 (London, 1963), 35. F. Swinnerton (ed.), *The Journals of Arnold Bennett* (London, 1954), 3 July 1897.

15 C. Mackenzie, *My Life and Times*, Octave 2, 173, 267.

16 K. Silverman, *Houdini!!! The Career of Ehrich Weiss* (London, 1996), 162–3.

17 C. B. Cochran, *Secrets of a Showman* (London, 1925), 135–42.

18 B. Mallon, I. Buchanan, *The 1908 Olympic Games: Results for All Competitors in All Events, with Commentary* (North Carolina, 2000).

19 R. H. Gretton, *A Modern History of the English People, 1880–1922*, 825.

20 D. Russell, *Football and the English* (Preston, 1997), 30–73.

21 W. Besant, 'The amusements of the people', in *Contemporary Review*, March 1884, 343–53. W. Besant, 'From thirteen to seventeen', ibid.

22 G. R. Sims (ed.), *Living London*, vol. 2 (London, 1901), 191–2. D. E. B. Weiner, 'The People's Palace. An image for East London in the 1880s', in D. Feldman, G. S. Jones (eds), *Metropolis – London. Histories and Representations since 1800* (London, 1989), 40–55.

23 London County Council, *London Statistics*, vol. 3, *1892–3* (London, 1893), 611.

24 G. Rowell, *The Victorian Theatre, 1792–1914* (Cambridge, 1978), 82–102.

25 Henry James, 'The London Theatres', 1877, at www.blackmask.com/thatway/books141c/lonthedex.htm.

26 C. Mackenzie, *My Life and Times*, Octave 2, 113. P. Horne (ed.), *Henry James. A Life in Letters* (London, 1999), James to Henrietta Reubel, 10 January 1895; Henry James' notebook, 23 January 1895.

27 M. Holroyd, *Bernard Shaw, volume 1, 1856–1898. The Search for Love* (London, 1990), 355.

28 M. Holroyd, *Bernard Shaw, volume 2, The Pursuit of Power* (London, 1989; Penguin ed., 1991), 335–41.

29 L. Bailey, *The Gilbert and Sullivan Book* (London, 1952, 1956), 284.

30 N. Temperley (ed.), *Blackwell History of Music in Britain*, vol. 5, *The Romantic Age* (London, 1981), 98–107. E. Partridge, *A Dictionary of Catch Phrases* (London, 1977), attributes the phrase to a song of the same name, published in 1907.

31 M. Holroyd, *Bernard Shaw*, vol. 1, 254–6, 279. M. Peters, *Bernard Shaw and the Actresses* (New York, 1980), 54–62.

32 M. Holroyd, *Bernard Shaw*, vol. 1, 302–7.

33 Ibid., 328–35. F. Harris, *My Life and Loves* (London, 1964; one-volume Corgi ed., 1967), 767–71.

34 J. Davis, 'The East End', in M. R. Booth, J. H. Kaplan (eds), *The Edwardian Theatre: Essays on Performance and the Stage* (Cambridge, 1996), 201–19.

35 S. Hicks, *Between Ourselves* (London, 1930), 35–44.

36 E. Pennell, 'The pedigree of the Music Hall', in *Contemporary Review*, April 1893. *Baedeker's London and its Environs* (Leipzig, 1898), 66–7. London County Council, *London Statistics*, vol. 22, *1911–12* (London, 1912), 239–40. C. Waters, 'Progressives, puritans and the cultural politics of the Council, 1889–1914', in A. Saint (ed.), *Politics and the People of London* (London, 1989), 59.

37 F. Anstey, 'London music halls', *Harper's New Monthly Magazine*, vol. 82 (488), (January 1891), 190–202.

38 A. Horrall, *Popular Culture in London, c. 1890–1918* (Manchester, 2001), 39–41, 217–25. E. Adeler, C. West, *Remember Fred Karno? The Life of a Great Showman* (London, 1939).

39 C. Carrington, *Rudyard Kipling. His Life and Work*, 190, 415–21.

40 W. Rothenstein, *Men and Memories. Recollections of William Rothenstein, 1872–1900* (London, 1931), 168–70, 237.

41 F. Swinnerton (ed.), *The Journals of Arnold Bennett*, 207.

42 W. Archer, 'The County Council and the music halls', in *Contemporary Review*, March 1895, 317–27.

43 D. Russell, *Popular Music in England, 1840–1914* (Manchester, 1997), 108–13, 131.

44 R. H. Gretton, *A Modern History of the English People, 1880–1922*, 305.

45 S. Pennybacker, 'The London County Council and the music halls', 126–30, in P. Bailey, *Music Halls: The Business of Pleasure* (Milton Keynes, 1986), 118–40.

46 C. Waters, 'Progressives, puritans and the cultural politics of the Council, 1889–1914', in A. Saint (ed.), *Politics and the People of London*, 58–66. S. D. Pennybacker, *A Vision for London, 1889–1914* (London, 1995), 210–17.

47 J. Stokes, *In the Nineties* (London, 1989), 54–67. K. Beckson, *London in the 1890s. A Cultural History* (London, 1992), 115–28. L. Bland, *Banishing the Beast. English Feminism and Sexual Morality, 1885–1914* (London, 1995), 95–7, 105–8, 114–15.

48 My sources for this and the next two paragraphs are the essays in B. Walker (ed.), *Frank Matcham, Theatre Architect* (Belfast, 1980), especially the useful list of Matcham theatres on pp. 166–73.

49 For this and the next paragraph I have drawn on the excellent website at www.victorian-cinema.net, by Stephen Herbert and Luke McKernan, which is based on their book *Who's Who of Victorian Cinema: a Worldwide Survey* (BFI, London, 1996).

50 Information from the British Film Institute's website, www.screenonline.org.uk, and www.victorian-cinema.net.

51 Programme reproduced in H. E. White (ed.), *The Pageant of the Century* (London, 1933), 147.

52 M. Webb, *The Amber Valley Gazetteer of Greater London's Suburban Cinemas, 1946–1986* (Birmingham, 1986), identifies many London cinemas that were founded before the Great War and still open in the 1940s.

53 London County Council, *London Statistics*, vol. 22, *1911–12*, 240–3, 250. *The New Survey of London Life and Labour*, vol. 1, *Forty Years of Change* (London, 1930), 290–5. D. Field, *Picture Palace, A Social History of the Cinema* (London, 1974), 13–23.

54 C. Booth, *Life and Labour of the People in London*, Industrial series, vol. 4, table preceding p. 108.

55 R. Pearsall, *Edwardian Popular Music* (London, 1975), 134–40.

56 N. Temperley (ed.), *Blackwell History of Music in Britain*, vol. 5, *The Romantic Age*, 87–9.

57 P. J. S. Richardson, *The Social Dances of the Nineteenth Century in England* (London, 1960), 117–21. B. Quirey, *May I Have the Pleasure? The Story of Popular Dancing* (London, 1976), 78–83.

58 R. Machray, *The Night Side of London* (London, 1902; Edinburgh, 1984), 135–59. C. Mackenzie, *My Life and Times*, Octave 3 (London, 1964), 137–9.

59 W. MacQueen-Pope, *Twenty Shillings in the Pound* (London, 1948), 370–83.

TWENTY-TWO: LONDON BEFORE 1914

1 A. Marwick, *The Deluge. British Society and the First World War* (London, 1965), 7.

2 A. Briggs, *The Birth of Broadcasting* (London, 1961), 26–33.

3 A. Horrall, *Popular Culture in London c. 1890–1918* (Manchester, 2001), 77–100.

BIBLIOGRAPHY

PERIODICALS

Contemporary Review
Illustrated London News
Nineteenth Century
Strand Magazine

PARLIAMENTARY PAPERS

42nd Annual Report of the Local Government Board. Second Report on Infant and
    Child Mortality, PP1913 xxxii.
Annual Reports of Chief Inspector of Factories and Workshops, 1900–1913.
Annual Reports of the Commissioner of the Metropolitan Police, 1883–1914.
House of Lords Select Committee on the Sweating System, evidence and report,
    1888–90.
Royal Commission on the Housing of the Working Classes, evidence and report,
    1884–5.
Royal Commission on London Traffic, evidence and report, 1905–6.
Select Committee on the London Building Acts, 1905.

INTERNET SITES

http://www.shu.ac.uk/schools/cs/teaching/sle/london/resources.htm (London:
    Literary and Historical Perspectives 1728–1914)
http://www.victorianlondon.org/ (Victorian London)
http://cityofshadows.stegenga.net/london.html (City of Shadows)
http://booth.lse.ac.uk/ (Charles Booth Online Archive)
http://www.british-history.ac.uk/ (for *Victoria County History of Middlesex*)
http://www.history.ac.uk/cmh (for *London's Past Online*, Heather Creaton's excellent
    bibliography)

BOOKS AND ARTICLES

A. Adburgham, *Shops and Shopping, 1800–1914* (London, 1964).

A. St J. Adcock, *London from the Top of a Bus* (London, 1906).

E. Adeler, C. West, *Remember Fred Karno?. The Life of a Great Showman* (London, 1939).

R. Allen (ed.), *The Moving Pageant. A Literary Sourcebook on London Street-Life, 1700–1914* (London, 1998).

G. Anderson (ed.), *The White Blouse Revolution* (Manchester, 1988).

B. Arnold, *Orpen. Mirror to an Age* (London, 1981).

F. Anstey, 'London music halls', *Harper's New Monthly Magazine*, vol. 82 (488), (January 1891).

W. Archer, 'The County Council and the music halls', *Contemporary Review*, March 1895, 317–27.

W. Ashworth, *The Genesis of Modern British Town Planning* (London, 1954).

Baedeker's London and its Environs (Leipzig, 1898).

L. Bailey, *The Gilbert and Sullivan Book* (London, 1952, 1956).

P. Bailey, *Music Hall: the Business of Pleasure* (Milton Keynes, 1986).

P. Bailey (ed.), *Popular Culture and Performance in the Victorian City* (Cambridge, 1998).

M. Ball, D. Sunderland, *An Economic History of London, 1800–1914* (London, 2001).

H. H. Ballin, *The Organisation of Electricity Supply in Great Britain* (London, 1946).

F. Barker, *Edwardian London* (London, 1995).

T. Barker, D. Gerhold, *The Rise and Rise of Road Transport, 1700–1990* (London, 1993).

T. C. Barker, M. Robbins, *A History of London Transport* (2 vols, London, 1963, 1974).

F. Barret-Ducrocq, *Love in the Time of Victoria* (London, 1991).

P. Bartley, *Prostitution. Prevention and Reform in England, 1860–1914* (London, 2000).

S. Beattie, *A Revolution in London Housing. LCC Housing Architects and their Work, 1893–1914* (London, 1980).

A. H. Beavan, *Imperial London* (London, 1901).

K. Beckson, *Arthur Symons. A Life* (Oxford, 1987).

———, *London in the 1890s. A Cultural History* (London, 1992).

M. Beerbohm, *The Incomparable Max* (ed. S. C. Roberts, London, 1962).

A. Bennett, *The Grand Babylon Hotel* (London, 1902).

J. Benson, *The Rise of Consumer Society in Britain, 1880–1980* (London, 1994).

H. T. Bernstein, 'The mysterious disappearance of Edwardian London fog', *London Journal*, vol. 2, (1975).

W. Besant, *All Sorts and Conditions of Men: an Impossible Story* (London, 1884)

———, 'The amusements of the people', *Contemporary Review*, March 1884, 343–53.

———, 'From thirteen to seventeen', *Contemporary Review*, March 1886, 413–25.

———, *East London* (London, 1901).

———, *South London* (London, 1901).

C. Black (ed.), *Married Women's Work* (London, 1915).

L. Bland, *Banishing the Beast. English Feminism and Sexual Morality 1885–1914* (London, 1995).

N. Blewett, 'The Franchise in the United Kingdom, 1885–1918', *Past and Present*, vol. 32 (December 1965), 27–56.

C. Booth, *The Aged Poor in England and Wales* (London, 1894).

———, *Life and Labour of the People in London* (17 vols, London, 1902)

M. Booth, *The Doctor, the Detective, and Arthur Conan Doyle* (London, 1997).

M. R. Booth, J. H. Kaplan (eds), *The Edwardian Theatre: Essays on Performance and the Stage* (Cambridge, 1996).

W. Booth, *In Darkest England and the Way Out*, (London, 1890; reprinted 1970).

B. Bowers, *Lengthening the Day. A History of Lighting Technology* (Oxford, 1998).

M. Bowley, *The British Building Industry* (Cambridge, 1966).

W. F. Brand, *London Life Seen Through German Eyes* (London, 1902).

J. H. Brazell, *London Weather* (London, 1968).

A. Briggs, *The History of Broadcasting in the United Kingdom*, vol. 1, *The Birth of Broadcasting* (London, 1961).

———, *Victorian Things* (London, 1988).

A. Briggs, A. Macartney, *Toynbee Hall. The First Hundred Years* (London, 1984).

A. Briggs, D. Snowman (eds), *Fin de Siècle. How Centuries End, 1400–2000* (London, 1996).

P. Brimblecombe, *The Big Smoke: A History of Air Pollution in London since Medieval Times* (London, 1987).

Britain at Work. A Pictorial Description of Our National Industries (London, 1902).

Sir J. Broodbank, *The History of the Port of London* (2 vols, London, 1921).

T. Burke, *The Streets of London Through the Centuries* (London, 1940).

———, *Son of London* (London, 1947).

E. G. Burrows, M. Wallace, *Gotham. A History of New York City to 1898* (Oxford, 1999).

I. C. R. Byatt, *The British Electrical Industry, 1875–1914* (Oxford, 1979).

B. Caine, 'Feminism in London, c. 1850–1914', *Journal of Urban History*, vol. 27 (6), (2001).

S. Calloway, *Aubrey Beardsley* (London, 1998).

J. Caplin, *The Rise of the Plutocrats* (London, 1978).

G. Carnaffan, 'Commercial education and the female office worker', in G. Anderson (ed.), *The White Blouse Revolution.*

C. Carrington, *Rudyard Kipling: His Life and Work* (London, 1955, 1978, 1986).

J. Cassis, 'Financial elites in three European centres: London, Paris, Berlin, 1880s–1930s', *Business History*, vol. 33, (1991).

Y. Cassis, *City Bankers, 1890–1914* (Cambridge, 1994).

H. N. Casson, *The History of the Telephone* (Chicago, 1910).

D. Cecil, *Max. A Biography of Max Beerbohm* (London, 1964).

C. Chaplin, *My Autobiography* (London, 1964).

G. E. Cherry, *The Evolution of British Town Planning* (Leighton Buzzard, 1974).

G. K. Chesterton, *Autobiography* (London, 1936, 2001).

J. Child, *Industrial Relations in the British Printing Industry* (London, 1967).

J. H. Clapham, *An Economic History of Modern Britain*, vol. 3 (London, 1938).

W. S. Clarke, *The Suburban Homes of London. A Residential Guide* (London, 1881).

G. Clifton, 'Members and Officers of the LCC, 1889–1965', in A. Saint (ed.), *Politics and the People of London. The London County Council 1889–1965.*

H. P. Clunn, *London Rebuilt, 1897–1927* (London, 1927).

—————, *The Face of London* (Feltham, 1970).

C. B. Cochran, *Secrets of a Showman* (London, 1925).

Mrs E. T. Cook, *Highways and Byways in London* (London, 1903).

D. F. Croome, A. A. Jackson, *Rails Through the Clay. A History of London's Tube Railways* (2nd ed., London, 1993).

T. W. H. Crosland, *The Suburbans* (London, 1905).

G. Crossick, 'Shopkeepers and the state in Britain, 1870–1914', in G. Crossick, H. Haupt (eds), *Shopkeepers and Master Artisans in Nineteenth-century Europe* (London, 1984).

G. Crossick (ed.), *The Lower Middle Class in Britain, 1870–1914* (London, 1977).

H. Cunningham, 'The Metropolitan fairs: a case study in the social control of leisure', in A. P. Donajgrodski (ed.), *Social Control in Nineteenth-century Britain* (London, 1977).

L. P. Curtis, *Jack the Ripper and the London Press* (London, 2001).

K. Daniels, 'Emma Brooke, Fabian, Feminist and Writer', *Women's History Review*, vol. 12 (2) (2003).

S. Dark, *London* (London, 1924).

M. Daunton, *House and Home in the Victorian City. Working-class Housing 1850–1914* (London, 1983).

M. Daunton (ed.), *The Cambridge History of Urban Britain*, vol. 3 (Cambridge, 2000).

L. Davidoff, *The Best Circles* (London, 1973, 1986).

A. Davin, *Growing Up Poor. Home, School and Street in London, 1870–1914* (London, 1996).

J. Davis, 'The East End', in M. R. Booth, J. H. Kaplan (eds), *The Edwardian Theatre: Essays on Performance and the Stage* (Cambridge, 1996).

—————, *Reforming London. The London Government Problem, 1855–1900* (Oxford, 1988).

R. Dennis, '"Hard to let" in Edwardian London', *Urban Studies*, vol. 26 (1989).

S. Dohrn, 'Pioneers in a dead-end profession', in G. Anderson (ed.), *The White Blouse Revolution*.

T. Dreiser, *A Traveller at Forty* (New York, 1913).

F. Driver, D. Gilbert (eds), *Imperial Cities. Landscape, Display and Identity* (Manchester, 1999).

I. Dunlop, *The Shock of the New: Seven Historic Exhibitions of Modern Art* (London, 1972).

H. J. Dyos, *Victorian Suburb. A Study of the Growth of Camberwell* (Leicester, 1977).

W. von Eckardt, S. L. Gilman, J. E. Chamberlin, *Oscar Wilde's London* (London, 1987).

The Economic Club, *Family Budgets: Being the Income and Expenses of 28 British Households, 1891–1894* (London, 1896).

P. J. Edwards, *A History of London Street Improvements, 1855–1897* (London, 1898).

C. Ehrlich, *The Piano: A History* (Oxford, 1990).

R. Ellmann, *Oscar Wilde* (London, 1987).

R. Emmons, *The Life and Opinions of Walter Richard Sickert* (London, 1941).

D. Englander (ed.), *A Documentary History of Jewish Immigrants in Britain, 1840–1920*.

D. Englander, R. O'Day (eds), *Retrieved Riches: Social Investigation in Britain, 1840–1914* (Aldershot, 1995).

Encyclopædia Britannica, (11th edition, London, 1910–11).

T. Escott, *Society in London* (London, 1886).

H. and D. Evans, *Beyond the Gaslight. Science in Popular Fiction, 1895–1905* (London, 1976).

D. Feldman, *Englishmen and Jews. Social Relations and Political Culture, 1840–1914* (London, 1994).

D. Feldman, G. S. Jones (eds), *Metropolis–London. Histories and Representations since 1800* (London, 1989).

D. Field, *Picture Palace. A Social History of the Cinema* (London, 1974).

R. A. Fellows, *Edwardian Architecture: Style and Technology* (London, 1995).

W. J. Fishman, *The Streets of East London* (London, 1979).

———, *East End 1888* (London, 1988).

P. Fitzgerald, *Picturesque London* (London, 1890).

D. Flower, H. Maas (eds), *The Letters of Ernest Dowson* (London, 1967).

F. M. Ford, *The Soul of London: a Survey of a Modern City* (London, 1905).

W. H. Fraser, *The Coming of the Mass Market, 1850–1914* (London, 1981).

G. S. Frost, *Promises Broken. Courtship, Class, and Gender in Victorian England* (1995).

P. Fryer, *The Birth Controllers* (London, 1965).

L. P. Gartner, *The Jewish Immigrant in England, 1870–1914* (London, 1960).

P. Geddes, *Cities in Evolution. An Introduction to the Town-Planning Movement and to the Study of Cities* (London, 1915).

Sir G. Gibbon, R. W. Bell, *History of the London County Council, 1889–1939* (London, 1939).

B. B. Gilbert, *The Evolution of National Insurance in Great Britain. The Origins of the Welfare State* (Aldershot, 1993).

G. L. Gomme, *London in the Reign of Victoria, 1837–1897* (London, 1898).

C. Gordon, *Old-time Aldwych, Kingsway and Neighbourhood* (London, 1903).

W. J. Gordon, *How London Lives* (London, 1890).

T. R. Gourvish, A. O'Day (eds), *Later Victorian Britain, 1867–1900* (London, 1988).

P. Grammond, *The Oxford Companion to Popular Music* (Oxford, 1991).

T. Gray, *A Peculiar Man. A Life of George Moore* (London, 1996).

R. H. Gretton, *A Modern History of the English People, 1880–1922* (London, 1930).

T. R. Gurr, P. N. Grabosky, R. C. Hula (eds), *The Politics of Crime and Conflict. A Comparative History of Four Cities* (London, 1977).

L. A. Hall, *Sex, Gender, and Social Change in Britain since 1880* (Basingstoke, 2000).

P. Hall, *Cities in Civilization* (London, 1998).

L. Hannah, *Electricity before Nationalisation: A Study of the Development of the Electricity Supply Industry in Britain to 1948* (London, 1979).

A. Hardy, *The Epidemic Streets* (Oxford, 1993).

A. Hare, *Walks in London* (London, 1884).

F. Harris, *My Life and Loves* (London, 1964; Corgi ed., 1967).

J. Harris, *Unemployment and Politics. A Study in English Social Policy, 1886–1914* (Oxford, 1972).

———, *Private Lives, Public Spirit: a Social History of Britain 1870–1914* (Oxford, 1993).

B. Harrison, *Peaceable Kingdom* (Oxford, 1982).

M. Harrison, *London by Gaslight, 1861–1911* (London, 1963).

E. Harwood, A. Saint, *Exploring England's Heritage: London* (London, 1991).

R. A. S. Hennessey, *The Electric Revolution* (Newcastle upon Tyne, 1972)

S. Herbert, L. McKernan, *Who's Who of Victorian Cinema: a Worldwide Survey* (London, 1996).

S. Hicks, *Between Ourselves* (London, 1930).

High Buildings in the United Kingdom (London, nd [1954?])

P. Hollis, *Ladies Elect. Women in English Local Government, 1865–1914* (Oxford, 1987).

M. Holroyd, *Bernard Shaw, volume 1, 1856–1898, The Search for Love* (1988).

————, *Bernard Shaw. volume 2, The Pursuit of Power* (London, 1989; Penguin ed., 1991).

P. Horn, *High Society. The English Social Elite, 1880–1914* (Stroud, 1992).

P. Horne (ed.), *Henry James. A Life in Letters* (London, 1999).

A. Horrall, *Popular Culture in London, c. 1890–1918* (Manchester, 2001).

E. Howard, *Garden Cities of Tomorrow* (London, 1945).

E. G. Howarth, M. Wilson (eds), *West Ham: A Study in Social and Economic Problems. A Report of the Outer London Committee* (London, 1907).

W. D. Howells, *London Films* (New York, 1905).

T. P. Hughes, *Networks of Power: Electrification in Western Society, 1880–1930* (Baltimore, 1983).

S. Humphries, *Hooligans or Rebels? An Oral History of Working-class Childhood and Youth, 1889–1939* (Oxford, 1981).

W. W. Hutchings, *London Town Past and Present* (2 vols, London, 1909).

P. Hutchins, *Ezra Pound's Kensington: an Exploration, 1880–1914* (London, 1965).

A. H. Hyatt (ed.), *The Charm of London* (London, 1920).

A. Hyman, *The Gaiety Years* (London, 1974).

H. M. Hyndman, *The Record of an Adventurous Life* (1911).

S. Hynes, *The Edwardian Turn of Mind* (Oxford, 1968).

K. S. Inglis, *Churches and the Working Classes in Victorian England* (London, 1963).

S. Inwood, *A History of London* (London, 1998).

A. A. Jackson, *Semi-Detached London* (London, 1973).

H. Jackson, *The Eighteen Nineties* (London, 1913).

K. Jackson, *George Newnes and the New Journalism in Britain, 1880–1910* (Aldershot, 2001).

P. Jackson, *Walks in Old London* (London, 1993).

H. James, *English Hours* (London, 1905, 1960).

J. B. Jefferys, *Retail Trading in Britain, 1850–1950* (Cambridge, 1954).

D. Jones, 'Crime in London: the evidence of the Metropolitan Police, 1831–92', in *Crime, Protest, Community and Police in Nineteenth-century Britain* (London, 1982).

G. S. Jones, *Outcast London* (Oxford, 1971).

P. Keating, *The Haunted Study: a Social History of the English Novel, 1875–1914* (London, 1989).

J. R. Kellett, *Railways and Victorian Cities* (London, 1969).

T. J. Kelly (ed.), *The London Building Acts, 1894–1926* (London, 1928).

S. Kemp, C. Mitchell, D. Trotter, *Edwardian Fiction. An Oxford Companion* (Oxford, 1997).

S. Koss, *The Rise and Fall of the Political Press in Britain* (London, 1990).

D. Kynaston, *The City of London*, vol. 1, *A World of its Own, 1815–1890* (London, 1994).

———, *The City of London*, vol. 2, *Golden Years, 1890–1914* (London, 1995).

B. Lancaster, *The Department Store: a Social History* (London, 1985).

C. H. Lee, *British Regional Employment Statistics, 1841–1971* (Cambridge, 1979).

———, 'Regional growth and structural change in Victorian Britain', *Economic History Review*, vol. 34, (1981).

J. London, *The People of the Abyss* (London, 1903).

The London Building Acts, 1894–1926 (London, 1927).

London County Council, *London Statistics*, vol. 3, *1892–3* (London, 1893).

———, *London Statistics*, vol. 11, *1900–1* (London, 1902).

———, *London Statistics*, vol. 22, *1911–12* (London, 1912).

H. C. Long, *The Edwardian House* (Manchester, 1993).

S. J. Looker (ed.), *Richard Jefferies' London* (London, 1944).

S. Low, 'The rise of the suburbs', *Contemporary Review*, October 1891.

B. Luckin, G. Mooney, 'Urban history and historical epidemiology: the case of London, 1860–1920', *Urban History*, vol. 24 (2) (1997).

K. Lunn (ed.), *Hosts, Immigrants and Minorities: Historical Responses to Newcomers in British Society, 1870–1914* (Folkestone, 1980).

A. Machen, *The Autobiography of Arthur Machen* (London, 1951).

R. Machray, *The Night Side of London* (London, 1902; Edinburgh, 1984).

C. Mackenzie, *My Life and Times*, vols 2–4 (London, 1963–5).

J. Mackenzie (ed.), *Cycling* (Oxford, 1981).

N. and J. MacKenzie, *The First Fabians* (London, 1977).

N. and J. MacKenzie (eds), *The Diaries of Beatrice Webb* (London, 2000).

H. Macmillan, *Winds of Change, 1914–1939* (London, 1966).

W. MacQueen-Pope, *Carriages at Eleven. The Story of the Edwardian Theatre* (London, 1947).

———, *Twenty Shillings in the Pound* (London, 1948).

P. Magnus, *King Edward VII* (1964; Penguin, 1967).

B. Mallon, I. Buchanan, *The 1908 Olympic Games: Results for All Competitors in All Events, with Commentary* (North Carolina, 2000).

L. V. Marks, *Model Mothers. Jewish Mothers and Maternity Provision in East London, 1870–1939* (Oxford, 1994).

J. Marriott, 'West Ham: "London's Industrial Centre and Gateway to the World", Part 1, 'Industrialisation', *London Journal* vol. 13, (1988); 'Part 2, Stabilisation and Decline, 1910–1939', *London Journal* vol. 14, (1989).

A. Marwick, *The Deluge. British Society and the First World War* (London, 1965).

M. Mason, *The Making of Victorian Sexual Attitudes* (Oxford, 1994).

———, *The Making of Victorian Sexuality* (Oxford, 1994).

H. and P. Massingham (eds), *The London Anthology* (Feltham, 1950).

C. F. G. Masterman, *The Condition of England* (London, 1909; 1960 edition).

C. F. G. Masterman (ed.), *The Heart of Empire* (London, 1901).

A. McLaren, *Birth Control in Nineteenth-century England* (London, 1978).

———, *A History of Contraception, from Antiquity to the Present Day* (Oxford, 1990).

H. McLeod, *Class and Religion in the Late Victorian City* (London, 1974).

A. Mearns, *The Bitter Cry of Outcast London* (ed. A. S. Wohl, Leicester, 1970).

H. Meller, *Towns, Plans and Society in Modern Britain* (Cambridge, 1997).

A. Meynell, *London Impressions* (London, 1898).

K. Middlemas, *The Pursuit of Pleasure. High Society in the 1900s* (London, 1977).

Minority Report of the Poor Law Commission (2 vols, London, 1909).

B. R. Mitchell, P. Deane, *Abstract of British Historical Statistics* (Cambridge, 1962).

H. Montgomery-Massingberd, D. Watkin, *The London Ritz. A Social and Architectural History* (London, 1980).

G. Mooney, 'Did London pass the "sanitary test"? Seasonal infant mortality in London, 1870–1914', *Journal of Historical Geography*, vol. 20 (2), (1994).

A. Morrison, *Tales of Mean Streets* (London, 1894).

———, *A Child of the Jago* (London, 1896).

R. Mudie-Smith, *The Religious Life of London* (London, 1904).

F. Muirhead (ed.), *The Blue Guide to London and its Environs* (London, 1918).

S. J. Murphy, *Continuity and Change. Building in the City of London, 1834–1984* (London, 1984).

L. Nead, *Victorian Babylon. People, Streets and Images in Nineteenth-century London* (London, 2000).

J. G. Nelson, *Publisher to the Decadents* (Pennsylvania, 2000).

A. H. Nethercot, *The First Five Lives of Annie Besant* (London, 1960).

R. Nevill, *Night Life* (London, 1926).

A. Newman, 'Trains and shelters and ships', paper for the Jewish Genealogical Society of Great Britain, 2000.

S. Nicholson, *A Victorian Household* (Stroud, 1994).

T. R. Nicholson, *The Birth of the British Motor Car, 1769–1897*, vol. 2, *Revival and Defeat, 1842–93* (London, 1982).

———, *The Birth of the British Motor Car, 1769–1897*, vol. 3, *The Last Battle, 1894–97* (London, 1982).

P. Norman, *London Vanished and Vanishing* (London, 1905).

S. Nowell-Smith (ed.), *Edwardian England, 1901–1914* (London, 1964).

M. O'Brien, J. Holland, '"Picture Shows". The early British film industry in Walthamstow', *History Today*, vol. 37 (February 1987).

A. O'Day (ed.), *The Edwardian Age. Conflict and Stability, 1900–1914* (London, 1979).

R. O'Day, D. Englander, *Mr Charles Booth's Enquiry. Life and Labour of the People in London Reconsidered* (London, 1993).

A. Offer, *Property and Politics, 1870–1914* (Cambridge, 1981).

H. Oliver, *The International Anarchist Movement in Late Victorian London* (London, 1983).

D. Owen, *The Government of Victorian London, 1855–1889* (London, 1982).

Sir Alexander Paterson, *Across the Bridges* (London, 1911; new ed. 1914).

R. Pearsall, *Edwardian Popular Music* (London, 1975).

G. Pearson, *Hooligan. A History of Respectable Fears* (London, 1983).

H. Pelling, *Social Geography of British Elections, 1885–1910* (London, 1967).

E. Pennell, 'The Pedigree of the Music Hall', *Contemporary Review*, April 1893.

S. D. Pennybacker, *A Vision for London, 1889–1914* (London, 1995).

H. Perkin, *The Rise of Professional Society: England since 1880* (London, 1989).

S. Petrow, *Policing Morals. The Metropolitan Police and the Home Office, 1870–1914* (Oxford, 1994),

N. Pevsner, *The Buildings of England: Middlesex* (Harmondsworth, 1951).

———, *The Buildings of England: London (except the Cities of London and Westminster)* (Harmondsworth, 1952).

———, *The Buildings of England: London, I. The Cities of London and Westminster* (Harmondsworth, 1957).

N. Pevsner, J. M. Richards, *The Anti-Rationalists* (London, 1973).

E. R. Pike, *Human Documents of the Age of the Forsytes* (London, 1969).

W. Plowden, *The Motor Car in Politics in Britain* (London, 1971).

M. H. Port, *Imperial London. Civil Government Building in London, 1851–1915* (London, 1995).

B. Porter, *The Origins of the Vigilant State* (London, 1987).

R. Porter, L. Hall, *The Facts of Life. The Creation of Sexual Knowledge in Britain, 1650–1950* (London, 1995).

R. Pound, G. Harmsworth, *Northcliffe* (London, 1959).

J. Pudney, *London's Docks* (London, 1975).

E. Pugh, *The City of the World* (London, 1912).

M. Pugh, *The March of the Women* (Oxford, 2000).

B. Quirey, *May I Have the Pleasure? The Story of Popular Dancing* (London, 1976).

L. Radzinowicz, R. Hood, *The Emergence of Penal Policy in Victorian and Edwardian England* (Oxford, 1990).

E. D. Rappaport, *Shopping For Pleasure: Women in the Making of London's West End* (Princeton, 2000).

E. T. Raymond, *Portraits of the Nineties* (London, 1921).

M. Pember Reeves, *Round About a Pound a Week* (London, 1913).

P. J. S. Richardson, *The Social Dances of the Nineteenth Century in England* (London, 1960).

D. C. Richter, *Riotous Victorians* (Athens, Ohio, 1981).

M. Robbins, *Middlesex* (London, 1953).

C. H. Rolph, *London Particulars* (Oxford, 1980).

C. Rook, *The Hooligan Nights* (London, 1899, 1979).

E. Ross, 'Survival networks: women's neighbourhood sharing in London before World War I', *History Workshop Journal*, vol. 15, (1983).

———, 'Hungry children: housewives and London charity, 1870–1918', in P. Mandler, *The Uses of Charity* (London, 1990).

———, *Love and Toil. Motherhood in Outcast London, 1870–1918* (Oxford, 1993).

W. Rothenstein, *Men and Memories. Recollections of William Rothenstein, 1872–1900* (London, 1931).

G. Rowell, *The Victorian Theatre, 1792–1914* (Cambridge, 1978).

D. Rubinstein, *School Attendance in London, 1870–1914. A Social History* (Hull, 1969).

———, *Before the Suffragettes. Women's Emancipation in the 1890s* (Brighton, 1986).

W. D. Rubinstein, *Elites and the Wealthy in Modern British History* (Brighton, 1987).

D. Rumbelow, *The Houndsditch Murders and the Siege of Sidney Street* (London, 1973).

D. Russell, *Football and the English* (Preston, 1997).

————, *Popular Music in England, 1840–1914* (Manchester, 1997).

D. S. Ryan, 'Staging the imperial city: The Pageant of London, 1911', in F. Driver, D. Gilbert (eds), *Imperial Cities. Landscape, Display and Identity* (Manchester, 1999).

A. Saint, *Richard Norman Shaw* (London, 1976).

————, '"Spread the People": The LCC's Dispersal Policy, 1889–1965', in A. Saint (ed.), *Politics and the People of London. The London County Council, 1889–1965*.

A. Saint (ed.), *Politics and the People of London. The London County Council, 1889–1965* (London, 1989).

Lady St Helier, *Memories of Fifty Years* (London, 1909).

R. Samuel, *East End Underworld. Chapters in the Life of Arthur Harding* (London, 1981).

G. Sanger, *Seventy Years a Showman* (London, 1910).

S. B. Saul, 'House building in England, 1890–1914', *Economic History Review*, vol. 15 (new series) (1962), 124–36.

————, *Studies in British Overseas Trade, 1870–1914* (London, 1960).

J. Schlor, *Nights in the Big City. Paris, Berlin, London, 1840–1930* (London, 1998).

J. A. Schmiechen, *Sweated Industries and Sweated Labor: A History of the London Clothing Trades, 1860–1914* (London, 1984).

J. Schneer, *London 1900. The Imperial Metropolis* (London, 1999).

P. A. Scholes, *The Oxford Companion to Music* (London, 1938).

G. R. Searle, *A New England? Peace and War, 1886–1918* (Oxford, 2004).

A. Service, *London 1900* (London, 1979).

A. Service (ed.), *Edwardian Architecture* (London, 1975).

H. A. Shannon, 'Migration and the Growth of London, 1841–91. A statistical note', *Economic History Review*, vol. 5 (1934–5), 79–86.

A. Sherwell, *Life in West London* (London, 1897).

E. Showalter, *Sexual Anarchy. Gender and Culture at the Fin de Siècle* (London, 1990).

K. Silverman, *Houdini!!! The Career of Ehrich Weiss* (London, 1996).

G. R. Sims (ed.), *Living London: its Work and its Play, its Humour and its Pathos, its Sights and its Scenes* (6 vols, London, 1901–3).

G. R. Sims, F. Barnard, 'How the poor live', *Pictorial World*, 1883.

R. Sindall, *Street Violence in the Nineteenth Century* (London, 1990).

C. Singer, E. J. Holmyard, A. R. Hall, T. I. Williams, *A History of Technology*, vol. 5, *The Late Nineteenth Century, c. 1850–1900* (Oxford, 1958).

D. H. Smith, *The Industries of Greater London: Being a Survey of the Recent Industrialisation of the Northern and Western Sectors of Greater London* (London, 1933).

F. B. Smith, *In London Town* (London, 1906).

Sir H. L. Smith (ed.), *The New Survey of London Life and Labour*, vol. 1, *Forty Years of Change* (London, 1930).

————, *The New Survey of London Life and Labour*, vol. 2, *London Industries 1* (London, 1931).

P. T. Smith, *Policing Victorian London* (Westport, Conn., 1985).

H. Snell, *Men Movements and Myself* (London, 1936).

F. Spalding, *Roger Fry. Art and Life* (Norwich, 1990).

W. S. Sparrow (ed.), *Flats, Urban Houses and Cottage Homes* (London, 1906).

R. V. Steffel, 'The Boundary Street Estate: an example of urban redevelopment', *Town Planning Review*, 1976.

M. D. Stetz, 'The New Woman and the British periodical press of the 1890s', *Journal of Victorian Culture*, vol. 6 (2) (2001), 272–85.

J. Stokes, *In the Nineties* (London, 1989).

J. Stokes (ed.), *Fin de Siècle, Fin du Globe. Fears and Fantasies of the Late Nineteenth Century* (London, 1992).

M. Sturgis, *Passionate Attitudes. The English Decadence of the 1890s* (London, 1995).

Sir J. Summerson, 'London, the artefact', in H. J. Dyos, M. Wolff (eds), *The Victorian City. Images and Realities* (London, 1973), vol. 1, 311–32.

Survey of London, vol. 42, *South Kensington: Kensington Square to Earl's Court*. General editor, H. Hobhouse (London, 1986).

Survey of London, vol. 45, *Knightsbridge*. General editor, J. Greenacombe. (London, 2000).

A. Sutcliffe, *Multi-storey Living. The British Working-class Experience* (London, 1974).

A. Sutcliffe (ed.), *Metropolis, 1890–1940* (London, 1984).

F. Swinnerton, *The Bookman's London* (London, 1951).

F. Swinnerton (ed.), *The Journals of Arnold Bennett* (London, 1954).

A. Symons, *London, a Book of Aspects* (London, 1909; New York, 1984).

S. Szreter, 'Victorian Britain, 1831–1963: towards a social history of sexuality', *Journal of Victorian Culture*, vol. 1, (1996).

———, *Fertility, Class and Gender in Britain, 1860–1940* (Cambridge, 1996).

S. Szreter, G. Mooney, 'Urbanization, mortality, and the standard of living debate: new estimates of the expectation of life at birth in nineteenth-century cities', in *Economic History Review*, vol. 51 (1998).

M. Teich, R. Porter (eds), *Fin de Siècle and its Legacy* (Cambridge, 1990).

N. Temperley (ed.), *Blackwell History of Music in Britain*, vol. 5, *The Romantic Age* (London, 1981).

F. M. L. Thompson, 'Nineteenth-century horse sense', *Economic History Review*, vol. 29, (1976).

F. M. L. Thompson (ed.), *The Rise of Suburbia* (Leicester, 1982).

P. Thompson, *Socialists, Liberals and Labour. The Struggle for London, 1885–1914* (London, 1967).

———, *The Edwardian: the Remaking of British Society* (London, 1992).

J. Thorne, *Handbook to the Environs of London* (London, 1876, 1930).

R. Trench, E. Hillman, *London Under London. A Subterranean Guide* (London, 1993).

C. Tsuzuki, *H. M. Hyndman and British Socialism* (Oxford, 1961).

E. S. Turner, *The Shocking History of Advertising* (Harmondsworth, 1965).

R. Turvey, 'London lifts and hydraulic power', *Transactions of the Newcomen Society*, vol. 65, (1993–4).

———, 'Street mud, dust and noise', *London Journal*, vol. 21 (2), (1996).

———, 'Office rents in the City of London, 1867–1910', *London Journal*, vol. 23 (2), (1998).

Victoria History of the County of Essex, vol. 2, ed. J. H. Round, W. Page (London, 1907).

Victoria History of the County of Essex, vol. 6, ed. W. R. Powell (London, 1973).

D. Wainwright, *The Piano Makers* (London, 1975).

E. Walford, W. Thornbury, *Old and New London* (6 vols, London 1883–5).

B. Walker (ed.), *Frank Matcham, Theatre Architect* (Belfast, 1980).

J. D. Walkowitz, *City of Dreadful Delight. Narratives of Sexual Danger in Late Victorian London* (London, 1992).

M. Warner (ed.), *The Image of London: Views by Travellers and Emigres, 1550–1920* (Barbican Art Gallery exhibition catalogue, London, 1987).

C. Waters, 'Progressives, puritans and the cultural politics of the Council, 1889–1914', in A. Saint (ed.), *Politics and the People of London.*

Sir Aston Webb (ed.), *London of the Future* (London, 1921).

B. Webb, *My Apprenticeship* (London, 1926, 1971).

————, *Our Partnership* (London, 1948).

M. Webb, *The Amber Valley Gazetteer of Greater London's Suburban Cinemas, 1946–1986* (Birmingham, 1986).

D. E. B. Weiner, 'The People's Palace. An image for East London in the 1880s', in D. Feldman and G. S. Jones (eds), *Metropolis – London.*

————, *Architecture and Social Reform in Late-Victorian London* (Manchester, 1994).

B. Weinreb, C. Hibbert (eds), *The London Encyclopaedia* (London, 1983).

C. Welch, *London at the Opening of the Twentieth Century* (London, 1905).

H. G. Wells, *The Wheels of Chance* (London, 1896).

————, *Ann Veronica* (London, 1909).

————, *Tono Bungay* (London, 1909).

————, *The New Machiavelli* (London, 1911).

————, *Experiment in Autobiography* (2 vols, London, 1934).

H. E. White (ed.), *The Pageant of the Century* (London, 1933).

J. White, *Rothschild Buildings. Life in an East End Tenement Block, 1887–1920* (1980).

————, *London in the Twentieth Century. A City and its People* (London, 2001).

F. Whyte, *The Life of W. T. Stead* (2 vols, London, 1925).

M. J. Wiener, *Reconstructing the Criminal. Culture, Law and Policy in England, 1830–1914* (Cambridge, 1990).

O. Wilde. *Selected Works* (ed. R. Aldington, London, 1946).

M. Williams, *Round London: Down East and Up West* (London, 1892).

S. C. Williams, *Religious Belief and Popular Culture in Southwark c. 1880–1939* (Oxford, 1999).

G. Wilson, *London United Tramways: a History, 1894–1933* (London, 1971).

T. Wilson (ed.), *The Political Diaries of C. P. Scott, 1911–1928* (London, 1970).

J. Winter, *London's Teeming Streets* (London, 1993).

A. S. Wohl, *The Eternal Slum. Housing and Social Policy in Victorian London* (London, 1977).

————, *Endangered Lives* (London, 1983).

R. Woods, *The Demography of Victorian England and Wales* (Cambridge, 2000).

E. L. Woodward, *Short Journey* (London, 1942).

W. B. Yeats, *Four Years* (Churchtown, Dundrum, 1921).

K. Young, P. Garside, *Metropolitan London. Politics and Urban Change, 1837–1981* (London, 1982).

M. Zimmeck, 'Jobs for the girls: the expansion of clerical work for women, 1850–1914', in A. V. John (ed.), *Unequal Opportunities: Women's Employment in England, 1800–1918* (Oxford, 1986).

INDEX